Homer

Homer

*His Art
and
His World*

Joachim Latacz

Translated by James P. Holoka

Ann Arbor

THE UNIVERSITY OF MICHIGAN PRESS

Foreword for English edition and English translation
copyright © by the University of Michigan 1996
Originally published in German by Artemis Verlag
All rights reserved
Published in the United States of America by
The University of Michigan Press
Manufactured in the United States of America
℗ Printed on acid-free paper

1999   1998   1997   1996   4   3   2   1

A CIP catalog record for this book is available from the British Library

Library of Congress Cataloging-in-Publication Data

Latacz, Joachim.
    [Erste Dichter des Abandlands. English]
    Homer, his art and his world / Joachim Latacz ; translated by
James P. Holoka.
        p.   cm.
    Includes bibliographical references and index.
    ISBN 0-472-10657-0 (hardcover : alk. paper) — ISBN 0-472-08353-8
(pbk. : alk. paper)
    1. Homer—Criticism and interpretation. 2. Epic poetry, Greek—
History and criticism. 3. Civilization, Homeric.   I. Title.
PA4037.L436   1996
883'.01—dc20   95-42481
                                                                   CIP

Vxori Patientissimae

Contents

Foreword

The First German Edition, 1985

A few years ago, the following comment appeared in a professional journal for teachers of ancient languages at the high school level: "In the scholarly bibliographies of recent years, there is hardly to be found a publication on Homer's *Iliad* or *Odyssey* that offers a synopsis of the actual epic and provides a comprehensive appreciation" (W. Klug in *Anregung* 27, no. 1 [1981]: 30). In fact, Homeric scholarship for about the last three decades has been so preoccupied with working up new theories and discoveries—among others, the sensational decipherment of Linear B—that there was hardly time to catch one's breath and sum up. But if even teachers of Greek are complaining, perhaps a short guide to current perspectives on Homer will be of yet more interest to a wider public. Thus this book is directed less to my colleagues than to all who are lovers of Homer generally and to all who would like to be. For them, I will try to bring Homer out of the preserve of specialists. For that reason, many narrowly philological questions are deliberately avoided. Also the whole vast area of so-called Homeric realia (that is, the particulars of social structure, economics, commerce, warfare, religion, and so on) has been excluded. Its systematic treatment would have required at least another whole volume (as the citations in the selected bibliography make abundantly clear). The chief emphasis here lies on the delineation of Homer's historical background (on developments of the Homeric era) and on the *Iliad* and the *Odyssey* as poems.

Underlying this selectivity is a desire to bring Homer closer to the modern audience as a poet and not as a historical source. This desire is sustained by the conviction that whoever sees Homer as representative of his epoch—that restless eighth century B.C., when the Greek people, after a long dormancy, gradually shifted to an ever accelerating dynamism—will most readily understand how to appreciate the sagacity, the artistry, and the charm of the poet.

It is impossible in an introductory work to offer a thorough explication of the *Iliad* and the *Odyssey* with their approximately 28,000 lines. Nothing more than a foundation can be given. Perhaps it may awaken in the reader a yearning to make for himself or herself a deeper journey of discovery into Homer, armed with the outline provided here. The needed translations and other sources that might prove useful are listed in the selected bibliography.

To all the colleagues who were helpful to me in various ways (especially my colleague at Basel, Josef Delz, as well as the archaeologists Professor Sakellarakis in Iraklion and Professor Korfmann in Tübingen) I am deeply indebted. A special thanks is owed to my assistant Edzard Visser and to my student aides in the Basel Seminar für Klassische Philologie, Martha Spiro and Renate Müller. May a little of our delight in Homer be transmitted to others!

The Second German Edition, 1989

I am delighted that the title of my first chapter, "The New Relevance of Homer," has found confirmation in the surprisingly strong response that my book has drawn from the general public as well as from students and teachers in academia. For this new edition, I have corrected minor misprints and oversights and updated the citations of scholarship in both the text proper and the selected bibliography.

The English Edition, 1996

It is a special joy to me that, following translations of this book into Italian (1990) and Dutch (1991), my views on Homer and his superb poems will now reach an English-speaking readership as well. Since 1928, Homeric scholarship in the United States and Great Britain—specifically, Milman Parry's theory of oral composition and Michael Ventris' decipherment of the Linear B script—has lent a decisive impetus to the quest for a better appreciation of Homer's epics. With this book, I hope on the one hand to demonstrate that German-speaking Homer scholars have been grateful for that impetus and have even here and there contributed to it a bit. On the other hand, I would be gratified if my exposition were to furnish proof that German-speaking scholars have left behind the era of stultifying disputes between Analysts and Unitarians; that they are now able to integrate appropriately an array of critical methodologies to make significant contributions precisely to the interpretation of the *Iliad* and the *Odyssey*. A few years ago, I spoke of the "reservations" that "American (and to an extent British) Homer scholars [have] with regard to the traditional European interpretation of Homer" (Latacz 1991b, ix). It would be a source of particular satisfaction to me if the present book were to dismantle some of those reservations.

I must thank the University of Michigan Press and especially Dr. Ellen Bauerle for the confidence they showed in me by undertaking to publish this book. I also thank a number of American friends for the encouragement they have shown me—above all, my old friend Ludwig Koenen, for the unstinting and selfless manner in which he has fostered cooperation between the Classics Departments at the Universities of Michigan and Basel; he also had a hand in the realization of this translation. Especially warm thanks go to James P. Holoka for his devotion to the project; with incredible efficiency and in cordial cooperation with me, he rendered the German original into a finely nuanced and, in my opinion, quite elegant English version. I am also thankful to him for helping to update citations of Homeric scholarship to 1994 and for expanding the bibliography to accommodate the needs of English-speaking readers.

No one who writes about Homer can expect that his view of the origins of the poems or his understanding of their meaning will convince all readers. That has not been my intent here. Rather, my goal has been to make modern readers so familiar with a great poetic work of the past that they might better understand their own lives. Nietzsche was surely correct to say that learning as an end in itself is incomplete. To be complete, learning must serve life.

Joachim Latacz

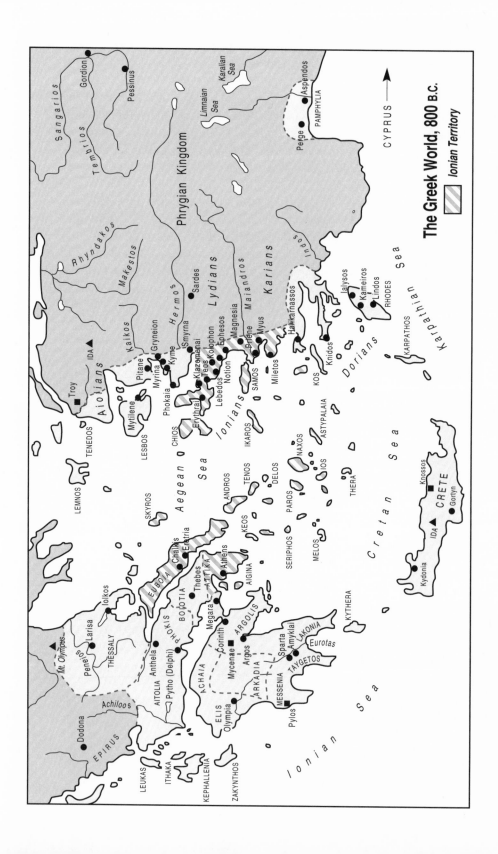

The Greek World, 800 B.C.

Ionian Territory

Introduction

The Immediacy of Homer

For more than twenty-five hundred years—first in Greece, then in the Roman and Byzantine Empires, and, since the Renaissance, in the culture of all European nations—the name *Homer* was synonymous with great poetry. Today, especially among the younger generation, it conjures up very few specific images. Since the Second World War, the number of students and lovers of literature who have read Homer in the original Greek has fallen off dramatically. Among the thousands who have become familiar with him through translations, those who have read his lengthy works in their entirety are probably in the minority.

The general public still associates with Homer the following essential elements (often acquired in a diluted form from secondhand sources): endless heroic combats with sword, shield, and spear, between Greeks and Trojans, in a war at Troy that lasted ten years—that is, the *Iliad*—and a long series of folkloric adventures experienced by the Trojan War veteran Odysseus during his homeward sea journey to the island of Ithaca, where his faithful wife Penelope awaited him for twenty years—that is, the *Odyssey*. To these may be added vaguely recalled bits, mostly of uncertain source and hard to localize: the Trojan horse, the beautiful Helen, the Cassandra story, the Achilles heel—these from the *Iliad*; the song of the Sirens, the Cyclops, the choice between Scylla and Charybdis, the temptation by Circe (the sorceress who turns men into swine)—these from the *Odyssey*. And over all this, finally, stands Olympus, with its strangely imminent gods, who speak with mortals, actively helping them but also cruelly deceiving them, gods who in the end have only "Homeric laughter" for these mortals: Zeus and Poseidon, Ares, Apollo, Hermes; Hera, Athena, Aphrodite, Artemis; the Muses, Nymphs, and Graces.

This list of such associations could be lengthened. What they make clear, despite their superficiality and sparsity, is ultimately something quite reassuring: how deeply rooted Homer still is in our language and our imaginations despite the decline in direct acquaintance with his work. It is nearly impossible to assess just how influential his position is in our literature and art. A glance at the small handbooks of Herbert Hunger (1988) and Betty Radice (1973) under, say, "Homer," "Helen," "Odysseus," and "Troy" reveals hundreds of works from the Middle Ages down to the present that revolve around themes from the *Iliad* and the *Odyssey*—paintings, dramas, stories, novels; cantatas, operas, ballets; and nowadays films and television programs. Among them are masterworks by Rubens, Tiepolo, Picasso, Joyce, Giraudoux, and Sartre; the most recent offspring is Christa Wolf's *Kassandra*. In reality, Homer's influence is much more pervasive, and all these individual works are only crystallization points within a broad tradition that has for centuries repeatedly given new stimulus to Western sculpture, painting, music, and literature. In regard to the history of Homer's influence, George Finsler's compendious reference work, *Homer in der Neuzeit von Dante bis Goethe* (1912), clarifies the mass of associations, which, in their number and their ramifications, are quite extraordinary. Nonetheless, Finsler's work is admittedly only a first attempt. The true history of Homer's influence remains to be written.

The present book has a different aim. It is intended to show not whom Homer influenced or how but by what means he did so. It aims to make Homer's epics speak directly to present-day readers. This is particularly necessary because the twenty-seven hundred years between Homer and ourselves have witnessed the evolution of literary conventions quite alien to those of Homer and his public.

Homer's Language

Homer's language poses the greatest obstacle for the modern reader. Homer speaks the language of early Greek epic—he speaks in verse. His verse is unrhymed but has a fixed meter. Each line must conform to the hexameter pattern, that is, it must consist of six dactyls (— uu), each replaceable by a spondee (— —):

1	2	3	4	5	6
— uu	— uu	— uu	— uu	— uu	— —

All the forms of speech that Homer chooses to use—narrative, description, direct address, dialogue, and so on—all that he wishes to express in every nuance of feeling must be transformed into this six-dactyl rhythm. This was a rigid restriction, which Homer certainly did not invent. When he began to compose verse, it had already existed for several centuries. Generations of freely improvising singers (in Greek, ἀοιδοί, *aoidoi*) had learned, practiced, and refined this style of speaking, or more precisely, of composing spontaneously, without any copy of a text, and of accompanying themselves on the *phorminx*, a four-stringed instrument. An art (τέχνη, *tekhnē*) thus originated that, like all arts, had a solid craftlike basis. Because of this art, the singer did not seek for new words each time he had to sing extempore to his audience of the routine matters, the actions, processes, and situations of life and the world. That would have been not only too difficult but much too risky. One could not have found instant-by-instant just the metrically correct words and word combinations for a given meaning. The flow of the narrative would have been arrested and—more damaging still—creativity would have been impeded. For how could one have spoken of the extraordinary and the unique if one had to search for a new expression even to recount the commonplace? One was relieved of that burden insofar as one retained in memory metrically suitable (that is, dactylic and spondaic) words, word forms and combinations, and even verses and verse groups. These convenient elements would be joined in a common fund, stored in the mind and extended from one generation of singers to the next, constituting a reservoir of prefabricated formulas. Whenever one had to speak of a person, situation, circumstance, or event for which a formula was available in the stock of prefabrications, this formula could be used (but did not have to be: Visser 1987, 1988; Latacz 1992b).

This technique, which first made possible sustained, regular hexameter improvisation, engendered a language in which the same structural elements were repeated much more frequently than in everyday speech (or in any post-Homeric literary language). Thus we hear again and again of "hollow ships," "the shining of the sun," "the shepherd of the people," "brilliant Hektor," "tall Olympos," "all (my, his, their, etc.) days," and so on. Speeches are repeatedly introduced with "and he spoke winged words," and responses are announced with "he spoke in answer to him." Wonderment is expressed with "what sort of word has escaped the barrier of your teeth?" The beginning of a meal is signaled with "and they raised their hands to the deliciously prepared meal."

These repetitions strike the typical reader as odd; their rendering in translation is often somewhat comic. Do not composition courses in school inculcate the practice of avoiding the repetition of words and of expressing oneself in general with as much variation of phraseology as possible? Against such an ideal, Homer's style seems childish, awkward, naive, even primitive. Can there be anything worthy of reflection behind this formulaic rigidity of a language that, vis-à-vis modern variation of expression, sounds like a call from a distant primitive era? Must not the inflexibility of the language imply a concomitant lack of discrimination in the thought expressed by it and therefore also in Homeric people and their problems? It is understandable that for many basically interested readers, and especially for the young, even when only turning over the pages of Homer for the first time, there is a sense of alienation and an inclination to turn away.

Against this reaction, I shall attempt to show that the linguistic/stylistic distance is merely a superficial phenomenon, though it demands a bit of effort to overcome it. The regular workings of the Homeric language must be understood, penetrated, and assimilated. How much effort we expend on learning the rules of games whose mastery brings much less gratification than does mastery of the rules of Homer! Once the linguistic/stylistic barrier has been hurdled, Homer's poetic world, with its really very distinct personalities and its (in essence) permanently relevant conflicts, can provide modern readers with a profound literary and human experience even in translation.

The introductory chapters attempt not only to rehearse but also to document briefly the current state of research into the historical background of Homer. The intent of this deliberately detailed exposition is to free Homer's poetry as much as possible from the still present odium of an indulgently recognized primitive origin. As long as Homer is seen under such categories as "still undeveloped, simplistic, archaic, clumsy," and so forth, the proper explication of his art is not possible, for in light of the supposed inception of this poetry, any sensitive interpretation may be suspected as a projection. To counteract this tendency, the findings of recent research in archaeology and cultural history had to be combined to provide a clearer image, one that reveals the work of the singer Homeros as a literary product of the last full flowering of a centuries-old aristocratic culture. This clarity was not achieved by reference to the Greek song tradition alone; the whole historical development had to be taken into account.

A Historical Sketch of Homeric Scholarship

Homer's works have been analyzed with scientific methods in modern times for roughly two hundred years. The research has gone down many dead ends and has often wasted energy. To review this extensive history of scholarship in a separate segment seemed inappropriate to the purpose of this book. The very perceptive Homer scholar Albin Lesky passed this judgment on modern Homeric scholarship over forty years ago: "the treatment of the Homeric question since F.A. Wolf may be labeled the most dubious chapter of philological research" (Lesky 1954, 1). That sounds harsh, but it is justified. Nonprofessional readers who would like to get to know Homer the poet may be spared a questionable body of research that would only distance them from their goal. A brief sketch of the most significant phases and tendencies of scholarship may serve them better.

The first phase of reflective concern with and not just enjoyment of Homer extends from the "publication" of the epics toward the end of the eighth century down to the beginning of the systematically conducted philology in Alexandria in the third century B.C. This period of roughly four hundred years was marked by the first intensive engagement of Greek intellectuals (poets, philosophers, statesmen) with the Homeric conception of the world, with his image of humans and gods, with his view of human existence and human society, and not least with his poetic art. In the course of this dialogue of minds, which reached its acme in the fourth century with Plato and Aristotle, a practical necessity first made itself felt: to have a common starting point for debate, one had to have more than mere familiarity with the text—which could be achieved in school, for Homer was the nation's primer from the very beginning. One also had to have a deeper understanding of the language and of the motivation for statements. Even a century later, many of the words, usages, and even inflectional forms of the old language of song in which Homer had versified were obsolete or misunderstood. Moreover, the stylistic peculiarities of this poetry often required explication. In the beginning no one was more adept in providing such explication than those who continually recited Homer's poems, in most cases as professionals—namely, the rhapsodes, particu-

larly the *Homeridae*. In their circles originated, already in the sixth century, the first word inventories (γλῶσσαι, "glosses") to meet the needs
of the classroom and of performance; there were also commentaries,
and biographical essays, of which traces have survived even up to the
present in the form of explanatory notes for students (σχόλια, *scholia*)
and *Vitae* or "Lives" (see chap. 1, "Homer as the Founder of Western
Textuality").

The tendency toward text normalization should also be seen in this
context. We may fix a very important moment in this process in the culturally and politically significant directive of the Athenian head of state
Peisistratos (or one of his sons, in the second half of the sixth century),
who mandated that a team of alternating rhapsodes publicly perform
the Homeric epics *in their entirety* at the Athenian state festival known
as the Panathenaia. The obvious conclusion is that an authorized unified text must have been created, which could take the place of what
had up to then been freely circulating copies. This was a significant
stage in the process of text fixation. On the basis of this text, the first
specialized studies of Homer were produced already during the fifth-
century enlightenment associated with the Sophists. These studies
dealt with his language, his homeland, his life, and so on (cf. Alkidamas
and Hippias of Elis, among others). While these sophistic writers on
Homer were deeply preoccupied with language in general as the fundamental tool for the motivation of men, they gave rise to an independent specialized Homeric scholarship by the fourth century. So far as
we know, Antimakhos of Kolophon (ca. 400 B.C.) was the first Homer
scholar to prepare an edition of the text, including an introduction and
glossary (Pfeiffer 1968–76, 1:94).

The second phase of work on Homer may be labeled scientific. It
began in the third century in the research institute known as the
Museion (Μουσεῖον) established in Alexandria by the successors of
Alexander the Great. It extended through the Greek and Roman Homer
scholars of the Roman Republic and Empire up to the great Homer
commentators of the Byzantine Empire in the twelfth century. In
Alexandria there were available in the library of the *Museion* both pri-
vately and publicly owned Homer manuscripts; these were accessed,
collected, ordered, and compared. On this basis was conducted the
extremely productive textual, editorial, and explicatory work on which
all of Homeric scholarship for fifteen hundred years (ca. 200 B.C.–A.D.
1300) was to feed by either appropriation or polemic and to which it

only seldom added anything of significance. Famous Alexandrian Homer scholars included Aristophanes of Byzantium (third century) and Aristarkhos of Samothrace (second century). During the principate of Augustus, Didymus of Alexandria made a name for himself as an epitomizer of Alexandrian Homer studies. Among Byzantine Homer scholars at least the two most industrious savants may be mentioned: Johannes Tzetzes, for his *Commentary on Homer's Iliad* (1143) and *Homeric Allegories* (1145), and Eustathios (ca. 1110–92), the bishop of Thessalonika, for his voluminous commentaries on the *Iliad* and the *Odyssey* (these are extant in autograph manuscripts). Real progress in understanding the epics, beyond the insights of the Alexandrians, was scarcely achieved in this fifteen-hundred-year phase; the great service of the epoch was the preservation of the heritage of the original Alexandrian research.

The third phase is the reception of Homer in western Europe (Italy, France, England, Germany, the Netherlands, Switzerland) in late medieval and early modern times. It began with Petrarch (1304–74), who, at a time when no one in the West knew Greek, commissioned the first translation of Homer into Latin (by Leonzio Pilato in 1360), and it ended with the establishment of modern Homeric scholarship by Friedrich August Wolf (1759–1824). This phase is distinguished for

1. the learning of the Greek language in the West: Manuel Chrysoloras taught Greek in Florence beginning in 1396 and published the first Greek grammar;
2. the production of printed texts of Homer (the editio princeps in 1488, by Demetrios Chalkondyles in Florence; the first Aldine edition in 1504)—Homer became the common possession of educated people;
3. the devising of a first, independent, modern theory of poetry (as one of the foundations of intellectual reanimation) by reference to Horace, and later to Aristotle, on the basis especially of the comparison of Homer and Vergil (Vida's *Poetica*, 1527; J.C. Scaliger's *Poetice*, 1561; Boileau's *L'Art poétique*, 1674; Gottsched's *Critische Dichtkunst*, 1730; among others);
4. the appropriation of Homer in the form of the production of individual national epics in his footsteps (Tasso's *Gerusalemme Liberata*, 1575; Spenser's *Faerie Queene*, 1590–96; Desmaret's *Clovis ou la France chrétienne*, 1657; Milton's *Paradise Lost*, 1667,

and *Paradise Regained*, 1671; Klopstock's *Messias*, 1748–51; among others);

5. the entry onto the scene of historical and philological Homeric criticism and the first formulation of the "Homeric Question" (Bentley's rediscovery of the letter *vau*, or *digamma*, in Homer around 1730; Blackwell's *Enquiry into the Life and Writings of Homer*, 1735; Lessing's *Laocoön*, 1766; Wood's *Essay on the Original Genius of Homer*, 1769; the *Conjectures académiques ou Dissertation sur l'Iliade* of the Abbé d'Aubignac, written by 1664, but not published until 1715 [which argues that Homer never lived and that there is no plan in the *Iliad*]).

In addition, there appeared toward the end of the eighteenth century the very insightful studies of Homer from the vantage point of poetic theory by Herder, Goethe, Schiller, W. von Humboldt, and Friedrich Schlegel.

At the end of this phase came a breakthrough that inaugurated the new era of Homeric scholarship—the discovery and publication of the tenth-century Homer manuscript known as *Venetus A* by de Villoison (first published in 1788): the manuscript's margins and interlinear spaces are filled with textual commentary of every sort that go back to the Alexandrians. This made possible for the first time an extension of knowledge beyond what had been attained already in antiquity. (The most recent and best edition of these so-called A-scholia, together with all the remaining *Iliad* scholia, is Erbse 1969–88.)

The fourth and, for the moment, last phase is that of systematic philological (historical, archaeological, linguistic) textual analysis and literary criticism of Homer's works in connection with comparative epic studies and, most recently, modern narrative theory. It begins with F.A. Wolf's *Prolegomena ad Homerum* (1795), enters a new phase with Milman Parry's Paris dissertation *L'Epithète traditionnelle dans Homère* of 1928, and reaches its newest stage following Michael Ventris' decipherment of the Greek Linear B script in 1952 (see Chadwick 1967). This phase is distinguished for the protracted scholarly struggle that is known even to a wider public by the designation "the Homeric Question" and for the gradual supersession of this struggle in the past two decades or so.

The Homeric Question, after various preliminary stages (d'Aubignac, Heyne), was newly formulated by a professor of philology at Halle—Friedrich August Wolf—in the subsequently famous 1795 prologue to his 1794 edition of Homer (*Prolegomena ad Homerum*). The Question consisted in the uncertainty produced by certain logical incongruities in the narrative of both epics as to whether one or more than one storyteller had composed them. It went overlooked until very recently that this formulation of the Question arose from quite specific historical conditions of knowledge vis-à-vis Homer and literature generally. Therefore, it really ought to be repeatedly reexamined for validity with every significant change, broadening or deepening, of knowledge of literature in general and of Homer in particular. This reexamination did not happen for a long while, so that an independent branch of research—concerned with the Homeric Question—was able to evolve. In the quest to carry off the prize for discernment, scholars still strove industriously to arrive at a solution even when the changing state of literary knowledge and thus of the intellectual landscape had rendered the Question obsolete. The formulation of the Question had itself issued from a conception of literature current in the seventeenth and eighteenth centuries, according to which a literary work was always, from beginning to end, the creation of a single individual. Already by the mid-nineteenth century, it had been established that a literary work could only very conditionally be seen as the creation of a single individual from beginning to end; in particular, the early, pre-literate national epics were the product of the handing on, with very slight changes, of preexisting material rather than of original invention. So actually, the question whether Homer had invented the *Iliad* from verse 1 of book 1 to verse 804 of book 24 had already been superseded. It nonetheless continued to be debated. The result was wholly unprofitable as regards the quest for a "solution"; however, as regards knowledge of the epics themselves, the repeated plowing of the same fields had its benefits.

By the doctrine of individual creativity, the incontestable existence of logical inconsistencies was a definite indication that the *Iliad* (like the *Odyssey*) was a work of several, or at least two, poets. One of these poets was "authentic" (that is, "good"), the others (or other) "secondary" (that is, "inferior"). The complete work could have come about in two ways: (1) later poets had enlarged a primal (or kernel or basic) story by new additions; (2) a single poet had at some point collected together—

or, according to one's aesthetic assessment of the final product, "patched together," "pieced together," "stitched together," "glued together," or "smelted together"—several smaller, self-contained stories. Ulrich von Wilamowitz-Moellendorff sought a compromise between the two solutions in his 1916 book, *Die Ilias und Homer*: smaller stories in the beginning phase; collection in the middle phase (with Homer as the compiler); further additions in the later phase. The task for Homeric research, according to the champions of this Wolfian line of inquiry, consisted in discriminating, or "analyzing" (ἀναλύειν), the various poets (or "hands") active in the complete work handed down to us. Consequently, this line of inquiry is designated "Analysis," and its proponents "Analysts." The opponents of this "dissolution" of the epics incorporated under the title "Unitarians" ("Unitarianism"). Not wanting to let their unified Homer be eliminated, they sought to argue away the logical inconsistencies discovered by Analysts as only *apparent* inconsistencies.

The argument was fruitless, because, as even the disputants themselves often recognized, it was conducted with subjective criteria on the basis of individual scholars' preconceptions about logic, aesthetics, ethics, and so forth. Put succinctly, each scholar revealed by his treatment of Homer only the proportions of his own standards of logic, aesthetics, ethics, and so forth. This accounts for the often unforgiving sharpness of the debate. The *Iliad* and the *Odyssey* as poetry receded ever further from view.

The impetus to a new conception of the whole issue came in 1928. In that year, Milman Parry verified something that had been foreshadowed in the work of many "outsiders" ever since Herder (Latacz 1979, 25–44)—namely, the realization that the language of the Homeric epics is a rigidly standardized poetic "secondary language." This language had been developed and used by generations of pre-Homeric singers to facilitate the free oral improvisation of hexameter songs before an actually present listening audience, not a reading public. The technique of such improvisation rested on the principle of the repetition of abundantly available metrical and semantic structural elements on all levels of composition from word to scene. Parry (and his collaborator Lord) in their day could most readily observe and study this technique in the still living improvisational epic tradition of modern Yugoslavia. (This tradition lives on even today in annual singer festivals supported by the state until recently as folk culture [Leuze 1986].) Improvisational epics of the same type could also be recorded in Russia, in many African tribal societies, in Polynesia (*Oralità* 1985), and elsewhere.

These investigations, which are still in progress, have sharpened our awareness of the typical versus the atypical and the conventional versus the individual generally in improvised epics. They have facilitated the discrimination of traditional from nontraditional elements in the *Iliad* and the *Odyssey* also. The search for the "individual" poet, whom most Homer scholars today equate with Homer, has been relieved of a great deal of ballast. The individual poet, as he revealed himself and continues still to reveal himself, is to be sought less in the mostly normalized sphere of language and style than in outlook and organization of the whole construction (by the use of prefabricated structural elements and patterns). With this conclusion, oral poetry research (the Parryist line of inquiry) supported at the outset the results of two other lines of inquiry that later evolved quite independently of it: (1) neo-unitarian analysis of composition (Schadewaldt 1938; Reinhardt 1961), and (2) so-called neo-Analysis or *Motivforschung* (Pestalozzi 1945; Kakridis 1949; Kullmann 1981, 1991; Clark 1986).

More recently, the initially restrictive standpoint of oral poetry theory has gradually been overcome (Finnegan 1977). By applying the procedures of modern narrative theory to the Homeric epics, scholars have sought to reconcile the difference between oral and written compositional methods. They have paved the way to the insight that Homer, even within the parameters of his oral technique, followed universal norms of narration. In view of this, the very plausible supposition presents itself that the *Iliad* and the *Odyssey* are in fact the well-planned monumental compositions of a single hand (Griffin 1980; Latacz 1981a, 1981b; de Jong 1987; Richardson 1990; Schwinge 1991).

The Homeric Question in its original form no longer exists. It had been possible only under the assumption of the comparability of Homer and Vergil as epic poets at the same stage of poetic technique; that is, the Homeric Question was asked ultimately from the perspective of the poetic technique of Vergil. From the perspective of Homer's (now adequately understood) poetic technique, the Homeric Question must be otherwise formulated. What did Homer do with the oral poetry of his predecessors and contemporary singer colleagues, poetry that he knew and mastered so thoroughly (Latacz 1984b)? In short, just what in Homer is Homeric? The answer to this question as it is now understood is to be sought not in ingenious argumentation but in patient interpretation. To this end, the findings of all the phases of Homeric scholarship down to the present are of great use.

The translations in this book do not attempt to follow the meter of the original, but where possible they do hint at the rhythm. Insofar as the style of Homer is concerned, all efforts to modernize it seem misguided. The strange must remain strange and should not be assimilated to what is already familiar. Otherwise a broadening of outlook is impossible.

All proper names are transcribed in their original Greek forms, not Latinized (*Akhilleus*, not *Achilles*; *Kirke*, not *Circe*; and so on). The name of the poet himself (Ὅμηρος) was originally pronounced *Homēros*; the Romans Latinized it to *Homḗrus*, whence the French made *Homère*, which has become *Homḗr* in German; English, following Latin rules of accentuation, stresses the first syllable (and lengthens its vowel)— *Hómer*.

The belligerents in the *Iliad* are always indicated in this book as Trojans and *Akhaians*, never as Trojans and *Greeks*. This is only to adopt Homer's own usage, since Homer speaks of the non-Trojan side exclusively as Akhaians, Danaans, and Argeioi. In this regard, he no doubt adhered to the practice of the old tradition of saga and song. The substitution for these earlier ethnic names of the later ethnic label preferred by inhabitants of Italy—namely, *Greeks* (from Γραικοί, a west Greek tribe)—persists for no better reason than that it easily connects with the associations of a national (or even nationalistic) perspective (in the sense of a struggle between West and East, Europe and Asia, and so on). This notion was quite alien to Homer. He never refers to the inhabitants of Troy as *barbaroi* (βάρβαροι, "foreign speakers"); only the Trojans' allies in Asia Minor are remarked on as belonging to non-Greek-speaking communities (*Il.* 2.805, 4.437 f.). This hints that the saga of the Trojan War was originally conceived not as an international but as a national conflict, possibly between Mycenaean centers. The hypothesis of Carl Blegen, the American excavator of Troy, that the founders of the sixth settlement level of Troy (so-called Troy VI) around 1800 B.C. (a level lasting into the thirteenth century B.C.) may have been *Greeks*, in the context of a general southward migration of Greeks at that time, is not to be dismissed out of hand (Blegen 1963, 145 f.). That the eighth-century audience, in light of the intervening Greek colonization of Asia Minor, will have received the story rather as an *inter*national conflict remains unaffected by Blegen's hypothesis.

Greek literary scholars (φιλόλογοι, *philologoi*) of the third century B.C. divided the *Iliad* and the *Odyssey* into twenty-four books and designated them by the twenty-four letters of the Greek alphabet. To simplify printing here, numerals are used in place of the Greek letters.

1

The New Relevance of Homer

The *Iliad* as the First Written Work of Art in the West

Homer is the first poet of the West whose work (or parts of whose work) has come down to us. According to our present state of information, he is at the same time the first author in Western culture whose works (or large segments of them) were created through the use of writing. For four hundred years before Homer, the poems of the Greeks—epic as well as lyric—were exclusively oral compositions. Still earlier, in the first flowering of Greek culture in the second millennium B.C. (the so-called Mycenaean era of Greek history, which had come to an end about four hundred years before Homer), there was certainly writing and poetry, but whether there was also written poetry is not clear on our current evidence. We must, therefore, proceed on the assumption that Homer's epics were the first Greek poems to be written down.

The momentous first transcription of poetry in western civilization occurred around twenty-seven hundred years ago. The exact moment cannot be specified, but it was in all likelihood in the second half of the eighth century B.C. The site was a city on (or an island along) the west coast of Asia Minor (which at that time—and down to 1922—was settled by Greeks). In antiquity, several works were attributed to Homer, among them the *Homeric Hymns*, the *Margites*, the *Batrakhomyomakhia* (*Battle of Frogs and Mice*) and the *Thebaid*. But of all the works ascribed to Homer, only two have a valid claim to be his authentic creations and thus to be the first poems in the West conceived in writing: the *Iliad* and the *Odyssey*. (Some scholars even maintain that only the *Iliad* belongs to him.)

The *Iliad* and the *Odyssey* are extensive narratives in verse (monumental epics). The *Iliad* is about sixteen thousand hexameter lines, the *Odyssey* about twelve thousand. Both works belong as distinct variants to the genre of heroic poetry. In the context of this sort of poetry, which is represented in the early eras of many peoples as the praise of the great deeds of a long-ago nobility (Bowra 1952), the *Iliad* and the *Odyssey* stand out by reason of two specific functions: (1) in the West, literature—the composition by writing of texts with a higher purpose than mere practicality—begins with them; (2) they introduced an altogether new epoch in the history of Western culture—the epoch of textuality (that is, the regulation of social relations through fixed written texts).

According to our present state of knowledge, the Greeks, in a milieu of commercial interactions, adopted a consonant script from the Phoenicians in the first half of the eighth century, possibly before 776, the traditional beginning of the Olympic victor lists (Johnston 1983, 66; 1990). They improved it to fashion the complete phonemic script that we still use today (Heubeck 1979, 100; 1984, 549; Burkert 1992, 25–29). There immediately came into use the specific text types of everyday activity: merchandise lists, bills, and business correspondence, as well as private transactions of every sort, some in the form of inscriptions (Heubeck 1979, 94 f., 153 f.; 1984, 550). Indeed, writing had been adopted to meet just such practical requirements of communication. This does not mean, however, that all areas of life were instantaneously permeated by texts as a ubiquitous means of communication, record keeping, archiving, administration, education, and so on. Life was not yet "textualized." Though already making use of writing in specific areas, society was not at this point altogether dominated by it.

This slow evolution is quite understandable in terms of historical development: the Greeks at the moment of their adoption of the alphabet had behind them about four hundred years of illiteracy. Their first phase of literacy had broken off between 1200 and 1100 with the collapse of their highly developed system of central administration. The skills of reading and writing not only had been lost but in most areas were forgotten even as a cultural technique. In this long phase of illiteracy, the communicational and behavioral forms of an oral society had again developed (the so-called *condicio humana oralis,* "oral human condition"). These forms could not, of course, vanish instantly upon the revival of writing in the eighth century. First, the new, writing-determined styles of life had to evolve again; the many potential uses of the new medium had to be discovered. This process, contrary to earlier assumptions, seems to have gone on quite continuously (Heubeck

1979, 87) but should still be reckoned at a few decades (Burkert 1992, 27). A whole series of consistent speech forms (including noncommercial ones) typical of oral cultures will certainly have been transferred into written forms already during this period. Examples are the list— with its variants the catalog and the genealogy (Goody 1977, 74 ff.)— the prayer, and the proverb, among others. (It is improbable that Homer himself first brought such speech forms over into writing all at once.) These initially rather isolated usages do not seem, however, to have led to a regular *system* of text use (one of the first forms of intertextuality). This same conclusion can be reached on the basis of the nature of earlier examples of alphabetic writing. There has come down to us from this opening phase of literacy only what were originally marginal variants, mostly graffiti on potsherds (Heubeck 1979, 152). Clearly, in this period, writing was still "primarily an activity relevant only to the actual moment, whose products, in the usual course of things, could and even should disappear as soon as they had served their purpose" (Heubeck 1979, 152). Such a moment-to-moment function of literacy, however, does not yet provide the basis for textuality.

Homer as the Founder of Western Textuality

Textuality is achieved only with the institution of text use for the purposes of preservation: the notation and storing of data, occurrences, judgments, achievements, and so forth, in the form of records, registers, law codes and collections, chronicles, and so on. For these steps in literacy to be perceived, aspired to, and attained requires, psychologically speaking, a "will to recollection" through "compilation and preservation" (Wimmel 1981, 6, 9). This desire to preserve occurs sooner or later in all literate cultures. In the literate Near Eastern and Egyptian cultures, it expressed itself in, among other things, kings' inscriptions, reports of governmental acts, and the recording of old, often poetically framed saga traditions. It cannot be established just how and when it expressed itself for the first time in literate *Greek* culture. However, it seems certain that the *Iliad* and subsequently the *Odyssey* owed their notation in writing precisely to this will to preserve. For at least behind the *Iliad* there clearly exists the desire of the social stratum whose value system the poem portrays and propagates to erect itself a monument (Heubeck 1979, 159; Latacz 1984a). But once this notion of saving the otherwise transient by fixing it in writing is born and visibly realized, it finds adherents and spreads by the proliferation of texts throughout all areas of social life suited to it: textuality begins.

The *Iliad* (and in its wake the *Odyssey*) played the role of harbingers in this process. This conclusion issues from a reliable indication: the beginning of textuality in early literate cultures can regularly be deduced from a sudden increase in the quantity of texts. This increase in texts is not the same as an (always chronologically preceding) increase in items that document the use of writing; the latter merely indicates the spreading of the mastery of script, that is, the mere facility in writing and reading. In Greece, this ensued already around 750 at the latest ("A cultural explosion has happened here," Burkert 1992, 28). By comparison, the moment of increase in the quantity of texts was apparently reached around 700. From that point forward, the quantity not only of literary texts (Hesiod, Kallinos, Tyrtaios, Arkhilokhos, Alkman [Latacz 1990, 237–39, with fig. 3 on 258]) but also of practical texts, such as statutes and decrees (Hölkeskamp 1992, esp. 97–102), grew by leaps and bounds. Now the period *after* ca. 700 was, by nearly all indications that we have (see chap. 2, "Homer's Work: When and How") demonstrably already post-Iliadic and, somewhat less certainly, post-Odyssean. The inference is that Homer first brought about the actual breakthrough of eighth-century Greek culture to textuality with his extensive body of work (or at least with the *Iliad*).

This significance of Homer—the foundation of Western textuality—secures a high degree of interest in his work today, especially among ethnologists, anthropologists, sociologists, cultural historians, and communication theorists. But even in the actual authorized fraternity of classical philology the first signs of this new interest in Homer are making themselves felt. Walter Wimmel, a philologist at Marburg, writes:

> because the basic themes of our intellectual household have been furnished by the record we associate with the name Homer, "Homer" has achieved a continuous preeminence in the development of the major text [western textuality]. . . . Our literature with all its emanations has remained "Homer-determined" right up to the present. (1981, 23)

Similarly, though with a somewhat different emphasis, the American Hellenist and oral theorist Eric A. Havelock had three years earlier put it as follows:

> [The writing out of the *Iliad* and the *Odyssey*] was something like a thunder-clap in human history. . . . It constituted an intrusion into culture, with results that proved irreversible. It laid the basis for the destruction of the oral way of life and the oral modes of thought. . . . What set in with the alphabetization of Homer was a process of erosion of "orality," extending over centuries of the European experience. (1978, 3–4)

The importance of the turning point in cultural history that Homer signifies can in fact hardly be overestimated. Since the *Iliad* and the *Odyssey*, the culture of the West has been a writing and text culture, one that conserves in writing all its science, knowledge, and desire, constantly storing layer upon layer. It is thereby protected against forgetfulness but also condemned to supersession. The consequences of this textuality for the evolution, the present condition, and the outlooks of modern society are currently the subject of intensive debate, especially in the United States (Goody and Watt 1963; Havelock 1978, 1986; Wimmel 1981; Goody 1982, 1986, 1987; Ong 1982; Murray 1993, 92–101).

Naturally this newly established relevance of Homer as regards his function in cultural history has also provoked renewed interest in the individuality peculiar to his poetry. The trait profile and the course of development of a literate culture are often predetermined by the character of the text that stands at its beginning. In the case of the *Iliad* and the *Odyssey*, a prior decision distinctively shaped the character of this text. When the Greeks in the eighth century B.C. established (unawares) the particular form of textuality and literary mentality that remains with us today, they did so by an act of choosing. Two literate cultures with more than two thousand years in development offered themselves for emulation—the Near Eastern and the Egyptian; each had produced literary texts of no mean quality. The existence of both literatures was quite well known to the Greeks at this time, as is evidenced in the importing of motifs from them into the *Iliad* and the *Odyssey* (Burkert 1992, 88–100). The Aramaic and Phoenician variants of these literate cultures in particular must have forced themselves on the attention of the Greeks. For the Greeks took over from the Phoenicians the very instrument of literature—writing. The extent of Aramaic-Phoenician literature (mostly recorded on leather rolls) was already considerable in the eighth century (Burkert 1992, 30–31). The development of the literary mentality of the West might have followed another course, had the Greeks acted in the same manner as their Etruscan, Roman, and medieval successors later did; all these adopted the literature as well as the script of their respective schoolmasters. They thereby made possible the unified literary mentality of the West from Homer to the literature of the present. The Greeks alone decided otherwise. They isolated the instrument from its products and used it for the creation of a literature of their own. The works that they installed at the beginning of this new line of literary development were not foreign imports; they were the creations of their own genius: the *Iliad* and the *Odyssey*.

The Poetic Quality of the Homeric Epics

Of course, only the preconditions for Homer's influence were established by this decision. Homer's epics might have been specific to their time to such an extent that a generation or two later they would no longer have been perceived as relevant and attractive. That even today, twenty-seven hundred years later, one may speak of the "Homer-determined current of our literacy" (Wimmel 1981, 24) shows that just the reverse was true. Homer's influence, right from the start, had rested on his very freedom from direct time conditioning, that is, on time-independent qualities. The history of Homer reception among the Greeks themselves, the Romans, and modern readers is proof of Homer's obvious quality for all times, especially when an attempt was made to deny it. The decision of the Greeks of the eighth century appears less a stroke of luck than an inevitability.

But if the true basis for Homer's enduring power to impress is his poetic quality, then the real "Homeric Question" must address not the genesis of the *Iliad* and the *Odyssey* but what constitutes this quality. Accordingly, the work as poetic construct and aesthetic phenomenon is situated at the center of this book. The question of the manner in which the work originated is kept in the background. Thus, only that aesthetic attitude according to which Homer created in the beginning will be suggested to the modern reader.

Homer's Nearness

In recent years, much time has been spent, especially in Germany, explaining how distant Homer is from us. The talk was of the "alterity" or "otherness" of Homer, of his "nonrelevance," of the (for us) "last extremity of incomprehensible foreignness" of Homeric society (Wickert-Micknat 1982, 4). Behind such expressions lies above all an overestimation of our inherent uniqueness, which strikes one as absurd against the background of the six hundred thousand years of human history. The period that divides us from Homer amounts to not much more than eighty generations. The foreignness between Homer and ourselves, apparent chiefly in external forms, shrinks away in the face of the obvious constants taken together. Each reader will discover for herself or himself what is immutable in human thoughts, values, and aspirations (perhaps a striving for a high degree of achievement, success, beauty, pleasantness of social forms and fluent expression; perhaps a sense of pride and a consciousness of dignity and self-worth). In the chapters that follow, impressive parallels in the artistic sphere will, I hope, appear: the desire and ability to compose judiciously, to construct logically but not plainly or simplemindedly, to motivate rationally and yet with exquisite discrimination, to delineate complete characters of diverse complexity, to devise conflicts and to resolve them convincingly—in short, to reflect the world in all its characteristics in a work of verbal art and to explain it meaningfully.

Were Homer really foreign to us, then our present world could hardly be recognized in him so consistently as has occurred in the modern reflection of cultural history on the beginnings of our Western identity. The new interest in Homer thus finally reveals itself as a renewed awareness of a substantial proximity of the ancient and the modern, a proximity sometimes lost sight of in talk of irreversible historical alienation. It is a secondary aim of this book to enhance the awareness of this proximity.

2

The Person, Environment, Time, and Work of Homer

The Source Situation: Nothing Authentic

"Homerus caecus fuisse dicitur" [Homer is supposed to have been blind.] This insignificant little example sentence, accepted on faith by generations of students of Latin grammar, contains in a nutshell the crucial qualification that applies to all statements about Homer's person and career: he is *supposed* to have been blind. So even the ancients knew nothing for certain about the greatest of all poets. Modern research has hardly improved matters. Mostly we are dealing with guesswork.

The case of Homer in this regard has sometimes been compared to that of Shakespeare, but the comparison is not apt: some two hundred entirely contemporary original documents provide information about Shakespeare. These range from the entry in the baptismal registry in Stratford-on-Avon to the signature in his own hand on the pages of his will. The dates of his birth and death (1564 and 1616, respectively) have been handed down. Entries in church registries, records of sale and transfer of property, legal documents, letters, and public notices of the performances of Shakespeare's theater company inform the biographer about family relations, property ownership, and occupational circumstances.

About Homer's personal life, by contrast, there exists not a single contemporary document. Even the earliest extant sources that name Homer—references in poets and philosophers of the seventh and sixth centuries B.C.—speak of him as a man of a past era. Moreover, these sources themselves do not stand in a firm chronological order; there existed no absolute, consistent reckoning of time, so one did not date what one wrote. Thus we cannot say precisely when Homer lived. Understandably, this total lack of documentary evidence led to a tendency among nineteenth-century philologists, with their faith in empirical data, to deny altogether the existence of a historical person Homer. Conjectures were rife: possibly the name *Homer* did not refer to an individual but was a collective designation, which indicated "only in a general way an arranger of old songs or a member of a singers guild" (Christ 1905, 32). The twentieth century has rejected such speculations and reestablished Homer as a historical personage. A mainstay in this rehabilitation of the historical Homer has been the ancient *vitae* (Latin *vita*, "life" or "biography"), despite their problematic value as documentary evidence.

The Homer Legend: A False Track

Seven Greek-language *Lives* of Homer have come down to us. In addition there is a substantial treatise known as the *Agon Homeri et Hesiodi* (*Contest of Homer and Hesiod*). To be sure, these narratives all originated in the era of the Roman Empire, more than five hundred years after Homer. Still, some scholars have thought that rigorous source criticism might enable one to determine the provenance and thus the original source of particular elements in these narratives. In fact, it has proven likely that parts of these texts—for example, the debate over Homer's birthplace—date back to the seventh century B.C. This likelihood has prompted renewed critical examination of the stories. Results have not as yet repaid the efforts expended in this direction. Essentially, there have been two, regarding Homer's name and regarding his home.

As for the name, inscriptional evidence for *Homāros* (an Aeolic dialect variant of *Homēros*) shows that Greek parents could in fact at one time name a male child "Surety" or "Pledge" (terms that comprise Aristotle's explanation of the meaning of *Homeros*). As for the place where the poet lived and worked, the region of Greek settlements along the coast of Asia Minor has emerged as most probable (see, most recently, West 1988, 172; Vogt 1991, 375), especially the zone where Ionian Greek and Aeolian Greek areas abut: Smyrna; Erythrai and the neighboring island of Khios; Phokaia; Kyme and the region of the Hermos River southward from Smyrna, perhaps along the whole coastal strip past Kolophon to Miletos. (This is the present-day area extending from Izmir, near Smyrna, about fifty kilometers north and about 100 kilometers south; from Izmir to the ruins of Kyme is no more than 40 kilometers along the coast road.) The celebrated quarrel of the seven cities, however, is most easily decided in favor of Smyrna. ("Seven cities contended to be the home of Homer. Even those generally lacking in education know enough to adduce this as the flower of their erudition," Wilamowitz 1916, 367.) This was the conclusion achieved by the sum of the efforts of Ulrich von Wilamowitz-Moellendorff, who made lasting contributions in this subcategory of Homeric scholarship also: "thus there can be no doubt of the existence of the poet Homaros or Homeros of Smyrna" (Wilamowitz 1916, 372). For the rest, however, Wilamowitz warned, in this area "confident answers can be given only if they overlook the unsatisfactory premises on which every conclusion rests" (Wilamowitz 1916, 376). Unfortunately, this warning was ignored and the material continued to be worked over.

In 1940, a far more important Homer scholar took an interest in this "chaos of the anecdotal" (Lesky 1967, 690 [3])—namely, Wolfgang Schadewaldt, in his *Legende von Homer dem fahrenden Sänger* ["Legend of Homer the Traveling Singer"], which appeared in 1942 and then reached a large public in a 1959 reprint (Artemis-Verlag). Schadewaldt undertook first of all to arrange the *Lives* in an at least somewhat meaningful totality and to link that reconstruction to the aforementioned *Contest of Homer and Hesiod.* He then translated the whole into German in a style that was consciously legendary. Finally, an appended "Commentary" sifted out the "Reality of the Legend." Schadewaldt's results, compared to those of Wilamowitz, were quite positive. They culminated in the conviction that "the image of Homer in the legend should not be held in contempt" (Schadewaldt 1959a, 61). Accordingly, Schadewaldt was inclined to accept as true not only the name and home but also the whole *manner of life* that the stories attribute to Homer: "If we willingly follow the deeds and sufferings of the blind itinerant, we may still ultimately glimpse the countenance of the poet between the lines of the legend" (Schadewaldt 1959a, 61).

That assessment was overly confident, as we see today. (In other works, furthermore, Schadewaldt himself reached other conclusions; see Schadewaldt 1943.) Whoever follows Schadewaldt in this opinion runs the risk of creating a false image of Homer. The "deeds and sufferings" of the blind itinerant, as more careful consideration quickly shows, cannot represent the experiences of the poet of the *Iliad* and the *Odyssey;* the singer of the legend is not the singer of our epics. To recognize this is the essential precondition of a proper evaluation of Homer's location and perspective and, therefore, the prerequisite for a proper determination of the level and status of Homeric epic as opposed to others. It is necessary, then, to provide an accurate rehearsal of the Homer legend, based here on the *Vita Herodotea* (Herodotean Life [of Homer]) (Wilamowitz 1929).

In Kyme, Melanopos and his wife have a daughter, Kretheïs, who, after her parents' death, grows up with a friend of the family; there, lacking proper supervision, she becomes pregnant by an unnamed man. Thereupon, because of the shame, her angry foster father sends her to a friend in the newly founded city of Smyrna. There, at a feast being held outside town by the river Meles, she brings Homer into the world, naming him Melesigenes, because he was "born at the Meles" River. Clearly discernible here are two of the principal tendencies of the legend: (1) to balance competing claims (if Kyme and Smyrna strove so intransigently for the honor of being Homer's birth city, this could have only one cause: Homer must have been born at both places—to wit, conceived in Kyme, delivered in Smyrna; here we see the razor-sharp logic of the Sophists and ask ourselves for the first time how seriously the inventor meant us to take this material); (2) to lower Homer's social status (his mother was a child of simple folk and grew up in irregular circumstances; his father was unknown and Homer was conceived out of wedlock, his birth rather a casual incident, like "dropping a litter").

The boy Melesigenes is certainly not blind. His mother, being quite destitute, hires out to do spinning and other housework for an unmarried schoolmaster named Phemios (this is the name of the singer at Odysseus' house in Ithaka; here we have a third basic tendency: to represent the poems of Homer as crudely autobiographical). Here the boy becomes an enthusiastic student and seizes the opportunity to learn reading and writing "and all the other arts of the Muses." He does this so well that, after the death of Phemios (who has of course married the boy's unattached mother in the meantime), he is able to take over the school and make it prosper even more. By this time he has become famous (we are not told how), and the merchants and sailors from the harbor of Smyrna often sit with him and listen to him in the evenings.

One day a certain Mentes from Leukas (again a character from the *Odyssey*) persuades him to go to sea with him, while he is still young, "to see lands and cities" (at the beginning of the *Odyssey*, it is said of Odysseus that "he saw the cities of many men" [*Od.* 1.3]). The young man agrees and goes along with him to sea. He "everywhere undertakes investigations" and "certainly makes himself written memoranda about everything." On his return journey from Etruria (!) and Spain, they come to Ithaka also. There Melesigenes is afflicted by a disease of the eyes, so that Phemios must leave him behind with his friend, the Ithakan Mentor (still another character from the *Odyssey*): "There Melesigenes had the opportunity to make extensive researches and inquiries about Odysseus." One day Mentes comes to take him from Ithaka and he again sails around in the world with him.

Finally, Melesigenes stays in Kolophon, where he finally goes blind. Then he goes back to Smyrna and "takes up the poet's craft." But he soon falls into poverty and decides to move to Kyme. On the way, however, he stops in a settlement near Kyme at a shoemaker's workshop. There, he treats the shoemaker Tykhios (!) to poems about the Theban War and to hymns to the gods, and he wins a great reputation. But soon it goes badly for him again (we are not told why), and he sets out for Kyme. There he presents his poetry in a public hall in the marketplace where the elders spend time; he wins respect and ultimately asks for public maintenance. But the council of the city refuses him after a heated session: "if we choose to support the blind, we will soon have to deal with a great horde of useless people" (in the *Odyssey*, this is the reaction of the suitors to the concern that Penelope, Telemakhos, and Eumaios show for the strange beggar). Melesigenes thereafter bears the name Homeros, because the Kymeans allegedly call blind men by this name (a pure linguistic fabrication).

He curses Kyme and moves again, first to Phokaia, where he once more presents his poems in the public halls, and where he falls into the trap of a certain Thestorides, who offers him room and board in return for all his poems. After he has transcribed all of Homer's dictated poetry, he absconds with the manuscripts to Khios. Homer then journeys to Erythrai and from there with some fishermen to Khios, intending to call Thestorides to account. On Khios, however, he gets lost and ends up on the farm of a goatherd named Glaukos, where he is menaced by dogs (as in the scene of Odysseus with Eumaios in the fourteenth book of the *Odyssey*). Glaukos then leads Homer to his master at Bolissos, where he is engaged as tutor. He composes "light verses" for the two young charges he is to instruct; among these is the *Battle of Frogs and Mice*.

Finally, he moves to the capital city of the island (Thestorides vacates just in time!), opens a school, and teaches interested parties how to compose poetry. He takes a wife and has two daughters by her and also works on the *Odyssey* and the *Iliad* (while still serving as schoolmaster!). Into the epics, he "inserts" all those who have done him kindness during his travels: Mentes, Mentor, Phemios, the shoemaker Tykhios, and finally—in anticipation, because he would like to visit Athens—even the Athenians. On the journey to Athens, he winters on Samos, where he spends his time among the people of the city, composes a song for some potters, and begs before the houses of the wealthy with a petition song of his own inventing. Finally, he comes to the mainland, where he visits Athens, Corinth, and Argos; he then recites his *Hymn to Apollo* at the great Ionian festival on Delos.

At length, he somehow arrives at the small island of Ios, where he falls ill on the seashore and becomes a "tourist attraction" for the people of the city. One day a few young fishermen come to him there. They pose him and the people standing around him on the beach the so-called Louse Riddle: "What we caught, we left behind; what we missed, we bring along." Thereupon, some say, he supposedly died out of chagrin at not being able to solve the riddle. The townspeople of Ios bury him and set up a tombstone with an epitaph that praises him as "divine Homer."

Obviously, most of this "biography" is woven out of material taken from the epics, especially the *Odyssey*. More important, the author who concocted the whole thing took no trouble to camouflage his intent. The enterprise actually tends toward the grotesque: we have the schoolmaster from Khios giving to the leather-worker who made Aias' shield (*Il.* 7.220) the name of his benefactor in the area of Kyme, Tykhios the shoemaker; and we have the author, in connection with the story of the Louse Riddle, expressing—in the formulaic style of the "poet's *Life*"— his doubts about the factual content in this particular case, with the apparently serious attitude of a scholar.

The whole "tradition" besides contains much that is laughable, as in the verses that are imputed to Homer as sporadic proofs of his ability, which brought Schadewaldt himself to a suspicion of "parody" (Schadewaldt 1959a, 57 f.), though he immediately rejected the notion. Possibly we have at work less of the people's naive delight in storytelling, as Schadewaldt envisages it, and more of the satire of an intelligent wag who is mischievously making fun of the conventional forms of the tradition of a poet's *Life* (and the credulity of the masses). Be that as it may, this is not a seriously meant biography. Such a work could serve for entertainment, not instruction (the term *folk book* has been applied to it with justice and it has been compared to the *Till Eulen-spiegel* [a medieval German tale of a merry prankster]).

This is the essential fact: the image of the poet sketched in the *Lives* has hardly anything in common with the one that confronts us in the epics. The Homer of this legend is a blind, begging singer who hangs around with little people: shoemakers, fishermen, potters, sailors, elderly men in the gathering places of harbor towns. Being a school-teacher, who teaches reading and writing, he associates above all with children. He is a clever versifier, who amazes members of the middle class and only once, with the Khian in Bolissos, comes in touch with the upper classes, before whose homes he is accustomed to beg for hand-outs with original short poems. It has been observed quite correctly that all this "stands in peculiar opposition to the sphere in which we envisage the poet of the *Iliad*" (Lesky 1967, 692 [5]).

Whoever constructed this image of the poet—whether or not with parodic intent—had in mind a kind of verse maker who pursued his vocation on a relatively low social stratum. This vocation first emerged when business and trade, the state and the community, were in full flower, and when the culture of the nobility had been pushed to the periphery. It was a time when the middle class was trend setting and the spirit of enterprise counted for more than wealth (witness the founding of schools). This was the occupational situation of the rhap-sodes, performing artists comparable to modern concert singers, who, then as now, gained fame by going "on tour"; they presented no origi-nal compositions, only reproducing the masterpieces of others. The Homer legend anachronistically depicts the greatest poet of an earlier time as such a rhapsode, since its inventors knew no other type of singer at their time. But they also had to depict the famous creator of the *Iliad* and the *Odyssey* as improvising, not merely reproducing, his verses. This involved the mixing of two incompatible modes of exis-tence; even Schadewaldt fell afoul of this when he spoke of the "rhap-sode Homer" who at the same time is supposed to have been "a much-admired virtuoso" and a "fast-thinking extemporaneous poet" (Schadewaldt 1959a, 65 f.).

On the whole, it is clear that the inventors of the legend had as little authentic information about the historical Homer as we do: "Antiquity knew nothing definite about the life and personality of Homer" (Kirk 1985, 1). The image substituted for the reality takes its complexion from

(1) the epics themselves and (2) the circumstances of a singer's life in the contemporary world. The latter were completely unsuitable. The former were much more appropriate in themselves, but, in their day, the inventors of the legend lacked the means and method to interpret them adequately.

Firm Ground: Homer's Indirect Self-Representation

Modern Homeric scholarship, armed with word indexes and concordances, makes deductions from the *Iliad* and the *Odyssey* altogether different from those made by the creators of the legendary Homer. In both epics, professional poets appear alongside many other occupation groups. They are called singers, *aoidoi*. It is obvious that, in depicting them, the poet of the *Iliad* and the *Odyssey* made use of his own experiences as a singer, mostly unconsciously, sometimes consciously. This has long since been recognized by such scholars as Wolfgang Schadewaldt (1943), Hermann Fränkel (1973; originally published in 1951), Walther Marg (1957), and Herwig Maehler (1963). From the manner in which the fictive singers are formed from the real singer, we may deduce a good deal about Homer's existence and self-conception.

Four singers appear in the *Odyssey*. All work at the courts of great lords and thus are court singers, not folksingers. The first is found at the court of Agamemnon in Argos: "the son of Atreus, when he set out for Troy, enjoined him to safeguard his wife" (*Od.* 3.267 f.); this singer thus functions as a confidant and almost as a proxy for the king. The second is found at the court of Menelaos at Sparta: when Menelaos celebrated the marriages of both his daughter and his son on the same day, "there sang among them the inspired singer, playing his lyre" (*Od.* 4.17). The third is found at the court of Alkinoös, the king of the Phaiakians; his name is Demodokos. The fourth is found at the court of Odysseus on Ithaka—namely, Phemios, the son of Terpios (that is, "Speaker," son of "Rejoicer").

All four are obviously well established in the service of a court, enjoy great respect (in the first case, even as a personal confidant of the prince himself), and have nothing whatever to do with shoemakers, potters, fishermen, and their kind. To be sure, the *Odyssey* does make mention once (in book 17) of a singer from another social stratum. It is an instructive case: the suitor Antinoös angrily demands of Eumaios the swineherd why he has brought in this beggar (Odysseus in disguise):

"do we not already have enough vagabonds and troublesome beggar folk hereabouts to spoil our feasting?" Eumaios responds: "Who would willingly invite a stranger into the land, unless he were one of those who work for the good of the whole people (*dēmioergoi*)—a seer or one who heals the sick or a wood-worker or even a blessed singer who can give pleasure with his song!" (*Od.* 17.375–85). Here the singer is grouped together with other "public workers," who place their skill at the disposal of everyone, not only of the court and the wealthy with their special needs. It is, of course, the swineherd who speaks of this type of singer. The poet himself never mentions such singers, nor do men of station in his poems. Concealed behind this is a sense of distance, perhaps not exactly arrogance, but a clear awareness of difference. Of course, that is hardly surprising in the world of the *Iliad* and the *Odyssey*, where differences in achievement and gradations of rank are unfailingly significant. Just as warriors differ one from another, so too singers differ. Naturally, in this world there are competitions not only at the festival contests; in daily life, in every occupation, at every moment, it is a matter of winning out and excelling. Thus, the singer is tested and rated not only at official competitions but above all in the challenge of everyday life.

The testing and rating of singers are shown quite explicitly in the singer scene with Demodokos and the Phaiakians. There, the singer is unexpectedly called into the palace (*Od.* 8.43–45). After he is first permitted to sing a song of his own choosing (8.73–82), he is suddenly presented with two very dissimilar extempore requests: the king asks him for a dancing song (8.250–55), while the guest Odysseus wants a heroic song about the fall of Troy, more specifically, about the wooden horse (8.488–98). To begin with, this reflects the extreme demands on his repertoire to which the poet of this singer scene was accustomed. Demodokos meets both demands with bravura. Thereupon, the poet has Odysseus bestow the following words of praise: "Yes, indeed, it is good to listen to a singer of this sort, like this one, whose gift of song is godlike!" (9.3 f.).

This sharp differentiation of singers of unlike quality ("a singer like this one") is clearly a projection of the *Odyssey* poet's own professional experience. (The poet has proven himself a master singer by his poetic ability to create both such a "star" singer and his songs.) With the obvious localizing of the highest caliber singer at the prince's court, the poet furthermore lets it be known that he assumes a social scale of singers, within which, for him, "the palace-singer" is the pinnacle. When one refers this projection back to Homer's own reality, it is clear whose horizon of expectations and level of demands he had in mind: those of an upper-class audience. This upper class, which was also the ruling elite, was, right into the fifth century, composed of aristocrats, that is, of people we call the nobility.

Further Clarifications: Homer's Identification with His Foremost Public, the Nobility

That Homer addressed himself to nobles is reflected not only in the criteria by which the creations of his fictional colleagues (and therefore also his own creations) are judged in the epics; it is reflected above all in the general themes of the *Iliad* and the *Odyssey*, in the atmosphere of the events they narrate, and in the thoughts, feelings, and not least the manners of the poetic characters (Hohendahl-Zoetelief 1980). The world of social strata beneath the nobility, down to slaves and laborers, is of course included, but only as a background seen always through the eyes of the nobility. Thus, in the epics, the vulgar, the base, the banal, and the truly sordid are deliberately excluded; where ugliness does appear (for example, in the Thersites episode in *Iliad* 2), it is "dematerialized" through a kind of aesthetic of ugliness. This accords with the goal of this art, which by displaying beauty (in the broad sense of a manifestation of the reality of existence) seeks to captivate the susceptible listener in a pleasurable experience (Marg 1957, 16 ff.). The singer could find an appreciation for such an artistry only among those from whose manner of life it originated and of which it was now an indispensable element—among the nobles. Their freedom from the necessity to earn a living by the sweat of their brow had given them leisure time, which they had long used not only for dancing, games, hunting, and sport, but also for aesthetic delights associated with personal adornments, care of the body, cosmetics, and so on, and for the art of song.

The poet illustrates this link between art and nobility in the *Iliad*, even though the subject matter of the poem—warfare—did not lend itself to the presentation of a singer; in book 9, Akhilleus, the strongest warrior, a member of the highest nobility, and the son of the goddess Thetis, is shown as a singer:

they met [Akhilleus] as he was delighting his mind with the lyre,
   the clear-sounding,
beautiful, well-wrought lyre; and it had a bridge of silver.
He had chosen it for himself out of the spoils when he had
   destroyed the city of Eëtion.
With this he was trying to cheer himself, and he sang of the
   famous deeds of long-ago heroes.

(Il. 9.186–89)

The strongest warrior chooses from the booty not the best sword but
the lyre; and with it he sings of the same things as the *Iliad* poet (with,
of course, a shift in time frame): the famous deeds of long-ago heroes.
This would be acceptable only to a public that saw its own ideal of the
highest form of self-realization reflected in this combination of warrior
and artist.

Homer could not have made clearer the natural link between nobility and heroic song, nor could he have declared more clearly his own
membership in this social sphere. The self-identification of the poet of
the *Iliad* and the *Odyssey* with the ideals of the nobility is more indispensable to an appreciation of his poems than most concrete biographical details might be. It makes the irreplicably high quality of the poems
comprehensible and can only have originated from a total concentration and a consistent ends-oriented thinking typical of the aristocratic
view of life and humankind (Latacz 1984a). This feature of Homer's
poems explains in large part the constant fascination that the works
have exerted over the ages on the most receptive minds. It also sets a
standard for the comparisons commonly made in the past fifty years
between Homeric epic and that of other peoples and cultures. While
the results of such comparisons have repeatedly shown a startling similarity in the techniques of the singers, a no less startling dissimilarity in
quality has also been revealed. The explanation for this dissimilarity
lies precisely where it has least been sought: in the disparity of social
status among the composers. Serbian coffeehouse singers, modern
Greek farmers, shepherds, and water carriers (Kakridis 1971, 114),
Russian fishermen (Bowra 1952, 417), and other, similar singers belong
to an altogether different social stratum from Homer. They can continue the old heroic sagas in the old techniques of singers; they can, by
sound basic training in the craft and by long practice, sometimes even

cast new material in the old style of song. But they can never imbue their productions with the spirit of the aristocratic mode of living. That spirit makes heroic poetry the living self-justification of a social class instead of mere storytelling. To this spirit belongs a type of singer who has much in common with the singing Akhilleus of the *Iliad*, a singer who can depict the milieu and lineaments of the characters he sketches with such flawless consistency and genuineness, because the poet himself so evidently thinks and feels in such terms.

Such mastery is attainable in two ways only: either (1) the poet himself belongs to the aristocracy (this is the oldest situation among the Greeks as among other peoples [Bowra 1952, 410 ff.; Schmid 1929, 59–60; Fränkel 1973, 9 f.]) and devotes himself to poetry on the strength of a special love for the art, a special talent for it, or a special situation in life—many researchers have in fact assumed this for Homer (Nestle 1942; Schadewaldt 1943, 63; Marg 1957, 16, 36); or (2) the poet lives permanently in the milieu of nobles. In support of the first interpretation one may refer to the aristocratic lineage of many post-Homeric ancient Greek poets (for example, Arkhilokhos, Alkaios, Pindar, Aiskhylos). In Homer's case, we lack the means to choose between the two alternatives, but it is clear in general that he did not belong to the category of singer that Wilhelm Schmid—based on the results of research in comparative epic—had characterized in his *History of Greek Literature* as "poor, old, blind, otherwise unemployable itinerant folk," who "carried the ideals of the aristocracy to a broader range of people and . . . yet, in so doing, were less hindered from making use of a certain criticism, because of their distance from the court" (1929, 60). By including Homer in just this category of individual, the Homer legend—as Schmid put it in the same place—proves itself to be false.

Even today the nobility's style of living jumps out with directness and vigor at the reader of the *Iliad* and the *Odyssey*. To be sure, this vividness could only have been achieved by a singer who belonged to a time when that style of living was so dominant and prevalent that it could, so to say, disclose itself in the composition of the singer. Specific styles of life in works of art have an authentic effect only when their reflection proceeds from their time of flowering. Here we have the decisive criterion for the dating of Homer. Such other dating criteria as the mentioning (or not) of particular objects, customs, practices, institutions, stylistic features, and so on in the epics can have only a supporting function. The time of Homer's life and creative work is restricted to the era of the fullest flowering of the nobility in Greece.

Based on the results of current archaeological and historical research, this full efflorescence of the Greek aristocracy, as Homer sketches it, took place in the second half of the eighth century B.C. The eighth century is nowadays designated the time of the Greek Renaissance, and with good reason (Hägg 1983b). The parallels with the European Renaissance lie not in matters of economic and social structure but in the general character of an absolute resurgence of prosperity. More than fifty years ago, Wolfgang Schadewaldt, in his daring and trenchant essay "Homer und sein Jahrhundert," [Homer and His Century] (1942; cf. Heubeck 1974, 216), adduced specific phenomena to show how this renewal of prosperity manifested itself in the Greek world. Since that time, many new finds and discoveries have made the picture considerably clearer. The unique dynamism of this era can come to life, of course, only against the background of past developments. Therefore, a historical retrospective is necessary at this point.

An Approach to Homer's Audience: Prosperity, Collapse, and Resurrection of the Greek Aristocracy

The So-Called Mycenaean Era (Second Millennium B.C.)

The Indo-European ethnic group we call Greeks wandered into the Balkan Peninsula around 2000 B.C. It first experienced a period of rapid cultural improvement in the more highly developed Mediterranean environment under the influence of the advanced cultures of Sumerians, Babylonians, Hittites, Egyptians, and Minoan Cretans. Especially along the shores of the east coast of mainland Greece and in the Peloponnesos, this led to small "plain-states" with fortresslike administrative and distribution centers under the authority of a monarch ("king," "prince")—for example, eastern Thessaly with Iolkos; Boiotia with Orkhomenos, Gla, and Thebes; Attika with Athens; Argolis with Mycenae and Tiryns; Lakonia with Amyklai; Messenia with Pylos. In the fifteenth century, a first heyday was reached during a time of expansion that culminated in the conquest, annexation, and occupation of the Minoan royal seat of Knossos and of large parts of Crete. The Greeks took over many elements of Minoan culture, including its writing system, which they used for the transcription of their own language. This script was the more recent of the two syllabaries that the excavations of Arthur Evans had brought to light on baked-clay tablets found at Knossos in 1900: the so-called Linear B script. After going unread for three thousand years, these tablets were deciphered in 1952 by the British amateur archaeologist Michael Ventris, who identified them as representing the Greek language. By their adoption of the writing system and of the Minoan administrative exactitude that went with it, the Greeks strengthened the central authority, which now held in its hands all the strings of economic life in a given area of jurisdiction. This central authority determined the conditions not only of economic but also of military, religious, and artistic life. All sorts of measures to promote trade, including the construction of a road network (as revealed by recent extensive excavations), facilitated a definite economic boom. In various types of commercial endeavor, especially pottery manufacture, the production of surpluses led to the development of a thriving foreign trade. The export trade necessitated the establishment of entrepôts (emporiums). At many places in the Mediterranean region, these succeeded Minoan installations.

Archaeology has had particular difficulty in the discovery of these settlements (Mellink 1971 is fundamental), not least because the sites have often been inhabited without interruption so that many and various modern accumulations lie over the ancient strata. Nonetheless, some trading settlements on the Aegean islands, Cyprus, Rhodes, and especially the west coast of Asia Minor have already been discovered and evaluated. These include Miletos (from 1400 at the latest), Iasos (north of Bodrum), Müskebi (near Bodrum, ancient name unknown), Bayrakli (Old Smyrna), and Liman Tepe (Klazomenai); there are definite traces also near Ephesos, Kolophon, Knidos, and some other coastal sites. Greek pottery of this period has been found throughout the Mediterranean area and, to some extent, at such inland locations as Sardis, Masat in the contemporary Hittite Empire, and Troy. Imported in exchange were copper and tin, precious metals (gold and silver not only in ingots but also in finished goods, especially jewelry and finery), textiles, spices and aromatics, ivory, and the like.

In the central palaces, this trading resulted not only in the amassing of extraordinary riches but also in a refinement in style of living, as evidenced most impressively in paintings (frescoes) from Knossos, Pylos, and Thera/Santorini. Many indications make it safe to assume that verbal art, too, played its part (see "Heroic Song as Self-Validation"), at least in the form of oral heroic poetry, which was an ancient Indo-European inheritance (Schmitt 1968). Constituting the audience for such art were the members of the royal family and of the ruling elite. We encounter these individuals in various capacities and with various titles in the Linear B tablets; they are a court nobility but also apparently a landed aristocracy—a midlevel ruling class in the regional centers of a given "province." Whether and to what extent the individual monarchies or "principalities" cooperated with one another is impossible to say at present, since up to now, other than in the eastern area, no correspondence of any kind between the centers has been found. (It is likely that nondurable writing materials were used for this purpose.) That contacts existed is clear from the similar writing systems, administrative organizations, and so forth. It is hardly plausible that such ventures as the invasion of the Minoan kingdom of Crete, which at this point still possessed naval dominance in the Aegean, occurred without the formation of an alliance.

This first Greek "advanced civilization" reached its pinnacle in the thirteenth century. It has been designated Mycenaean ever since Schliemann's excavation of Mycenae, under the influence of the *Iliad*, in which Mycenae is the home of Agamemnon, the commander in chief of all the Greek leaders. This designation has been thought inappropriate, and of late it has increasingly been replaced by the term *Akhaian civilization*, especially among English-speaking scholars. The Greeks are called Akhaians (*Akhaioi*) in Homer; Aḫḫijawā appears to be named as their settlement area or at least a part of it in contemporary Hittite texts (Page 1959; Güterbock 1984); *Akhaiwijā* turns up in a Linear B tablet from Knossos as the destination for a delivery of cattle (Gschnitzer 1971, 95; 1983, 153); and *Aqaj(ja)waša* in an Egyptian royal inscription of ca. 1200 designates some three thousand men who make up half of an attack force of "northern warriors" (Lehmann 1985, 50–56; 1991, 112). *Akhaians* is likely to be the label that at least a portion of these early Greeks of the Bronze Age applied to themselves (Latacz 1994a). However, as long as this designation is not universal in English-language scholarship or yet very common in the German-language literature or elsewhere in the international scholarly community, *Mycenaean* must continue to be used.

Internal military conflicts among these Mycenaean principalities certainly occurred during the centuries-long life of this civilization; these are reflected in later Greek myth, especially in the Theban War saga. Nevertheless, the overriding impression is one of peaceful coexistence. This situation came to a sudden end around 1200. Most of the royal establishments went up in flames. Since the destruction was more or less simultaneous everywhere, an invasion by outsiders must be assumed.

The identity of these invaders and destroyers is, however, still unknown, despite intensive research. More recent researchers no longer regard the so-called Dorian migration as the primary cause of the catastrophe of ca. 1200. (The migration was a sudden incursion of a culturally backward ethnic Greek subgroup, the Dorians, who had previously remained in the northern part of the Balkan Peninsula.) There was a striking synchronicity of destruction at Mycenaean sites, at widely dispersed centers of civilization outside the Greek world—such as Hattušas, capital of the Hittite Empire, and Ugarit, chief site of Hittite vassal principalities in the area of present-day Syria—at many centers in the Levant, and in Canaan as well as on Cyprus. This suggests a vast migratory movement, motivated by the extraordinary affluence of the civilizations of the eastern Mediterranean region; possibly, as the migrating people moved through a region, a variety of ethnic elements (including the Dorians in the Balkan area) traveled with them. The well-known historical phenomenon of "migration avalanche" has been cited in this connection (Dobesch 1983, 60). Contemporary Egyptian texts speak of a dangerous threat by the "Sea-Peoples," to whom they also ascribe the destruction of Hattušas. The Egyptians of the heartland itself were able to repulse the attackers, who arrived in two great waves before and after 1200. But they lost the Levant (to the Philistines, hence the later name *Palestine*) and suffered a considerable weakening. Although the Egyptian sources include some ten different names of individual groups under the general term "Sea-Peoples," a clear identification of these ethnic groups and determination of their origins remains elusive. In the present state of scholarly research, it is a plausible assumption that a more or less backward people from central Europe set the migration in motion. It is increasingly obvious that ethnic groups from the Italian Peninsula (especially in the area of the Adriatic) as well as (by sea) from Sardinia participated in the migration (Deger-Jalkotzy 1983a; Lehmann 1983, 1991); the people called Serds are clearly to be connected with the Sards—this would better account for the Egyptian terms "Sea-Peoples," "People of the Sea," and "People of the Islands"; Linear B texts from Pylos also speak of a threat by sea (Hiller and Panagl 1976, 117 ff.).

Particulars of the development, course, duration, numerical size, striking power, manner of attack, and goals of the whole movement are still unclear. With respect to the part of the migration that affected Greece, we may have a case of a relatively quick, temporary devastation by a foreign horde in whose wake a northern Greek ethnic group moved into the Mycenaean homelands, or perhaps the northern Greeks, simply stimulated by the movement, flocked southward more or less on their own initiative. In any case, no settlement of a foreign people took place on Greek soil, and the continuity of Greek settlement was not interrupted.

Also scarcely apparent as yet are the internal relations of the Mycenaean principalities at the time of this occurrence. They suffered a total military defeat despite (on the evidence of Linear B texts) the enlargement of their military and naval forces and defensive installations in general, including a considerable strengthening of the fortifications of the Mycenaean citadels toward the end of the thirteenth century. This seems to presuppose a prior weakening, whose causes we cannot discern at present. Was it a case of internal strife or one of foreign expeditions that drained their strength? In our present state of knowledge, we can only conclude that around 1200 a concerted attack by "Sea Peoples" occurred over all the eastern Mediterranean civilizations and a portion of their hinterlands in Asia Minor. This thoroughly upset the relative stability of the region and so convulsed its international political and economic relations within a comparatively brief time that we must speak of the end of an entire era of cultural development.

The So-Called Dark Ages: (ca. 1200–800 B.C.)

For Greek, as well as for Hittite, civilization the effects of the catastrophe of ca. 1200 were especially far-reaching. The destruction of the palaces, which represented the nerve centers of a finely exfoliated system of operations, caused a sudden rupture in the highly evolved life cycle in the affected areas. This rupture was final: the palaces were never rebuilt (the ruins were first excavated in modern times). This complete abandonment of the palaces and the regions under their control was in sharp contrast to the reconstruction that usually occurred in the Mediterranean area after periods of occupation or natural disasters.

This clearly points to a dramatic decimation through death and expulsion of the palace dwellers in particular, that is, of the Mycenaean ruling elite.

In fact, archaeology has demonstrated the existence in the twelfth century of a rapidly increasing number of Mycenaean foundations (refugee settlements) outside the homeland, especially on Cyprus and on the west coast of Asia Minor, where there had already been Mycenaean footholds. That Athens, the only center remaining undestroyed, was a refuge would also have to be accepted on the basis of the historical probabilities of expulsion and flight, even if later Greek texts reported nothing about it. Other places of refuge were the mountains of Arkadia, the Ionian islands (Kephallenia, Zakynthos), and certain islands of the Cyclades (for example, Naxos). Future excavations will hopefully shed more light on this matter. In no instance, however, do the new settlements appear to have led to a restitution of the old structures. Instead, they were evidently founded by relatively small groups of refugees, who of course lacked in their new settlement areas the large-scale operational basis of the homeland.

In the homeland, the loss of the upper level of the ruling elite and the cessation of central planning led to a far-reaching disintegration of overall operational coherence and thereby to the separation and isolation of population elements on the regional and local levels. There were displacements owing to flight, immigration, emigration, and assimilation. In addition there was clearly a considerable decline in population generally as a consequence of defensive struggles and associated disturbances. All these things undoubtedly led to an immediate, severe deterioration in the scale and quality of economic life. A highly efficient, surplus-producing society became for a long period a merely primitive, self-reproducing society. The old conditions of land possession had been nullified owing to the death, flight, or expulsion of earlier owners, especially the upper aristocracy, who, to judge from the Linear B texts, had owned a high proportion of the land. Also, the population had shrunk too drastically for the now masterless estates to be cultivated to the same extent and degree as in earlier times. For these reasons, the agrarian economy apparently gave way to a pastoral economy. (This explains the retention of Mycenaean place-names, themselves often taken over from the pre-Greek population, even in some areas where there now no longer were settlements [Sarkady 1975, 121;

followed by Snodgrass 1980, 35]). The very distinctive crafts and decorative arts of Mycenaean times, designed to satisfy the tastes chiefly of
landed aristocrats, now decayed or adapted themselves to new circumstances. In pottery, for example, the simple forms of the Geometric style
took the place of the more extravagant earlier designs. Metallurgists
responded to the cessation of imports of raw materials—copper and
tin—and to the closing of armament- and chariot-producing facilities
by opening more and more sources of the new raw material—iron. This
brought the transition from the Bronze to the Iron Age also in Greece.
All in all, then, the dominant image of the postcatastrophe era is one of
a general social retrogression.

Along with the central governments, there disappeared, at least in
the homeland, the most important administrative tool of those governments—writing (this was not the case on Cyprus, as is shown by the
new find of a late eleventh-century specimen of Greek writing at Kouk-
lia [Karageorghis 1980]). Since the archaeological finds bearing on this
issue were relatively scant, the lines of development of the so-called
sub-Mycenaean and proto-Geometric era long remained in darkness
for modern researchers. Consequently, this period, some three hundred to four hundred years in duration, was given the designation
"Dark Ages" (Tsountas and Manatt 1897, 363 ff.) Originally, this was
meant as a subjective judgment—they were "dark" *for us;* but many historians, philologists, and archaeologists right up to the present have
often used the term in an objective sense. They have used the label as if
the Greeks, throughout their entire settlement area in these centuries,
were hopelessly impoverished and benighted, if not extinct. Contributing to the prevalence of this misconception was an inexact formulation
of the so-called problem of continuity. Thus, Oswyn Murray, even in
1993, wrote: "the result of the collapse of Mycenaean culture was a dark
age, lasting for some three hundred years. Discontinuity with the past
was virtually complete" (8). It would perhaps be more correct to speak,
with Snodgrass, of a "profound economic, social and demographic
recession" (1980, 31), because continuity is obviously the salient fact of
the development. This is true of the basic configurations of ethnicity,
language, settlement, sustenance, and so on, as well as in such spheres
of higher culture as religion, where we find the same gods, and mythology, where we find the same subject matter, and very likely also in verbal artistry, where we find the same forms and techniques and the same

fundamental attitudes regarding values and reality. Rather than a matter of continuity versus discontinuity, the question is, How great is the
degree of discontinuity in the elements of high culture?

Even assuming this more precise reformulation of the question, we
find that spectacular archaeological finds of the past few years clearly
show that answers given in the past have proceeded from a false sense
of certainty and have been much too negative in character. In 1980, the
Cambridge archaeologist Anthony Snodgrass, discussing the meager-
ness of the Greek settlements in the "Dark Ages," adduced as his prime
example Lefkandi on Euboia. Based on the number of grave sites then
known, he estimated the average number of inhabitants of Lefkandi
between 1000 and 900 B.C. at some fifteen to twenty-five persons (Snodgrass 1980, 18). In the same year, at the very same site, excavators
revealed a magnificent tomb of a lord in a monumental apsidal structure 45 meters by 10 meters in area with an enclosing colonnade, all
clearly datable to between 1000 and 950 B.C. There were two graves.
One held the skeletons of four horses, the other that of a woman
adorned with gold and faience ornaments; beside her was the funerary
urn of the cremated lord, a bronze amphora graced with pictorial dec-
oration—a lion hunt. The numerous grave-gifts included pieces evidently imported from the Near East, Egypt, and Cyprus (Winter 1982).
Judgments about Lefkandi and its significance had to be radically
revised overnight: "there must have commenced in the later eleventh
century a prosperity that for the next two centuries made Lefkandi,
together with Athens, the richest state in Greece"; and, more to the
point for us, "there existed here a princely court where destitution did
not prevail and where merchants from the Levant were welcomed
guests" (Blome 1984, 9, 12; see also 1991). This shed new light also on
the importance of Euboia in the centuries between the Mycenaean collapse and the cultural resurgence of Greece: "in the tenth and ninth centuries, luxury goods from the Near East flowed into Euboia to an extent
we could hardly have imagined during the seemingly 'dark ages'"
(Blome 1984, 10; see also 1991; Latacz 1994a; Antonaccio, forthcoming).

Wolfgang Schadewaldt, already in 1942, brought about a general
awareness of the preeminent role that Euboia, with its two principal
ports, Khalkis and Eretria, played in the *eighth* century; he noted among
other things its sea power and commercial influence in the hinterland
of Boiotia, its founding of the first Greek colonies in Italy and Sicily,
and its transmission of the alphabet to the Etruscans, the Romans, and

thereby to ourselves. That this prominent role extends back into the eleventh century was first revealed in the excavations of 1979/80. We had actually known nothing about Lefkandi.

It appears, as the finds of the next few years disclosed, that when we spoke of the "Dark Ages," we did not know what we were talking about. In 1982, the ephor of Crete and director of the Herakleion Museum, Professor Jannis Sakellarakis, made a discovery that could decisively alter our image of the era between 1200 and 800 in the Greek motherland. In the grotto of Zeus, famous in myth, on the edge of the Lassithi Plateau on Crete, with the aid of modern, high-intensity flood-lights, he found in previously untouched strata thousands of votive offerings of all types and materials from all parts of the Greek world. Some 70 percent of the objects found in the campaigns of 1982 and 1983 derive from the period from 1100 to 725. Comparison of these objects with analogous contemporary items found previously on the Greek mainland will permit us to infer, among other things, the pilgrims' places of origin and thereby to provide data regarding distribution of population, commercial traffic between the mainland and Crete, the level of artistry on the mainland, and so forth (Winter 1984; Stock 1984; Sakellarakis 1988; and personal conversation with Professor Sakel-larakis).

These and numerous other, less sensational but still informative dis-coveries (on the mainland as well, especially in Phokis, Macedonia, and Thrace), justify the hope that the "Dark Ages" will in the foreseeable future be so thoroughly illuminated that the whole concept may be consigned to the annals of the history of scholarship (Deger-Jalkotzy 1991; Latacz 1994a). At this point, it has been confirmed that Greece in the period between the collapse of its first (Mycenaean) efflorescence and the beginning of its second cannot possibly have been impover-ished to the shattering degree previously supposed. As Lefkandi now shows, already by 1000 (if not before) in many sites in the motherland, a new prosperity, concentrated in the hands of aristocrats, had already been attained. This has lent welcome support to Sarkady's 1975 recon-struction (followed in part by Snodgrass 1980) of developments in the interval between 1200 and 800: after a temporary regression to simpler economic and social conditions, there was a gradual recuperation, driven by the Greek spirit of enterprise and spearheaded above all by the surviving members of the old aristocratic class. A lively sense of past greatness will have been a final stimulus. After a transitional

period of leveling in the distribution of wealth there was a renewal of
the diversification of property ownership. However, there was no concomitant restoration of an overall royal authority, with easily explained
exceptions in certain districts that for various reasons had experienced
no sudden interruption in development, such as Athens and later the
new Dorian foundation of Sparta. Instead, there was a desultory evolution of limited local aristocracies that furnished leadership in war and
in peace and derived their authority from family lineage and property
ownership. Replacing the absolute decision-making power of the earlier supraregional lord (*wanax*) was a kind of participatory administration, with a council of nobles and a communal assembly. After a temporary regression to isolated, nomadic modes of existence during the
chaotic times of war and flight, there was a preference for resuming old
customs by grouping homes together in relatively close proximity. The
designation for these communities was "polis," a term encountered in
related forms already in Linear B texts (cf. Mycenaean and Homeric
πτόλις). Of course, the word at first carried only the superficial meaning "place of habitation." The meaning "city-state" evolved only later.
The new foundations were sometimes situated on the remains of pre-
war settlements, but they were more frequently on new sites.

Using archaeological evidence, reconstructions like these attempt to
bridge the gaps between well-known situation "A" (cultural heyday
and collapse around 1200 B.C.) and well-known situation "B" (reflower-
ing of culture in the eighth and seventh centuries) by a complex method
of deduction, sometimes drawing on analogies from the history of
other nations, in a manner that satisfies our desire for logical argument
and synthesis. Of course treatments of particular developments in various regions of Greece will proceed differently depending on the current state of the data (Lehmann 1985, 62–66), and certain significant
aspects may be overlooked, overemphasized, or misconstrued. So long
as no outright contradictory evidence comes to light and, as in the case
of Lefkandi, archaeology even provides corroboration, one must proceed from these reconstructions. In this regard, the position of the aristocracy is especially important for our purposes.

Nearly all attempts at reconstruction in recent scholarship assign the
aristocracy a critical role in the recovery of Greece. In fact we see aristocrats in key positions in both the Mycenaean social system and, later,
that of the eighth and seventh centuries. And now an unexpected find
like the burial at Lefkandi demonstrates the aristocracy's key position

also between these two eras in the tenth century. It is unlikely that other social forces could have dislodged it from its leading role at any time between 1200 and 800 B.C. The forms of dominance within which it played this leading role during the time of anarchy and migration will have varied from place to place and case to case. There are hints that in some areas of Greece aristocrats were "overlords," whose supremacy was hereditary (somewhat as in the case of Odysseus on Ithaka in the *Odyssey*). Elsewhere, and possibly in a different stage of development, the aristocrats seem early on to have exercised a collective authority, which tolerated only a primus inter pares (like Alkinoös in the *Odyssey*'s description of Phaiakian political structures, though the episode is folkloric). There may have been a great abundance of manifestations and there are obvious distortions of actual conditions in the poetic renditions found in the *Iliad* and the *Odyssey*. Nonetheless, it remains clear that the aristocracy was the leading power (Deger 1970). This role is reflected also in the Greek tradition regarding the first (post-Mycenaean) colonization of the coastal areas of Asia Minor. According to the tradition, the new settlements both of the Ionian coastal region and offshore islands of Khios and Samos and of the Aeolian region, from the Kaïkos Plain in the north to the Gulf of Smyrna in the south (the offshore island of Lesbos constitutes a special case), were led by the sons or relatives of kings. Excavations have placed the beginning of these undertakings in the mid-eleventh century (Cook 1975). The names and genealogies of the individual expedition leaders may be uncertain, but that members of the aristocracy led these endeavors is suggested not only by the nature of the case but also by analogy with the second phase of Greek colonization, during the eighth and seventh centuries.

As the theory in fashion for a time—that the Greeks of the period after the catastrophe of ca. 1200 began at point-zero and gradually progressed from there—loses ground (see, for example, Sarkady 1975, 113; Gschnitzer 1981, 26), the pertinent question now becomes, Who were the actual carriers of tradition? The answer—the aristocrats—cannot be in doubt (Latacz 1994a). In many cases, there must have been continuity in family history, not only where excavations indicate it (for example, at Salamis on Cyprus), but precisely where they will never indicate it, because there was no continuous habitation at one location. It was precisely in the anarchy and migrations of the postcatastrophe period that the members of the old aristocracy proved their worth. That the word βασιλεύς (*basileus;* Mycenaean *qa-si-re-u*), which had been the functional designation of the representative of central authority in individual Mycenaean sites, survived as the designation of the leading personalities in the ranks of "the best" or "nobles" (*aristoi, esthloi*), both in epic poetry and in reality, cannot be a matter of chance. The reuse of this term in most cases likely resulted from the identity of the persons rather than from any "logical choice" (Deger 1970, 179). Once again, we conclude that the interruption of the Mycenaean palace culture involved the ruin of administrative structures, not genocide. The Greeks survived the era of catastrophe. We would be very mistaken to assume that specifically the aristocratic elite was totally exterminated, especially in view of the relatively large area of Greece and the inaccessibility of many of its districts. Add to this the geographical knowledge and seafaring expertise of the longtime inhabitants, who undertook demonstrably successful emigrations even to places as distant as Cyprus. Also, we should not underestimate the tenacious cohesion of just this ruling elite across local and regional boundaries (Antonaccio, forthcoming). That a rich nobleman was buried around 1000 B.C. in Lefkandi with costly grave-gifts imported from Cyprus proves that the old connections—even by sea—had never been forgotten. One must presume that the seafaring of which the Greeks had been masters for centuries prior to the catastrophe was never altogether disrupted (Kurt 1979).

The importance of the aristocracy, the proven carrier of continuity and tradition, was doubtless considerably increased by its leadership of the colonization of the coast of Asia Minor. This effort amounted to the foundation of a "New Greece." (As usual in such undertakings, names from the old homeland were transferred to the new.) Based on what we know so far, this colonization was not the action of desperadoes but clearly a well-planned operation, requiring considerable matériel and intelligent preparations. If the colonists' ultimate motivation remains as yet undetermined, the immediate goal was clearly land acquisition and an increase of wealth. In large measure, this goal appears to have been reached. The cities that the colonists founded or refounded—Ephesos, Miletos, Kolophon, Klazomenai, Erythrai, Myus, and Priene, among others, as well as the settlements on the islands of Samos and Khios—were soon the richest in Greece. In Kolophon there even came about the extraordinary circumstance that, in the eighth century, the "wealthy and noble" (that is, the aristocrats) constituted a majority of the population (as Aristotle noted even in the fourth century, at *Politics* 1290b15). This wealth was acquired through agriculture. The fertility of the land and the quantity of possessions and estates, which were probably cultivated with the help of the indigenous population, around 700 B.C. led to great surpluses, especially of wine (Khios and Samos) and olive oil (which acquired new importance as lamp fuel, in place of the old pine-torches and brands). The resulting export trade added a new dimension to pottery manufacturing in the sense of a package-production industry (excavators have spoken of "fragments of standard containers"; see Cook 1975, 801). Ship building, the expansion of harbor installations, the construction of associated buildings, and so on stimulated skilled crafts and professions (see in general Rostovtzeff 1930, 189–204).

The engine of this development was the aristocracy. It was an immigrant, not an autochthonous, nobility. That it had set out from Athens is attested in later sources that see in the first colonists the sons of the Athenian King Kodros (the historicity of this origin from the king is not relevant to our inquiry). The same origin is also suggested by close linguistic affinities: one speaks today of an Ionic-Attic dialect. Thucydides (1.6.3) states, toward the end of the fifth century, that there was a uniformity in the entire manner of living (including dress and hair style) among the "well-to-do" (εὐδαίμονες), owing to their "common ancestry" (κατὰ τὸ ξυγγενές). Athens was, as mentioned, the only undamaged principality remaining from the period prior to the catastrophe of ca. 1200, and like other undamaged or reconstructed Mycenaean centers (Cyprus, Naxos, possibly Lesbos), it served as a place of refuge for the Mycenaean upper class. Later eras of Greek history recalled that the refugees had come chiefly from the center at Pylos. A historical fact may underlie this reminiscence: at any rate the Pylian origin of certain Ionian nobles can hardly be doubted (Heubeck 1983, 1984). There were also connections early on from Athens to nearby Euboia, which, as we know from excavations, was likewise already settled in the Mycenaean era. After the catastrophe, new settlers also seem to have arrived there; in at least one case—Lefkandi—we now have confirmation of this (Themelis 1983, 152). These new arrivals were, from the beginning, in close contact with Cyprus, known to us as the other great refuge for Mycenaean displaced persons. It is improbable that this was a contact between peoples originally unfamiliar with each other. Furthermore, already around 1000, the pottery of Lefkandi shows such close connections with Thessaly, Boiotia (Delphi, Thebes), and Naxos that one of the excavators has spoken of a *koine* (Themelis 1983, 154). Already by 1000 at Lefkandi, a nobleman was buried with a splendor that previously seemed unthinkable. About fifty years earlier the resources seem to have been available in Athens to carry out so expensive an endeavor as the new settlement of an entire coastal area in Asia Minor.

The combination of all these individual data leads to the conclusion that the Greek aristocracy retained unbroken the will to survive, a spirit of enterprise, and the pluck to make a new beginning. These qualities led to the establishment of a new and differently structured cultural unity in eastern Greece, from Thessaly in the north through Boiotia, Euboia, and Attika, and farther across the Cyclades to Cyprus in the south, and across the Anatolian coastal islands Lesbos, Khios, and Samos to the newly settled areas of the north and west-central coasts of Asia Minor. Strictly excluded from this cultural unity were a people who had first immigrated *after* the catastrophe and who thus shared no part of the glorious past—the Dorians. They were intruders, misfits. The Peloponnesos, now the land of the Dorians, remained, in the idealizations of the nobles of eastern Greece, the land of their forefathers, of princes residing in splendor at Argos, Mycenae, Sparta, and Pylos. In their hearts, they could not accept the present reality, which was far different.

Heroic Song as Self-Validation

Such is the attitude toward past and present that we see reflected in Greek epic. Its language remained free from Doric influence over the centuries up to Homer's time. Its basis is Ionic, with strong traces of Aeolic. Its subject matter is the momentous deeds of ancestors—exclusively Ionian and Aeolian aristocrats—in that great era *before* the catastrophe of ca. 1200. The catastrophe itself was ignored; being a document of defeat, it was an unwelcome topic, as was the period that followed, when the upstarts from the north inundated the land of the forefathers. The singer was allowed at most to hint at a discussion of this. Our *Iliad* contains a reflection of it: at 4.52 ff., Hera offers Zeus, as recompense for the destruction of Troy that she is demanding, the destruction of "Argos and Sparta and Mycenae of the wide ways"— and Zeus accepts. This is a final reflex of an interpretation based on the principle of compensatory justice. The name *Dorian* appears only once in the epics, clearly inadvertently, in a geographical detail in one of Odysseus' false stories (*Od.* 19.177). The singer should give delight and not spoil the mood ("and at the stately feast, there will be no pleasure if vile things prevail," *Il.* 1.575).

That is the mentality of an aristocracy that not only rediscovers itself in its heroic poetry but also wishes to feel validated and inspired by it. We must not underestimate the hortatory power of heroic poetry, whose sole theme is essentially achievement and honor, quite apart from its function as entertainment. This power is greatest in that type of epic poetry that C.M. Bowra, in his panoramic *Heroic Poetry*, placed at the top of the scale as "aristocratic" heroic poetry, above both "primitive" and "proletarian" heroic poetry, with Homer as the high point (1952, 476–81). It has rightly been stressed that such poetry must have accompanied and stimulated the Greek nobility as it recovered from the catastrophe and constructed a new aristocratic culture (Ritoók 1975). Milman Parry's theory of oral poetry and associated research in comparative epic have taught us that in language and meter, in form and content, Homer's epics had a centuries-long history as a genre. Heroic epics of the same form and the same or similar content (though not of the same magnitude and level of perfection) no doubt had been recited in the citadels of nobles on Euboia around 1000 (West 1988, 166 f.; Latacz 1994a, 361). (About 700, Hesiod, the second Greek epic poet whose works have survived, reports that he had won a tripod in a "contest" held at Khalkis on Euboia to honor the deceased Amphidamas, "skilled in warfare" [*Works and Days* 654 f.]; similar contests could have been held in honor of that great lord who was buried around 1000 at Lefkandi [Blome 1984, 21].) However, the history of heroic epic goes back further still: "there is every likelihood that the epic singer had an established place in Mycenaean strongholds" (Lesky 1967, 695); "almost everyone accepts that the Greek epic tradition goes back at least to late Mycenaean times" (West 1988, 151).

Also indicative of an early provenance for heroic epic was the fact that many elements contained even in *our* (very late) examples of the genre—the *Iliad* and *Odyssey*—refer back to the era before the catastrophe of ca. 1200; and these references were made at a time when events prior to the catastrophe could have been known only very sketchily (Nilsson 1950). When this era became better understood, with further excavations (at Pylos, Thera/Akrotiri, Cyprus) and with the recovery of its language (Linear B was deciphered in 1952), the evidence accumulated for the existence of Greek heroic epic long before the fall of the Mycenaean centers. But the question could not be decided on the basis of external evidence, such as the so-called singer fresco from Pylos, which depicts a man dressed as a "musician," sitting on a rock and playing a large five-stringed lyre. Nor could it be decided on the strength of material objects and practices that were no longer produced or current after the catastrophe but that appear in our epics and are verified archaeologically for the time before the catastrophe. Examples are the so-called Nestor's cup, boar's-tusk helmets, metal-inlay work, man-sized convex rectangle shields, the military use of chariots, and so on (Webster 1958, 168–74; Kirk 1960; Lesky 1967, 744 ff. [58 ff.]). It is very likely that all such objects and practices were in fact current only before the catastrophe and must therefore have arrived in the poems of Homer from that time. But they could either have been transmitted in nonpoetic narratives from generation to generation or—in the case of objects—have been preserved as family heirlooms up to Homer's day.

Homer's mentioning of these things proves only that he is singing about the time before the catastrophe; they do not prove that there was at that time also a *poetry* of the same type as Homer's. This would be verified only if we were to find analogous texts, even a solitary heroic hexameter verse. Unfortunately, archaeology has not yet provided such a find. The Mycenaean Linear B texts inscribed on the tablets at the palaces are (so far) devoted exclusively to administrative and technical matters; here, too, we have only hints, of which a large number have been investigated. Scholars have discovered a series of linguistic phenomena in the *Iliad* and the *Odyssey* that were very probably current only in Mycenaean Greek and thereafter vanished from normal speech. These must have been transmitted to Homer via a linguistic medium that preserved archaic forms under stylistic constraints (cf. biblical language in German, which has continually led in recent times to "modernized Bibles"). In the nature of things, this linguistic medium can only have been epic poetry (Lesky 1967, 712 ff. [26 ff.]; West 1988, 156–59).

An instructive example is the famous bronze sword with silver nails on its hilt—in Homer, the φάσγανον ἀργυρόηλον (*phasganon argyroēlon*). Archaeology up to now has placed a weapon of such description only in the fifteenth century and then not again until the seventh. The word *phasganon* appears on a (fifteenth-century) Linear B tablet from Knossos as an everyday designation of a weapon. In post-Homeric Greek literature it appears only as a poetic word, naturally in keeping with Homeric usage. The term for sword in common use then was *xiphos*. This can only mean that after the fifteenth century the weapon was no longer in use and therefore that the term designating it was no longer employed either. But the word combination *phasganon argyroēlon* comprises a metrical unit especially suited to the end of a hexameter line, and in fact, in both its Homeric occurrences, it stands at precisely this position in the verse (*Il.* 14.405, 23.807). The obvious conclusion is that we have here "a tiny piece of Mycenaean poetry" (Webster 1958, 92), which at least since the fifteenth century survived as a repeatedly used verse ending right up to Homer's time, even though the object so designated had long since passed out of use and, as a result, was unmentioned in normal language, apart from poetry.

The assumption of a tradition of Greek heroic poetry in the time of the first flowering of Greek culture, that is, long before the catastrophe of ca. 1200, recommends itself on many other grounds. One of the most telling is the linguistic similarity of expressions and concepts to those found in the poetries of other individual Indo-European languages (Old Indic, Old Persian, Slavic, Hittite, Italic). This hints at the presence of an "Indo-European poetic language" prior to the dispersal of the several language groups (Schmitt 1967, 1968; Risch 1969, 324; West 1988, 152–56). From the standpoint of the history of conditions *within* Greek culture, one final question has to be asked: How are we to explain the emergence of epic singers and the creation of a poetry highly distinctive in meter, style, and themes depicting long past events, legendary figures, remote objects, and so on, in geographically widely separated sites, precisely at a time of very severe recession? It is easier to believe in the creation and cultivation of an aristocratic, polished literary artistry, analogous to other, contemporary artistic productions, *prior* to the catastrophe, for it was then that "in the vicinity of the vast palaces a refined courtly society emerged and rose above the common folk" (Gschnitzer 1981, 18), not in the first decades *after* the catastrophe, when the society was thrown back to the level of bare subsistence.

Thus much suggests that the poetry of "the famous deeds of men" (κλέα ἀνδρῶν), as Akhilleus sings it to the accompaniment of his lyre in the *Iliad*, belonged among the small treasures that the Greek aristocracy had saved from the catastrophe and to which it clung with special affection. As long as external conditions were miserable, however, the singer's old heroic songs only made his audience bitterly aware of the immense decline it had undergone, and epic poetry—subsisting only on memories—could merely repeat its familiar themes. It was able to take flight again only after the style of life that sustained it had once more become a reality.

The Renaissance of the Eighth Century

This stage appears to have been reached in Ionia in Asia Minor in the eighth century. On the basis of our reconstruction of general historical developments, let us grant that the new settlers had brought heroic song over from their old homeland to the new. The recently founded agricultural settlements enjoyed relative tranquillity in a colonial area of great extent and affluence. In this context, the arts and their patrons could proceed, as it were, hand in hand toward new prosperity. Early on, the wealth of the Ionians was well known throughout Greece. The author of the *Hymn to Delian Apollo* speaks of it in the seventh century (151–52): "a man might think that they were immortal and ageless were he to come among the Ionians when they gather together" (that is, for the athletic and musical games in honor of Apollo at Delos). Of course, the poet means by "Ionians" not only those of Asia Minor but also those of Attika, Euboia, the Cycladic islands, and so on; still, the communities in Asia Minor embraced the largest space in his enumeration of Ionian settlements in the Greek world.

Around 800 B.C. the originally much more numerous coastal settlements combined to form a *dodekapolis* (twelve-city union). They began a festival, the Panionia, at the site of the communal shrine of Poseidon Helikonios, the Panionion, at Mount Mykale, north of Priene. It is enough to list the names of the member cities, all of which commanded extensive territories in the fertile coastal plains and inland river valleys, to form a conception of the prosperity that prevailed in the region (from south to north): Miletos, Myus, Priene, Ephesos, Kolophon, Lebedos, Teos, Klazomenai, Erythrai, Phokaia, the large, rich islands of Samos and Khios, and, in a broader sense, also Magnesia on the Maiandros (Meander) and Smyrna. Here there evolved an upper class of wealthy landowners who managed their property from an estate house (οἶκος, *oikos*; cf. *economy*) with the help of farm laborers, stewards, herdsmen, and domestic servants. Since in these early days businessmen and merchants were regarded with contempt (see *Od.* 8.158–64) and craftsmen worked mainly for the estate lords, the latter comprised the "aristocracy." In the political sphere, in the eighth century, this landed aristocracy also maintained an unchallenged position of leadership in the assembly and in the judicial system. The aristocrats were not untouched by the general changes and innovations that swept through Greece in this century, but their effects were only indirectly felt.

Euboia was the hotbed of innovation from the beginning of the eighth century. The city of Lefkandi (old Eretria?) on the island had been almost completely abandoned around 825 in favor of the new city of Eretria. Then Eretria and Khalkis, even before 800, started the maritime activities that triggered a whole chain reaction of alterations in the conditions of life. Apparently together with Cypriot Greeks and Phoenicians, they founded the commercial entrepôt Al Mina at the mouth of the Orontes River (near present-day Antakya in Turkey): "this was the main port for Greek trade with the east from about 800 until at least 600; and it remained important for a further 300 years" (Murray 1993, 73). The Greeks were exchanging pottery and possibly silver for iron, finished metal products, textiles, and wrought ivory. The imported wares point to specific needs in the homeland: a need for iron ore for weapons and armor and a need for luxury items. The consumers in both cases were the aristocrats, whose wealth must therefore have greatly increased.

These contacts with the east, facilitated by the Phoenicians, brought innovations of many kinds to Greece. Writing is perhaps the most significant development. Its adoption from the Phoenicians was likely prompted in the course of dealings at Al Mina by its obvious utility for matters of long-distance trade. It is unimaginable that Greek merchants looked on idly for thirty to fifty years while their Phoenician counterparts simplified their own work by the use of writing. The adoption of writing probably followed on the heels of the building of harbor warehouses and offices. At the same time appeared writing tablets and leather rolls, as well as instruction in writing (Burkert 1992, 29–30). Cyprus may have played the part of entrepôt in this process of adoption and perfection of the alphabet (Burkert 1992, 27; Heubeck 1979, 84–87). Contact with the Phoenicians had a further consequence in the Greek expansion to the west, where Phoenician merchants had long since felt at home. Around 775 the first settlers from Khalkis and Eretria appeared on the west coast of Italy and established themselves first on the small island of Pithekussai (present-day Iskhia in the Bay of

Naples). The purpose of the settlement here, too, was commerce, in this case with Etruria, which supplied metals but also served as entrepôt for trade in tin and amber from the north. Pithekussai was itself the center of extensive iron-smelting operations and, based on the evidence of grave-finds, was already a flourishing city around 750 (Murray 1993, 74–76). The famous "cup of Nestor" was found here in 1953. It bears an inscription in three verses, including two epic hexameters, datable to 735–720 B.C.; this has established the possibility that heroic verse could have been transcribed already in the middle of the eighth century (see below, "Homer's Work: When and How").

Further innovations whose penetration into Greece must be dated to the beginning of the eighth century include religious customs from Phoenicia and the east generally (for example, the cult of Adonis), eastern myths of the creation of the world and its development to the present (attested in epics written around 700 by Hesiod of Askra, by Mount Helikon in Boiotia), themes from ancient eastern and Egyptian literature, a familiarity with magic and eastern purification rites, many new words for previously unknown objects and practices, techniques of craftsmanship (thus, for example, the appearance of embossed metalwork and the changeover in Greece during the eighth century from the usual Geometric style of vase-painting to the Orientalizing style with lavish use of plant and animal forms), and a fundamental improvement in ship construction with the adoption of the Phoenician trireme (three banks of rowers arranged one above the other). All this has been extensively treated by Walter Burkert (1992).

At the moment it is not possible to date with precision the arrival of such innovations in Greece during the eighth century. It is, however, indisputable that the transferral of these things was feasible at any time after the commencement of regular long-distance trade via the route from Al Mina/Cyprus to Rhodes (to Crete) to Euboia (and Attika) to Corinth to Pithekussai. In another sense, this profusion of new experiences and new knowledge in Greece led not only to an extraordinary and dramatically rapid broadening of horizons but also to the emergence of the Greeks' awareness of their own identity.

Via Samos, the traditional intermediary, innovations and information that were transforming everyday life across mainland Greece soon reached Ionia in Asia Minor. At the sanctuary of Hera on Samos—the Heraion—the earliest "one-hundred-foot temple" (*hekatompedos*) in

Greece had been built at the beginning of the eighth century; it measured 32.86 meters (100 Samian feet) by 6.5 meters, and had a row of twelve roof-supporting wooden columns down the center of its interior (Coldstream 1977, 97; might this have been the first common undertaking of the Dodekapolis?). Objects of eighth-century provenance found at this site include, besides votive gifts of strongly Attic character, great masses of items from the east: wrought ivory from Egypt and the Levant, terracottas from Cyprus, and bronzes from Egypt, the Levant, north Syria, Cyprus, and Phrygia (Coldstream 1977, 267). Though not at the focal point of innovation, Ionia did take part in all the changes: "Levantine trade hardly touched the Greek cities of Asia Minor. For them the eighth century was a time of consolidation, punctuated by minor commotions. . . . These Greek cities were indeed fortunate, in that they were able to consolidate their power during this period without being threatened by any large and organized Anatolian state" (Coldstream 1977, 268). Unfortunately, excavation projects in Ionia at this time are still relatively scanty. Thus there is a particular dearth of archaeological indications vis-à-vis social structure. Nonetheless, two things do point to a firmly entrenched aristocracy: first, the extraordinarily strong city wall at old Smyrna, the earliest Geometric era example known to us (ca. 850); and second, the numerous votive gifts bearing horse motifs found in the Heraion (Coldstream 1977, 254 f.). Wall construction and horse breeding are evidence of military activity, which, at this early date, was the bailiwick of the aristocracy.

Archaeological material to date offers little testimony regarding the proportions of aristocratic land and livestock ownership or the conditions of daily life. Inferences drawn from conditions obtaining at settlements like Emporio on Khios and Zagora on Andros (Coldstream 1977, 304 ff.) may be misleading, since these are little villages having small populations. Still, even here, there is a discernible difference in the construction of the many "normal" and the rare aristocratic houses. The latter are relatively larger and more carefully built and have more rooms. The most important room was the *megaron*, equipped with a hearth and often featuring stone benches running along the walls. Systematic, well-designed excavations in the Ionian coastal cities may bring to light other dimensions, though unfortunately this is often impossible owing to continuous habitation up to the present day. Consider, for example, the discovery of a bathtub at Miletos: it is the earliest known bathtub in the post-Mycenaean era, although "a separate bathroom, in the Geometric world, would have been an inconceivable luxury" (Coldstream 1977, 308).

Of very great interest is a proposition put forward by Oswyn Murray: that the dramatic increase in the number, size, and quality of kraters (mixing bowls) and drinking cups in the eighth century bespeaks the increasing importance of the never completely abandoned aristocratic institution of the symposium, which at this time constituted a kind of unofficial political steering committee (Murray 1983; on symposia generally, see also Murray 1990, 1991, and 1993, esp. 1993, 207–13; Latacz 1990). (Only in the seventh century did symposia begin to degenerate into more private drinking parties as the political influence of the nobility declined.) This interpretation of the finds accords perfectly with the relevant evidence of the Homeric poems and will have to be tested against the Ionian material (still largely unpublished).

Despite the unsatisfactory archaeological situation in Ionia, we are able to say that, from the very beginning, a population enjoying especially favorable and affluent living conditions achieved a continually increasing level of prosperity during the eighth century. That a general increase in population in Ionia took place concurrently follows in the first place from the construction projects in old Smyrna, where we may discern several eighth-century phases of additional construction as well as improvements to existing buildings (Coldstream 1977, 304 and passim). Moreover, Ionia in fact sent out no colonies at all until the middle of the seventh century, when Miletos began its expeditions to the Black Sea. By contrast, mainland Greece had been engaging in continuous colonizing operations since 734. So extensive were the territories and resources available in Ionia. We may therefore conjecture that here a well-to-do aristocracy, quite conservative in outlook, observed the innovations of the era with a certain complacency from its position of security.

Plausible Hypotheses: Homer's Time and Place

Homer grew up in this world in these years. Precisely when and at what location (or locations), we cannot say. That it was in an upper-class social milieu is clear from all his descriptions of beautiful objects, houses, and persons, and from the formulation of his speeches and dialogue ("some of the finer speeches display tact and comprehension of a sort that even in a more sophisticated age would help make this vale of tears a pleasanter place to pass through," Cook 1975, 801).

Like every traditional singer, he no doubt from his youth followed with special fascination the heroic songs that accomplished *aoidoi* recited in the *megara* for audiences of aristocrats. An exceptional musical talent and an exceptional sensibility, combined with a lively intellect and an uncommon feel for proportion and organization, must very soon have led him onto the path of the artist. Much later, in the figure of Paris in the *Iliad*, he exhibited many of the difficulties entailed by the inescapability of an artistic gift in an aristocratic world where physical achievements were so highly valued. One could guess from the basic optimism of his view of the world and of humankind that his younger years fell in a time of renaissance and revitalization of ancient splendor and ancient ideals. This contrasts very distinctly with the distrustful pessimism of Hesiod. This difference in worldview helps us define Homer's era more exactly.

Homer and Hesiod confront us not only as two entirely different characters but also as representatives of two different stages of historical development. Hesiod's pessimism is less a personality trait than an expression of an age. Around 700, Hesiod in Boiotian Askra leveled bitter accusations against "gift-devouring lords" (δωροφάγοι βασιλῆες; *Works and Days* 39, 264). By this time, the aristocracy to which these "lords" belonged had already passed the apogee of its power. By its very leading role in opening new routes, the aristocracy had set in motion developments that worked to its own disadvantage. The advent of long-distance trade had accelerated the rise to social prominence of a new class of merchants, businessmen, and producers of export goods. The broadening of horizons generally and the adoption of writing had strengthened the capacity for autonomy and the self-reliance of non-aristocrats. Colonization, with its multifarious communal problems, had fostered public spiritedness through individual responsibility. Furthermore, under the conditions of a constantly growing population, the customary restriction of armed conflict to a nobility that possessed weapons and raised horses could no longer be maintained. A concomitant of the need to arm broader segments of the population was the technical perfection and institutionalizing of a new battle tactic. This was the phalanx, a massing together of infantrymen shoulder-to-shoulder in a thick wall of human bodies. The expansion of the phalanx from relatively small groups of nobles to large companies of men (Latacz

1977; cf. Raaflaub 1991, 226–30) led to a diffusion in the consciousness of individual duty, which had previously been delegated to nobles. Increasing self-confidence in turn brought serious demands for the abolition of aristocratic privileges, for justice, for equality, and ultimately for self-determination. The journey to democracy had begun.

This process in fact goes unmentioned in the *Iliad* and the *Odyssey*. Still, the epics survived. This indicates that they originated at a time when they could still be widely accepted and welcomed, a time when there was still no danger of their being discarded as the self-portrait of an incipiently marginal elite class. This time was the second half of the eighth century.

At that time, the negative results of aristocratic leadership either had not emerged or were not yet apparent. On the contrary, broad segments of the population appear to have acquiesced in the nobles' leading role at the time and to have sympathized with their efforts to revive the aristocratic mode of life. We nowadays cannot speak as easily as Wolfgang Schadewaldt did, over fifty years ago, about the "high aristocratic sensibility" and the "elevated spirit" of the eighth century. It seems to us overly idealistic to say that "Homer's century is the century of a wonderful second youth of his people, a time enlightened by memories, full of expectations, and still capable of high aspirations" (Schadewaldt 1959b, 127; first published in 1942). Nonetheless, the reasoned diagnosis that underlies such descriptions has frequently been confirmed since Schadewaldt wrote. It is true, for example, that at the great Panhellenic festivals that arose in the eighth century (at Olympia, Delphi, Delos) "the germ of an overarching Greek self-consciousness took shape" (Schadewaldt 1959b, 125; cf. Rolley 1983). It is true that at this time, because of "the fusion of ancient recollection with a vital outlook to the future, the first historical consciousness stirred beneath the surface" (Schadewaldt 1959b, 125; see also Hiller 1983; Hägg 1983a). Archaeological research in the past thirty years has in fact uncovered things that can be understood as typifying a revolutionary mentality in the culture as a whole, not exclusively in a specific social stratum. One example is the discovery of ancient graves and sanctuaries from former (Mycenaean) times and the widespread observance of a "cult of heroes" throughout Greece (Antonaccio 1987; Calligas 1988). Many phenomena of this kind have been summed up under the concept of "recollection of a heroic past" (Coldstream 1977, chap. 14). Homer has been considered a catalyst of this trend (Coldstream 1977, 356 and passim).

Of course, this interpretation seems too neat and mechanistic. Homer did not set this process in motion with his poems. Rather the signs of renewed material and intellectual progress, which were becoming clear and palpable everywhere, had evoked a new, optimistic feeling for life, which displayed itself in all fields as creativity. It was manifest in the vigor of the old cults and the founding of new festivals, in the renewed veneration of ancestors (to whom people now again felt close), in the acquisition of new living space in foreign lands, in the stimulation of commerce, in the intensified construction activity in both religious and secular spheres (the first large temples were produced, and the Ionian cities were renovated), and also in the revival of the ancient heroic poetry in a spirit of understanding for which the prerequisites had been lacking during long centuries. Homer's *Iliad* and *Odyssey* are a part of this general movement. On the other side of the coin, the poems stimulated and influenced the general movement. This process of mutual interaction distinguishes eras of such dynamism (Hiller 1983).

Homer's Work: When and How

These reflections place the birth of Homer's poems in the second half of the eighth century. The work of scholars over the past few decades has assembled a plethora of evidence for this date from various spheres of Greek cultural development before and after 700. The result has been a battery of corroborative arguments.

The earliest extant non-Homeric Greek epic and lyric clearly show the influence of the *Iliad* and the *Odyssey* (and obviously in the very same form that both epics exhibit in our texts); at some points, we can identify direct citations. This influence is visible in Hesiod, who wrote around 700; in Kallinos of Ephesos (that is, one of Homer's Ionian "neighbors"), who may be dated by his mention of the invasions of Kimmerians in 652 and 645; in Arkhilokhos of Paros, who may be dated by his allusion to the eclipse of 6 April 648; and in Alkman, Alkaios, and Sappho, all firmly datable in the seventh century. There are quotations in Semonides of Amorgos (likewise seventh century), Alkaios of Mytilene on Lesbos (ca. 600), and Stesikhoros (ca. 600; see Burkert 1987,

51), among others. The quotation in Semonides, for example, runs as follows:

> one thing, however, the most lovely, the man from Khios said:
> "as is the generation of leaves, so too is that of humankind."

This is a verbatim quotation of line 146 from the sixth book of the *Iliad*. If Semonides knows the author of these verses as a "man from Khios" (Χῖος ἀνήρ), this means that around the mid-seventh century Homer was already known as a poet from the island of Khios, exactly the region of Ionia that other evidence identifies as the home of Homer. The reference by Alkaios (frag. 44 Voigt) does not quote a verse but alludes to a specific Homeric scene; it runs (in the reconstruction by Denys Page 1968):

> calling his mother by name, he summoned her, the highest of the
>   Naiads,
> the nymph from the sea; and she, embracing the knees of Zeus,
> implored him [to avenge?] the anger of her beloved son.

This is a conflation of the scene in which Akhilleus on the seashore calls his mother Thetis, the highest of the nymphs (*Il.* 1.348–59) and the scene in which Thetis on her knees asks Zeus on Olympos to avenge her son on the Greeks (*Il.* 1.495–533). In Alkaios' day, this combination of scenes, as he cites them, could hardly have been found outside the first book of the *Iliad* as we know it (Meyerhoff 1984, 46–53; West 1988, 151 n. 5).

Toward the end of the eighth century, elements from Homeric epic begin to appear in Greek vase-painting, as pictorial art responded to poetry (Schefold 1975, 42). Because the earliest of these vase-paintings do not yet carry name labels for the depicted figures in them, we cannot be as certain as we are with literary allusions that they refer to already fixed texts of the *Iliad* and the *Odyssey*. Though they seem to our eyes to illustrate Homer's epics, they may actually be depicting scenes from heroic epic in general, which, as we have shown, was enjoying a vogue in this time of renewed interest in the great traditions of the past. Nonetheless, there can be only one explanation for the fact that, of the many different cycles of legend in circulation at the time, the heroic scenes on vases between 725 and 600 illustrate characters and incidents drawn exclusively from the saga of the *Trojan War*: we must assume that the vase painters were dependent on a preeminent literary version of the subject matter then in vogue. Such a version can only have existed in the *Iliad* and the *Odyssey* (Kannicht 1979). The earliest picture that relates to the *Iliad* may be a representation, on a late eighth-century *oinokhoe* (wine pitcher; Agora P 4885), of Siamese twins, shown standing in a chariot while fleeing before the attack of a hero. This illustrates *Iliad* 11.750–52, where Poseidon rescues Siamese twins, the Moliones, scions of Aktor, from the attack of Nestor (Coldstream 1977, 352). The earliest picture that relates to the *Odyssey* may be a representation of a hero who, with a warding-off gesture, holds out a plant toward a woman (fragment of a pot from Ithaka). This illustrates *Odyssey* 10.291 ff., where Hermes gives Odysseus the magical plant moly, to protect him against the sorceress Kirke (Brommer 1983, 70, 120). Beginning about 675, there appear the famous, widespread representations of the blinding of Polyphemos, which are generally seen as allusions to the Cyclops episode in the ninth book of the *Odyssey* (Andreae 1982, 27 f.). Still more important than these concrete signs of influence, as regards the dating of both epics, may be the "structural equivalencies between the Homeric epics and early Greek vase-painting" analyzed by the archaeologist Bernard Andreae and the Hellenist Hellmut Flashar. Both scholars are convinced that these structural similarities go back to a "craving for symmetry" underlying both literary and pictorial art in this era (Andreae and Flashar 1977).

Beginning probably around 650, at various locations in the Greek world, Troy epics written in an additive, episodic style ("and then . . . and then . . .") set down in hexameters all those parts of the Trojan Cycle that, in the chronology of the saga, either precede or follow the events narrated in the *Iliad* and the *Odyssey*. These works include the *Kypria, Aithiopis, Iliupersis, Little Iliad, Nostoi,* and *Telegony.* On the one hand, these epics do not even in the smallest particular overlap the *Iliad* and *Odyssey*; on the other, they do refer to the smallest particulars of the *Iliad* and *Odyssey* to explain and justify them (Lesky 1966, 79–84). All this presupposes written versions of the *Iliad* and the *Odyssey* (Kullmann 1981, 33); and, since Homer's epics present only parts of the Troy story, these later epics were intended to complement them by filling out the full cycle (*kyklos*) of the Trojan saga (hence the rubric *cyclic epics*).

In 1953, a potsherd bearing a three-line inscription in the alphabet of

Kalkhis—a single iambic verse followed by two hexameters—was discovered in an excavation at Pithekussai. In the first verse, a piece was unfortunately broken off, causing a gap of two or three letters. The remainder runs as follows (in a normalized transcription and reading left to right—the original read right to left):

νεϲτοροϲ : ε̣[2–3]ι̣ : ευποτ[ον] : ποτεριον
hοϲδαντοδεπιεϲι : ποτερι[ο] : λυτιϙακον
hιμεροchαιρεϲει : καλλιϲτε̣[φα]νο̣ : αφροδιτεϲ

The most tenable translation at this time reads:

Nestor had a certain cup, good to drink from.
But whoever drinks from *this* cup, will immediately
be seized with desire for Aphrodite of the beautiful crown.

The cup and the inscription are at the present time generally dated to ca. 735–720 (Hansen 1983 and corrigenda). The inscription presupposes a certain level of cultural sophistication: only a person familiar with the story to which it alludes can appreciate the witticism. In the eleventh book of the *Iliad*, we read the following: Makhaon and Nestor are recuperating in Nestor's tent; the captive girl Hekamede prepares a potion for them consisting of wine, cheese, and barley meal in an obviously immense mixing bowl (*krater*):

and next to it [she placed] the wonderfully beautiful cup, which
    the old man had brought from home
fixed with golden nails; it had four eared handles
on both sides of each a dove was pecking,
made from gold, and beneath it were two firm legs:
another man could only with effort have moved it a bit from the
    table,
if it was full, but the old man Nestor lifted it on high effortlessly.
                                                              (*Il.* 11.632–37)

As soon as both heroes drank from the potion, it goes on, they had "slaked their strong thirst" and they delighted in conversation.

The author of this verse inscription (not necessarily either the potter or the owner of the vase) in the first line calls to mind "Nestor's cup" to set the stage for his joke. This reference would have made sense only if "Nestor's cup" was an object familiar to the reader of the inscription. But that could only happen if it appeared in a story known to everyone at the time the inscription was written and read. It also had to be a story in hexameter verse, since that would be the only point of continuing the inscription in hexameters after its iambic beginning. We deduce that this hexameter story was precisely that of our *Iliad* passage. To avoid this deduction, we would have to establish the existence of one (or more) widely known hexameter versions of the story apart from the *Iliad*. But since all the other indications of date that I have previously discussed suggest that no hexameter poetry was better known at that time than the *Iliad* and *Odyssey*, an inscription like the one on the cup is highly unlikely to have referred to a poem other than the *Iliad*. Apart from the explanation of the point of this inscription (Heubeck 1979, 112 f.), it also represents a further corroboration of a date in the second half of the eighth century for the origin of the *Iliad*. It even contributes to a still more precise dating: if around 735–720 a reader of an inscription in remote Iskhia could be assumed to be familiar with a particular Iliadic passage, then the *Iliad* must have been a sort of "best-seller" at this time. It must therefore have been composed in the 730s or 720s.

This estimate of date, nowadays accepted as the most probable by the international community of Homeric scholars, raises new questions. The most important bear on the form of composition and method of distribution in the 730s and 720s and on the size of the *Iliad* (and also the *Odyssey*) at the time. These questions are closely linked.

The composition of a large epic poem in writing during the eighth century long seemed inconceivable, for the following reasons: literacy, it was said, did not yet exist; suitable writing materials were lacking; and there was no incentive to write. These doubts led to the assumption of a purely oral method of composition (and centuries-long verbatim oral transmission) and/or an originally very short work, which would have been expanded by a succession of later poets until it reached the dimensions of the canonical texts of the third-century Alexandrian philologists. The inscription on the Iskhia cup makes such assumptions unnecessary. It is apparent that both of the hexameters on the cup had been composed originally for this cup (or for this cup pattern—there are indications that a series was produced): "whoever drinks from *this* cup . . ."; that is, they emanated from a method of composition already based on writing. The object was from the first to realize at any moment a concept that, thanks to writing, had become independent of the author in the act of reading, an act that already at the moment of composition was assumed to be the normal form of reception. It cannot be maintained that the cup inscription represents a first instance of a type of composition that assumes an "implied reader." Graffiti are a casual, secondary result of the ability to read and write, not the first form of its application. The composition of hexameters in writing (not their mere recording) was thus already in practice at the moment when the cup inscription was devised.

Facility in writing was very advanced already at the time of the inscription's composition. Here we have whole hexameters produced flawlessly and in a regular script, on a writing surface as unsuitable as the curvature of a ceramic vase. We must infer a more common dexterity in writing on the regular surfaces of standard writing materials (Jeffery 1990, 64 f.).

Our case entails a further special expertise in writing, resulting from the developed technique of verse notation. Both hexameters are (correctly) rhythmically articulated ("phrased") by two separation lines. A practice current at the time of the vase inscription and customary on another sort of writing material (to facilitate recitation or learning, like musical notation) has been unthinkingly adopted (Alpers 1970; Heubeck 1979, 115; Latacz 1990, 233–35).

Therefore, the question of the original size of the epics is no longer bedeviled by technical considerations about writing. If strictly internal analysis of the works leads to a recognition of an organic, large-scale structure and requires us to assume a quite expansive composition right from the outset, nothing from the standpoint of writing technique disallows that assumption. The number of the hexameters is irrelevant. It was possible around 725 to write two hexameters in a technically sophisticated special notation on the curved surface of a ceramic vase. It must then have been possible some time before this to produce any number of hexameters on a normal writing surface. From a technical point of view, it was simply a matter of diligence. Many a Greek merchant, in the course of his professional life, will have written business documents of a total quantity far exceeding that of our *Iliad*. The *Iliad* comprises about five hundred thousand letters; by comparison, Herodotus' history comprises about one million. It is certain that around 700 the Boiotian part-time singer Hesiod wrote at least three thousand hexameters (and very likely more than that). That the professional Ionian singer Homer could not have possessed a like facility in writing down hexameters only thirty years earlier can be ruled out thanks to available epigraphic evidence for such transcription.

The question of writing material also no longer obstructs the assumption of an earlier transcription of the *Iliad*. As Albin Lesky noted in 1967, "The state of our knowledge does not permit us to exclude the possibility that papyrus was known and used in the Homeric period" (708 [21]). Egyptian papyrus exports to Phoenicia are attested already around 1050 (five hundred papyrus rolls were exported to Byblos in exchange for lumber; see Pritchard 1969, 28; Heubeck 1979, 155 f.). It is extremely unlikely that Greek merchants in Al Mina, in connection with the adoption of the alphabet, would have persistently overlooked available writing materials (papyrus besides leather; see Heubeck 1979, 156).

All available indications lead to this conclusion: anyone in Greece around 730 (especially in the more developed area of eastern Greece) who wanted to transcribe or to compose in writing a hexameter poem—even a relatively long one—had at hand the basic technical prerequisites for such an undertaking.

The Homeric *Iliad* as the Poetry of Renewal and Self-Celebration

There remains the question of motive. The purely psychological motivations of an individual do not suffice to explain a phenomenon like the very first written composition of a monumental epic of the stature of the *Iliad*. Behind it there must lie something larger, specifically a social necessity. Parallels from the earlier history of other national literatures suggest this (Latacz 1984a, 18). Seen against the background of our reconstruction of the history of Greece and particularly of the Greek aristocratic class, the creation of the *Iliad* was certainly part of the general revolutionary trend of the eighth century; it met a pervasive need on the part of the nobility to celebrate its accomplishments. Growing prosperity, expanding geographical knowledge, increasing importation of luxury goods, refinements in manner of living, a renewal of ancient religious beliefs (seen in worship and in temple building), the overcoming of centuries-old territorial limits through colonial expansion—all this must have led to a new self-awareness and concomitantly prompted a need for self-justification. A method of satisfying this need was at hand—heroic song. In the centuries following the catastrophe of ca. 1200, epic had survived rather than flourished as a celebration of the Greek upper class's noble origin and ancient tradition of leadership. Now once more the glorious contents of the epic poetry bore some resemblance to present realities, though in novel ways. For the aristocracy in the eighth century, the glorious past reflected in the mirror of epic was no longer so shamefully different from present reality. At the same time, the efficacy of this instrument of self-representation (as compared with local phenomena like symposia, games, festivals, etc.) was unsurpassed. Epic combined the widest distribution with the most lasting impression. Such early examples of influence as the "Nestor's cup" inscription confirm this.

Thus, many things attest that the creation of the *Iliad* may not have been an isolated or unique endeavor. Although we cannot speak of commissioned poetry, still the connections between the aristocracy and poetic art, as they can be traced from the earliest choral lyric of Terpander and Alkman through Simonides, Pindar, and Bakkhylides up to Attic drama, must have had their precedents. Literary master works have originated in this manner in all ages. We do Homer no disservice in thinking he was encouraged and patronized by an aristocratic clientele (to whose class he himself may have belonged; see Janko 1992, 38). This association was only natural in an undertaking that demanded not only talent but also much energy, time, material expense, and—not least—pioneer spirit.

Homer: A Feasible Portrait

It is risky to push on past these probabilities into the realm of more concrete details. Nevertheless, the place where the *Iliad* originated was most likely one of the Ionian coastal or island cities. That, among these cities, old Smyrna is so far the only one where writing is attested already in the eighth century (Johnston 1983, 65) may be put down to coincidence. It is very likely that, as many have conjectured (Dihle 1970; Kullmann 1981, 34 ff.), preliminary work in writing (notes, outlines, early drafts of particular sections of narrative) was indispensable. The actual writing down of the composition is to be attributed to Homer himself, not to a literate assistant, as Albert Lord (1953) romantically inferred from his own experiences in modern Yugoslavia (a notion still persuasive to some scholars [for example, see Powell 1990; Janko 1992,

37 f., 99 f.; Janko 1994]). (The supposed blindness of Homer, though some scholars even today think it worthy of consideration as a bit of tradition, is patently fanciful in light of the extraordinary visual sensitivity of Homer's depiction of the world and of human beings.)

The size of the *Iliad* that Homer composed can be deduced only indirectly and remains, in the last analysis, uncertain. The decisive criterion for the attribution of individual portions of the work is their indispensability to the structural harmony of the whole. Authentically Homeric then are the "weight-bearing" parts of the structure, namely, all those episodes that clearly forward the plan of action announced at the beginning and whose omission would leave rifts in the overall pattern. Conversely, *Iliad* 10 as a whole, the so-called Doloneia, which is not designed into the plan of the plot and is relatively superfluous in the overall structure, may have been added later by another hand. The same applies to shorter embellishments that here and there may have found their way into the poem still later on. Even Attic drama of the fifth century was still not secure from such interpolations (Page 1934; Lesky 1967, 831 [145]). As will be shown, however, all these instances count for little in the big picture. In essence, the *Iliad* as we have it may be labeled the work of Homer.

For the *Odyssey*, the question of authorship remains open. That the *Odyssey* as a whole is "more modern" need not entail different authorship. As will be shown, there are numerous structural correlations between the two epics. Moreover, it is hard to believe that in eighth-century Ionia two equally gifted geniuses composed monumental epics within one generation. So long as compelling contrary evidence is lacking, we, like the ancients, may see the work of Homer in the *Odyssey* also.

We cannot determine precisely how Homer's epics were disseminated in the earliest times. I have argued in chapter 1 that textuality in Greece began with the transcription of the *Iliad* and the *Odyssey*. If this is correct, then there was no stage of purely oral dissemination reliant on memory alone in the absence of a fixed text. Rather, the *Iliad* and the *Odyssey* gave rise to a revolution in the traditional profession of the singer. The singer changed from improviser to reciter: in Greek terms, he changed from *aoidos* to *rhapsodos*. Repetition replaced free-form composition. For the first time in European intellectual history, the preservation of the original sequence of words became possible through the use of manuscripts. These were at first safeguarded by associations or "guilds" of rhapsodes. It is likely that copies were soon made. It goes without saying that "in the early phases of the tradition, we need not think [these written exemplars] were very numerous" (Lesky 1967, 831 [145]). To procure a copy required considerable initiative and expense on the part of interested persons (aristocratic families or communities whose prehistory was glorified in the epics). The same was true of humanists during the European Renaissance prior to the invention of printing. Still, it would be a mistake to underestimate the extent of the dissemination of copies at this early stage. The absence of a regular book trade, which only the modern intellectual considers imperative, was no hindrance. Hesiod, also, and Alkman, Tyrtaios, Sappho, Alkaios, and many other early poets were preserved without benefit of a book trade. And it is out of the question that, for example, the nine books of Sappho's songs collected in the third century could possibly have been learned by heart (we know that the first book alone contained 1,320 lines).

In addition, school requirements will have played a part in the early dissemination of the Homeric epics. Xenophanes of Kolophon, another Ionian compatriot of Homer's, near the end of the sixth century indignantly remarked, "since from the beginning, all have learned in accord with Homer . . ." (frag. B 10). By this he undoubtedly meant Homer as a school text and, as "from the beginning" shows, a school text as long as one could remember. Even if only the teachers of aristocratic children in the larger settlement areas had written copies of the epics (or portions of them) at their disposal, the production of manuscripts must have begun early on.

Also to be considered is the political significance of the epics. The *Iliad* and the *Odyssey* were recognized as masterpieces from the very beginning; their immediate effect on their contemporary audience proves this. Unlike early Greek lyric, with its personal quality and local impact, Homer's epics joined the Greeks together in a new, accelerating consciousness of their own identity. They did so through their embodiment of a common history, a common belief-system, a common morality, and a common set of great achievements. The wish to have these documents of a new national self-definition available not only sporadically in the recitations of rhapsodes must have prompted the procuring of copies in many locations in Greece. Here were the roots of those "city manuscripts" so often cited by third-century Greek philologists in their editions as "the manuscript of Marseilles," "the manuscript of Sinope," and so on (Kirk 1985, 38–43). Homer, unlike the early Greek lyric poets, appealed to *all* Greeks. From the beginning, his dissemination in written form extended to the whole of Greece.

Those who love sharp pictures may believe that Homer was born to a good home around 770 B.C. in a coastal or island city of Ionian Asia Minor. He listened to the old heroic songs from the mouths of *aoidoi* from an early age and soon made efforts of his own. His education was good. He learned to read and write perhaps as a youth, certainly by young manhood. His travels (facilitated by the far-reaching family connections of the nobility) took him far and wide in the Greek world. (Schadewaldt [1942] vividly characterized the smallness of the Greek world at the time and thus how easily it could be experienced: from Troy in the north to Crete in the south is a distance no greater than from Berlin to Munich [about 325 miles].) By 730, at around age forty, the singer Homer had become famous. In keeping with the general enthusiasm of the times, after various poetic experiments, he gave fresh expression to the new aristocratic self-consciousness by a timely revival of the ancient songs celebrating the Trojan War. It is not inconceivable that Homer, in about 710, at age sixty or so, encouraged by the unexpected success of the *Iliad* and struck by the swift pace of the further developments he witnessed around him, set down in words a second great interpretation of the world, the *Odyssey*, a poem that reflected traditional images of the world, of humankind, and of the ideals of the nobility, all of which were undergoing rapid transformation owing to colonization and commerce. The fame of Homer's works had spread so quickly throughout the Greek world even in his own lifetime that his name, when he died around 700, remained so closely linked to the *Iliad* and *Odyssey* that it was never forgotten thereafter.

Many elements of the preceding portrait of Homer are only conjectural, but they are not simply plucked out of thin air.

3

The *Iliad*

The Theme: The Wrath of Akhilleus

The *Iliad* begins with an eleven-line *prooimion* (προοίμιον, "proem" or "prelude"). This component traditionally combines three functions: invocation, statement of theme, and exposition. Invocation and theme statement are regularly interwoven with each other. The singer asks the deity by whom he hopes to be inspired—the muse—to "sing" (or "tell" or "make known" or the like) a specific theme through his mouth. The audience by convention is construed to be witnessing this transfer rather than itself being addressed. From the singer's request for inspiration, it learns the narrative program and gains an initial, though still indistinct, notion of the poem's content and the planned course of the narrative. The singer tries to arouse the interest of the audience and generate suspense at the outset by emphasizing the originality of the tale he plans to tell. This technique of attracting and holding the attention of the audience was later consolidated as a literary topos—chiefly in rhetoric as the Greek prooimion and the Latin exordium (with its *captatio benevolentiae*), and in drama as the *prologos* (πρόλογος), or prologue. It survives to this day.

In the case of the *Iliad*, the form of the prooimion is plainly bipartite. The first seven verses, in the guise of an invocation of the muse, announce the theme and provoke interest in it by a first, still dim foreshadowing. The next four verses supply a transition to the narrative proper.

The theme is announced with the very first word of the poem (in the original Greek): *mēnin* (μῆνιν), "wrath." (The frequently encountered rendering "anger" does not convey the meaning of this thematic word. We are dealing not with a sudden emotion, an "access of anger," but with a lasting, festering, embittered hostility on account of an inflicted insult, the aftereffect of a "suppressed" anger. Thus, in English, "wrath" is the best rendering, even if it does sound somewhat archaic.)

After the announcement of the theme comes a long relative clause. This gradually particularizes the theme through a series of more and more specific details. At the same time, the general context is obscured (and unsettling questions are raised) by these very details.

> Sing the wrath, goddess of Akhilleus son of Peleus,
> the accursed wrath that brought infinite pain to the Akhaians
> and hurled many strong souls down to Hades—souls of
> heroes!—and left them to be booty for dogs
> and a banquet for the birds, but this was the will of Zeus being
>   accomplished,
> from that moment when there stood against each other in
>   opposition
> the son of Atreus, lord of men, and godlike Akhilleus.
>
>   (*Il.* 1.1–7)

We see immediately that this theme sketch must stir more puzzlement than suspense in the modern reader lacking prior knowledge. Suspense cannot arise in an audience that lacks information presupposed in a text. Or if it does, it will be misdirected (in relation to the original auctorial intent). This confusion is, in general, precisely the problem today. The text evokes false questions for the modern reader: What is the setting of the action? What is the time of action? Who are the main characters? What does "Hades" refer to? What does "Zeus" refer to? Who is the "goddess" in the first line? These questions did not occur to the contemporary audience when it heard the opening of the epic, because it already knew the answers. By contrast, the modern reader, accustomed to the modern form of narrative—mainly fiction— is at risk of going astray right here at the outset. While preoccupied with the search for answers to these false questions, he or she falls into a fundamental misunderstanding of the recipient role intended for the reader by the author and begins to read the *Iliad* "falsely." He or she may, for example, believe that here is a so-called abrupt opening that will be set in an overall context by a later recapitulation of the argument. The modern reader might then focus on the expected resolution of a prologue kept fragmentary (supposedly) by design. Such a reader would then, of course, be a complete failure in his or her role as a recipient of the poem.

The purpose of a work of literary art is attainable only if its recipients rightly comprehend the work. In the case of an ancient work, accordingly, the modern reader must reclaim the position of a member of the contemporary audience. The first prerequisite for this and thus for a "proper" understanding of the *Iliad*, beginning with its prooimion, is to realize that the epic, in its basic subject matter, was offering its public not a newly invented fiction but a treatment of a long since familiar topic; that is, the general background and the larger context of the tale announced in the prooimion were well known to the audience. The specific knowledge that the *Iliad* poet required of his public for a proper comprehension of his story was identified and elicited by the very elements of the prooimion that mean little or nothing to the modern reader—the proper names. "Akhilleus, son of Peleus," "the son of Atreus, lord of men," "the Akhaians," "Hades," "Zeus"—all these identifiers triggered definite associations for contemporary listeners. The names, together with the information that the son of Atreus and Akhilleus "had a falling out and quarreled," would resonate in them just as the names "Moses," "Aaron," and "the children of Israel," together with a mention of "dancing around the golden calf," strike a chord today in those who know the Bible: the curtain rises before the listener's eyes, the stage is the Sinai desert and the action is set in the time of the Exodus—all this the listener knows for himself or herself. In both cases, the narrator, with a few signals, guides the audience onto familiar ground: on the one hand, into the biblical story, on the other, into the myth of the war at Ilios, that is, into the Trojan saga.

The Troy saga was an indispensable common element in the education of Homer's public—the aristocracy; they had taken in the saga with their mother's milk. The story of the mighty Akhaian naval expedition against Ilios/Troy (the names derive from those of mythical kings of the city, Ilos and Tros), the bloody battles during the ten-year siege of the city on the Hellespont (present-day Dardanelles), the stubborn resistance of the city's inhabitants and their allies from neighboring regions, and finally the only stratagem by which the city could be taken in the tenth year of the war, the wooden horse—this story had been so often narrated and recounted in the songs of the *aoidoi* that its basic structure and the sequence of its narrative elements were known to contemporary Greeks from childhood in the way biblical stories are known to Christians today. Thus the principal characters of the story were also familiar. The most prominent of these could be identified merely by their father's name. (German heroic sagas are not comparable in this respect; Tolstoy's *War and Peace* is a possible analogue: for

aficionados, Nicholas Andréevich suffices to identify Prince Bolkón-
ski.) Thus the two Atreidai (sons of Atreus) automatically called to
mind Agamemnon and Menelaos, Peleiades (or Peleides) meant
Akhilleus, Laertiades meant Odysseus, Tydeides meant Diomedes,
Telamoniades (or Telamonian) meant Aias, and so on. The deeds and
functions of these heroes in the story, as well as their respective personalities, were well known. If the singer began to sing of Akhilleus,
son of Peleus, and Atreides, lord of men (of the two sons of Atreus, only
the elder, Agamemnon, carried this honorific title), and of how these
two quarreled in the Akhaian army, then the general locale, the scene of
the action, and the historical moment would be instantly apparent. But
that also means that the *Iliad*, with its opening words, identified itself to
its contemporary audience (though not to its modern one) as the
retelling of a story. But it would not have been identified as a verbatim
repetition, because memorizing and reciting by heart were unknown
for Greek epic before the introduction of writing. It was rather repetition of a known story in different words—that is, a rendition.

This sense of recognition that attended every hearing of epic renditions of the Troy saga (as well as other ancient sagas) evoked in the
ancient audiences of the Greek *aoidoi* a sort of interest as the story
unfolded that was quite different from that aroused in a modern reader
of the *Iliad*. The ancient audience was concerned less with the facts and
general shape of the story than with its distinctive style in any given
immediate performance by a singer. (Two hundred years later, Attic
drama held the same interest for its audience.) Because both the story
itself and the medium in which it was presented (the formulaic language of hexameter verse) lacked for ancient listeners the charm of
novelty that they hold for us, their interest could be roused and sustained only by the display of a very high level of narrative quality.
Every narrator who reworked traditional stories (folk tales, sagas,
myths) had to reach that level to be successful. The singer had to tell his
story as beautifully as possible. So beautifully that an audience would
be fascinated anew by an old tale and would find it more beautiful than
any rendition it had ever heard. Now "beautiful" in this context could
mean many things: a more nuanced and facile control of the formulaic
language and the techniques of delivery, more compelling motivation
of events, better structural organization, greater vividness, enhanced
realism (since the stories were accepted as basically true accounts of
actual events), and in general the creation of stronger suspense and

deeper enjoyment. All these criteria formed the basis for judging the quality of the singer and his song, as may be seen from the indirect literary criticism (the "immanent poetics") implied, for example, in the scenes involving the singer Demodokos in the *Odyssey* (cf. Kannicht 1980, 16–19).

Homer's *Iliad* surely met all these criteria in an especially high degree. In fact, many versions of the Troy saga must have been recited during the eighth century, but only the rendition represented by Homer's *Iliad* was found worthy to be set down in writing. This suggests to us that a further criterion may have decisively swayed the judgment of the audience of epic poetry—originality of perspective.

No other epic renditions of the Troy saga prior to or contemporary with Homer's version, that is, our *Iliad*, have come down to us. We cannot, then, say for certain whether or how the perspectives of these renditions differed from that of Homer's *Iliad*. Nevertheless, some likely conclusions can be drawn from the fact that these other renditions were not preserved. The most plausible explanation is that these other versions—allowing for individual variations in length, amount of ornamentation, and so on—never strayed far from a traditional framework, one that also dictated a standard perspective. Homer, however, exploded that framework with a spectacular revolution in perspective. We may support such a conclusion by examining the structure of some post-Homeric versions of the Troy saga written in hexameter verse and accessible in fragments and later prose summaries. These works, of the seventh and sixth centuries, responded to the tremendous popular success of the *Iliad* and the *Odyssey* by rounding them out with portions of the saga omitted from Homer's epics or only briefly alluded to. They provided a supplementary narrative or, as the Greeks saw it, a completed cycle of saga, of which Homer's *Iliad* covered only a relatively small portion. These are the so-called cyclic epics.

It is altogether unclear whether the perspective of these post-Homeric, written Troy epics in fact corresponded to that of the oral versions of pre-Homeric singers who dealt with the same subject matter. For the composers of the cyclic epics had the object of embedding the *Iliad* and *Odyssey* in the overall story of Troy. This may have led them to concentrate on the sheer chain of events and to ignore digressions, ornamentation, and even possible special perspectives that may have typified individual singers' recitations in pre-Homeric practice. The prose narratives, to which in the main we owe our knowledge of the

content and plot construction of the cyclic epics, made further adjustments for practical and pedagogical reasons (synopses of them were
later attached to editions of the *Iliad* and *Odyssey* to furnish essential
introductory background). Nevertheless, it is likely that the cyclic epics
tightened and compressed the material they used but still basically
retained the standard perspective of the pre-Homeric song versions of
the Troy saga. In this case, the cyclic epics offer us a means of arriving
at the perspective of renditions made in and before Homer's time; this
in turn enables us indirectly to compare these perspectives in the same
way that Homer's first audience automatically did.

What then is the perspective of the cyclic epics? A good example is
preserved for us in the extant beginning of one of these poems, which,
in its original form, narrated in four books the events at Troy from the
death of Akhilleus to the bringing of the wooden horse into the city.
The title *Little Iliad* distinguishes it from Homer's (great) *Iliad*. The
beginning runs as follows:

> I sing Ilios and the land of the Dardanians [= Trojans], good
>   horse-land,
> for which the Danaans [= Akhaians, Greeks], followers of Ares
>   [= strong warriors], suffered much grief.

Here, too, the first word, *Ilios*, states the theme and thereby fixes the
perspective of this epic as relating to externals. Gross constituent units
provide the points of departure for this narrative: city ("Ilios"), land
("land of the Dardanians"), two peoples ("Dardanians" and
"Danaans"), and gruesome warfare. A large canvas spreads before the
reader's eye, almost a tableau: there is a city in a wealthy foreign land,
and the Akhaians are embroiled in a protracted war ("they suffered
much grief") to gain possession of the city ("for which . . ."). The narrative begins here with the totality; it will thereafter proceed in its later
development from the external to the internal, from the large-scale to
the small-scale.

Numerous singers will have presented the Troy saga or segments of
it to their listeners in this normal way of telling a tale. Homer chooses a
different perspective. He begins his rendition of the saga thus:

> Sing the wrath, goddess, of the son of Peleus, Akhilleus!

The theme here is not the city and the struggle for it. The theme is, moreover, no external event at all. It is rather a process that takes place within an individual: a wrath. The narrative begins then not with major elements. Instead, it is restricted to the small-scale and—as it seems— the private, within the soul of an individual hero in the Akhaian army: the son of Peleus, Akhilleus. This perspective then is unlike that of the "normal" beginning. It offers a "view from within": the narrative gradually proceeds step-by-step from an internal point to the external. It embraces ever enlarging areas until the whole finally comes into view.

It is doubtful whether the mere reversal of perspective, that is, the change from an external to an internal perspective, was entirely new to Homer's audience. The presentation of large sequences of events from an individual's point of view is a very common narrative technique (seen in the form of direct discourse even in narratives told from an external perspective). Thus, we cannot go so far as to attribute its invention to Homer. What may be new, however, is the consistent "deepening" of this perspective, the shift "to a deeper level" within the individual hero.

Indeed, the *Iliad* commences not with the whole person "Akhilleus" but with the designation of a state of mind—to wit, "wrath." Homer does not begin, "Sing, goddess, of how the son of Peleus, Akhilleus, once grew wrathful"; rather, precisely the *mēnis*, or wrath, itself becomes an agent: "Sing the wrath, goddess, that brought pain to the Akhaians, sent many heroes' souls on the way to Hades, and made them the spoils of scavenging dogs and birds of prey!" The state of mind, too, not just the person, is valued here: "the wrath, accursed wrath!" (such translations as "the destructive wrath" or "the ruinous wrath" do not convey the sense of the word *mēnis* in the original [Kirk 1985, 53]). The wrath "does" something, it is to blame for something and is for that reason accursed. We see here an announcement of the story not of a noble hero and his deeds but of the inner condition of a human being and its effects. The interest is not so much in what the man does but in what transpires within him (and forms the basis for his action). It has rightly been suggested that we are witnessing a process of "internalizing" and a tendency to "psychologize the facts of the saga" (Kullmann 1981, 26). This tendency pervades the *Iliad*. It shifts the mythical incident to a deeper, interior level; and insofar as it deepens, it also clarifies. The *Iliad* becomes an interpretation of the Troy saga. This is Homer's first innovation—an innovation in the *direction* of focus.

Constituting a second innovation is the *manner* in the *Iliad* of looking at things, one might even say of judging things. The wrath of a hero is accursed; it reveals itself not as a positive, praiseworthy thing but as a negative force:

> . . . that brought infinite pain to the Akhaians
> and hurled many strong souls down to Hades—souls of
>   heroes! . . .

In the world of epic poetry, the anger of heroes is normally directed against the enemy and spurs the heroes to momentous deeds. Here, the wrath of Akhilleus is directed toward his own people and causes the death of his own comrades. The vector of action is thus reversed. What should be directed outward as a strength is directed inward as a weakness. The heroic appears not in its customary brilliance but bedimmed, even ominous. This impression is intensified by a further movement toward the negative—the death of the heroes is not merely stated but portrayed in horrific terms:

> . . . and left them [viz., the heroes' bodies] to be booty for dogs
> and a banquet for the birds. . . .

(The Greek *dais* [banquet], which denotes not a quick snack but a formal common meal, conjures up the macabre image of a festive dinner of birds of prey.) For a man of standing in Homer's time nothing was more disturbing than the prospect of lying dead and unburied in an open field to serve as food for dogs and vultures. Later in the *Iliad*, truces are regularly concluded for the sole purpose of recovering corpses. Therefore, this repulsively graphic image of dogs and birds ripping pieces from corpses stands at the beginning of our *Iliad* by design. It sends this message: so shockingly did the wrath of Akhilleus affect his comrades!

It is hard to imagine that this was the usual perspective on the heroes of the glorious Trojan expedition. The song of the war fought by noble ancestors around the citadel of Troy begins here with a profoundly repugnant image, void of any human dignity. This could hardly have failed to impress the audience. Emotions were stirred. Certainly an ancient commentator on this passage was right to say, "the violent emotions that the prooimion triggers [in listeners] are quite exceptional" (BT scholia; see Griffin 1980, 118). Above all, indignation will have been aroused, indignation toward the responsible party—Akhilleus—and toward this "accursed wrath" of his. The audience's need for decorum was supplanted by revulsion—against perhaps not only the character but also his creator. From the author's point of view, this was an infallible method of building suspense. At this point, we recognize the motive for the novelty of the perspective adopted in the *Iliad:* what one was hearing in this rendition was no longer an old-fashioned heroic song. If it had taken only an individual as its subject, its beginning would have run: "I wish to praise Akhilleus and his great deeds (as well as sufferings)." Instead, we read: "I wish to sing of the wrath of Akhilleus, which caused horrible and unseemly death for many of his noble people." Let us grant that even before Homer, as some scholars have thought, Akhilleus may already have been the hero of a version of the Troy saga. Let us grant also that even before Homer there may have been an ancient "Akhilleid," in which perhaps even the motif of an insulted and angry hero boycotting his comrades played a roll. Nonetheless, it is very unlikely that a personal feeling and its public repercussions could ever previously have been so pointedly linked and announced as the theme of a heroic epic pertaining to the saga of Troy. An enormous dramatic energy informs the prooimion; it transmutes a feeling into a personage and with a few words raises it to an all-pervading active force with negative, indeed lethal, results. Although nothing can be proven beyond doubt in this matter, such things can scarcely have been typical of the traditional creations of epic singers.

As if this beginning, so out of character with the customary tone of saga, were not forceful enough, a further heightening of tension follows at this point:

. . . but this was the will of Zeus being accomplished.

Was Akhilleus then ultimately not responsible for this extraordinary situation? Was he merely an instrument? Was the wrath of Akhilleus, with its shocking consequences, ultimately the contrivance of the supreme Greek god? The urgency of the question peaks at this point. How could it have come to this? Where did the cause lie? How did one thing follow from another? And, above all, why had Zeus willed it so? What were the deeper interconnections among these things?

The poet consciously creates this tense atmosphere of concern and then immediately returns to his point of departure—the wrath. Up to the end of line 5, he has pushed ever forward into the future consequences of this wrath and allowed us to glimpse its always enlarging compass: first the Akhaian army, then the underworld ("Hades"), and finally, with the naming of Zeus as a prime mover, even Olympos. The poet has fostered the impression that the whole universe is filled with Akhilleus' wrath. From this "cosmic" view of the anticipated future field of play, the poet turns back in line 6 to the "present time," specifically to the precise moment when the wrath originated:

> from that moment when there stood against each other in
> opposition
> the son of Atreus, lord of men, and godlike Akhilleus.

The listener is transported to the mise-en-scène of the sharp quarrel during which the flashpoint was reached.

At this point, the poet redirects or channels the suspense of the audience over critical questions into paths of his choosing. By a clever stratagem he transfers to himself the feelings he has aroused in his audience. He himself asks the question that he has evoked in the listener:

> Who among the gods set these two into conflict with each other?
>
> (*Il.* 1.8)

This is the first question: how did this quarrel ever come to pass at all, this quarrel that caused such a wrath? It is the quintessential Greek inquiry into origins, into the *archē* (ἀρχή). With it, the poet guides the work and its audience from the wrath back into the past. The question elicits three answers, each of which, by clarifying an implied question, refers back before the preceding one and thus anchors the event to be described ever deeper in the past:

> The son of Leto and Zeus [= Apollo]!—who, full of anger at the
> king [= Agamemnon]
> caused a grievous pestilence to rage among the host, and the
> soldiers were perishing

because the son of Atreus had treated the priest Khryses
   dishonorably.
This man had come beside the swift ships of the Akhaians,
   to ransom his daughter. . . .

$$(Il. 1.9–13)$$

Here then are the three answers: (1) Apollo was the author of the quarrel (and therefore of Akhilleus' wrath). Why and how? (2) He was angry at the leader of the Greek army, Agamemnon, and for that reason inflicted a pestilence on the army, causing many deaths. Why did Apollo become so angry at Agamemnon? (3) Agamemnon had not respected Khryses, the priest of Apollo. The next question follows logically: how did this disrespect come about and what was its nature? The answer launches us finally into the narrative proper: Khryses enters the Akhaian camp, holding the insignia of his priestly status and bearing abundant ransom. Before the assembled host, he officially appeals to the two sons of Atreus to be allowed to purchase the freedom of his daughter, Khryseis, whom the Akhaians have taken captive. Agamemnon harshly rejects this humble request. The priest of Apollo asks the god for his assistance. Apollo becomes enraged, sends the pestilence, and so on.

The prooimion has thus fulfilled its function.

1. In the form of an invocation of the Muse, it has announced the theme: Akhilleus' wrath.
2. It has provided a preliminary narrative plan, with emphasis on three points: presentation of the events leading up to the wrath; the origin of the wrath itself—that is, the quarrel between Agamemnon and Akhilleus; the consequences of this wrath for the army.
3. It has created a transition to the beginning of the narrative.

But the prooimion has done even more than this. Significantly, it has not announced itself as a rendition of the whole Troy saga or of particular parts of it. Rather, it has concentrated on a singular point—the wrath of Akhilleus—which the audience cannot easily place within the overall framework of the saga. It has dramatically heightened the importance of that singular point by investing it with an emotional charge, thereby reaching an extraordinary level of suspense. Modern readers can appreciate the unique and intense quality of that suspense only by bearing in mind the contemporary audience's horizons of knowledge and expectation in the realm of the epic of Troy.

The Framework of the Theme: The Troy Saga and the Trojan War (Myth and History)

For eighth-century audiences, the Troy saga was only a small portion of a large repertoire of saga, itself only part of an immense pool of stories of various kinds (folk tales, legends, short stories, adventure stories, etc.). Some of these stories originated in a common Indo-European heritage prior to the Greek migration to the Balkan Peninsula. Others originated after the migration either under the influence of the stories of the indigenous population or as a result of new experiences and adventures of the Greeks themselves. Saga as a narrative type formed its own category within the domain of storytelling. In their earliest forms, sagas about heroes and gods (besides other types of saga) were molded to the service of the elite class, that is, the warrior nobility. This is clear from the common Indo-European terminology of praise. By their transmission in the medium of a special (Indo-European) poetic language, these sagas became an instrument of ennobling self-representation. Later, in the new homeland of the Balkan Peninsula, much new material replaced the old, irrecoverable topics of the earlier common Indo-European heritage. This occurred during the years of independent cultural development between the immigration of the Greeks around 2000 and the catastrophe of around 1200. This new material was related to the sensational accomplishments of the new centers of civilization (Nilsson 1931; cf. Bowra 1952, 25). Thus there evolved a whole complex of saga in connection with the military conflicts around Thebes (the sagas of Oedipus and the Seven against Thebes, among others). Another complex related to the first voyages of discovery in the Black Sea, voyages evidently originating at Iolkos (the saga of the Argonauts, including the Golden Fleece, and the characters Jason and Medea). A third complex centered on the undertakings of the town of Pylos (the Neleus-Nestor sagas); a fourth centered on the hostilities between the towns of Tiryns and Mycenae (the Amphitryon-Alkmene-Herakles sagas). That other great centers like Argos/Mycenae or Athens likewise provided material for saga is evident from such reflexes as the Athenian Theseus saga (annual tribute of Athens to Minoan Crete; the escape of Theseus from the labyrinth of the Minotaur, that is, the palace at Knossos, with the aid of Ariadne) or the Argive Atreus-Pelops saga ("Pelopon-nesos" = island [scil. peninsula] of Pelops).

Many of these stories, which became intricately interwoven myths as the original incident receded in time, must have been taken over into epic poetry or undergone epic transformation soon after the event (Ritoók 1975). The common notion that this epic transformation could have occurred only after the collapse of Mycenaean civilization proceeds from the tacit assumption that an exceedingly interesting event would have to become myth before it could form the subject matter of poetry. But, on the contrary, research in the field of comparative epic has adduced many examples to show that wherever a living tradition of epic poetry exists, important events are very quickly converted into song. Thus, for example, the famous Russian poetess Marfa Kryukova (b. 1876), a composer of *byliny* (heroic songs), felt compelled to compose a *bylina* about Lenin and Stalin very soon after the immense upheaval of the Russian Revolution of October 1917 (Bowra 1952, 116–17). Many comparable examples from modern Greek folk epic are cited in the works of James Notopoulos (Holoka 1973, 268–69, 282–83, 288; Latacz 1979, 606). Homer's *Odyssey* furnishes the explanation for this stress on the topical (in an era without mass media!): the singer Phemios at the house of Odysseus sings of the "unlucky homecoming of the Akhaians from Troy" (*Od.* 1.326 f.)—that is, a very recent event in the time frame of the *Odyssey* (at most nine years in the past). When Penelope tries to prevent his singing that particular song, her son Telemakhos objects on the grounds that "people always give the highest praise to the song that comes newest to their ears" (*Od.* 1.351–52). Of course, poets in times less abounding in noteworthy occurrences undoubtedly prefer to rework old tales in fresh variations as shining examples of past greatness. Thus the productive phase of many epic transformations—and also of sagas, for sagas do not always "presuppose ruins" (Lesky 1967, 756 [70]; 1981, 21), but only great events and deeds—is to be placed in the period prior to the catastrophe. The phase of the most intensive elaboration of epic came afterward (Latacz 1988c).

Not only "heroic sagas" but also Greek sagas and epic poems in general typically "announce a historical event" that, however, "they routinely conceive of in the light not of their historical reality but of 'fame,' of personal deeds and achievements, of sufferings, of the struggle with destiny, and so on" (Schadewaldt 1970, 39 f.). Therefore, as historical sources, they are only indirectly useful: they reveal much that is authentic about the thought of the times they describe; they are less reliable regarding the actual events that underlie them. They are thus documents of intellectual and cultural history rather than factual records. Undoubtedly, the sagas and epics take their point of departure from historical incidents, because historicity is an integral ingredient of saga, as opposed to folktale (Schadewaldt 1970, 40; cf. Lesky 1967, 755 [69]). But by themselves they do not as a rule permit us to reconstruct the original shape and dimensions of the initiating event. The reason lies in the character of their intended effect: sagas—be they prose or verse—are not told with the object of fixing outstanding events in the consciousness of humankind as stages in "world history." Rather, they aim (not without pedagogical intent) to pass on such events to future generations as paradigms of extraordinary challenges and trials. They are thus highly susceptible to elaboration and transformation. Succeeding epochs see the ancient sagas as new at any given time, because they can only see them in light of their own experiences, needs, and value systems. Thus, they also variously estimate the significance of particular elements, characteristic traits, and correlations within a given saga. Consequently, in the course of a narrative tradition, sagas are reinterpreted, remotivated, abridged, expanded, condensed, diluted, interpolated, extrapolated, and regrouped to the point where their original form soon becomes indiscernible. Still, a saga remains identifiable, because its basic constellation of elements is not altered. Despite any changes in particulars, Oedipus still always comes to the same fate: he will kill his father and wed his mother, effecting, in the process, what he wants to avoid (Graf 1993, 7).

The original form of the Troy saga also is irrecoverable. This was doubtless the case already in Homer's day, too. Nonetheless, its basic premises and the pivotal events of the story were well known to the eighth-century public, as we can clearly see from internal allusions in the *Iliad* and *Odyssey* (Kullmann 1981). The "raw form" of the saga ran as follows:

In the prosperous citadel of Ilios/Troy, in Asia Minor near the Hellespont (present-day Dardanelles), there reigns a powerful king named Priam. One of his sons, Paris, sails on a friendly mission to the land of the Akhaians, specifically the Peloponnesos. He arrives at Sparta, where Menelaos, the son of Atreus (Atreides), rules. Paris abuses the hospitality shown to him there by abducting Helen, Menelaos' wife, to

Troy. Menelaos seeks the help of his brother Agamemnon of Argos/Mycenae. A delegation of Akhaians goes to Troy to demand Helen's return but is rejected. Thereupon, Menelaos and Agamemnon (the Atreidai) make the decision to force the release of Helen through a military operation. Agamemnon invites all the more important powers on the mainland and on the islands to send contingents for a joint expedition to Troy. This call to arms is answered far and wide.

The ships gather at the harbor of Aulis in Boiotia, each contingent under its own commander. Agamemnon is assigned the supreme command. The fleet sails across to the Hellespont (ca. 350 km), via the islands of Lemnos and Tenedos, and lands on the coast of the Troad (territory surrounding Troy). Initial attempts to take the city by storm or to negotiate a solution end in failure. The Akhaians then commence a siege, but the stubborn resistance of the city's people and their allies from the neighboring peoples of Asia Minor causes an unexpected prolongation of operations over a number of years. These operations involve continual efforts to cut off Troy from its sources of aid and to bring about its surrender by conquering, sacking, and destroying neighboring cities, island settlements, and communities in the environs of Troy. This strategy is unsuccessful, not least because the gods are divided over the fate of Troy. In the tenth year of the war, after the pro-Trojan faction of gods has given up its opposition, the Akhaians manage to take the city by trickery. An immense wooden horse is constructed at the urging of the clever Odysseus. It is filled with picked fighting men. The besieging Akhaian warriors, seemingly demoralized, board ships and sail away. But in fact they lurk out of sight, awaiting a signal from the city during the night. The Trojans take the horse to be a gift-offering to the gods and, despite the warning of the priest Laocoön, drag it into the city to secure its supposed protective power. During the night, the Akhaian heroes climb out of the horse's belly and direct a fire-signal to the fleet standing off Tenedos. Together with the main force, which quickly sails back, they put Troy to the torch. King Priam and the adult male population are slain, and the women and children are abducted as slaves.

The return home (*nostos*) does not proceed in so orderly a fashion as had the outward expedition ten years before. Some contingents and ships go far off course. Some heroes, including Odysseus, reach home only years later, after wanderings fraught with adventure. Troy, however, is forever destroyed.

Apart from such fabulous elements as the wooden horse and the activities of the gods, which may be "rationalized away" as generic conventions of Greek heroic saga, this sequence of events seems completely realistic, largely due to the verifiably precise geographic details. Thus, the tale was sometimes considered historical not only by ancient audiences of the eighth century and later but also by modern readers, including even some in the twentieth century. The *Iliad*, which relates a good portion of the story, often seemed to be a slightly exaggerated poetic war report. With the skeptical attitude of our own time, the pendulum has swung far to the other direction in the past fifty years. The whole tale is nowadays often taken as pure fantasy.

A reasonable compromise position may perhaps be attained in view of the following considerations: It would obviously never have occurred to the first audience of the *Iliad* to compare the singer's recitation with a reliable report of the war. This audience did expect the epic singer to reach the highest level of authenticity (Kannicht 1980, 16–19). But the required authenticity, in the sense of the need to maintain narrative consistency, could refer only to a core event whose alteration would impede the audience's recognition of the story. However, the audience regarded it as the business of the individual singer to fill out the narrative framework imposed by unchanging essential material. The epics themselves bear this out. Thus, Odysseus, while still an unidentified stranger at the court of the Phaiakians, sets the singer Demodokos the topic of "the wooden horse" in the following terms:

> but now turn to another theme and sing the song of the horse
> of wood, which Epeios readied together with Athena
> and which the ruse of godlike Odysseus brought up to the
>   citadel
> after it was filled with men, who then laid waste to Ilios.
>
> (*Od.* 8.492–95)

With an extensive song, Demodokos fleshes out Odysseus' four-line sketch of the framework of the narrative "from the construction of the horse to the conquest of the city." The *Odyssey* poet takes twenty-one verses to describe this song (8.500–520). In formulating this synopsis, the poet makes it clear that the "actual" tale of Demodokos was significantly more elaborate (and much longer than twenty-one lines): "and he sang of how the sons of the Akhaians utterly destroyed the city, streaming out of the horse, leaving their hollow hiding place; he sang how one here and another there laid waste the high city . . ." (*Od.* 8.514–16).

Both the singer and his public were well aware that an element of creative imagination, of what we call "fiction," had now come into play. That is, different singers would flesh out the narrative structure in different ways. An awareness of this was vital to any evaluative discrimination among singers. The poet's use of direct discourse, which the audience will have considered an indispensable feature of epic narration, points to the same conclusion. The fictional quality of the speeches could hardly escape the notice of anyone who heard at least two versions of the same story. In such a context, then, authenticity did not mean accuracy in an unchanging documentation of reality. The audience had no notion of such a reality anyhow. Rather, it meant accuracy vis-à-vis a specific, current conception of "truth" in the mind of the audience.

The singer's public at any given time thus construed authenticity as one thing respecting the overall framework and as another respecting the fleshing out of that framework. Modern scholars have often ignored that distinction and consequently come to the mistaken conclusion that the manifestly fictional character of the fleshing out proves the fictional character of the very structure as well. This is the result of false reasoning.

The admittedly fictional nature of various novels about, say, Napoleon's Russian campaign does not entitle us to deduce that the campaign itself was fantasy. This is not the way to prove or disprove the historicity of the story or specifically the historicity of the Trojan War (a topic that has, by the way, recently enjoyed great vogue at scholarly conferences and in the pages of special issues of journals). Certainty in this matter could come only from evidence independent of saga and epic. At this point, we can only build a case based on "circumstantial evidence," with all its attendant imponderables.

However, the proportion of history to fiction in accounts of the event that forms the *Iliad*'s point of departure is irrelevant to an appreciation of the poem as a work of art. The *Iliad* would remain a literary masterpiece even if the Trojan War had never occurred. Still, the modern reader of the *Iliad* does well to accept the epic on the presumption that the war was a historical reality. Only so can one recapture the outlook of Homer's public, the poem's original recipients, and thus get a feel for the effect the *Iliad* must have had on that audience. It would be pure intellectual vanity to adopt an ironic attitude of self-conscious superiority based on rational criticism. Whoever prefers to view the text consistently from such a stance forgoes any chance of experiencing the work of art in an authentic manner.

It is impossible to summarize briefly the current state of the "case from circumstantial evidence" previously mentioned. The rediscovery of Troy in 1870 by Heinrich Schliemann (who followed topographical details in the *Iliad*) has, it is true, proved the historicity of the citadel at Ilios/Troy. But it cannot support this further chain of reasoning: that the historicity of a military conflict between the city's inhabitants and the Akhaians follows necessarily from the mere historical existence of the two parties. Only archaeological evidence (if that) can bring proof of the historicity of the war. So long as that is lacking, any decision for or against historicity can only be speculative.

Proponents of the historicity of a particular conflict can today, however, work with analogies drawn from the conditions of power politics within Akhaian civilization; this has only become possible since the decipherment of Linear B in 1952. Beginning in the fifteenth century, Mycenaean civilization had embarked "on a course of conquest and colonization . . . on Crete and farther afield on Rhodes and Cyprus, encroaching also on the coast of Asia Minor" (Gschnitzer 1981, 10). The citadel at the south entrance to the Dardanelles on the hill of Hissarlik in the vicinity of Çanakkale has left impressive fortification ruins indicating continuous habitation from ca. 3200 until ca. 1200. Its commanding position above the (then as now) important straits giving access to the Black Sea region may have attracted the interest of the Greeks prior to the catastrophe of ca. 1200. That it became, like Crete two centuries earlier, the target of a military expedition is likelier than not. The notion that a singer, standing in awe at the ruins of Troy after the catastrophe, composed a poem about the undertaking in a systematic way, conjures up a rather romantic image.

It is, of course, conceivable that the saga might have arisen in many other ways. It is advisable to concentrate on the *Iliad* as a work of art and to leave to one side the question of the historicity of the Troy story, as long as conclusive archaeological evidence is lacking. It should be noted, however, that important new light is being shed by the work of the Tübingen excavation-team under the direction of the prehistorian Manfred Korfmann. On the basis of results achieved in the area of Troy after 1981 (Korfmann 1984–1989; Latacz 1988.a, 1988.b), the government of the Republic of Turkey in 1988 granted Korfmann permission to resume the excavations of the Cincinnati expedition, directed by Carl Blegen and broken off in 1938, on the citadel itself (Korfmann 1991 and esp. 1993, 25–28). In the excavation campaigns of 1993, 1994, and 1995, Korfmann has made finds that strengthen the case for historicity. Before the citadel in Troy VI, in the very settlement stratum where a conflict between Trojans and Akhaians comes into question, there is an extensive lower city, protected by a strong enceinte wall and two deep trenches (Korfmann 1994, 28–37; Jablonka 1994). In 1995, substantial remains of defensive armaments were found in the area of the southwest gate of the citadel, through which a road led to the harbor of Troy. Since there is no indication whatever that defenders were able to use these armaments, we likely have to do with a surprise attack. Korfmann's 1996 excavations may provide a definitive answer to this question.

The "raw form" of the Troy saga, summarized earlier in this section, gives some notion of the possibilities inherent in this extensive complex of narrative material for an epic reformulation. The singer could round off interconnected parts of this material in self-contained "chapters," such as the "Destruction of Troy" (*Iliupersis*) sung by Demodokos at *Odyssey* 8.500–520 or the "Homecoming of the Akhaians" (*Nostos*) recited by Phemios at *Odyssey* 1.326 f. He could also trace a continuous narrative line, highlight the fate of an individual, or elaborate individual episodes (thus Demodokos at *Od.* 8.75–82 sings of a "quarrel between Odysseus and the son of Peleus, Akhilleus," which likely belonged to the prehistory of the Trojan War, that is, in the subject area of the later *Cypria*).

But it was possible to tell the entire story in the epic manner at one go only at the beginning of the saga's evolution. The initial version of the story was very quickly inflated by the invention of new characters and episodes; it soon became impossible to tell the entire tale within the time limitations that any epic narration must abide by. A complete narration, in the sense of a systematic, chronological presentation of action, could occur only when the availability of writing freed the composer from any concerns about the receptive powers of a listening public. Even then definite conventions about the division of material were inherited from the routines of pre-Homeric oral performance. This is apparent in the subdivision of the saga in the post-Homeric cyclic epics:

1. *Cypria* = prehistory of the war, and the war up to the beginning of the *Iliad* (eleven books).
(2. the *Iliad*.)
3. *Aithiopis* = the story subsequent to the *Iliad*—that is, continuation of the story of the war up to the death of Akhilleus at the hands of Paris and Apollo (five books).
4. *Little Iliad* = continuation from the quarrel of Odysseus and Aias over the weapons of the fallen Akhilleus to the bringing of the wooden horse into the city (four books).
5. *Iliupersis* = continuation from the Laocoön-scene at the wooden horse, through the destruction of Troy, to the departure of the Akhaians for home (two books).
6. *Nostoi* = events subsequent to the war: the homecoming of the Greek warriors up to the return of Agamemnon and of Menelaos and Helen (five books).
(7. the *Odyssey* = the story of the homecoming of Odysseus specifically.)
8. *Telegony* = continuation of the *Odyssey* from the return of Odysseus to his death (two books).

Even if one puts down much in these written epics to the tendency of their conservative-minded authors to systematize and tidy up, the richness of material in the pre-Homeric Troy saga is obvious. No singer could have covered it all in a typical oral recitation.

It required a whole new narrative strategy and technique to achieve a seemingly exhaustive version of the Troy saga. This was in fact one of the great accomplishments of Homer. The novel perspective of the *Iliad* appears to be the manifestation of this new technique.

The Development of the Theme: The Plan of Action

For audiences that knew the whole of the Troy saga, the prooimion of the *Iliad* must have seemed to announce a poem about an individual episode. The theme—wrath resulting from a quarrel—was nothing unusual in itself. In the aristocratic world, honor occupied a high position and consisted, for example, of respect shown to an individual on the strength of his achievements or possessions. Given this, there were, naturally, unavoidable conflicts among members of the same house, clan, military camp, and so on. This much was assumed as a central theme in the poetry of heroic epic. Thus, for example, in Homer, the quarrel of Odysseus and Akhilleus, mentioned in passing in the *Odyssey* as the subject of a song sung by Demodokos (*Od.* 8.75–82), hints at an episode that had long had its place somewhere in the overall structure of the Troy saga. So too, the portentous quarrel of Odysseus and Aias over Akhilleus' weapons, which we learn of in the *Little Iliad*, was surely fixed in the epic tradition of Troy from time immemorial, for it is linked to Akhilleus' death. Likewise a familiar subject in heroic epic was an anger or wrath stemming from a quarrel or latent difference of opinion and resulting in the angry man's hindering or frustrating the cause of his adversary even if that cause was also his own (Bowra 1952, 123–25; Patzer 1972, 46). In the *Iliad*, for example, Paris "sulks" in book 6 (see lines 326 ff.; an aborted theme in the context), and in the ninth book the Aitolian hero Meleager refrains from fighting, "cooking up his heart-offending wrath [against his mother]" (Schadewaldt), and lies apart with his wife Kleopatra, while the enemy are already scaling the walls of his home city Kalydon (*Il.* 9.553 ff.). In the world of the gods, moreover, always mirroring human conditions, anger and wrath are the order of the day (Irmscher 1950).

It is not impossible then that a quarrel between the supreme commander Agamemnon of Argos/Mycenae and the son of Peleus, Akhilleus, from Phthia in Thessaly was an element of the epic of Troy even before Homer. It may indeed have centered on a gift of honor (γέρας, *geras*)—a captive girl (Reinhardt 1961, 56–63). Even a temporary boycott of the fighting by Akhilleus may already have been present in pre-Homeric poetry. Many a peculiar thing about the opening of the *Iliad*—for example, the astonishing fact that the time of the events being narrated (the ninth year of the war) is first indicated only in the second book and then as something entirely self-evident (2.295)—would be less odd if Homer could have relied on specific prior knowledge in the minds of his auditors. But it is far less likely that this segment of the saga, the quarrel of Akhilleus and Agamemnon and the wrath of Akhilleus, had ever previously been anything more than a way station in the narrative, let alone the announced exclusive subject of an entire epic. It is still less plausible that any singer before Homer had taken as his theme not the quarrel per se but the representation of the aftermath of such a quarrel in the mind of a hero, together with the effects it exerted on the hero himself and his world.

The suspense of the audience was stimulated by Homer's novel

approach. The poet followed this up with another surprise in the elaboration of his theme. For he embodied the theme in a plan of action that
far exceeded the parameters of a poem dedicated to a single episode.
His "new perspective" was distinctive in a structural sense as well. The
psychological dimension enabled him to handle the entire saga within
a part of it, chiefly through compression and reflection. Compression
occurs when a character whose nature is gradually disclosed through a
series of individual scenes and situations in the overall saga is
restricted in the *Iliad* to a few appearances, or even to one, in which
nonetheless all the salient traits of that character are displayed. Reflection is employed when Homer cannot directly include those stages of
the saga that fall chronologically before or after the action of the *Iliad*.
Such material is "mirrored" along the way in the *Iliad* in various fash-
ions, including the use of symbolic substitutes. Thus, the *Iliad* is able to
be both a treatment of a single episode and a rendition of the saga as a
whole. The particulars of how this is done can be seen precisely in the
way the theme evolves.

The development of the theme begins with the realization of the
three programmatic points announced in the prooimion.

The Events Leading up to Akhilleus's Wrath

On one of their plundering forays, the Akhaians have abducted the
daughter of Khryses, a priest of Apollo. The priest goes to the camp and
petitions the Akhaians en masse—"all the Akhaians" (*Il.* 1.15), "but
especially the two sons of Atreus" (1.16)—to return his daughter in
exchange for a considerable ransom. "All the other Akhaians," we are
told, "consented to heed the holy man and to accept the shining ransom." (1.22–23)—only Agamemnon bluntly denies him. He drives away
the old man with a speech that is not only insulting but blasphemous:

> Let me not find you, old man, beside the high ships
> (either tarrying now or returning again later)!
> lest your staff and the ribbons of the god not protect you!
> The girl, for her part, I will not release to you! Sooner will old
>   age overtake her
> in our court in Argos, far from her home,
> working at the loom and meeting my bed!—
> Get out! Do not anger me—that way at least you may return
>   home safely!
>
> (*Il.* 1.26–32)

This is the first instance of a specific type of direct address that figures prominently in Homeric poetics. It eliminates the need for direct characterization of individuals; it sets a course for future action; it injects drama into the narrative; it brings the current habits of thought and feeling of the audience into the ancient story; and it subtly guides the audience's manner of reception. Agamemnon's speech characterizes this highest ranking Akhaian as an overbearing and cynical ("and meeting my bed") autocrat. It motivates the intervention of a divine agency (Apollo) by the contempt and disdain shown for the priestly status of the petitioner. It forges, both externally and internally, the causal links leading to the conflict with Akhilleus. It elicits examples of the same personality traits from the audience's own experience, and it evokes sympathy for the victim, the rejected Khryses, while stirring initial feelings of antipathy toward Agamemnon.

The priest goes along the shore of the sea and beseeches his god, Apollo, to avenge him against *the whole body* of the Akhaians. Resonating here for the first time is the fundamental theme of the *Iliad*: how the misbehavior of an individual damages the common good. Like Khryses, Akhilleus, three hundred lines later, will go along the shore and ask his divine mother Thetis to take vengeance against *the whole body* of the Akhaians (*Il.* 1.348 ff.). In both cases, the person responsible for the subsequent horrendous reprisals is Agamemnon. The complex problem of leadership becomes apparent for the first time: leadership based on power alone courts disaster. It is hard to imagine that this lesson does not stem from Homer's own experience. The warning may reflect the threat to aristocratic leadership that sharp eyes were already discerning on the horizon in Homer's day (Nicolai 1983, 1984, 1987; Effe 1988; Latacz 1991a, 100 f.; 1992a, 205–7; Janko 1992, 38).

Apollo hears Khryses and helps him, as later Thetis hears and helps Akhilleus. He strides down from Olympos, with "anger in his heart" (*Il.*1.44); the arrows, signifying the pestilence, rattle menacingly in his quiver, as he approaches "like the night" (1.47). He sits a little apart from the ships and shoots the first disease-arrow,

> and terrible was the thrum of the silver bow.
>
> (*Il.* 1.49)

He strikes first at the mules and dogs, but then at the heroes themselves,

> and the pyres of corpses burned constantly, close by.
>
> (*Il.* 1.53)

The idea of casting the father of the abducted girl as a priest proves to be very well conceived: the insult to Khryses in this way becomes a violation not only of human but also of divine conventions. The divine sphere is thereby included in the story and a systematically two-tiered sequence of events is set in motion in the *Iliad*: action on the human plane runs parallel to action on the divine plane. These levels are quite discrete but repeatedly overlap at particular points or sections of the narrative. Humans appeal to the gods, and the gods, once implicated, take part on their own initiative as well. The result is a complex and intricate web of reciprocal interests and interdependencies. The poet who oversees all this has at hand a unique method of motivating and remotivating actions, of accelerating or retarding the tempo of action through divine intervention, of indirectly passing moral judgment on human actions, and of directing his audience toward a proper interpretation of his stated intentions (Griffin 1980, 179–204; Kullmann 1985; Erbse 1986; Janko 1992, 2).

The pestilence continues for nine days. On the tenth, Akhilleus summons an assembly of the army,

> since white-armed Hera had put this in his mind,
> because she worried about the Danaans when she saw them
>   dying.
>
> (*Il.* 1.55–56)

Why does Hera, the mother of the gods and wife of the most high Zeus, show concern for the misfortunes of the Akhaians? Again, the prior knowledge of the audience is assumed. Hera, like Zeus' powerful daughter Athena, is a mortal enemy of Troy because of the judgment of Paris. Paris, at the time a shepherd on Mt. Ida in the Troad, had been asked to judge which of three goddesses—Hera, Athena, or Aphrodite—was the most beautiful. He awarded the prize to Aphrodite, because she promised him the most beautiful woman in the world—Helen. Since then, the two slighted and humiliated goddesses have hated and persecuted Paris and his people (Reinhardt 1948, 19). The poet masterfully controls the instrument of myth, playing on several keyboards at the same time: Apollo intervenes in answer to an impulsive prayer, and his impetuous actions jeopardize the siege of Troy; Hera intervenes on her own initiative because this current accident imperils many long-standing, intense interests—especially, her desire to see Troy fall; the poet has Hera choose precisely Akhilleus as her tool, to involve him in a bitter dispute with Agamemnon and consequently to make him aggrieved and enraged. We see the poet pulling the strings of the story.

With the summoning of an assembly of the army, the narrative embarks on the second of the three programmatic points made in the prooimion.

The Origin of the Wrath

Akhilleus addresses Agamemnon as a concerned commander of the Myrmidon contingent in the army and is representative of the general mood in the Akhaian camp:

> Son of Atreus! Now I think that we, beaten back,
> must return home again—assuming we escape death
>   at all—
> if evidently both war and sickness overcome the Akhaians!
> So then! Let us ask a seer or priest,
> perhaps even an interpreter of dreams (for a dream, too, comes
>   from Zeus),
> who may tell us why Phoibos Apollo has become so angry. . . ."
>   (*Il.* 1.59–64)

The seer Kalkhas stands up. Akhilleus had deliberately avoided naming him (why will soon become apparent), but naturally Kalkhas, like everyone present, knows that he is meant. Before he speaks, Kalkhas is expressly called

>   the best of bird-watchers,
> who had knowledge of the present, the future, and the past,
> and who had guided the ships of the Akhaians on their way to
>   Ilios
> by his seercraft—which Phoibos Apollo had granted him.
>   (*Il.* 1.69–72)

Kalkhas thus represents a "spiritual" power. He, like Khryses, is a priest of Apollo, but a much higher ranking one, and he is especially esteemed by the Akhaians in general—an implicit counterweight to the authority of Agamemnon, it seems. Everyone realizes that whatever Kalkhas might say will be significant. Still, he hesitates to speak, for he knows perfectly well whom he must name as the party responsible for the epidemic. The truth is dangerous, so he wants Akhilleus to guarantee his safety beforehand. Akhilleus obliges him:

> Boldly speak the word of the gods, which you know!
> By Apollo, beloved of Zeus, to whom you, Kalkhas,
> pray when you disclose the will of the gods,
> so long as I am alive and look upon the earth,
> no one beside the hollow ships shall lay heavy hands on you,
> no one of all the Akhaians, even should you name Agamemnon,
> who now declares he is far the best of the Akhaians!
>
> (*Il.* 1.85–91)

Here again we have a speech that serves several purposes. First, with regard to characterization, we see Akhilleus as the intrepid protector of the weak, but also as impulsively quick to take on weighty personal obligations. Next, with regard to the program of action, Kalkhas, as the listener realizes, will of course speak out after receiving his guarantee. The great conflict is unfolding. Finally, with regard to the implicit control of the listener's reactions, does this not appear to be a case of tacit collusion? First, the name *Kalkhas* is cleverly avoided; then, as if this were his cue, Kalkhas promptly stands up. Then the guarantee of safety is made by the very man who has called together the assembly and proposed consulting some "seer or priest" or "interpreter of dreams." Finally, in giving his guarantee, Akhilleus makes an apparently offhand mention of the name *Agamemnon,* as if only to strengthen the guarantee by referring to a risibly unlikely possibility. Is there not at work here an unspoken alliance between insightful persons who have the best interests of the group at heart? Persons who know from long experience the volatile temper of their leader, so obstinately proud of his position of supreme authority, and who wish unobtrusively to guide him back onto the right path? To achieve this, someone must say what the misguided individual would never recognize or admit on his own.

Kalkhas says it: the guilty party is Agamemnon. Because he dishonored Khryses, Apollo's priest, "the far shooting Apollo sent sorrows and will send yet more" (*Il.* 1.96), until the maiden Khryseis is given back to her father in Khryse (and now without ransom) and Apollo himself is appeased with a great sacrificial offering.

Now the truth is out. Agamemnon rises, "his heart black with rage" (*Il.* 1.103–4) and his eyes flashing. First he makes a sharp thrust at Kalkhas, a thrust that bespeaks latent animosity:

> You seer of misfortune! You have never yet said anything pleasing to me. And now this! I must be the guilty one, because I would not take ransom for Khryseis! To be sure, I wouldn't. I dearly wanted her in my home. I preferred her even to my wife Klytaimestra, since she is not at all inferior to her. . . . But now, despite all that, I will give her back, because *I* desire that the soldiers be well and not die. But give me immediately a prize of honor to take her place, lest I alone of the Argives lack a prize! That would be unseemly!
>
> (*Il.* 1.106 ff.)

Akhilleus is very upset and answers in angry disapproval:

> Atreus, most glorious and greedy of all! How are the brave Akhaians to give you a gift? The prizes have long since been allotted; do you mean to take something back from its possessor? You must now return this maiden *at the god's bidding*! We will compensate you three- and fourfold, once Zeus has granted us to take the high-walled city of Troy!
>
> (*Il.* 1.122 ff.)

The controversy still might have ended at this point. Akhilleus' proposal is reasonable, and Agamemnon will presently comply with it. But Akhilleus has made a mistake (had he not, he would not have been Akhilleus); he has disclosed a little of what he thinks of Agamemnon in general, in a way uncalled for in the dispute at hand: "most . . . greedy of all!" he calls Agamemnon, and he insists that one cannot reclaim what has already been apportioned. We detect a note of disdain and almost of contempt: touching a nerve, he goes on to call Agamemnon "grasping," "small-minded," "petty."

The quarrel has now come to the nitty-gritty. The girl is no longer the central issue; she will shortly board ship for Khryse. The heart of the matter now is the profound hostility between these two different kinds of men, clearly a hostility that both have felt and endured for a long while. It erupts in an explosion of long-suppressed tensions:

> *Agamemnon*: Do not try to trick me! You only want to have a gift of honor and look on gloating as I sit by without one. No! Either the Akhaians give me an equivalent prize or I myself will take one— from you or Aias or Odysseus! We will get to that later!

> *Akhilleus*: Oh shameless one, grasping for gain! How can you still keep your leadership? I have not come here to battle on account of the Trojans, those spear-fighting men, since they are not blame-worthy *to me*! They have never once driven off *my* cattle or horses; never in the broad fields of fertile, man-nourishing Phthia have they destroyed the crops. . . .
>   *You* were the one we followed, oh most shameless one, so that *you* might gain satisfaction! to procure honor for Menelaos and for *you*, dog-eyes! Honor from the Trojans!
>
>   (*Il.* 1.131–60)

A long suppressed account is being settled here: Akhilleus has fol-lowed the commander of his own volition and not as a subject, but he has never enjoyed the same rights as Agamemnon. He far surpasses Agamemnon in achievement yet is always fobbed off with an inferior share of booty. Now comes the threat: "Enough of this! I am going home to Phthia. I do not think I shall any longer go on enriching you while I go without honor!" (1.169–71).

The quarrel now reaches its climax. Agamemnon accepts Akhilleus' threat to resign:

> Go on, then! Do as you wish. I will not ask you to stay here for my sake. There are plenty of others who respect me, Zeus above all! You, however, have always been the most hateful of princes to me! You are always keen on strife and war and battle! Don't pride yourself on your power! For that is given you by a god. Go on home with your ships and rule over your Myrmidons. I do not trouble myself over you *or care a whit about your anger*. Now here is my threat: I will send Khryseis home, to please Apollo. But in recompense I will in person take for myself your Briseis, she of the

beautiful cheeks. With my own hand I will take your prize of honor from your tent . . . so you may well know how much greater I am than you, and so another man hereafter will shrink back from contending with me or likening himself to me!

(*Il.* 1.173–87)

Akhilleus, beside himself, grasps his sword. The poet now has Athena appear (visible only to Akhilleus). In a brief exchange, he has her dissuade the hero from killing the king. In line 194, we read that

he was drawing the great sword from its sheath, and then
    Athena came. . . .

and in line 220

he pushed the great sword back into the sheath, and followed
   . . . .

This fleeting moment on the razor's edge, which epic renditions before Homer would simply have touched on ("named," in narratological terminology), is here filled with inner action, brought to light in the form of a divine intervention.

Of course, Akhilleus must not kill Agamemnon, and not only because the Troy saga tradition would not allow it. For how could the wrath—the theme of the whole epic—come into being without anger being repressed? The wrath, as the dramatic *basso ostinato* of the action of the *Iliad*, was possible only if total dissension came at the very beginning. Furthermore, it was possible only if Akhilleus was so deeply insulted that only the slaying of the offender could bring satisfaction, yet no such slaying takes place. In short, Akhilleus must *repress* both his sword and himself, in the literal sense of the word (that is, "press back"). The very idea of not having reacted spontaneously, of having instead repressed one's feelings—the idea, that is, of having passively suffered a humiliation—must constitute a permanent self-reproach for Akhilleus. This is what makes him so implacable. The insult went so very deep, because the insulted man could not forgive himself for having swallowed such indignities. This is what makes the wrath so very plausible. But how was the poet to bring this off? An Akhilleus who simply yielded to Agamemnon would be no Akhilleus at all. He must be made to obey a superior force. That force could come only in the form of a divinity. The epiphany of Athena offered the solution.

With this compelling account of the origin of the wrath, the poet has made the transition to the third of his programmatic points.

The Consequences of the Wrath for the Larger Group

Akhilleus has sheathed his sword, aware of his public humiliation. The poet now has him bind himself by the terms of "a great oath," terms that will restrict his actions for a long time to come:

> Still I say this to you, and swear a great oath on it:
> as surely as this scepter will never again put forth leaves or
>   buds,
> having left the cut stump behind in the mountain forest,
> and will never sprout again . . .
> truly a day will come when all the sons of the Akhaians will
>   yearn for Akhilleus!
> Then, though hard-pressed, you will be able to accomplish
>   nothing,
> when many fall to the ground, dying at the hands of death-
>   dealing Hektor.
> But you will eat out the hearts within you,
> full of remorse, because you did no honor whatever to the best of
>   the Akhaians!
>
> (*Il.* 1.233–44)

Among the functions of direct address in Homer, the programmatic is most prominent in this instance. To be sure, Akhilleus' words serve to characterize the hero—his passionate impulsiveness, his burning desire for satisfaction. But more importantly, they point far beyond Akhilleus and the whole situation in which he finds himself. Akhilleus' words adumbrate the structure of the work. In the terminology used by E. Lämmert in his *Bauformen des Erzählens* [Structural Patterns of Narrative] (1980), the speech provides an indistinct but inevitable anticipation of the future. In it, the poet for the first time gives concrete information about the results of the quarrel and of the wrath stemming from it: Akhilleus will no longer take part in the war ("the sons of the Akhaians will yearn for Akhilleus") and the Trojans will consequently gain the upper hand. Their leader, Hektor, will rampage among the Akhaians. And Agamemnon—deeply aware that he can do nothing alone against Hektor—will rebuke himself, knowing that he is to blame for all this because of his tyrannical behavior during the quarrel with Akhilleus. The vague prediction of the prooimion regarding "the wrath of Akhilleus . . . that brought infinite pain to the Akhaians" (*Il.* 1.1–2) now acquires definite contours. Into the mouth of a principal character—Akhilleus—the poet puts a statement whose confirmation in an oath assures the listener that it will be accomplished. The poet thus conveys to his public that the consequences of Akhilleus' wrath will consist of the ever-worsening plight of the whole Akhaian army. But the listener at this point learns neither how these events will transpire in detail nor how they will arise at all. The listener thus continues to be in suspense.

There eventually comes a dead point in the quarrel:

So spoke the son of Peleus. He threw the scepter down to the
    ground,
with its golden studs, and sat down himself.
The son of Atreus still raged on the other side. . . .
                                                (*Il.* 1.245–47)

Nestor intervenes, Nestor "the clear-voiced Pylian counselor with his fair words; from his throat the words flowed sweeter than honey. He had already seen two generations of men pass away . . . in sacred Pylos, and he now ruled over the third" (*Il.* 1.247–52). Nestor is a "gray eminence." He represents the wisdom of age, born of experience and reason. With all his psychological means, he tries to settle the quarrel: he points out the immense military advantage for the enemy of a rift between their two strongest and most intelligent attackers, with the attendant division of the besieging army. He recalls that many important heroes have accepted his mediation in the past. He calls on the parties of the quarrel to be reasonable and to acknowledge how crucially important their cooperation is for the whole army and how indispensable each is to the common welfare of the army. But all his efforts are frustrated by the extreme incompatibility of the two personalities. It even seems that Nestor's whole speech has been inserted chiefly to underscore the implacability of the two parties. The listener can better gauge the real depth of Akhilleus' wrath by witnessing the cogency of the arguments he rejects. At the same time, this speech also performs the programmatic function of making the poet's structural plan somewhat clearer. The stress on the military advantage that Akhilleus' wrath gives to the Trojans shows that the scope of the wrath reaches far beyond one episode and that the whole Trojan expedition is at stake. In this epic the matter of Akhilleus' wrath speaks to a larger issue—the entire war.

After the failed attempt to mediate, matters take their course. With his friend Patroklos and the rest of his "staff," Akhilleus withdraws into his own area of the Akhaian camp. Agamemnon allows Khryseis to be returned to Khryse on a ship under the command of Odysseus. Immediately afterward, his two heralds, Talthybios and Eurybates, proceed to the tent of Akhilleus with official orders to bring away his captive girl Briseis. Akhilleus gives up the girl, but not before calling on the two messengers as witnesses of this injustice

> before the blessed gods, mortal men,
> and also this brutal king [Agamemnon], if ever hereafter
> there should be need of me to ward off shameful destruction
> from the others, because that man [Agamemnon] of course rages
>   now in his ruinous heart
> and lacks utterly the wit to look before and behind him
> so that the Akhaians might fight safely beside the ships.
>
> (*Il.* 1.339–44)

Here again, we have a foreshadowing. Fixed even more firmly in the mind of the listener—again, by means of an oath—is the certainty that the army will be gravely endangered by the misbehavior of its leader and will desperately need rescue by Akhilleus. At the same time, we see the opinion of the audience being molded: Agamemnon clearly lacks the foresight essential to a leader in his position; lacking "the wit to look before and behind him," he is not the man for his job. This is true of him not only at the moment of this quarrel in the ninth year of the war, but throughout the whole Troy saga; his personality is displayed in a concentrated way by the sharp contrast with Akhilleus. "One expects in the *Iliad* that this man will come to a bad end" (Kullmann 1981, 27); his own wife will suffocate him in his bath!

The heralds leave with Briseis. Akhilleus, however, goes in tears to the seashore (as had Khryses earlier). "Looking out over the boundless sea" (*Il.* 1.350), he stretches out his arms and beseeches his mother to hear him in his need. His mother, Thetis, a goddess of the sea, comes and asks what is wrong. Akhilleus tells her. He tells her everything that the listener already knows, but this time from his own point of view, stressing Agamemnon's *hybris* (insulting arrogance). He concludes:

> If you are able, protect your son:
> Go to Olympos and petition Zeus . . .
> if he might be willing to help the *Trojans*,
> pressing the Akhaians back to the sterns of their ships along the
>   sea,
> dying, so that they may all have the benefit of their king,
> and so the son of Atreus, the great commander Agamemnon,
>   may recognize
> that he was blind when he did not honor the best of the
>   Akhaians!
>
> (*Il.* 1.393–94, 408–12)

Akhilleus speaks here with sarcasm ("so that they may all have the benefit of their king"), asking that Zeus assist his mortal enemies while wreaking death and destruction on his own comrades.

Akhilleus is not, of course, actuated by a simple longing for vengeance. Were that his motive, then he would have wished for Agamemnon's own death above all. But he is interested in a subtler punishment. If Agamemnon were simply killed, then he would go—still blind—to Hades. Akhilleus would in that case have technically avenged himself, but he would not have extracted satisfaction. Agamemnon must realize that he was wrong and Akhilleus was right and that Akhilleus is indispensable to the expedition. Akhilleus' ascendancy is contingent on Agamemnon's abasement. Thus, Agamemnon himself must not die. He must live, but he must live so that his blindness may gradually be brought home to him in its consequences. But because this autocrat is demonstrably lacking in true intelligence and therefore also in the imagination needed for abstract calculation, he can comprehend his blindness only indirectly through a truly macabre series of experiences. He who is convinced that he acts in the interest of the whole army must come to the painful awareness that his actions have brought down the army to ruination. The Akhaians must die so that their leader's eyes may be opened.

The poet who had Akhilleus conceive this strategy apparently had a conception of the character of the hero unlike that found in older sagas. In the latter, Akhilleus appears to have figured as an ambitious, honor-craving, unreflective, somewhat naive prototype of the "young hot-head." The hulking Akhilleus in his helmet and armor is a common-place picture in our modern storybooks, a much imitated favorite of playful, hero-worshiping boys in heated schoolyard battles. But Homer's Akhilleus is a young man who knows his destiny is to die in the attainment of greatness. He sees himself hindered on his course by a mediocre official who has not once noticed the brilliance of the flame that burns within Akhilleus. Akhilleus is not only physically stronger than his commander; he comprehends, while Agamemnon only calcu-lates his own interest. This is only one example. Homer never portrays truly simplistic individuals. Limited or one-sided individuals, yes, but still always self-aware human beings. Because Homer is not simple, neither are his poetic creations. Nothing could be more mistaken than to read Homer as representative of a "naive epoch."

The plan of action in the *Iliad* has again been further elucidated in the request of Akhilleus. It had already been disclosed in the oath of Akhilleus that this epic would not take the form of a mere episode. The story of the wrath of Akhilleus would be one of ever-increasing mortal peril for the Akhaians. While the perspective in the oath remained quite general, in the request we find a ray of light illuminating the darkness. The creator of the Akhaians' peril is visible—Zeus himself. *He* will help the Trojans. More specifically: he will drive the Akhaians back to the sterns of their ships (which have been drawn onto land stern-first), back to the breaking waves of the sea. This augurs not only the failure of the whole expedition but the very annihilation of the army. Then indeed Agamemnon will be aware of his blindness.

Thus the planned course of events has become a little more concrete. But here, too, we are dealing with only a partial revelation. Certain questions remain open: How, for example, will Zeus help the Trojans? Has not the fall of Troy been decided, and by this same Zeus? How can Zeus contradict himself? The still more pressing question is, What will happen when Agamemnon undergoes his "recognition"? Will there be a reversal? Will it be too late? But it cannot be too late, because, accord-ing to the saga, Troy must ultimately fall. How, then, will there be a reversal?

The poet clearly intended this uncertain element in his elucidation. It

is one of his principles of composition. The listener has already tra-
versed three stages in the revelation of the narrative plan. First—the
whole general statement of the prooimion—the wrath of Akhilleus has
brought "infinite pain" to the Akhaians. Then Akhilleus in his oath
graphically prophesied that the army would yearn for him in a situation of dire adversity. Now there is the prospect of the Akhaians being
driven back into the sea, coupled with the as yet indefinite prediction
that *then* Agamemnon will come to his senses.

The request of Akhilleus is immediately succeeded by the pledge of
Thetis. It provides another small increment in the clarification of the
narrative plan. It will explain the interconnections among the previously divulged parts of the plan. Thetis says:

> I will go myself to snow capped Olympos, if he [Zeus] might
>   comply.
> But you wait, sitting by the swift ships,
> in anger at the Akhaians, and stay away from the fighting
>   altogether!
>
> (*Il.* 1.420–22)

This reveals the general outlines of the subsequent course of events.
The poet has devised a plot that will progress to the same result along
two parallel planes—human and divine. On the divine plane, Zeus *will
act*, while on the complementary human plane, Akhilleus *will not act*.
Akhilleus will sit in wrath beside the ships, and Zeus will drive the
Akhaians back to these very ships. For the overall narrative plan to succeed, both component plans must intermesh fully. That means that
Akhilleus' wrath is now compulsory. If he were to take part in the fighting again, the design of Zeus would come to naught. Thus new compli-
cations and narrative threads are introduced. Being the hero he is,
Akhilleus will not long endure having to sit aside in wrath. It is just not
possible. His "fingers will itch." What will win out? His desire for satisfaction or his desire to see Troy fall (and to win undying fame)? For he
has acted from an unqualified wish to see Troy fall; that was why he
summoned the assembly of the army! The listener is far from certain
about these things.

Thus the poet's technique consists of an incremental disclosure of the
overall narrative plan of the *Iliad*. The individual increments are,
nonetheless, relatively small and shed light on only so much of the larger

plan. This leads listeners to ask new questions and thus to experience growing suspense: "The poet's formulation of a narrative program, if it is to foreshadow events and create suspense, must never divulge everything the poet has in mind. If it makes one thing manifest, it must shrewdly conceal others. It reveals the general direction and the ultimate goal of the action, but it leaves the precise route in darkness. Above all, it says nothing about delays or setbacks. For setbacks entail an element of surprise in all narrative and dramatic art" (Schadewaldt 1938, 54 f.). Therefore, the poet only hints at the complete narrative plan. The listener can see only far enough into the future to be conscious that there is a plan. He or she cannot discern in detail how it will play out. This is what creates suspense. Moreover, there should be room within his own plan for the poet to surprise even himself. It would be impossible to sketch every last detail of such an immense construction on the drawing board. The good architect leaves much open. No one has seen this more clearly than the great Homer scholar Karl Reinhardt: "thus new elements are successively added to an underlying pattern or matrix, emerging in part from that matrix itself, in part from circumstances arising outside it, and growing more or less in step with the main trunk" (Reinhardt 1961, 210). Of course, the *Iliad* poet's exact processes of creation can no more be reconstructed than those of any other poet. What reader even today does not automatically know that works of art begin with a concept, an original plan that is then gradually elaborated, at some times very successfully, at others less so?

The Execution of the Narrative Plan: "Akhilleid" and *Iliad*

The listener who has followed the *Iliad* poet carefully up to this point has not only a *basic* structural concept of the further course of action but also the sense that the structure delineated to this point will take up considerable space. In the first 427 lines, the course has been set, and the listener feels that the actual "journey" is now beginning. It will leave far behind the spatial and temporal confines of previous incidents. To this point, everything has transpired in a small area: the Akhaian camp (the meeting place and the tent of Akhilleus) and along the shore where the ships have been dragged to land. The action has involved only a few characters: Khryses, Agamemnon, Akhilleus, Nestor, Patroklos, and fleetingly also Aias, Odysseus, Hektor, Khryseis, Briseis, the two heralds, Zeus, Apollo, Hera, Athena, and Thetis. The events since the poem's opening have occupied only a few hours: on the first day of action the brief altercation between Khryses and Agamemnon occurred; then the passing of nine days of pestilence is simply indicated or "named"; on the tenth day we have the assembly, the quarrel, the wrath of Akhilleus, the return of Khryseis to her father at Khryse, the fetching of Briseis from the tent of Akhilleus, and Akhilleus' conversation with Thetis.

The listener is now aware that the framework of action will enlarge. We foresee that Zeus himself will be taking matters in hand; he will allow the Trojans to drive the Akhaians back to the sea. Therefore, the Trojan side also will now figure in the action. The city of Troy, until now only an abstraction, will be depicted concretely. The number of actors will increase. Battle will resume. The static character of the action to this point will come to an end. Events will acquire momentum. Great things are in the offing.

There is now a brief interlude for the expiatory embassy to Khryse; this is essential from a technical, narrative standpoint, since the action at Troy can proceed only when the pestilence in the Akhaian camp ceases, and this in turn will happen only after the appeasement of Apollo, as Khryses has made plain (Latacz 1981b). Starting in line 493, events begin to take on dimensions that are difficult for a modern reader to grasp. (Naturally, the ancient audience, steeped in saga, will have had an easier time of it.) The next 15,205 lines of the epic recount—more or less exhaustively—the incidents of a further thirty days and five nights.

Before discussing how Homer structured this massive narrative, we must set out a synopsis of the events in the *Iliad*. In table 1, the flow of action has been segmented into individual scenes, which are defined and labeled in the interest of gaining the clearest possible conception of the poem's organization. (Other divisions might serve other interests.) The letters *a* and *b* added to line numbers indicate the first and second half of the line. Line numbers in the "day" column indicate the point at which a day or night begins or ends. The Greek terms designating particular books or parts thereof (for example, τειχοσκοπία, "view from the wall," for book 3) go back for the most part to ancient Homer scholars, and perhaps in some cases to the practice of rhapsodes. The causal connections between the most important complexes of scenes are discussed after the synopsis.

TABLE 1. Scene-Distribution in the *Iliad*

Day	Scene	Lines

Book 1

Day	Scene	Lines
	Prooimion	1–12a
9th year	I. Quarrel between Akhilleus and Agamemnon:	
of the war	background	12–53
(2.295)	(1) Khryses before Agamemnon—his appeal is rejected	12b–32
1st day	(2) Khryses on the shore: he appeals to Apollo for	
	vengeance on the Akhaians	33–43
	(3) Apollo sends the plague	44–53

> Days 1–9: plague

Day	Scene	Lines
10th day	II. The Quarrel and its consequences	54–492
(1.54)	(1) Council of the chief Akhaians (ἀγορή, *agorē*):	54–187
	(2) Escalation of the quarrel almost to the killing of the king	188–94a
	(3) Intervention of Athena: killing of the king forestalled; Nestor's fruitless attempt to mediate; partial concession of Akhilleus; Agamemnon sends heralds to Akhilleus	194b–326
	(4) The heralds with Akhilleus and Patroklos; they take Briseis with them	327–348a
	(5) Akhilleus and Thetis on the shore: Akhilleus' petition (407–12)	348b–430a
	(6) The embassy under Odysseus in Khryse	430b–476
11th day	(7) Return of the embassy from Khryse	477–487
(477)	(8) Akhilleus' anger (μῆνις, *mēnis*)	488–492

> 11-day absence of the gods, including Zeus,
> with the Ethiopians

Day	Scene	Lines
21st day	III. Intercession of Thetis, the promise of Zeus, and the council of the gods (θεῶν βουλή, *theōn boulē*; 493–611)	
(493)	(1) Thetis with Zeus: her petition; Zeus promises to fulfill it	493–533a
	(2) Zeus and Hera quarrel	533b–570
	(3) Hephaistos reconciles his quarreling parents; "Homeric laughter"; banquet of the gods; the gods retire to sleep	571–611

TABLE 1—*Continued*

Day	Scene	Lines

Book 2

The testing of the Akhaian army (διάπειρα, *diapeira*);
the catalogs

Day	Scene	Lines
Night	I. Zeus sends Agamemnon a dream: "Attack!"	1–47
before	II. Council of the Akhaian elders (βουλή, *boulē*);	48–483
the 22nd	assembly of the Akhaian army	
day	(1) Testing-speech of Agamemnon: tumultuous	48–210
(1.605)	departure of the army for the ships; intervention	
22nd day	of Athena and Odysseus; return of the army into assembly	
(2.48) =	(2) Thersites scene; attempt at mutiny	211–278
1st day of	(3) Calming speeches of Odysseus, Nestor, Agamemnon	279–393
combat	(4) Sacrifice and breakfast in the camp	394–483
	III. Catalog of Ships (marching order of the	484–785
	Akhaian contingents)	
	IV. Zeus sends Iris, messenger of the gods, to the	786–815
	Trojans: the Trojan army marches forth	
	V. Catalog of the Trojans (marching order of the	816–877
	Trojans and their allies)	

Book 3

Truce—view from the wall (τειχοσκοπία, *teikhoskopia*)

Scene	Lines
I. Request and preparations for a truce: the resolution of the war to come through single combat of Menelaos and Paris	1–120
(1) Encounter of both armies	1–14
(2) Paris and Menelaos	15–37
(3) Conversation of Hektor and Paris; agreement between Hektor and Menelaos regarding truce and decisive single combat of Paris and Menelaos	38–120
II. View from the wall, *teikhoskopia* (Helen "spots" the Akhaian heroes from the wall for Priam)	121–244
III. Conclusion of the truce between Agamemnon and Priam	245–313
IV. The single combat of Menelaos and Paris: Paris in dire need, rescued by Aphrodite	314–382
V. Aphrodite forces Helen to the bed of the defeated Paris	383–448
VI. Result: Agamemnon claims victory for Menelaos, restitution of Helen and the stolen treasure, and payment of reparations	449–461

(continued)

TABLE 1—*Continued*

Day	Scene	Lines

Book 4

Bow-shot of Pandaros

I. Breaking of the truce — 1–219

(1) Council of the gods: decision—continuation of — 1–73
the war and destruction of Troy; Zeus sends Athena
to the Trojans—she is to induce the Trojans to
break the truce

(2) Pandaros wounds Menelaos with a bow-shot at the — 74–147
urging of Athena

(3) Agamemnon's concern for his brother Menelaos; — 148–219
the physician Makhaon treats the wound

II. Agamemnon reviews the assembled Akhaian troops — 220–421
(ἐπιπώλησις, *epipōlēsis*)

III. Beginning of the battle — 422–544

(1) The armies advance and engage: individual — 422–516
combats (exemplifying the battle on a wider scale:
technique of selection); Apollo encourages the
Trojans, Athena the Akhaians

(2) Further individual combats leading to the full — 517–544
development of battle

Book 5

Aristeia of Diomedes (Διομήδους ἀριστεία)

I. Superiority of the Akhaians by Athena's influence — 1–453

(1) Aristeia of Diomedes

(a) the deeds of Diomedes up to his wounding by — 1–113
Pandaros' arrow

(b) his fight against Aineias and Pandaros and — 114–418
his wounding of Aphrodite

(2) Athena derides Aphrodite; Apollo saves Aineias — 419–453

II. Superiority of Trojans under Ares' leadership — 454–710
in Athena's absence

(1) Recovery of the Trojans through Ares and — 454–626
Hektor; Diomedes gives ground

(2) Fight between Lykian Sarpedon and Rhodian — 627–710
(Akhaian) Tlepolemos; further deeds of Hektor

III. Intervention of Hera and Athena on behalf of — 711–846
the Akhaians

IV. Diomedes wounds even Ares — 847–906

V. Hera and Athena return to Olympos — 907–909

TABLE 1—*Continued*

Day	Scene	Lines

Book 6

Conversation (ὁμιλία, *homilia*)

I. The battle: individual combats; many Trojans fall; Nestor urges the Akhaians to energetic pursuit and slaughter of the Trojans — 1–72

II. Conversation of Helenos and Hektor; Helenos' advice: "Go into the city and arrange for the women to make a state sacrifice for Athena" — 73–118

III. The Lykian Glaukos and Diomedes meet — 119–236

IV. Hektor in the city (ὁμιλία, *homilia*) — 237–529

(1) Hektor with his mother, Hekabe — 237–311

(2) Hektor with his brother, Paris, and his sister-in-law, Helen — 312–369

(3) Hektor with his wife, Andromakhe, and his small son, Astyanax — 370–502

(4) Hektor returns with Paris to battle — 503–529

Book 7

The building of the Akhaian wall

I. The Trojans gain ground — 1–16

II. Single combat of Hektor and Aias (inconclusive outcome; respectful exchange of gifts) — 17–312

III. Council of the leaders (βουλή, *boulē*) in Agamemnon's tent; result: request for a truce for the purpose of burial of the dead (and the erecting of a wall around the ships) — 313–344

IV. The Trojan army assembles (ἀγορή, *agorē*) on the Acropolis; result: assent to the Akhaian proposal, additional offer of the stolen treasure (but not Helen) — 345–380

23rd day (7.381) — V. Truce and burial of the dead; the Akhaians refuse the Trojan compromise offer — 381–432

24th day (7.433) — VI. The Akhaians build a wall (Poseidon and Zeus watch from Olympos: Poseidon may destroy the wall after the Akhaians depart (anticipatory rebuke) — 433–464

VII. Meal in the Akhaian camp; thunderclap of Zeus—omen of a difficult battle — 465–482

(continued)

TABLE 1—*Continued*

Day	Scene	Lines

Book 8

Broken-off battle (κόλος μάχη, *kolos makhē*)

Day	Scene	Lines
25th day (8.1) = 2nd day of combat	I. Assembly of the gods: the gods will not participate in battle; Zeus goes to Mt. Ida	1–52
	II. The second day of battle	53–565
	(1) Inconclusive battle	53–67
	(2) Midday intervention of Zeus (weighing of the destiny of both parties [κηροστασία, *kērostasia*]): superiority of the Trojans	68–77
	(3) Advance of the Trojans under Hektor; Zeus drives back Diomedes	78–197
	(4) Hera angered by the course of the fighting; prayer of Agamemnon to Zeus; change in the battle	198–252
	(5) Advance of the Akhaians	253–315
	(6) Hektor pushes the Akhaians back	316–349
	(7) Zeus forestalls an attempt by Hera and Athena to intervene in the battle on behalf of the Akhaians despite his prohibition	350–484
	(8) Nightfall ends the battle; the Trojans encamp for the first time in the plain outside their walls; dire straits of the Akhaians	485–565

Book 9

The embassy to Akhilleus (Λιταί, *Litai*)

Day	Scene	Lines
Evening and night before the 26th day (8.486)	I. Council meetings of the Akhaians	1–181
	(1) Assembly of the army: crisis situation (ἀπορία, *aporia*)	1–88
	(2) Advice (βουλή, *boulē*) of the elders (γέροντες, *gerontes*) in the tent of Agamemnon: an embassy to Akhilleus	89–181
	II. Unsuccessful embassy to Akhilleus (Akhilleus' mind unchanged by the speeches of Odysseus, Phoinix, and Aias)	182–668
	III. Announcement of Akhilleus' refusal and the reaction of the Akhaians	669–713
	(1) Odysseus announces Akhilleus' answer	669–691
	(2) The angry Diomedes disperses the assembly; summons to further battle on the next morning	692–713

Book 10

Doloneia (Δολώνεια)

Day	Scene	Lines
	I. Both sides plan a nighttime spying expedition	1–339
	(1) Preliminaries of the Akhaian spying expedition	1–298

(continued)

TABLE 1—*Continued*

Day	Scene	Lines
	II. Battle at the center	126–205
	III. Renewed intervention of Poseidon; preparation for battle on the left flank	206–329
	IV. Intense fighting in the sector of Idomeneus and Meriones	330–344
	V. Zeus and Poseidon in opposition on the battlefield	345–360
	VI. Aristeia of Idomeneus	361–454
	VII. Battles over the corpse of the Trojan Alkathoös	455–575
	VIII. Single combats of Menelaos	576–672
	IX. Trojans prepare for a new general assault; the Akhaians stand firm	673–837

Book 14

	The deception of Zeus (Διὸς ἀπάτη, *Dios apatē*)	
	I. Nestor and the three wounded Akhaian heroes (Diomedes, Odysseus, Agamemnon) reenter battle; Poseidon incites the Akhaians	1–152
	(1) Nestor takes stock of the situation	1–26
	(2) Nestor's encounter with the three wounded heroes	27–40
	(3) The four leaders take counsel	41–134
	(4) Poseidon encourages the leaders and the army	135–152
	II. Hera seduces Zeus, with the help of Aphrodite and Hypnos, the god of sleep, to assist the Akhaians	153–362
	III. Continuation of fighting up to the (temporary) victory of the Akhaians	363–522
	(1) Preparation for battle by both sides	363–388
	(2) Poseidon now personally leads the Akhaians	389–401
	(3) Aias fights Hektor; Hektor dazed	402–439
	(4) New onslaught of the Akhaians; successful single combats of the Akhaians	440–505
	(5) Flight of the Trojans back over the camp trenches	506–522

Book 15

	I. Restoration of the earlier situation	1–389
	(1) Zeus awakes; argument with Hera	1–77
	(2) Hera goes to the gods on Olympos and tries to instigate them against Zeus	78–156
	(3) Zeus, through Iris, orders Poseidon to leave the battle	157–219

TABLE 1—*Continued*

Day	Scene	Lines
	III. Battle for the horses of Akhilleus	424–542
	IV. Return of the Akhaians with the corpse of Patroklos	543–761

Book 18

	The arms of Akhilleus	
	I. Announcement of Patroklos' death and its aftermath	1–147
	(1) Antilokhos informs Akhilleus of Patroklos' death	1–34
	(2) Lament of Thetis for her son	35–64
	(3) Akhilleus informs Thetis of his intention to avenge Patroklos; Thetis promises him new arms	65–147
	II. Rescue of the Akhaians, who are retreating with Patroklos' corpse, by Akhilleus' appearance at the trench	148–238
Night before the 27th day (18.239–242)	III. Events in both camps during the following night	239–368
	(1) End of the battle owing to premature sunset	239–242
	(2) Poulydamas' advice to return is overruled by Hektor	243–314
	(3) Akhilleus by the corpse of Patroklos; vow of vengeance	315–355
	(4) Dialogue of Zeus and Hera	356–368
	IV. Thetis with Hephaistos; Hephaistos makes a new set of arms for Akhilleus; the shield of Akhilleus	369–617

Book 19

	Quelling of the wrath (μήνιδος ἀπόρρησις, *mēnidos aporrhēsis*)	
27th day (19.1) = 4th day of combat	I. Thetis gives Akhilleus his new arms	1–39
	II. Settlement of the quarrel between Akhilleus and Agamemnon; Briseis given back to Akhilleus	40–281
	III. Laments for Patroklos (Briseis and the women; Akhilleus and the chief Akhaians)	282–351a
	IV. Preparations for the battle for vengeance	351b–424
	(1) Akhilleus arms for battle; the army goes forth	351b–398
	(2) His horse, Xanthos, informs Akhilleus of his approaching death	399–424

TABLE 1—*Continued*

Day	Scene	Lines

Book 20

The *Aeneid*
I. Council of the gods; participation of the gods in the approaching battle — 1–75
II. Single combat of Aeneias and Akhilleus — 76–352
(1) Apollo encourages Aeneias to engage Akhilleus — 76–111
(2) Hera tries in vain to stir Poseidon and Athena to intercede on Akhilleus' behalf; the gods draw back — 112–155
(3) Conversation of Aeneias and Akhilleus; they fight — 156–287
(4) Poseidon rescues Aeneias — 288–352
III. Akhilleus' battle-rage and the flight of the Trojans — 353–503

Book 21

The river battle; battle of the gods (Θεομαχία, *Theomakhia*)
I. Akhilleus fights the Trojans beside and in the river Skamandros — 1–232
II. Skamandros fights Akhilleus; Hephaistos overpowers Skamandros (fire against water) — 233–384
III. The battle of the gods — 385–520
(1) Ares vs. Athena — 391–417
(2) Athena vs. Aphrodite — 418–434
(3) Apollo vs. Poseidon — 435–469
(4) Artemis vs. Hera — 470–496
(5) Hermes vs. Leto — 497–504
(6) Artemis on Olympos with Zeus — 505–514
(7) Apollo goes to Ilios; the other gods go back to Olympos — 515–520a
IV. Flight of the Trojans into the city under Apollo's protection — 520b–611

Book 22

The death of Hektor
I. Preliminaries to the encounter of Akhilleus and Hektor — 1–130
II. Hektor's flight before Akhilleus — 131–166
III. The gods decide Hektor's destiny — 167–247
(1) The gods deliberate — 167–187
(2) Akhilleus continues his pursuit of Hektor; the scales of Zeus weigh against Hektor — 188–213

(continued)

TABLE 1—*Continued*

Day	Scene	Lines
	(3) Athena, in the guise of Deiphobos, persuades Hektor to stand his ground against Akhilleus	214–247
	IV. The battle between Akhilleus and Hektor; Hektor's death	248–394
	V. Akhilleus' mistreatment of Hektor's corpse; dirges for Hektor	395–515
	(1) Akhilleus drags Hektor's corpse back to his camp	395–404
	(2) Hektor's father Priam and his mother Hekabe lament his death	405–436
	(3) Andromakhe hears Hekabe's lament and hurries to the tower	437–474
	(4) The lamentation of Andromakhe	475–515

Book 23

Day	Scene	Lines
	Funeral games (Ἄθλα, *Athla*)	
	I. The burial of Patroklos	1–255
	(1) Akhilleus drives around Patroklos' corpse; the funeral meal	1–58
Night before the	(2) Patroklos appears in a dream to the sleeping Akhilleus and asks to be buried quickly	59–110a
28th day	(3) The burning of Patroklos' corpse	110b–225
(23.62)	(4) The burial of Patroklos' bones	226–257a
28th day	II. Funeral games in honor of Patroklos	257b–897
(23.109)	(1) Chariot race: Eumelos, Diomedes, Menelaos,	257b–652
29th day	Antilokhos, Meriones	
(23.226)	(2) Boxing: Epeios and Euryalos	653–699
	(3) Wrestling: Aias and Odysseus	700–739
	(4) Foot race: the lesser Aias, Odysseus, Antilokhos	740–797
	(5) Armed combat: Diomedes and Aias	798–825
	(6) Discus throwing: Polypoites, Aias, and Epeios	826–849
	(7) Archery: Meriones and Teukros	850–883
	(8) Spear throwing: Akhilleus stops the contest between Agamemnon and Meriones	884–897

Book 24

Day	Scene	Lines
	The ransom of Hektor (Ἕκτορος λύσις, *Hektoros lysis*)	
	I. Preliminaries to the ransoming of Hektor's corpse	1–467
	(1) Akhilleus' mistreatment of Hektor's corpse	1–21

TABLE 1—*Continued*

Day	Scene	Lines
	The mistreatment goes on for 11 days	22–30
41st day (24.31)	(2) Council of the gods: Zeus instructs Thetis to persuade Akhilleus to release Hektor's body	31–142
	(3) Zeus, through Iris, commands Priam to go into the camp of Akhilleus	143–187
Night before the	(4) Priam goes into the Akhaian camp; Hermes guides him to the tent of Akhilleus	188–467
42nd day (24.351)	II. The encounter of Akhilleus and Priam; the ransom of Hektor	468–676
	(1) Priam's appeal; they join in sorrow; Akhilleus promises to give back the corpse	468–571
	(2) Akhilleus accepts the offered ransom; he washes, anoints, and clothes Hektor's corpse and then bids Priam join him in a common meal	572–627
	(3) Akhilleus prepares a bed for Priam and agrees to an 11-day truce for Hektor's funeral	628–676
42nd day (24.695)	III. Hektor's corpse is brought home; mourning and burial	677–804
	(1) Hermes urges Priam to depart in safety during the night; he leads him to the Skamandros	677–697
	(2) Priam arrives at Troy with Hektor's body; Kassandra's cry of grief; general mourning	698–718
	(3) Solemn laments of Andromakhe, Hekabe, and Helen in the palace	719–776
	9 days to build Hektor's pyre	777–784
51st day (24.785)	(4) The burial of Hektor's corpse	785–804

In all, 51 days' events: the occurrences of 15 days and 5 nights are narrated action; the rest of the time is, in narratological terms, only named.

Despite the, at times, large magnitude of some of the scenes we can always discern the main line of development through all phases of the *Iliad*'s action. (Though we should not forget that, as with all large-scale epics in world literature, there is normally also a "hidden" agenda present.)

In conformity with the plan of action laid down in book 1, Akhilleus refrains from joining in battle, and Zeus drives the Akhaians ever farther back toward the sea. As the situation of the Akhaians becomes more dire (at the end of book 8), they appeal to Akhilleus for help. Akhilleus refuses because his condition for rejoining is far from fulfilled: the Akhaians, and thus Agamemnon, are not yet standing on the brink of disaster (book 9). As the battle takes an ever higher toll (book 11), Akhilleus can no longer bear merely to look on (this eventuality, too, was anticipated already in the program outlined in book 1). He sends his friend Patroklos to gather information (at the end of book 11). Patroklos goes to the tent of Nestor. There, the old man urges him to ask Akhilleus if he might at least send Patroklos into battle in his stead (*Il.* 11.796). Patroklos is slow to return, because he stops to care for the wounded Eurypylos. By the time he gets back to Akhilleus, the Trojans are already throwing torches on the ships of the Akhaians (end of book 15)—this latest critical turn of events was something that Patroklos himself, however, had not observed during his return; he reports to Akhilleus only of the "extreme peril" of the Akhaians. Repeating the words of Nestor's request at 11.796 almost verbatim (16.38), Patroklos asks Akhilleus to send him into battle in his place along with the now well rested Myrmidons (about twenty-five hundred men, as we know from *Il.* 2.67 f.). Akhilleus consents, provided that the Akhaians "are actually already pushed back against the sea surf and hold only a narrow strip of the shore" (*Il.* 16.67 f.). Patroklos dons Akhilleus' armor and the enemy takes him to be Akhilleus. He drives the Trojans back to the walls of Troy but is then killed by Hektor (16.855). The Trojans now finally have a free hand.

When Akhilleus learns of his friend's death, all his previous arrangements are null and void. His wrath, "accursed" in view of its outcome, is now inconsequential and obsolete. He settles his dispute with Agamemnon as a mere irksome formality (19.270–75) and plunges back into battle (end of book 19). With his Myrmidons, he drives the Trojans back to the city walls. Then he avenges Patroklos by killing Hektor (22.361). He buries the body of Patroklos with all honors, but he desecrates the corpse of Hektor in a frenzy of vengefulness that alienates him from himself (24.39–54). The gods intervene. They prompt the old king Priam to go in person to Troy's mortal enemy, the killer of his son, to ask for Hektor's body. Priam dissolves Akhilleus' nearly inhuman obduracy by an act of nearly superhuman self-effacement: Priam kisses the hands of Akhilleus, "the dreadful, manslaughtering hands that had cut down so many of his sons" (24.478 f.). Akhilleus gives back Hektor's corpse, which is brought home to Troy and buried.

This is the baseline of the action that throughout the whole plot stays fixed in the listener's consciousness as the "reality." It is the Akhilleus line with which the work began: the wrath and its consequences. By the end, these consequences have amassed such "infinite pain"—and not only physical pain—as to obscure and submerge the point of the wrath. These consequences abate only gradually, and finally, with the ransom of Hektor's body, they die away altogether. This is the *mēnis* (wrath) plotline. It is rightly dubbed the *Akhilleid*.

The *Akhilleid* does not, however, encompass the entire work. Other elements are combined, mixed together, and merged with it. There are narrative sequences that seem only indirectly relevant to the *Akhilleid:* for example, certain of the scenes at Troy—Helen with Priam on the wall, identifying the Akhaian heroes; Aphrodite forcibly bringing Helen and Paris together in bed; Hektor's lengthy conversations with his mother, his brother, Paris, and his wife, Andromakhe. Then there are the long battle scenes of the third day of combat, which fill nearly all of books 11 through 18; the description of the shield of Akhilleus (*Il.* 18.478–607); the detailed account (639 lines) of the funeral games in book 23. The *Akhilleid* by itself could be quickly presented. It is the expansions (which Analyst scholars prefer to call "ornamentations," "accretions," "poetic augmentations," "patchwork," "insertions," "interpolations," and so on) that lengthen what might have been a short narrative, as it were—a novella—and make it into an epic; in short, they make an *Iliad* out of the *Akhilleid*. How are we to interpret the relation between the two?

Is the *Iliad* a river along which the narrator travels, regarding the landscape beyond the shore and including sections of it in his narrative? Is the *Iliad* a more or less accidental unity, held together only by the will of a poet selecting material according to his own whim or the preferences of his public? Superficially, we are dealing with the question posed by F.A. Wolf and all Analyst scholars after him. If one scratches the surface, however, one ultimately comes to the fundamental issue that has motivated Analytic scholarship—the poetic quality of the *Iliad*. This issue was already indirectly raised by Aristotle in the context of his comparison of tragedy and epic at *Poetics* 1462b3–11 (unfortunately a somewhat lacunose passage). Aristotle evaluates Homeric epic very positively: "And yet [though the length of epic necessarily makes it seem less unified than drama] *these* poetic works [the *Iliad* and *Odyssey*] are put together [composed, organized] as well as can be and are nearly the representation of a *single* action." The rationale for this judgment is provided in another passage (*Poetics* 1455b13): the episodes (that is, "added elements") in the *Iliad* and the *Odyssey* are "intrinsically related" (οἰκεῖα, *oikeia* = integral constituents). Is Aristotle correct? We cannot here decide the issue with respect to the immense structure of the whole *Iliad*. But perhaps we may give a few indications of how carefully the structure of the work has been contrived and arranged.

The *Mēnis* Theme

The plan of action laid out by the *Iliad* poet by line 427 of book 1 may be completed only when both of the principals involved in it—Zeus and Akhilleus—act in conformity to that plan. In other words, Zeus must help the Trojans, and Akhilleus may *not* help the Akhaians. But both parties must first be induced to act in these ways. For both in reality wish to do quite the opposite: Zeus actually desires the fall of Troy, and Akhilleus in fact wants to fight along with the Akhaians (even though he is in a different mood at the moment). Both must therefore be compelled to reverse their genuine instincts. Thetis effects this reversal in Akhilleus by her advice to "sit beside the swift ships in anger at the Akhaians and keep far away from the fighting!" (*Il.* 1.421–22). She achieves it with Zeus by her petition (1.503–30). But only when both reversals are actually realized can the narrative shift into the anticipated course. The poet must therefore report the reversals.

He describes the first reversal (Akhilleus) at *Iliad* 1.488–92:

But he waited in anger, sitting beside the swift ships,
the divinely born son of Peleus, swift-footed Akhilleus:
Now he went neither to the assemblies where men gain honor
nor into battle. But he constantly wasted his heart

holding out in his camp, yet longing always for the fighting and
din of battle.

This amounts to a very literal implementation of the advice that Thetis
gave at 1.421–22. Thus one of the two complements of the plan of action
is fixed once and for all in the listener's mind; it is a component that
provides the substructure of books 2 through 19: Akhilleus' wrath and
abstinence from fighting, and the suffering (including his own) caused
thereby. The wrath of Akhilleus—a mere abstraction in the first line of
the poem—has now taken on concrete form in the mind of the listener:
it consists of utter passivity and suffering.

Of course, this entailed a problem for the poet. To support the overall structure of the plot, the poet had to keep his listeners continuously
aware of both of the, so to say, weight-bearing members of the construction—the divine as well as the human. This was not difficult as
regards the divine complement of the plan: it was easy to translate into
action the behavior of Zeus in helping the Trojans and driving back the
Akhaians. The same was not true as regards the human complement of
the plan, because in this case he had to show how Akhilleus was *not* acting. This could not be accomplished simply by having Akhilleus disappear, for the listener would tend to forget him—precisely what must
not be allowed to happen. Then the listener would not perceive the
structural tension in the fabrication of the following narrative. Rather,
the listener had to be made to think, "All that I am witnessing here and
now—the battles, the woundings and deaths of men, even the hopes
and disappointments on both sides—is possible only because Akhilleus
is passive." Akhilleus, then, far from vanishing from the narrative, had
to remain as present as possible, but as a nonparticipant. The listener
had to be aware of Akhilleus' passivity as passivity. Only then could
the listener distinguish what was happening as a conditional,
ephemeral, inconclusive state of affairs, a reversal of momentum that
would persist only so long as Akhilleus was passive. It had to be very
clear that, if Akhilleus renounced his passivity, the reversal would be
undone and the true state of affairs reinstated. Only such an awareness
of conditionality could generate suspense in the deeper sense; that is,
the point of view must be one of constantly maintained expectancy.
Thus the *Iliad* poet faced the task of presenting the inaction of Akhilleus
as one of the *most forceful* actions of the epic.

Homer solved the problem by a certain process of reiteration. He repeatedly flashes on the passivity of Akhilleus in the intervals between the passages in which it is the main focus (books 1, 9, 16, 18, 19). Thus the structural efficacy or energy of the basic theme of the action of the *Iliad* could not be forgotten even in those portions of the story that otherwise might have seemed to be loose episodes. This stratagem of reiteration had the further effect of showing the apparently loose episodes to be parts of the action made possible only because of the wrath of Akhilleus.

It is not possible here to quote all the relevant passages at length. They include: *Iliad* 2.239 ff., 2.769 ff. (the catalog of ships), 4.512 ff. (where Apollo encourages the Trojans), 5.788 (where Hera encourages the Akhaians), 6.99 (where Helenos mentions Akhilleus in the presence of Hektor), 7.228 ff. (where Aias threatens Hektor). Two examples will illustrate the type. In the first, Thersites accuses Agamemnon before the assembled army of lacking the qualities of leadership:

> he who has now insulted even Akhilleus, a man better by far
>   than he:
> he has taken away his gift of honor, seizing it himself!
> But there is no gall in Akhilleus, the weakling!
> Else you would have behaved disgracefully for the last time, son
>   of Atreus!
>
> (*Il.* 2.239–42)

In the second, Hera addresses the Akhaians:

> Shame on you Argives, good-for-nothing pretty boys!
> Indeed, so long as godlike Akhilleus used to go into battle. . . .
>
> (*Il.* 5.787–88)

The wrath of Akhilleus, the underlying theme of the action, is referred to in this way no less than six times between books 1 and 9—once by the poet in propria persona, and five times by various Akhaian, Trojan, and divine characters. Akhilleus is present even in his absence. Every character (and thus also the audience) remains fully aware of Akhilleus' abstention from fighting and thereby of the temporary nature of the present situation. There is a concomitant sense of the retardative character of the *Iliad* within the Troy saga as a whole.

Clearly, an organizing intellect wishes to maintain a unified action and seeks to prevent a collapse into fragmentation.

Hand in hand with this technique of conjunction goes a technique of disjunction. By distinctively anticipating later flashbacks, the poet is able to expand the scope of action and include complexes of material that initially seem irrelevant but suddenly prove pertinent. This technique is most in evidence in books 2 through 7.

The Theme of the Thetis Petition

It required a strong force to reverse in a lasting way the true desires of both the major figures in the plot the poet had devised. The poet provided such a force in the form of Thetis. As a goddess and the mother of Akhilleus, she was able to move on both the divine and the human levels of action. Thus she could plausibly bring about on both levels the change in circumstances demanded by the poetic plan. With her son Akhilleus, Thetis could simply give a command: "Stay sitting by the ships and fight no longer" (*Il.* 1.421–22). Akhilleus obeys, at first, of course, with pleasure, because the command coincides with his own wishes, but soon, the poet tells us, his compliance brings ever increasing inner turmoil. For Akhilleus is acting against his own true nature, which impels him not to sit around but to perform heroic deeds: "he sat in wrath beside the ships and went neither into the assembly of the army nor into battle, but his heart languished unceasingly while he stayed there and he longed unceasingly for battle and the sounds of battle" (1.488–92). Moreover, the listener will later be apprised of Akhilleus' destiny, which had to be known to him since it was a basic element of the saga. As Akhilleus himself puts it: "My destiny prescribes alternative paths to death for me: if I remain here and fight around the city of Troy, then my homecoming is lost, but undying fame will be mine; if I return to my house in my beloved homeland, then glorious fame will be lost for me and my life will continue for a long time" (9.411–15). Akhilleus, of course, has long ago opted for the former, that is, the fame. He *must*, therefore, wish to fight, and he must wish to destroy the city of Troy. Consequently, he must also be troubled and tormented by the present developments, which run contrary to all he desires. Nonetheless he obeys. His sense of honor and his mother's command constrain him.

Thetis could not simply command Zeus, the other actor who had to "play along," if the plan was to succeed. Him she had to entreat. She presents her request in book 1, lines 503–10: "Zeus, if I have ever served you well in word or deed in the past, grant this wish to me. Honor my son, who has been born to die so long before his time. The lord of men Agamemnon has utterly dishonored him. He has taken away his gift of honor with his own hands! Therefore, do grant him honor, Olympian Zeus, in your great wisdom. Grant supremacy to the Trojans until finally the Akhaians show respect to my son and overwhelm him with honors!" Zeus gives his consent, although he has reservations in view of what he knows to be the diametrically opposed objectives of his extremely emancipated wife, Hera. In one of the most majestic scenes of the *Iliad*, Zeus nods assent and Olympos trembles (1.524–30; by such means the poet customarily underscores the importance of particular items in his narration). It signals also the accomplishment of the second reversal. The two complementary motive forces of the narrative can now begin to function. Akhilleus is wrathful and Zeus helps the Trojans.

But, surprisingly, the expectations of the listener are met only with respect to the first motive force of the narrative. Akhilleus is in fact wrathful and the listener is alerted to this fact repeatedly in the subsequent books, as I have shown. But Zeus does *not* help the Trojans in these subsequent books. In books 2 through 7, the action runs quite contrary to the expected reversal; that is, the Akhaians are winning. They drive the Trojans into such dire straits that, toward the end of the seventh book, they make an offer of partial capitulation: to wit, the return of all the treasure that Paris had once taken with him from Troy. Beyond that, they also offer to make an additional payment by way of reparation. Paris wishes only to keep Helen. The Akhaians refuse and the battle continues the next day.

At this point, Zeus suddenly begins to fulfill the request of Thetis. He in fact gives supremacy to the Trojans and prevents the pro-Akhaian goddesses Hera and Athena from intervening on behalf of their favorites. And toward the end of the eighth book, Zeus announces his long-range plans in precisely the way we would have expected him to do immediately after Thetis made her request:

Tomorrow morning, you will see the powerful son of Kronos
 [= Zeus] become yet stronger,

if you have the stomach for it, ox-eyed lady Hera,
destroying a numberless host of Argive spear-fighters.
Because the mighty Hektor will not leave off from battle
till swift-footed Akhilleus bestirs himself beside the ships,
at that time when battle rages around the very sterns of the ships
for the body of Patroklos in the frightfully narrow space
　　remaining to the Akhaians.

　　　　　　　　　　　　　　　　　　　(*Il.* 8.470–76)

This passage is known to students of Homer under the rubric "the first announcement of Zeus." In it, the poet sketches in broad outline the actual course of events of the next day of battle, detailed in books 11 through 18: Hektor will drive forward to the ships of the Akhaians; Patroklos will be sent against him; Patroklos will fall. Akhilleus will bestir himself beside the ships to avenge his friend. From the stance of narrative technique, this announcement is a foreshadowing by the poet; but it is also a veiled allusion to and reiteration of the actual terms of Thetis' request. The catchword is "sterns" (πρύμναι, *prymnai*). In the first formulation of his petition to Thetis, Akhilleus had used this word to designate the spatial limit of his desire for vengeance. She in turn used the same word in conveying the request to Zeus. He was to allow the Akhaians to be driven back to the "sterns" of their ships (*Il.* 1.409). Now here the poet picks up the same catchword again in Zeus' announcement: "at that time when battle rages around the very sterns of the ships" (8.475). Obviously, one and the same poet is at work here: he picks up in book 8 the thread of the narrative line begun with the request of Thetis in book 1, without overlapping, lapses in logic, or gaps.

　　But what are we to make of books 2 through 7? Why is the request of Thetis not mentioned in them? Furthermore, why is the request of Thetis apparently inoperative in them? Why does the action in these books run precisely counter to the direction of events that the request of Thetis must dictate? Has the poet in these books forgotten the promise that he has had Zeus give to Thetis in the first book? Or—the interpretation preferred by Analyst scholars—was the poet of books 2–7 not the poet who composed the request of Thetis?

　　The latter explanation is not possible. For the request of Thetis and the wrath of Akhilleus form a bipartite structural unity. The request has been indissolubly linked to the wrath since book 1, lines 419–22. Now the structural correlative of the request of Thetis, namely, the wrath of Akhilleus, is a recurrent motif in books 2 through 7, as I have shown. That the poet of the wrath (*mēnis*) is identical to the poet of the request is undeniable in light of the indissoluble connection of these two components of the overall narrative plan. Therefore the poet who constantly invokes one of the two complements in books 2 through 7 cannot conceivably have "forgotten" the other in these same books. Rather, he must have merely avoided it. That is, the *Iliad* poet, in books 2 through 7, must deliberately have faded out, postponed, and suspended all traces of the request of Thetis and the promise Zeus gave in response. Themes are suppressed in narrative to make room for others. What then did the *Iliad* poet fade into this free space or "breathing room" that he created for himself?

After Zeus has given his promise, he immediately thinks of a way to fulfill it. On the following night (beginning of book 2), he sends a dream to Agamemnon. The dream, at Zeus' instigation, deludes Agamemnon into thinking the conquest of Troy will occur the next day. Nothing could be more welcome to Agamemnon than such a vision, which promises to free him from all his current difficulties. He clutches at the straw held out in the dream. The poet stresses Agamemnon's self-delusion and desperation by one of his very rare uses of auctorial commentary: "for he believed that he could take the city of Priam on that very day—fool that he was, who knew nothing whatever of the things Zeus was plotting" (*Il.* 2.37 ff.). At dawn, Agamemnon persuades the fairly skeptical members of his general staff to mobilize the men (though the pestilence has only just ceased and one of the most important contingents—that of Akhilleus—has gone on strike). An assembly of the army is summoned. Agamemnon then tries to restore the motivation of the troops by means of a ruse that is often effective in military settings. He feigns a disgraceful defeatism with the aim of shocking the men; this is the famous *diapeira* or "test," of the army, which he had discussed early during the conference with his general staff. In the course of his long "testing" address (2.110–40), the poet has Agamemnon make a statement that radically alters the direction of the entire narrative to this point: "nine years of mighty Zeus have already gone by, the timbers of our ships have disintegrated and the ropes have rotted, and our wives and young children sit at home longing for us, while the task we came here to perform remains utterly undone" (2.134–38).

This indication of time introduces a development that accounts for the suspension of the request of Thetis in books 2 through 7. For it introduces a whole new dimension to the narrative: the dimension of the past, of history. To this point, it has seemed that only an excerpt of the saga would be presented, within a discrete time frame, while the background, the larger context, and the depth of the story would be presupposed. In other words, the narrative seemed to be synchronic. Now, however, a diachronic perspective comes into play. A few lines later, the poet mentions Helen. This not only pushes the temporal envelope further back into the past (the reason for the war, the period prior to the war) but also introduces an element of causation. From the current situation before Troy, an arc extends back to the first beginnings. A background emerges.

In the following books, the poet consistently follows the narrative line established here. The first instance comes a little later in book 2 itself, when Odysseus gives his long speech to boost morale (*Il.* 2.284–332). Not only does he too speak of the "ninth year of the siege" (2.295), but he tries to stir new hope for victory by a graphic picture of the wonderful omen that the Akhaian army had received at Aulis at the outset of the expedition. The prophet Kalkhas, as everyone well knows, had construed it to signify the conquest of Troy in the tenth year of the war. The listener is imperceptibly transported back through nine years to find himself suddenly at the start of the expedition. The circumstances of book 1—the quarrel and the wrath—begin to lose their insularity; they have become a pivotal moment in the context of events occurring over a span of ten years. The story of the entire Trojan War has been absorbed, inserted, and interwoven into the story of the wrath of Akhilleus. The listener remains in the plain before Troy, but with a small part of his consciousness he is also at Aulis. This small part of his consciousness will expand in the following parts of the narrative—first, in the so-called catalog of ships that almost immediately follows. Leaving aside the thorny questions associated with this piece of the narrative, we may take the following as certain: the present context of the narrative does not call for a catalog of ships that once arrived at Aulis for the expedition to Troy; rather, it calls for a plan of the marching order and battle formation of the regiments being positioned for an infantry attack in the plain before Troy. Chronologically speaking, the list of ships belongs to the beginning of an *Iliad*, not of an *Akhilleid*. The poet has inserted it here for just this reason. It offered him the chance to augment in a natural way his projected leap back into the past.

The point of this stratagem is apparent. It allowed the poet to transform what initially seemed to be merely an episode—the wrath of Akhilleus—into a grand epic of the Trojan War, in short, into an *Iliad*. He accomplished all this without abandoning his true theme—the *mēnis Akhilēos* (wrath of Akhilleus). The same technique is evident in the structure of the *Odyssey* as well. The antecedents of the story being narrated by the poet are mirrored into the current story in the form of Odysseus' first-person flashback narrative among the Phaiakians. This is, of course, a universal technique. In later Greek literature, we first encounter it in its perfected form in Herodotus, where the subject proper is the history of the Persian War and the flashback narrative encompasses the prior national history of the principal belligerents. Here in the *Iliad*, we find the technique at an evidently early stage in its development, since the flashback is not truly made explicit, as it is in the *Odyssey* by the use of first-person narration. Still, it is patently a flashback.

This becomes still clearer in the following books. After the "troop review" of the two catalogs, the listener is expecting a first clash of the armies. Instead, in the area between the two assembled armies, Paris offers to duel Menelaos; that is, the offending party challenges the offended party (*Il.* 3.67–75). As he informs his brother Hektor, Paris would like to fight Menelaos, with the winner taking home both the entire treasure and Helen. All the other combatants would have to conclude a treaty of friendship. By its terms, after the ensuing duel, the besiegers would return home again and the Trojans would finally enjoy peace once more. This is an attempt to settle the conflict by a duel of the two opponents who have a personal stake in the outcome; it amounts to a judgment of the gods. Logically, this should have come up not in the ninth year of the siege but at the beginning of the war. The same is certainly true also of the ensuing scene sequence known as the *Teikhoskopia*, or "view from the walls."

While Menelaos is agreeing to Paris' proposal to duel and Hektor is sending a herald to the acropolis of Troy to summon King Priam for the authorization of the truce, the messenger-goddess Iris fetches Helen, who sits modestly weaving at her loom. When she comes into the presence of the curious old men along the city wall by the Skaian gate, they whisper among themselves: "this woman is incredibly beautiful, like a goddess! Still, it were better she should return home, lest she bring misfortune to our sons hereafter" (*Il.* 3.158–60). It most certainly would have occurred to these wise elders to make such an exhortation to Helen, the cause of the war, long before its ninth year. This raises the expectation of the listener to hear related further incidents from the beginning of the war.

The view from the wall follows (*Il.* 3.160–244). Priam calls Helen to his side and has her identify by name the individual Greek leaders who are present in the plain. It turns out that he does not recognize Agamemnon, Odysseus, or Aias—something utterly impossible, of course, in the ninth year of the siege. In terms of the chronology of saga and epic, the *Teikhoskopia* likewise belongs to the beginning of the war.

After the duel of Paris and Menelaos comes the famous scene where Aphrodite compels Helen to join the loser, Paris. The irrational character of the mutual attraction of Helen and Paris is well illustrated by their coming together just here in the immediate aftermath of the complete humiliation of Helen's lover at the hands of her husband. The saga of the rape of Helen is, as Karl Reinhardt used to put it, transported into an epic situation.

The temporal and causal dimensions of this retrospective line of narrative have now been repeatedly increased. At the beginning of book 4 there is a council of the gods on Olympos. Zeus considers ending the war between the Akhaians and the Trojans (*Il.* 4.16). There are several indications in the context of the passage that Zeus is not being disingenuous. This scene cannot, then, come from the same chronological stratum as book 1. If it did, Zeus, bearing in mind his promise to Thetis, could not entertain any such ideas of terminating the war at this point. The Trojan Pandaros then must maliciously break the truce that has been concluded and thereby open the way for further warfare and the conquest of Troy. Clearly the mythic (that is, individual and human) motivations for the war handed down in ancient saga are corroborated here by rational (that is, legal and moral) motivations. This whole complex of attempts to settle rationally the question of responsibility for the war obviously belongs to its beginnings.

In the fifth book, the Akhaians behind Diomedes push forward so successfully that in the sixth book the Trojan opposition collapses altogether and salvation can be expected only in the form of divine assistance. Hence Hektor visits Troy, which gives an opportunity for a deeper analysis of the situation in a city under siege and of the feelings of the heroes' families. When Hektor returns to his forces in book 7, the dire situation there has not changed one whit (*Il.* 7.4–7). Only a divine intervention (Athena and Apollo in collaboration) brings a temporary reprieve. Then comes the offer of capitulation mentioned earlier (7.385–97).

In looking back on books 2 through 7, we may say this much is clear: with the opening of book 2, the poet gradually begins to fade out the request of Thetis and concomitantly to open the perspective of the work to include the prior history of the war and the events of the war's opening phases. In this way, he makes an *Iliad* out of the *Akhilleid*. The technique by which this broadening of the narrative horizon is achieved consists of a gradual, oblique redirection of the listener's attention back to the very beginnings of the course of events. A sudden disruption or an abruptly explicit flashback is thus avoided. The technique entails an ever more detailed depiction of the opening stages of the war. To speak in terms of the genesis of the poetry—though that is not our express purpose—we may conjecture that we are seeing portions of the general Troy epic being adapted for use here, portions that the *Iliad* poet had himself previously used in many recitations. The advantage of this mirroring of prior history consists, on the one hand, of a general deepening of the subject matter of the *mēnis Akhilēos* through the integration of the general subject matter of the saga of Troy and, on the other, of laying the basis, in terms of dramatis personae and mise-en-scène, for the ensuing wrath-poem.

This tactic of "mirroring in" ends, as I have shown, in book 8, where the narrative thread begun in book 1 is again picked up. We immediately see what effects the wrath of Akhilleus is having: the Trojans have for the first time encamped for the night in the plain rather than inside the city walls. Akhilleus' services are obviously indispensable for the Akhaians. Thus their decision to send an embassy to petition him. With the completion of the extended narrative parenthesis, the poet's partially suspended structural plan once more becomes fully operative: the Akhaians are gradually driven back, ultimately to their very ships. It is understandable that Akhilleus should not have been petitioned for help till the ninth book. For only in the eighth book have the Akhaians come to a full realization of his importance. From this perspective, the first day of combat in the *Iliad*, which begins in book 2, does not seem to the listener to be the first day of combat in the tale of the wrath of Akhilleus. The first day of combat in the *mēnis* movement is rather that of the eighth book.

It is evident that we have here a careful first attempt to fashion a narrative that is at once both taut (employing the technique of conjunction by recalling the wrath) and loose (dropping and then later picking up one strand of the double narrative thread). The *Odyssey* exhibits a further stage of development in the same strategy. Homeric scholars still cannot say whether, as Karl Reinhardt (1961) believed, this represents the ongoing efforts of one and the same poet to perfect the technique.

Analysis of this obviously well conceived mode of incorporating material shows we are dealing with a relatively high level of technical narrative skill on the part of the *Iliad* poet. This carries important methodological implications. Attempts to excise seemingly irrelevant portions of the narrative as later "interpolations" to an earlier original structure are now only a last recourse. Before resorting to such attempts, we must first exhaust every conceivable possibility that such portions of the narrative are better understood as deliberate structural enhancements, enlargements, additions, and so forth. Thus, for example, it is ill advised to label the long descriptions of the third day of battle (books 11–18) "confused," "chaotic," or the like. Careful analysis reveals a premeditated structural design underlying these narrative sequences as well (Latacz 1977). The length of the battle descriptions poses no difficulty. An aristocratic audience would be quite happy to have the deeds of its heroes "trotted out" in great detail. They would not have been bored, any more than modern sports fans are bored while listening to or watching sometimes hours-long radio or television broadcasts of, say, five-set matches at Wimbledon. The audience follows every serve, return, slice, lob, and so on with rapt attention. Of course, in this domain, it was still well within the realm of possibility to "enrich" an already finished work by adding this or that detail, scene, or character. It is a fair judgment, however, that, in its intrinsic form and content, the work as a whole was still unaffected by such things. The *Iliad* exhibits a thoroughly premeditated unity from first to last: there are no overlappings, no actual reduplications, no lapses in logic, no inconsistencies in the basic plan. If one were to have asked the *Iliad* poet whether he (like his modern interpreters) had paid special attention to this and whether he had taken special pains to achieve this, he would likely have reacted with surprise. He was preoccupied with creating not a unified epic—that was a given—but one that would make the world more comprehensible and more beautiful.

4

The *Odyssey*

The Homecoming of Odysseus: The Theme and Its Framework

The *Odyssey* begins in a less-focused way than the *Iliad*. With the first word of its prooimion, it designates as its theme not a specific episode in the life of its hero but the hero himself: "tell me of the man, O Muse, the man of many turns. . . ." Then the theme is narrowed down; only a well-defined section of the man's life will be recounted: "the man who wandered much after he sacked the sacred city of Troy." Only the post–Trojan War part of the hero's life is to be included. But within these limits, no further boundaries are drawn at first.

> He saw the cities of many people and learned their thoughts,
> undergoing many pains on the sea and in his heart,
> striving tirelessly to preserve his life and the homecoming of his
>   comrades.
> But even so he did not save his comrades, though he yearned to:
> they perished through their own unruly deeds,
> the fools! who devoured the cattle of the sun god Hyperion. . . .
> Tell us, too, about these things, starting anywhere, goddess,
>   daughter of Zeus.
>
> (*Od.* 1.3–10)

The thematic open-endedness of this invocation of the muse contrasts sharply with that of the *Iliad*: "tell us about these things, starting anywhere. . . ." It seems as though this poet has no definite plan. His opening is much less focused, less portentous, less dramatic and suspenseful. The muse is asked only to tell the story of this much-traveled Trojan War veteran to the poet's audience too (as she has already done to so many others before). It is the story of a hero who endured many sufferings during his return from Troy, who alone of his whole company reached home at last, because he did not act so recklessly as his companions.

Although all this has a generic ring to it, this is not due to a lack of a definite objective on the part of the poet. Rather, it is an attribute of the material. The public that heard these opening verses of the epic was familiar with the material, possibly even more familiar than it was with that of the *Iliad*. It did not even have to hear the name of the implied hero (mentioned first in line 21). The clever veteran of the Trojan expedition, the man of many turns, much "turned round" by the forces of destiny, the hero who returns home at last, having survived all dangers thanks to his practical intelligence—this character was a symbol. All the intelligence, resourcefulness, diplomacy, pragmatism, irrepressible will to survive, inventiveness, and instinctive hope to be found in humanity had been attributed to this hero—to Odysseus—in countless stories for centuries. A song about Odysseus, unlike one about Akhilleus, could in fact begin "anywhere," because, whatever the specific subject matter, the same story was always being told in an exemplary and comforting manner: the ultimate triumph of the human spirit.

Odysseus is not a Greek name. The form *Olysseus* (cf. Latin *Ulixes*) is also attested. On the basis of other evidence, we know that *d* was substituted for *l* in words borrowed by Greek from the language of the pre-Greek population in the Aegean region. Thus Odysseus must have been a figure in the sagas of the indigenous people, a figure who became familiar to Greeks only after their immigration into the Aegean area. From the beginning, Odysseus was a seafarer, at home on the sea and on the islands; he himself was an islander with a home on Ithaka. The Greeks—landlubbers originally—became sailors themselves in their new homeland. They no doubt acquired from the indigenous population a knowledge of shipbuilding and its terminology, maritime geography, and nautical science (Kurt 1977). From the same source, they will also have taken the sagas and yarns of seafarers. Odysseus belonged to that narrative realm.

All the magicians and giants, mermaids and mermen, and the ghost ships and floating islands that these seagoing people thought they had seen, all the adventures in distant lands and on remote islands that they had come through triumphantly—all these things were attributed to Odysseus. He had always come home again, through every kind of danger.

Naturally, Odysseus also had to have taken part in the Trojan War.

The cleverest man of all could not be left behind. Of course, he tried to avoid recruitment—else he would not be the cleverest—but the madness he feigned for that purpose was exposed as a pretense. Before Troy, he again demonstrated that the decisive weapon of humankind is the intellect. When all the military force had been exerted in vain, he conceived the stratagem of the wooden horse: physically, the Trojans had held out for nine long years; intellectually, they were checkmated in a few hours.

The return home of a sailor like Odysseus could not be the same as that of an Agamemnon or Diomedes. We cannot now ascertain when exactly an epic singer first hit on the idea of shifting the adventures associated with the *seafarer* Odysseus to the time of the *warrior* Odysseus' homecoming. We may be certain, however, that it was not done first by the poet of our *Odyssey* (Lesky 1967, 803 f. [116 f.]).

Still a third narrative theme seems to have been connected with Odysseus long before the composition of our *Odyssey*—that of the belated homecoming. This theme was a perfect fit for a sailor. Embarked at the mercy of the sea, tossed by storms, repeatedly detained by various obstacles, reduced to penury on foreign shores, destitute, down at heel, and lacking the means to continue his journey home, this husband is away so long that he is taken for lost or perhaps even dead. Affairs at home take their course. Suitors for the hand of the "widow" make their appearance. She strives long and hard to remain true (since she has no certain report of her husband's death). Because there is a son who is now growing up, the suitors press her. Gradually, she loses hope and begins to give in; the wedding date is set. But, at just the last moment, the husband given up for dead returns home.

Long before Homer, the tradition of oral song had woven together sailors' stories, tales of homecoming, and accounts of the returns of the Trojan War veterans, into a great complex of narrative centered on Odysseus (Lesky 1967, 803 f. [116 f.]). Thus the singer could in fact reach in and produce a song "starting anywhere." The audience could be relied on to reconstruct the context. Thus, the poet of our *Odyssey* begins his version in the customary fashion, at least initially: "Tell us, too, about these things, starting anywhere, goddess!"

Then, however, the poet abruptly becomes clearer and more concrete. As in the prooimion of the *Iliad*, the theme is suddenly sharply defined and a program is outlined:

Then all the others who had escaped sheer destruction
were at home, having survived the war and the journey by sea.
Only this one, who so longed for his homecoming and his wife,
was held fast by the queenly nymph, Kalypso, the noble
    goddess
who wanted him for her spouse, in her vaulted cave.
Even when the year had come in the cycle of seasons,
in which the gods had granted his wish to return home
to Ithaka, even in that place he was not free from struggles,
among his own loved ones. . . .

                                                    (*Od.* 1.11–19)

With these words, the poet of *this* version fixes in both space and time
the theme he wishes to deal with in the story. The starting point will be
Odysseus' detention with the nymph Kalypso; the end point will be his
struggles on his home island of Ithaka. The time frame is the year of his
homecoming. The connoisseur knew that this was the twentieth year
after Odysseus had set out for Troy (this chronological point is often
repeated in the epic itself). As in the *Iliad*, so also here the poet has chosen a very opportune moment. He begins not just "anywhere" in the
universe of the story; and he does not seize on just anything in it. Contrary to the impression he gives in his opening, which seemed to conform to customary past practice, the poet begins at a point where matters are just about to come to a head; he begins at the decisive moment
in a critical phase of the story.

   Beyond these external facts, the poet reveals more of his program in
the expanded prooimion. Of the sea adventures that would come to the
mind of anyone who heard the name *Odysseus* there is no mention.
Instead, the poet alludes to the "struggles" (the Greek word is *aëthlos*,
which means "trial" or "contest"; cf. *athletics* in English), which the
hero will have to endure even in his own homeland of Ithaka, even
"among his own loved ones." The poet is clearly interested in the
homecoming rather than adventures. He focuses on tests of intelligence, strength, perseverance, cunning, and self-control that the hero
must pass in the presence of his own people before he can be truly "at
home" again. This is what made the story intriguing for the poet and
sparked his interest: to tell how a man refused even a "queenly nymph"
and "noble goddess," because he so longed for home and for his wife.
To tell how such a man had to prove himself in the presence even of his

own wife, the person most beloved to him, for whom he had endured all the misery of warfare and the sea, so that he might win the struggle to regain his own loved ones—his son and his wife.

The listener might not grasp right at the beginning of the narrative precisely what is actually meant by the passage. The "struggles" seem, at first sight, to refer only to the battle against the suitors, in which the hero of the story, having returned home, must overcome the many competitors for his wife who have appeared in his absence. Many singers had already told of this. Only later will the audience realize that the poet of *this* epic has other struggles in mind. The poet is not interested in the external, superficial aspects of the struggle. He is captivated by the question of what it meant *psychologically* to have to "win" one's wife again; what it meant to the wife and son and those others who had remained at home to have to accept back again the man who had gone away twenty years before. It will become evident that the poet of the *Odyssey*, like the poet of the *Iliad* (whether one and the same person, we cannot say), is really interested not in the factual details of the story but in what the saga demands of its heroes in terms of the human spirit. In each epic, the poet describes not how it was but how it could have been. Each says, "it was this way," but actually means, "I imagine it was this way." By tapping the potential for understanding, they charge the old sagas with relevance to the present. Thus their interpretations of the saga help listeners to see and contemplate in a new light both their fellow human beings and themselves.

The Elaboration of the Theme

The structure of the *Odyssey* is easier to grasp than that of the *Iliad*. A detailed synopsis is not necessary. The events are played out in three primary and two secondary locales. Appropriately enough in a tale of a seafarer's return home, all three primary locations are islands: Ogygia, the island of Kalypso; Skheria, the island of the Phaiakians; and Ithaka, Odysseus' homeland. The two secondary locales are Nestor's palace at Pylos and the palace of Menelaos and Helen at Sparta.

As in the *Iliad*, the action encompasses only a few days, forty in all. Again as in the *Iliad*, the events of some of these days (sixteen days and eight nights) are narrated, while the events of the others are only indicated. The *Odyssey* gives the impression of encompassing a very long time. Two things contribute to this sensation. One is Odysseus' first-person narrative among the Phaiakians, in which he reports on his adventures between the fall of Troy and his arrival at Skheria (covering nearly ten years). The other is the thoroughness with which the poet recounts the incidents since the day (the thirty-fifth in the chronology of the poem's action) following the night of Odysseus' arrival on Ithaka. At the beginning of book 13 Odysseus arrives—this is his first day on Ithaka. At the end of book 23—during his fifth day back home—Penelope recognizes him. The chronicle of only five days (and, to be exact, parts of four nights) extends over eleven books, nearly half of the entire epic. Here and there, the poet's account even approaches real-time narration (that is, coincidence of time narrated and time of narration). Thus, for example, the fifth and decisive day after Odysseus' return to Ithaka occupies no less than four books (20–23), 1,701 verses in all. Conversations, interior monologues, the thoughts of various individuals—all these things contribute to a sense that much time has passed. But, in fact, these things actually reflect the efforts of the poet to portray a reality fuller, deeper, and more textured than the bare reality of everyday life. Familiarity with the modern narrative techniques of twentieth-century literature has put us today in a better position than most scholars during the heyday of Analytic criticism in the nineteenth century to appreciate this sort of representation of reality.

The action of the *Odyssey* consists of five large blocks:

		Book
Initiation of the action: council of the gods		
I.	Ithaka prior to Odysseus' return	1 and 2
II.	Telemakhos' journey to Pylos and Sparta to ascertain the whereabouts of his father (parts I and II, together with the return of Telemakhos in book 15, are designated the Telemakhia)	3 and 4
III.	Odysseus drifts by raft from Ogygia to Skheria	5
IV.	Odysseus on Skheria with the Phaiakians (the so-called Phaiakis): Odysseus recounts his adventures from the fall of Troy to his arrival at Skheria	6 to 12
V.	Odysseus on Ithaka	13 to 24

A fundamentally bipartite structure is quite apparent:

A. Twelve books in which all the participants at Ithaka are (unwittingly) prepared for the homecoming, with appearances by wife, son, domestics, suitors, the people of Ithaka, the outside world of the houses of friendly nobles, the gods, and Odysseus himself.
B. Twelve books of the homecoming itself: reacquisition and securing of possessions once taken for granted.

The Program of the Poem

The poet begins with a council of the gods. This was anticipated in the expanded prooimion with the information that now "the year had come . . . in which the gods granted his wish to return home" (*Od.* 1.16 f.). Zeus begins speaking and, with his mention of the murder of Agamemnon by Aigisthos and its avenging by Orestes, brings up the topic of the homecoming of the veterans of the Trojan War. Athena, Odysseus' protectress, immediately seizes on this opening: "and what of Odysseus? He must suffer griefs for so long far from his loved ones on the wave-ringed island. The daughter of Atlas (= Kalypso) detains the unlucky man, lamenting piteously,

> and always with smooth and flattering words
> she plies him to forget Ithaka. But still Odysseus,
> pining only to see the smoke rise
> over his land, longs to die. Does even that
> not stir your heart, Olympian?
>
> (*Od.* 1.56–60)

Zeus explains that Poseidon is the obstacle to Odysseus' homecoming. Poseidon is angry at Odysseus for having blinded his son, the Kyklops Polyphemos. But Poseidon at the moment is off on a journey, and the matter of Odysseus' homecoming can now be taken up. Poseidon will resign himself to it later. Athena seizes the opportunity:

> Our father, son of Kronos, you are the highest lord!
> If then this is now really pleasing to the blessed gods,
> that clever Odysseus should set out on his journey homeward,
> then let us bid the messenger Hermes, the famed slayer of Argos,
> to go to the island Ogygia, that he might very quickly

tell the fair-haired nymph of this ineluctable ruling:
that long-suffering Odysseus should in fact return home!
But I myself shall set out for Ithaka, to encourage
his son further and to put greater resolve in his mind,
to call the longhaired Akhaians into an assembly
to forbid the suitors from the house, who are always
slaughtering the sheep and the shuffling cattle with their curved
     horns.
Then I will send him to Sparta and to sandy Pylos,
to inquire about his father's return, if he might hear something,
and so he may have a good renown far and wide among men.
                                        (*Od.* 1.81–95)

Thus the immediate plan of the epic is clarified for the listener. First Athena will go to Ithaka and rouse Odysseus' son Telemakhos to action (the Telemakhia); then Hermes will go to Kalypso on Ogygia and deliver the directive to allow Odysseus to leave (book 5).

The execution corresponds precisely to the plan, just as it does in the *Iliad*. It has, of course, struck some as odd that the gods assemble on Olympos again at the beginning of book 5 and that Athena again complains to Zeus that Odysseus is languishing on Kalypso's island, whereupon Zeus—only now!—sends Hermes to Ogygia (*Od.* 5.1–42). The explanation (of, for example, Lesky 1967, 810 [124]; 1971, 69–70) that the poet, following the order of succession in narrative, could only recount seriatim two actually simultaneous actions (the Telemakhia in books 1–4 and the journey of Odysseus from Ogygia to Skheria in book 5) is unconvincing for a variety of reasons. It does better justice to the poet to credit him with having wished to make the two actions appear as distinct, nonintersecting, continuous blocks, each with its own motivations, two unified episodes moving toward convergence. Undoubtedly, there were precedents for both plot sequences in the rich and varied materials of the Odysseus saga. It is also clear that the fusing of these disparate elements within such a frequently treated and multifaceted theme posed a special problem. But an important circumstance is often overlooked. If written versions of the *Iliad* had already been in circulation for some two or three decades, the *Odyssey* poet was living in an era of advanced textuality. With him, more so than with the *Iliad* poet (even if they were one and the same), we may assume the existence of written drafts of both his own work and that of others. In view of these complexities of the poem's origins, we must marvel even more at the poet's achievement in fashioning such a monumental whole.

The First and Second Major Segments: The Telemakhia

The Telemakhia is the foundation of the epic. It lays out in detail the situation at home and prepares the listener for the appearance of Odysseus. (The same technique is found later in Attic tragedy: Herakles in Sophocles' *Women of Trakhis* and Philoktetes in his *Philoktetes* are seen first through the eyes of third parties before they themselves actually appear on stage.) The poet does not describe the situation on the island to his listeners. Rather, they enter into the setting step-by-step together with Athena, who comes to the master's house on Ithaka disguised as Odysseus' old guest-friend Mentes. The situation here has recently become critical. For about three years, the clever spouse of a clever man has staved off her numerous suitors. She said she would decide among them after she had completed a piece of weaving (a shroud for Odysseus' aged father, Laertes). But she secretly unwove every night what she had woven during the day (Heubeck 1985). After the exposure of this scheme, the suitors, feeling tricked and cheated, put ever greater pressure on Penelope. They "occupy" the palace and inflict all the economic disasters associated with their daily abuse of a coerced "hospitality." And now finally they say she must give up her absurd hopes for the return of her husband, the rightful lord of the island, and consent to marry one of them.

Penelope no longer knows what to do. Telemakhos, her son by Odysseus, is neither still a child nor yet a full-grown man. He is at just that point where he is beginning to sense how unjust and intolerable the situation is and to chafe at his mother's indecisiveness. Penelope sees this with anxiety. For she is constantly aware of something she will later tell the suitors (and the audience): when Odysseus set out for Troy, he said to her on his leave-taking (*Od.* 18.259 ff.): "I do not think that all of us who are going to Troy will return again. The Trojans, too, know how to fight. Thus, I know not whether I shall return. So, in the future, you must take care of everything here":

"Remember my father and my mother here in the house
as you now do, or even more so, while I am away.
So soon as you see that our son grows a beard,

marry whom you please and go out of the house!"
These were his words. And now all these things are come to
    pass.

(*Od.* 18.267–71)

It has been speculated, and with justification, that the stipulation "so soon as . . . our son grows a beard" formed the central motif of the old story of the homecoming. The *Odyssey* poet has transformed it into a concrete situation, into an action and a state of mind (Hölscher 1978, 60). What happens, he asks, when that moment has actually arrived? And he gives an answer, in that he has the son first of all seek definite information about his father. The son has never known who his father actually was; because he was an infant when his father left, he has only heard stories.

Friend [Mentes/Athena], my mother says indeed I am his son,
    but I
do not know. For no one has witnessed his own begetting!
Would that I were the son of a prosperous
ordinary man, whom old age overtook among all his
    possessions.
But I am the son of the most ill-fated of men.
That is the man from whom they say I am sprung!

(*Od.* 1.215–20)

Telemakhos does not know what he ought to do, because he does not know who he is. He must first find his identity. Only then can he act with force and conviction. And only then can he encounter his father, because to recognize his father as truly his father, he must first recognize himself as his son. The poet of the *Odyssey* is aware of this. For this reason, he has Athena send the young man into foreign parts, after his fruitless attempt to clear up the situation in the community assembly on Ithaka. Although the heads of the aristocratic houses that had previously been friendly with his father in Pylos (Nestor) and Sparta (Menelaos and Helen) cannot say whether Odysseus still lives or not, they can tell the young man what is most significant for him at this moment: that he is the son of Odysseus. They knew Odysseus. They are therefore able to discern Odysseus in both the physical features and the nature of Telemakhos. That is compelling. When Telemakhos returns, he has found himself. He has matured and grown in self-awareness. Now he is ready to be his father's partner when he returns, something he could never have done before.

The Third and Fourth Major Segments: The Phaiakis

The poet can now attend to the return of Odysseus. But another problem presents itself. It is basically a variant of the Telemakhos problem, as in fact the theme demands. Odysseus has not only been away from home for years; he has of late also been utterly isolated. On the island of Kalypso, "where the navel of the sea is" (*Od.* 1.50), he has lived a life without purposeful activity, a life of surrender to the love and care of an affectionate goddess, a life, however, of heartache and yearning. In large measure, he has lost his vitality and autonomy together with his own image of himself. He has almost entirely forgotten that he is a hero of the Trojan War, who has triumphantly accomplished so many world-renowned feats. He must "relearn" all this. Before he can face his last great trial, he must first "grow into" himself once again. To this end, the poet does not have him return nonstop from Kalypso to Ithaka. Instead, he diverts him to an intermediate way station—the land of the Phaiakians.

In the first council of the gods, when the initial plan of action was presented in the words of Athena, there was no mention of the Phaiakians. That comes now for the first time, just before the actual departure from Ogygia in book 5. In the form of instructions to Hermes, Zeus prophetically reveals the poet's further plan of action. (The technique of disclosing the structure of the work through prophecy—prophecy certain of fulfillment because pronounced by a god—is familiar to us already from the *Iliad*.)

Hermes!—for you are my messenger in all other matters—
tell the fair-haired nymph of this ineluctable ruling:
long-suffering Odysseus shall return home!
Escorted home by neither gods nor men
but enduring troubles on a securely bound raft, he must
come to the fertile land of Skheria on the twentieth day out,
the land of the Phaiakians who are close to the gods.
They will revere him like a god from their hearts
and carry him by ship to his homeland,

giving him bronze and abundant gold and many clothes
(Odysseus would not have brought so much back from Troy
had he returned safely home straightway with his share.)
In this way, it is destined for him look upon his loved ones
and come back to the high-roofed house in his fatherland.

(*Od.* 5.29–42)

The poet clearly states here the purpose of the Phaiakis, the fourth major segment of the *Odyssey*: the stay among the Phaiakians restores to Odysseus a sense of his own self-worth. These people, who are "close to the gods" (thus especially trustworthy), show him great respect and bestow material gifts on him. Thus, he does not return to his fatherland a broken and destitute man. (Ironically, he chooses to return disguised as a beggar.)

The poet leaves indistinct the details of the process of Odysseus' psychological rehabilitation among the Phaiakians. He is employing the same technique of adumbration familiar to us from the *Iliad*. Tension is heightened and interest is sharpened anew.

But before this resurrection comes a fall—to the lowest point imaginable: "enduring troubles on a . . . raft, twenty days on the sea." In the course of events, Odysseus first feels renewed hope after his splendid achievement of building the raft in four days (*Od.* 5.228–61). But his reawakened self-confidence is utterly annihilated during his solitary raft-voyage to Skheria. Poseidon in his anger sends a storm and shipwrecks him; Odysseus, in fear for his life and nearly drowning, clings to the last of the raft's timbers. He swims for it and (again with divine aid) finally reaches land, but in what a state!

He bent his knees and his strong arms,
because the saltwater had subdued his heart;
his whole body was drenched, and a flood of water
gushed from his mouth and nose. Breathless and speechless,
he lay there, barely living, and an awful exhaustion gripped him.

(*Od.* 5.453–57)

Having had to strip off his clothes, Odysseus arrives among the Phaiakians naked, debilitated, and unsightly—a man at the limit of his physical and psychological resources; he will depart three days later fully recovered, well groomed, well clothed, and—most important—

armed with a new awareness of himself. All this is brought about by the friendship, admiration, and love of the Phaiakians for the hero, and for the man, Odysseus. It is no accident that he is repeatedly aided and restored to courage by women: above all, Athena, but also Kalypso; then, during the sea journey, the nymph Leukothea (5.333–53); and now, on Skheria, Nausikaa, the king's daughter, a girl in the flower of her youth. Nausikaa is attracted to this mature, much-traveled man, so different from her age-mates, whose chief preoccupation is games. This contributes not a little to Odysseus' rediscovery of his own self-worth. Of the greatest importance in this process of recovery, however, is Odysseus' successful self-validation, first in his quest for social approval during a dispute with the king's son Laodamas and in the ensuing athletic competition (8.143–255), and then—climactically—in the restoration of his honor as a hero through his account of his deeds and tribulations between the fall of Troy and his arrival at Ogygia, in the so-called apologues (tales) of books 9 through 12.

The adventures of Odysseus, recounted first-person over the space of four books, are not simply topics that the *Odyssey* poet could not pass over because tradition and his audience demanded their inclusion. In *his* version of the story, they had a crucial function to perform: Odysseus had to reconstitute in them his own mighty deeds and tribulations. The function of the adventure tales within the *Odyssey* of the *Odyssey* poet coincided neatly with their function within the *saga*: by demonstrating the triumph of the human spirit they strengthened the faith of the listeners in themselves. But this deeper significance of the adventures could be made obvious only by their placement in a new context within this epic. By making the adventures fulfill a specific function within the *Odyssey*, the poet revealed their true meaning.

A detailed account of the adventures is unneeded here; instead, a sketch of their general outlines follows:

Odysseus' departure from Troy with twelve ships

1. The land of the Kikones: destruction of the city of Ismaros. Battle with the neighboring Kikones. Loss of seventy-two comrades. A storm off Cape Malea (in the extreme southeast of the Peloponnesos) drives them past the island of Kythera and beyond for nine days. Departure from the real world into the realm of sailors' yarns.

2. The land of the Lotophagoi (Lotos-Eaters): the enjoyment of the drug Lotos almost causes them to forget their homecoming.

3. The island of the Kyklopes (one-eyed ogres); the Kyklops Polyphemos (*polyphēmos*, "the notorious one"): Odysseus shut up in the giant's cave with twelve companions, six of whom are devoured by the Kyklops. They bore out the giant's one eye with a sharpened, burning hot olive-wood stake. The "Nobody" trick. They escape under the bellies of sheep tied together three-by-three, even though Polyphemos, now blind, guards the opening of the cave. Incautious taunting of the giant from the boat. Polyphemos petitions his father Poseidon for revenge.

4. The floating island of Aiolos, the lord of the winds: he gives them the bag of winds. As they come within sight of home, the foolish comrades open the bag of winds. A whirlwind carries them back to Aiolos, who utters a curse against Odysseus.

5. The land of the Laistrygones (giants): the giants destroy eleven ships in the harbor by throwing boulders down on them; the comrades swimming for it are fished out and devoured. Only Odysseus' ship now remains.

6. The island Aiaia and the sorceress Kirke (daughter of the sun god Helios): Kirke transforms twenty-two comrades into swine. Hermes gives Odysseus the apotropaic herb moly (μῶλυ, *moly*, a wonder plant). Odysseus succumbs to Kirke's attractions. A year's life of leisure with Kirke. Kirke sends Odysseus to the seer Teiresias in the land of the dead.

7. Conjuring up of the dead along Okeanos, the river that circles the earth: the prophecy of Teiresias; Odysseus encounters his mother, Agamemnon, Akhilleus, Patroklos, Aias. He observes Minos, the judge of the dead; the malefactors Tityos, Tantalos, and Sisyphos; and the beneficent Herakles. Return to Kirke, who forewarns Odysseus about the Sirens, the planktai (wandering rocks), Skylla and Kharybdis, and the cattle of Helios.

8. The island of the Sirens: Odysseus is tied to the mast (and his companions' ears stopped with wax); thus Odysseus escapes the temptation of absolute knowledge.

9. Skylla and Kharybdis (a maelstrom): six companions are lost.

10. Thrinakia, the island of Helios: out of hunger, Odysseus' comrades slaughter the forbidden cattle of Helios. Helios demands vengeance from Zeus, who blasts the ship with his lightning. All the comrades drown. The sole survivor, Odysseus, arrives at Ogygia, Kalypso's island, by riding the lashed-together mast and keel of the ship.

The Fifth Major Segment: Homecoming on Ithaka

The first half of the *Odyssey* has created a background of ten years for events of six days' duration. Thus, the audience already knows the personal history of each of the leading characters in the story: Odysseus, Penelope, Telemakhos, and the suitors. The whole first half of the epic has made it unnecessary to offer explanations of their conduct.

So, too, the audience understands why Odysseus cannot go directly to his house after he awakens on Ithaka. The motif of his arrival back home in disguise was firmly fixed in the old return stories. The *Odyssey* poet shows why it has to be this way. No one actually believes that the master of the house is still alive. That is the real reason why everyone— the people of Ithaka, the house servants, Telemakhos, even Penelope— tolerates the behavior of the suitors, albeit with displeasure and a troubled conscience. Whoever arrives on the scene at this point and says, "I am Odysseus," will have to bear the burden of proof.

The whole second half of the epic provides this proof. The traditional tale of the homecoming typically employed signs to facilitate the hero's recognition: the scar, the trees Odysseus planted with his own hands, and the bed he built himself. The poet of the *Odyssey* finds these insufficient. Is it that simple? he asks. Is it so easy that, away for twenty years, the hero returns and says "Here is the scar, look! I am Odysseus"? How does it really take place when layers of mistrust, fear of disappointment, and disbelief must be penetrated?

Odysseus would not be the man the poet has presented in the great adventures of books 9–12—circumspect, farsighted, and therefore truly daring—if he failed to realize that he should dissemble his identity when he first arrives back on Ithaka. When he meets a young man of noble bearing along the shore, he regales him with a tale of woe: he is (he says) a fugitive from Crete (and yet a Trojan War veteran), where he killed the king's son. He has drifted off course to Ithaka with a group of Phoenicians. When the young man, ostensibly an aristocratic shepherd,

reveals himself as Athena, the strongest intellects on both the divine
and the human levels enter into alliance. As Athena puts it:

> "It would take a crafty and deceitful one to surpass you
> in all your machinations, even if a god went against you!
> You naughty, shifty-minded, habitual trickster. . . .
> Not even in your own land have you been willing to give up
>   your tricks
> and deceptions that so thoroughly please you!
> Let us speak no more of this. We both know how to
> beguile. For you are far the best of all mortals
> in planning and speaking, while I among all the gods
> am renowned for counsel and cleverness. . . .
>
> (*Od.* 13.291–99)

A plan is formulated: Odysseus must first go to the faithful swineherd
Eumaios at his "ranch" outside of town and reconnoiter the situation
from there. Athena will fetch Telemakhos from Sparta. Next, both
Odysseus and his son will plot the destruction of the suitors. But
Odysseus, for reasons of security, must be rendered unrecognizable.
Athena disguises him as a ragged and ugly old beggar.

Everything now proceeds according to plan. On the first day,
Odysseus learns from the ever-loyal Eumaios how matters stand in the
city and in the house of Odysseus. (Eumaios, like everyone else, does
not recognize the beggar, but he has an odd feeling when in his presence.) On the third day, Telemakhos arrives from Sparta, having been
guided by Athena past the ambush set for him by the suitors. He also
proceeds to the "Eumaios-base." Odysseus then reveals himself to Telemakhos, who recognizes him *without* external distinguishing signs. On
the fourth day, Odysseus arrives at his own house and continues to
play the role of beggar. He maintains his "cover" despite all the insults
he receives at the hands of the suitors and his own household servants
and despite the almost superhuman self-control that the role demands
of him when he first meets with his wife after his twenty-year absence.
On the fifth day, he finally reveals his true identity, first to the loyal servants Eumaios and Philoitios, and then to the suitors. He kills the suitors and then is also able finally to break through the cool reserve of his
wife Penelope. On the sixth day, he is reunited with his old father

Laertes out in the country. Together with Laertes, wondrously rejuvenated by joy at his son's return, Odysseus settles the dangerous situation on the island arising from the punishment that he has inflicted on the sons of the leading houses of Ithaka. Here, too, Athena steers things along. She first initiated the action during the council of the gods (book 1) and she has seen it all the way through to the end. Why? Athena says to Odysseus:

> thus I cannot abandon you when you are in trouble,
> because you are wise and quick-witted and insightful.
>
> (*Od.* 13.331–32)

This is the new ideal of the human being, whose glory is sung in the *Odyssey*. The nobility has changed its outlook on the world. Strength, military preparedness, a dogged sense of honor, and excessive obstinacy now count for much less. Now, whoever is ingenious like Odysseus enjoys the favor of the gods. The gods no longer love the strong arm more than the clever head.

The Recognition of Odysseus and Penelope

The recognition of the two spouses is the true objective of the epic; the poet's narrative strategy has been leading to this from the very beginning. It is cited right at the start, in the (expanded) prooimion:

> [Odysseus], who yearned for his homecoming *and for his wife*.
>
> (*Od.* 1.13)

The *Odyssey* is actually complete when this goal is reached in book 23. (Nonetheless, book 24, in which the poet, by way of epilogue, reports on the *securing* of all the things Odysseus has finally won back, is not simply a superfluous appendage [Stössel 1975, 150].)

The longing of the two spouses for each other spans the whole epic, appearing repeatedly in a manner and with an effect reminiscent of the technique of reiteration employed in the *Iliad*. Penelope's longing is first mentioned in book 1. Phemios has been singing of the returns of the Trojan War heroes; Penelope overhears from her rooms upstairs and comes down:

> yet stop this sad song,
> which always casts down the spirit in my breast,
> because an unforgettable sorrow oppresses me grievously,
> since I must yearn for such a person,
> for a man whose fame reaches far throughout Hellas and the
>   heartland of Argos.
>
> (*Od.* 1.340–44)

Odysseus' yearning is brought home to the listener in book 5 with images that will remain fixed in the memory throughout the rest of the narrative. Kalypso, coming upon Odysseus,

> found him sitting along the shore; his eyes
> were never dried of their tears, since he passed his life
> in lamentation for his homecoming. . . .
> . . . .
> All day he sat on the rocky beach
> and looked continuously out over the barren sea, shedding tears.
>
> (*Od.* 5.151–53, 156–58)

Like the wrath in the *Iliad*, this yearning of husband and wife in the *Odyssey* resonates as the recurrent, fundamental theme throughout all that happens. Because Penelope cannot forget Odysseus, she cannot summon the nerve to leave home. Because of her inability to bring matters to a close, she must continue to live in a state of intolerable uncertainty, which impels her son to make his journey and to risk death. Because she longs so very much for Odysseus, who left twenty years earlier, she cannot recognize Odysseus in the flesh when he has been living for two days under the same roof, though she does have peculiar sensations. Because Odysseus cannot forget Penelope, no other woman can hold him, neither goddesses like Kirke and Kalypso, nor human women like Nausikaa among the Phaiakians.

During the first day Odysseus spends inside his own home in twenty years, the suitors humiliate and revile him and pelt him like a stray dog. During the evening of that same day, Odysseus meets his wife for an audience. Penelope wishes to ask this beggar, who seems so unlike a beggar, whether he knows anything about Odysseus. He tells her a story of how he once entertained Odysseus on Crete (because he is actually the brother of the king of Crete, etc.; we know the story already). Penelope cannot keep back her tears:

> As she listened, the tears flowed down and her skin melted,
> as when the snows melts and flows down from the high
>   mountains,
> when the east wind thaws what the west wind has heaped up,
> when the snowmelt, running down, fills the rivers,
> so her fair cheeks melted, spilling over with tears,
> as she wept for her man, who was sitting right beside her.
> Odysseus, meanwhile pitied his wife in his heart, as she
>   sobbed,
> but his eyes stood fast as horn or iron,
> unmoving inside their lids; cleverly he hid his tears. . . .
>
> (*Od.* 19.204–12)

This superhuman self-restraint nearly goes for naught when his old nurse Eurykleia, on Penelope's command, washes the beggar's feet. The scar! She recognizes the scar. In the traditional versions of the homecoming, this apparently signaled the beginning of the recognition. The poet of our *Odyssey* makes something else altogether out of the scar motif—another test for Odysseus, who forestalls a premature revelation by grabbing Eurykleia by her throat (Erbse 1972, 96 f.). This shows the same presence of mind he displayed inside the wooden horse, when one of his companions nearly gave everything away by making a noise that could be heard outside the horse. The time is not yet ripe. But this had to be a near miss! The listener had to recognize that Odysseus was in terrible danger. The resolution of twenty years of suffering and striving could have been wiped out in a few seconds. Not for nothing is the *Odyssey* laced with references to the counterexample of the homecoming of Agamemnon; he had been too trusting, too forthright. He simply came home. He did not think of the perils that a long absence might breed. His wife's suitor, Aigisthos, had struck him down. And it had been easy for him. Agamemnon had conquered Troy—but he died in his own bath.

The *Odyssey* poet delays the recognition. First, the suitors must be eliminated. Odysseus must again become master of his home. Success must not be imperiled by haste. It is risky to allow anyone to be "in on" his secret.

When the suitors have been shot through with spears and arrows and their corpses cleared away, the proper moment for the recognition has come. Husband and wife sit before each other. Penelope still cannot believe it. She had had a presentiment, to be sure. But what if it is all a trick? The clever Penelope is not so naive as to fall on the neck of the beggar just because he has killed the suitors. What possibilities for subtle deceptions still remain! No one is more mindful of this than the woman who has for years led a whole horde of grown men around by their noses. No, there must be greater certainty. She feels that this is indeed Odysseus, but can Penelope allow herself to give in to a mere feeling, a hunch? Would that be worthy of her husband, of a man of Odysseus' intelligence? Then, one last time, she puts him to the test, a test that will also show him how truly unique his wife is:

> You strange man! I do not flatter myself or snub you!
> Even so, I am not terribly impressed. I know very well how you
>   [!] were
> when you [!] sailed away from Ithaka on the long-oared ship.
> Now then, Eurykleia, lay out for him the stout bed,
> *outside* the well-built bedroom, which he himself constructed.
> Carry out there for him the stout bed and put upon it the
>   bedspread,
> sheepskins, sheets, and gleaming coverlets.
>
> (*Od.* 23.174–80)

This is too much. Not that he is being quartered outside the house, but that the bed evidently no longer stands in its place. *That* provokes him to respond: "I myself constructed the bed using an olive tree that grew there as one of the four bedposts! Has some other man . . . ?"

> This loosened her knees and her heart on the spot:
> she had recognized the irrefutable signs that Odysseus had
>   shown her.
> She broke into tears, ran to him, flung her arms
> around Odysseus' neck, and kissed his head. . . .
>
> (*Od.* 23.205–8)

The *Odyssey* poet has been working toward this moment right from the start. He has prepared for it in various ways; he has brought it close and then put it off. This serves to make it credible.

The *Odyssey* derives its inner unity from this ultimate goal. As Peter Von der Mühll said in his splendid article on the *Odyssey*: "It is obvious and needs no proving that the *Odyssey* as a whole follows a well-conceived plan and is a unity" (1940, 698). True, it does not really require proof. But one must know how to listen. Even the Greeks themselves, in the centuries after Homer, could no longer listen particularly well. Art shows this: no incident mentioned in the *Odyssey* was as frequently depicted by artists as the blinding of Polyphemos. As if this one adventure among many so typified either Odysseus or what the poet of the *Odyssey* wanted to make of the myth of Odysseus in *his* version. But it was spectacular. Much more spectacular than the construction of the raft in book 5, a man's self-control in the presence of his wife as she weeps for him, or the gripping of his own nurse's throat (book 19). This superficial interpretation of the *Odyssey* continued in Roman times, the Renaissance, and even our own day. Countless books have been written about "the adventures of Odysseus" and "the wanderings of Odysseus." Countless hypotheses have been put forward to determine which island of the Mediterranean or the Black Sea or the North Sea was really Kirke's Aiaia, where the Lotos-Eaters or the Laistrygones really lived, or where Odysseus' raft broke up. It is as if the poet of our *Odyssey* had not made clear the shift of emphasis that he was striving for when he ingeniously adapted to his own purposes the whole series of traditional Odysseus adventures by transforming them into first-person narrative! No, those who read the *Odyssey* in this superficial way will not be able to divine its unity. They are hearing only the old yarns of sailors; they are not hearing Homer.

Abbreviations and Works Cited by Author's Name and Date

AA   *Archäologischer Anzeiger*
AAntHung   *Acta Antiqua Academiae Scientiarum Hungaricae*
AJA   *American Journal of Archaeology*
ArchHom   *Archaeologia Homerica: Die Denkmäler und das frühgriechische Epos.*
            Ed. F. Matz and H.-G. Buchholz. Göttingen 1967–. [Projected are
            three volumes embracing some twenty-eight monographs as
            chapters; now nearly complete.]
CW   *Classical World*
JHS   *Journal of Hellenic Studies*
RE   *Paulys Real-Encyclopädie der klassischen Altertumswissenschaft*
ST   *Studia Troica*
WJA   *Würzburger Jahrbücher für die Altertumswissenschaft*

Alpers, K. 1970. Eine Beobachtung zum Nestorbecher von Pithekussai. *Glotta*
    47:170–74.
Andreae, B. 1982. *Odysseus: Archäologie des europäischen Menschenbildes.* Biele-
    feld.
Andreae, B., and H. Flashar. 1977. Strukturäquivalenzen zwischen den home-
    rischen Epen und der frühgriechischen Vasenkunst. *Poetica* 9:217–65.
Antonaccio, C.M. 1987. The Archaeology of Early Greek "Hero Cult." Diss.,
    Princeton.
———. Forthcoming. Lefkandi and Homer. In *Homer's World: Fiction, Tradition,
    Reality,* ed. O. Andersen. Athens.
Blegen, C.W. 1963. *Troy and the Trojans.* New York.
Blome, P. 1984. Lefkandi und Homer. *WJA* 10:9–21.
———. 1991. Die dunklen Jahrhunderte—aufgehellt. In Latacz 1991c, 45–60.
Bowra, C.M. 1952. *Heroic Poetry.* London.
Bremer, J.M., I.J.F. de Jong, and J. Kalff, eds. 1987. *Homer, beyond Oral Poetry:
    Recent Trends in Homeric Interpretation.* Amsterdam.
Brommer, F. 1983. *Odysseus: Die Taten und Leiden des Helden in antiker Kunst und
    Literatur.* Darmstadt.
Burkert, W. 1987. The Making of Homer in the Sixth Century B.C.: Rhapsodes
    versus Stesichoros. In *Papers on the Amasis Painter and His World,* 43–62. Mal-
    ibu.
———. 1991. Homerstudien und Orient. In Latacz 1991c, 155–81.

———. 1992. *The Orientalizing Revolution: Near Eastern Influence on Greek Culture in the Early Archaic Age.* Trans. M.E. Pinder and W. Burkert. Cambridge, Mass., and London.

Calligas, P.G. 1988. Hero-Cult in Early Iron Age Greece. In Hägg et al. 1988, 229–34.

Chadwick, J. 1967. *The Decipherment of Linear B.* 2d ed. Cambridge.

Christ, W. 1905. *Geschichte der griechischen Literatur bis auf die Zeit Justinians.* 4th ed. Munich.

Clark, M.E. 1986. Neoanalysis: A Bibliographical Review. *CW* 79:379–94.

Coldstream, J.N. 1977. *Geometric Greece.* London.

Cook, J.M. 1975. Greek Settlement in the Eastern Aegean and Asia Minor. In *Cambridge Ancient History,* vol. II, part 2, 773–804. 3d ed.

Deger, S. 1970. Herrschaftsformen bei Homer. Diss., Vienna.

Deger-Jalkotzy, S. 1983a. Das Problem der "Handmade Burnished Ware." In Deger-Jalkotzy 1983b, 161–78.

———. 1983b. *Griechenland: die Ägäis und die Levante während der "Dark Ages" vom 12. bis zum 9. Jh. v.Chr.: Akten des Symposiums von Stift Zwettl (NÖ), 11.–14. Oktober 1980.* Sitzungsberichte der Österreichischen Akademie der Wissenschaften in Wien 418. Vienna.

———. 1991. Die Erforschung des Zusammenbruchs der sogennanten mykenischen Kultur und der sogenannten dunkeln Jahrhunderte. In Latacz 1991c, 127–54.

De Jong, I.J.F. 1987. *Narrators and Focalizers: The Presentation of the Story in the Iliad.* Amsterdam.

Dihle, A. 1970. *Homer-Probleme.* Opladen.

Dobesch, G. 1983. Historische Fragestellungen in der Urgeschichte. In Deger-Jalkotzy 1983b, 179–239.

Effe, B. 1988. Der Homerische Achilleus: Zur gesellschaftlichen Funktion eines literarischen Helden. *Gymnasium* 95:1–16.

Erbse, H., ed. 1969–88. *Scholia Graeca in Homeri Iliadem [Scholia vetera].* 7 vols. Berlin.

———. 1972. *Beiträge zum Verständnis der Odyssee.* Berlin and New York.

———. 1986. *Untersuchungen zur Funktion der Götter im homerischen Epos.* Berlin and New York.

Finnegan, R. 1977. *Oral Poetry: Its Nature, Significance and Social Context.* Cambridge.

Finsler, G. 1912. *Homer in der Neuzeit von Dante bis Goethe.* Leipzig and Berlin. Reprint, Hildesheim, 1973.

Foxhall, L., and J.K. Davies. 1984. *The Trojan War: Its Historicity and Context.* Bristol.

Fränkel, H. 1973. *Early Greek Poetry and Philosophy.* Trans. M. Hadas and J. Willis. New York.

Goody, J. 1977. *The Domestication of the Savage Mind.* Cambridge.

———. 1982. Alternative Paths to Knowledge in Oral and Literate Cultures. In *Spoken and Written Language: Exploring Orality and Literacy,* ed. D. Tannen, 201–15. Norwood.

————. 1986. *The Logic of Writing and the Organization of Society.* Cambridge.

————. 1987. *The Interface between the Written and the Oral.* Cambridge.

Goody, J., and I. Watt. 1963. The Consequences of Literacy. *Comparative Studies in Society and History* 5:304–45. Reprinted in *Literacy in Traditional Societies,* ed. J. Goody, 27–68. Cambridge, 1968.

Graf, F. 1993. *Greek Mythology: An Introduction.* Trans. T. Marier. Baltimore.

Griffin, J. 1980. *Homer on Life and Death.* Oxford.

Gschnitzer, F. 1971. Stammesnamen in den mykenischen Texten. In *Donum Indogermanicum: Festgabe für A. Scherer,* ed. R. Schmitt-Brandt, 90–106. Heidelberg.

————. 1981. *Griechische Sozialgeschichte: Von der mykenischen bis zum Ausgang der klassischen Zeit.* Wiesbaden.

————. 1983. Zur geschichtliche Entwicklung des Systems der griechischen Ethnika. In Heubeck and Neumann 1983, 140–54.

————. 1991. Zur homerischen Staats- und Gesellschaftsordnung: Grundcharakter und geschichtliche Stellung. In Latacz 1991c, 182–204.

Güterbock, H.G. 1984. Hittites and Akhaeans: A New Look. *Proceedings of the American Philosophical Society* 128:114–22.

Hägg, R. 1983a. Burial Customs and Social Differentiation in 8th-Century Argos. In Hägg 1983b, 27–31.

————, ed. 1983b. *The Greek Renaissance of the Eighth Century B.C., Tradition and Innovation: Proceedings of the Second International Symposium at the Swedish Institute in Athens, 1–5 June, 1981.* Stockholm.

Hägg, R., et al., eds. 1988. *Early Greek Cult Practice: Proceedings of the Fifth International Symposium at the Swedish Institute at Athens, 26–29 June 1986.* Stockholm.

Hansen, P.A., ed. 1983. *Carmina epigraphica Graeca saeculorum VIII–V a.Chr.n.* Berlin and New York. [Corrigenda in *Zeitschrift für Papyrologie und Epigraphik* 58 (1985): 234.]

Havelock, E.A. 1978. The Alphabetization of Homer. In *Communication Arts in the Ancient World,* ed. E.A. Havelock and J.P. Hershbell, 3–21. New York. Reprinted in *The Literate Revolution in Greece and Its Cultural Consequences,* 166–84. Princeton, 1982.

————. 1986. *The Muses Learn to Write: Reflections on Orality and Literacy from Antiquity to the Present.* New Haven and London.

Heubeck, A. 1974. *Die homerische Frage: Ein Bericht über die Forschung der letzten Jahrzehnte.* Darmstadt.

————. 1979. *Schrift. ArchHom* 3.X.

————. 1983. Review of *Gründungsmythen und Sagenchronologie,* by F. Prinz. *Anzeiger für die Altertumswissenschaft* 36:212–20.

————. 1984. Zum Erwachen der Schriftlichkeit im archaischen Griechentum. In *Kleine Schriften zur griechischen Sprache und Literatur,* ed. B. Forssman et al., 537–54. Erlangen.

————. 1985. Penelopes Webelist. *WJA* 11:33–43.

Heubeck, A., and G. Neumann, eds. 1983. Res Mycenaeae: Akten des VII. *Inter-*

nationalen Mykenologischen Colloquiums in Nürnberg vom 6.–10. April 1981. Göttingen.

Hiller, S. 1983. Possible Historical Reasons for the Rediscovery of the Mycenaean Past in the Age of Homer. In Hägg 1983b, 9–15.

Hiller, S., and O. Panagl. 1976. *Die frühgriechischen Texte aus mykenischer Zeit.* Darmstadt.

Hohendahl-Zoetelief, J.M. 1980. *Manners in the Homeric Epic.* Leiden.

Hölkeskamp, K.-J. 1992. Written Law in Archaic Greece. *Proceedings of the Cambridge Philological Society* 38:87–117.

Holoka, J.P. 1973. Homeric Originality: A Survey. *CW* 66:257–93. Reprinted in *The Classical World Bibliography of Greek Drama and Poetry,* ed. W. Donlan, 37–75. New York and London, 1978.

Hölscher, U. 1978. The Transformation from Folk-Tale to Epic. In *Homer: Tradition and Invention,* ed. B. C. Fenik, 56–67. Leiden.

Hunger, H. 1988. *Lexikon der griechischen und römischen Mythologie, mit Hinweisen auf das Fortwirken antiker Stoff und Motive in der bildenden Kunst, Literatur und Musik des Abendlandes bis zur Gegenwart.* 8th ed. Vienna.

Irmscher, J. 1950. *Götterzorn bei Homer.* Leipzig.

Jablonka, P. 1994. Ein Verteidigungsgraben in der Unterstadt von Troia VI: Grabungsbericht 1993. *ST* 4:51–66.

Jahn, T. 1987. *Zum Wortfeld "Seele-Geist" in der Sprache Homers.* Munich.

Janko, R. 1992. *The Iliad: A Commentary.* Vol. 4. Cambridge.

———. 1994. Review of *Homeri Odyssea,* ed. H. van Thiel. *Gnomon* 66:289–95.

Jeffery, L.H. 1990. *The Local Scripts of Archaic Greece: A Study of the Origins of the Greek Alphabet and Its Development from the Eighth to the Fifth Centuries B.C.* 2d ed. Oxford.

Johnston, A.W. 1983. The Extent and Use of Literacy: the Archaeological Evidence. In Hägg 1983b, 63–68.

———. 1990. Supplement. In Jeffery 1990, 423–82.

Kakridis, J.T. 1949. *Homeric Researches.* Lund. Reprint, New York and London, 1987.

———. 1971. *Homer Revisited.* Lund.

Kannicht, R. 1979. Dichtung und Bildkunst: die Rezeption der Troja-Epik in den frühgriechischen Sagenbildern. In *Wort und Bild: Symposion des Fachbereiches Altertums und Kulturwissenschaften zum 500-jährigen Bestehen der Eberhard-Karls-Universität Tübingen 1977,* ed. H. Brunner et al., 279–96. Munich.

———. 1980. Der alte Streit zwischen Philosophie und Dichtung. *Der altsprachliche Unterricht* 57:6–36.

Karageorghis, V. 1980. Chronique des Fouilles et Découvertes Archéologiques à Chypre en 1979. *Bulletin de la Correspondance Hellénique* 104:761–803.

Kirk, G.S. 1960. Objective Dating Criteria in Homer. *Museum Helveticum* 17:189–205. Reprinted in Kirk 1964, 174–90.

———. 1985. *The Iliad: A Commentary.* Vol. 1. Cambridge.

———, ed. 1964. *The Language and Background of Homer: Some Recent Studies and Controversies.* Cambridge and New York.

Korfmann, M. 1984. Beşik-Tepe: Vorbericht über die Ergebnisse der Grabung von 1982: Die Hafenbucht vor "Troia" (Hisarlik), Grabungen am Beşik-Yas-sitepe. *AA* 99:165–76.

———. 1985. Beşik-Tepe: Vorbericht über die Ergebnisse der Grabung von 1983: Grabungen am Beşik-Yassitepe und Beşik-Sivritepe. *AA* 100:157–72.

———. 1986. Beşik-Tepe: Vorbericht über die Ergebnisse der Grabung von 1984: Grabungen am Beşik-Yassitepe, Beşik-Sivritepe, und Beşik-Gräberfeld. *AA* 101:303–29.

———. 1988. Beşik-Tepe: Vorbericht über die Ergebnisse der Grabung von 1985 und 1986: Grabungen am Beşik-Yassitepe und im Beşik-Gräberfeld. *AA* 103:391–98.

———. 1989. Beşik-Tepe: Vorbericht über die Ergebnisse der Arbeiten von 1987 und 1988: Auswertungsarbeiten Beşik-Sivritepe, Beşik-Yassitepe, Beşik-Gräberfeld, Grabungen am Beşik-Sivritepe. *AA* 104:473–81.

———. 1991a. Der gegenwärtige Stand der neuen archäologischen Arbeiten in Hisarlik (Troia). In Latacz 1991c, 89–102.

———. 1991b. Troia: Reinigungs- und Dokumentationsarbeiten 1987, Aus-grabungen 1988 und 1989. *ST* 1:1–34.

———. 1992. Troia: Ausgrabungen 1990 und 1991. *ST* 2:1–41.

———. 1993. Troia: Ausgrabungen 1992. *ST* 3:1–37.

———. 1994. Troia: Ausgrabungen 1993. *ST* 4:1–50.

Kullmann, W. 1981. Zur Methode der Neoanalyse in der Homerforschung. *Wiener Studien* 15:5–42.

———. 1984. Oral Poetry Theory and Neoanalysis in Homeric Research. *Greek, Roman and Byzantine Studies* 25:307–23.

———. 1985. Gods and Men in the *Iliad* and the *Odyssey*. *Harvard Studies in Classical Philology* 89:1–23.

———. 1991. Ergebnisse der motivgeschichtlichen Forschung zu Homer (Neo-analyse). In Latacz 1991c, 425–55. Reprinted in *Homerische Motiv: Beiträge zur Entstehung, Eigenart und Wirkung von Ilias und Odyssee*, 100–134. Stuttgart, 1992.

Kurt, C. 1979. *Seemännische Fachausdrücke bei Homer unter Berücksichtigung Hesiods und der Lyriker bis Bakchylides*. Göttingen. [See review by Latacz in *Kratylos* 31 (1986): 110–25; reprinted in Latacz 1994b, 625–38.]

Lämmert, E. 1980. *Bauformen des Erzählens*. 7th ed. Stuttgart.

Latacz, J. 1977. *Kampfparänese, Kampfdarstellung und Kampfwirklichkeit in der Ilias, bei Kallinos und Tyrtaios*. Munich.

———. 1981a. Der Planungswille Homers im Aufbau der Ilias. *Die Alten Sprachen im Unterricht* 28, no. 3:6–16.

———. 1981b. Zeus' Reise zu den Aithiopen (Zu Ilias I, 304–495). In *Gnomosyne: Menschliches Denken und Handeln in der frühgriechischen Literatur: Festschrift für Walter Marg*, ed. G. Kurz et al., 53–80. Munich. Reprinted in Latacz 1994b, 175–203.

———. 1984a. Das Menschenbild Homers. *Gymnasium* 91:15–39. Reprinted in Latacz 1994b, 71–94.

———. 1984b. *Perspektiven der Gräzistik*. Freiburg and Würzburg.

———. 1988a. Neues von Troja. *Gymnasium* 95:385–413.

————. 1988b. News from Troy. *Berytus* 34:97–127.

————. 1988c. Zu Umfang und Art Vergangenheitsbewahrung in der mündlichen Überlieferungsphase des griechischen Heldenepos. In Ungern-Sternberg and Reinau 1988, 153–83. Reprinted in Latacz 1994b, 37–69.

————. 1990. Die Funktion des Symposions für die entstehende griechische Literatur. In *Der Übergang von der Mündlichkeit zur Literatur bei den Griechen*, ed. W. Kullmann and M. Reichel, 227–64. Tübingen. Reprinted in Latacz 1994b, 357–95.

————. 1991a. Hauptfunktionen des antiken Epos in Antike und Moderne. In *Dialog Schule-Wissenschaft: Klassische Sprachen und Literaturen*, vol. 25, *Die Antike im Brennpunkt*, ed. P. Neukamp, 88–109. Munich. Reprinted in Latacz 1994b, 257–79.

————. 1992a. Homers Ilias und die Folgen: Wie der Mythos Troia entstand. In *Troia: Brücke zwischen Orient und Okzident*, ed. I. Gamer-Wallert, 201–18. Tübingen.

————. 1992b. Neuere Erkenntnisse zur epischen Versifikationstechnik. *Studi italiani di filologia classica* 10:807–26. Reprinted in Latacz 1994b, 235–55.

————. 1994a. Between Troy and Homer: The So-Called Dark Ages in Greece. In *Storia, Poesia e Pensiero nel Mondo Antico: Studi in onore di Marcello Gigante*, 347–63. Naples.

————. 1994b. *Erschliessung der Antike: Kleine Schriften zur Literatur der Griechen und Römer*, ed. F. Graf et al. Stuttgart and Leipzig.

————, ed. 1979. *Homer. Tradition und Neuerung*. Darmstadt.

————, ed. 1991b. *Homer: Die Dichtung und ihre Deutung*. Darmstadt.

————, ed. 1991c. *Zweihundert Jahre Homer-Forschung: Rückblick und Ausblick*. Stuttgart and Leipzig.

Lehmann, G.A. 1983. Zum Auftreten von "Seevölker"-Gruppen im östlichen Mittelmeerraum: eine Zwischenbilanz. In Deger-Jalkotzy 1983b, 79–97.

————. 1985. *Die mykenisch-frühgriechische Welt und der östliche Mittelmeerraum in der Zeit der "Seevölker"-Invasionen um 1200 v.Chr.* Opladen.

————. 1991. Die "politisch-historischen" Beziehungen der Ägais-Welt des 15.–13. Jh.s v. Chr. zu Ägypten und Vorderasien: Einige Hinweise. In Latacz 1991c, 105–26.

Lesky, A. 1954. Mündlichkeit und Schriftlichkeit im homerischen Epos. In *Festschrift für D. Kralik*, 1–9. Horn. Reprinted in *Gesammelte Schriften*, 63–71. Bern, 1966. Also reprinted in Latacz 1979, 297–307.

————. 1966. *A History of Greek Literature*. Trans. J. Willis and C. de Heer. 2d ed. New York.

————. 1967. Homeros. *RE* supplement 11:687–846. Reprint, Stuttgart, 1967.

————. 1971. *Geschichte der griechischen Literatur*. 3d ed. Bern and Munich.

————. 1981. Epos, Epyllion und Lehrgedicht. In *Neues Handbuch der Literaturwissenschaft: Griechische Literatur*, ed. E. Vogt. Wiesbaden.

Leuze, G. 1986. Guslari u Jugoslaviji: Volksgesang im heutigen Jugoslawien. *WJA* 12:21–33.

Lord, A.B. 1953. Homer's Originality: Oral Dictated Texts. *Transactions of the*

American Philological Association 84:124–34. Reprinted in Kirk 1964, 68–78. Also reprinted in Latacz 1979, 308–19.

Maehler, H. 1963. *Die Auffassung des Dichterberufs im frühen Griechentum bis zur Zeit Pindars.* Göttingen.

Marg, W. 1957. *Homer über die Dichtung.* Münster. 2d ed. 1971.

Mellink, M.J. 1971. Archaeology in Asia Minor. *AJA* 75:295–317.

Meyerhoff, D. 1984. *Traditioneller Stoff und individuelle Gestaltung: Untersuchungen zu Alkaios und Sappho.* Hildesheim, Zurich, and New York.

Murray, O. 1983. The Symposion as Social Organisation. In Hägg 1983b, 195–99.

———. 1991. War and the Symposium. In *Dining in a Classical Context,* ed. W.J. Slater, 83–103. Ann Arbor.

———. 1993. *Early Greece.* 2d ed. Cambridge, Mass.

———, ed. 1990. *Sympotica: A Symposium on the Symposion.* Oxford.

Nestle, W. 1942. Odyssee-Interpretationen, I–II. *Hermes* 77:46–77, 113–39.

Nicolai, W. 1983. Rezeptionssteuerung in der Ilias. *Philologus* 127:1–12.

———. 1984. Zu den politischen Wirkungsabsichten des Odysseedichters. *Grazer Beiträge* 11:1–20.

———. 1987. Zum Welt- und Geschichtsbild der Ilias. In Bremer, de Jong, and Kalff 1987, 145–64.

Nilsson, M.P. 1933. *Homer and Mycenae.* London.

———. 1950. *The Minoan-Mycenaean Religion and Its Survival in Greek Religion.* 2d ed. Lund.

Ong, W.J. 1982. *Orality and Literacy: The Technologizing of the Word.* London and New York.

Oralità, Cultura, Letteratura, Discorso: Atti del Convegno Internazionale Urbino 1980. 1985. Ed. B. Gentili and G. Paioni. Rome.

Page, D.L. 1934. *Actors' Interpolations in Greek Tragedy.* Oxford. Reprint, New York and London, 1987.

———. 1959. *History and the Homeric Iliad.* Berkeley.

———, ed. 1968. *Lyra Graeca Selecta.* Oxford.

Parry, A., ed. 1971. *The Making of Homeric Verse: The Collected Papers of Milman Parry.* Oxford. [See review by J. Russo in *Quaderni Urbinati di Cultura classica* 12 (1971): 27–39.]

Parry, M. 1928. *L'Epithète traditionnelle dans Homère.* Diss., Paris. [English translation in A. Parry 1971, 1–190.]

Patzer, H. 1972. *Dichterische Kunst und poetisches Handwerk im homerischen Epos.* Wiesbaden.

Pestalozzi, H. 1945. Die Achilleis als Quelle der Ilias. Diss., Zurich.

Pfeiffer, R. 1968–76. *History of Classical Scholarship.* 2 vols. Oxford.

Powell, B.B. 1990. *Homer and the Origin of the Greek Alphabet.* Cambridge.

Pritchard, J.B., ed. 1969. *Ancient Near Eastern Texts Relating to the Old Testament.* 3d ed. Princeton.

Raaflaub, K.A. 1991. Homer und die Geschichte des 8. Jh.s v. Chr. In Latacz 1991c, 205–56.

Radice, B. 1973. *Who's Who in the Ancient World: A Handbook to the Survivors of the Greek and Roman Classics*. Rev. ed. Harmondsworth.

Reinhardt, K. 1948. Das Parisurteil. In *Von Werken und Form: Vorträge und Aufsätze*, 11–36. Bad Godesberg.

——. 1961. *Die Ilias und ihr Dichter*. Ed. U. Hölscher. Göttingen.

Richardson, S. 1990. *The Homeric Narrator*. Nashville, Tenn.

Risch, E. 1969. Review of Schmitt 1967 and 1968. *Gnomon* 41:321–27.

Ritoók, Z. 1975. Stages in the Development of Greek Epic. *AAntHung* 23:127–40.

Rolley, C. 1983. Les grands sanctuaires panhelléniques. In Hägg 1983b, 109–14.

Rostovtzeff, M.I. 1930. *A History of the Ancient World*. Vol. 1, *The Orient and Greece*. Trans. J.D. Duff. 2d ed. Oxford.

Sakellarakis, J.A. 1988. Some Geometric and Archaic Votives from the Idaian Cave. In Hägg et al. 1988, 173–93.

Sarkady, J. 1975. Outlines of the Development of Greek Society in the Period between the 12th and the 8th Centuries B.C. *AAntHung* 23:107–25.

Schadewaldt, W. 1938. *Iliasstudien*. Leipzig. 3d ed. 1966. Reprint, Darmstadt, 1987.

——. 1942. Homer und sein Jahrhundert. In Schadewaldt 1959b, 87–129.

——. 1943. Die Gestalt des homerischen Sängers. In Schadewaldt 1959b, 54–86.

——. 1959a. *Legende von Homer dem fahrenden Sänger*. 3d ed. Zurich.

——. 1959b. *Von Homers Welt und Werk*. 3d ed. Darmstadt.

——. 1970. *Hellas und Hesperien: Gesammelte Schriften zur Antike und zur neuen Literatur*. 2 vols. Zurich.

Schefold, K. 1943. *Die Bildnisse der antiken Dichter, Redner und Denker*. Basel.

——. 1975. Das homerische Epos in der antiken Kunst. In *Wort und Bild: Studien zur Gegenwart der Antike*, 27–42. Basel.

Schmid, W. 1929. *Geschichte der griechischen Literatur*. Vol. I, part 1. Munich.

Schmitt, R. 1967. *Dichtung und Dichtersprache in indogermanischer Zeit*. Wiesbaden. [See Risch 1969.]

——, ed. 1968. *Indogermanische Dichtersprache*. Darmstadt. [See Risch 1969.]

Schwinge, E.-R. 1991. Homerische Epen und Erzählforschung. In Latacz 1991c, 482–512.

Snodgrass, A.M. 1980. *Archaic Greece: The Age of Experiment*. Berkeley.

Stock, W. 1984. The Secrets of Crete. *New York Times Magazine*, 19 August, 94–112.

Stössel, H.-A. 1975. Der letzte Gesang der Odyssee: Eine unitarische Gesamtinterpretation. Diss., Erlangen-Nuremberg.

Themelis, P.G. 1983. Die Nekropolen von Lefkandi-Nord auf Euböa. In Deger-Jalkotzy 1983b, 145–60.

Tsountas, C., and J.I. Manatt. 1897. *The Mycenaean Age*. London and Boston.

Ungern-Sternberg, J. von, and H. Reinau, eds. 1988. *Vergangenheit in mündlicher Überlieferung*. Stuttgart.

Ventris, M., and J. Chadwick. 1953. Evidence for Greek Dialect in the Mycenaean Archives. *JHS* 73:84–103.

Visser, E. 1987. *Homerische Versifikationstechnik: Versuch einer Rekonstruktion.* Frankfurt, Bern, and New York.

———. 1988. Formulae or Single Words? Towards a New Theory on Homeric Verse-Making. *WJA* 14:21–37.

Vogt, E. 1991. Homer—ein grosser Schatten? Die Forschung zur Person Homers. In Latacz 1991c, 365–77.

Von der Mühll, P. 1940. Odyssee. *RE* supplement 7:696–768. Reprinted in *Ausgewählte Kleine Schriften*, ed. B. Wyss, 27–121. Basel, 1976.

Webster, T.B.L. 1958. *From Mycenae to Homer.* London. Reprint, New York, 1964.

West, M.L. 1988. The Rise of the Greek Epic. *JHS* 108:151–72.

Wickert-Micknat, G. 1982. *Die Frau. ArchHom* 3.R.

Wilamowitz-Moellendorff, U. von. 1916. *Die Ilias und Homer.* Berlin.

———. 1929. *Vitae Homeri et Hesiodi.* Berlin.

Wimmel, W. 1981. *Die Kultur holt uns ein: Die Bedeutung der Textualität für das geschichtliche Werden.* Würzburg.

Winter, N.A. 1982. News Letter from Greece, Lefkandi. *AJA* 86:550–51.

———. 1984. News Letter from Greece, Lefkandi. *AJA* 88:54.

Wolf, F.A. 1795. *Prolegomena ad Homerum sive de operum Homericorum prisca et genuina forma variisque mutationibus et probabili ratione emendandi.* Halle an der Saale. English ed. *Prolegomena to Homer.* Trans. A. Grafton et al. Princeton, 1985.

Selected Bibliography

1. Editions

Allen, T.W., ed. 1912. *Homeri Opera.* Vol. 5, *Epic Cycle, Hymns,* and *Lives.* Oxford. [Oxford Classical Text.]

Munro, D.B., and T.W. Allen, eds. 1920. *Homeri Opera.* 3d ed. Vols. 1 and 2, *Iliad.* Oxford. [Oxford Classical Text.]

Wilamowitz 1929.

Von der Mühll, P., ed. 1962. *Homeri Odyssea.* 3d ed. Basel. Reprint, Stuttgart, 1993. [Teubner edition.]

Barnabé, A., ed. 1987. *Poetae epici Graeci: Testimonia et fragmenta.* Part I. Leipzig. [Teubner edition.]

Thiel, H. van, ed. 1991. *Homeri Odyssea.* Hildesheim, Zurich, and New York. [See Janko 1994.]

2. Translations

The *Iliad*

The Iliad of Homer. 1951. Trans. R. Lattimore. Chicago. Often reprinted. [The most literal verse rendition, with an excellent introduction by Lattimore.]

Homer: The Iliad. 1974. Trans. R. Fitzgerald. Garden City, N.Y. [Verse.]

Homer: The Iliad. 1987. Trans. M. Hammond. Harmondsworth. [Prose; a great improvement over E.V. Rieu's Penguin edition.]

Homer: The Iliad. 1990. Trans. R. Fagles. New York. [Verse, with introduction and notes by B.M.W. Knox.]

The *Odyssey*

Homer: The Odyssey. 1961. Trans. R. Fitzgerald. Garden City, N.Y. [Verse.]

The Odyssey of Homer. 1965. Trans. R. Lattimore. Chicago. [The most literal verse rendition.]

Homer: The Odyssey. 1967. Trans. A. Cook. New York. [Verse.]

Homer: The Odyssey. 1980. Trans. W. Shewring. Oxford. [Prose; preferable to E.V. Rieu's Penguin edition.]

The Odyssey of Homer: A New Verse Translation. 1990. Trans. A. Mandelbaum. Berkeley.

Epic Cycle and *Lives* of Homer

Hesiod, The Homeric Hymns, and Homerica. 1936. Trans. H.G. Evelyn-White. Rev. ed. Cambridge, Mass. [Includes the *Epic Cycle* and the "Contest of Homer and Hesiod," with facing Greek text; Loeb Classical Library edition.]

Lefkowitz, M. R. 1981. *The Lives of the Greek Poets.* Baltimore. [Appendix 1, pp. 139–55, is a translation of the pseudo-Herodotean *Life of Homer.*]

3. Commentaries

The *Iliad*

Willcock, M.M. 1976. *A Companion to the Iliad, Based on the Translation by Richmond Lattimore.* Chicago.

Willcock, M.M., ed. 1978–84. *The Iliad of Homer.* 2 vols. London.

Hogan, J.C. 1979. *A Guide to the Iliad, Based on the Translation by Robert Fitzgerald.* Garden City, N.Y.

Macleod, C.W., ed. 1982. *Homer: Iliad, Book XXIV.* Cambridge.

Kirk, G.S., et al. 1985–93. *The Iliad: A Commentary.* Cambridge. Vol. 1, bks. 1–4, by G.S. Kirk, 1985. Vol. 2, bks. 5–8, by G.S. Kirk, 1990. Vol. 3, bks. 9–12, by B. Hainsworth, 1993. Vol. 4, bks. 13–16, by R. Janko, 1992. Vol. 5, bks. 17–20, by M.W. Edwards, 1991. Vol. 6, bks. 21–24, by N. Richardson, 1993.

Griffin, J., ed. 1995. *Homer: Iliad IX.* Oxford.

The *Odyssey*

Stanford, W.B., ed. 1958–59. *The Odyssey of Homer.* 2d ed. 2 vols. London.

Heubeck, A., et al. 1988–92. *A Commentary on Homer's Odyssey.* Oxford. Vol. 1, bks. 1–8, ed. A. Heubeck, S. West, and J.B. Hainsworth, 1988. Vol. 2, bks. 9–16, ed. A. Heubeck and A. Hoekstra, 1989. Vol. 3, bks. 17–24, ed. J. Russo, M. Fernández Galiano, and A. Heubeck, 1992.

Jones, P.V. 1988. *Homer's Odyssey: A Companion to the Translation of Richmond Lattimore.* Carbondale, Ill.

Rutherford, R.B., ed. 1992. *Homer: Odyssey, Books XIX and XX.* Cambridge.

Hexter, R. 1993. *A Guide to the Odyssey: A Commentary on the English Translation of Robert Fitzgerald.* New York.

Garvie, A.F., ed. 1994. *Homer: Odyssey, Books VI–VIII.* Cambridge.

4. General Bibliographies and Surveys of Scholarship

For exhaustive listings of Homeric studies after 1983, the reader should consult the annual volumes of *L'Année philologique*.

Dodds, E.R., L.R. Palmer, and D. Gray. 1968. Homer. In *Fifty Years (and Twelve) of Classical Scholarship*, ed. M. Platnauer, 1–49. Oxford.

Hainsworth, J.B. 1969. *Homer*. Oxford.

Holoka 1973.

Heubeck 1974.

Packard, D.W., and T. Meyers. 1974. *A Bibliography of Homeric Scholarship: Preliminary Edition 1930–1970*. Malibu, Calif.

Holoka, J.P. 1979. Homer Studies 1971–1977. *CW* 73:65–150.

Clarke, H. 1981. *Homer's Readers: A Historical Introduction to the Iliad and the Odyssey*. Newark, N.J., and London.

Heubeck, A. 1982. Zur neueren Homerforschung (VII). *Gymnasium* 89:385–447.

Holoka, J.P. 1990. Homer Studies 1978–1983. *CW* 83:393–461; 84:89–156.

5. Books and Articles

Historical Background

Webster 1958.

Page 1959.

Chadwick 1967.

Chadwick, J. 1976. *The Mycenaean World*. Cambridge.

Finley, M.I. 1978. *The World of Odysseus*. 2d ed. New York.

Gschnitzer 1981, 1991.

Foxhall and Davies 1984.

Burkert 1991.

Deger-Jalkotzy 1991.

Lehmann 1991.

Raaflaub 1991.

Murray 1993.

Oral Poetry

A new scholarly journal devoted to this subject area is *Oral Tradition* (founded 1986).

Bowra, C.M. 1952.

Lord, A.B. 1960. *The Singer of Tales*. Cambridge, Mass. Reprint, New York, 1965.

Kirk, G.S. 1962. *The Songs of Homer*. Cambridge.

Parry 1971.

Finnegan 1977.

Latacz, J. 1979. Spezialbibliographie zur Oral Poetry-Theorie in der Homerforschung. In Latacz 1979, 573–618.

Kullmann 1981.

Foley, J.M. 1985. *Oral-Formulaic Theory and Research: An Introduction and Annotated Bibliography*. New York and London.

Shive, D. 1987. *Naming Achilles*. Oxford.

Boedeker, D. 1988. Amerikanische Oral-Tradition-Forschung: Eine Einführung. In Ungern-Sternberg and Reinau 1988, 34–53.

Holoka, J.P. 1991. Homer, Oral Poetry Theory, and Comparative Literature: Major Trends and Controversies in Twentieth-Century Criticism. In Latacz 1991c, 456–81.

Archaeology

ArchHom.
Blegen 1963.
Vermeule, E. 1964. *Greece in the Bronze Age.* Chicago.
Mylonas, G. 1966. *Mycenae and the Mycenaean Age.* Princeton.
Wood, M. 1985. *In Search of the Trojan War.* London and New York. [Based on the BBC television series.]
McDonald, W.A., and C.G. Thomas. 1990. *Progress into the Past: The Rediscovery of Mycenaean Civilization.* 2d ed. Bloomington, Ind.
Blome 1991.
Buchholz, H.-G. 1991. Die archäologische Forschung im Zusammenhang mit Homer: Gesamtüberblick. In Latacz 1991c, 11–44.
Hiller, S. 1991. Die archäologische Erforschung des griechischen Siedlungsbereiches im 8.Jh. v.Chr. In Latacz, 1991c, 61–88.
Korfmann 1991a.

Literary Criticism

Schadewaldt 1938, 1959b.
Owen, E.T. 1946. *The Story of the Iliad.* Toronto. Reprint, London, 1994.
Stanford, W.B. 1963. *The Ulysses Theme: A Study in the Adaptability of a Traditional Hero.* 2d ed. Oxford.
Erbse 1972.
Eisenberger, H. 1973. *Studien zur Odyssee.* Wiesbaden. [See the review by J. Latacz in *Göttingische Gelehrte Anzeigen* 232 (1980): 29–42; reprinted in Latacz 1991b, 406–17.]
Page, D.L. 1973. *Folktales in Homer's Odyssey.* Cambridge, Mass.
Fenik, B. 1974. *Studies in the Odyssey.* Wiesbaden.
Schadewaldt, W. 1975. *Der Aufbau der Ilias: Strukturen und Konzeptionen.* Frankfurt am Main.
Latacz, J. 1979. Homer. *Der Deutschunterricht* 31:5–23. Reprinted in Latacz 1991b, 1–29. Also reprinted in Latacz 1994b, 13–35.
Clay, J.S. 1983. *The Wrath of Athena: Gods and Men in the Odyssey.* Princeton.
Schein, S.L. 1984. *The Mortal Hero: An Introduction to Homer's Iliad.* Berkeley.
Edwards, M.W. 1987. *Homer: Poet of the Iliad.* Baltimore and London.
Murnaghan, S. 1987. *Disguise and Recognition in the Odyssey.* Princeton.
Siegmann, E. 1987. *Vorlesungen über die Odyssee.* Ed. J. Latacz, E. Simon, and A. Schmitt. Würzburg.
Hölscher, U. 1990. *Die Odyssee: Epos zwischen Märchen und Roman.* 3d ed. Munich.

Richardson 1990.

Latacz 1991b.

Lowenstam, S. 1993. *The Scepter and the Spear: Studies on Forms of Repetition in the Homeric Poems.* Lanham, Md.

Schwinge, E.-R. 1993. *Die Odyssee—nach den Odysseen: Betrachtungen zu ihrer individuellen Physiognomie.* Göttingen.

Stanley, K. 1993. *The Shield of Homer: Narrative Structure in the Iliad.* Princeton.

Segal, C.P. 1994. *Singers, Heroes, and Gods in the Odyssey.* Ithaca and London.

Index

Table of Contents

A HISTORY OF CHRISTIAN, JEWISH, HINDU, BUDDHIST, AND
MUSLIM PERSPECTIVES ON WAR AND PEACE
Volume I: THE *BIBLE* TO 1914

Table of Contents

A HISTORY OF CHRISTIAN, JEWISH, HINDU, BUDDHIST, AND MUSLIM PERSPECTIVES ON WAR AND PEACE
Volume II: A CENTURY OF WARS

PREFACE

I wrote this book for individuals who are intelligent, curious, and sophisticated about many subjects but not specialists on the history of religions, the evolution of wars, and the relationships between them. Those seeking a brief survey of the impact of religion at a given time period can use the book for reference. Advanced undergraduates and seminary students could read selected chapters as a textbook, although the professor will probably need to provide additional materials on the initial sections dealing with the origins of religious traditions. This book is also designed to appeal to clergy, laity, and those who believe that lessons can be learned by seeing how faith communities in the past dealt with issues of war and peace similar to those we face today.

The close linkage between the practices of religions and political wars is as old as recorded history and shows few signs of ending any time soon. I began teaching a course on the history of religious ethics on war and peace in 1974. I have been reading on these subjects ever since, and have devoted most of my research time for the last fourteen years to this book. Teachers of undergraduates in liberal arts colleges offer survey courses on topics that cover immense spans of time: philosophy, political theory, ethics, English literature, Western or World civilization, European, Chinese or American history. Most of us divorce our teaching from our research and hope to offer one course on our specialty. My specialty is Quakerism, a topic discussed here in one-third of one chapter. As a professor I read and have written monographs, but I teach fields. This book seeks to link two fields: war and religion. Even this limits the scope because religion here is often in dialogue with secular ethics and realpolitik. Early on I concluded that the best approach was not to do intensive research on one time period or one war, but to survey the actions and interpretations of many religions over a long time period. This decision allowed me the pleasure of reading in areas for which I had no formal training and little background and has necessitated relying upon secondary sources. Now that the book is finished, I wonder at my presumption and naïveté in undertaking so massive a task and ask for the readers' reasonable expectations and even charity in judging the fruits of my labors. My defense is simple: there is now no other survey of the interactions between religions and wars and the topic is too important to be left to journalists and "talking head" pundits on television. My hope is that this book will stimulate scholars to fill in the gaps in literature, help teachers to create courses on the history of religions, wars, and peaces, and aid citizens to deal responsibly with the challenge that organized violence continues to present for those who wish to apply religious ethics to politics.

My first acknowledgement is to Roland Bainton, whose *Christian Attitudes to War* (1960) I often used as a textbook. When asked by a friend whether he should throw away Bainton's book, my response was "No way!" Bainton's study is gracefully written and well researched, but it is now over forty years old, deals only with Christianity, and spends little time on the twentieth century. A second debt is to Arthur Holmes, whose edition of original sources entitled *War and Christian Ethics* (1975) I used for years before it went out of print.

At Swarthmore my colleagues have attempted to educate an American historian in the discipline of religious studies. Several have read chapters of this book, and I have profited from, and often, but not always, followed their advice. I received grants from the U.S. Institute of Peace, a Lang fellowship and an additional year of leave from Swarthmore College for this project. Two reference librarians, Steve Sowards and Edward Fuller, provided major assistance, as did student assistant Jean Quinn. Over the years my students read chapters of the book, and their questions and comments required many revisions. Those who have read this manuscript in whole or in part include: Howard Kee, James Kurth, Martin Ostwald, David J. Smith, P. Linwood Urban, and Melvin B. Endy, members of the Religion Departments at Swarthmore College and Haverford College, the staff of the Friends Library, and Susan K. Frost. Claire Whitehill copy-edited the manuscript. They deserve my thanks for their many helpful suggestions. Charlotte Blandford, who accurately prophesied that the U.S. would get into another war, but not two, before I finished, deserves special thanks for putting up with repeated revisions, inaccurate citations, incomplete directions, and my constant battle with the workings of computers.

My thanks to the University of Chicago Press for permission to use lines from the *Iliad of Homer*, translated and edited by Richmond Lattimore, in Chapter 3 of the text.

The image on the book cover is a reproduction of a post card from the National Council for Prevention of War Records, circa 1929, artist Louise Rochon Hoover. Its use is courtesy of the National Council for Prevention of War, Postcard Collection, Swarthmore College Peace Collection.

Introduction:
The Past in the Present

Shakespeare knew his audience. Those who gathered at the Globe Theater in 1599 could recite the story of Henry V's famous victory at Agincourt just as we talk about D Day. Shakespeare could also assume that the playgoers accepted Just War theory, the ideology that distinguishes a fair fight from a brawl or massacre. The theory requires just cause for the war and right conduct during battle. *Henry V* is about a battle that the English but not the French thought was just.

In Act I the King before entering into the war requires assurance from the Archbishop of Canterbury and other bishops that his cause is just. The bishops, who in the opening of the play are seeking to dissuade the King from taxing or seizing their estates, see in the possibility of hostility with France an opening to divert the King's attention. So in answer to Henry's query, the Archbishop enters into a long and complex discourse as to why Henry's claim to the French throne, though coming through a woman, is valid because the Salic law applies to Germany and not to France. The conclusion, sought by the King, is that legal and moral precedence is on his side and that waging war for his right is just. So Henry in the play asserts that he is innocent of any guilt. The bishops then offer to make a generous contribution to the war. Both sides leave happy: the bishops have preserved the wealth of the church and the King prepares to venture to France with God on his side. The Dauphin of France insults Henry's claim as well as his masculinity by sending him a gift of tennis balls, establishing by this gesture that the war is also about chivalric honor.

Henry V assumes that there is a correct, moral way to wage war. The play is about chivalry and honor since the King promises before battle that the commoners who fight at Agincourt will have a nobility equivalent to that of those born with the right to bear arms. Henry instructed his soldiers when marching through France to pay for all supplies and to abuse no French; he even executed a man who plundered a church. Yet Shakepeare's attitude to fighting is ambivalent. Fighting is an ultimate test of character and there is glory in battle, yet there is hatred of war and nostalgia for peace.[1]

With an outnumbered English army in France, on the night before the battle of Agincourt in 1415, common soldiers, in the presence of the disguised King, insist that they need not know the justice of the cause, for the responsibility for the war is the King's and their duty is simply to obey. However, the men worry about the possibility of facing a judging God when their last act will have been shedding of blood. So they rationalize that God will judge the King and hold him solely responsible for the killing in battle. Henry strongly disagrees and proclaims that God judges all soldiers according to their lives before the war. The King's understanding of church teachings is correct but he has also diverted the issue from his responsibility for the war or the morality of actions in battle. Yet Henry had earlier placed responsibility for the rightness of the war onto the clergy; so he can legitimately according to Just War theory reassure the men that God will make the unjust side, the French, responsible for deaths.

During the course of the battle, after the English have obtained victory (though Henry does not know it) the King orders the massacre of French prisoners. Shakespeare gives two motivations for Henry's actions. In one, the French have attacked the unarmed boys who cared for the English baggage in an attempt to gather spoils. So English retaliation for an unjust act is required; this is a weak argument, which may be why Henry does not say it. The other motivation, coming from Henry, is that the French are mobilizing for another attack, and he does not have enough men to guard the prisoners of war and fight

---

[1] In 1943 Laurence Olivier obtained backing from the British war office to use the play to create a propaganda film intended to rouse the public's patriotism for the war against Hitler. Kenneth Branagh's 1989 *Henry V* emphasized the chaos and suffering in battle and had a much darker tone. R.A. Foakes, *Shakespeare and Violence* (2003), 96-106 sees Henry as a model Christian king, determined to have God and the Church on his side and, therefore, able to conquer.

the French. So as an act of necessity he orders all French prisoners killed, but soon countermands the order. Shakespeare, following the medieval chronicles, did not suppress the knowledge of this blot upon the character of his chivalrous hero. At the end of the battle Henry refuses to take credit for the victory, ordering a *Te Deum* mass exalting God who fought on the side of England.[2]

Shakespeare's account of the clergy's and Henry's actions before and during the war follows closely the information found in the Holinshed's Chronicles - which he almost paraphrases. The ambiguities between organized religion's proclamation of peace and full involvement in the origins, course, and conclusions of the war presented in the medieval chronicle and the play are echoed in contemporary questions about the relationship between religion, morality, war and peace. We, like Shakespeare, know how often religion supports war. At issue in this book is whether the opposite has also been true: does religion support peace? At the very least, has it restrained conduct in order to guarantee an ethical fight?

II.

The historical distance between the religious world of 1415 and our times seemed unbridgeable until the events of September 11, 2001, made us turn to religion for assurance that our cause was just. The terrorists had reinterpreted the meaning of Islamic *jihad* (holy war) to legitimize the killing of 3000 non-combatant men and women who thought the U.S. was at peace. The attack occasioned a debate in the Muslim world on the meaning of *jihad,* with many Islamic scholars insisting that their religion required submission to Allah who brought peace. In America the President drew upon Just War theory to distinguish between war and a massacre, a soldier and a terrorist, and insisted that

---

[2]Michael Hattaway, "Blood is their Argument: Men of War and Soldiers in Shakespeare and Others" (1994); Paul Jorgensen, "Theoretical Views of War in Elizabethan England," *Journal of History of Ideas* (1952), 469-481; and "Moral Guidance and Religious Encouragement for the Elizabethan Soldier," *Huntington Library Quarterly* (1950); Peter Saccio, *Shakespeare's English Kings: History, Chronicle, and Drama* (2000), 65-89 recounts where Shakespeare follows or changes the chronicle and where both distort history.

our battle was not with Muslims but only with those who perverted Islam to attack the innocent. Against those "evil" people he proclaimed a "crusade."

Journalists noted that the American people turned to organized religion for consolation in mourning their dead and to sanction a war against the Taliban and all others who provided refuge for terrorists. Singing the "Battle Hymn of the Republic" and Irving Berlin's "God Bless America" in worship services, at sports events, and on radio showed the continuing potency of linking God and country. Flags and signs proclaiming God bless America appeared on cars, mailboxes, banks, and restaurants. Religious patriotism was used to sell almost any product. For example, a large billboard near a parkway in Philadelphia offered a special of three adult (pornographic) movies followed by "God bless America." I saw only one sign that reversed the sequence: "America bless God." The ubiquity of the slogans allowed a wide variety of meaning. Was the invocation of God a product of a deep-seated insecurity that the bombing showed that America might not be blessed? Very few accepted Rev. Jerry Falwell's sermon that God had punished America because of our secularism, immorality, and toleration of homosexuality. Or was the slogan a call to war, an assertion that God was on our side and would guarantee victory against immoral terrorism? Or a recognition that the sacred land of America had been violated by the bombing and bringing the terrorists to justice would re-establish a moral order? Had God bestowed on America a new manifest destiny to rid the world of terrorism?

President Bush vowed that the U.S. would pursue terrorists and those who gave succor to them. At first the focus was on the Taliban in Afghanistan, but after their defeat the President denounced an "axis of evil'" including North Korea, Iran, and Iraq. ("Axis" reminded people of the German-Italian Axis of World War II and "evil" was selected for its religious connotation.) Now if the security of the U.S. was threatened by a rogue nation acquiring or seeking to obtain weapons of mass destruction, a new policy called for pre-emptive or preventive war. The obvious target was Iraq where Saddam Hussein had for ten years thwarted UN demands for disarmament. When the U.S. claimed a right to attack Iraq with or without UN sanction, a worldwide debate ensued on the ethics of such an action. The British Prime Minister and American President, both men known for their frequent church attendance and conspicuous piety, emerged as the two strongest defenders of the morality of a pre-emptive war against Iraq. Many American evangelicals and Pentecostals supported the President. The Pope, the American Catholic Bishops, the Archbishop of Canterbury, and leaders of the National Council of Churches opposed. Clearly, church authorities, but not necessarily the laymen, see a religious obligation to speak on issues of war and peace.

An issue central to this book is simply: was Al Qaeda's use of religion a normal use of religion? The same question should be asked about the American response to 9/11. Did using God to sanctify a defensive or pre-emptive war distort the teachings of Jesus? What in the nature of Islam and Christianity would allow such divergent interpretations? It is clear that a Judaic-Christian response to a crisis remains imbedded in American culture. Islam functions in the same way in the Arab world, and so does Judaism for Jews in Israel and the diaspora. For all our modernity, we remain very close to the worlds of Henry V and Shakespeare. Today as in the past, organized religion remains a potent influence for and in war and peace and we need to understand why this is so.

III.

War is defined for this book as "a period of armed conflict between political units" and peace is the absence of armed conflict. A "cold war" is something in between, but is here classified as a war. Morality is "principles or considerations of right and wrong action or good and bad character." Moral or ethical behavior is that which is "good or right." Religion is a system of faith and worship involving an "institutionalized expression of sacred beliefs, observances, and social practices within a given cultural context."[3]

---

[3] *Webster's Third New International Dictionary* (Chicago: Encyclopedia Britannica, Inc., 1971), II, 1468, 1918, III, 2575. Jeremy Black, *Why Wars Happen* (1998), 15-45 is an excellent evaluation of various definitions of war and the difficulties in using either a systemic/structural

Readers should be aware of the inadequacies of these working definitions. Throughout most of recorded history, revolution was not considered a war because the rebels were not a political unit. "Peace" as defined above is a negative concept, the absence of armed conflict, and many believe that positive or real peace is attainable only after an end to structural oppression. A society practicing structural war can be ostensibly at peace, but the masses live in such poverty and under such political duress that they cannot fulfill their potential.[4] Using structural peace as a definition would mean that virtually all societies have been at war constantly. Political peace for many religions is only an image or a prefiguring of true peace or union with God. Ethical behavior is grounded in a theological or metaphysical affirmation, for example, natural law, or a philosophical doctrine like utilitarianism, the greatest good for the greatest number. Even the concept of religion has western cultural baggage making it difficult to apply to Islam, Hinduism or Native American customs. The separation of religious from political authority is a basic theme in the West, but distorts Islam where the caliph's responsibility was to enforce the laws of the *Qur'an* for Muslims. Rather than worry about precise nomenclature in considering what constitutes a religion, this book concentrates on what most people assume are the prevalent faiths of the world: Judaism, Christianity, Islam, Hinduism, Buddhism, as well as secularism.

I have used historical narrative rather than theoretical precision to examine religion and war. There is little attempt to assess the causes of war, because even for the modern period, political scientists cannot agree, and their studies of the causes of World War I or the Vietnamese War end with a list: political leadership, economics, balance of power, hegemonic pretensions, internal discontent, class conflict, ideological dissimilarity, arms races, the role of the military. Religion normally comes far down the list. Karl Marx, Sigmund Freud, and René Girard are

approach or concentrating on personalities, fate, or mentalities in seeing whether hostility will continue for generations, ease, or lead to war. See also the "Introduction" to T. Harry Williams, *The History of American Wars* (1981), xi-xvii.

[4] Johann Galtung in *A Reader in Peace Studies*, ed. Paul Smoker, Ruth Davies, and Barbara Munske, 9-14.

among the many who authored major interpretations of the relation between religion and war; I find their explanations simplistic, distorting the variegated roles of religion within societies and ignoring the nuances of the past.[5] To put it baldly, there is no theoretical shortcut by which history can be ignored. Religions arise in history and flourish in the culture of many societies and how they evolve influences the relationships between faith communities and war.

Those who attempt to predict the weather encounter a scientific phenomenon known as chaos. That is, even if it were possible to instill a monitoring device on every square mile of earth, air, and ocean, there would still be sufficient unknowns to make accurate weather forecasting impossible. Unlike weathermen, historians of religion and war know in advance the final outcomes, but understanding why is like attempting to master chaos. Deciphering the relationship between religion and war is not easy in contemporary settings and becomes even more difficult in the remote past. How, for example, does one separate religious, political, and economic factors in conflicts in Kashmir, the West Bank, the Balkans, or Central America? Albert Einstein postulated that the test of a scientific theorem was whether it was the simplest explanation congruent with the phenomenon.[6] Our result will seem the opposite: the simpler and clearer the explanation, the more likely it is to ignore the realities of history.

The reader should keep in mind six major variables that influence the relationships among religions, moralities, and wars: 1. The nature of the religion. Does it have sacred writings and how are they interpreted? Is there a set of

---

[5]Sigmund Freud, "Why War" (1932), reprinted in *War: Studies from Psychology, Sociology, Anthropology,* ed. Leon Bramson and George Goethals (1968). Many explanations of war in pre-literate society are better at dealing with the links between religion and violence than religion and war. An explanation for the religious impact on war would have to deal with the motivations of the leaders who decide on war, the men who fight, those at home who support them, and the diplomats who eventually make peace. Different perspectives on the relation of religion and war are found in René Girard, *Violence and the Sacred,* tr. Patrick Gregory (1977); Barbara Ehrenreich, *Blood Rites: Origins and History of the Passions of War* (1977); Bobbi Low, *Why Sex: A Darwinian Look at Human Behavior* (2000), 230-245; a summary of the evidence from pre-history is John O'Connoll, *Ride of the Second Horseman: The Birth and Death of War (1995).* A good bibliography on theoretical issues of war and religion is Mark Juergensmeyer, *Terror in the Mind of God: the Global Rise of Religious Violence* (2000).
[6]Albert Einstein paraphrased in Low, 11-12.

official teachings and one creed, or are there several voices within, and how do they coexist? 2. The institutionalization of the religion. Who are the religious authorities or professionals and how do they maintain their positions? What is the relationship of lay women and men to the religious institution and what does the institution demand of them? 3. The impact of the religion upon peoples and individuals. Is this an age in which religious rightness is of prime importance? What is the class of the believers? It is, for example, normally more significant for world history to have a devout emperor than a playboy son of a merchant, but not if that young man is later canonized as St. Francis. What is prescribed as ethical behavior for a sultan may not be required or admirable in a monk or soldier. Buddhist traditions, position in society, and numbers of Buddhists in Thailand, China, and Sri Lanka will have a direct impact on the practice of religion and how the religious community views civil and foreign war. 4. The relation of the dominant religion with other religions. Hinduism prides itself on a syncretic attitude, while Judaism claims to be exclusive. Medieval Islam recognized the legitimacy of Christianity, but Christianity viewed Islam as heretical. 5. The role of religion in the political culture. Are the political and religious boundaries coterminous? How does the religion utilize the political culture: for security, to spread the faith, to exterminate heretics, or to support the institutional framework? In return, what does the political culture demand: loyalty, taxes, or intercession with the deity? 6. The relationship between religious ethics and other sources of morality.[7] Religions require social and cultural practices that they label as good, and yet there have always been independent sources of value like philosophy and the state whose standards can be used to judge religious practices or even to assess the religion's adherence to its own precepts. We must remember that even within a given society each of these six factors is subject to history; that is, change can occur rapidly as in war or conquest or slowly over centuries.

---

[7]These variables will not be directly referred to in the text, but the last chapter attempts to assess their impact on when organized religion facilitates and when it restrains war.

Finally, it should be recognized that war and religion either separately or in concert are not politically correct or an equal opportunity employer. Until recent times with a few notable exceptions - Queen Elizabeth I, Catherine the Great, Maria Theresa - men made the decisions to war and did the fighting. Female monarchs relied upon male chief ministers, religious advisers, and the military. Men created virtually all the literature about military affairs and about religion, morality, and war. They also wrote the history of war. Males were the human role models (Jesus, Muhammad, Buddha) of religions, writers of sacred texts, theologians, philosophers, dramatists, military strategists, and political theorists. Even the writers of stories about fictional women - Judith, Antigone, and Lysistrata, for example - were men. The spiritual leaders who ran religious institutions that influenced political authorities were men. The church, government, and army have remained patriarchal institutions until the present, although within this framework enormous variation occurred.

The neglect of women in the sources does not mean that they had no influence.[8] Women bore the sons, accepted the absence of soldier husbands, and endured the pain of widowhood. There could have been no war had not the women at least silently acquiesced, for we know that politicians in ancient Israel and Greece attempted to gain their support. Men proclaimed that they fought for the security of families, even as they sought as spoils the women and children of their opponents. Not until the nineteenth century, when women began working for social reform and suffrage, did peace become a women's issue and it is only then that they emerge into view in this book. Those who argue that the

---

[8]Jean Elshtain, *Woman and War* (1967); Adrienne Harris and Ynestra King, eds., *Rocking the Ship of State: Toward a Feminist Peace Politics* (1989); Jeanne Vickers, *Women and War;* (1993); Ruth Pierson, ed., *Women and Peace: Theoretical, Historical and Practical Perspectives* (1987). Sara Ruddick, *Maternal Thinking: Toward a Politics of Peace* (1993) Carol Kohn, "Sex and Death in the Ritual World of the Defense Intellectual," in *Gender and Scientific Authority,* ed. Barbara Laslett, et al. (1996). Unlike the anthropological literature, where discussions of religion are a crucial ingredient in accounting for the origins of war, the role of religion in causing war is often underplayed in gender analysis. For example, *The Women and War Reader,* ed. Lois Ann Lorentzen and Jennifer Turpin (1998) focuses on contemporary events where religions have often exercised enormous influence, but there are only a few discussions of Christianity, Islam, and Judaism.

patriarchal nature of human society causes war have strong supporting evidence from history. War as an instrument of politics has always been and still remains a masculine preserve.

IV.

This book is organized chronologically in order to understand the sources for, creation of, dissonance within, and alternatives to traditions that earlier shaped European and American attitudes towards war and that still control contemporary societies. By "tradition" I mean people relying upon common sources and knowledge of each other's works.[9] A traditions approach works well for the West, since there is continuity from the ancient Hebrews and Greeks to the present. Judaism and Christianity were also present in the Arabian Peninsula and known by Muhammad and early Muslims. Islam, Hinduism, and Buddhism created their own traditions and, while in contact with each other, had little direct influence from Western Europe before colonialism. Still, the precepts of these religions on war and peace often agreed with the teachings of Judaism and Christianity. This convergence indicates the universality of organized religions' attempts to deplore, limit, end, and justify war. Today religious traditions interact with each other as well as with secular international law.

A disproportionate attention in this book is placed upon European and American materials, in spite of the fact that Jews and Christians constitute a minority of the world's populations. There are three explanations for this orientation. One is that I am by training an historian of America and her religious traditions and a teacher in a peace studies program, and this book originated from a need for a relevant survey for my courses that concentrate upon the West. A second is that this book is designed for students in U.S. colleges and seminaries and for ministers and laity whose primary concern is America's encounter with the world. The third is that Rome, modern Europe, and America practiced

---

[9]A critique of a traditions approach from a post-modernist perspective is found in Kathryn Tanner, *Theories of Culture: A New Agenda for Theology* (1977), 128-38.

imperialism ably and successfully imposed elements of their culture on the world, and the United Nations reflects their heritage. The fourth is that the most costly arms races and wars in human history have occurred among nations whose shared histories shaped the political and religious traditions accented in this book. Powerful movements of the contemporary world - Islam, Christianity, democracy, fascism, communism, and capitalism - all grew out of cultures conversant with Jewish, Greek, and Roman civilization.

A final difficulty comes from the nature of the sources. This book attempts to focus on the theological, institutional, and social manifestations of religion and war, including the opinions of ordinary persons. Pursuing these objectives is often frustrating because religious communities preserved frequently only the thoughts of the priests, saints, and governmental authorities. The theologians and lawyers interpreted the basic foundation texts (scriptures) to guide all in their encounter with war. We do not know how many knights or generals read, discussed, or were even aware of the subtle distinctions in the writings of religious leaders. Nor is it clear how much monks and bishops knew about war. However, certainly there was an intimate relationship between evolution of religious traditions, political power, and innovations in the practice of war. Frequent discussions of changes in the manner of conduct in battle throughout this book are designed to illustrate the symbiotic relationship between religion and war.

Even in ancient times "realists" concentrated upon natural factors to assess the causes and results of war and ignored religious categories of God's favor and moral conduct. We should not assume without more evidence than we now have that soldiers were either religious or realists or that realpolitik becomes more prevalent the closer we approach the twentieth century. My hope is that presentation of the thought of the realists and of the evolving nature of battle will allow a critical evaluation of the continuity and change in the interactions of religion and war.

V.

Each chapter seeks to answer three questions: At a given time, what in the religion fostered peace, what facilitated armed conflict, and was there an impact upon the conduct of war? The juxtaposition of war and religion in this book is not an artificial construct; rather, it grows from the reality that for thousands of years war has been too important to leave to soldiers and politicians. As a general rule, only those dynasties, states, and nations that make war successfully endure.[10] No advanced country or nation ever loved peace so much that it ruled out the possibility of making war. States that in the modern world appear peaceful, like Sweden and Switzerland, escaped direct involvement in two world wars, but remain heavily armed and ready to fight. No matter what the state's religion, there is no such entity as a peaceful political entity; there are only more or less belligerent states. A vision of a world at peace, like a glimpse of a deer in the woods, is enticing but fleeting.

Religions can cause war. Peoples find it easier to wage war if they believe they are doing good and will be aided by the supernatural so that right will prevail. Seeking a means for understanding success and failure in battle led ultimately to gods and their priests. Because there seems to be a natural revulsion against causing death, men have to be trained into becoming soldiers. Part of that conditioning involves objectifying the enemy, making the fighter feel that because the opponent deserves to die, there will be no moral opprobrium attached to killing. Religion can create a boundary between communities so that actions proscribed within the group can become praiseworthy when done to outsiders. By dividing humanity into those who are within the faith, who are good, and those who oppose the truth, who are evil, religion makes it easier to kill the bad to save the good. Making war accompanied by or on behalf of the gods overcomes moral

---

[10]Jared Diamond, *Guns, Germs, and Steel: the Fate of Human Societies* (1999), 278, 290 argues that states are created "by conquest" or the "threat of external force." Religion is then used to justify rulers, stop the inhabitants from killing each other, and give motives for self-sacrifice in aggression or self-defense.

qualms, and can make killing an acceptable act. A religion joined with a nationalism centered on a sacralized land or ethnic group remains a dominant force in our time.

In addition, the immediate consequences of war, the destruction of property, and the sacrifice of lives, are horrible to contemplate. Even if a society feels no compassion for the slain enemy, its inhabitants grieve for their own dead sons and civilian casualties. Organized violence either ends in stalemate, with both sides unhappy, or in a victory with one side balancing the fruits of winning against the costs, and the loser left to face the death of its soldiers with no compensation. No state or nation always wins. So humans have sought for reassurance that death and destruction are not the real purpose, that their sacrifices are not caused because of insatiable blood lust or an intrinsic human flaw. Instead, the suffering is endurable because war's objectives are praiseworthy: love of neighbor, honor, security, prosperity, justice, and peace. Religions embody and sanctify these objectives, make them higher than just self-interest.

By sacralizing the political arrangement of a society, religion sanctifies its objectives, and the gods become warriors, or at least enlist on the side of soldiers. The cliché still remains apt: "there are no atheists in foxholes," because to individual soldiers -- but not to the generals -- his or her survival or death may be random, a product of luck or fate, and wearing a cross or remembering God might provide security.[11] For those at home, religion offers a means through prayers of prolonging a son's life or an army's success or, at worst, a framework to make death and defeat less final. By providing reasons to fight, easing the burden during conflict, and making losses seem worthwhile, faith makes war more likely. Because the state requires warfare, all the major religions of mankind have found means of blessing war.

Has religion ever prevented or stopped a war? An obvious answer is that it is impossible to prove a negative, but that is clearly a rhetorical device rather

---

[11] In World War II, 74% of American soldiers said they prayed before going into battle. John Appel, "My Brush with History," *American Heritage* (Oct. 1999), 28.

than a scholarly answer. Many would defend the perceptiveness of Shakespeare's view of a self-serving clergy who, because of their privileged position in society, see that kings or presidents desire to go to war and invoke God to sanctify their decision.

The question could be phrased in different ways: does religion cause or influence the situation that most nations and people are most of the time at peace? Is asking whether religion should prevent war analogous to wondering whether codes of laws stop murder or theft? Or is the function of law (and religion) to condemn and punish those who commit such acts? What is the relationship of law and punishment in shaping behavior? After all, there are so-called primitive societies without law codes in which theft and murder are virtually nonexistent. Some of these are also societies in which there is no war.[12] All such societies have religions. Does that mean that religions work in these cultures but not our own? I think not and conclude that religion is one of many and not the most important factor in why modern nations go to war. Inevitably, however, men and women who find meaning in faith try to understand and evaluate the war using categories derived from religion.

For a positive answer to the question as to whether religion has ever prevented or stopped a war, what evidence would be required? Using Henry's war as a test case, we would need to know that Henry wanted to go to war and thought that he could win. For if he believed he was likely to lose, the decision would be based upon self-interest and not religious and moral grounds.[13] But

---

[12]Signe Howell and Roy Willis, ed., *Societies at Peace: Anthropological Perspectives* (1989); Jonathan Haas, ed., *The Anthropology of War.* (1990); Paul Turner and David Pitt, *The Anthropology of War and Peace: Perspectives in the Nuclear Age* (1990); Thomas Gregor, ed., *Natural History of Peace: A Positive View of Human Nature* (1996). Leslie E. Sponsel & Thomas Gregor, eds., *The Anthropology of Peace and Nonviolence* (1994); S. P. Reyna and R. E. Downs, eds., *Studying War: Anthropological Perspectives* (1994); Keith F. Otterbein, *Feuding and Warfare: Selected Works of Keith F. Otterbein* (1994).

[13]The value of the lives of soldiers plays a role in realpolitik as well as Just War theory. In realpolitik, a loss of lives is a weakening of an army and loss of national power; so there is a prudential calculation. In Just War theory, the deaths of soldiers on both sides are a moral evil that must be proportional to the good that results from punishing a fault; so again there is a prudential calculation. The *Chronicle* gives no indication that Henry before going to war weighed the value of his claim to the French throne against the lives of soldiers.

before attacking, he needed to have his conscience clear, and Shakespeare has Henry remind God of past good deeds while praying for God's help. (Note that in France before the battle Henry does not ask God's advice on whether to fight or surrender. He decides to fight and offers credit to God.) The prophet Jeremiah told two kings not to wage war. There are instances in Greek history of generals delaying a battle because the omens were wrong. We have examples from American history to show that presidents have found positive answers to prayers before going to war. Sometime after the wars were over two presidents - McKinley before the Spanish American and Bush Sr. before the Gulf War - testified publicly to their earlier prayers. Roosevelt's radio address on the morning of D-Day was a prayer to God for victory as well as justification (directed both to God and the American people) of the morality of the war. Clinton says he prayed before sending troops to Haiti. Lincoln, on the other hand, in the midst of the Civil War wondered why the Almighty spoke more clearly after prayer to others who did not have the power to act than to himself. One difference was that McKinley and Bush won their wars easily. It may be that success in the war showed that God was on their side.

Henry may also have prayed before invading France, though Shakespeare did not say so, but he also turned to the clergy who could have told him that the war was immoral either because his claim was unjust or because the good sought - becoming King of France - was disproportionate to the evil caused by the war. They could have even said that being King of England provided enough glory and power for any individual and that wise kings overlook insults from foolish dauphins. (The chronicler, unlike Shakespeare, makes Henry disingenuous, for he had already asserted his claim to the French throne before consulting with the clergy.)[14]

---

[14]*Holinshed's Chronicles As Used in Shakespeare's Plays* (1940), 71-74.

There is no evidence from history that such a dialogue between a king and his religious advisers has ever occurred, at least I know of no such instance.[15] What I am looking for at a minimum is something like the debate of Spanish theologians before Charles V about the treatment of the Indians in the New World, a discussion that resulted in changing policy on moral grounds. Just War theory requires that councilors give monarchs true advice. Still, that does not mean that the search for such a debate is misguided for it is important for kings and presidents (and even the United Nations) to be able to receive accurate ethical guidance before a war; otherwise, they would not be able to convey moral certainty to the soldiers, anticipate God's help in victory, and justify their actions to posterity.

A second model for religious creation for peace focuses not on states but on how people live. Thomas More in *Utopia* and Voltaire in *Candide,* as a way of satirizing their societies' proclivities to war, described peoples living at peace. St. Augustine saw heaven as the only realm of true and enduring peace. Monasteries in East and West served as refuges from war, and poets and city dwellers often idealized isolated villages and farms as peaceful. Peasants in many wars past and present sought only to be left alone. For a brief period, Japan sought isolation from the world as a way of preserving peace. Within large empires conquered peoples have been able to ignore distant wars over boundaries and small states have preserved some independence and ostensible peace by appeasing powerful neighbors.

Classic religious attitudes towards war, Just War theory and holy war, assume that some wars should not be fought. Religious pacifism asserts that no wars are ethically permissible. One focus for this book is attempting to assess the political effects of these doctrines. For if pacifism can't prevent war, it should not be argued for on political grounds; and if justified and holy war theories have not

---

[15]Billy Graham has met with Presidents Johnson, Nixon, and Bush Sr. and Jr. before or during a war. We don't know what he said to them or what Roman Catholic priests said to kings in the confessional booth.

in practice found wars to oppose and serve only to engender hatred of an allegedly immoral enemy, then they have no religious value. Of course, an historian cannot really determine beyond a reasonable doubt whether religion causes war; nor can she prove that religion is instrumental in preserving the more frequent times of peace. What an historian can do is to survey the interactions between religion and war at selective times in world history seeking an answer to the question: how have religious people dealt with war? This book seeks to answer the question: is there historical evidence that peoples' faiths caused wars, stopped wars from beginning, shortened their duration, changed conduct, and fostered peace after the end?

VI.

Section I of the book on "Origins" (chapters 1-7) relies chiefly upon sacred scriptures: the *Bible*, the *Qur'an*, and *Vedas* and the *Mahabharata* to assess the attitudes towards war and peace in the formative period of the major religions of the world. The Western attitudes were also shaped by Greek epic poetry, drama, philosophy, and history as well as the practices of Rome.

The Hebrew Scriptures recounted God's relationship to a people who through military conquest created a kingdom, but then experienced civil war, defeat, exile, and subjugation. The Lord of Hosts (armies), a war deity of the Jews, became the God who controlled all history. The New Testament described a Jew whose followers claimed he was the messiah inaugurating a new transcendent kingdom. The Romans executed Jesus because they thought he was a revolutionary bringing war, not peace.

Greek civilization provided the third set of images of war and peace. Homer, Thucydides, Aristophanes, Plato, and Aristotle sought to understand their gods and wars through concepts like fate, glory, justice, and nature. After Constantine's conversion, the Church merged biblical texts and practices of the Roman world to create a way for Christians to deal with war.

Hindus and Buddhists created alternative perspectives on war and violence that played a crucial role in India under Asoka and in southeast Asia. Islam drew upon a classical heritage, the Hebrew Scriptures, the New Testament, the practices of Arabs, and the revelation of Allah to Muhammad to create an alternative method of reconciling a religious desire for peace with holy war (*jihad*). The clash between Islam and Christianity, analogous to what had occurred earlier between Christianity and Judaism, resulted in both sides espousing traditions of justice in cause and conduct of war and engaging in crusades.

The second section (chapters 8-10) entitled "European Traditions" deals with Europe from the Middle Ages through the nineteenth century. Medieval Europe originated Just War theories as part of an attempt to limit the frequency of war and to tame its practice. The sixteenth century saw Protestant and Catholic versions of Just War theory, Anabaptist pacifism, and international law emerge as ways of coping with guns, larger armies, and constant war. Machiavelli stands as an exemplar of a realist tradition whose advocates also appear in ancient Greece and Rome, Sunni Egypt, and Puritan England. When the rise of monarchies brought no peace, men of the Enlightenment advocating creating a European parliament to foster harmony. Colonial Pennsylvania served as an experiment to see if not preparing for war was the way for peace.

"The Rise of Nationalism," a sub-section comprising chapters 11-13, begins with a comparison of the peaceful English Glorious Revolution of 1688, which provided an ideology used to legitimate the violent American and French Revolutions. These political upheavals changed the way countries justified war and their manner of fighting. The French radicals before Napoleon disdained the help of Christianity in war, the first time such a rejection had occurred since Constantine. The Napoleonic Wars and nationalism had very different impacts on two already dissimilar countries: Prussia and America. Prussia created an ideology glorifying war and deifying the state but remained at peace until 1860 after which she rapidly defeated Denmark, Austria, and France and created a German empire. The U.S., with an ideology insisting that democracies were peace loving, fought Native Americans, the British in 1812, the Mexicans, and then each other in a Civil War. After 1870 America and Europe refrained from major wars as diplomats, peace workers, churchmen and women, industrialists and socialists sought to tame nationalism and create a brave new world in which civilized nations would settle their differences through international law. Generals disdained the peace movement and prepared for war.

"The Twentieth Century: An Age of War" (chapters 14 -18), the longest section of the book, witnessed the eclipse in practice of the restraints built up over centuries; yet the new reality was so frightening that the traditional approaches to controlling war have appeared in both religious and secular guise. World War I showed that the churches and socialists had a greater commitment to nationalism than love of peace. The general staffs' acquiescence in slaughter in the trenches demonstrated incompetence. The seeming bankruptcy of Western idealism prompted Gandhi and Indian nationalists to turn to Hinduism where they found non-attachment and nonviolence. However, the Japanese alliance of Shintoism with the cult of the emperor indicated that Eastern religions did not necessarily lead to peace. In Europe and America, those who sought to prevent World War II utilized a cosmopolitan internationalism, symbolized by the League of Nations and World Court, disarmament, and a Tolstoyan nonresistance. The Roman Catholic Church faced but never solved the issue of how religious people could deal with dictators. The end of the 1930's witnessed a debate between pacifists and Christian realists over the necessity of resisting fascist states by war if necessary. The savagery of World War II with fascist attacks on neighboring states, widespread civilian casualties, saturation bombing, the Holocaust, and the atomic bomb marked a low point of world civilization. No religious groups could prevent the erosion of whatever standards had remained intact after World War I.

In the Cold War atheistic Communist USSR and China confronted democratic and nominally Christian U.S. and Western Europe with both sides insisting that they could preserve the peace by threatening to destroy the world in a nuclear war. The possibility of annihilation occasioned a revival of moral concern about the efficacy of possessing and threatening to use atomic weapons. Members of religions throughout the world drew upon the peace emphases in their traditions to demand a cessation of nuclear testing and disarmament. Scientists, moral philosophers, and political theorists sought to create a non-religious foundation for restraint in war.

Guerrilla wars against colonial powers in Algeria and Vietnam occasioned the greatest popular outcry against ongoing wars in recorded history. Governments and people debated whether the same standards about civilian immunity should be applied to wars of liberation or if Just War traditions favored corrupt regimes. What would be permissible tactics in struggles in South Africa and Latin America?

Section IV, the "Middle East" focuses on modern wars involving Islam. Using a Zionist and religious ideology, Jews created and armed the state of Israel, and Arabs responded with war. Religion also fueled a bloody eight-year war between Iraq and Iran. This was followed shortly by the Iraqi invasion of Kuwait and a war led by the U.S. and fought under the UN's auspices. The debates over the Gulf Wars in the United States, Europe, Middle East, Asia, and the United Nations showed that categories derived from the ancient world now received the allegiance of all the nations of the world. What remained uncertain, however, was whether those inherited traditions rationalized war or fostered peace. The chapter on Iraq should be updated as current events unfold.

The end of the Cold War brought a resurgence of religious/ethnic conflict. A horrendous price in lives resulted from the failure of state systems in the Congo, Liberia, and Rwanda, and these events showed a lack of resolve by Western powers to intervene, even in the face of genocide. In the 1990s religious-motivated violence appeared in Sudan, Israel, Pakistan-India, Sri Lanka, Bosnia, Chechnya, and Afghanistan. The creation of a fragile peace in Northern Ireland was overshadowed by the failure of the Oslo peace process between Israelis and Palestinians and the bombing of the World Trade Centers in New York City. The belief, dominant in the West since the Peace of Westphalia in 1648, that wars over religion were illegitimate, now appeared naïve. Practitioners of the new discipline of peace studies sought to understand whether domestic, patriarchal, and economic violence had the same root cause and could be eased by conflict resolution.

My conclusions or "final thoughts" returns to themes raised in the introduction of why religions have so often supported wars and have been unable to implement their teachings on peace. Are these conditions systemic and so will continue indefinitely? To those who insist that linking religion, morality, and war is an oxymoron, my answer is that these have been linked since the beginning of civilization and should be studied together.

A few years ago a prospective student visited Swarthmore College where I taught and attended a class, which was on Gandhi. At the end he complained that the discussion left many questions and considerable ambiguity about nonviolence and war. My answer might help those who struggle with the issues raised in this book: "If war were simple and easily abolished, humanity would have done it long ago."

I.
The Hebrew Scriptures and War

I. Reading the Scriptures

In the beginning was chaos, and God tamed this warlike condition to make the world.[1] So begins Genesis, and our exploration begins with the Hebrew Scriptures, partially because they embody many traditions of the ancient world on the relation of war and religion. The Hebrew Scriptures, books originally written in Hebrew, which Christians call the Old Testament, are sacred to three faiths: Judaism, Christianity, and Islam. Adherents of these faiths agree that these Scriptures witness to a revelation of God in history, but their interpretations differ on the precise meaning of what was revealed and the extent that the Hebrew *Bible* is normative or final. Over the centuries Jews, Christians, and Muslims have built up distinctive traditions or patterns of understanding the Hebrew Scriptures. Today arriving at one agreed-upon meaning is further complicated because, in addition to the three major faiths, there are deep cleavages within each of these religions -- Orthodox, Conservative, and Reform within Judaism; Sunni, Sufi, Shiite within Islam; Roman Catholics, Orthodox, and Protestants in Christianity; with each group bringing different standards to determining beliefs and practices.

Since the late nineteenth-century archaeological discoveries, increased knowledge of civilizations of Mesopotamia and Egypt, new techniques for analyzing historical documents, sophisticated theories of the relationship of texts to their original creators, and a non-religious institutional setting (the modern

---

[1] The Hebrew word translated "deep" is related to Tiamat, a goddess who was the dragon slain by Marduk. Several passages in Scripture refer to a "primeval struggle between Yahweh and the forces of chaos." An interpretation of Genesis 1:1, linking the killing of the dragon with the drying up of the "waters of the great deep," is supported by references to the "deep" in the flood story and Isaiah 51:9 where God "cut Rahab in pieces, that didst pierce the dragon. Was it not thou that didst dry up the sea, the waters of the great deep?" This act is linked to God's parting the Red Sea in the Exodus. *Interpreter's Dictionary of the Bible* (1962), I, p. 813. See also Thomas B. Dozeman, *God at War* (1993), p. 131, 157.

university) have added new dimensions to the study of sacred texts. Those who embrace the new methods of study insist that the *Bible* is a product of history and reflects surrounding cultures.[2] Faith communities have responded either by embracing, modifying, ignoring, or rejecting the techniques and conclusions of modern scholars.

Readers of this book should not assume that the account of the ideas of war and peace in the Hebrew Scriptures presented here will exemplify a universally agreed-upon objective meaning or will satisfy any of the faith communities. Our interest is not in determining, for example, whether the walls of Jericho actually tumbled down as described in the book of Joshua, but how the Israelites saw that event and how they reinterpreted that conquest of a city as their history changed. For the Hebrew Scriptures show that the Israelites reenacted and reinterpreted their history. This process of reliving and rethinking the original sacred myths, begun by the Hebrews while they were still an independent nation before 630 B.C.E. (before the Christian era), continues to this day. The early Christians engaged in a similar process with the Hebrew Scriptures and their own traditions, though with different premises, and so did Muhammad and his followers. Our concern is both with what the *Bible* originally said of the events and why many peoples over the centuries have interpreted it as requiring different practices.

Reading about the scriptures and war is an exercise that should take place on several levels. Imagine how the event was perceived when first described, then how that narrative evolved through history, and finally how that original event preserved in tradition is used today by people seeking insight who know both the original scriptures and presently participate in the religious ceremonies. If this seems difficult, think of the different roles all of us play, often at the same time:

---

[2] A readable introduction to contemporary scholarship on the *Bible* is Richard Elliott Friedman, *Who Wrote the Bible (1997)*. Two good textbooks are Bernhard W. Anderson, *Understanding the Old Testament (1997)* and Norman K. Gottwald, *The Hebrew Bible: A Socio-Literary Introduction* (1985).

child, parent, friend, roommate, employee, and citizen. These roles change as we age; yet successfully operating as one of these does not diminish the ability to be all. That ability to live simultaneously at many levels of consciousness is analogous to knowing the several sacred times occurring concurrently and appreciating the influence of holy texts on war. The reader should try to be an ancient Hebrew and modern Jew, a disciple of Jesus, a medieval priest and a modern fundamentalist, an ancient Greek and a contemporary student, a seventh-century Sunni and a modern Shiite. She should try to imagine what Gandhi would say to Joshua, Muhammad to Clausewitz, and what all would say to the Secretary General of the United Nations. This asynchronistic mixture is the way religion and war have actually functioned.

II. The Hebrew Scriptures

Our approach to the Hebrew *Bible* will be selective, concentrating on issues of war and peace and ignoring such central themes as the content of the ritual and moral law, religious festivals and temple worship, changes in the way the Hebrews interpreted the nature of God, and the responsibilities brought by their election. The creation stories, proverbs, psalms, devotional literature, prophecies -- i.e., the texts most often used by contemporary faith communities -- are not our primary concern. Instead, we shall concentrate on the history of the Israelites from Moses through the creation, flourishing, and fall of Israel and on those prophets who declared Yahweh's counsel on foreign policy before and during rule by Babylon, Persia, and Rome. Our focus will be on the Hebrews' understanding of the role of God and their responsibilities in times of victory and defeat. The stories about God, man, and battle are complex and confusing, but for 2000 years the faithful knew and relied on their biblical precedents.

The Hebrew Scriptures record the stories of the acts of Yahweh in history; virtually all of these events are described in detail in no other documents because in the ancient world the Jews seemed unimportant. The *Bible* claims that God selected the Israelites as a chosen people to serve Him (the male pronoun is appropriate insofar as God was perceived to have gender) and bestowed upon them the land of Canaan. The Hebrews' exodus from Egyptian slavery and their deliverance from the chariots of Pharaoh during the crossing of the Red Sea were the formative events in the creation of the Jewish peoples.

The Exodus stories contain two kinds of holy war motifs, both designed to show that the Lord God was more powerful than Pharaoh and Egypt's gods. After witnessing the oppression of the Hebrews, Moses appeals and brings plagues to distress the Egyptians, but Pharaoh will not relent. Finally, God destroys the first born of all Egyptians and the Israelites are allowed to depart after despoiling their captors of silver, gold, and clothing - a war booty. God "passed over" the Hebrew houses because Moses had instructed to the Jews to sprinkle lamb's blood on the lintel above the door. The blood is a sacrificial theme, linking the Passover to Succoth, the festival of first fruits.[3] A second holy war motif is the destruction of Pharaoh's army by God's parting of the Red Sea, holding back the Egyptian chariots by a pillar of fire, allowing the Hebrews to walk through the sea on dry land, and then destroying the Egyptians by allowing the waters to return. These miraculous acts demonstrated that "Yahweh is a man of war . . . Pharaoh's chariots and his host He cast into the sea . . . Thy right hand, O Yahweh, shatters the enemy" (Exodus 15: 3-6).

Israel literally meant "El (God) does battle," and Yahweh was the Hebrews' war god.[4] In the early traditions a pantheon of gods existed, and Yahweh, who warred only for the Hebrews, demonstrated His superiority when the Jews prevailed in battle. The Lord God of Hosts was the commander of the legions of heaven who intervened in miraculous fashion. The Hebrews were only one of many ancient peoples who claimed a special relationship with a god who fought for them and who used sacrifices (including humans) and propitiatory actions to insure his or her help in battle. What is unique is that the victory God

---

[3] Thomas B. Dozeman, *God at War: Power in the Exodus Tradition* (1996), 46-51.
[4] Julius Wellhausen quoted in "Introduction" to Gerhard von Rad, *Holy War in Ancient Israel* (1991), 3. See discussion of "El," and "Israel" in *Mercer Dictionary of the Bible,* ed. Watson Mills (1990), 240, 417.

of the Hebrews survived their political defeat and the destruction of the Kingdom of Israel.

Yahweh was also the lawgiver who, after the deliverance from Egypt while the Israelites moved towards Canaan, bestowed on them the Ten Commandments at Sinai, one of which forbade killing. Murder in the community was outlawed, but not in war. Yahweh demanded obedience from the Israelites, and although His election of them was unconditional, their successes in battle depended upon their faith and trust.

The stories of Gideon and Joshua in the books of Judges and Joshua show how Yahweh fought for Israel. In the book of Judges, the Hebrews dwelt in the hills of Canaan, and the cities in the plains below belonged to their enemies. The book of Joshua described the conquest of those cities. One either must assume that the Israelites took the cities and then lost them, of which there is no mention, or that some of the stories in Judges pre-date Joshua. Judges described the Hebrews as being oppressed by their Canaanite neighbors and God's inspiring a leader to deliver them. Barak, for example was called by the priestess Deborah, and he then summoned the tribes of Hebrews, not all of whom joined the army. (In Judges the twelve tribes never fight as a unit, showing that the definition of who was an Israelite comes later.) Barak led the forces into battle against enemy general Sisera, but the victory belonged to Yahweh, who caused even "the stars . . . to fight against Sisera" (Judges 5:20).[5] As in the Exodus deliverance, the *Bible* preserved no record that the Hebrews did any fighting. After Sisera's army was destroyed, he fled and accepted hospitality and refuge with Jael, the wife of a Kenite. While he slept in Jael's tent, she took a mallet, struck him on the head shattering his temple, and he died: "So perish all thine enemies, O Lord." Though she was not a Hebrew, Jael's act made her the "Most blessed of women" (Judges

---

[5]Millard Lind, *Yahweh is a Warrior: The Theology of Warfare in Ancient Israel* (1980), 59, 64, 82 stresses the motif of Yahweh doing the fighting in a supernatural event as a central motif in the holy war starts with the Exodus. See also Von Rad, Chapter 2.

5: 24, 31). The Barak/Jael story combined God's victory with a woman's murder of a sleeping man.

The book of Joshua's description of the conquest of the Holy Land contained all the essential ingredients of Yahweh's war. After leaving Egypt, Moses led the Hebrews to the River Jordan where they could see the Promised Land. However, because they were fearful of the Canaanites and did not trust Jehovah, the Lord sentenced the Israelites to wander in the wilderness for forty years. At the end of that time, Joshua, the successor to Moses, led the Hebrews in a miraculous crossing of the Jordan River (analogous to the parting of the Red Sea) and prepared them ritually (through circumcising all males) to conquer Jericho. The inhabitants of Jericho stayed behind their fortified walls. Following instruction from an angel of the Lord, Joshua instructed a group of priests, carrying ram's horn trumpets, and soldiers to circle the city silently once a day for six days. On the seventh day, the procession circled the city seven times, then the priests blew the horns, and all the people shouted. At this instant the walls of the city tumbled down and the Hebrews burned the city, keeping no booty for themselves but preserving silver, gold, bronze, and iron for the treasury of the Lord. The Jews killed all the people of Jericho, excepting the family of the prostitute Rahab who had previously aided Jews spying out the city. The inhabitants of Jericho and their wealth became God's possession and were sacrificed to God.

Under the Lord's direction, Joshua conquered several cities. His only military failure came after Achan, one of the soldiers, kept for himself some booty designated for Jehovah; this disobedience caused God to withdraw His favor and resulted in a defeat. Killing that soldier, his family, even his animals restored the blessing of God, who in the next battle even caused the sun to pause to enable the Hebrews to pursue opposing kings to their deaths. Unlike the victories of Gideon and Barak and the fall of Jericho, the other battles of Joshua required the Hebrews to fight, and even on one occasion to stage an ambush. The writers of Judges and

Joshua made clear that the Hebrews' success in battle came only through Yahweh's intervention.

In Deuteronomy 7:1-3; 20:1-20 God spelled out exactly how the Hebrews were to fight. When the war occurred over the land that Yahweh had promised the Hebrews, then all who dwelt there -- men, women, and children -- were to be put to death. If, however, the war involved land outside the Promised Land, women and children were enslaved and the men were either killed or enslaved.[6] A woman captive was not to be raped, but could become a wife after living for a month in a man's household. Still, there was one restriction on fighting: trees that produce food were to be spared -- "Are the trees in the field men that they should be besieged by you?" Non-food trees could be cut to build siege works. In Deuteronomy, the Hebrew warriors were a holy caste: no one should serve who was afraid or who had a new house or vineyard or who was betrothed to wed. (All these restrictions are observed in Gideon's war described in Judges 6:11 – 7:23.) Since the war was a holy event, no one was to fight to gain possessions, and any spoils not burnt were reserved for Yahweh. Deuteronomy made no distinction between offensive and defensive war and granted to civilians no special status.

Lacking in the Deuteronomic code of war was the emphasis upon a charismatic leader, or judge, who called the Israelites together. That missing element, along with the mention of siege works when neither Judges nor Joshua showed the Hebrews able to besiege cities, has led scholars to see the code as a later distillation during the monarchy of traditions of early and late holy war practices.[7] In the latter, the men in an opposing army would be killed, but women, children, and property would be treated as a spoil of war. Still the essential ingredient was the same: that God delivered the Hebrews from Egypt and, if they

---

[6]This distinction in kinds of war may show the survival in ancient Israel of two traditions of holy war, which are here joined. See Susan Niditch, *War in the Hebrew Bible: A Study in the Ethics of Violence* (1993), 66-68. This is best secondary source for those who wish to study in more depth the problem of war in the Hebrew Scriptures.

[7] Gerhard von Rad, *Studies in Deuteronomy* (1953), 45-55.

remained faithful, would give them victory in battles and possession of the Holy Land.

Note that early Hebrew wars were for conquest, not self-defense. God had elected the Hebrews and his blessings were a scarce commodity, available to only one people.[8] The Canaanites who already lived on the land had no legitimacy either to life or land there because God owned and gave it to the Jews. In fact, their worship of other gods and their attempt to corrupt the obedience of the Hebrews to God justified their total destruction. And yet there is an ironical tone in the Yahweh war motifs of the conquest of the Holy Land because the scriptures also record that there were always non-Jews in Israel; the Moabites were present because they deceived Joshua who granted them permission to stay; the descendants of Rahab and many Israelites and non-Jews worshipped rival deities of Yahweh. The Israeli people were the elect of God and given the land, yet the boundaries of the land or who was included in the children of God remained cloudy, because the inhabitants of Israel often ignored God's commandments.

The Yahweh or holy war ideology in Deuteronomy enabled the religious leaders to deal with both victory and defeat. Victory came because Yahweh helped the Hebrews; defeat could be explained by the failure of Yahweh to aid the Hebrews because they were not loyal to Him or did not observe His law. Holy war could become a preaching device, useful to remind the Israelites that their survival required remaining faithful to the commandments.

Although at first glance the Deuteronomistic interpretation of war prevails in Judges and Joshua, a closer reading reveals major differences in emphases, leading some scholars to conclude that the *Bible* encompasses a wide variety of practices and interpretations of war. For example, stories about Samson in Judges

---

[8]Regina M. Schwartz, *The Curse of Cain: The Violent Legacy of Monotheism* (1997) argues that violence in the Hebrew Scriptures comes from the scarcity model of God's arbitrary blessing, a tradition beginning in the Cain/Abel stories and continuing through the history of Israel and later Christianity. Such a model for the relation of religion and war does not work well when applied to Hinduism. Connor Cruise O'Brien, *God Land: Reflections in Religion and Nationalism* (1988), 2-7 sees the Hebrews as exemplifying a land nationalism.

did not evoke holy war motifs; nor is there an ethical tone to his victories over the Philistines. He is a strong man, a warrior like the heroes in the *Iliad*, who marries a non-Jew, Delilah, who tries to destroy him. Samson's riddles and hot temper are far removed from the priest-warrior Joshua. Strength for Samson depends on long hair, a subject not mentioned in the Deuteronomic code. Gideon, after his initial victory over the Midianites in a holy war, acts like a warrior hero who seems to observe a kind of soldier's code. Two captive kings desire to be killed by Gideon, rather than by his young son, because there is honor involved with who kills whom. Samson, Gideon, Saul, and David are mighty warriors. By contrast, Jael and Ehud are trickster figures who assassinate Israel's opponents by devious actions.[9]

Wars in the first books of the Hebrew Scriptures are bloody affairs during the fighting and in the treatment of humans and spoils. In Numbers 30, which uses none of Deuteronomy's holy war motifs, an army of 10,000 led by priests destroys the Midianites and slays all male captives. When the army returns to camp carrying the females and children and booty, Moses is furious and has all the male children and the non-virgin females killed. The spoils are ritually purified and then divided among the soldiers and priests. The preservation of the maidens seems to be related to a desire for ethnic purity, since presumably they will become the brides of Hebrew soldiers. By contrast, after the fall of Jericho all humans are killed and the booty reserved to God. In the Gideon sagas, he takes gold from the enemy and makes an ephod, or golden image. The image leads to false worship, but Gideon is -- unlike Achan and his family -- not punished. In the book of I Samuel, King Saul loses the divine blessing because he allows the King of the Amalekites to survive and keeps the cattle to divide among warriors.

The variety of religious emphases, ethical awareness, actions of heroes, causes of wars, kinds of battles, and treatment of human and material spoils, has led scholars to insist that there is no one attitude toward war in the Hebrew *Bible*.

[9] Susan Niditch, *War in the Hebrew Bible: A Study in the Ethics of Violence*, ch. 4.

The ban on the killing of captives after battle is sometimes justified as a sacrifice to the Lord God; at others as a just punishment for evil deeds.[10] The author of Chronicles is more concerned with a moral cause for a war than the author(s) of I Kings or Judges. The layers of traditions reflect different religious, political, social and cultural phases in the life of Israel. While there is an historical core to the stories, there is also interpretation and re-interpretation as time progresses.

The victories of Joshua did not guarantee security. In I Samuel the Philistines waged incessant successful war against the Hebrews. When the Hebrews attempted to guarantee security by carrying the Ark of the Covenant housing the Ten Commandments into battles (a motif of holy war that Deuteronomy did not mention, again suggesting that its formulation, while using earlier motifs, was drawn up later), they were totally defeated and the Ark captured. Israel's response to defeat was to demand a king. The Hebrews blamed their weakness on the lack of a Canaanite institution, kingship, not a failure of faith, another indication that the Deuteronomic formulation on war was imposed on earlier traditions.

III. The Unified Kingdom: Saul, David, and Solomon

The first two kings, Saul and David, bridged the transition from charismatic war leadership to hereditary monarchy, generals, and standing armies. Before the monarchy, the Lord God was Israel's king, and He summoned leaders who called the army into being. God in essence declared the war, set the strategy, and gave the victory. Now the king kept a standing army of mercenary soldiers who had to be paid either from taxes or the spoils of war. The monarch, after consultation with priests or prophets, decided on the war, decided on tactics, and either led the army himself or employed generals. Unlike other Mesopotamian rulers, Israel's kings were not divine figures and God required obedience from both king and people for success in war. Eventually the right to rule came from

---

[10] Ibid., ch. 1, 2, 28, 51-53, 56, 77.

dynastic legitimacy (David's lineage), not godliness, and the *Bible* tells that many monarchs showed neither piety nor obedience to God's law.

The first kings, Saul and David, became rulers because they were successful charismatic warriors. "Saul has slain his thousands, David his tens of thousands" (I Samuel 21:11). The changes in the nature of war are illustrated by the familiar story of David and Goliath. This war with the Philistines was not like Gideon's. David visited his brothers who were serving in King Saul's standing army and saw the Hebrews' fear of the giant. As a shepherd, David had previously shown valor by killing a lion and a bear, and he shamed the soldiers by offering to attack Goliath who was taunting the Israelites for cowardice. After declining Saul's offer of armor, David took his sling. The Lord's power protected David and gave him victory, but David was the primary actor. He took the stone in the sling, hurled it at Goliath, and struck him in the forehead -- knocking him out. David then took the fallen Goliath's sword and cut off his head. With the Philistines demoralized, the Israelites attacked and won. Previously, under the Yahweh war motifs, the army was almost superfluous. In the Samuel narratives, Yahweh's presence gave victory to Saul and David, but the soldiers now waged war. Note that except for David, who was a fighting hero unlike Moses or Joshua (he most resembles Samson), holiness was a minor matter. The Hebrew soldiers were afraid of Goliath; David's act gave them courage; the morale of an army was now crucial, and the Lord God's presence gave courage.

The monarchs created a permanent core of soldiers who needed to be paid. So the spoils in war went to the warriors rather than being destroyed or earmarked for Yahweh. Friction over the spoils of war led to the prophet Samuel's denunciation of King Saul and the choice of David to succeed him. After the monarchy was established, those who spoke for the Lord God's demand for faithfulness and promise of victory had to contend with the practice of statecraft: dynastic alliances including marriages with foreign princesses, prudent calculation of actions, and even sacrifices to foreign fertility deities like Ba'al. Becoming a state under Saul and then an empire under David subjected Israel to new practices in the traditional worship of God as well as new ideals of war. The wars of Israel, whether of conquest of neighbors or putting down revolts, were still fought under God's banner, and He guaranteed security, prowess in fighting, and victory. "Blessed be the Lord, my rock, who trains my hands for war, and my fingers for battle: my rock and my fortress, and my stronghold and my deliverer, my shield and He in whom I take refuge, who subdues the people under Him" (Psalms 144: 1-2).

Victory in battle remained the clear sign of favor with God and evidence of obedience to the law. The Philistines killed King Saul in battle because he sinned in not dedicating all the spoils to Yahweh. David succeeded in battle, even though he committed adultery with Bathsheba, the wife of the warrior Uriah who was absent fighting for the King. (Uriah's refusal to sleep with his wife while he was a soldier tells us about a practice of holy war mentioned nowhere else in the Hebrew Scriptures.) David's punishment for his sin was not failure and death in war, but the death of his child, rebellion of his sons, and the necessity of fighting throughout his reign. David maintained his kingdom by quelling a rebellion towards the end of his reign, an indication of the fragile unity of Israel. The King's repentance and faithfulness to Yahweh were rewarded in the promise that his dynasty would endure. To the covenant of a Promised Land to his people, Yahweh now added a secondary pledge to the Davidic dynasty.

The Kingdom of Israel attained its greatest glory under David, who conquered and then made Jerusalem his capital, and his son Solomon (961-922 B.C.E.). The boundaries of the Promised Land became the areas conquered by David, even though these areas included many non-Jews. As a way of unifying the twelve tribes of Israel under the dynasty, the center for worship became the temple in Jerusalem built by David's heir, King Solomon who, the *Bible* declared was a man of peace rather than a warrior who had shed blood. Yahweh who had earlier been encountered on mountains and in the wilderness now dwelt in the temple on Mount Zion. Temple worship, like kingship, was an alien feature the Hebrews imported from neighbors. A rivalry between those Israelites who preferred to worship at traditional holy sites like the mountain at Shechem and the royally sponsored new temple in Jerusalem would become a prominent feature of Jewish life. If the kingdom had stayed united, the tension over where to worship might have been a minor irritant.

Unfortunately for the long-term prospects of Israel, Solomon's centralized kingdom and building program required heavy taxation and forced labor, and his making a place in Jerusalem for the gods of his many wives irritated tribes in the northern areas of Israel. After the death of Solomon, rebellion resulted in the division in 937 B.C.E., with the northern areas becoming a new kingdom of Israel with worship centered at Shechem and a small southern kingdom called Judah, containing Jerusalem, remaining loyal to the Davidic line. The resulting wars over boundaries, dynastic instability in the northern kingdom, and weaknesses in both states created immense political and religious discontent.

Scholars now believe that the present form of the historical books of the Hebrew Scriptures reflect the emphases of several editors. These anonymous editors are labeled J, E, P, and D.[11] J and E date from the division of Israel into northern and southern kingdoms. Attempting to gain popular support for the Davidic dynasty, an editor or historian in the southern kingdom or Judah, referred to by scholars as the J or Yahweh source (J in German sound like Y), compiled many of the stories from Genesis chapter 2 through Judges, and I Kings and centered the last portion of his narrative on the history of David and Solomon. J's narrative stressed the patriarchs, Ark of the Covenant holding the Ten Commandments, covenant of God with the Davidic line, and the Aaronic priesthood in Jerusalem. J did not stress ethics in war and his account of David shows a complicated hero with virtues and flaws.

A comparable document termed the E source because the name for God is Elohim (often translated as Lord God in English versions) came from the northern kingdom of Israel (both the unified kingdom of David and the area of the Ten

---

[11]Richard Elliott Friedman, *Who Wrote the Bible* (1997), ch. 2, J & E, ch. 6, 7D, ch. 11P.

Tribes were called Israel). E's emphasis was on the conquest of the land, Moses, Joshua, Samuel, and the Levite priesthood of Shiloh. After the fall of the northern kingdom, these histories would be merged because the redactors of J and E told many of the same stories, though from different perspectives reflecting the political and religious needs of the two kingdoms.

IV. Judah and Israel: Prophecy and Destruction

The kings of Israel and Judah sought to utilize the prestige of Yahweh through court-approved rituals and sacrifices conducted by priests in Jerusalem and Samaria. The Yahweh cult had existed before kingship, and both the monarchs and the people believed that a successful reign depended upon the favor of God. With the establishment of the monarchy, political and religious authority divided. The king symbolized the rule of God over Israel, priests conducted the sacrifices and rituals of common worship, and prophets advised the king and people on Yahweh's desires.

The prophets continued an earlier pattern as inspired or charismatic individuals in declaring the mind of Yahweh. The prophets did not prove by action or reason that they spoke for God; they proclaimed God's will and demanded acceptance. The *Bible* describes a constant contest between true and false prophets, with the kings facing the dilemma of deciding whose prophecy was correct. So they often listened to court prophets who could be expected to provide advice congruent to the kings' wishes. Just as the monarchy in Israel/Judah was a religious/political institution, so was prophecy. The prophets, initially concerned mostly with the behavior of the king, during the crisis after the division of the kingdom broadened their focus to judge the social conditions and religious actions of the entire population. They drew upon common themes in Israel's past -- a chosen people, Exodus, holy war, law, and the Davidic dynasty, the Promised Land -- and interpreted the relevance of these teachings for contemporary issues. When the prophets discussed God's future actions, they conditioned those actions on the behavior of the king and the people.[12]

The Hebrew prophets also discussed foreign policy. The rise of the Kingdom of Israel under David and Solomon around 1000 B.C.E. occurred while surrounding states remained weak. Now the Hebrews lived in two antagonistic and vulnerable states subject to threats from larger neighbors. Israel and Judah sought to preserve their independence by war with neighboring states, by alliance with a coalition of states, or by the payment of tribute to powerful empires. Palestine was a strategic area located between Egypt and Syria.

In the eighth century B.C.E. the prophets Amos and Isaiah saw the threat posed by the rise of Assyria. They also saw within the two kingdoms worship of false gods, a lack of justice, and the exploitation of the poor by the rich. They denounced those Hebrews who believed Yahweh provided security for Israel in spite of internal oppression. The prophet Amos saw God's wrath falling upon Judah and Israel because "they trample the head of the poor into the dust of the earth, and turn aside the way of the afflicted," and "have rejected the law of the Lord." (Amos 2:4, 7) Amos proclaimed that Yahweh did not accept the sacrifices and burnt offerings of the people. Israel had placed its confidence in foreign gods, and the Lord God would bring punishment. Yahweh still had a special claim on Israel, but His dissatisfaction would result in destruction. For Amos, God's election of Israel as a chosen people was not unconditional, and Yahweh's wrath might end in the destruction of the northern kingdom and the exile of its people. Yahweh was still the God of battles. However, holy war no longer meant that God fought for Israel against foreign deities. Instead, for Amos and Isaiah, Assyria could become the "rod of my (God's) anger" (Isaiah 10:5) and, because the Jews had not repented and changed their ways, God would fight for the Assyrians against His chosen people.

---

[12] Good introductions to the subject of prophecy are found in the standard *Bible* commentaries on

Because the prophets spoke to concrete situations, their advice changed according to the circumstances. Amos, when he spoke to Israel's king, saw only destruction; by contrast, Isaiah told King Hezekiah of Judah to resist the Assyrians, and argued that -- in spite of God's anger which would bring desolation -- Yahweh would preserve Mount Zion, the site of the temple in Jerusalem. There would be lamentation in Judah, but there would also be a new day in which swords would be beaten into plowshares, the lion and the lamb would lie down together, and a Davidic son would establish a government that would bring justice and peace and righteousness "from this time forth and forevermore." (Isaiah 9:7) Unlike Amos, Isaiah found in the promise to the Davidic dynasty and dwelling place of God on Mount Zion the link guaranteeing that present catastrophe would climax in future exaltation. Isaiah's definition of a future peace depended upon Yahweh's holy war activities. *Shalom* was not a human created political condition.

Amos and Isaiah were right; Assyria did invade. "Your country lies desolate, your cities are burned with fire." (Isaiah 1:7) The Northern Kingdom of Israel fell in 721 B.C.E. and the ten northern tribes disappeared from history. Judah, however, survived. The Assyrians laid siege to Jerusalem, but it was not laid waste. Isaiah's prophecy was not completely fulfilled, however. He was correct that Jerusalem and Judah would endure and that the Assyrians would withdraw. II Kings, Chronicles, and Isaiah use the exalted language of holy war, claiming that the Lord's direct intervention brought victory. "And an angel of the Lord went forth, and slew a hundred and eighty-five thousand in the camp of the Assyrians." (Isaiah 37:36) However, II Kings: 18: 13 recounted that Assyria conquered all the fortified cities in Judah, and King Hezekiah paid tribute including all the gold within the temple. An Assyrian document boasts of victory and money received, but also indicates that Jerusalem survived a siege. What seems

---

individual books included in series such as *The New Interpreter's Bible VI* (1999), general reference works including the *Anchor Bible Dictionary* (1992), as well as works of introduction such as the *Cambridge Companion to the Bible* (1997).

certain was that, however occurring, the survival of the city led to a re-emphasis upon holy war and to belief in impregnable Mount Zion as the dwelling place of Yahweh.

Within the *Bible* a prophet was more than a successful fortuneteller. Sometimes the prophecies were fulfilled completely; at other times partially; sometimes not at all. The prophets claimed to bring the counsel of Yahweh to an issue. The king and his advisers had the problem of deciding who, from among the many prophets, or schools of prophets, declared the will of God correctly and gave wise counsel. The career of Jeremiah demonstrated the difficulties for both king and prophet.

Assyria's ascendancy was short-lived. During its decline before the fall of Nineveh in 612 B.C.E., the Kingdom of Judah experienced a revival, and under king Josiah (638-609) recaptured much of the land of the former Northern Kingdom. A revitalization of the worship of Yahweh accompanied the return to outward prosperity. The book of Kings described the discovery of the old scroll of laws in the Temple. When the laws were read, the Israelites learned how much they had departed from true worship; they repented, and began observing the law correctly. Modern scholars believe that scroll contained the sections of the book of Deuteronomy describing holy war.

A redactor, termed the Deuteronomistic historian (D), took the earlier histories of J and E and reshaped the history of Israel from Moses' farewell in the book of Deuteronomy through the conquest in Joshua, Judges, Samuel, and Kings. The D editor saw in King Josiah a second Joshua, restoring the Kingdom of Israel, centralizing worship in Jerusalem, and emphasizing observance of the law. The Deuteronomic war code explained why Yahweh had been so powerful in the creation of a unified monarchy, and yet had later allowed the defeat and destruction of the Northern Kingdom. The Hebrews had not kept the law, had worshipped other gods, and had not trusted in Yahweh. Joshua's conquest of Jericho showed all Israel how to be successful in war. The message to the revitalized state of Judah: survival depended upon keeping the Lord's laws.

The prosperity and power of Judah did not endure. In spite of his religious fervor, King Josiah was killed battling the Egyptians. Judah now faced a new threat: the Babylonians. Judah's kings again sought a policy of survival, debating whether to join in a coalition led by Egypt or to pay tribute to the Babylonians. Again the religious tensions in the kingdom surfaced as priests and prophets advocated contrasting policies. Isaiah had at an earlier period proclaimed the inviolability of Mount Zion in Jerusalem and advocated resistance to Assyria. Now the prophet Jeremiah did the opposite, finding no hope for survival in either the covenants of God on Promised Land or with the Davidic dynasty motifs that had been so prominent in the Deuteronomistic interpretation of Israel's history. If, as some scholars believe, Jeremiah agreed with or even wrote the D source, he now changed his perspective.

Jeremiah looked internally in the kingdom and saw decay, injustice, and idolatry; he looked externally and saw disaster coming. Against the nationalists, Jeremiah advocated surrender. Judah faced destruction, for the Lord was backing the enemy and nothing could be done. Even the prophet did not like the message God commissioned him to bring. For appearing to support the Babylonians, patriotic Jews plotted against Jeremiah's life and had him thrown into a cistern. The only hope for Judah that Jeremiah foresaw was that in the future God might initiate a new covenant where He "will put my law within them, and I will write it upon their hearts; and I will be their God, and they shall be my people" (Jeremiah 31: 33). But at present all was desolation as Yahweh declared, "I will make Jerusalem a heap of ruins, a lair of jackals; and I will make the cities of Judah a desolation without inhabitant" (Jeremiah 9:11).

One king resisted Jeremiah's advice and challenged the Babylonians; he was deported. The Babylonians left another puppet Hebrew king on the throne. When he also spurned Jeremiah's counsel of submission and led a revolt, King Nebuchadnezzar of Babylon returned with an army, took the city, burned the temple, and forced many of the leaders into exile. Except for a period of semi-autonomy under the Maccabean leaders in the second and first centuries B.C.E., Jewish independence ended in 586 B.C.E. and would not come again until 1948.

V. The Rebirth of Judaism

The prophets' divorcing holy war from the success of the state and asserting the primacy of observance of the law and ethical behavior enabled the worship of Yahweh to survive the destruction of both kingdoms. The seventy years of Babylonian captivity before the Persians allowed the Jews to return to Jerusalem witnessed great creativity as the exiles transformed Judaism from a political cult into a people's religion stressing festivals like Passover, ritual purity, and observance of the law of God. A rebuilt temple remained the center of cultic worship, but kingship of the Davidic line ended. During this period the *Bible*'s history books from Joshua to Kings received their final written form. The only changes in perspective that needed to be made to the Deuteronomistic formulation was to assert that Judah also deserted Yahweh who then terminated the political covenant.

An editor scholars call the Priestly (P) historian shortly after the return from exile during Persian Empire ca 540 B.C.E. recast the oral and written traditions from creation to the founding of the kingdom into the present form of the first five books of the Bible, often termed the Pentateuch. The Priestly historian emphasized the role of God as creator (the first chapter of Genesis), sabbath observance, obedience to God, the importance of the priesthood and cultic worship, the wilderness, the creation of the Ark of the Covenant, circumcision as a means of preserving religious-ethnic purity, keeping the law, and Yahweh's power over all nations and peoples.) The account of war in Numbers 30 (see p. 31) represents the Priestly historian's view of an ancient battle. In the Books of Chronicles the history of Israel was retold from a priestly point of view. In many instances the Priestly editor merely added his perspective to older accounts so that it is sometimes possible to find ancient traditions as well as perspectives from J E D and P within the same story.

The Jewish belief that God determined the success or failure in war also survived the fall of the two kingdoms, and was a theme of the prophet known as Second Isaiah whose oracles date from the reign of the Persian Cyrus the Great (ca 539 B.C.E.). For Second Isaiah the Lord God had pardoned Israel's iniquity (40:2) and had restored the Hebrews as a people of God, but without political power. Second Isaiah reiterated many of the themes of the earlier Isaiah (he may have viewed himself as continuing Isaiah's perspective), but his concern was not with Assyria but with the creator God who shaped world history. Jehovah was still a war god, but he was no longer only a warrior for Israel. Instead, the Lord God established and destroyed empires. Yahewh's dwelling place remained Mount Zion and from here he controlled history. The prophet affirmed that God created the world and would re-create Israel through a new exodus. Second Isaiah declared that God determined all history but provided no details as to how God created the world, acted to raise and destroy empires, or would restore the Promised Land.

For Second Isaiah, Israel was still the elect of God, but her role was as a suffering servant, whose present ordeal would prepare her for future renewal. In time God who created and rules the world of empires would re-create Israel. The New Jerusalem would be a city of justice, obedience to the law, prosperity, and eternal peace. "For you shall go out in joy, and be led forth in peace . . . Instead of the thorn shall come up the cypress . . . and it shall be to the Lord for a memorial, for an everlasting sign which shall not be cut off." (Isaiah 55: 12-13). There will be "no peace . . . for the wicked" but for the righteous "Peace, peace, to the far and to the near." (Isaiah 58: l9, 24).

Peace is a word frequently mentioned in the Hebrew Scriptures with a wide range of meaning, most of which do not refer to politics.[13] The most frequent use is as a greeting or blessing (Numbers 6:20 "The Lord bless you and keep you, and

---

[13] *Interpreter's Dictionary of the Bible*, ed. G. W. Bromiley (1979) III, 705-7; *Anchor Bible Dictionary*. For longer discussions of the meaning of peace in the Old and New Testaments, see the essays in Perry Yoder and Willard Swartley, eds., *The Meaning of Peace: Biblical Studies* (1992).

give you peace"). Here *shalom* refers to outward or material factors in a social context - prosperity, health, general well-being in a community - all of which are gifts of God. Because Israel was often threatened by hostile neighbors, the wish for peace in the Psalms could mean the security provided by God's holy war protection, and on occasion even Yahweh's war is called a peace. At the same time, a battle undertaken in God's direction would bring victory and the re-establishment of peace. While occasionally used as a treaty relationship between two nations, peace more often meant an absence of conflict or right order in the society in which the king, the people, and God are in harmony. However, the modern conception of a continuing state of war that contrasts with a normal relationship of peace among kingdoms is alien to the *Bible* where a war is a battle.

For the prophets, peace requires that society reflect the order of Yahweh's creation. So the poor must receive succor and the rich dispense true justice. The prophets condemned the rise to power of the rich and the growing oppression of the poor in the Northern and Southern Kingdoms as a false peace. For the writers of First and Second Isaiah, God in a new Exodus will create a new salvation, a new peace that is both a present event and a promise for the future. So in the Hebrew Scriptures peace is a gift of God with past, present, and future dimensions.

VI. Wisdom Literature

The Jews in exile prayed for the restoration of the temple and the right to return to Jerusalem, and yet they seemed to lead quiet lives first under Babylon and then Persia. Religious persecution was not a characteristic of life of subject peoples in the empires of the ancient world. So long as religion did not lead to political rebellion, subjects could practice their religion in peace. For our purpose, which is to understand the evolution of ideas of war, the most important contribution of this period was the development of the "wisdom" literature of Proverbs, Job, and Ecclesiastes -- none of which deal directly with war, but which provide counsel on how to live.

The book of Jonah provided a transition between the prophets and wisdom literature. Jonah's story was a fable with a message, and with their knowledge of what Assyria had done to Israel and Judah, the ancient Jews would not have taken the tale as literal fact. Jonah was a prophet whom the Lord told to go preach to the Assyrians in their capital Nineveh. The Assyrians who twice invaded Israel were not very popular with Jews. So Jonah decided to run away from God by boarding a ship going in the opposite direction from Nineveh. A storm occurred and the sailors searched for a cause. Jonah confessed that he was the culprit and told the sailors to throw him overboard. They did so and the storm ceased. A big fish swallowed Jonah and carried him to Nineveh. Jonah then denounced the sins of the Assyrians and foretold their impending destruction, but to his surprise and dismay, all the Assyrians repented. The Lord repented his anger and spared Nineveh. Jonah, however, was unhappy because he did not like Assyrians and saw his prophecy of desolation unfulfilled; so he retreated to the edge of the city where he sulked, mad at God for not killing the Assyrians. A little gourd plant grew up next to where Jonah rested and brought him shade. A worm ate the plant and it died. Jonah complained to the Lord about the worm; the Lord answered Jonah, "You pity the plant . . . Should not I pity Nineveh . . . in which there are more than a hundred and twenty thousand persons?" (Jonah 4:10-11). The book of Jonah ends with this rebuke of exclusiveness and a claim for God's compassion for all.

The book of Job questioned the Deuteronomistic historian's vision of the relationship between sins and evil. Job was a good man delivered up by God to be tested after Satan argued that Job was good only because he was prosperous, healthy, and with a good family. So God allowed Satan to test Job by taking away everything, including his children, his wealth, and his health. The false comforters of Job echoed the Deuteronomic historian's thesis that sin caused evil and blamed all Job's losses on his lack of repentance. Job rejected the false comforters' advice, insisted on his own goodness, and had the audacity to demand an explanation from God. God answered Job's complaint not by explaining the origin of evil but by showing all the wonders of creation. Job's experience of conversation with God convinced him to submit to God's actions and to worship even in the face of evil.

During the experience of exile and then return to Jerusalem during the reign of the Persians (540-330 B.C.E.), priestly Judaism gradually replaced prophetic Judaism. The emphasis was upon temple worship, the preservation of Jewish religious identity, observance of the sabbath, and performance of the law. The Jews defined themselves not as a political entity but as a religious community bound together by the priesthood. Not all Jews had gone into exile. Now under King Cyrus the Persians allowed those exiles who so desired to return to Jerusalem, rebuild the temple, and even fortify the city. Judea became a province of the empire, with a governor who was a descendant of the Davidic dynasty. The prophet Zechariah envisioned this ruler as the messiah who would inaugurate the era of peace in which Jerusalem would be restored to pre-eminence. This restoration would be done "Not by might, not by power, but by my Spirit, says the Lord." (Zechariah 4:6). Yahweh as Israel's warrior had re-emerged from the remote past, but in a tempered form.

VII. Responses to Greek Conquest: Apocalyptic and Maccabean Wars

The re-emergence of holy war as a motif occurred after the conquest of Persia by the army of Alexander the Great in 333 B.C.E. After Alexander's death his empire was divided between his generals, and in time Palestine came under the rule of Alexander's generals, first the Ptolemies, and then the Seleucids. The Seleucids came promoting Greek culture, and Jews were both attracted and repelled by Hellenistic civilization. Jerusalem, the site of the rebuilt temple and center of the culture, soon had a citadel of pagan soldiers and also boasted of a gymnasium in which young males competed in the nude. After what may have been some kind of an uprising, the Greek king Antiochus Epiphanes in 169 B.C.E. attacked and plundered the temple. This trauma caused a re-interpretation of the ancient teaching on war.

The later portions of the book of Daniel, written after Antiochus' profanation of the temple, contain a description of apocalyptic war. Daniel experienced a mystic vision of four beasts, which referred to four periods or empires into which history is divided. The Seleucids represented the fourth or final beast. The end of history was imminent and as time came to its conclusion, there would be a period of troubles followed by a great battle in heaven fought between angels and demons. Each nation had a good or evil force to rule over it until the final battle when the Lord God triumphed over all. The Lord God of hosts or his archangel Michael would lead the forces of good and destroy the reign of evil. After the final battle, there would be a time of judgment involving the reward of the good and the punishment of the wicked in a life beyond death. In the apocalyptic war spelled out in Daniel, Antiochus would be broken, but not by human hands. An individual had no role to play in the battles of the gods. Nor did he or she have a responsibility for history. All was pre-determined by God.[14]

Jewish apocalyptic war was a response to the feeling of powerlessness of in the Seleucid Empire. The older themes of Deuteronomistic holy war reappeared in apocalyptic war: Yahweh was a warrior, a people's faithfulness would be rewarded, victory and everlasting peace would be attained at the end. Even the miraculous intervention, like Yahweh's actions against the Egyptians at the Red Sea, reoccurred. At the end there would be a new Israel, a new creation. Yet apocalyptic holy war was very different from either holy war as pictured by Isaiah and Jeremiah or Deuteronomy because no national army or independent state or any human activities were required. Conditions were so hopeless that faithful humans could do nothing but wait for God's initiative.

The Maccabean revolt was an active response to the desecration of the temple by Antiochus Epiphanes. In the Apocrypha, the book of Maccabees

---

[14]John J. Collins, *Daniel, First Maccabees, Second Maccabees with an Excursus on the Apocalyptic Genre* (1981), 1-6, 131-145. John and Adelay Collins provide an analysis of apocalyptic literature in the *Anchor Bible Dictionary* ((1992), I, 279-292. A more detailed study is Jonathan A. Goldstein, *I Maccabees and II Maccabees* (1976, 1983) in the Anchor Bible Commentaries. A good introduction to the role of apocalyptic literature is in *International Standard Bible Encyclopedia*, ed., G. W. Bromiley (1979), I, 151-60. An interpretation of the role of apocalyptic prophecy in modern America is Paul Boyer, *When Time Shall Be No More* (1992).

portrayed an uprising of the people of Israel led by the sons of Mattathias against the corruption of Judaism, the influence of Greek culture, and the rule of Antiochus and the Seleucids.[15] Judas, who became the military commander of the Hebrews was portrayed as a composite of Moses, who observed the law, and Joshua, who led the people in war. Motifs taken from Judges characterized the war. For example, when Judas' army captured a Gentile city, he burned it, killed all the male inhabitants, and took spoils. Judas' small force's engaging in guerrilla warfare against far larger armies was analogous to Gideon's victory. Still, the portrayal of the Maccabean war differed from Deuteronomistic holy war and apocalyptic war. Judas won battles because of his strategy. He prevailed because of the Lord's help; but when he was defeated, there was no reflection on the sins of Israel causing Yahweh to turn away. On one occasion Judas' younger brother Joseph disregarded counsel not to fight and was defeated. According to the book of Maccabees, Joseph's fault was imprudence, not evil doing.

After Judas' death, his brothers Jonathan and Simon carried on the struggle, and eventually by shrewd diplomacy between various claimants to the Seleucid throne, created a semi-autonomous Jewish state, rid Jerusalem of the Gentile garrison, and purified the temple. Jonathan became both high priest and governor before he was treacherously killed. Then his brother Simon carried on the struggle for autonomy, again combining in his person the roles of high priest and political/military leader. The triumphs of the Maccabees today are commemorated in the feast of Hanukkah.

In First Maccabees the victories of Judas and his brother came from human agency. Yet Second Maccabees described the same battles by emphasizing the miraculous intervention of Yahweh. The leaders recalled Yahweh's defeat of the Assyrians; the motto of the Hebrews was "The Help of God,'" and victory came because "the Almighty fought on their side" (II Maccabees 8: 1-3). War here was a religious event and the soldiers celebrated victory by keeping the sabbath and

---

[15] The Apocrypha are writings included in the Greek and Latin (Orthodox and Roman Catholic)

giving the spoils of their victory to the maimed, widows, and orphans. When Antiochus sought to invade Israel, Yahweh "smote him with a fatal and invisible stroke." Antiochus was so impressed with the power of God that he repented and had a deathbed conversion. In Second Maccabees the temple existed for the sake of the nation, not just as a dwelling place for God. The cult of Yahweh now served as a unifying ideology to justify revolution and Jewish freedom.

Judith was a third book of the Apocrypha dealing with war. Unlike the interpretation of history in First and Second Maccabees, Judith appeared as a work of fiction in which King Nebuchadnezzar, the conqueror of Judah, was an Assyrian from Nineveh. Any good Jew would know that the current destroyer of Jerusalem was a Babylonian. In the story, the Jews defied Assyria, so the king sent his general Holofernes to force them to submit. Holofernes came with an enormous army, but refrained from a direct attack upon Jerusalem because he heard a prophecy about the power of God. Instead he laid siege to the city. The elders of the city held out for a time, but finally concluded they must surrender.

Judith, a pious and beautiful young widow, learned of the elders' decision and gained a postponement for five days. She then took off her widow's garb and dressed herself beautifully. With a basket of food and her maid, she left Jerusalem and went to Holofernes' camp. She was so gorgeous that the soldiers allowed her to come to Holofernes. She told the Assyrians that the Israelites had broken the law, and the Lord would deliver them up, and so she had left Jerusalem. Holofernes welcomed her to his camp. As an observant Jew, every morning Judith left the camp carrying food in a basket to pray, bathe, and eat. Finally, Holofernes, determined to get Judith drunk and seduce her, invited her to a banquet. He drank too much, and fell into a deep sleep; Judith, Jael-like, took his sword, cut off his head, and put it in her basket. She left the camp the next morning and took the head to the Hebrews. They put the head on a pike and displayed it as they prepared to attack the Assyrians. The Assyrians, seeing the

---

versions of the Old Testament but are excluded from Jewish and Protestant versions.

head, experienced the fear of Yahweh and were defeated by the Hebrews. The Lord gave victory, and the spoils were dedicated to him. The moral is clear: "Woe to the nations that rise up against my people: the Omnipotent Lord Almighty will take vengeance on them in the day of judgment, He will consign their flesh to fire and worms, and they will wail with pain forever" (Judith 16: 17).[16] Judith earned renown for her devotion to God and her willingness to assassinate an enemy of Israel.

Deliverance, conquest, preservation, captivity, re-creation, domination - from these events grew the Hebrew Scriptures' description of God's dealing and human responsibility for war and peace. The Hebrews' attitudes toward war evolved with external conditions because God entered into a covenant and bestowed upon them a land. The people of Israel saw themselves as selected, defended, rebuked, sustained, defeated, and restored through God's power. In their search for understanding of God and themselves, the Israelites interpreted present and past events in light of what they saw as Yahweh's continuing actions in history. So there was no one constant definitive Jewish attitude to war in the Hebrew Bible and different books even provide various interpretations of the same event.

After unsuccessful revolts against Rome in 70 and 115 C.E., Jews had virtually no direct influence in shaping Western traditions of war. Jews lived in the Diaspora as a subject people seeking to preserve their identity as a distinct religious community living at peace with their neighbors. Rabbis in commentaries termed Midrash treated every verse of the Hebrew Scriptures, now regarded as "holy" because inspired by God, as important and worthy of study, but they ceased to regard the Lord God's wars to create and the monarchs' wars to preserve the Kingdom of Israel as relevant or deserving of emulation. Instead, commentators argued that the war practices in Judges and Joshua, undertaken in

---

[16] Carey A. Moore, *Judith* in *The Anchor Bible* (1985), 245, 256. The hymn of praise of Judith echoes themes in the Exodus, particularly the Song of Miriam.

response to Yahweh's direct command were unique occurrences that were no longer possible. The commentators agreed that God also authorized the wars of the kings of Israel, whether they were defensive or offensive, so long as the intent was to protect the Holy Land. Such wars levied by Jewish kings required the consent of the Sanhedrin, a court of elders in Jerusalem.[17] Since neither Hebrew kings nor the Sanhedrin nor a Jewish state now existed, there was no possibility of having a God initiated war. The rabbis did not advocate pacifism either. Rather than talk about an abstract right to wage war, Jewish scholars focused on a person's right of resistance when pursued. If there were no alternatives except yielding or martyrdom, the rabbis distinguished between permissible submission on minor issues and when to defy the oppressors even if it meant death.[18] In the meantime, the Jewish people waited for the return of the messiah who in a holy war would end the reign of evil and restore the Davidic dynasty in the Kingdom of Israel and inaugurate a reign of God's perpetual peace.

The impact of the Hebrew Scriptures on Western norms for war and peace did not come from firsthand contact with Jewish warriors. Instead, the Christian Church interpreted the Old Testament as fulfilled by the New Testament and saw God's will in both. Christians cited selected stories, verses, and precedents from the Hebrew Scriptures depending upon the external circumstances and their understanding of what happened to the Jews. The re-interpretation of the significance of the history of Israel continues to this day in the Jewish and Christian faith communities. The ideas of war and peace derived from the Hebrew Scriptures have been used to justify aggressive war, defensive war, pacifism, barbarity, and gentleness. After all, although the prophet Isaiah said to beat swords into plowshares, the prophet Joel advocated making plowshares into swords.

---

[17] This interpretation of the earlier role of the Sanhedrin is a post-second century understanding of earlier texts. In actuality, the Sanhedrin or court was a Greco-Roman institution whereby the high priests collaborated with the political authorities.

[18] Michael Walzer in *The Ethics of War and Peace: Religious and Secular Perspectives*, edited by Terry Nardin (1996), 95-114.

II.
The New Testament and War

Unraveling the various strands of the New Testament's teaching about war is no easy task. Analyzing a few verses and stories might seem the simplest method and certainly through the centuries the Church on occasion has done this. Our task is to understand how Christians using the biblical narratives have been able to justify crusades, Just Wars, pacifism, as well as seeing politics and war as irrelevant to the search for true peace. In the past and present, Christians' attitudes to peace and war depend upon their understanding of the meaning of Jesus' actions and teachings, that is, of the essence of the faith. So this chapter will discuss at length the literature and different ways of interpreting the New Testament.

Compared with the Hebrew Scriptures, the Christian Scriptures, or the New Testament, were highly compressed in time of composition and event. Jesus died about 33 in the Christian era (C.E.), and the latest books of the New Testament date from no later than the early second century C.E. Except for the birth narratives and a childhood appearance in the Temple, the four gospels dealt with events in the adult teaching and ministry of Jesus over a period of three or four years. Acts, a continuation of Luke's gospel, described happenings of the disciples and early Church after the resurrection through Paul's summons to Rome. Paul's letters, the first written books of the New Testament dating from 50 C.E., provided virtually no additional details about the life and teachings of Jesus of Nazareth and emphasized, rather, his significance as messiah or Christ.[1]

The three synoptic gospels, Mark, Matthew, and Luke, and to a lesser extent John, provide the data available on Jesus and none of these writings

---

[1] General introductions to the New Testament include Howard Kee, *Understanding the New Testament* (1993), and Dennis Duling and Norman Perrin, *The New Testament, Proclamation and Parenesis, Myth and History* (1994).

conforms to the modern norms of what a biography or history should be. There was no tradition of "objective" history in the first century; rather, the books in the New Testament made religious claims and sought to persuade readers to become Christians. Followers of Jesus wrote the New Testament books to be of service to the early Church, and the churches found them useful, preserved them, and continued to be guided by them. The canonical New Testament contains some of the writings about Jesus and the early Church that later Christians saw as authoritative. The earliest surviving manuscripts of portions of the New Testament date from the turn of the third century.[2]

The New Testament, containing a record of the Church's understanding of Jesus, was written by Christians to guide those who sought salvation through Christ. The Church proclaimed that Jesus was the unique Son of God, sinless in all his thoughts and actions, the only redeemer of humanity, and the normative interpreter of God's will to mankind. The New Testament was the record of Jesus' first followers' seeking to understand the implications of the life, teachings, death, and resurrection of the man they called Lord. Because Jesus' life and teachings summarized the ethical pattern of life, the way he acted and what he said should determine the Christian responses to war and peace.

Because Jesus and his first disciples remained devout Jews and esteemed and lived by precepts in the Hebrew Scriptures, the Church would also esteem and utilize them, but it would reinterpret their meaning. The Hebrew Scriptures would become the Old Testament, and the Church cited the prophecies of the

---

[2]The writings in the Hebrew *Bible* received authoritative status over a long period, with copies of the Torah and Deuteronomy referred to in II Kings, the prophets accepted in final form during and after the Babylonian captivity, and the wisdom literature written before the Greek conquest. The final compilation occurred in the second century B.C.E. Not all parts of the Hebrew Scriptures have the same status in Judaism, and Jews stress a continuing revelation contained in a series of commentaries termed the *Mishna* and *Talmud*. Canonicity is a Christian term used to limit the number of sacred writings in the Old and New Testament. The twenty-seven books in the New Testament received canonical status - that is, were considered to be apostolic in origin, correct in doctrine, and of universal application for the Church – in the second century, but there were still disagreements between Western and Eastern Christianity until the fourth century.

Davidic lineage, of the messiah, his role as the suffering servant, and the redeemer of Israel to prove the unique status of Jesus. When by the time of the fall of Jerusalem in 70 C.E. it became clear that most Jews rejected belief in Jesus as the messiah, Christians insisted that the blessings of God's election once given to Israel now was transferred to the Church. So the history of Israel and its wars became the heritage of the Church, and Christians read the Old and New Testaments as the record of God's will for humanity and saw Jesus fulfilling the prophecies of the coming messianic age.

Our task in understanding the relation of Christianity to war and peace is to learn what in the gospels relates to these conditions, to see how the early Church interpreted those teachings, and how modern scholars have attempted to go behind both the Church's and the gospel writers' message to re-create the historical Jesus. Our purpose in understanding the New Testament is not religious; that is, there is a summary here of what the scriptures say about Jesus using the biblical text as our only source, but no evaluation of the claims the gospel writers made that Jesus was the messiah. This initial portrait of Jesus will be based upon the assumption, which was universal until the nineteenth century and is still the belief of many Christians, that the gospels were written either by the apostles (Matthew and John) or by those whose information came from those who knew Jesus firsthand (Luke and Mark), that Paul wrote all the epistles to which his name is attached, that the apostles James, Peter, and John wrote pastoral epistles and Revelation. Since the accounts in the four gospels emphasized different parts of Jesus' career, one task of traditional biblical exegesis was to harmonize them into a unified biography. The first section of this chapter uses the gospels as an eyewitness description of the life and teachings of Jesus. The next section will look at the views of scholars who argue that the gospel accounts were written by Christian authors years after the events relying upon oral and written traditions preserved by the Church.

Neither the traditional nor the recent study of the New Testament has led to agreement on the Christian view of war and peace, even among those who agree on methodology. Readers should remember that for our purposes the New Testament, like the Hebrew Scriptures, functions on various levels: as the only record of the formative events of one of the world's important religions, as an influence on later understanding of politics by both churchmen and warriors, and for millions of people today as the most important documents for determining ethically correct behavior; in short, as the way to discover the will of God.

II. The Kingdom Is Not of This World

The gospels proclaimed that Jesus came to bring peace. Jesus is identified as the person who fulfills Isaiah's prophecy of a messianic bringer of peace that is salvation. In addition, peace (Greek, *eirene*) carried the same multiplicity of meanings as in the Hebrew Scriptures: a greeting, a blessing, a condition of health, a relationship with neighbor, and a description of harmony with God. The Hebrew Scriptures also described peace as a condition of non-war among kingdoms. Whether peace in the New Testament continued to have a political connotation is one of the topics of this chapter, because the gospel writers - according to the traditional view - presented the kingdom of God as a spiritual entity.

In Luke the angels praised God to the shepherds saying "Glory to God in the highest, and on earth peace among men" (Luke 2:14). Luke uses the term "peace" fourteen times in order to indicate that peace is an essential attribute of the gospel brought by Jesus and offered to all those willing to accept it. Those who follow Jesus gain peace in this world and the next. Yet living in this condition of peace is also compatible with martyrdom, a paradox in which to lose one's life is to save it.

In Matthew, in the Sermon on the Mount, Jesus blessed the peacemakers. He told his followers to be merciful, to "Love your enemies and pray for those who persecute you." The Ten Commandments said, "You shall not kill." Jesus proclaimed that even one who was angry or insulted his brother was "liable to the hell of fire"(Matthew 5:9, 21-23). "You have heard that it was said, 'An eye for an eye and a tooth for a tooth.' But I say to you, Do not resist one who is evil.

But if anyone strikes you on the right cheek, turn to him the other also; and if anyone would sue you and take your coat, let him have your cloak as well, and if anyone forces you to go one mile, go with him two miles" (Matthew 5:38-42). In none of these commandments did Jesus directly discuss politics, say whether such activities he recommended were practical, or would have an effect on earthly success. The reward he promised was a religious blessing or life in heaven. Even so, the Church concluded that the Sermon on the Mount contained guidelines for Christian living down to the present.

On two occasions Jesus discussed paying taxes, clearly a political subject. After Peter was questioned as to whether Jesus paid the temple taxes, Jesus told Peter that in order to avoid offense he should go catch a fish. The fish would have a coin in its mouth that Peter could use to pay the tax for both Jesus and Peter. As a guide to policies on Roman taxation, the moral of this incident is not clear, but the story could be used to indicate Jesus' support for the Jewish temple authorities who were allowed by Rome to tax all Jews.

The other occasion occurred during the final week in Jesus' life. When, in the Temple in Jerusalem, the Pharisees and Herodians attempted to trap Jesus into rejecting payment of taxes unto Caesar, he asked for a coin and received a Roman denarius. Jesus asked his questioners whose image was on the coin. "Caesar's," they replied. Jesus retorted, "Give unto Caesar what belongs to Caesar; give unto God what belongs to God." This clever saying left the rulers of the Temple confused (Mark 12: 14-17). It may also do the same to us, since Jesus did not define what belonged to Caesar and what to God. This saying was as close as Jesus ever came to giving political advice. He provided no opinion on the legitimacy of Roman rule of Judea, but did have a sardonic view of the taxation policies of rulers of the earth and termed Herod Antipas, the son of King Herod and ruler of Galilee for Rome, "that Fox" (Luke 13:32).

Since Israel was part of the Roman Empire, Jews could not avoid contacts with Roman officials. John the Baptist instructed soldiers to "be content with your wages" (Luke 3:13). Jesus healed the daughter of a Roman centurion and commended the man's faith. In the garden of Gethsemane on the occasion of his arrest, when one of Jesus' followers took a sword and cut off a soldier's ear, Jesus healed the man and rebuked Peter: "Put your sword back into its place; for all who take the sword will perish by the sword" (Matthew 26:52). Jesus forecast his arrest and crucifixion, but made no effort to resist arrest or to counter the claims of his accusers either before the Jewish council or the Roman prefect, Pontius Pilate. In his ministry Jesus often criticized the Jewish authorities; Roman officials were not similarly singled out.

Throughout the gospels, Jesus proclaimed the coming of the kingdom of God. This kingdom was the reign of God, but it was not a political entity. Mark pictured Jesus, before beginning his public ministry, as going into the wilderness where he was tempted by Satan. One of the temptations rejected by Jesus was for worldly power and honor. In none of the four gospels was there any explicit discussion of government or political theory.

Jesus' reticence on politics contrasted with his teachings about the social and religious conditions of his day. He frequently condemned the wealthy, and advised the rich young ruler to give away all his goods to the poor. He associated with a tax collector who then returned his ill-gotten gains to the poor. In the Gospel of Luke Jesus compared a rich man gaining entrance to heaven to a camel going through the eye of a needle. A rich man who enjoyed a life of luxury but gave no charity to the poor neighbor was pictured suffering the torments of hell, but angels carried the beggar to enjoy the blessings of heaven. Luke's Jesus, born to a poor family in a manger and worshipped by poor shepherds, identified with the poor. In Matthew's Beatitudes, Jesus blessed the poor in spirit; in Luke, Jesus blessed the poor and announced "woe to you that are rich, for you have received your consolation" (Luke 6:20, 24).

The main opponents of Jesus in all the gospels were the Jewish religious leaders: the temple authorities in Jerusalem, the Sadducees, and the Pharisees. These men resented Jesus' attack upon their legalism, their hypocrisy, and what he depicted as false religion. They disliked his non-observance of the sabbath, his working of miracles, his claim to inaugurate the kingdom of God, his forgiving of sins, and his prophecy of the destruction of Jerusalem and the Temple. The popularity of Jesus with the Jewish people posed a threat to their religious power, and so the chief priests and temple hierarchy in Jerusalem and the members of the Jewish council, along with the Sadducees and Pharisees, plotted against Jesus.

When Jesus journeyed to Jerusalem to celebrate the Passover, the Jewish people on Palm Sunday acclaimed him as the messiah. They welcomed him in triumph in his entrance to the city and marveled at his wisdom in teaching. The gospels insist that the common people's understanding of his role was mistaken and that even the disciples did not grasp that Jesus' reign was to be as a heavenly, not an earthly, king.

In the final week of his life, Jesus visited the Temple and threw out the moneychangers and those selling sacrifices, complaining about the profanation of God's house. Jesus taught and acted with authority, but because he so often spoke in parables, his real status remained hidden. Still, the wisdom of his teaching confounded the religious authorities and attracted more followers. Jesus' popularity meant that the chief priests and the council could not arrest him openly. Finally, Judas Iscariot, one of the twelve disciples, betrayed Jesus for thirty pieces of silver. In a final supper with his disciples, Jesus again forecast his death and told his followers how to commemorate it. He also again prophesied his resurrection. The disciples still misunderstood and disputed about who was to be greatest in the coming kingdom. In a garden outside of Jerusalem, soldiers arrested Jesus who had been praying. He was brought before the high priests and elders in the council who listened to false charges. Then the high priest asked whether Jesus was "the Christ, the Son of the Blessed" and Jesus said, "I am, and you will see the Son of Man sitting at the right hand of Power, and coming with the clouds of heaven" (Mark 14:61-62). The chief priests, elders and scribes concluded that Jesus was guilty of blasphemy and deserved the death penalty. They then delivered him up to Pontius Pilate, the Roman prefect, who asked if Jesus was

"King of the Jews." Jesus made no answer. Pilate found no fault with Jesus, and even offered to the crowd to release either Jesus or Barabbas, who had committed murder during an insurrection. The crowd demanded the release of Barabbas, and Pilate, who washed his hands of responsibility, condemned Jesus to be scourged and then crucified.

Jesus was crucified between two thieves or bandits, and the Romans placed a tablet above him with the words "King of the Jews." Seeing Jesus' behavior and the wonders that accompanied the crucifixion (the darkness and the earthquake), the Roman centurion in charge realized that "Truly this man was a son of God." Jesus having died on the cross and been put into a tomb on Friday, Mary Magdalene and another Mary discovered the empty tomb on Sunday and encountered the risen Christ. Jesus appeared to various disciples who now believed that he was the messiah.

According to the traditional interpretation, Jesus in his life, death, and resurrection was an apolitical figure. His kingdom was a spiritual kingdom, and the ethic he preached concerned the reign of God, not the reign of Caesar. Everyone misunderstood the nature of his ministry until after the resurrection. Jesus was crucified because he opposed the abuses in Jewish religion, and the Romans along with the high priests, scribes, and Pharisees bore responsibility for his death.

The spiritualized Jesus of the New Testament stood in striking contrast to the violence that permeated the gospels. The angels proclaimed peace, but after the visit of the magi to Jerusalem, King Herod, in an effort to destroy the newborn king of Israel, killed all the infants under three years of age living in Bethlehem. It was the first example of the authorities' misunderstanding of Jesus' spiritual reign. Years later Herod Antipas, the son of King Herod, had John the Baptist beheaded. Jesus told his followers to expect persecution and insisted that ever since the preaching of John "the kingdom of heaven has suffered violence, and men of violence take it by force." When Jesus approached Jerusalem, "He wept" over the future of the city, saying "Would that even today you knew the things that make for peace ... For the days shall come upon you, and hem you in on every side, and dash you to the ground, you and your children within you, and they will not leave one stone upon another" (Luke 19:41-44).

In a crowd which had come to see Jesus were some "who told him of the Galileans whose blood Pilate had mingled with their sacrifices" (Luke 13:1), i.e., men who had been killed by the Roman authorities in Jerusalem. A disciple, during the last week of Jesus' ministry, carried a sword into the Garden of Gethsemane, evidently seeing no incompatibility with following Jesus and bearing arms. He was willing to use the sword to defend Jesus from arrest. Luke recorded that when instructing the disciples at the time of the Last Supper, Jesus said, "And let him who has no sword sell his mantle and buy one ... And they said, 'Look, Lord, here are two swords.' And he said to them, 'It is ... enough' (Luke 22:36-38). In Matthew, Jesus preached, "Do not think that I have come to bring peace on earth; I have not come to bring peace, but a sword" (Matthew 10:34). The context was the cost of discipleship, and Jesus brought disruption in the household and required placing love of himself above father, mother, wife, or child.

The conclusion of those accepting the eyewitness version of the gospels is that in a violent age, Jesus taught, healed, forgave sins, and demonstrated that his messianic powers threatened no political realm. His kingdom was to be God's rule in earth and heaven, and by his death and resurrection he demonstrated a hope for an eternal life. Over the centuries, agreement on the implication of a spiritual apolitical Jesus for Christian views of war has been elusive. Some traditional exegetes see Jesus as a pacifist; others see non-participation in the military as part of a counsel of perfection observed by priests or monks but not practical for daily existence in this imperfect world. Jesus' ethic in the Sermon on the Mount then is interpreted as one of intention, not specific actions. Since no one can be perfect, Jesus wanted his followers to do their best, and they could rest assured that their failures would not interfere with salvation through God's grace. An alternative interpretation stressed Jesus' example of resisting evil and his command to love thy neighbor. A Christian, who would willingly accept his own martyrdom, may be required to show his love of neighbor by taking the sword to defend him. After all, Jesus nowhere specifically condemned a soldier's life. Among traditional exegetes there is agreement that the gospels present an accurate portrait of Jesus, but the sparsity of comments on politics and war allow for substantial variation in interpretation of whether the gospels condemn war or allow war in order to achieve peace.

III. The Historical Context

Most non-fundamentalist New Testament scholars today do not believe eyewitnesses or men who had firsthand knowledge of Jesus wrote the gospels of Matthew, Mark, Luke, and John. These writers were Jewish and Gentile converts of the Church whose primary language was Greek. Paul's letters to various churches are the other major component of the New Testament. Paul made no claim to having known personally the human Jesus of Nazareth and included few biographical details, but boasted of his encounter with the spiritual risen Christ. The first of Paul's letters, the earliest writing in the New Testament, dates from around 50 C.E. or twenty years after the crucifixion. The Gospel of Mark was probably written about the time of the fall of Jerusalem in 66-70 C.E.; Matthew and Luke date from around 100; John came somewhat later, perhaps 115. Matthew and Luke had read Mark's gospel, but not each other's. Both also used a now lost early summary of Jesus' teachings, termed Q, though whether Q was a written document or oral tradition remains controversial. The sources for the gospel writers were the stories about Jesus' life and teachings preserved by the early Church. Each gospel writer had specific theological or religious agendas, and he interpreted the traditions in light of the Church's needs at the time he was writing. All knew the story ended with the creation of the Church, and so interpreted the teaching and life of Jesus in terms of the post-resurrection faith. Because the gospels differ on many issues, recreating an agreed-upon summary of chronology, actions, and teachings is virtually impossible. Rather, each gospel writer must be considered in isolation in order to assess his viewpoint as well as comparatively to see what all agreed upon. A second task of contemporary New Testament scholarship is to distinguish different layers of tradition used by these writer/editors in order better to understand the historical Jesus and the evolution of the early Church.

Modern scholars insist that the first part of the gospel tradition written was the passion narrative; accounts of Jesus' final week of life, trial, and execution make up nearly one-third of the gospels. All the gospel writers agreed that Romans executed Jesus, even though all shift some or all responsibility to the Jewish regional council. Jewish courts may have had the right to inflict the death penalty, but in such cases the manner of execution was stoning. The Romans reserved crucifixion for serious criminals, often those guilty of political offenses, because it was a particularly heinous form of death.

The Roman authorities had reason to be worried about religious/political messianic figures. Rome had conquered Israel relatively easily in 63 B.C.E., snuffing out the quasi-independent Hasmonean or Maccabean dynasty. Rome ruled either indirectly through appointed puppet kings and governors, like Herod and his sons, or directly through consuls or prefects like Pontius Pilate. Roman sources indicate that Pilate was prefect from 26-36 C.E. and that he earned notoriety for arbitrary justice. Jesus would have been under direct Roman justice only when he was in Judea. Most of Jesus' ministry occurred in Galilee, which was ruled by a son of King Herod, Herod Antipas, who went to Jerusalem for the Passover, and Pilate, according to Luke, turned Jesus over to him. Herod questioned and scourged Jesus before returning him to Pilate.

Judea was under direct Roman rule, with a garrison of soldiers in Jerusalem, and the countryside seethed with revolt. John Crossan, a Jesuit scholar, analyzing peasant unrest in early Roman Palestine, listed seven cases of protest, ten cases of prophets, eleven instances of bandits, and five messiahs. These disturbances could be religious, political, or social, or all three, and could be directed solely against Rome or against the social conditions prevailing in Israel. The messiahs claimed to pattern themselves after King Saul or David, proclaimed themselves Israel's kings, formed religious and political leadership, gained substantial followings, invoked the traditions of holy war, and succeeded for a brief time in driving out the Romans. The messiah could begin as a bandit, serve as a focus for agrarian unrest, and through charisma become identified as God's anointed. In 4 B.C.E. after the death of King Herod, Judas of Galilee led a major revolt that was brutally suppressed, with 2000 of his followers being crucified. Since the crosses remained by the roadside for years, the boy Jesus could have seen them. Zealots or bandits led various disturbances throughout the period in which Jesus was alive. The Galileans whose blood Pilate shed could have been engaged in a revolt or political disturbance.[3]

Eventually, in 67-73 C.E., about thirty years after the death of Jesus, in a major revolution, several messianic claimants seized Jerusalem, purified the Temple, and executed the high priests as Roman collaborators. The Jews fought each other as well as Rome, showing that the struggle was internal class warfare as well as opposition to foreign rule. The Jews had success at first, taking control of Jerusalem as well as much of the surrounding countryside. After a long siege, Rome recaptured Jerusalem, destroyed the Temple, burned the city, exacted a bloody vengeance on the populace, and dispersed the people. Jerusalem ceased to be a Jewish city. Still, discontent continued, and in 113-115 and 132-135 C.E. the Jews rose again. There was again a messianic claimant in this final attempt to throw off the Roman yoke.

The writings of the pro-Roman Jewish historian Josephus contain the most detailed analysis of the Jewish uprising of 67 C.E. Josephus' accounts made clear that there were basic conflicts in Palestine within Judaism over the interpretation of scriptures, observances of the law, and relations with Rome. Josephus, who was writing for a Roman audience, enumerated the rivalries between the various Jewish groups: the Sadducees, who controlled the Temple, denied the resurrection of the body, and insisted upon strict observance of the law; the Essenes, who withdrew into the wilderness and preached repentance; and

---

[3]John Dominic Crossan, *The Historical Jesus: The Life of a Mediterranean Jewish Peasant* (1991), 168-224. 451-52.

the Pharisees, the group whose interpretation of the observance of the laws and resurrection of the body seems similar to what the gospels tell of Jesus' attitudes. Two of these groups, the Sadducees and Pharisees, are mentioned in the New Testament. Josephus also talked about bandits or zealots who worked for the overthrow of Rome.[4] Josephus did not mention the Jewish community at Qumran whose writings, now termed as the Dead Sea scrolls, were discovered in a cave in 1948. The Qumran community was a sect of Judaism that had withdrawn from temple worship in Jerusalem because of alleged corruption. The Qumran scrolls show a group practicing strict discipline, contempt for outsiders, and belief in the imminence of apocalyptic war. More recently, the excavations of Sepphoris, a town the Romans were building at the time Jesus grew up in Nazareth only four and a half miles away, indicate the presence of Greek-Roman ideas, and a Hellenized Judaism.[5] So Jesus may have known Hebrew, Aramaic, and even some Greek. What seems clear is that in the first centuries there were many Judaisms or, more accurately, that the Jews had enormous variations in beliefs and practices, and to outsiders like the Romans, Jesus and his followers would have seemed just another sectarian group.

In ancient Israel religious and political authorities often shared power. The Romans relied upon local authorities to control the people, and in Judea the chief priests and scribes mediated between the occupation forces and the Jews. The high priests in Jerusalem cooperated with the Romans so that worship in the Temple could be carried on. The Romans did not interfere with religious observances in areas they controlled, and the Roman authorities allowed the

---

[4]Flavus Josephus, *History of the Jewish Wars* (C.E. 75-79) and *Jewish Antiquities*. A discussion of the difficulties in determining the accuracy of conflicting accounts provided by Josephus is in Crossan, 92-98. John Meier, *A Marginal Jew: Rethinking The Historical Jesus* (1991), I, chapters 2-6 is an excellent introduction to the sources biblical scholars use in defining the historical Jesus.
[5]The archeological evidence can support various interpretations. King Herod rebuilt the Temple in Jerusalem, but his capital Caesara Martima shows pervasive Roman influence including a temple to the goddess Roma and Augustus. The city of Sepphoris built by Herod Antipas shows more appreciation of Jewish sensibilities. Nazareth was a poor village of a few houses. John Crossan and Jonathan Reed, *Excavating Jesus: Beneath the Stones, Behind the Texts* (2001), 56, 62, 64-66.

Temple priesthood to levy a tax to support worship at the Temple. Jewish religious courts handled many offenses involving both religious and secular affairs. Any challenge to the Temple hierarchy could easily be broadened to include the Roman authority. Having seen the power and cruelty of Rome, the religious leaders in Jerusalem might wish to make sure that no revolution occurred. Wealthy landowners, tax collectors, and merchants would oppose any prophet who criticized their manner of living and mobilized the people against them. A careful reading of Josephus, the Apocrypha, and the gospels shows that there was reason for the Romans to worry about Jesus of Nazareth.

IV. The Politics of Jesus

The gospel narratives show that Jesus enjoyed great support among the people and that he criticized abuses in the Temple worship, upbraided the religious authorities, and attempted during the final week of his life to reform practices in the Temple. The synoptic gospels do not portray the disciples as a very perceptive group. Even after prolonged exposure to Jesus' teachings and miracles, the disciples misunderstood his mission and reinterpreted his significance after his death and resurrection. During his lifetime, Jesus was identified as a teacher, a prophet, Elijah, and a magician. There was speculation that he might be the long-awaited messiah, a member of the Davidic lineage, a king of Israel. Jesus may have encouraged such speculation and claimed to be a messiah. At the least, his actions were such that after his death and resurrection, his followers proclaimed him the messiah.

The Jews had long sought for a religious/political figure to liberate them from oppression, and there were several models as to what this messiah would be. He could be like Judas Maccabeus, a man of conspicuous piety and a military leader. The Maccabean revolt had as its goals a purifying of the Temple, throwing out of corrupt high priests, a re-invigorating of religious life, expelling the foreign oppressor, and instituting national independence under a king dedicated to the reign of God. Jesus' denunciation of the priestly hierarchy in Jerusalem, his prophecy of the destruction of the Temple, and his symbolic cleansing of the Temple could all be interpreted as messianic acts.

An alternative form of deliverance would come through apocalyptic war as described in Daniel, a book cited in the gospels and especially in Matthew. Here a heavenly figure, a son of God, often also called the Son of Man, would lead the angels in the war against the forces of evil. Their victory over evil would lead to a resurrection of the dead and a final day of judgment for humans. The term "Son of Man" is used forty times in the gospels, sometimes by Jesus and also to refer to him. In addition, Jesus used apocalyptic language to describe the destruction of Jerusalem (Luke 21) and to enforce ethical norms. At the final judgment, the separation of the good from the bad would be based upon giving charity to the poor; "inasmuch as you have done it unto the least of My brethren, you have done it unto Me" {i.e., Jesus} (Matthew 25:40). A consistent theme in the preaching of both John the Baptist and Jesus was the imminence of the kingdom of God, referred to forty times in the gospels (Matthew 24). The Lord's Prayer, for example, says, "Thy kingdom come; Thy will be done on earth ..." (Matthew 6:10). The kingdom meant God's direct rule over his people, and the messiah was to inaugurate this rule. What is currently much debated by New Testament scholars is whether Jesus saw himself as essentially a Jewish apocalyptic prophet proclaiming the last days and his own role as "Son of Man" in them, or whether the early Church after the death and resurrection applied the prophecies of Daniel to Jesus.[6]

Jesus' popularity, his denunciation of the religious authorities, his proclamation of the coming kingdom, the messianic claim made either by his followers or by Jesus himself would have been sufficient for the Romans to fear an armed insurrection. The authorities acted after the events of Holy Week. Jesus' entrance into Jerusalem on a donkey with his followers spreading their

---

[6]Paula Fredriksen, *From Jesus to Christ: The Origins of the New Testament Images of Jesus* (1988), 98-102, 112-13, 125-30.

garments and leafy branches on the road fulfilled a messianic prophecy, so also did his cleansing the Temple, claiming the authority to heal the sick, and forgiving sins. Finally, there was the previously mentioned dispute in the Temple over paying taxes to Caesar in which Jesus said, "Render unto Caesar the things that are Caesar's and to God the things that are God's" (Mark: 12:13-17).

Virtually all scholars insist that this saying is authentic. A recent archaeological discovery of denari in Palestine shows that this particular coin was in general circulation.[7] The inscription to Caesar asserted that he was a god; the other side had the portrait of a Roman deity. Both sides of the coin were idolatrous and symbolic of Roman imperialism. To carry such a coin would be to profane the Temple. If for Jesus' questioners to produce such a coin showed their ill will and subservience to Rome, for him to assert "give unto God what belongs to God" was to claim that all Israel belonged to God. Jesus, therefore, was denying the legitimacy of Roman rule. No wonder the Romans arrested and executed Jesus. Here was a popular leader, considered by many to be a potential messiah, at a celebration of a Passover feast commemorating God's past deliverance of Israel from Egyptian slavery, showing the temple authorities to be Roman dupes, perhaps also advocating non-payment of taxes. Was Jesus also calling for revolution? And if he envisaged a new order, how was it to come about?

Scholars who dispute the portrait of Jesus as an apocalyptic prophet also cite the coin story. For them, Jesus was a wandering teacher of wisdom, a person whose style of life was like Greek cynic philosophers who sought to provoke thought by phrasing questions in a new way. Here Jesus is a wise person who broke down social barriers by associating with all sorts of people.[8] All three gospels use the coin story as a dispute in which Jesus confounds hostile questioners by making the issue deeply relevant, and none spell out any political

[7] F. F. Bruce, "Render to Caesar," *Jesus and the Politics of His Day* (1984), 249-265.
[8] Crossan, 421.

implications for the answer. So Jesus' distinction between God and Caesar was not a call to revolt or an attack upon the temple hierarchy, but a clever debater's attempt to force both questioners and listeners to consider what were the legitimate claims of God and Caesar. The image on the coin was Caesar's; humans were made in the image of God. What are the implications for human behavior of being made in the image of God? No wonder that the authorities were confused and the people amazed at Jesus' subtlety.

V. Jesus and War

For the later Christian community searching the gospels for divine guidance on issues of war and peace one issue is crucial: did Jesus advocate political violence, resistance, or pacifism? Was the kingdom of God to be initiated by an apocalyptic war? Were his practices and teachings congruent? Did the Gentile writers of the gospel understand the social/religious situation in Jerusalem? Did the disciples and the early Church understand Jesus' ethics? Does the present form of the gospel present an accurate image? What did John the Baptist and Jesus mean when they proclaimed that the kingdom of God was at hand? There likely never will be a scholarly consensus on the answers to these questions.

The issue of the historical Jesus' attitude towards war can be determined only by a decision as to the reliability and the meaning of the writings in the New Testament. The gospel writers proclaimed that Jesus was innocent of the crimes for which he was crucified. Some scholars have asked if they had reason to distort the record. Their answer is yes. The early Church proclaimed that Jesus was the messiah, the Son of God, risen from the dead. A salient feature of Jesus' life was that he was crucified as a Jewish rebel. The Church wanted to present Jesus as attractively as possible to Gentiles (i.e., non-Jews): playing down the Roman element in Jesus' trial and emphasizing Jewish opposition to him served this purpose. After the major Jewish revolt from A.D. 67 to 73, the center of Christianity moved from Jerusalem to Gentile cities. The Gentiles would not be attracted to an earlier unsuccessful Jewish religious/political leader. None of the writers of the synoptic gospels knew Jesus, and so they may not have grasped all the political significance of the sayings and stories about Jesus preserved in the traditions of the early Church. The Gospel of Mark, written after the destruction of Jerusalem, had to convince Romans that Jesus was not just another Jewish rebel or one of many messianic claimants. The resulting picture of Jesus' ministry played down the political context and made the kingdom of God purely spiritual. So Mark's Jesus threatened neither Roman Judea nor the continuing power of Rome. The later-written gospels increased the continued emphases on the Jewish responsibility for Jesus' crucifixion. Compared with the Gospel of Mark, for example, both Matthew and Luke were less sympathetic to Jewish leaders and more pro-Roman. In Luke Pontius Pilate not only washed his hands of responsibility for Jesus' sentence, but he did not even pronounce sentence. By the time John wrote, Jesus' controversies are not with selected chief priests and Pharisees (some of whom other gospels portray as sympathetic to him) but with "the Jews." This divorcing of Jesus from his Jewishness and making the Jews solely responsible for his trial and execution ("His blood be on us and on our children" Matthew 27:25) served to differentiate a new Christianity from an emergent Pharisaic Judaism as both traditions sought to legitimate themselves through an appropriation of the Hebrew Scriptures. The gospel accent on Jewish plotting to kill the Son of God also provided a scriptural warrant for the constant anti-semitism that has haunted Christianity's relationship with Judaism.

VI. Millennialist or Revolutionary?

Many scholars insist that the central core of Jesus' message was that the kingdom of God was at hand; humans were living in the final days and should prepare for the end.[9] In assessing the relation of Jesus' teachings on the final days, there are four distinct issues: was Jesus a millennialist and did the early Church continue his teaching; did the early Church create the millennial emphasis in an effort to understand Jesus' role as messiah; is millennialism anti-political; must

---

[9] The classic statement of the eschatological core of Jesus' teaching is Albert Schweitzer, *The Quest for the Historical Jesus* (1907). Stressing the eschatological core of Jesus' teachings has

millenialism be violent? Those scholars who emphasize Jesus' eschatology insist that he designed his ethical teachings on loving enemies not for a political realm, but for a community of his followers who were to wait expectantly during an interim period until the war in heaven occurred. Humans need do nothing in this heavenly war. Jesus allegedly provided no specific instructions on political actions during this time of troubles; rather, he exhorted his disciples on how to endure, and to expect their reward in heaven. He saw either himself or another heavenly figure (a Son of Man) coming to lead the forces of good because the kingdom of God was a supernatural creation that would mark the end of human time and the creation of God's realm of peace. Jesus' actions, therefore, can be used neither as support nor denial for political war.

A few scholars claim that Jesus was a political and religious revolutionary.[10] He attacked directly the leadership of Israel and the Romans. The gospel writers, who were attempting to appeal to Gentile converts, either did not understand or consciously played down the political aspect of his career, but preserved and incorporated in the present gospels is an early tradition of statements about war, carrying a sword, and violent actions. The Romans were not mistaken; Jesus in his final week claimed to be the messiah who would lead his people in revolution. An armed uprising would also bring Yahweh's direct intervention again in Israel's history. Jesus, like Judas Maccabeus, would be a new Joshua. The ambiguity in the Hebrew Scriptures' teachings on holy war reappeared in Jesus. That is, either Jesus' and his followers' violent acts could begin the process, or God alone could usher in the final days, or God's actions would follow Jesus' proclamation, the repentance of the people, and a few symbolic deeds. In this scenario neither Jesus nor his followers had to take

---

become characteristic of biblical exegesis in this century. An excellent summary of the issues is in John Meier, *A Marginal Jew*, II, all of chapters 14-16, and particularly 348-51 and 451-54.
[10]S. G. F. Brandon, *Jesus and the Zealots: A Study of the Political Factors in Primitive Christianity* (1967); Oscar Cullman, *Jesus and the Revolutionaries* (1970).

violent actions to initiate the parousia. Either way, God's response to the violent evil of his day was to bring violent good and, thereby, usher in the millennium of peace.

An alternative modern interpretation agrees that Jesus was a revolutionary, but insists that Jesus radically reformulated what God's rule over Israel might mean.[11] His demands on his followers undermined the legitimacy of temple and state and would create a new form of society. His attacks upon wealthy landowners, the law courts, and his emphasis upon love of neighbor, service to enemies, and the value of the poor were to bring about a nonviolent transformation of society. The kingdom of God was already present, and Jesus sought to actualize it among the poor who were his followers. The kingdom was also a future reality, and the person of Jesus linked the present and future rule of God. God's rule would bring a political revolution, but Jesus by preaching a new ethic was inaugurating a social revolution. Richard Horsley argues that Jesus was nonviolent, but to term him a pacifist is incorrect. The Sermon on the Mount contained an ethic binding upon his followers, but it was not about politics. The liberation Jesus promised to his followers was spiritual and social. Politics were not discussed because the spiritual and social transformation would make them irrelevant. Jesus was not a realistic politician, but he was a servant of God. His example and teachings were one, and he both preached and practiced denunciation of wrong, living of good, and loving of enemies.

Finally, some modern scholars argue that theological agendas of the gospel writers did not distort their picture of Jesus and that the conclusions of traditional Christians on the non-political nature of God's kingdom are right. John Howard Yoder, a Mennonite theologian, insisted that Jesus was a non-resistant pacifist

---

[11]Richard Horsley, *Jesus and the Spiral of Violence* (1987), 318-326; Richard J. Cassidy, *Jesus, Politics, and Society: A Study of Luke's Gospel* (1978); John Ferguson, *Politics of Love: The New Testament and Non-Violent Revolution* (1973).

who rejected an appeal to physical violence.[12] Jesus did not provide political counsel or advocate a violent revolution, but neither were his teachings restricted to a purely spiritual realm. In his precepts and in his attitudes to the Romans, Jesus practiced love of enemies while resisting evil and his followers sought to imitate his life, even to suffer martyrdom to create the kingdom of God. The kingdom that Jesus proclaimed and that his disciples continued put people, priests, and kings under the reign of God. Caesar's realm could continue to exist because God could use it to fulfill his purposes. God through Jesus liberated humans from sin and death and brought the possibility of eternal life with God. The ethic in the New Testament is confidence in God and love of neighbor, which will create a community of peace. Neither by precept nor example is war endorsed.

The possibilities for agreement among modern scholars on the precise meaning of Jesus' teachings on war and peace seem remote. All serious scholars have access to the same documents and a major discovery of new sources seems unlikely.[13] Unfortunately, gaps in historical knowledge do not disappear because of what contemporaries want to know. Considering the sources available on other figures of the ancient world, Jesus is well documented. The Church preserved the information it thought important, and we operate within those limits.

VII. The Early Church's Understanding of War and Peace

In the New Testament politics, war, and peace are discussed in epistles of Paul, the epistle of James and Revelation. These writings provide evidence as to

---

[12]John Howard Yoder, *The Politics of Jesus: Vicit, Agnus Noster* (1972); C. J. Cadoux, *Early Christian Attitudes to War: A Contribution to the History of Ethics* (1940); G. H. C. Macgregor, *The New Testament Basis of Pacifism* (1936); Martin Hengel, *Was Jesus a Revolutionist?* tr. William Klassen (1971); Perry Yoder and Willard Swartley, eds., *Meaning of Peace: Biblical Studies* (1992).

[13]There is new evidence from archeological excavations in Israel, Gnostic texts like the "Gospel of Thomas," and the writings of the Qumran community labeled "Dead Sea Scrolls." Crossan and Reed, *Excavating Jesus*, 172-79 integrate new archeological findings with textual criticism. They argue that against a process of Romanization resulting in commercialization and increasing disparity between rich and poor, Jesus sought a nonviolent transformation of a covenanted society emphasizing communal sharing and social justice. The Romans executed only Jesus and not his disciples because they considered him a minor and not a violent threat.

how the early Church dealt with these subjects. Paul gave advice similar to the Beatitudes about loving one another, repaying evil with good, and living peacefully with all, but with a different conclusion. "Vengeance is mine, I will repay, says the Lord" (Romans 12:20). Paul required paying taxes to the Romans, for all authority came from God, and "he who resists the authorities resists God." The magistrate is "the servant of God to execute his wrath on the wrongdoer" (Romans: 13:1-6). The same emphasis upon being "submissive to authorities" and to avoid quarreling appears in the pseudo-Pauline epistle to Titus, and here the context is clearly on behavior within the Church. Although Paul did not discuss political war, he (and those who wrote in his name, such as the author of Ephesians) used military metaphors in describing faith. Christians were to "Put on the whole armor of God" so that they could resist the "wiles of the devil." Fortified with the "breastplate of righteousness," "the shield of faith," "helmet of salvation," and (in spite of the mixed metaphor) having feet "shod" "with the equipment of the gospel of peace," a believer would be able to withstand the "spiritual hosts of wickedness" (Ephesians 6:10-17). The context is clearly apocalyptic war. Paul associated the imminent return of Christ with the final battle against evil and last judgment.

The Acts of the Apostles, which many scholars believe was written as a continuation of the Gospel of Luke, shows violence to Christians by Jewish authorities (the stoning of Stephen), converts from and conflict with Jews living in diaspora, and an uneasy relationship with Roman and Jewish authorities, but does not discuss war.

However, the story of Ananias and Sapphira parallels the account of Achan in Joshua. The early Church initially practiced a form of communism in which converts donated all their property to the Church, a practice similar to what went on in the Qumran community. Ananias and his wife sold property and allegedly gave the proceeds to the church, but kept some back. How Peter learns about this deception *Acts* does not say. When Peter confronts Ananias who lies, the apostle denounces him as under Satan's rule. Ananias dies and the body is carted away. A short time later Sapphira comes and has a similar confrontation about the property with Peter who informs her that her husband has just died. She also dies. Acts does not indicate the manner of death, but it seems clear that the Holy Spirit of God is responsible.[14] The parallels between Achan's violation of God's ban on war spoils and Ananias' voluntary contribution are not exact; the Hebrews put Achan and his family to death. For our purposes one lesson is clear: in the Ananias story there is no clear contrast between a humanitarian New Testament God and a judging Old Testament Jehovah. For the early Church, the God of Holy War is the same God who exercises apocalyptic judgment.

The New Testament frequently refers to disputes within the Church, but the solution advocated is not death but forgiveness and tolerance. Paul's paean to love in I Corinthians is one of the most famous passages in Scripture. James (4:1-4) argues, "What causes wars, and what causes fighting among you? Is it not your passions that are at war in your members? You desire and do not have; so you kill. And you covet and cannot obtain; so you fight and wage war." It is unlikely that James here referred to political war; the more likely context was passionate conflicts within the Church. James rebuked Christians who wished their ill-clad brethren "peace," but did nothing to clothe them. The wisdom from God is "first pure, then peaceable, gentle, open to reason . . . " (James 3:17).

The final book in the New Testament, the Revelation of John, dealt extensively with apocalyptic war. Traditionally this John was identified with the apostle of Jesus, but modern scholars date Revelation from the time of Roman persecution. Like the contents of the book of Daniel, the visions in Revelation were in graphic but cryptic language and spelled out a blueprint of the future time of troubles of plague, famine, and war, followed by a time of peace. "Now war arose in heaven, Michael and his angels fighting against the dragon, and the dragon and his angels fought, but they were defeated" (Revelation 7:8). And a blasphemous beast "was allowed to make war on the saints and to conquer them.

---

[14]Luke Timothy Johnson, *Acts of Apostles* (1992), 87-93

And authority was given it over every tribe and people" (13:7). As in earlier apocalyptic visions, the separation of the pure from apostates was a prominent theme. Those who faced persecution or were martyred and held true to the faith would see the wrath of God poured out on the forces of evil while the saints put on white robes and worshipped at the throne of God. Revelation juxtaposed descriptions of horrendous conditions on earth with the final victory of the Lord.

The leader of the heavenly host, termed "King of Kings and Lord of Lords" wore "a robe dipped in blood," a clear reference to Jesus Christ. But the Lord here was no passive resister who turned the other cheek; rather he was a leader of the "armies of heaven," and "from his mouth issues a sharp sword with which to smite the nations, and he will rule them with a rod of iron; he will tread the wine press of the fury of the wrath of God the Almighty" (Revelation 19:13-17). Paul in *Romans* had insisted that earthly authority came from God; Revelation identified earthly kingdoms with the reign of the anti-Christ. Christians should follow God, not Caesar, but in the final book of the *Bible* taking the sword is the prerogative of the heavenly host. In the final days, God will wage war on earth against supernatural forces of evil, but the Christians will be spared and join Christ in a New Jerusalem.

A normal reaction to the maze of scriptural texts and interpretations presented in these first two chapters would be to ask: why do I need to know this? An answer is that the complexities within the text have allowed Christianity to survive and influence behavior in a multitude of social contexts, to be a force for war and for peace and for right conduct in battle. Those who wish to see their actions as ethical can easily find a text or interpretation to suit their purpose - whether their goal is saintliness, worldly power, absolution from guilt, or a combination of motives difficult to unpack. Political and religious authorities have often assured their followers that there is a simple Christian attitude to war and peace: believe and do what we tell you is right.

Even if the reader should conclude that Jesus never addressed the issues arising from political war, he or she is still confronted with ethical dilemmas. Does an interpretation of the Kingdom of God as a spiritual realm mean that there can be no religious response to war? Or can one extrapolate from the life and teachings of Jesus an ethic that can be applied to war? This has been the normal response of the Church. Throughout Christian history, the various texts and traditions have allowed an ongoing debate on the permissibility for those who follow Jesus to participate in war.[15] The New Testament is clear that peace – in the Church, in the society, and with God – is the goal, but is using violence a necessary means or a betrayal of the ultimate purpose?

---

[15]The conclusions of scholars of the *Bible* often reflect their positions in society or views of human nature. For example, Roman Catholic priests are not to shed blood and therefore do not serve in the army, except as chaplains. Pacifism in the late nineteenth and early twentieth centuries was associated with an optimistic view of humanity as basically good or whose evil could be overcome by grace or Christian love. Those who stressed the pervasive power of sin and were more pessimistic about the power of good to overcome evil in society tended to accept the necessity of the military. Another variable has been the extent to which the tradition justified the political power of Christians. In general, those sects least interested in political power, like the Anabaptists, have been pacifists. Roman Catholics, Lutherans, and Calvinists have downplayed anti-war implications of the New Testament.

III.
The Greeks and War

Imagine being a tourist in modern Athens. When you go outside the hotel in the early morning, the first sight is the sun rising on the Acropolis, a mountain fortress in which the primary temple, the Parthenon, arguably the most beautiful building in the world, is dedicated to Athena, chaste goddess of wisdom and war participant in the *Iliad*. The Parthenon still symbolizes the most creative period of Western civilization when Athens with a population less than 250,000 produced exquisite architecture, sculpture, and drama, and gave birth to modern ideas of philosophy, political theory, and historical writing.

The Greeks even shaped our understanding of the value of athletic competition; for example, we still use the Greek terms -- discus, marathon, gymnastics, and Olympics. The Olympic ideal of competition among the best athletes of all nations stems from the ancient Greek festival at Olympia where men from many city-states gathered to show their prowess by racing and throwing a spear, skills that were also useful in war.

The ancient Olympics required a truce or suspension of war among the independent and autonomous Greek states, because religion, culture and language, not political unity, bound the Hellenes together. The Panhellenic ideal asserted cultural identity among the Greeks that might bring them together in time of crisis, but their political rivalries resulted in frequent wars and debate on characteristics necessary for success in battle.

The Greeks shaped Western civilization by adding ethical and literary vocabulary to the biblical perspectives on war and peace. We still employ the concepts the Greeks used in dealing with war: honor, glory, fame, heroism, natural law, just and unjust war, war for the sake of peace. Their legacy contained an exaltation and a critique of war. In addition, some credit the Greeks with inventing the Western way of war, a strategy of risking heavy casualties for a decisive battle. Peace, however, received little attention. This chapter examines Greek contributions on war and peace through four genres: the epic poetry of Homer, the history of Thucydides, the drama of Aristophanes and Euripides, and philosophy of Plato, Aristotle, and the Stoics. The questions these authors posed are perennial: if the gods decree victory and defeat, what do such actions show about the character of the gods? What is the effect of war on people? Is there a distinction among civilizations that legitimates war? What makes a war just?

I. The *Iliad:* Heroism and War

The *Iliad* is an epic poem about war, heroism, death, and the gods. Composed as early as the eighth century B.C.E. in oral form by a poet known to the ancients as Homer, and about whom there is no certain biographical information, only a tradition that he was blind, the poem was written down by the seventh century B.C.E. The poem describes a few incidents in the ten-year war between the Achaeans and their allies (who inhabited modern day Greece although the term "Greeks" was never used in the poem) and the Trojans who lived in today's Turkey. Whether orally recited from memory or read aloud, the listeners were expected to remember the causes of the war and its outcome. They also knew the myths about the gods, so originality in the plot was not the essence of the epic. Rather, Homer intermingled myth and history into a compelling portrait of a heroic age in which the gods, children of the gods, and humans interacted.

The *Iliad*, often ranked with Shakespeare as the greatest literature of the West, had immense influence on shaping Greek and then Roman ideas in religion, drama, and philosophy. For example, Virgil's *Aeneid,* an epic like the *Iliad,* claimed that the Romans descended from refugees of Troy. Homer also pioneered many of the literary conventions used ever since in the portrayal of war. The *Iliad* was not a sacred book to the Greeks, but its stories of the gods and humans in the battle for Troy are second only to the *Bible* in shaping western attitudes towards soldiers and war.[1]

The Greek gods of the *Iliad* bear little resemblance to the Lord God of the Hebrews. Homer's gods are like physically perfect immortal humans who eat, drink, marry, quarrel, have sex, bear children, and experience emotions of love, jealousy, and rage. Homer treats the gods with reverence, because they are more powerful than men and can bring harm if left unacknowledged, but they also provide comic relief from the drama of the war. In a way they are like cartoon characters, because the gods could be disappointed temporally, but nothing bad can harm them. They watch humans, intervene in their affairs, reward and punish them, respond to their prayers and devotion, but also ignore them. People can cause gods to suffer at least temporary anguish, but human action also serves as a spectator sport to keep the gods from boredom. Neither consistency nor morality characterizes the gods who from their dwelling in Mount Olympus buffet humans by their fickleness and conflicts. The *Iliad* juxtaposes the feasting and joy of the gods with the bitterness of human existence.

At a cosmic level, the gods cause the Trojan War, determine its duration, and select the victims and winners. Once Zeus has decided the outcome, no prayers, devotions or pattern of conduct by humans or lesser gods will change fate. Yet the Trojans and Greeks also cause the war by their feckless actions and both sides forfeit chances to end the conflict. If for the gods war is like watching and participating in a championship football game, for the human participants war is like an unending Russian roulette, filled with exhilaration but ultimately ending in agony for both winners and losers.

The *Iliad* embraces the warriors' code of honor and glories in the cruelty and gore of war but also depicts the tragedy, even the futility, of all the heroism.

---

[1] Most influential in the interpretation presented here are the essays in Harold Bloom, ed., *Homer: Modern Critical Views* (1986) and *Homer's Iliad: Modern Critical Interpretation* (1987); Jasper Griffin, *Homer on Life and Death* (1980); Carl Rubino and Cynthia Shelmerdine, eds., *Approaches to Homer* (1983); and Simone Weil, *The Iliad: A Poem of Force* (1956).

Both the Trojans and Achaeans are presented as worshiping the same gods, and Homer does not present either side as more deserving of the gods' favor. Instead the epic praises both sides, preserves impartiality between them, and presents them as very similar peoples, not civilized Greeks and Asian barbarians.

The cause of the war, not described in the *Iliad*, was the wife-stealing of the most beautiful mortal woman, Helen. When courting her, all her suitors vowed that they would aid anyone who won her hand. King Menelaus married Helen. Later when the Trojan Paris visited Sparta, Menelaus offered him hospitality. Aphrodite (Venus) put a spell on Helen and Paris so that they fell in love, robbed Menelaus of his wealth, and fled to Troy. Remembering their vow, Menelaus' friends from all over Greece sailed to Troy to avenge the abduction of Helen. King Agamemnon of Mycenae became commander of the army.

During the course of the *Iliad,* the hearers learn the complete history of the war, but the poem opens with the siege of Troy having lasted for eight years with inconclusive results. Most of the soldiers have no personal stake in the outcome of the war, except for the possibility of taking as booty the women and children of Troy and the wealth of the city. When the war-weary Achaeans are offered a chance to return home without victory, the soldiers rush back to their ships, and only the intervention of Athena and Hera stops a flight home to Greece.

The central protagonists in the *Iliad* are Achilles, mortal son of a goddess, invulnerable everywhere except his heel, with the strength and ferocity of a god, and Hector, also a mighty warrior and the son of King Priam and Queen Hecuba of Troy. Both warriors exalt in battle and love killing; they also know that they are destined to die in battle, and in the *Iliad* there is no sentimentality about death or afterlife. Hector and Achilles die for their reputation as heroes, believing that the afterlife in Hades is miserable. Achilles prefers to be home with his aging father, but instead risks his life in what he knows is a worthless cause. Hector realizes that his death will lead to the destruction of Troy, the murder of his son and father, and the slavery of his wife as a concubine, but he still cannot make peace. When in battle, Achilles and Hector lose their thoughtfulness and become possessed by uncontrollable rage. The gods doom both men, but the heroes' irresponsible actions cause their deaths.

Throughout most of the epic Achilles refuses to fight because he has been humiliated by King Agamemnon. Achilles even resists the plea of his dearest friend, Patroclus, to fight. He does loan Patroclus his armor. Patroclus wears the armor and rallies the Greeks until he encounters Hector, who kills him. Achilles, whose sulking doomed Patroclus, now becomes so wrathful that, after obtaining new armor from the gods, he goes out to challenge Hector.

Hector's father, King Priam, mother, Hecuba, and wife plea with him to stay secure within the walls of Troy, but the hero refuses. He ventures out to fight Achilles, but the sight of Achilles' shining armor causes Hector's courage to desert him and he flees. Achilles chases Hector around the walls of Troy three times before the goddess Athena appears in a false vision telling Hector to stand and fight. Hector begins the battle, realizes that the goddess had betrayed him, and still fights until his death. Achilles kills Hector, ties the body to his chariot and drags it around the walls of Troy, and other Achaeans mutilate the body. But the gods restore Hector's body.

For both Greek and Trojan, when a body lies unburied without appropriate funeral rites, the warrior is doomed to an agonized wandering on earth. King Priam decides to approach Achilles and pay ransom for the body. The god Hermes brings Priam safely through the Achaean lines to Achilles' tent.

> Great Priam entered and approached,
> And took Achilles by the knees, and kissed
> His hands, the dreadful slaughterous hands that had
> Slain many of his sons . . . Then
> Spoke Priam and entreated him, and said: . . .
> Revere the gods,
> Achilles, and remembering thy father
> Have pity on me; I am more piteous;
> I have endured what never mortal man
> On earth has yet endured, to stretch my hand
> Unto the mouth of him who slew my son.'
> He spoke, and roused a longing in Achilles

To sorrow for his father. By the hand
He took and gently pushed the old man back;
And for remembrance both wept bitterly;
Priam, sunk down before Achilles' feet,
Wept for manslaying Hector, but Achilles
For his own father, and anon Patroclus:
And through the house their lamentation went.[2]

The reconciliation of Priam and Achilles is the climax of the *Iliad*. Here, as the two men weep over the deaths of Patroclus and Hector and face their own deaths, Homer portrays the futility of war. In the epic, war is a heroic act that ended in a misery caused only by the prospect of glory.

Ethics play virtually no role in the Trojan War, and battles occurred without restraint. Agamemnon slaughters without qualms captives who no longer threaten him and who beg for mercy. The heads of warriors are cut off and carried on spears to taunt the enemy. Agreements are violated with no negative repercussions. In an attempt to settle the war amicably, both sides agree to determine the victor by a duel between Paris and Menelaus. Menelaus wounds Paris and is winning when the goddess Aphrodite intervenes and spirits Paris away. The Trojans do not abide by the verdict.

Homer did not describe the fall of Troy, the famous horse, or even the death of Achilles in the *Iliad*, but his audience knew that eventually the cowardly Paris killed Achilles by hitting his heel with a dart, a most inappropriate death for a mighty warrior. Homer mentions large forces in both armies, but most of the characters of the *Iliad* appear only as they die in agony after having been stabbed by some hero. A focus on a few individuals and their duels mitigates the impersonality of war. The method of fighting is for the heroes to ride up in chariots, dismount and attack each other with sword or spear. Their glory comes from the quality of other heroes they killed.

---

[2]Homer, *The Iliad*, tr. Richmond Lattimore, Book XXIV, l. 488. Homer's epic was composed 500 years after the Trojan War, so his description of battles, though containing valuable information, may not be an accurate description of practices of war.

War in the *Iliad* is a very masculine enterprise and is contrasted to family values. His infant son does not recognize and is frightened by the sight of Hector in his helmet, but when Hector removes it, the child smiles for his father. The descriptions of Hector and Achilles stress their gentleness to women and family. Hector's idyllic relationship with his parents and love of his wife contrasts with the barrenness of war, and the grief exemplified by his mother Hecuba and wife Andromache vividly exemplify the pathos of death. Achilles' respect for his father is why he grants King Priam the body of Hector. Though there was no personal reason for Achilles to stay in camp after his humiliation by Agamemnon, he could not return home and desert the Greeks. Agamemnon would not leave because of the humiliation of returning home without victory and booty. In the *Iliad* old men exist to grieve for their sons killed in battle. Women represent family and - through the bearing of children - continuity of the city. Men quarrel over the possession of women and fight to preserve their families and cities. Still, ultimately, heroes fight because they are heroes with their honor and fame more important than life. To risk one's survival in a battle against a heroic opponent is the essence of the warrior's code, even if the resulting glory is an empty delusion.

The *Iliad* is in a sense mythical and timeless. However, there may have been a city of Troy sacked by Achaeans, even a Trojan horse, and some parts of the epic contain valuable historical information. During the classic portion of Greek history - beginning with the war against Persia and ending with the conquest by Alexander the Great - the *Iliad's* framework of gods, half-gods, and heroes made the epic appear even to the Greeks as the by-product of a golden age of the past. Still, the religious traditions that shaped the *Iliad* influenced Greek and Roman history while playwrights, philosophers, and artists continued to use the myths to comment on the relationship between the gods and war. Alexander the Great, for example, saw himself as a descendant of Achilles and, in his conquest of Asia Minor, visited and sacrificed at his alleged tomb. Medieval chivalry built on images derived from Greek and Trojan heroes. From the Renaissance through the twentieth century, educated persons have known the story of the *Iliad* and admired Hector. The verb "to hector" (meaning "to boast") and the name Hector with heroic connotations still are used. The American landscape is dotted with towns called Troy and football teams called Trojans. The *Iliad* is right: the memory of heroes does endure.

The literary conventions used in the epic - concentration upon a few characters and using other men as cannon fodder, contrasting home with battlefield, portraying women as loved ones to show the humanity of the heroes but making them marginal to the action, reveling in the gore of battle, admiring the strength and courage of the central characters - remain the formulas of war literature and movies. Today, however, the role of the gods has been replaced by fate or luck and Homer's empathy for men on both sides has disappeared.

II. Greek Religion and War

The political unit of the Hellenes was the city-state or *polis*, an independent political entity consisting of the town and its immediate surrounding countryside. The most famous of these *poleis* (the plural of *polis*) were Athens, Sparta, Corinth, and Thebes; and their small size, vulnerability, and constant attempts to expand their power either in cooperation or competition with their neighbors meant that Greek politics brought constantly shifting alliance systems and wars. Military prowess was crucial, for defeat in battle for a city-state could result in subordination or, even worse, a conquest which meant the extinction of independent existence, slavery for women and children, and death for men. Greek poets pictured a golden age of peace at the beginning of time, but pacifism was not a viable option so long as all citizens' primary obligations were to strengthen the city-state.

Two major wars, the defeat of Persia (in 480-479 B.C.E.) and the Peloponnesian conflict (431-404 B.C.E.), correspond in their impact on Greek thought to the different American responses to World War II and Vietnam. The Persian Empire was an eastern despotism ruling from the borders of India to modern-day Turkey. When the Persians moved west, Athens, sometimes acting alone and occasionally with the aid of other the city-states, beat back the Persians in the land battle of Marathon and the sea battle of Salamis. Considering the overwhelming numbers of Persians, estimated as high as 250,000 troops and 1000 ships, the Greeks believed the preservation of their independence rested upon superior strategy, better fighting techniques, good morale, and the favor of the gods. They had an annual thanksgiving for the victories at Marathon and Salamis.[3]

Military historian John Keegan argues that the Greeks began the Western way of war. The tactics used in the various Greek battles did not resemble the kind of individual duel pictured in the *Iliad*. The basic fighting unit was the infantry in a phalanx, composed of soldiers marching close together whose shields - held on their left arms - and extended spears created a barrier, a kind of moving porcupine. Battle conformed to a kind of ritual with fighting confined to a small space about the size of a football field. The two armies in full readiness would first stare at each other for an hour or so and then slowly march at each other, seeking to preserve their solid formation. In battle, the units of infantry would attack each other and use three-feet-long swords to hack their way through. The morale of the whole unit was crucial, for breaking rank or the retreat of one section could lead to panic and defeat. A land battle required no strategy. Naval warfare entailed either ramming ships or opposing ships grappling together, after which the soldiers on board engaged in hand-to-hand combat. A "war" lasted only one day with the victor erecting a battlefield trophy and the loser asking for the return of the bodies of the dead. Ancient battles could involve many casualties, and Greeks saw the hands of the gods both in mass panics and retreats and in overwhelming victories.[4]

---

[3] Pierre Ducrey, *Warfare in Ancient Greece (1985)*; W. Kendrick Pitchell, *The Greek State at War* (1974), 173-178. Graham Shipley, "Introduction: The Limits of War," in *War and Society in the Greek World*, eds. John Rich and Graham Shipley (1993), 3.

[4] John Keegan, "First Blood" in "War and Civilization," documentary on Arts and Entertainment, Aug. 2, 1998 that is based on his *A History of Warfare* (1993), 244-256. Gwynne Dyer, *War* (1985), also derived from a television series, in chapters 1 and 2 is a readable introduction to the history of war.

Because all Greeks worshipped the same pantheon of gods, religious differences played no role in the cause of war. But each city-state sought the sanction of the gods as necessary for victory. Like the Hebrews, the Greeks sought to learn the message of the supernatural forces before and during a war, but their techniques were very different. Rather than religious figures analogous to the Hebrew prophets, the Greeks used sacrifices, oracles, and omens. Often before declaring war or even engaging in battle, priests or diviners accompanying the forces sacrificed an animal; they then assessed the chances for success based upon the shape of the animal's liver. All Greeks relied on the words of the oracle at Delphi, where the priest spoke the words of the god Apollo, even though the prophecies were sufficiently ambiguous as to allow alternative interpretations.

Soldiers in the field encountered epiphanies, or apparitions of local divinities or heroes, which proved that a god was on their side. They interpreted as omens the direction of the flight of birds and the weather (fogs, thunderstorms, earthquakes, meteorites, eclipses). The message of a dream could be clear or could be so ambiguous that diviners, analogous to the Hebrew prophet Daniel, had to provide the meaning. Generals took particularly skilled diviners with them into campaigns.

Before a battle, armies sacrificed a lamb and would not fight without a favorable omen. The sacrifices could be designed to win approval of the gods or to see if the gods were favorable. Obviously it behooved a general to gain a positive omen because having supernatural aid would provide a great boost to morale and should make the soldiers fight better. The temptation to rig the sacrifice or to make sure the diviner interpreted the message of the dream positively must have been immense. Still, there were many instances where omens determined strategy. Greek history contained examples of armies retreating, refusing to battle, and postponing actions until the omens were favorable. Since both sides in a battle wanted favorable omens, there could have been a credibility gap on the loser's side, but this did not seem to have occurred.

Those *manteis,* or diviners, who successfully predicted the outcome received substantial financial reward. Individuals and cities believed that "gifts move the gods and gifts persuade dread kings" and made vows of a tithe or actions if victory should occur.[5] These vows were conditional; that is, they were fulfilled only if the gods granted victory. Warriors dedicated a portion of the spoils of war to the gods; such booty could be used to build a temple. Soldiers could also dedicate their weapons or armor to a god.

Although military elements were important in religious celebrations, they were not the central focus. The Romans made the cult of Mars, god of war, second only to that of Zeus. In contrast, the Greeks had only a few celebrations of Ares, god of war, or of Nike, god of victory. Sparta sacrificed to Phobos, a war god who inspired panic and flight in soldiers and symbolized the constitution. Even in Sparta, a *polis* organized to create an efficient military, the war god was not a prime figure. All the Greek gods symbolized basic features of Greek life, but there was neither celebration of nor a cult for Eirene (peace) at Athens until after the Peloponnesian war (375 B.C.E.). Accounts of war throughout the entire period of Greek and Hellenistic history show that war remained a religious act.[6]

The issue then becomes: did their religious attitudes restrain aggressiveness in the cause or conduct of war? There is no easy answer to this question, because the Greeks distinguished between how they should fight other Greeks in war and the way non-Greeks or barbarians should be treated, and in both cases restraints were sometimes ignored. Even in war to the death against the Persians, both sides observed some limitations. The Panhellenic ideal insisted that all wars among Greeks should be fought with moderation and restraints: wars should be declared, truces observed, there should be no disruption of religious festivals, and priests should not be killed. Heralds received safe conduct and at the end of battle declared who had won. The Delphic priesthood issued certain rules of war, e.g.,

---

[5] Quoted in Pritchett, III, 230.
[6] Ibid., III, 155-63.

prohibiting the poisoning of the enemy's water supply, and sparing prisoners who surrendered voluntarily. The breaking of a treaty was an offense against the gods. Prisoners of war should be offered for ransom rather than executed; noncombatants were not the primary targets. Pursuit of defeated opponents was limited.

Historian Josiah Ober argues that these restraints, established by custom rather than treaty, were generally observed during the period of 700 to 400 B.C.E.[7] Limited war served the interests of the *hoplite* (farmer) class of warriors and meant that the conflicts did not threaten the basis of the *poleis*. However, the limitations broke down in the Peloponnesian wars. Thucydides' *History of the Peloponnesian War,* written sometime around 400 B.C.E. records the Greeks observing but also sometimes breaking of ritual taboos of wars. The nature of weapons, the class of the soldiers, and planning for long-term strategic emphases eroded the informal but observed conventions on limiting war.

III. Realism in War: Thucydides

Thucydides' perspective differs so radically from Homer and the *Bible* that he can legitimately be called the first "realist" in describing war. Given the prevalence of religious rituals before and during the Peloponnesian War, described several times by Thucydides, it was remarkable that in his history the gods played no role. Instead, skill, strategy, morale, and numbers determined victory. Even so, the plans of both sides often went awry, and chance, luck, or necessity occupied the position that earlier and later writers ascribed to the gods. Thucydides' purpose in writing his history was to allow "those who want to understand clearly the events which happened in the past and which (human nature being what it is) will, at some time or other and in much the same way, be repeated in the future."[8]

Thucydides wanted to portray the causes, conduct, and effects of the war. He described his method as recounting those events for which he was an

---

[7] Josiah Ober, "Classical Greek Times," *The Laws of War* (1994), 12-26.

eyewitness or had credible evidence, but he did not operate like a modern journalist. For example, he inserted many important speeches by important politicians on both sides, and shorthand had not yet been invented. So scholars debate whether the speeches represented a summary of what Thucydides heard, thought was appropriate to, or might have been said on the occasion. Thucydides was an Athenian general and supporter of the policies of Pericles, but he presented a sympathetic and credible account of the motives and actions of both Athens and Sparta.

Athens, after the defeat of the Persians, engaged in a series of actions that seemed to threaten potential rivals. It turned a league of friendly or allied *poleis* (city-states) into an empire of allied states. Out of desire for prestige, self-interest, and fear, Athens began to treat its allied states as subordinates and seized the treasury of the Delian League to spend on increasing its military strength. Athens' policy of allowing its citizens to colonize other areas while keeping their Athenian citizenship also contributed to its strength. Further, Athens changed its form of government into a direct democracy for all who were citizens. (Women, children, and slaves were not citizens.) The citizens gathered at a central hill termed the *Pnyz* where, after listening to orators present significant policy options, they voted on actions. The subject allies of Athens operated in the same way. By contrast, an aristocracy or traditional oligarchy remained in control in Sparta and other cities of the Peloponnesian peninsula. Thucydides did not assume that democracies were inherently peace-loving and oligarchies war-loving. Just as much as Sparta, Athens welcomed the war.

Thucydides distinguished between the immediate and long-range causes of the war. "What made the war inevitable was the growth of Athenian power and the fear which this caused in Sparta." Because of their situations, actions that appeared reasonable to each struck the other as threatening. The squabbles of subordinate states allied with Athens or Sparta grew into attempted subversive

---

[8]Thucydides, *The Peloponnesian Wars*, tr. Rex Warner (1959), 24-25.

takeovers and battles. The losing side appealed to either Athens or Sparta for support, and their interventions to counter each other escalated what could have remained localized conflicts. "The cause of all these evils was the desire for power which greed and ambition inspire."[9]

Major differences in culture between Athens and Sparta contributed to hostilities. Sparta, ruled by an aristocratic oligarchy, attempted to preserve older agrarian patterns; democratic Athens, by contrast, located in an area with poor soil, gained its wealth from trade. Sparta's whole way of life centered on the training of its youth for military success, and there was little concern with the arts. The Athenians relished the intellectual excitement occasioned by the questioning of traditional ways of thought and worship. Both *poleis* had more in common than either had with surrounding non-Hellenic peoples and Persia, but their rivalries and differences resulted in a war to the death. Thucydides wrote the story of the impact of what happened when the struggle that both had assumed would be a short glorious campaign turned into a twenty-seven year war.

At the end of the first year of struggle, when the Athenian navy reigned supreme at sea but the land forces of Sparta put Athens under siege, the Athenians gathered to commemorate their dead. Pericles, their political leader and architect of the war policy, gave the funeral oration. His speech remains the model for an effective discourse rallying a democracy to war. It could have been delivered with little modification by every American president during the Cold War.

Pericles presented the war as not over power or material interest, but over the preservation of the Athenian way of life, a continuation of the struggle of the ancestors who through "blood and toil" (notice the similarity to Churchill's "blood, sweat and tears") had given to their children a "free country."[10] Pericles did not

---

[9]Ibid., 25; Book Three; Edith Hamilton, *The Greek Way to Western Civilization* (1960), 132-39. Charles Robinson, *Athens in the Age of Pericles*, tr. Richard Dunn (1973) offers an analysis of the two sides.
[10]Thucydides, 115-23.

describe the wars of the fathers - after all, they had won their battles - but dwelt on the Athenian constitution bequeathed by their victory. The ancestors had created in Athens a "democracy," where everyone was "equal before the law," and citizens openly made decisions. No one was kept in obscurity from poverty or lack of rank in birth; talent enabled a man to rise to prominence. Disgrace came not by poverty at birth, but from not taking advantage of opportunity to rise. Just as Athenian political life was free, so social life was open. "We are free and tolerant in our private lives; but in public affairs we keep to the law." The Athenians found themselves praised by Pericles as hard-working, enjoying recreation, exercising good taste in the arts, and participating vigorously in sport.

Pericles went on to say that the contrast was with Sparta. Athens believed in a liberal education; Sparta trained only for military virtue, though such training made them no more adept in battle than the Athenians. During war, the Athenian soldiers willingly met danger. They knew the risks and were brave, not out of ignorance, but based on knowledge. "The man who can most truly be accounted brave is he who best knows the meaning of what is sweet in life and of what is terrible, and then goes out undeterred to meet what is to come." Athens was composed of heroes, and future ages would wonder at their accomplishments. "We do not need the praises of a Homer" in the *Iliad* for "our soldiers," because the Athenian empire itself was a comparable monument to the men who died.

Those who died while facing the uncertainty of battle without flinching showed "the meaning of manliness," Pericles insisted, whatever their faults, they gallantly defended their native land. Those now living "must resolve to keep the same daring spirit against the foe . . . It is for you to try to be like them. Make up your minds that happiness depends on being free, and freedom depends on being courageous."

For the mothers of the sons who died, Pericles suggested taking "comfort in the thought of having more children." For those too old to bear more children, remember the "fair fame of the dead." In Pericles' oration, the praise of women proved how irrelevant they were to the war. The greatest glory of women, he claimed, "is to be least talked about by men." That is, they were to send their husbands and sons off to battle and to suffer their dead in silence. Thucydides, like Homer and Pericles, saw women's position as supporting and suffering from the war, not from fighting in it. When women threw stones from the tops of houses against an invading army, he recorded such conduct as an unusual instance

The honor and glory Pericles saw in Athens' conduct was severely tested the next year when the siege continued and the plague struck. The plague affected the good as well as the bad and was particularly prevalent among those who nursed the sick. The illness was long and debilitating, and death often agonizing; with the realization that they could do nothing to prevent or cure the plague, the Athenians succumbed to despair. Honor, worship of gods, and duty were replaced by "unprecedented lawlessness" and "self-indulgence."[11] The plague undermined that disciplined love of liberty and willingness to sacrifice that had characterized the Athenians.

The war was partly an ideological conflict between an Athenian democracy guaranteeing "political equality for the masses" and a Spartan oligarchy or aristocracy providing "safe and sound government." Thucydides recounts how as the war dragged on year after year, supporters of rival versions of government, convinced of the moral superiority of their system, attempted to seize power in smaller city-states. Personal ambition allied with fanaticism for democracy or oligarchy allowed success to justify any means. Moderates were destroyed; people of principle thrown aside; vengeance and party victory ruled. The result of a war for ideals was that those who were the least scrupulous and less intelligent triumphed. The ordinary conventions of honesty and honor disappeared. The result was "a general deterioration of character throughout the Greek world" as the "ordinary conventions of civilized life" disappeared. "Human nature . . . showed itself proudly in its true colors, as something incapable of

---

[11] Ibid., 123-27, 180-91.

controlling passion, insubordinate to the idea of justice, the enemy to anything superior to itself."[12]

By the time the war was in its sixteenth year, the consequences of pure power politics ruled. Melos was a neutral island of strategic importance coveted by the Athenians, who brought a huge fleet and army and laid siege to the town. The Athenian generals asked to address the town's people. Here they demanded that the Melians surrender. The leaders of Melos asked for a debate on "fair play and justice," seeing that the Athenians offered as alternatives only war or slavery. The Athenians responded that justice was irrelevant to the issue at hand; the one significant issue was the "safety" of Melos. The Athenians offered two alternatives: Melos could surrender, after which the inhabitants would be enslaved, or they could resist, but the Athenians would conquer and then destroy the inhabitants and seize all lands. Resistance was a foolish alternative considering the disparities of power.

When the Melians complained about a lack of justice, the Athenian answer was "the strong do what they have the power to do and the weak accept what they have to accept." Then the Melians appealed to the Athenians' self-interest in building good will and asked what would happen if in the future the Athenians ever needed compassion. The Athenians' rejoinder was they did not care about the future and were prepared to take the risk; the present issue was only the strength of the empire, and a friendship with the Melians would be a sign of weakness: "Hatred is evidence of our power." The Melians invoked the power of the gods; the Athenians retorted, "It is a general and necessary law of nature to rule wherever one can." Any nation with power would act just like the Athenians. Melos rejected the Athenian terms, placing their faith in the gods and help from Sparta. After a siege of over a year, Melos fell, and the Athenians killed all men of

---

[12]Ibid., 211.

military age, sold the women and children as slaves, and seized the land and settled it with colonists.[13]

Thucydides' story is so compelling that it makes all succeeding military histories appear derivative. Strategy, ideology, heroism, cowardice, competence, greed, self-aggrandizement, national-interest, ideology, alliances, cruelty, arrogance, piety, suffering -- all played a role as the war ground on. The original causes came to seem minor as the grievances against both sides mounted. Eventually, even the victors lost.

Thucydides provided the first example of the "realist" tradition, which sees wars as caused by disputes over power. The gods played no discernable role, and right and wrong were irrelevant to cause or victory. Even he himself recognized his omission from his history of what he termed the "romantic" or the human dimension to the conflict. Even though Thucydides shows the characters of different leaders as ruthless, incompetent, brave, ambitious, or moderate, Homer's Hector and Achilles are more compelling figures than any of the generals or orators of Athens or Sparta. Thucydides lamented the moral degeneration of character of both people and leaders as a consequence of the war but, while he described abortive peace feelers, nowhere did he discuss alternatives to fighting or whether a peaceful settlement was possible. Instead, he insists that not just this one but war as a phenomenon was "inevitable," because of "human nature."

IV. The Dramatists

The reactions of the people at home to the long duration and immense cost of the Peloponnesian War can be deduced from the indirect comments in two plays: Aristophanes' *Lysistrata* and Euripides' *The Trojan Women*. These plays were performed in Athens, possibly as a part of a religious festival which included sacrifices to the gods. *The Trojan Women* dates from after the sack of Melos and at the time of the expedition to Sicily; *Lysistrata,* after the crushing Athenian defeat at Syracuse. That a state at war and fighting for survival would allow

---

[13] Ibid., 350-66.

dramatists such freedom of expression is extraordinary and a tribute to the democracy of Athens. Both men continued to write plays and have them performed. Certainly, governments allowed nothing of comparable satirical tone in America, Great Britain, and Germany during either World War I or World War II. There is far more bite, for example, to the *Lysistrata* than to the American television show *Mash* produced during the war in Vietnam but set in Korea. Like *Mash*, these plays showed that the most effective way for an artist to oppose war was to ignore politics and concentrate on the human cost, and all of them illustrated that literary satire in comedy or tragedy would not change war policies.

The premise of *Lysistrata* was simple. Led by the heroine Lysistrata, the women of Athens, joined by women representing the major cities on both sides, stopped the war by using the one weapon at their disposal: sex. Lysistrata persuaded all the women, first in Athens and then in the neighboring *poleis*, to refrain from sexual intercourse until the fighting stopped and the men made peace. The women enforced mutual chastity on themselves and the men by blockading themselves in the Acropolis, the location of the temple to the chaste goddess Athena. The play was in no sense realistic drama. The women resented the war because their men were absent and they had no sex. Yet their weapon was to refrain from having sex, which they were not doing anyway. Historically, the play's premise was nonsense since there were always men available in Athens.

In the midst of double entendres and ribald comments, Aristophanes presented a series of images of war and death and contrasted them with symbols of family, children, and prosperity. The war was being fought to protect families, but because the men were absent fighting, no children were being produced, husbands and wives could not aid each other, and parents mourned their lost sons. Aristophanes managed to make the women spokesmen for peace by relying upon their traditional role in the home. Any subversive quality of women's rights and abilities was probably vitiated by the ribaldry that permeates the play.[14] Except for Lysistrata and the woman representing Sparta, other characters - male and female - were not too bright or moral or praiseworthy. What they had in common is that they were horny, a condition that may have been represented by the men on-stage wearing under their tunics leather phalluses so long that they had difficulty walking. Eventually, the erections on all the men so debilitated them that they could not fight; reluctantly they surrendered to the ladies, and made peace. The play probably ended with some kind of fertility festival dedicated to the goddess Peace, who may have appeared in the nude.

The play never discussed causes or purposes of the war and contained no realistic advice on how to end it. The play has been called a pacifist tract, but there is no certainty that this was the case. It was clearly anti-war. Aristophanes satirized demagogic political leaders, war profiteers, and military leaders, and called upon the common people - artisans, farmers, and small traders -- to change policy. In several of his anti-war plays, Aristophanes contrasted fertility and the bounty of nature in peace with the barrenness of war and evoked the unity of the Greeks as a way of opposing the Peloponnesian War.

The *Iliad* had established the precedent of juxtaposing the heroism of the warriors with agonizing death scenes and the suffering of women. The Greek tragedians Aeschylus, Sophocles, and Euripides continued this tradition. Aeschylus' *The Persians* contrasted the glory of the Greek resistance with the sufferings of the defeated Persians. In Euripides any glory and heroism receded and war was a barbaric butchery and a senseless activity: "When a community votes in favor of war, no one thinks of the possibility of his own death. Everyone is quite sure that only others can be killed. But if the real implications were properly realized, nobody would ever succumb to the temptation to fight."[15]

---

[14] Aristophanes, *Five Comedies*, tr. B. B. Rogers (1955); Cedric Whitman, *Aristophanes and the Comic Hero* (1961); Kenneth Reckford, *Aristophanes' Old-and-New Comedy* (1987), and Lauren Taafe, *Aristophanes and Women* (1993).

[15] *The Suppliants* quoted in Geraldo Zampaglione, *The Idea of Peace in Antiquity* (1973), 77.

The story of Euripides' *The Trojan Women* begins just after the *Iliad* had ended. Troy had fallen, and the play centered on the fate of Hector's mother, Hecuba, his sister, Cassandra, his wife, and his son. When the play opens, Queen Hecuba already knows that Hector and her husband have been killed. She remains a stoical figure, telling the other Trojan women to accept their fate and offering to lead the mourning. During the course of the play she learns that the Greeks are so afraid of Hector that they have decided to sacrifice his infant son. When the Greek heralds come to seize child from his mother, they warn that if the women curse them, they will not even allow the child's body a proper burial.

Hecuba later learns that Odysseus, who advocated killing the child, will become her master. Hector's sister, Cassandra, who has a form of madness that allows her to forecast the future but to have no one believe her, will become the concubine of King Agamemnon. Cassandra foretells that he will be killed by his unfaithful wife and her lover on his return to Greece. Hector's wife, renowned for her virtue and loyalty, longs for death, but her good character makes her a prized commodity, and she becomes the slave of the son of her husband's killer, Achilles. Hecuba vows that at least she will get the satisfaction of seeing Helen punished, and persuades King Menelaus to kill Helen. But when the King confronts his wife, he is again smitten by Helen's beauty and does nothing. Helen is stupid and Menelaus a dolt. They go home to bed and to prosperity. The rest will continue to suffer. As the play ends, Hecuba prepares the body of Hector's infant son for burial while Troy burns in the background.[16] The play offers no hope. The gods are irrelevant or sadistic; the Greeks are cruel; the results of the war for all except Helen and Menelaus are disaster.

In the *Iliad* Homer always pictured the gods reverently, even when their actions were comic. For Thucydides and Euripides the gods provided no solace from the ills of wars. The anti-war plays of Aristophanes and Euripides seem to have had no effect on the actions of Athens during the Peloponnesian War. The

---

[16] Euripides, *The Trojan Women* in *The Bacchae and Other Plays*, tr. Philip Vellacott (1981).

dramatists could picture a horrendous war and a utopian peace, but had no way to bridge the gap. The fate of the plays was to have been often performed, but, Cassandra-like, to have had little effect on the desire of politicians and people to make war.

V. The Philosophers

The Greeks and Hebrews preserved their ideas about the relation of the gods, war, and ethics through a great variety of literary genres: myths, epics, histories, dramas, and poems used in religious ceremonies. One Greek form that had no parallel among the Hebrews until after the time of Alexander the Great was the philosophical treatise. Some of the most distinctive Greek contributions to the western traditions of evaluating war come from the abstract thought contributed by philosophers. The philosophers asserted that the essence of nature, society, and humans could be discovered by thinking. Using human reason provided a way to discover true reality, with a corollary that right or ethical living consisted of conformity to nature's dictates.

The Greek philosophers did not write formal treatises on war, but in their discussions of the state Plato (427-347) and Aristotle (384-322) dealt with civil and external conflict. Both men taught in Athens after the conclusion of the Peloponnesian War and designed their political theories to preserve the Greek city-state. For them virtue was not an abstract entity divorced from society; rather, a citizen's ethics contributed to the political survival of his city. A well-ordered human society was a moral good and merited defense from its citizens. Plato and Aristotle believed in the inevitability of war, saw the abilities of the warrior as necessary for the preservation of the *polis*, and worried about the dangers for the society of uncontrollable urges for war. They also distinguished between just and unjust wars.

For Plato a human being was made up of body and soul; this duality or division occasioned striving, first for food, then for surplus, then for other goods. Such strife created civilization, because the desire of a person for goods was essentially unlimited, and he would seek to accumulate and preserve surplus.

Surplus allowed civilization, but obtaining it occasioned conflict with other people because the supply of goods was finite. War was, therefore, a product of civilization, and some of the virtues necessary for civilization were necessary for war. It followed that wars were inevitable.[17] Aristotle, like Plato, linked the need to acquire with the attributes for war, but he never speculated on the ultimate cause of war. Aristotle argued that the state's survival depended upon a virtuous citizenry, and military virtues were the most widespread but not the most important qualities. The rulers must have the war virtues like courage and valor, plus other positive attributes like prudence and wisdom.

While for Plato war was inescapable, that did not mean all wars were good. Plato distinguished between disorder and war. Disorder was related to faction within a city-state or among relatives. He condemned any war of Greek versus Greek because of the Panhellenic ties between them. Wars that were not disorder were Greeks versus barbarians, i.e., the Persians. Even among the Greeks, defensive wars were not disorder. Aristotle assumed that leaders could know the intentions of the enemy, and so he drew no moral distinction between preventive and defensive war.

For Aristotle, just wars sought to prevent men from becoming slaves to others, to seek leadership to be used for the benefit of all, and to become masters over those who deserved to be slaves. The issue became: who deserved to be a slave? For Plato, no Greek should be a slave, but an offensive war against non-Greeks who deserved to be slaves was permissible because the Greeks and non-Greeks were enemies by nature. Aristotle also assumed that those who were destined to be slaves could be warred against, but he was not sure that Greeks and non-Greeks were enemies by nature. Any war against those not destined by

---

[17]A good introduction is provided by the selections from Plato in *War and Christian Ethics*, ed. Arthur F. Holmes (1975), 13-23. Plato, *The Republic*, tr. Francis Cornford (1958), ch. XVII. My analysis of Plato and Aristotle's perspective on war is based on Martin Ostwald, "Peace and War in Plato and Aristotle," in *Scripta Classica Israelica* vol. XV (1996), 102-18.

nature to be slaves was unjust.[18] A prisoner of war could be made a slave only if the original purpose of the war was just.

Plato and Aristotle insisted that war was not an end in itself; that is, it was not a good. Civilization created war and also brought ways to control it. One responsibility of a good ruler was to avoid unnecessary war. Plato repudiated the doctrine of the Sophists (which also resembles the arguments that the Athenians used at Melos) that all life was a series of wars at different levels: the state, the village, the family, the individual. Instead, for Plato a well-ordered society consisted of a natural hierarchy in which the higher ruled the base, a condition analogous to the role of virtue in a moral person. In the *Laws* Plato argued that the goal of society was to reward the best, not the most violent. A society characterized by internal peace and friendship was better than one in civil war. Therefore, war was not the means to create the good life; it was a method to preserve it.

The goal of war was not war, but peace: "War, whether external or civil, is not the best, and the need of either is to be deprecated; but peace with one another, and good will, are best ... No one can be a true statesman ... who looks only, or first of all, to external warfare; nor will he ever be a sound legislator who orders peace for the sake of war, and not war for the sake of peace." The same thought is found in Aristotle's *Politics*: "War must be ... only a means for peace; action as a means for leisure; and acts ... merely necessary or ... useful ... as means to acts which are good in themselves."[19] This insight of the value of preserving a well-ordered society lies behind all ethical theories that distinguish just from unjust wars.

VI. The Hellenistic World

The Peloponnesians led by Sparta granted generous terms of surrender to defeated Athens, but they then proved unable to hold their victorious coalition

---

[18] Aristotle, *The Politics of Aristotle*, tr. Ernest Baker (1946), 14, 319-322.
[19] Plato, *Laws*, quoted in Holmes, 23; Aristotle, *Politics*, tr. Ernest Banker, (1968), VII, 12, 317. *Nicomachean Ethics*, X, 7.

together. Even though weakened by the long war and watched by neighboring ambitious Persia, the Greek *poleis* continued to feud. Under King Philip II (382-336), Macedonia, a kingdom bordering Greece on the north, involved itself in Hellenic affairs and eventually came to exercise hegemonic control. After the assassination of Philip, his son - known to history as Alexander the Great - asserted Macedonian dominance over the individual city-states. Alexander, whose tutor for three years was Aristotle, admired Greek culture, worshiped the gods of Mt. Olympus, and showed no appreciation for the value of peace. Instead, in an eight-year period beginning in 334, he defeated and conquered the Persian Empire and marched with his armies to Egypt and eventually to India.

Philip and Alexander revolutionized the practice of war. They created a professional standing army, found a way to utilize cavalry as a kind of shock troops, changed the phalanx formation (lengthened the spears to fourteen feet and reduced the size of shields), improved a catapult which could be used against fortifications, made greater use of archers, and planned logistics so that an army could journey thousands of miles from home. In his campaigns Alexander's actions toward his opponents could be ruthless, involving total annihilation, and yet on occasion, seeing the need for allies, he could be gentle. A mystic who saw himself as having a divine mission or even being a god, Alexander respected and observed the religious practices of all his conquered peoples, but saw Greek civilization as providing a common bond for his empire.

After Alexander's conquest, the foundation of ethical thought changed. The political theories of Plato and Aristotle rested upon an absolute distinction between Greek and barbarian and based ethical behavior upon the needs of the *polis*. Even before the Peloponnesian War, some Athenian Sophists had begun to question whether the polis was the most desirable form of political life. The names of the various philosophical alternatives remain part of everyday language, though often with a meaning that distorts the original intent: from the Sophists, sophomores; from the Cynics, cynicism; from the Stoics, stoicism. The Sophists' main goal was to undermine traditional Greek religious and political values by questioning the value of the *polis*, heroism, ethics, and the gods. The dialogues of Socrates, written down by Plato, often aimed at refuting the Sophists by insisting upon the value of order, virtue, and knowledge. The Cynics and Stoics provided ethical theories for the new world empires.

The Cynic view of life is exemplified by a conversation between Alexander the Great and the Cynic Diogenes. The young conqueror, impressed with the ascetic way of life of Diogenes, asked the philosopher, who wore rags and rarely bathed, if there were anything he could give to him. Diogenes, who was sitting sunning himself, replied, "Stand out of my light."[20] The Cynics criticized wealth, nationality, law, status, possessions, politeness, physical pleasures, and the family - anything that was an external form of value. They desired to live naturally, which they interpreted as in extreme simplicity and with no possessions. The modern term cynicism comes from the Cynics' attacks upon the pretensions of alternative systems of values and the goals of most people. The relationship of war to ethics was clear: an individual should avoid any kind of involvement with the state or with war because they were irrelevant. Yet the Cynics would not lead an anti-war campaign because they opposed politics. To Hellenistic civilization the Cynics contributed an individual ethic independent of politics.

The Stoics, like the Cynics, originated in third-century B.C.E. Athens, but their primary significance came in the Hellenistic Age after the conquests of Alexander and in Rome in the last century of the Republic. In the fourth century C.E., Stoicism influenced how Christians formulated their ethic of war. Stoicism was a philosophy treated by its adherents as almost a religion; that is, they subordinated logical and metaphysical aspects to the quest for virtue. The Stoics were monists and believed that the entire universe - Zeus, man, soul, emotions, animals, plants, rocks, water - was material composed of various degrees of *pneuma* (spirit). The active principle of spirit - fully realized in God, to a smaller

---

[20]Laertius Diogenes, *Lives of Eminent Philosophers*, tr. R. D. Hicks (1965), 41.

degree in humans, and even less in animals - which they termed *logos*, or reason, bound together all creation. For humans, virtue was action in accordance with spirit, or living according to nature, or reason, or Zeus' will - all four were the same.

In Stoic metaphysics human nature or law replaced the *polis* as the source of virtue. A universal brotherhood linked all peoples as part of a *cosmo-polis* (cosmopolitan). The customs, race, nationality, and religions that divided people were all artificial - not in accord with nature. So Aristotle and Plato were wrong, and there was no natural division between Greek and barbarian; and no one by nature was designed to be a slave. Instead, all had equal rights and should exist in brotherly harmony in a peaceful universal state.[21]

The fragmentary surviving treatises of the early Stoics make it difficult to know whether they did more than condemn war in the abstract and advocate love as the structuring principle for life. Later Roman Stoics like the philosopher-statesman Cicero and Emperor Marcus Aurelius stressed that a law of nature was self-preservation, and this law legitimated wars of defense. Stoicism gave to inhabitants of the Alexandrian and Roman empires an ascetic ethic mandating indifference to external vicissitudes. There is a legend that the master of the Roman slave Epictetus (50-13 C.E.) sought to see if he really was indifferent to pain. So the master took Epictetus' leg and began twisting it. Epictetus responded calmly, "You are breaking it.'" and when he had broken it he said, "Did I not tell you that you were breaking it."[22] It is easy to see how a philosophy advocating peace and love could also appeal to soldiers taught to endure pain stoically while fulfilling their duty.

War for the Greeks was a religious enterprise in which the gods gave victory, and yet it was also a human enterprise in which the virtues and flaws of kings and warriors determined events. Such ambiguity with gods and people

---

[21] Brad Inwood, *Ethics and Human Action in Early Stoicism* (1985); Margaret Reesor, *The Nature of Man in Early Stoic Philosophy* (1989); Lionel Pearson, *Popular Ethics in Ancient Greece* (1962).

responsible for war appeared in the *Iliad* as well as later dramatists and in the actions of generals and common soldiers. The Greeks bequeathed vocabulary, methods, and conclusions in dealing with the glory of war and the desirability of peace. The Roman Christians faced the task of integrating the conflicting insights of the Hebrew Scriptures, the New Testament, and the classical world into an ethic suitable for emperors and subjects attempting to follow the will of God.

---

[22]Origen, *Contra Celsum*, tr. Henry Chadwick (1965), 440; Zampaglione, 145-71.

IV.
Rome: Pagan and Christian

I. The Roman Way of War

The successful conquest by Rome's legions provided the lands around the Mediterranean Sea nearly four centuries of stability and relative peace. The imperial system exploited subject peoples, but also created a cultural unity. Although initially little concerned with the ethics of war, Rome would create and bequeath to the West a religious evaluation of war combining Greek, Jewish and Christian motifs. This chapter, the story of the creating of that tradition, will focus on Roman attitudes to fighting, Cicero's analysis of Just War, Julius Caesar's account of the Gallic wars, the responses of early Roman Christians to war, the merger of Christian and traditional Roman attitudes after Constantine, and the divergent traditions of evaluating war in two sections of the empire - Augustine in the West and the Byzantines in the East. Our theme is the adaptation of Christianity to the empire's need for a justification for war that preserved the Church's witness for peace. Still debated is whether the prevailing synthesis allowed Rome or Jesus to triumph, or whether it was, rather, a creative response allowing the best of each to prevail.

My mother used to exhort me to hard work citing the old adage "Rome wasn't built in a day." As a motivational device the saying did not work, but it is a succinct description of the long period, strenuous efforts, and sacrifices required for an obscure city to create an empire. Unlike Alexander's twelve-year conquest from Greece to India, the Roman Republic between 370-27 B.C.E. mobilized the army each spring to be prepared to fight that summer's battles.

The military was the foundation of Roman society and politics. Aristocrats who wanted high political office had to complete at least ten campaigns; soldiers in the professional army of Augustus served for twenty years and were forbidden to marry during that time. In the Republic, forty-five percent of the male population of Rome served in the army for ten years. Not until the French Revolution or later would a larger percentage of the population serve in the military. The constant warring took a heavy toll on the Roman population: from 200 to 150 B.C.E. perhaps 100,000 died in war out of a total adult population of less than one million.[1] Yet until the end of the Republic, there was little difficulty in recruiting soldiers - even when there was no serious external threat to Rome.

During the Republic, the common people never successfully resisted a demand for war by the patricians, and they were often more belligerent than the magistrates. Citizens remained preoccupied by war, sought glory, and served because of patriotism, booty, and the land bonus given to veterans. The population of Rome supported a government that subsidized the price of grain and, after 58 B.C.E., provided it free, and also gave entertainments - the games or circuses.

The Romans fought to expand the area in which they exercised power, conquering first Italy, then Carthage, Greece, Palestine, Egypt, and eventually much of what is now Turkey, Spain, England, France, and Germany. Julius Caesar's, "I came, I saw, I conquered" confirmed the Roman attitude toward war. Peace meant not a negotiation between equals, but conquest. One Roman general is quoted by the historian Livy as claiming, "I do not negotiate for peace, except with people who have surrendered."[2]

The Romans' successes came because they modified the Greeks' tactics of war. Every soldier carried a two edged shortened sword better for dueling and thrusting. The Romans lightened the spear to make it better for throwing in order to break up an enemy formation, made the size of the legions smaller, which

---

[1] William V. Harris, *War and Imperialism in Republican Rome* (1977) 44; Keith Hopkins, *Conquerors and Slaves* (1978), 25-28, 30-35. Nathan Rosenstein "Republican Rome" and Brian Campbell "The Roman Empire" summarize recent research on motivations, composition, tactics, and changes in the Roman army. *War and Society in the Ancient and Medieval Worlds* (1999), 193-240.

[2] Hopkins, 25-27.

allowed fighting in all terrains, and trained constantly, learning from the tactics of successful gladiators. By allowing non-landowning peasants to serve, they created a professional, disciplined army that was always ready for war and, because they built fortified camps every night, was difficult to surprise. Roman cavalry remained subordinate to the armed legionaries, which eventually meant that the horsemanship of the tribes like the Huns remained superior.

Roman ferocity in war was unmatched in the ancient world, and a conquest could result in indiscriminate killing. The legionaries often killed all adult males and raped and enslaved women; children were just another form of booty. On occasion, they even killed dogs in captured cities. War and brutality were so regular under the Republic that one historian has argued that the Romans appeared almost pathological.[3]

A. Julius Caesar on War

Julius Caesar wrote *The Conquest of Gaul* around 52 B.C.E. as personal political propaganda intended to impress his contemporaries with his abilities as a military commander and to persuade the Senate to elect him consul again. Caesar intended his account as a running commentary on his successful campaigns in what is now France. The book's economy of language and straightforward narration, which have made it useful as a basic text for teaching Latin, may stem from its origin in the style used for dispatches from the general in the field to the Roman Senate.

The Conquest of Gaul assumed the legitimacy of the Roman pattern of total war waged in the name of security for profit (mostly from the sale of slaves) to the soldiers, the commander, and the city. Although Caesar waged a war of conquest, he presented the conflict as a series of actions intended to defend Rome and its allies and portrayed the various tribes of Gauls as aggressors. Caesar

---

[3] Harris, 53; John Keegan, *A History of Warfare* (1993), 265; *War and Civilization,* Part II, Rome and China; Adam Ziolkowski, "*Urbs direpta,* or How the Romans Sacked Cities" in *War and Society in the Roman World* (1993), 77-90.

boasted of his clemency, always done for political purposes, but after a siege and conquest of a city, he wrote that left alive were only 800 out of 40,000 people. Once to impress on the enemy the futility of rebelling against the Romans, he cut off the hands of prisoners of war so that they could not fight against the Romans in the future. Women and children of resisting towns or tribes became slaves; one victory alone brought 53,000 slaves. Such routine cruelty came not because Caesar hated the Gauls or deviated from normal Roman customs; on the contrary, he commended the Gauls often and praised their valor in fighting for freedom - even if only to magnify his own victories. Caesar wrote as if he need not justify using any method necessary to break the Gauls' resistance to Roman rule.

According to Caesar, the gods played almost no role in the Gallic wars. Victory was gained by the general's strategy, the number of troops, the courage of the men, the speed of maneuvers. Caesar never thanked the gods for victory and did not mention divination or religious ceremonies in camp. In the entire book, he recorded only one instance of a valiant soldier invoking the gods as he carried the legion's standard into the midst of the enemy's force. On the contrary, Caesar belittled religious superstitions that hurt the Gauls and cost the Romans their only defeat. The closest that Caesar came to invoking a religious framework was in a few comments about the god Fortune: "Fortune is indeed powerful in all things, and especially in military affairs." "Fortune had shown her strength by the sudden arrival of the enemy."[4] Fortune was like fate; impersonal, giving good and ill, and decipherable only after the events. Caesar never sought divine help, but his opponents explained their losses because the gods aided the Romans.

Caesar's neglect to give the gods credit for his victories need not mean that he was irreligious. After all, earlier he had campaigned for and been elected Pontifex Maximus (chief priest), and he described the "barbarian" Germans as worshipping and sacrificing to the same gods as the Romans, showing that he imposed his cultural norms on other peoples. In accounts of Caesar's deeds and

---

[4] Julius Caesar, *Seven Commentaries on the Gallic War*, tr. Carolyn Hammond (1996), 133, 140.

assassination written by Roman historians, he appears very conventional in his religious attitudes.[5] Yet whatever the reasons for his omissions, Caesar, like Thucydides, gave the gods no role in war.

Julius Caesar became one of the heroic figures of Western civilization, though some condemned his ambition that helped to lead to the end of the Republic and rise of the Empire. The schoolboys, scholars, and military commanders who read *The Conquest of Gaul* learned that Caesar's personal qualities: shrewdness, unscrupulousness, intelligence, and courage, when combined with the fighting prowess of the Roman legions, brought victory over much more numerous barbarians whose lives had been dedicated to becoming warriors.

Rome bequeathed to the world a strategy of constant vigilance and unlimited war. The most influential military treatise in the West until the beginning of the nineteenth century was Vegetius' *Of Things Military,* written in the fourth century, a time when its prescriptions for reinvigorating Rome's legions would be obsolete. Used by commanders of Charlemagne, carried by Crusaders, printed in the Renaissance, the treatise's advice for conducting sieges, the value of heavy infantry, and training methods would prove useful after the invention of gunpowder. In Germany alone in the nineteenth and twentieth centuries forty commentaries on the treatise were published. Vegetius, like Caesar, sought victory through superior strategy and ignored the role of gods and morality in war:

> It is the nature of war that what is beneficial to you is detrimental to the enemy and what is of service to him always hurts you ... He who aspires to peace should prepare for war ... An army unsupplied with grain and other necessary provisions will be vanquished without striking a blow ... Few men are born brave; many become so through training and force of discipline."[6]

---

[5] Suetonius, *Lives of the Caesars,* tr. J. C. Rolfe (1960), 81, 99, 107-11. "No regard for religion ever turned him from any undertaking, or even delayed him. Though the victim escaped as he was offering sacrifice, he did not put off his expedition against Scipio and Juba."

[6] Vegetius, *The Military Institutions of the Romans,* tr. John Clarke, in Roots of Strategy, ed. Thomas R. Phillips (1940), 68-72, 171-75.

B. Attempted Restraint in Roman War: The Fetials

Before the end of the first century B.C.E., it is rare even to find a Roman writer enthusiastic about peace. Only after their empire was created and the Republic threatened with civil war did Romans began to ponder if peace were not better than war and whether their conquests were legitimate. The only limitation on the Roman drive for empire came from the religious ceremonies involving the fetial observances. The fetials were Roman priests who visited the enemy and laid out the grievances of Rome before an official declaration of war. Under fetial law an envoy had to visit the enemy three times in order to state Rome's grievances and to give a chance for response. At issue is whether fetial practices actually restrained Rome or only provided a method of justifying past Roman actions.[7] In actuality, Rome ignored the fetial conditions if it was attacked, or if the enemy was weak, or if the enemy lived too far away to make three visits practicable. Often the envoy's demands were more about blackmail than about negotiation, with the Romans making the conditions outrageous, assuming that the results would be rejection. The Romans may have assumed that they were seeking redress for injury, but they were really issuing non-negotiable conditions. The Romans used words like "injury" and "injustice," but it was not the content but the form of the fetial observance that established the rightness of the Roman cause. The justice sought was not a part of a universal system of equity to which actions had to conform, but was rather a declaration intended to gain the support of the gods. The conclusion of the war, a Roman victory, showed the justice of the initial demands. The fetials were a formulaic device whose effects were psychological but not a restraint on action.[8] In the Empire the fetials became less prominent even in theory, for the divine status of the emperor guaranteed the righteousness of the war and the favor of the gods.

---

[7] John Rich,"Fear, Greed and Glory: the Causes of Roman War-making in the Middle Republic," in *War and Society in the Roman World* (1993), 61-66. Rich argues that the Romans often used moral arguments, which on occasion may have restrained them because their consciences were not "infinitely elastic."

[8] Harris, p. 35, 166-72.

The fetials do show that for the Romans, like the Greeks, religious rituals undergirded war. Cicero even claimed that the Romans won their victories not because they were better soldiers, but because they were more religious. Classical civilizations did not separate functions of church from state. In Rome religion was a civil ritual, and sacrifices to the gods sanctified the existence and policies of a state and brought success in war. The *sacramentum*, the soldiers' oath to the Republic and later to the emperor, was a religious act reaffirmed several times a year. Each legion had a standard or pole topped by a golden eagle, representing Jupiter, Rome, and the unit. The legionnaire who carried the standard, a kind of early flag, into battle knew it should never be captured.

A soldier entering a Roman military camp was entering into a sacred space. In the exact center of the camp stood the standards. A fortified military camp was laid out in a manner that represented a recreation of the sacred city, Rome, the center of the world. Each Roman camp followed a prescribed calendar of sacred festivals to various deities. In addition to the state cults, which included emperor worship, officers and soldiers carried on unofficial cults outside the precincts of the camps.[9] Continuing the pattern begun by Alexander and his successors, Roman officials welcomed all religions as useful to the state, so long as their adherents did not claim exclusive truth or try to undermine other religious practices.

C. Cicero

Cicero (l06-43 B.C.E.), a soldier, politician, consul, and provincial governor created an uneasy blend of the traditional Roman glorification of war with the ideals of the Stoics and Platonists. Cicero sought to limit unjust war, even though he actually defended all the previous wars of Rome that had created the Empire. Drawing upon principles of the Stoics, Cicero asserted that the reason structuring nature resulted in universal moral laws binding upon all peoples everywhere:

---

[9]John Helgeland, "Roman Army Religion," *Aufstieg und Niedergang der Romischen Welt* (1978), 1470-1505; for examples of Roman prayers for victory, see Harris, 118-24.

The moral law equaled right reason in agreement with nature." Nature endowed all living creatures with an instinct for self-preservation. Unlike animals, humans used reason to modify or tame this instinct in order to create civilization and norms for personal behavior, family life, and government.[10]

The natural law principles underlying correct behavior among individuals also applied to states. For example, an individual should receive justice, which Cicero, like Plato, defined as a person's giving and receiving one's due. Giving and receiving justice was also an imperative for the state. The state and individuals had a sacred obligation to prevent injury to themselves as well as others; each also had a duty to keep their agreements. If an injury occurred, the individual might run away or absorb an injury, even risk his own life. A state could not risk suicide, because it was obliged to preserve a good life for its citizens. So, unlike an individual, a state could not run away from or ignore or accept an injury. Cicero concluded, therefore, that according to natural law, any war the state fought for defense or to avenge an injury was just.

For Cicero the procedures that Rome followed to ensure that its wars were just derived from the fetial ceremonies; that is, the war had to be proclaimed, and fighting could begin only after the enemy received warning and had rejected the opportunity to redress the injury it had inflicted. Cicero, like Plato and Aristotle, insisted that the goal of life was not war but peace. The state was to create a well-ordered society in which beauty and order prevailed. The higher nature of man was against violence, so war became a last resort used only after diplomacy failed. The state's obligation was twofold: to punish those who inflicted wrong and to shield those who were wronged.

If Cicero had been consistent, his principles might have served as a rebuke to the way Rome fought. Instead, Cicero showed his commitment to the traditional Roman attitudes by adding the quest for supremacy and "glory" as

---

[10] Cicero, *De Officiis*, quoted in Holmes, 25-31. For the context of Cicero's discussion, see Thomas Mitchell, *Cicero: The Senior Statesman* (1991), 205-11.

allowable reasons for war; however, wars fought for glory should be conducted more mildly. In either case, promises made to the enemy must be kept. Examples of Roman wars cited by Cicero as illustration for his principles showed that any war decreed by Rome could be termed "just." He construed even the existence of an alternative powerful state as threatening the supremacy of Rome. Cicero knew that some of the Roman wars had been provoked by ambitious generals seeking glory. In theory, either the fetials or the natural law demand for self-defense should have restrained such power-mad individuals, but Cicero did not provide any mechanism or a clear enough exposition of what was a sufficient fault to create a significant check. Instead, like the fetial observances, Cicero's principles of injury, self-defense, supremacy, and glory provided a rationale to justify Roman expansion rather than a principle to restrain war.

During the Empire, there were many examples of Roman historians, philosophers, and poets - of whom the most famous is Virgil - praising peace, rejoicing in the closing of the doors of the temple of Janus during the peace in the reign of Augustus, and condemning war in the abstract. The *Aeneid* of Virgil (70-19 B.C.E.) became until the twentieth-century the most widely read secular poem in the Western world, studied by many generations of school children learning Latin. Virgil drew upon the themes of Homer's *Iliad* in tracing the interactions between gods and humans from the fall of Troy to the foundation of Rome. The first line proclaimed the subject as "of arms and man," but could also have added "and the gods." Jupiter, when he pays attention to events, like Fate, decrees final results, but individual gods cause war and bring victory or defeat. Virgil portrayed the gods as being in control but this brought no solace for humans living in a "vale of tears."

Neither Virgil nor the heroes in the epic question the value of public religious rites. They saw the gods as enabling Aeneas to found Rome; later they allowed the city to fulfill its destiny of ruling the world. Individual traits bring success or failure, and yet the decision of the gods is also responsible. Aeneas, the Trojan hero, is pious toward the gods, dutiful to his father, obedient to his destiny of going to Italy, and peace seeking - seeing the war he is forced to fight as unnecessary. Yet Aeneas and his major opponent Turnus are, like Achilles and Hector, mighty warriors, exalting in battle and succumbing to blood lust.

Virgil, like Cicero, rejoiced in the military discipline that allowed the rise of Rome from an obscure village to world power, but he also extolled the blessing of moderation and peace to his patron Caesar Augustus.[11] Virgil had lived through the civil wars at the end of the Republic and the beginning of the Empire, and his poem has a dual focus: rejoicing in heroism and bewailing the effects of war, the latter most prominent in sorrowful descriptions of the destruction of Troy and the deaths of young men in the battles in Italy. Like Virgil, for the citizens of Rome the benefits of a secure civilized peaceful existence foreclosed any questioning of the brutal methods used to create and sustain the "Pax Romana."[12]

Christians in the next three centuries would identify their interests with the survival of the Empire, accept Cicero's injury and self-defense, but reject glory and supremacy as just causes for war, and replace gods with the Lord God as the granter of victory. The Church's transition from obscurity to political power is our theme.

II. The Church in the Empire

The Christians who were subjects or citizens of Rome provide our first evidence on the early Church's attitude to war. As early as the Middle Ages, a debate began within the Church that continues to this day as to whether Roman Christians fulfilled, adapted, or betrayed the teachings of Jesus. The content of the early Church's teachings on war and peace takes on additional importance because of the first Christians' role in creating the New Testament and normative interpretations of religious belief and practices. Many Catholics and Protestants continue to assert that the actions of the Church Fathers (i.e., Patristics) are a

---

[11] Virgil, *Aeneid* (1984). For modern discussions on Virgil's war views, see R.D. Williams, *The Aeneid* (1987), 56-77.

[12] The "pax Romana" used to describe Augustus' reign distorts the fact that Augustus greatly expanded the Empire, and disorder and rebellion occurred frequently. Tim Cornell, "The End of Roman Imperial Expansion," in *War and Society in the Roman World,* 164-68.

source of authoritative teaching second in importance only to the Scriptures. After all, the apostles had known Jesus; the next generation could talk to those who had known the person who they believed was messiah. Our task in this section is to sketch out the different modern interpretations of Roman Christians' attitudes to war and peace, to show the kind of evidence available, and, finally, to analyze the teachings on war of two major early Christian writers Tertullian (ca. 155-ca. 240) and Origen (ca. 185-254). The last section will assess changes in both halves of the Empire after Christianity became the officially espoused religion.

The New Testament never directly addressed whether a follower of Christ should support the wars of Rome or become a soldier in the Roman army. While there are offhand comments about war in the literature of the early Church, there are no surviving treatises that discuss the issues in any depth. This lacuna results in scholars' drawing widely divergent conclusions. Because none can be proved even within striking range of beyond reasonable doubt, in the past as well as the present the social and religious views of the scholars themselves predominate.

There is general agreement that there is no certain reference to Christians serving in the Roman army before 173 C.E.; the evidence is mixed between 173 before 250; and there were significant numbers of Christians in the army by 300. Constantine's vision of the cross before his decisive battle of Milvian Bridge in 312 consolidated rather than initiated a major change in the Church's attitudes to war. The debate is then: was the early Church pacifist and began only in the late third century to accept the legitimacy of war? Or, alternatively, did the early Church have no position on war, but as its numbers of adherents and position in Roman society improved, come to see the need for defense of the Empire? Did most Christians choose not to serve because of opposition to all war, the danger of committing idolatry in military camps, or some combination of the two? Aggressive wars were not at issue because for the first centuries of Christianity the Empire was at peace or engaged in defensive war. So early Christians faced the question whether any war, even of self-defense, was moral.

116

The scholars who stress the anti-war tradition establish their case through numerous citations by Church fathers (all the literature was produced by men, most of whom were priests) of condemnations of war and its effects and their complaints about the sinful causes of war. They also find writers contrasting Jesus as the bringer of peace with the heathen deities who allegedly wanted war. War and death were the products of sin; peace and eternal life were the Christian message. Christians did not serve in the military because believers took literally the teachings of the Sermon on the Mount and blessed peacemakers, loved their enemies, and turned the other cheek. Allegedly, the reason there were no explicit treatises on the subject of war was that all Christians agreed to avoid such immoral activities. There are no writings calling upon Christians to join the army or exalting in killing in battle. Instead, Christians, whose mission was the imitation of Christ, not the service of Caesar, continued to trust God who controlled the destiny of the world and sought peace by what the Church preached as the only truly efficacious action - prayer.[13]

Those who find the pacifist interpretation inadequate explain the absence of sources justifying war in two ways. First, the early Church expected the imminent return of Christ. All kingdoms of this world were transitory, and Christians had no concern with any earthly powers. By the end of the first century, when Christ had not returned to usher in the *parousia*, Christians reinterpreted the meaning of the return of Jesus in a spiritual fashion and began to rethink their responsibility to the general society. Second, Rome considered Christianity a variant of Judaism. Jews were not required to serve in the army, and there was no need for volunteers. In addition, Christianity grew most rapidly

---

[13] The classic statement is John Cadoux, *The Early Christian Attitude to War* (1919); updated by G. H. C. MacGregor, *New Testament Basis of Pacifism* (1936). John H. Yoder, "War as a Moral Problem in the Early Church: The Historian's Hermeneutical Assumptions," in *The Pacifist Impulse in Historical Perspective* (1996) cautions that modern definitions of pacifism are not the same as the early church's moral condemnation of war and refusal to kill. John H. Yoder, *Christian Attitudes to War, Peace, and Revolution: A Companion to Bainton* (1983), 23-54 assesses the change in perspective required when the Church changed from a pacifist to pro-Roman war stance.

in cities, and these cities furnished few soldiers because they were far from the frontiers of the Empire.

For non-pacifist scholars the primary issue for the early Church was not love of enemy or imitating Jesus' nonviolent action, but idolatry. In the military camps worship of the emperor and pagan deities was an everyday occurrence. Because Christians strongly condemned idolatry, their absence from the military shows more about the exclusive nature of their religion than their views of war.[14] Anecdotes about Jesus in the non-canonical literature of the early Church (i.e., writings that were not included in the New Testament) were less concerned with portraying him as humble and merciful than as a powerful miracle worker. Stories of the childhood of Jesus show that those who tease or beat him up soon die. The mothers of Jesus' playmates appealed to Mary for help because playing with the Son of God was a high-risk activity.[15] The early Church advocated love within the congregation, but wanted judgment and apocalyptic war on opponents. Condemnation of war in the abstract and praise of peace by leading spokesman for the Church did not establish a pacifist Church, because such views have always remained common among those who see war as an evil, but still a necessary activity. During the first century the Church did not face the problem of war and never developed a consistent ethic.

As in the case of many other important historical problems, it may be impossible now to arrive at firm conclusions, but the remaining fragmentary evidence suggests that some second century Christians refused to serve in the military and others joined. One proposed compromise solution is that some Christians in the military served in areas far removed from the scene of hostilities and acted as a civil police or, as the Empire declined, a kind of bureaucracy.

---

[14] The classic statement is Adolf von Harnack, *Militia Christi: The Christian Religion and the Military in the First Three Centuries* (1905), tr. and introduction by David M. Gracie (1981). Two recent denials that the early church was pacifist are John Helgeland, "Christians and the Military from Marcus Aurelius to Constantine" and "Roman Army Religion," *Aufstieg und Niedergang der Romischen Welt* (1979), 724-834, and Louis Swift, *The Early Fathers on War and Military Service* (1983).

[15] "The Infancy Gospel of Thomas," *New Testament Apocrypha* (1963), 392-99, 409.

Unfortunately, though some Christian documents allow this interpretation (by telling Christian soldiers not to shed blood or commit idolatry and to withdraw in time of war), Roman accounts of army life show no such tolerance of tender consciences. Even after 300, it is scarcely credible that the army would allow soldiers to serve in peacetime but leave when there was a danger of war.[16]

Scholars on both sides of the debate assume that there was a Christian attitude to war. More likely, there were differences in applying Christian teaching to war because of regional variations or degree of commitment. Enormous diversity in doctrine and in practice marked the early Church. It took centuries of effort, many Church councils, and the power of the Roman state to define Christian orthodoxy, and even then the unity was superficial. So during the second century it seems plausible that Christians in some areas of the Empire stayed away from the army because they were opposed all wars and were afraid of idolatry, but in other places they joined the army, and some soldiers converted to Christianity and continued to serve. Although church leaders denounced the Roman religion as idol worship, a soldier might have considered the ceremonies to statues as insignificant because there was only one God.

The first evidence of Christians in the army is the story of the Thundering Legion. In 173 this legion, fighting the Germans, was allegedly saved from dying of thirst by rain brought about by the prayers of unarmed Christian soldiers. (Some sources claim that Jupiter brought the rain.) The importance of the story is not which god was efficacious or even if the story is true, but that Christians preserved a tradition about fellow believers serving in the military aided by the Christian God.[17]

---

[16] Roland Bainton, *Christian Attitudes Towards War* (1960), 79-81. During the Empire, the creation of permanent military camps, the use of foreign soldiers who married, and the settling of veterans in local communities meant greater integration of soldiers into local life. This also would have facilitated greater impact of Christianity on soldiers. Brian Campbell, "The Roman Empire," 226-27.

[17] John Helgeland, Robert Daly, and J. Patout Burns, *Christians and the Military: The Early Experience* (1985), 31-35. For a discussion of problems using the story to prove anything about early Christians, see Yoder, 100-101.

The accounts of Christians as military martyrs come from the end of the third century. For example, around 260 a soldier named Marinus served with such distinction that he was picked to become an officer. A fellow soldier complained that Marinus should not be chosen because he was a Christian, so Marinus was ordered to sacrifice to the emperor. After consultation with his bishop, Marinus refused and was beheaded. Another martyr soldier was Marcellus, a centurion, who threw down his sword and refused to take the oath. When questioned, Marcellus replied, "It is not proper for a Christian . . . to fight for the troubles of this world."[18] The stories of the Thundering Legion and the martyrs make sense only if many Christians supported Rome, served in the military, and did not wish to commit idolatry. The soldier martyrs show that worship and oaths to pagan gods caused Christians to disobey.

Our earliest source of the story of the Thundering Legion is Tertullian (ca. 160-220), who was not a sympathetic observer of Christian participation in war. In his *Apology* (ca. 197), Tertullian commented on the number of Christians in every walk of life. "Already we have filled . . . everything that belongs to you -- the cities, apartment houses, fortresses, towns, market places, the (military) camps themselves, your tribes, town councils, the imperial palace, the Senate." Since there is no record of Christians being in the Senate or the palace this early, maybe Tertullian was referring to the slaves serving the magistrates in these places. His second reference allows no ambiguity: "We, no less than you, sail the sea, serve in the army, farm the land, buy and sell." In both instances Tertullian boasted about the spread of Christianity and the numbers of the believers. He also stressed the loyalty of Christians to the Empire: "We pray without ceasing for all emperors, for their prolonged life, for a secure empire, for protection of the imperial palace, for brave armies . . . ."[19] Rome stood as a bulwark against the

---

[18] Ibid., 61; Louis Swift, *The Early Christian Experience of War* (1983), 71-79

[19] The salient passages are reprinted in Holmes, 39-47; Helgeland, et al., 21-30; Swift, 38-46. Tertullian, *Apology*, 17, 26, 40, 42; *On Idolatry*, 70-71, 73. *The Ante-Nicene Fathers*, III, tr. Alexander Roberts and James Donaldson (1885).

chaos that would accompany the *parousia*, and so, for Tertullian, Christians would support the state.

In later life Tertullian became a critic of what he saw as the compromises of the Church and demanded a more ascetic pattern of life. He also protested, not always consistently, against Christians serving in the military. Jesus' taking the sword away from Peter in the garden of Gethsemane, he argued, "disarmed every soldier." Joshua had a divine blessing to lead the Jewish nation into war, but Christ was a "son of peace." Because of the oaths, the idolatry, and the sacrifices, Christians should not join the army, and those who converted should leave "as many have done" because remaining would entail "so much quibbling it seems an impossibility." The moral obligation of a soldier and civilian was the same, and there was no dispensation for "wrongdoing" because of "necessity."

The most detailed account of Christians and warfare comes from Origen (ca. 185-254). Origen faced the most vexing problems confronting the Church in dealing with the ethics of war: the relation between Old and New Testaments, Christian revelation versus Greco/Roman learning, and the role of Christians in Roman society. For the earliest Christians the Hebrew Scriptures were holy writings; by the time of Origen the Church saw most of the books of what we know as the New Testament as equally authoritative. The writers of the Gospels had shown how Jesus' actions and teachings fulfilled Old Testament prophecies. Later apologists for Christianity, using a pattern earlier pioneered by Jewish philosophers, made the God of the Old Testament resemble a rational Greek deity. Philo of Alexandria, a Hellenized Jew, interpreted stories of God in the Hebrew Scriptures by stressing their deeper or allegorical meaning. Paul, in Acts, when visiting in Athens found near the Acropolis an altar to an unknown god whom he identified with God. First century Christians identified the Hebrew Lord God as the Platonic or Stoic Logos or Prime Mover, and asserted that the revelation found through Jesus fulfilled the best wisdom exemplified in Greek philosophy.

Pagan opponents who read the Hebrew Scriptures charged that Yahweh who caused the sun to stand still so the Israelites could kill Canaanite kings and forbade the eating of pork, was not a God of reason. Such views found sympathizers within the Church. In the second century Marcion asserted that the god of the Hebrew Scriptures was not the Christian God. He contrasted a god of violence with the God of love, and sought to divorce Jesus from Judaism. Marcion denied that the Hebrew Scriptures were sacred books and sought to make as the only Christian scriptures an expurgated version of Luke and the letters of Paul. Because none of Marcion's treatises have survived (knowledge of his ideas comes from quotations and refutations by his opponents), it is not possible to know whether he drew a contrast between the war in the Hebrew Scriptures and the New Testament.

Origen, unlike the pagan philosophers and Marcion, assumed that the stories in the Hebrew Scriptures were true, but he did not approve of the violence and irrationality associated with the Lord God. The God of Jesus would not require dietary commands or bloodthirsty war as described in Judges. Origen distinguished between the historical/literal meaning of Joshua's conquest and the real spiritual and moral meaning exemplified by Jesus. Christians engaged in a war, but did not fight with physical weapons. Instead, using the military metaphors of Paul, Origen pictured the real battle as inward and heavenly and the sword of Christ as prayer and love. Origen used a typological exegesis to link Joshua and Jesus; that is, Joshua's actions prefigured Jesus. Joshua led the Hebrews into a physical Promised Land through outward military victories; Jesus delivered Christians from sin, defeated the powers of evil by his crucifixion/resurrection, and led the new people chosen of God into the Promised Land of salvation. Christians imitated Christ, and Origen insisted that Christians

122

were forbidden to make use of the sword under any pretext whatsoever. Killing was forbidden whether for "self-defense" or "by reason of being in the army."[20]

The uncompromising tone of Origen's strictures against war seems to make him an absolute pacifist who did not oppose war because of emperor worship or the danger of idolatry, but because of Christ's express commands and actions. Such a stance left Christians open to the charge expressed fifty years earlier by Celsus. Celsus charged that Christians weakened Rome by refusing to serve in the army and by avoiding prayer for the emperor as a god. Since some Christians were in the military, Origen could have responded that Celsus' charges were untrue. Instead, he accepted them as descriptive of Christian conduct, and argued that Christians prayers to the one true God would bring the emperor victory in a just war. Prayer was more powerful than pagan soldiers. Origen never spelled out the criteria that would determine whether the war was just, nor did he imply, like Cicero, that all Roman wars were just.

Origen and most other second century Christian apologists asserted that the creation of the Roman Empire was providential, because the creation of its extensive area allowed for the peaceful spread of Christianity. Augustus Caesar had served the purposes of God in creating a land of peace. The Pax Romana was a pre-figuring or type of the peace within the Church.[21] The eventual spread of Christianity throughout the world would end the occasion for any war. Until that occurred, the non-Christians fighting in the army would be aided by the prayers of the faithful.

It is difficult to derive a consistent ethic of war from Origen. A complication in understanding Origen arises because he distinguished between right conduct for Christians inside and outside the army. Those outside the army must remain pure; those converted in the army must take care never to shed blood.

---

[20] Holmes, 48-50; Helgeland, 39-44; Swift, 52-59; Origen, *Against Celsus*, in *Ante-Nicene Fathers*, IV, 666-668; my interpretation of Origen is based on Gerald E. Caspary, *Politics and Exegesis: Origen and the Two Swords* (1979), 18-32, 125-34.
[21] Caspary, 127, 138.

Christians should refrain even from attending public executions. The passages in *Mark* where Jesus resisted political power, argued Origen, did not indicate that the state was illegitimate, but that Christians had a higher calling.

Origen had an almost secular view of the state. God created the political realm for the use of non-Christians and the Church for true believers. In what amounted to a separated church and state, the magistrate could use a carnal sword in order to preserve a "this worldly" and ephemeral peace.[22] For Origen, the "render unto Caesar" passage meant to give Rome the worldly gold and to preserve the soul for God. Christians would wield the spiritual sword within their own souls, the Church, and the society to destroy the evil forces or demons that caused war. For Origen all of life was a war against evil, Christ was the supreme leader in the only battle of eternal significance, and the weapons of his human soldiers were nonviolent.

Tertullian and Origen, like most Christian apologists before 300, saw the continued existence of the Roman Empire as a good. The Church contrasted evil and persecuting rulers like Nero and Diocletian with good emperors like Marcus Aurelius who left the Church in peace. Christian writers blamed sporadic Roman persecution on demons or evil advisers stirring up opposition, and did not criticize the government of Rome. Instead, they agreed with pagan writers that religion sustained the Empire, with the main difference being that the responsible deity was not Jupiter but God. Christian intellectual support for the Empire meant that Roman officials could become members, and the Church - particularly in urban areas - began to attract a higher class of converts.

The spread of Christianity also prompted new efforts by supporters of traditional Roman gods who recognized that that the exclusive nature of monotheism challenged the Empire's pattern of welcoming and utilizing all religions for the purposes of the state. Christianity in essence created a new paradigm of loyalty to one true religion, and advocates of traditional Roman gods

---

[22] Ibid., 142.

found there was no way to add worship of Christ to sacrifices to Jupiter as jointly supporting the state. Before, Rome welcomed all religions; now Christianity opposed syncretism. Defenders of an older Roman civilization felt threatened by Christianity, and between 250 and 312, brief periods of intense but largely ineffectual persecution followed edicts of toleration. Eventually the status of Christianity became a political issue in the struggles of various claimants to be emperor.

III. Constantine and the Triumph of Christianity

Constantine, before his decisive victory in the Western Roman Empire at the battle of Milvian Bridge in 312, claimed to have had a vision of the cross with the words "In this sign thou shalt conquer." So he had emblazoned on the shields of his soldiers the sign of the cross, and they fought with the support of the Christian God.[23] Roman armies carried into battle a standard with an imperial eagle representing the sun god or Jupiter. Constantine's soldiers soon carried into battle a standard made of gold and studded with jewels depicting either the initial letters of the name of Jesus or the cross. Bishop Ambrose, less than a century later, wrote that Constantine enclosed a fragment of the true cross in the golden cross carried to war and put relics of Christianity into the harness of the horse he rode in battle. The triumphal march after victory had previously climaxed with sacrifices to Jupiter. After Constantine's victories, a mass in church replaced such sacrifices. Instead of Roman priests and diviners, Christian priests or a bishop now accompanied armies into battle.

Constantine took the title Victor, because Invictus, or invincible, referred to the relation of the Emperor to Jupiter. Victor was a more neutral term, though for Christians it may have had a more positive connotation because it had been used to describe martyrs. The meaning of the terms was the same: Caesars before

---

[23] Pamphilus Eusebius, *Life of The Blessed Emperor Constantine* (1845), 26. Eusebius claimed that Constantine told him of the vision and also the appearance of Christ in a dream. Eusebius' account of Constantine's espousal of Christianity stresses the utilitarian nature of the decision for God as a guarantee of victory. Timothy Barnes provides the context for this vision in *Constantine and Eusebius* (1981), 43-44, 266-7. The probable form of the cross termed a labarum is an "XP."

had been Invictus because they had the support of the gods; now Constantine and his successors would be Victor because they had the aid of God. The language Christians used for martyrs who sacrificed their lives for a holy cause and gained an everlasting victory now vindicated soldiers who shed their blood in a war for God.[24]

Christianity, no longer persecuted or barely tolerated, now emerged as an official religion of the Empire, although its relationship to traditional Roman gods remained ambiguous. At first the invocation of Christianity in war celebrations existed on a parallel track with continued calls on traditional gods. Like the old gods, Christ brought victory in war and prosperity in peace. Defenders of Christianity, like Bishop Eusebius, identified the peace of Rome with the peace of Christ. Eusebius compared the Milvian Bridge victory with God's destruction of the Egyptians at the Red Sea. Just as earlier Christian apologists saw Augustus as chosen by God to create a peace allowing the true religion to spread throughout the Empire, now bishops asserted that God picked Constantine so that Rome could be reconstituted upon a new foundation of Christianity. The reign of Constantine supposedly fulfilled the prophecies of Isaiah about the coming reign of peace.[25]

The blending of Christian and Roman culture took centuries to complete. Constantine was pictured as a thirteenth apostle, but coins issued during his reign identified him sometimes with Jupiter and other times with a cross, and he retained the title Pontifex Maximus. Both Emperor and the Church had to adjust to the new situation. The Emperor wanted Christianity to unify the realm, not to create controversy with non-Christians. The Church received imperial patronage in building churches, creating a Christian art, defining correct doctrine, and

---

[24] Michael McCormick, *Eternal Victory: Triumphal Rulership in Late Antiquity, Byzantium and the Early Medieval West* (1986), 37-40,101-04. Eusebius, *Life of Constantine,* 69, 74.; Andrew Alfoldi, *The Conversion of Constantine and Pagan Rome.* tr. Harold Mattingly (1948), 21-23. A good introduction to the roles of Christianity in Rome and Byzantium, though devoting little attention to issues of war and peace, is Judith Herrin, *The Formation of Christendom* (1987).

[25] Eusebius, *Life of Constantine,* 4-8. Charles Cochrane, *Christianity and Classical Culture* (1957).

persecuting heretics. Should the Emperor have a role in defining doctrine? After all, Constantine was only a layman and recent convert, but he was also the Lord's anointed who summoned and attended the Council of Nicaea that promulgated the doctrine of the trinity, the co-equality of God the Father, God the Son, and God the Holy Spirit. Later emperors would also call Church councils in an attempt to standardize beliefs about the nature of God and Jesus.

The contrast, often drawn by later reformers within and outside the Roman Catholic Church, between the plain living and pacifism of the earlier Christians and the pomp and militarism of the Church after Constantine is now recognized to be an over-simplification. If the Church had not already become deeply imbedded in Roman society before 300, she could not have so easily become the handmaiden and also reformer of the state. For example, the Church from a position of weakness had long voiced support for the Roman Empire. Could she now from a position of strength do less? And if the Christian God were all-powerful and had intervened on behalf of the faithful Israelites, would not the Lord God also favor Rome in battle? The Hebrew Scriptures recorded God's intervention in Joshua's battles. Now Constantine and his successors, who would be identified with Moses and David as defenders of the one true faith, would have God on their side.

Constantine's wars now became holy; priests and emperor placed the sign of Christ on his helmet and prayed before battle in a kind of tabernacle similar to what the ancient Hebrews had used to house of the Ark of the Covenant. The militarization of Christianity can be illustrated in the changing composition of the army. A century after Constantine all non-Christians were barred from serving in the army.[26]

Still, the anti-war tradition in the New Testament and early Church did not disappear. Traditional Roman religion had distinguished the function of priests

---

[26] Eusebius, *Life of Constantine*, 28, 56. John Howard Yoder, *Christian Attitudes To War, Peace and Revolution* (1983), 39-45; Bainton, 88. The word "pagan" in Latin originally meant "a civilian;" now its meaning changed into "a non-Christian."

from warriors and had guaranteed the sanctity of temples. Christianity arrived at the same conclusions. Eusebius insisted that a priest who participated in the sacrifice of Jesus in the Eucharist should not shed blood. At around 400 a compilation of disciplinary rules told Christians not to volunteer for the army and allowed soldiers who had shed blood to gain admission to the Eucharist, but only after a long period of penance.

After Constantine's conversion, the social acceptability of being Christian grew, but the large number of new adherents also resulted in what some saw as a lowering of standards of acceptable religious behavior. The Church pondered how forgiving it would be of those who after conversion committed grievous sin or who under persecution had recanted or turned in their copies of the *Bible* to be burned. Not all the emperors after Constantine were pro-Christian. Julian, the Apostate (r. 331-363), attempted to revive traditional Roman religion and persecuted Christians. A group of North African Christians termed Donatists saw the Church in Rome as far too tolerant of lapsed Christians. Within a century bishops had to decide whether they would be tolerant of the Donatists, of others who threatened the unity of the Church, and of paganism. The answer, in each case, was no. The solution was to first use persuasion, but if that failed, to employ coercion, and to rely upon the power of the Roman state to enforce uniformity in the Church.

Christian Roman officials sought to reconcile their faith with their responsibilities in the Empire. Their response to the issues of war became easier because Rome was a status quo power, attempting to preserve and defend what it already controlled rather than to expand. And Roman rule looked positively benign when contrasted with the alternatives offered by the Vandals and the Goths, the Germanic or so-called barbarian invaders. Aristotle, Plato, and Cicero had allowed the legitimacy of self-defense. The Old Testament recorded the successful wars of kings who were faithful to God, and the Church saw itself as the new Israel and the Empire as a force for good. Christian apologists wanted to prove that their God could be more helpful in war than false pagan gods. If Christians were to provide the cement for the Empire, the Church needed to legitimatize its members' serving in the legions in a way that abrogated neither the New Testament nor the traditions of the early Church. The two bishops in the Western Roman Empire most influential in this process were Ambrose of Milan (ca. 339-397) and Augustine of Hippo (354-430), both of whom were later declared saints.

A. Ambrose and Augustine

Ambrose's writings merged traditional Roman learning with Christian emphases. After all, he was a layman serving as a provincial Roman governor who had not been baptized when he was chosen Bishop of Milan. Ambrose insisted that a Christian should not engage in self-defense and should put aside personal violence or seeking for gain. Yet the bishop also insisted that a Christian had a responsibility for his fellows and could engage in violence to protect them from harm. A violent act on behalf of one's neighbors did not negate Christian love, because one could love the person doing harm while still opposing his evil, even while killing him.[27]

Peace was always preferable to war, argued Ambrose, but under certain circumstances Christians could serve in the military. Citizens should not take up their weapons irresponsibly or on their own initiative. Ambrose strongly condemned any civil war against duly constituted authority. All wars were not wrong or God would not have initiated and fought in the wars of Israel. What then constituted Just War? Following Cicero, Ambrose insisted that the magistrate had authority from God to punish wrongdoing and defend the nation. Also like Cicero, Ambrose defended the wars creating the Roman Empire as just and, like Eusebius, saw the existence of the "Pax Romana" of Augustus as God's providential ordering of history to prepare the way for the spread of Christianity. When the Emperor Theodosius prepared to battle the Goths, Ambrose proclaimed a holy war in which Jehovah would vindicate his religion and celebrated a mass for victory. His confidence should have been shaken when the Goths destroyed a

---

[27] Selections from Augustine on war are in Holmes, 55-60; Helgeland, 74-75; Swift, 96-110.

Roman army. Ambrose identified God with the cause of Rome and Christianity and came close to asserting that any war with barbarians/infidels was just.

When the Emperor Theodosius in 390 killed 7,000 inhabitants of Thessalonica because they had murdered a Roman official, Ambrose required the Emperor to do public penance. In less than a hundred years after Constantine, a bishop had evolved from a purely spiritual leader of a persecuted minority to become an official with sufficient power to discipline an emperor. Such changes occurred because of a series of crises that beset the Western Roman Empire. The invasion of western Europe and north Africa by the Vandals and the sack of Rome by the Goths in 412 showed that the Roman peace was ending.

Augustine was the most important single figure in shaping the Western Christian traditions of war and peace. His influence came partially because he managed to combine the Greco-Roman, biblical, and Christian perspectives, but also because ambiguities in his writings allowed later generations to take passages out of context or to erode subtle distinctions. Augustine wrote an enormous amount, generally to meet a specific objective, over a long period of time, and his thoughts on war and peace reflect the unsettled times in which he lived. He never wrote a treatise in which he summarized all his thoughts about war and peace, and there is a danger of ignoring inconsistencies or of reading too much significance into what might have been an offhand comment. Augustine's thoughts on war and peace, like his political theories, grew out of his vision of the Christian life.

War, a symbol of all the ills of humanity for Augustine, was an inescapable part of human existence because people were deeply flawed and societies provided evidence of their weaknesses. The failures of mankind, which he termed "original sin," produced people's estrangement from God, their false evaluation of creation. Selfish impulses in the form of a lust for domination governed all humanity. Because humans were controlled by their sinful desires, the state needed to restrain these impulses. The state's survival required constraint, coercion, and hierarchy - all of which were contrary to human existence before the fall. Yet the state, or the City of Earth in Augustine's phrase, did provide the order necessary for civilized life and was, therefore, a good.

All human beings, according to Augustine, divided into two groups, or Cities, on the basis of their loves. Love here was not romantic passion, but a basic orientation of being. To love was natural to all humans; but the distinction between the members of the two Cities came on the basis of the real worth of the object they loved. Christians believed that the ultimate object of life was to know and love God, and those who inhabited the City of God structured the rest of their existence through that love. Inevitably, however, true Christians shared this world with those who loved only the earthly City. Augustine approved of a love of human life of happiness, beauty, and sensual delight, but condemned the failure to keep worldly values in true perspective. Humans were pilgrims here, and ultimate fulfillment would come in life after death. The inhabitants of the City of Earth took partial goods and made them ultimate, with the result that humans were always striving, always unfulfilled. Their false view, this estrangement from God that was an inescapable part of human existence, contaminated all human creativity and accomplishments, and was the ultimate cause of war.

History intermixed the two kingdoms or Cities. Assyria, Babylon, Persia, Greece, and Rome exemplified the City of Man. All these empires attempted unsuccessfully to create an ordered secure existence by dominating the world. Their wars were symptomatic of their prideful attempts to create peace. The City of God, existing in the midst of the City of Man, was the history of salvation embodied first in ancient Israel and more recently in Jesus and the Church. Israel had, like Jerusalem, both a natural and a spiritual existence. At times Augustine described the Church as a mixed body composed of saints and sinner, but also the embodiment of the City of God on earth. Yet he also wrote as if both state and Church were symbolic of the two cities. Augustine's writings are ambiguous about the extent to which the Church itself was tainted or whether its institutional form on earth could be identified with the City of God. The grace offered by the Church to believers was sufficient for salvation, but would not end the flawed nature of the Christian's actions in this life because all human deeds and institutions remained tainted by original sin. Jesus linked the institutional Church as a grace-dispensing institution to the ultimate, pure City of God in heaven, and a believer through the sacraments could obtain the peace of God on earth.

The members of both Cities desired peace. True peace, like true justice, was "the tranquility of order . . . which allots things, equal and unequal, each to its own place." The result was peace, a harmony within a person, a family, a society, a state. The goal of human society was to create peace. Peace was the symbol of all good, just as war was the symbol of all evils. The heavenly peace of God was eternal and perfect; through grace humans could achieve a taste or a glimmering of it, but not the full realization in this life. The heavenly peace that Jesus brought was "either peace in eternal life, or eternal life in peace."[28]

Because all institutional embodiments in this life are only proximate and cannot bring full peace, humans had created states. The City of God did not need hierarchy and coercion; the earthly City did because it must restrain human sinfulness. The states in the City of Earth served a valuable function: they brought an approximate peace so that the inhabitants of the City of God could find the true love. The best that a state could do was to provide not a perfect but an adequate peace for the citizens to live in a natural harmony close to justice and based upon its peoples' desire for the right ordering of society. The state was a Band-Aid to alleviate temporarily the misery of human life, but it could not heal the wounds.

Unlike Eusebius and the Christian apologists in the Eastern Roman Empire, Augustine did not identify Rome with the Kingdom of God. Sinful men whose wars were kindled by aggression created Rome, like all other states. The emperor should be a servant of God, but he was not the thirteenth apostle. The peace that Rome brought, like the earlier peace of Persia and Alexander the Great,

---

[28] Saint Augustine, *The City of God* (1950), Book XIX, 686, 690.

was a false peace that would not endure. Still, the peace that Rome gave was a natural good, even worth fighting and killing to preserve.

For Augustine war was so horrible that it should always be engaged in only as a last resort after diplomacy had failed. He was very eloquent in detailing the horrors that war brought: pain, poverty, destruction, injury, and death. Yet these were only symptomatic of a deeper malaise: "What is the evil in war? Is it the death of some who will soon die in any case, that others may live in peaceful subjection? This is mere cowardly dislike, not any religious feeling. The real evils in war are love of violence, revengeful cruelty, fierce and implacable enmity, wild resistance, and the lust of power . . . ."[29]

Like Ambrose, Augustine found the Sermon on the Mount to be a rationale for Christians making war. A member of the City of God should not engage in self-defense, but in the earthly city a person had an obligation to protect his neighbor's life. Loving one's neighbors might require not just prayer but outward or physical protection. The ethic of Jesus was an inward disposition of love that could not be limited to any specific external act, but it also did not preclude an active defense. Augustine confidently proclaimed that a member of the heavenly city could love God and do as he or she pleased because the love of God would create the love of neighbor and enemy.

Merging Cicero and Matthew, Augustine insisted that the purpose of going to war was to create peace, so a Christian warrior engaged in a just cause was a peacemaker, a restorer of the natural harmony, the right order. Jesus had said, "love your enemies" but he had also opposed evil. Just Wars were to "avenge injuries, when a nation or a city should be punished for failing to right a wrong done by its citizens, or to return what has been taken away unjustly." So Just War was a form of punishment, law applied outside of the state. The aim of

---

[29] Holmes, 64. In addition to the selections in Holmes, 61-84; see Helgeland,78-85; Swift, 110-48. *The Political Writings of St. Augustine,* ed. Herbert Deane (1963) contains important documents. The best summary is William R. Stevenson, Jr., *Christian Love and Just War: Moral Paradox and Political Life in St. Augustine and His Modern Interpreters* (1987).

a Just War was a just settlement as close to the natural harmony of God as could be obtained in this world. "Peace should be the object of your desire; war should be waged only as a necessity, and waged only that God may by it deliver men from the necessity and preserve them in peace."[30]

The scriptural precedents for going to war had become traditional by the time Augustine cited them. Joshua and David were God's elect who waged war by His explicit command. John the Baptist had instructed the soldiers to be content with their wages; Jesus had praised the centurion's faith. An angel of the Lord appeared to the centurion Cornelius and told him to contact the apostle Peter; Peter preached to and converted Cornelius with no word of rebuke for his military career. The imitation of Christ was a counsel of perfection to be followed by the few, priests and monks, but that way of life was neither suitable nor attainable for the laity. There was no holy war in Augustine, no attempt to glorify war or the warrior. Rather, war was a part of the agony of the human condition, a reflection of the uncertainty of this world.

Augustine spelled out the implications of his view of a soldier's responsibility in a letter to Count Boniface, the leader of the Roman garrison in the town in North Africa where Augustine lived. Boniface sought to leave military service and join a monastery, even though the Vandals were threatening. Augustine sought to persuade Boniface to defer his decision and proclaimed the legitimacy of military calling as approved by God and necessary for society, even though a priest's vocation was higher. The best that a soldier could do was to create temporal peace; a priest could, through the sacraments, bring eternal peace.

The responsibility for initiating war never lay with the private individual. Augustine insisted that a private citizen robbed by a highwayman should not defend himself by killing the robber. Such a deed would indicate that the citizen placed ultimate value on his material possessions. The legacy of civil war at the

---

[30] Augustine as quoted by Aquinas, based on the compilation by Gratian, Holmes, 62.

end of the Roman Republic and struggles for succession as emperor prompted Augustine to argue that rebellion and civil war could never be justified.

If a commander demanded worship of idols, soldiers should manifest their disobedience through passive actions and refusal to commit the sin. But if the ruler began an unjust war, the soldier should still serve. The ruler had power and, according to Paul, all power derived from God. If the ruler was corrupt, even if he persecuted Christians, he was still God's anointed. The inhabitants of the City of Earth could not always discern the purposes of God, particularly when He allowed an evil ruler, but the Christian knew that God's providence would always conquer. Unlike Eusebius, Augustine found no ultimate significance in the Christianization of Rome; the obedience owed to the emperor came irrespective of his support of Christianity. Even so, Augustine wrote as if he assumed that the emperor would attempt to be the obedient servant of God.

Early in his life Augustine reserved the use of the sword for purely secular matters. He opposed the use of military power to promote the expansion of Christianity and insisted upon the necessity of free exercise of faith. However, as a bishop of an embattled church in North Africa, he faced the responsibility of defending orthodox Christianity against the Donatists. Because they insisted upon purity of conduct, the Donatists could not be accurately charged with immorality. During the long Donatist controversy in North Africa, Augustine changed his mind, or perhaps more accurately, drew out the implications of his conclusions on the use of force in matters of conscience. He first advocated the use of power of the state provided the coercion was done as an act of love, and if life itself was not threatened. Augustine insisted that only the shock of real danger would convince the Donatist heretics to return to the true Church. The issue, as Augustine saw it, was that a heretic was a danger not only to himself but also to his neighbor. A neighbor contaminated by heresy would forfeit eternal life; it was better policy to be rid of the heretic, even at the cost of a life. A pagan could be deprived of a right to worship, but not forced to join the Church. However, a Donatist schismatic who had once been a Catholic could be compelled to rejoin the true faith. Neither Augustine nor the Roman Church advocated killing heretics; rather, they sought to utilize the power of Rome to suppress heretical and pagan worship. Even so, Peter Brown, the best modern biographer of Augustine, does not deny that his subject deserved his later title the "Prince of Prosecutors."[31]

Augustine can be regarded as the founding father of Just War theory. He popularized the usage of "just cause" as punishment for wrong or something unjustly taken, though he did not spell out the exact meanings of these causes. He denied the right of private war and rebellion, insisting that only those with legitimate authority could conduct a Just War. His exegesis provided a rationale incorporating Christian love and peacemaking as the purpose for waging war and seeing war as a mournful necessity, a sign of sin, to be avoided if possible. He exempted clerics from fighting because of their function, but made no distinction between civilians and soldiers in the conduct of war. Lacking was any clear definition of what was permissible in the course of battle, although -- like Cicero -- Augustine insisted upon the necessity of keeping ones word with the enemy. Perhaps his emphasis upon loving the enemy could be considered a limitation of conduct in war. His clear distinction between the responsibilities of the City of God (Church) and the City of Earth (state) provided a foundation for later developments in western Europe. Still, his writings assumed the existence of a Roman emperor and a centralized Roman state preserving a Pax Romana by defending citizens threatened by unchristian barbarian hordes who observed no limitations on the initiation or conduct of war. Augustine died as his city of Hippo was besieged by the Vandals.

IV. Byzantium

Augustine wrote in Latin and was little read in the Eastern or Greek speaking portions of the Roman Empire, the capital of which was Byzantium,

---

[31] Peter Brown, "St. Augustine's Attitude to Religious Coercion," *Religion and Society in the Age of Augustine* (1972), 260, 277.

later renamed Constantinople. The last victory celebration in Rome occurred in 410; barbarians deposed the last Roman emperor in the west in 476; and the Western and Eastern Roman Empires, though one in theory, went their separate ways.

The Eastern Roman Empire would survive and preserve the heritage of classical civilization for almost another 1000 years. Constantinople, unlike Rome, was founded as a Christian city, and the merger of Christianity and the state had far-reaching consequences. The Byzantine pattern of automatic church support for the Empire's wars continued throughout its history and spread with the conversion of eastern Europe and Russia to Orthodox Christianity.

The Byzantine Empire's theory and practice of warfare remained far closer to the framework of Eusebius and Constantine than to Ambrose and Augustine. That is, there was no tradition of support for a pacifist witness by the general population of Christians, no questioning of the emperor's right to make war, and no limitations on strategy. The Empire was Christian and legitimate, and the barbarians who were pagans or infidels were the aggressors. When the Emperor Justinian in the sixth century defeated the Vandals and re-conquered North Africa, he treated the Vandal kings not as fellow monarchs but as usurpers or rebels.

The mosaics in Justinian's new capital in Ravenna pictured the Emperor as a semi-divine figure, God's emissary on earth. All emperors sought to achieve the same status, and various court rituals pictured the caesar as the defender of the Christian faith. The use of relics, supernatural deliverances by the Virgin, special prayers before and after battles, thanksgiving services at Justinian's magnificent church Hagia Sophia, and liturgical processions which paid special homage at shrines of Constantine and the Virgin - all became part of the Christianization of Byzantine warfare.

A preparation for battle of one of Justinian's armies on a holy day began with a Eucharistic service at dawn to which the standards were brought for blessing. Then the soldiers sang hymns and prayed for forgiveness. The commander then prayed: "Look upon the Romans at last, look, O highest God, and succor them, O holy Father, and with your power, I beseech you, smash the proud pagans. Let the peoples recognize you alone as Lord and powerful, while you crush the enemy and save your own kind by battle."[32] The soldiers in the field before battle might observe a fast day, and carried shields picturing the Virgin or various military saints. Monks who did not fight would carry crosses into battle. Such religious observances became part of the routine of preparation for battle.

The Byzantines acted as if the army's ethical and theological purity were as crucial to victory as its size or its competence. Victory came because God was on the side of the Christians, and special readings from Exodus and Psalms confirmed God's participation in the battle. Defeat came from a lack of piety or the dawn of the time of troubles before the apocalypse and could be averted by earnest prayers. In 718 Leo III celebrated the role of the Virgin in saving Constantinople from an Arab siege.[33] In the eighth century, when Constantinople was again under attack, the patriarch of the Orthodox Church rallied the populace to the defense of Christianity by promising the aid of God. Byzantium's soldiers, who carried icons of the Virgin, saw death in battle as a kind of martyrdom.

While barbarians ransacked western Europe and Roman civilization became a hazy memory, Constantinople remained a cosmopolitan city and the kingdoms of western Europe sought to imitate its rituals. The Byzantines pictured themselves as crusading Christians defending the true faith against Goths, Vandals, and Saracens. The German Christian converts in new kingdoms of Italy, Spain, and France consciously emulated Byzantine zeal for God's war.

[32] Peter Brown, "St. Augustine's Attitude to Religious Coercion," *Religion and Society in the Age of Augustine* (1972) 260, 277.
[33] Ibid., 143, 162.

V.
The Religions of the East: Hinduism

I. Defining Hinduism

Hinduism is a term that in popular and scholarly usage defines the cultural, social, and religious practices of those living in India.[1] Hinduism is also now used to describe the beliefs of ethnic Indians living in many countries and of converts to faiths now practiced in India. The ancient Greeks created the word, and their usage was later adopted by Persians and Muslims, who referred to the peoples dwelling beyond the Indus River as Hindus. In the seventeenth century British imperialists called Hindu everyone in India who was not Muslim. The British, following a policy of indirect rule, sought to allow adherents of major faiths to follow their own customs and laws as a way of ensuring political stability, yet they also accentuated the animosities between religious groups in India in order to justify colonial rule and to keep control. So Hinduism is not a description that arose naturally from within religious communities, but was imposed from without by men with only a superficial knowledge of Indian religions.

In the late nineteenth century Indian nationalists adopted the word Hinduism to differentiate between indigenous religions that reflected the unity of Indian civilization as against foreign imports like Christianity and Islam. So in spite of enormous differences in beliefs, modern nationalists saw as parts of Hinduism the majority who worship Vishnu, Siva, Sakti, and countless local deities, as well as present-day minorities of Sikhs, Jains, and Buddhists.

History provides considerable evidence of long periods of cooperation and mutual influence, as well as times of rivalry and antipathy among adherents of differing religions of India. At the local level Hindus and Muslims even

---

[1]For example, the entry in *The New Encyclopaedia Britannica* (1975), VIII, 888. A good introduction is R.C. Zaehner, *Hinduism* (1970); more difficult but also more perceptive is Thomas Hopkins, *The Hindu Religious Tradition* (1971).

worshipped at the same shrines, and adherents of many faiths regarded India as a sacred land. Advocates of using Hinduism as an inclusive term defend the lack of precision as illustrative of the way religions developed in India. Over the centuries Hindus absorbed tenets and customs from many indigenous and foreign religions and now espouse tremendous variety in beliefs. However, at present and in the past Buddhists, Sikhs, and Jains would take offense at their religion's being called varieties of Hinduism. Scholars also see these as distinct religions from Hinduism, though originating in a matrix of Indian religious practices.

Today Hinduism remains a politically useful, myth-like concept of many meanings employed, much like Judaeo-Christian or Abrahamic religions in the U.S., in an attempt to create a tradition of Indian religious unity or to erect a cultural boundary excluding Muslims, Christians, and secularists. We will be using Hinduism in a protean sense to refer to the early religious practices of those living in the Indian subcontinent. Our task, as in previous chapters, is to provide enough introduction to the basic beliefs to show how religion structured the practice of war and the desire for peace. Rituals originally designed to guarantee success in war evolved into a division between warrior and priest classes, with an emphasis upon asceticism as the means for an elite few to obtain ultimate peace. The warriors also received divine sanction for an ethical conduct of war, although there was sufficient ambiguity as to whether a victory for a legitimate ruler excused using any means to prevail. Over the centuries Hinduism's creative borrowings gave the faith the flexibility to survive centuries of rule by outsiders and to become a powerful force in modern India.

Hinduism has no founder or authoritative interpreter of the faith or universal canon of beliefs or agreed upon ethics and practices, because there is no one theology and philosophy that unites all groups, but rather a continuity in social practices and ritual order. Because there is a variety in ways to be Hindu, tolerance of diversity, or at least acceptance of syncretism, is built into the religion. So Hinduism over the centuries has been able to combine elements of traditional village religions, the views of those living in the north and south of the subcontinent, the beliefs of conquerors like the Aryans, Persians, Mughals, and British, and ideals of newly created religions in India like the Jains and Buddhists. Hindus affirm that there are many avenues to truth, although that does not mean that all paths are equal, and are willing to use one or many vehicles: philosophical analysis, chanting hymns and mantras, rituals and sacrifices in elaborately carved temples, pilgrimages to sacred sites, asceticism, mysticism, and poetry as ways to a final goal which can encompass well-being, prosperity, liberation, salvation, and ecstatic union with a god.

Hinduism cannot be reduced to either monotheism or polytheist notions of the divine; many villagers worship only one or a few of the many gods in an elaborate pantheon, but others see all these gods as manifestations of an underlying uncreated reality termed *brahman*. *Brahman* is both being and non-being, the One who is All, present in every living creature of the Self (*atman*). So for some Hinduism expresses a monistic conception of the interrelationship of the entire universe of humans, other animals, vegetables, earth, gods, and *brahman*. *Brahman* (the creator) is a philosophical concept that undergirds Hinduism's religious observances but tends to be assumed rather than personified. Believers are less likely to worship *brahman* than its theistic emanation in Vishnu, the sustainer, or Siva, the destroyer and bringer of grace. For some the primary deity is Sakti, the Goddess. Vishnu appeared in human form, termed an *avatar*, in ten major incarnations (and in these, incarnations like Krishna and Rama, has many appearances) and can be worshiped in any or all of these manifestations. At one time Vishnu, Siva, and Sakti might have been separate sectarian streams, but for many centuries those who worship Vishnu have recognized the existence of Siva as well as other deities like Ganesa (patron of learning and new enterprises) or Varuna (upholder of moral law). In a contemporary family in India, the father, mother, son and daughter may each pay special homage to a different god yet come together in religious rituals and worship at home or at a shrine.

For our purpose, which is to examine issues of war and peace in the Hindu traditions, one way of viewing the development of Indian religions is to conceptualize the various layers as like Russian nesting dolls: the smallest doll would be the Vedic myths; the next size doll would incorporate a few features of the small doll but be changed into Brahmanic traditions (which is not the same as *brahman* mentioned above) whose scriptures would be the *Puranas* and *Upanishads*; larger dolls represent the main modern sects of Hinduism: Saivism, Vaisnavism, and Saktism, with the teaching found in the great historical epics, particularly the *Mahabharata* with particular emphasis on the section termed the *Bhagavadgita,* considered by many as the single most influential Hindu writing.

To continue the analogy, Jainism and Buddhism are like dolls with different faces and cloths. These faiths originated and flourished in India for several centuries beginning around 500 B.C.E., but by the first century C.E., suffered eclipse by a revival of Hinduism that had absorbed some of their teachings. Most of the approximately two million Jains live in India and their teachings about nonviolence are an appropriate topic for this chapter. Because of its origins in India, Buddhism could also be included here, but will be discussed in the next chapter because most of its adherents now live in Thailand, Burma, Japan, China, and Sri Lanka.

II. The Scriptures

In this chapter, our focus is on treatments of war and peace in texts modern Hindus consider sacred scriptures, termed "hearings" (*sruti*) for the most authoritative writings like the *Vedas,* and "remembering" (*smrti*) for the *Puranas,* and the still influential epics like the *Ramayana,* which have influence but less authority. Buddhists and Jains reinterpret or reject these writings.

The Hindu scriptures, formed over centuries and incorporating layers of traditions, are difficult to interpret because they contain different emphases and many elusive passages. Outsiders risk misunderstanding an individual Hindu's complex relation to the sacred if they ignore the different emphases in the layers of tradition, all of which are available to the believer depending upon his or her needs. For example, Vedic religion centered on sacrifice and the goal was primarily "this worldly." This was a religion for worldly goods, and a sacrifice that captured the power of *brahman* would bring wealth, power, health, prosperity, and - after death - immortality. In reaction to the emphasis upon material success in Vedic religion and influenced by the Jains and Buddhists, a reformulated vision of Hindu life with more emphasis upon individual accountability was spelled out in the *Bhagavadgita.* Here, depending upon a person's character, his or her search to experience ultimate reality can take a variety of forms, including the three major ways of duty: rituals or action (*karma*), knowledge or study of the sacred writings and meditation (*jmana*), and devotions (*bhakti*). The final goal is an escape from the rule of *karma* in this existence of birth, rebirth, and impermanence (*samsara*) into peace or union with a personal god and attaining heaven (*moksa*). A person's search for true knowledge is in order to escape the evil inherent in this existence. Renunciation as a way of life appealed to a few.

For most Hindus the four-fold religious life is characterized by *dhrama* or moral duty, *antha* or prosperity, *kama* or pleasure, and *moksa* or liberation. All of the religions of Hinduism draw upon common myths and history and share rituals and beliefs in *samsara, moksa,* caste, and rebirth or reincarnation.

As in Judaism, Christianity, and Islam, the past is very much alive in present day Hindu rituals as Indians recite Vedic hymns originating thirty-five hundred years ago or practice Brahmanic asceticism or link the *ahimsa* associated with the Jains and Buddhists with the nonviolence espoused by Gandhi. During this decade in a successful search for political power, a leader of the most important modern Hindu nationalist party appeared at a rally clothed like the god Rama, called for the destruction of an unused sixteenth-century mosque at Rama's alleged birthplace, and invoked India's warrior past to justify military armaments, and as Prime Minister fulfilled his pledge to resume testing of nuclear weapons. The recent broadcast on Indian television of versions of the epics *Ramayana* and *Mahabharata* became major events providing a sense of Hindu unity in a culturally splintered nation.

We will look at issues of war and peace as discussed in three kinds of classic texts of India: the hymns or *Vedas,* an epic the *Mahabharata* (including the

Bhagavadgita), and *Antha* or wisdom or advice literature designed for kings, one of which is the *Arthasastra* or political theory of Kautilya. The sacred writings refer to events taking place in the primeval past and yet occurring in history, and the rituals deriving from them reflect the justification for war in the societies that practiced and preserved them.

Scholars, well aware of the difficulties in using language originating in religious ceremonies to describe secular activities, in the absence of other written sources use these myths to recreate the social history of early India. Many of the practices described in the myths reappear in Kautilya's manual for a king, a source much easier to analyze because he prescribed a pattern of governing an empire that was already in existence.

Our emphasis is upon the relationship of religion to practices of war and peace during the formative period of Hinduism, from the *Vedas* (ca. 1500 B.C.E. until 400 C.E.). Hinduism continued to be the faith of the masses and to influence the rulers of various princely states, but from ca.1000 until 1948 invaders whose official religions were Islam and then Christianity ruled much of what is now modern India and Pakistan, and they shaped the practices of war.

III. The *Vedas*

The *Vedas* provide the most important source for knowledge of early Indian religion. The *Vedas* are hymns created by people termed Aryans, migrants from 2300 B.C.E. whose wealth was in herds of cattle.[2] They seem to have conquered and also to have absorbed part of the culture of what had been a sophisticated city-state civilization. Many small north Indian kingdoms that seem to have constantly warred with each other for plunder of cattle, land, and women, used similar hymns and mantras and over time joined their gods into a pantheon.

Priests through sacrifices linked humans with these Aryan gods who represented forces in nature. The fire in the sacrifice is Agni, who is also the sun, lightning, plants, and animals, and who links humans to all creation and brings strength to men; fire can also be a weapon of last resort in sieges. Agni captures the essence of the gods so he can be called many names. "You, O Agni, are Indra, the bull (strongest) of all that exist; you are the wide striding Vishnu . . . " Soma is a god and is also food given in sacrifice for the gods who will then bring rain to make human food. All the Vedic and Hindu gods carried weapons.[3]

Indra, the most important of the Aryan pantheon of gods, was a creator and sustainer and also a war god. His weapon was lightning (also identified with both a club and trident) that he used to kill the demon Vritna (literally, "obstruction"), thereby unloosening the waters of creation. Indra's battles against demons and other foes, in which he killed hundreds and even thousands, became a model to be invoked in time of war.

> He [Indra] who is invoked by both of two armies, enemies locked
> in combat, on this side and that side, he who is even invoked
> separately by each of two men standing on the very same chariot,
> he, my people, is Indra.
>
> He without whom people do not conquer, he whom they call on
> for help when they are fighting, who became the image of everything,
> who shakes the unshakeable [4]

Indra was the king of gods and the god identified with earthly kings who brought sacrificial goods to gain his support. Consecration hymns chanted at the time of coronation or investiture ask Indra to support the king and to make him firm and steadfast, suggesting that such qualities will "let the people want you." Prayers to Indra ask for the king's well-being and superiority over all foes: "Of lion-aspect, do thou devour all the clans; of tiger-aspect, do thou beat down the

---

[2]Klaus K. Klostermaier, *A Short Introduction to Hinduism* (1998), 7-9. B. G. Godhale, *Ancient India: History and Culture* (1962), 3-33.
[3]Quoted in Thomas Hopkins, *The Hindu Religious Tradition*, (1971), 17. V. Govind, *War and Ancient India* (1925), 27.
[4]*The Rig Veda*, tr. and ed., Wendy Doniger O'Flaherty (1981), 16. A better selection of militant poems to Indra is in V. R. Ramachandra Dikshitar, *War in Ancient India* (1987), 26-27.

foes: sole chief, having Indra as companion . . . "[5] According to some chants, the king in battle was not only symbolically identified with Indra but became the god.

The Vedic hymns of Indra seem to have been chanted at a time of sacrifice designed to enlist the god's favor but not to have required any particular moral stance by either king or the people. War was a ritual act, symbolizing the king's power over all the earth. The hymns are linked to the need for the king's power to control so much territory that his stallion can roam at will.[6] Wherever the horse goes, followed by the king's armies, opponents will pay tribute. Vedic religious ceremonies seem to have been utilitarian: Indra is a source of power to sanction the role of the king, to compel obedience, and to bring success in battle. In the sacrifice, the king represented the whole people; so his relationship with Indra will bring prosperity to the whole people. If the conquest is done righteously, the success will be permanent.

In both early and late Indian and Buddhist conceptions of kingship, the kings' power and law (*dharma*) is a function of their relationship to the gods, who will bring security and prosperity. The main difference is that in the *Vedas* the king's *dharma* is founded upon ritual observance of the sacrifice while later, for Hindus, Buddhists, and Jains, *dharma* will also depend upon the morality or justice in the king's actions. Here divine law served to put restraints upon the king's power.

The Vedic worship of Indra was also linked to the military role of a hereditary aristocracy, termed *Ksatriyas* or warriors whose duties included fighting, ruling, and gaining wealth. The Ksatriyas resemble medieval knights, another group whose profession was fighting. To die apart from battle or even worse, to be wounded in the back, became a sign of disgrace, but being killed while fighting was a kind of sacrifice that brought life in heaven. The warriors wore a

---

[5]Ibid., 64; quoted in Charles Drekmeier, *Kingship and Community in Early India* (1962), 25.
[6]The hymns for the horse sacrifice are in the *Rig Veda*, 85-96. Its significance is discussed in Drekmeier, 22, 46 and James Aho, *Religious Mythology and the Art of War: Comparative Religious Symbols of Military Violence* (1981), 63-64. Areas where the horse could roam acknowledged submission to the king, but a group seizing the horse defied his authority.

distinctive garb and had a special education that included study of the *Vedas*, knowledge of heroic ancestries, and training in the tactics of war.

Since being successful in making war brought a taint, sacrifices would appease the gods and end the fault. Priests, termed Brahmans - because they had the knowledge of the rites to harness the creative power of *brahman* - conducted the sacrifices to bring military success and legitimate the power of the various kings and warriors.

Originally the Vedic priests remained subordinate to the warrior aristocrats, but the Brahmans gradually increased their power as the rituals accompanying sacrifices became more elaborate. Studying the rituals for sacrifice and living in a way to ensure purity in everyday tasks became an occupation for specialists whose arcane knowledge was necessary to win the favor of the gods. Those who conducted the sacrifices had to observe many taboos. The Brahmans, like the warrior caste, became a hereditary elite whose status was decreed from birth. In fact, the Brahmans claimed superior status to the Ksatriyas because the ultimate reality they represented and could manipulate in the sacrifice determined the events in the world.

The divisions within society into caste were not man-made, but reflected the order of the cosmos. In the "Hymn to the Person," the primal Person or *Purusa* was the universe in past, present, and future, and actions within the sacrifice conducted by the priests corresponded to offerings of the gods. In the sacrificial division of the *Purusa* in the original creation, the mouth became the *Brahman*, the arms the ruler, the two thighs the merchants and farmers, and the feet the *Sudras*. Like the feet, which touch the earth, the *Sudras* are of the earth, basic but low. Part of the *Purusa* became the universe: the feet of the *Purusa* became the earth, the moon came from thought, the sun from the eye, and from the mouth Indra and Agni. The original *Purusa* sacrifice created the universe with its continued existence depending on the continuing performance of the sacrifice in its correct form.[7]

The caste system early became an enduring feature of Hinduism. Under the Aryans the early caste system was flexible and there are examples of men earning Brahman or warrior status and kings creating genealogies to justify their role as Ksatriyas. However, over the centuries the division of Indian society into superior castes hardened into the twice-born: priests or Brahmans, then warriors or Ksatriyas, then merchants and artisans called Vaishya. The peasants (Sudras) and the untouchables (who were outside the four orders) were the once born and ritually impure.[8] The caste system was an effective way to freeze society. No one could legitimately complain about his or her position in society, since where each was born depended upon deeds in a prior existence. So the untouchable deserved to be poor while the Brahman's ancestors brought him superior status. The Ksatriyas protected the Brahmans who preformed the religious rituals to preserve the stability of the realm. The highest duty for both warriors and merchants was to give gifts to the Brahmans, who were not, according to the scriptures, to value wealth. The Brahmans would through correct performance of sacrifice remedy the evil that was the inevitable concomitant of strife in war and, thereby, strengthen the *dharma* of the king.

In the Brahmanic reinterpretation of Vedic religion, ritual knowledge guaranteed access to power, and the *Puranas* devote much attention to metaphysical questions such as the unity of all creation, including man, animals, and the gods. Because they had knowledge of the origin and destiny of the universe, which guaranteed their access to ultimate reality, the Brahmans would be the supreme source of power. In the *Upanishads,* there was less emphasis upon the battles of old Vedic gods and more on abstract principles of *dharma,* justice or a moral order. A passage from the *Brhadaranyaka Upanishad* shows how

---

[7]Hopkins, 23-24
[8]Richard Gombrich, *Theravada Buddhism: A Social History from Ancient Benares to Modern Colombo* (1991), 38-40.

brahman as the source of all power temporarily exalts the prince but ultimately gives superiority to the Brahman priest.

> In the beginning this [universe] was *Brahman*, - One only, Being One only, he had not the power to develop. By a supreme effort he brought forth a form of the Good [namely], princely power - that is to say, those princely powers among the gods called *Indra*, *Varuna*, *Soma* ... Hence nothing higher than princely power, and so the Bráhman [priest] sits below the prince at the ceremonial anointing of a king, thereby conferring glory on the princely office. *Brahman* [the quality that makes a Bráhman a Bráhman] is the womb and source of princely power. Hence, even though the king enjoys supremacy, in the end he must return to *Brahman*, which is his [mother's womb]. And so whoever injures a [Bráhman] does violence to his [mother's] womb. He becomes more evil in that he has injured one who is better [than himself.]"[9]

Note that the warrior class to which the king belonged can be killed in battle, but no one should kill a Brahman. In the caste society emerging in India the priests who wrote the sacred literature proclaimed that the highest task was to obtain true knowledge or spiritual enlightenment. Each caste had obligations to other castes, but the hierarchical arrangement meant that worldly rule or business had less significance than attaining enlightenment. And only the Brahmans had the time to study the sacred writings and to meditate in order to attain true knowledge and ultimate power. Neither the *Vedas* nor *Puranas* contain information on the justification for or right conduct in war.

Creating a warrior caste favored both a pro and anti-war mentality. Making war became an honored profession; however, the other two upper classes and peasants lost competence to fight. Moreover, unlike medieval Europe where kings triumphed over priests, in India the Brahman became superior to the warrior.

IV. War and Peace in the *Mahabharata*

The *Mahabharata* "sums up . . . every shade and nuance of classical Hinduism."[10] A second saying is that everything worth knowing is in the

---

[9]*Hindu Scriptures*, ed. and tr., Dominic Goodall (1996), 50-51.
[10]Zaehner, *Hinduism,* 8.

Mahabharata. This epic, incorporating many traditions and stories from various sources, was composed about 400 B.C. but only written down eight hundred years later. Like the *Iliad* and *Odyssey* but eight times longer, the *Mahabharata* is a 100,000 line poem whose main plot line describes a war involving heroic mortals who are the children of the gods but whose ultimate destiny is determined by the gods or fate.

The *Mahabharata,* whose materials date from 400 B.C.E. to 400 C.E., has two kinds of war. One is an unrighteous war that involves trickery, the use of charms and spells, and allows any tactic. The second is ethical or just war and is fought according to the principles of *dharma.* Here war is proclaimed, the protagonists agree on how it is to be fought, and there is nothing secret. Instead, the warriors follow a well-developed code of allowable reasons for going to war as well as actions permissible in war. The first kind of war reflected the Vedic traditions; the second shows the impact of a powerful warrior aristocracy concerned with its survival and the moral rightness of making war.[11]

While in form and content the *Mahabharata* is more like Homer than the writings of medieval canon lawyers or Islamic commentators, the similarities in these three writings show that the attempt to control war through religion transcends cultural boundaries. In Christian Europe, the Muslim Middle East, and Hindu India, aristocrats and priests created an ethic of war designed to serve their class interests. The ideal of restraint in war is a product of many cultures and not just a western contribution to world history.

War in the *Mahabharata* is a seventeen-day affair between cousins Pandavas and the Kauravas who are fighting for universal sovereignty of earth. The Pandavas are clearly the "good guys" who enjoy the favor of the god Krishna and are destined to win, but only after strenuous activity. There are many brave and morally excellent heroes among the Kauravas, but most are generally also

---

[11]Dikshitar, *War in Ancient India,* 59-60.

"misguided, impure, and evil-minded men."[12]   The war is caused when the Kauravas, because of their pride, greed, and jealousy, refused a reasonable peace, even plotting to kidnap the god Krishna who is serving as ambassador - a clear violation of the rules of war. The epic insists that in the origins of the war (but not in conduct during) there was a right and wrong conduct and the Pandavas acted in self-defense and to protect what was rightfully theirs.

Like the *Iliad*, the *Mahabharata* celebrates war, feats of valor, and gore: "on the battlefield flowed an awful river whose current and waves were made up of blood." Like Achilles, the warrior hero Arjuna is a son of a god, in this case Indra, who gives him weapons but also instructs him in music, dancing, and the sacred scriptures (*Vedas*).[13]   So Arjuna is both godlike and human, a model of devotion and a superb killing machine.

The poem, reflecting as well as creating practices of war, contains a chivalric code agreed upon by both sides and reaffirmed throughout the epic. Chariot riders could fight only with other chariot riders; similar restrictions bound foot soldiers and those who rode on elephants. "It was also agreed that a combatant who was engaged in fighting with another, one seeking refuge, one retreating, one whose weapon was broken, and one who was not clad in armor should never be attacked. Likewise charioteers, animals, men engaged in carrying weapons, drummers, and conch-blowers should not be attacked." Fruit trees, flower gardens, and temples were not to be harmed.

The criteria were clearly that only warriors battled, and unarmed people were exempted, even if they were supporting the war effort. Neither wounded nor captured soldiers were to be killed. The concept of civilian immunity seemed to be implied but was not clearly spelled out. A fourth-century B.C.E. Greek observer of Indian war practices noted that "husbandmen are regarded as a class

---

[12]*The Mahabharata: An English Version Based on Selected Verses*, tr. and ed., Chakravarthi V. Narasimham, (1965), 104.
[13]Ibid., 63, 132.

that is sacred and inviolable, the tillers of the soil, [and] even when battle is raging in their neighborhood, are undisturbed."[14]

Only occasionally do the actual battles described in the epic conform to the ethical code of the knights. Instead, the two sides are so closely matched that the Pandavas win each crucial battle only by violating the code of fair practices in battle: they practice deception, strike below the belt, lie about the death of a warrior's child so that he will stop fighting and then kill him while he meditates. And the God Krishna approves and often instigates these actions and reassures the Pandavas they have not done wrong: "If I had not adopted such deceitful ways, you would never have been victorious, nor could you have regained your kingdom or your wealth . . . You should not mind the fact that your enemy has been killed deceitfully. When one is outnumbered by his enemies, then destruction should be brought about by stratagem. The gods themselves . . . have followed the same methods."[15]

Even while the listeners' sympathy is enlisted for the Pandavas, there are strong condemnations of war most often uttered by the most pure of the Pandava warriors, King Yudhisthira: "In all cases war is evil . . . Victory and defeat, O Krsna, are the same to one who is killed. Defeat is not very much better than death." "Peace is preferable to war. Who, having the choice, would prefer to fight." "Slaughter is never praised in the Vedas. It can never produce any good." [16] Neither side, however, can escape from his warrior caste's destiny, which is to fight. The epic insists that it is ethically better for a warrior to fight poorly than to follow the precepts for another caste. So kings who come from the warrior caste must study state polity and accept their duty of warring.

After much heroism, pain, carnage and duplicity of both sides, only the seven victorious Pandavas are left alive and ultimately the dynasty is saved only

---

[14]Ibid., 121; Megasthenes quoted in Dikshitar, who summarizes the law codes of traditional Indian wars, 66-71.
[15]Ibid., 175.
[16]Ibid., 94, 101-02, 122.

because a god preserves alive one child in the womb. The most righteous of the Pandavas, King Yudhisthira, has a vision where he goes to heaven. Here he does not find his brothers, but the Kauravas, the unjust side. They are in heaven because they fought according to the *dharmic* rules of war, but the Pandavas are in hell in order to do penance for their unjust tactics. The king awakes and says it's all a story or lie. But the epic by including the condemnation of the Pandavas' actions reflects an ambivalent attitude towards restraint in war as a necessary but perhaps unrealistic way to victory.

The poem ends with an elegiac quality, an eastern *Gotterdamerung* or "Twilight of the Heroes," as the war leads to an eclipse of heroism and the destruction of the old order. The war itself and the disreputable tactics necessary to prevail are a sign of the destruction or the decline of *dharma* into the present impure age. The corollary is that any contemporary king will need the wisdom of duplicity in war to preserve his realm.

V. *The Bhagavadgita*

The *Bhagavadgita*, described as "the most important, the most influential, and the most luminous of all the Hindu scriptures," is a short section of the *Mahabharata*, probably inserted later in the priestly attempt to sanitize the immoral tactics of the heroes.[17] This chapter of seven hundred lines describes events just before the beginning of the final battle with the two enormous armies drawn up facing each other.

The hero, Prince Arjuna, who elsewhere in the epic has gloried in gore and never shown any qualms about killing, realizes that the battle will end with relatives killing each other and will destroy family and law. He wonders whether victory for either side is worth the cost. Arjuna who has earlier done mighty acts of valor is not questioning the morality of all war, but only the sinfulness of this battle because it is a family affair. In his indecisiveness and awareness of moral ambiguity, Arjuna appears most human, unlike a hero or god. He is answered by

---

[17]Zaehner, 10.

his charioteer Krishna, a god who is an avatar of Vishnu. Initially Krishna counters with a variety of rationales for fighting, some of which contradict his later arguments. For example, Arjuna's qualms make him unmanly and like a coward filled with sentimental pity because he knows that the opponents are unworthy to succeed. Victory in battle will bring booty and fame.

Krishna's main argument is that this (and all) war is no sin if approached correctly. That is, Arjuna must act in such a fashion that he fulfills his duty as a warrior irrespective of the consequences. A warrior's destiny is to fight, no matter whatever his temporary qualms. Arjuna's nature, his deepest being, will compel him to fight. There is no hint of opposition to a warrior ethic: "heroism, vigor, steadiness, resourcefulness, not fleeing even in battle, generosity and leadership." For a warrior there is no greater good "than a battle enjoined by duty," and to fight and die in such a war is an "open door to heaven."[18]

However, there is a right and a wrong way to fight, and for Arjuna to escape a taint of sin, he must cultivate a right attitude of selflessness, acting not "for selfish ends, but as a conscious instrument of the Divine." The warrior's ethic is one of detachment from this impermanent world. Arjuna, like all good Hindus, must realize that victory, defeat, life, death, pain, and happiness - the impermanence structuring this world - are irrelevant to him. The fruits of victory, even wishing for a victory - all outward motives will make the war a sin. After he attains such an attitude of absolute detachment, Arjuna can fight secure in the knowledge that killing his cousins is no sin, because the final victory will not come from humans. Arjuna may not care about triumph, but he is still informed that Krishna will give "fortune, victory, welfare and morality."[19]

Death is not the evil in war. After all, life is merely a garment temporarily put on, and birth and death have no effect on the *atman* or soul within all humans. Humans live, die, and are reborn as a part of an eternal karmic cycle. So death is

---

[18]*Bhagavadgita,* 119, 336.
[19]Ibid., 337, 383

neither final nor a tragedy: "For to the one that is born death is certain and certain is birth for the one that has died. Therefore for what is unavoidable, thou shouldst not grieve."[20] Arjuna and the Kauravas will all die sometime and in the ever-recurring cycle time has no ultimate meaning. So Arjuna will not ultimately destroy the Kauravas because they will be reborn. In fact, he will not kill at all because all of Arjuna's previous kills were done not by his arrows but by the god Rada. Krishna announces that fate has already determined the course of the battle, who will live and die, who will prevail, and that Arjuna will fight. After Arjuna experiences a hieraphany of Krishna in all his glorious manifestations, he goes off to war. Nowhere in the *Bhagavadgita* is there a condemnation of war or of the warrior's ethic, so long as he remains detached.

In the *Bhagavadgita* war is not a central theme, and Krishna's dialogue with Arjuna is like bookends at the beginning and end of a long disquisition showing the three ways to escape from impermanence into reality. The epiphany of Krishna, not Arjuna's decision to fight, is the climax here. Elsewhere in the epic, Arjuna is the human hero, the godlike warrior; here he is the devotee and his relationship with Krishna exemplifies the love of God for man and man for God. Note the contrast between the emphasis upon sacrifice and ritual in the earlier Vedic and Brahmanical writings and the *Bhagavadgita*'s concentration upon an individual, his personal duty and his unity with the divine. This new element, which some scholars believe reflect influences of Buddhism and Jainism, would facilitate the revival of Hinduism in the cults of Vishnu and Siva following the decline of the Mauryan empire after 800 C.E.

Like the Muslim *jihad*, which can be either a personal or societal struggle, Hindus interpreted Arjuna's war as a charter for war or as a metaphor for an interior struggle to escape from the tyranny of self. Early Indian nationalists saw the entire epic and the *Bhagavadgita* as justifying independence and violent struggle against the British. A more common interpretation among Hindus and

---

[20]Ibid., 110.

among the Europeans who at the beginning of the twentieth century began appreciating classical Indian civilization was to spiritualize the advice. Here Arjuna's war morality was made subordinate to an ethic for daily living. Gandhi utilized the *Bhagavadgita* to provide a paradigm for a nonviolent warrior seeking God. He built upon a traditional Hindu interpretation of moral purification while revolutionizing the ostensible meaning by making the quest for truth politically powerful.

VI. Jainism.

The creation of the *Upanishads* and the emergence of the Jains and Buddhists during the sixth century B.C.E. show that many Indians did not find the sacrificial religion of the Vedas and the Brahmans satisfying. There is no scholarly consensus about the causes for the emergence at this time of many holy men teaching new religions that rejected traditional ideas of sacrifice and caste. Alternative explanations include the decline of small tribal states and the emergence of larger kingdoms, social dislocation caused by frequent wars fought by bigger armies, economic transformation with the decline of nomadic political power, and increased prosperity due to flourishing trade and artisan crafts, or even the unsatisfactory nature of Brahmanism for members of other castes.

Two of the most prominent new teachers, Sidharatta Gautama of the Buddhists and Mahavira of the Jains, were born into the warrior or Kastriya caste. Both religions used military metaphors to describe spiritual battles, and their language describing the ideal person to become a monk and life in the monastic communities (*sangha*) included terms used in earlier warrior guilds.[21] Yet both religions represent in their earliest stages a repudiation of the warriors' responsibility for the whole society. Initially, Jain and Buddhist teachings emphasized individual transformation, set a goal of escape from this karmic existence, and advocated life as a wandering ascetic or in monastic communities. Both religions exemplified a common tendency in Indian religious life for a

---

[21]Paul Dundas, *The Jains* (1992), 15.

spiritual elite to turn away from political responsibility for the general community.

The Jains' fundamental teaching was nonviolence: "All breathing, existing, living, sentient creatures should not be slain, nor treated with violence, nor abused, nor tormented, nor driven away. This is the pure, unchangeable, eternal law which the clever ones, who understand the world, have proclaimed."[22]

Two foci of this quotation are important. First, the Jain doctrine of Mahavira was not a new creation, but a discovery of ancient truth. A true interpretation of the Vedas and Brahmanic writings would prove that Jainism was a universal truth taught by a series of twenty-four teachers, termed "Jains" or "conquerors." Mahavira was the last of these fordsmen or builders of a crossing from this transient life into true knowledge. The result was that past religious beliefs were blended with the new and Indra now became a Jain deity, Rama and Krishna early Jain laymen, and all gods, even *brahman*, were of the same substance and subject to rebirth.[23] The Jains rejected the Hindu practice of sacrifice as cruelty to animals. They also rejected the power of gods to intervene in human affairs and insisted that there was no creator God. The second emphasis in the above quotation was *ahimsa*, or nonviolence. Jains sought to practice nonviolence in thought as well as action, because impure thoughts led to accrual of *karma*, a material substance that is attracted to the life force by action that binds *jiva* to rebirth. Jain practices involved the effort to sanctify thoughts from passion and to teach non-involvement through mortification of the flesh.

In Jainism there are two kinds of reality: inanimate matter, which is uncreated and exists forever, and life or soul. All life forms including the gods, devils, humans, insects and vegetables are one, and there are even microscopic life forms in the air and water. No life wants to suffer, but the world is a scene of sufferings caused by actions. For example, humans must eat, and even the vegetarian diet causes death. The Jainist pattern of life is to reduce the sufferings

---

[22]Quoted in Dundas, 36.

of all life forms in order to escape from the world of birth and rebirth (*samsara*) by enlightenment. The suffering is caused by *karma*. The particles of *karma* interfere with sensory and mental perception leading to false knowledge. *Karma* causes the endless cycle of suffering, death, and rebirth, but a monk can attain spiritual deliverance or a true knowledge of past, present, and future through a life style of mortification of the flesh and meditation.

After his enlightenment, Mahavira wandered as a beggar and underwent physical deprivation. Mahavira is often pictured as naked, and some sects of Janism have monks who remain completely naked and refuse to bathe, arguing that water would kill the life forms in dirt. Other less strict sects allow monks a loincloth and begging bowl. Monks and laity are vegetarians. *Ahimsa* restricts occupations for the laity; they do not farm, because plowing would kill minute organisms, or sell intoxicating beverages that weaken self-control.

Jain nonviolence seems logically to require an opposition to all military activities, but that did not happen because *ahimsa* remained a personal lifestyle rather than a political philosophy. The Jains insisted that death in battle did not bring rebirth in heaven. However, Jain monks received the patronage of kings who gave gifts and built temples. Jainism began in a warrior caste and soon became the creed of warriors, particularly in southern India, who saw the spiritual struggle, disciplined life style, and willingness to undergo hardship as analogous to the life of a soldier.

The Jains did not create a new ethic for practices in war, but instead merely claimed older Brahmanic manuals as their own. Treatises for an ideal Jain monarch stressed his obligation to protect himself and his subjects and the need to war to keep the kingdoms free from heretical Brahman influence. One model first-century king fought a war to retrieve a statue of a fordmaker. A later tale described a duel of two half-brothers over a kingship. At the moment of victory over the usurper, the hero Jain brother, defending what was his rightful throne,

---

[23]Ibid., 77.

renounced all worldly affairs, including kingship, and became enlightened. Note that his enlightenment coming after the battle occurred because he changed the form of his valor. His victory and apotheosis were commemorated in one of the largest Jain shrines in south India, dedicated by a victorious general in 981 C.E. Here the Jain warrior was pictured as a disciplined ascetic, like Arjuna, prepared to fight for the right in a just cause while recognizing the ultimate irrelevance of all worldly battles.[24]

The Jains today are known primarily as merchants, but until the Muslim conquest they were more frequently known as a warriors. Stories of rivalry between Jains and Hindus suggest that the reasons for the change may lie in persecution. The early history of the Jains illustrates that even a belief in the unity of all creation and practices designed to protect even tiny organisms from death can be adapted to serve the military needs of a society.

VII. Kautilya: Realism, Indian Style

A legend says that when the Chandragupta, the founder of the Mauryan dynasty and the man who would drive the Greeks out of India, went to meet Alexander the Great, he was accompanied by an official named Kautilya. Besides being a major minister at the court of Chandragupta, Kautilya is also reputed to be the author of the *Arthasastra*, a philosophical treatise about politics. The *Arthasastra* is a compendium of earlier Indian political advice as well as an original guide of conduct for a king who wishes to be a universal monarch but is instead an insecure head of a weak state. It is also a valuable source for information about the relationship of religion and war under Chandragupta, the Buddhist king Asoka's grandfather, and shows how ambivalence over norms of conduct in the religious writings could be incorporated into political theory.

Kautilya's king needs to be a moral being considerate of his subjects. A responsible king knows that, "in the happiness of his subjects lies his happiness, in their welfare is his welfare." The purpose of the state is the realization of

---

[24]Ibid., 192, 97, 101-03; Dikshitar, 79-80.

virtue through the maintenance of the moral order (*dharma*). A dissolute monarch because he is "the aggregate of the people" will have immoral subjects who will weaken the realm. Such subjects will betray the king when there is danger because there is no loyalty. Morality strengthens the king for it is both imprudent and "unrighteous to do an act which excites popular fury." The King prays every night and also observes the religious rites of sacrifice, listening to omens, supporting priests, and honoring holy men, particularly ascetics. He personally attends to the "business of gods, of heretics, of Brahmans learned in the *Vedas*, of cattle, sacred places, of minors, the aged, the afflicted, and the helpless, and of women." The king worships the gods and utilizes the Brahmans in order to avert providential visitations of fire, flood, disease, and famine.[25] However, such conventional piety plays a minor role in Kautilya's vision of a successful king.

Less concerned with devotion than utility, the *Arthasastra* has an ambivalent attitude towards the king and religion. Clearly, he must give the appearance of supporting the gods and not upset traditional religious practices. The moral basis of the state is crucial for success, because the gods are powerful but also because religion structures the society and makes people obedient and placid. Yet the king should not allow religious observances to interfere with his unceasing quest for security and power. Here the demands of the state are paramount, and religion becomes a tool to be manipulated.

Kautilya advocates exploiting superstition and religious belief for the king's purposes. If money is needed, the king can fake supernatural miracles, wonders like falling stars, or charge the people admission to see fabricated many-headed snakes. A king "in good faith" can assassinate a devout enemy king at worship or in pilgrimage. Bogus holy men can spread false rumors, spy out the enemy's intentions, or even poison opponents.

Before going into battle, the king must make sure that the omens are favorable to his purpose and that priests build the morale of his army. He can

---

[25]Kautilya, *Arthasastra*, tr., R. Shamasastry (1961), 38, 285, 352; Drekmeier, 199.

also attempt to give the opposing army unfavorable omens by bribing their priests or tampering with oracles as a way of destroying morale. A hollowed-out image of a god could contain an assassin or a person who during sacrifice or prayers could pour blood out of the god's mouth as a demonstration of defeat.

The *Arthasastra* embodies a pragmatic ethic and envisions a state policy based on force, advice followed by Chandragupta. In the *Arthasastra*, virtue (*dharma*) is pursued not for its own sake but because virtue is the basis of wealth, and wealth is the foundation of the state. Kautilya asks whether it is better for a king to have money or an army. The answer is money, because it will buy an army. Prosperity will allow the king to provide salaries and gifts that will make state officials and priests happy and satisfy the population. Money will allow the state to employ spies to see if the princes, the harem, the officials, and the generals are loyal. Spies can be prostitutes, holy men, traders, Brahmans, or peasants. They will investigate everyone; serve as the king's eyes and ears. Spies will allow the king to investigate tax collectors and criminals, but he must be careful that they are not corrupted and that the information he receives is accurate. His knowledge of the minutiae of the realm derived from spies will make his subjects and potential troublemakers believe in the "omniscient power of the King."[26] The King's essential task is punishment (*danda*), an activity that must be neither too severe nor too mild.

External enemies are everywhere and the king must be "ever wakeful" and energetic in assessing the strengths and weaknesses of his own kingdom and his neighbors. Nothing is constant in war and peace, and the king must calculate his actions according to his needs. If he is weak, he should seek peace. This can be done by an alliance with the enemy or with the enemy of the enemy. If these strategies do not work, then the weak king should pay tribute, even sending sons as hostages. Of course, if there is more than one son, he should send the dumb or disloyal one; if it becomes necessary to sacrifice them in this way, the king can

---

[26]Ibid., 240.

have more children. A weak king always has the option of assassination or fomenting rebellion, or he can bribe an agent to disrupt an enemy's court. If the agent is successful, the enemy is weakened, but if discovered and executed, the suspicion may poison relations between the enemy king and his court or subjects. Alternatively, a strong enemy can be exhorted to keep the peace on moral grounds because it is a sin to kill, war causes ill effects, and a king's primary duty is to be mindful of "virtue and wealth."[27]

The king's strategy differs if the enemy is weak. Then the king's policy should weaken him further either by open war, secret war, or treacherous war - whichever accomplishes the task with the least expenditure of wealth and power. If marching up and down, fomenting rebellion, assassinations, or invasions will contribute to power, then that becomes the right policy. Peace is normally better than war, not for moral grounds, but because its outcome is less problematic. No king can be sure he has compared accurately his own and his enemy's strengths and, in addition, in war fate can intervene.

Kautilya does not argue that there is more merit in making peace or preserving neutrality than in waging war and voices no concern about the moral effects of battle in killing soldiers and impoverishing civilians. The king's concern is with the morale of soldiers and the strength and loyalty of the army. For Kautilya the international realm is power politics in which the weak seek survival and strength and the strong try to dominate or conquer the weak, and virtue brings no reward.

The *Arthasastra* provides guidelines for fighting rather than detailed strategy. The kind of war depends upon the objective. If the land is to be incorporated into the king's realm, then the war should be mild, with physical damage kept to a minimum, and the defeated king or his relatives should be put in charge, although forced to pay tribute. Conquest is not intended to foment revolution because traditional social-political arrangements fostered stability. But

---

[27]Ibid., 32, 413.

if there is no thought to annexing the area and the people resist, then the invader should destroy "stores, crops, and granaries, and trade." Necessity justifies no restraint in the pursuit of advantage. The good of the realm allows using poisonous snakes, grasses that will cause madness, spreading leprosy and fevers, employing devices to put out eyes. If the war is to be fought in treacherous fashion, then false rumors, assassination, rebellion might succeed in terrorizing the enemy.[28]

If the ruler decides that he will benefit if the war is to be fought openly and fairly, then he should declare to his troops that brave men lost in battle go immediately to heaven but those whose cowardice makes them flee will go to hell.[29] And a virtuous king's decision to fight openly should depend upon whether his forces are stronger, his position better (i.e., the sun is in opponent's eyes), his army rested, and that there will be more gain from fighting quickly than stalling. The varieties of war like those of neutrality, peace, and alliances depend on circumstances. In external and internal affairs for Kautilya "uneasy is the head that wears the crown."

Kautilya's treatise contains conflicting advice, an indication that there may have been several authors and additions over the centuries. The king is instructed in everything from how to lay out a capital city, the administrative divisions of government, how much to pay different officials, even the prices to offer soldiers before battle for the head of an enemy king, general, or priest.

Unfortunately for scholars trying to assess the descriptive value of the *Arthasastra*, there is no discussion or even recognition of the long-term effects if all rulers, officials, and nobles followed Kautilya's formulas for success. Any king who took seriously the *Arthasastra* would be so insecure as to seem paranoid, worried to eat because of poison, afraid to meet with his wives and sons who might assassinate him, unable to rely on information from ministers or spies or

---

[28]Ibid., 443-53.
[29]Ibid., 395.

priests who might mislead him because they have been bribed. He must act in war and peace to maximize his strength, yet a lack of ethics will prompt rebellion from within and attack from without. A fear of anarchy permeates the treatise, yet the disorder from a society organized on its principles would create anarchy.

A later satire of Kautilya has a young prince starting to master the twenty-four thousand lines of *Arthasastra* and growing old while becoming so fearful that he cannot act. We don't know how seriously the treatise was taken or whether monarchs tried to keep its advice secret. Kautilya has been called the eastern Machiavelli, but considering that he predates the Italian by fifteen hundred years, it seems more accurate to term Machiavelli the western Kautilya. Realism, realpolitik or the subordination of religious ethics to necessity becomes an attractive alternative when states decide that to survive they must grow in power at the expense of their neighbors.

The diversity characteristic of Hindu religious traditions carries over into attitudes towards war. One dominant motif identifies the gods with victory in battle. A second tradition in Brahmanic Hinduism sees war as a symptom of a *samsara* existence, part of the ceaseless struggle of life that has no ultimate value. War, politics, even society have no relevance here, except insofar as the laity can gain merits by bring gifts to the monk.

The focus on nonviolence by the Jains and Buddhists, a teaching later taken up by some Hindus, could have led to an ethic of pacifism as a social philosophy. However, Jainism began within the military caste and extended the image of the warrior into asceticism. Its repudiation of material needs and espousal of a disciplined ascetic life resulted in Jainism's becoming the religion of south Indian warriors. The ideal Jain warrior resembles Arjuna in the *Bhagavadgita* where Arjuna sees the futility and costliness of war, but Krishna, by appealing to Arjuna's destiny as a warrior, convinces him to fight. The ideal warrior is heroic in action and detached in attitude, not subject to passions of anger and hatred. Arjuna fights neither for booty nor glory, though Krishna promised both, but as a devotee of the gods. A feudal or aristocratic code of war is espoused in other sections of the *Mahabharata*.

Flourishing in India along side the myths and epic chronicles was the political theory of Kautilya in which war is an act of state designed to enhance the security of the king. Religion here is a useful means to an end.

In India the only people who could opt out of war were those who had become enlightened and even here there are exceptions. For example, even ascetics participated in wars against demons in the *Ramayana*. Defended by kings and warriors who should not become ascetics, monks spent their days in meditation and study. For everybody else war was something to be endured, an unending and ultimately insignificant part of an unending cycle of life.

VI.
The Religions of the East:
Buddhist Nonviolence and Statecraft

When Alexander the Great invaded India in 327 B.C.E. after having defeated Persia, he encountered a sophisticated, rich, and religiously diverse civilization whose decentralization into many small kingdoms meant that there was no united opposition to his conquest. Alexander's triumphs proved ephemeral as a mutiny of his troops forced him to retreat, but his actions by disrupting traditional patterns paved the way for the creation of Indian political unity under the Mauryan dynasty (ca. 321), whose great King Asoka came to symbolize the ideal of a Buddhist monarch committed to religious purity and peace. Alexander's glorification of war contrasted with Asoka's views. Asoka renounced war and sought to rule in accordance with law *(dharma)*. However, Asoka became enamored of peace only after converting to Buddhism.

Nonviolence towards all living creatures had been an integral feature of the teaching of Gotama Siddhartha, the founder of Buddhism. The Buddha's first adherents became monks who renounced force and lived in separated communities, but his teachings also attracted kings. Rulers who sought to follow the Buddha had either to renounce political power or adapt the teachings to a political situation in which numerous principalities sought for power as a means of survival.

This chapter will focus first on the original vision of peace as taught by the Buddha and embraced by the monks, then discuss early Buddhist views of kingship, the policies of King Asoka who became the paradigmatic Buddhist ruler, the later blend of Buddhist nonviolence and *raison d'état* by the kings of Sri Lanka and Thailand, and the impact of Zen Buddhism in Japan. Buddhism, like Christianity, offers a fascinating blueprint for the ways in which a religion whose original ideas seem to preclude violence and political responsibility can be interpreted to allow warrior kings to claim to be holy men, even future Buddhas.

I. The Buddha

Gotama Siddhartha (ca. 563-480 B.C.E.), known to his followers as the Buddha or fully enlightened one, was the son of a minor north Indian king. According to tradition, eight fortune-tellers prophesied to the king that his son would become either a universal monarch or a holy man. The father, fearing the later, raised the prince in a secluded atmosphere in which the child never saw suffering. As a young prince, Gotama experienced a life of pleasure and aesthetic delight, married a beautiful woman, and had a son, but his happiness ended when he saw human suffering exemplified in an old man, a diseased man, a dead man, and a monk. Seeking to understand the origin of and to escape from suffering, Gotama renounced his family and kingdom and for six years sought knowledge by following the religious practices of holy men of his day - extreme self-mortification and asceticism or cultivation of the inward self or soul. Learning that neither sensual gratification, intellectual pursuit of self-knowledge, rituals and sacrifices, nor ascetic renunciation brought peace, Gotama adopted a Middle Way grounded in meditation.

One night, while seated under a fig tree, he discovered that the idea of the self was a false belief that "leads to all troubles of the world from personal conflicts to wars."[1] That is, violence results from acting on the false presumption that the things of this world have permanence and can bring happiness and security. All human relationships, all sensual and intellectual pleasure, all enjoyments are transitory - even the self has no ultimate reality. There is no human soul or eternal life in heaven; rather, all is in flux. Humans are caught in a never-ending karmic cycle of birth, death and rebirth in which a person's present condition is determined by actions in a prior existence, a view called the law of

---

[1] Walpola Rahula, *What the Buddha Thought* (1974), 51. Another excellent introduction to Buddhism is Donald Swearer, *Buddhism* (1977).

karma, and that all aspects of life are part of a process of interdependent co-arising.

To escape from *karma* requires correct knowledge of the true nature of things. The religious life begins with an intellectual understanding of the Four Noble Truths: 1. that misery is an inevitable component of life, 2. that suffering is caused by humans' craving for permanent satisfaction in this life of impermanence, 3. that this craving can be eliminated, and 4. that there is a way or path to escape from suffering. This path is termed the Middle Way because it rejects the extremes of worldliness and asceticism.

The Buddhists' goal is to transcend this life of birth and rebirth and its fleeting pleasures mixed with pain, to attain *Nirvana.* The final goal or *Nirvana* cannot be described but is the end of *karma,* attachment, birth and rebirth: "The extinction of greed, the extinction of anger, the extinction of delusion: this indeed is called *Nirvana.* And for a disciple thus freed, in whose heart dwells peace, there is nothing to be added . . . and naught remains for him to do." The Middle Path "leads to peace, discernment, to enlightenment, to *Nirvana.*"[2] However, the peace evoked as a first stage on the way to *Nirvana* has nothing to do with political peace or the absence of war, both of which are ultimately irrelevant: "If a man were to conquer in a battle a thousand times a thousand men, and another conquer one, himself, he indeed is the greatest of conquerors."[3]

The Buddha claimed neither special revelation from a supernatural being nor that he was a divine being. He told his followers that it was not the messenger, but the message that was important, for any person who followed the Middle Path could realize *Nirvana.* Having attained supreme enlightenment after which he could have withdrawn from the world, the Buddha instead began teaching "for the good of the many, for the happiness of the many, and out of compassion for the world."[4] During the rest of his long life, the Buddha instructed

---

[2] *A Buddhist Bible,* ed. Dwight Goddard (1994), 32-33.
[3] quoted in Balrisha Gokhale, *Asoke Maurya* (1966), 61.
[4] quoted in Rahula, 46.

his disciples on the meaning of his Truth. In addition, he provided guidance for right conduct within the monastic community.

After he died, and he taught there was neither eternal life in heaven nor any supreme God, the monks preserved his teachings in an oral tradition that was not written down for centuries. In Christianity, the quest for the historical Jesus is of prime importance because of his uniqueness as God-man. By contrast, in theory at least, the quest for the historical Buddha or for the exact original content of his dialogues is not critical to the truthfulness or survival of the religion. And because other Buddhas appeared in history before and after Gotama (though there can be only one fully enlightened Buddha, *Sammasambuddha*, at any time), the possibility of drawing upon earlier and later traditions is built into the teachings.

The *sutras* (dialogues) show the Buddha often affirming the truths in other religions and as tolerant of alternative beliefs. Buddhism resembles Hinduism in drawing upon and reinterpreting parts of the Indian religious traditions. For example, the Buddha utilized portions of the prevailing Brahmanic beliefs in *karma* and reincarnation and affirmed the existence of gods like Indra even while making sacrifices to them irrelevant to achieving *Nirvana*. Buddhism and the Jains, whose founder Mahavira lived in India about the same time as the Buddha, share a belief in *ahimsa* or nonviolence.

Over centuries stories of the Buddha's activities were joined to earlier folk tales, and there was intense curiosity about his personal history. Soon stories about the Buddha stressed the appearances of angels at his birth, physical signs of his extraordinary status, and his ability to do miracles and convert opponents. At times the Buddha becomes a transcendent figure throughout the cosmos. Images of the Buddha are found in all monasteries, and many homes have a shrine with a picture or statute of the Buddha. In modern Sri Lanka, although Theravada Buddhists insist that Gotama was a man who died, they also invoke the living presence of the Buddha when dedicating a shrine. One scholar concluded that "cognitively the Buddha is dead, but affectively he is alive."[5]

Soon after the death of the Buddha, a council attempted to preserve the purity of his teachings by agreeing upon a canon and standardizing the rules for a monastic life. Still, major divisions appeared early and today, in addition to a common core of beliefs, there are dozens of major schools of interpretation of which the most famous are Theravada, Mahayana, and Vajrayana with basic differences in the ritual practices and beliefs of Buddhists in Sri Lanka, Thailand, China, Tibet, Burma, Laos, and Japan. Few Buddhists now live in India, the country of origin of the faith.

For our purposes the variety in Buddhisms is less important than their common affirmation of the Middle Path, the way of virtue. Nonviolence is a major theme in the Eightfold Path, the first step of which is "Right Understanding" in which the obligation is to realize that "To abstain from killing is merit" and "Destruction of living beings is demerit." Doing meritorious deeds is important as influencing one's future karmic rebirth. The second step, "Right mindedness" requires having thoughts "free from ill-will" and "free from cruelty." In the fourth step, "Right Action," the person "avoids the killing of living beings . . . Without stick or sword, conscious, full of sympathy, he is anxious for the welfare of all living beings." There are two levels of "Right Action:" abstaining from killing, stealing, and unlawful sexual intercourse is "Mundane Right Action," which yields worldly fruits and brings good results. All Buddhists, lay as well as monks, must observe these prohibitions. A higher level called "Ultramundane Right Action," designed for monks aiming at becoming saints, had the same prohibitions but required the "mind becoming holy" and was not aimed at attaining worldly results.[6]

---

[5]Gombrich, "The Consecration of Buddha Image," *Journal of Asian Studies,* XXVI, 23-36.
[6]*Buddhist Bible,* 32, 42, 44.

Gotama, the Buddha, served as an exemplar of the Eightfold Path, holding himself "aloof from causing injury to seeds or plants" and laying aside the cudgel and sword; "putting away the killing of living things, . . . he dwells compassionate and kind to all creatures that have life." The Buddha instructed his monks to refrain from listening "to tales of kings, of robbers, of ministers of state; tales of war stories, of terrors, of battles."[7] They were not to witness military parades. Monks should not earn a living by following such "low arts" as "prophesying as to war and its results." For a layman, making military weapons and brewing alcohol were forbidden occupations. The community of monks should be uninvolved and unconcerned about war:

> The chiefs will march out./ the chiefs will march back/
> The home chiefs will attack,/ and the enemies' retreat./
> The enemies' chiefs will attack,/ and ours will retreat./
> The home chiefs will gain the victory,/ and the foreign chiefs suffer
> defeat.
> The foreign chiefs will gain the victory,/and ours will suffer defeat./
> Thus will there be victory on this side,/defeat on that./
> Gotama the recluse holds aloof from such low arts.[8]

His abhorrence of violence did not mean that the Buddha ignored political affairs, particularly kingship and the threat of war. On one occasion Gotama went to the field of battle to prevent a war between two kings fighting over a river and on another his words stopped a king from attacking a foreign realm. An allegorical tale about worthy "King Wide-realm," described this monarch as "powerful, in command of an army, loyal and disciplined, in four divisions (of elephants, cavalry, chariots, and bowmen) burning up . . . his enemies by his very glory." Having an army was a mark of sovereignty for Indian political theorists, including Buddhists. The Buddha did not instruct kings to disband their armies and seems

---

[7]*Dialogues of the Buddha,* in *Sacred Books of the Buddha.* tr. T.W. Rhys Davids (1966), 5-6, 13*The Middle Length Discourses of the Buddha. Majjhima Nikaya,* tr. Bhikkhu Bodhi and Bhikkhu Nanamoli, (1995), 114:5, 135:5 and 6.
[8]Ibid., 20.

to have recognized that the rules for laymen or monks could not easily be applied to affairs of state.[9]

Gotama Siddhartha was from a noble clan and, although welcoming disciples from all classes, he accepted the warrior caste's hereditary right to rule. Kingship was a lesser status than an *arhat* (saint), but monks and kings existed in a symbiotic relationship. Monarchs preserved society from anarchy, built monasteries and temples, and gave gifts. Monks in the monastery instructed kings in their duty. The king who called the First Council talked about two cooperating but distinct authorities, that of the spirit, belonging to the monastic order, and power, belonging to the king. [10]

Buddhist history postulated an original golden age when people maintained ethical norms and there had been no need for government. But when morality declined, chaos resulted and kingship was instituted to bring order. While affirming that government originated for the good of the people, Buddhists espoused neither social contract theory in which the people chose the king nor right of revolution against an unjust monarch. After all, a person became king because of *karma,* with his actions in a previous life determining his present status. However, unlike previous Indian kings, early Buddhist rulers did not claim descent from the gods but they were still semi-divine figures, a link between the forces of nature and other humans, and their virtue or lack thereof would result in good rains and favorable harvest or drought and famine. A good Buddhist king fostered virtue by practicing self-control. For example when King Agatasattu visited the Buddha and heard the teaching, he asked to be a "disciple" but confessed his sin of putting to death his father, "a righteous king," for the sake of supreme power. The Buddha accepted the confession and advised "self restraint in the future." After the King left, the Buddha said that had he not put his father

---

[9]Rahula, 84, *Dialogues of the Buddha,* 177; Gokale, *Early Buddhist Kingship,* 21; Richard Gombrich, *Theravada Buddhism: A Social History from Ancient Benares to Modern Columbo* (1991), 81-86 argues that the Buddha took no serious interest in politics and had no political theory, though kings are often mentioned as predators rather than protectors.
[10]Gokale, *Asoka,* 28.

to death, he would have entered into the path ending as a saint (*arahat*).[11] This possibility of sainthood existed even though the King had not become a monk.

Early Buddhism remained ambivalent towards kings, appreciating their roles in promoting morality and preserving justice without partiality but fearing their greed, cruelty, and tyranny. The goal was to limit a human being who had absolute power. A list of "Ten Duties of a King" ascribed to the Buddha focused on character rather than specific policies. A king should disdain wealth and property, observe the five precepts for all laymen, which including non-killing, and practice honesty, kindness, austerity, patience and tolerance. He should not oppose the will of the people, and should make their welfare his uppermost concern. He should practice nonviolence, meaning that he should harm nobody and try to preserve peace and avoid war. The king who ruled with impartiality and justice would bring prosperity and righteousness. Subjects had a religious duty to obey such a ruler who gained status as almost a semi-divine figure. [12] His personal example and the force of the moral law would enable him to rule without force and violence, "to burn up his enemies by his very glory."

There were two early ideals of Buddhist kingship, the *cakkavatti*, or "wheel-turning," and *dharmaraja*, or the monarch who lives and rules by the *dharma*. In one the king was parallel to the Buddha; just as the Buddha was the highest religious figure, the king was the highest lay figure. Such a king was, like the Buddha, a universal monarch who ruled the perfect world by the worth of his own merit. Here the king is a kind of supernatural being whose righteousness calls forth the "wheel of *Dharma*" and this spreading of the teachings legitimates his rule. This king does no violence because in this realm no one commits crime. Whether such a ruler could ever exist as anything more than an ideal type is unclear. The second kind of ideal king rules an imperfect world with righteousness

---

[11]*Dialogues*, 94.
[12]Rahula, 85; John Spellman, *Political Theory of Ancient India: A Study of Kingship from the Earliest Times to Circa A.D. 300* (1964), 210-215. Gokale, *Early Buddhist Kingship*, 18-19.

and exemplifies the *dharma*. He is a leader who by his charisma brings order out of chaos and he can do violence to obtain justice.[13]

II. Asoka: The Model Buddhist King

The Mauryan dynasty of King Chandragupta, whose adviser was Kautilya, reached its greatest height under his grandson, Asoka. King Asoka ruled ca. 265-238 B.C.E. a realm encompassing most of the Indian sub-continent. Asoka converted after he became king and his practice of nonviolence, support of monks, and piety made him the model for all later Buddhist kings. Our knowledge of Asoka derives from two sources: a series of edicts he ordered carved on pillars and rock monuments and erected throughout the empire and from stories preserved by monks. The stories have more details but less reliability, while the edicts date from the time of Asoka and show how he wished to be viewed.

The stories preserved by the monks stress the contrast between Asoka "The Fierce One" before his conversion and the *Dharma-asoka*, or the virtuous nonviolent monarch. Buddhists illustrated the two facets of Asoka's personality by recounting the story of how in his previous life when as a small child he saw the Buddha walking and offered him some dirt as a gift. The monks with the Buddha were horrified at this dishonor, but the child's happy innocence and generosity pleased the Buddha. Still, dirt was filthy and Asoka would have a dark side. He also would be physically unattractive, but his gift brought such karmic merit that in a later life he would be the Universal Emperor.

Other religiously motivated legends portray Asoka as a younger son of King Bindusara (299-273), called the Slayer of Foes, a title difficult to reconcile with this king's reputed sympathy with Jain asceticism and nonviolence. Bindusara sent Asoka as a young man to be a governor in a rebellious province that submitted to him voluntarily; allegedly, he brought unarmed soldiers but weapons miraculously sprang up from the ground before the walls. Asoka proved

---

[13]Frank Reynolds, "The Two Wheels of Dhamma: A Study in Early Buddhism" in *The Two Wheels of Dhamma: Essays on the Theravqada Tradition in India and Ceylon* (1972), 18. In Sanskrit the term is "Dharma," in Pali "Dhamma."

to be an able administrator, more competent than his elder brothers. After the death of Bindusara, there was a succession struggle in which Asoka won, putting to death ninety-nine brothers, according to the stories.

As a young king Asoka earned his reputation as "The Fierce" by burning alive 500 concubines for disloyalty and personally chopping off the heads of 500 ministers.[14] For people awaiting execution, he built a jail that was designed to resemble hell. Buddhists preserved such stories as illustrating the extraordinary transformation of the king. The legends also have Asoka converted by a miracle-working monk and being so grateful that he was prepared to surrender his throne to the monastic order and bow to monks.

The rock edicts make the crucial event in Asoka's transformation his war against the prosperous trading kingdom of Kalinga about eight years after he had become king. Victory was costly, with 150,000 deported as prisoners, 100,000 killed or wounded in battle, and even more civilians dead. After the war, there arose in the King "remorse for the conquest. For when an unsubdued country is conquered, there occur such things as slaughter, death, and deportation of people." In addition, Brahmans and ascetics, virtuous householders, and their "friends, acquaintances, relatives, and kinsmen" suffered injury. These were, of course, non-combatants. The King would have been grieved had the cost been only one hundredth or one thousandth part, for he "desires that all beings should be safe, self-restrained, tranquil in thought and gentle."[15] In his remorse at the carnage, Asoka decided to re-found his empire on Buddhist (and also Jainist) principles of moral virtue and nonviolence. In an edict, he declared "the sound of war drums has become the call for morality."

The new policy of nonviolence had limits. The army still existed and border people were warned that the King "has the strength to punish the

---

[14]John Strong, *The Legend of King Asoka: A Study and Translation of the Asokavadana* (1983), 210-215.

[15]Rock edicts quoted in Gokale, *Asoka Maurya,* Appendix, 157-158. A more thorough study of the concept of Dhamma under Asoka, which also reprints the edicts, is Romila Thapar, *Asoka and the Decline of the Mauryas,* (1961) 137-181, 255-266.

wrongdoers who do not repent." Capital punishment was retained, though those condemned were given three days to repent. Still, there is no record of additional wars by Asoka, and he sent ambassadors to the Seleucid and Ptolemaic dynasties established by Alexander's generals in Syria and Egypt promising peace and attempting to spread moral behavior.

Asoka sought to reform India in accordance with nonviolence. Royal edicts forbade animal sacrifice and told of the reformation in the King's kitchen where formerly thousands of animals were killed and eaten, but now the number was only two peacocks and one deer per day and sometimes not even that many. Asoka even refrained from the royal sport of hunting. Edicts from the King protected some species of animals from slaughter. The King boasted of planting trees, digging wells along roads, founding hospitals, and supporting holy men. The aim was to promote morality so that the King and his children, grandchildren, and subjects would live a righteous life.

Asoka in the rock edicts proclaimed that his "chief duty" was the "welfare of the people" as he sought to discharge his "debt to people, so that I may give happiness to some here and win heaven hereafter."[16] In his concern for promoting virtue, the King sought the common core of morality in all sects, upbraided those who boasted of their religion's superior morality, and proclaimed that the holy men of all sects were "worthy of reverence." Asoka gave donations to Brahmans and Jains, and his edicts praised all religions as promoting *dharma*.

Asoka is remembered in the legends as being the greatest benefactor of Buddhists. He made pilgrimages to the birthplace of the Buddha and honored the village by cutting its inhabitants' tax rate. He founded monasteries and sent missionaries abroad and allegedly erected 84,000 *stupas* for the relics of the Buddha, one for every atom in Gotama's body. As he became older, he gave away so much wealth to the monks that his advisers restrained his giving. During his

---

[16]Ibid., 155, 158.

final illness, Asoka had left only one half of a myrobalan fruit and he even donated this, becoming the greatest benefactor to Buddhism in all history.

Kautilya advocated using spies for knowledge and security; Asoka replaced spies with government-appointed censors who examined the practices of people and officials. His attempt to end hunting, protect certain species, promote vegetarianism, and abolish sacrifices may have appeared to his subjects as just another form of imperial authoritarianism. After all, he did not renounce war until after he had consolidated power and expanded the realm. Perhaps, given the limits of transportation and mechanisms for effective control, he concluded that ruling virtually the entire Indian subcontinent was sufficient. Even Asoka's promotion of religious toleration, public support of holy men, and advocacy of Buddhism can be seen as attempts to preserve the unity of his empire. Historians are not accustomed to taking proclamations of an emperor's piety at face value, particularly when they are carved on rocks for public display and serve a political purpose. Even granting normal skepticism, the rock edicts show that Asoka presented himself as a unique king, a father of his people committed to peace and their welfare. There was no boasting of conquest, claim of divinity, or exaltation of wealth. By contrast, he proclaimed a readiness at all times to serve the people and sought to hold his officials to high standards.

Buddhists (and Hindus and Kautilya) believed that a moral king ruling a religious people created a harmony with nature in which the whole kingdom became a *dharma* realm - a place of virtue, justice, law, order, peace, wealth and detachment. It is not surprising that Asoka continued to be an exemplar to Buddhists of the Universal Monarch turned saint long after Indians had lost the ability to decipher the language of the rock inscriptions.

Later Buddhist kings who modeled themselves on Asoka would know of his conversion, attempts to promote *dharma*, and gifts to monastic orders, but knowledge of the reasons for and effects of his renunciation of war would be lost. Europeans dismissed the stories of Asoka's piety as legends until the rock edicts were translated in the 1830s; today Asoka's symbol of kingship, four lions carved on the capital of one of his pillars, is the national symbol of India.

III. National Buddhism: Sri Lanka

According to a legend recorded in the chronicles of Sri Lanka, the Buddha visited this island off the coast of India three times. He came in order through his glory and miracles to vanquish and banish the Yakkas, the primordial inhabitants of the land, though whether these were chaos-personified, demons, or humans is unclear. The Buddha's presence in Sri Lanka allegedly sanctified the land, made it a place for his teachings (*dharma*) to flourish. Later kings would justify their wars of ascension as imitating the Buddha in defeating opponents who opposed the teachings. A victory would reaffirm the sacred order of life in Sri Lanka.

A second legend recruited Asoka in order to confer legitimacy and prestige upon Sri Lanka and its kings. The *Mahavamsa Chronicles*, written down about 518 C.E., recount that Asoka sent his son to introduce Buddhism to the island. Asoka also conferred the title "beloved of the gods" (*Devanampyatissa*) on the first Buddhist king, sent relics of the Buddha, and provided a twig from the original Bodhi tree which miraculously sprouted at Devanampyatissa's capital, Anuradhapura. By linking their religion, monasteries, and king with Asoka, the Sinhalese could insist that they practiced the pure form of religion. According to the chronicles, the land, the kingship, and the teaching had a uniquely Buddhist status.[17]

Sinhalese Buddhist kings faced challenges to the teachings on nonviolence when Tamils from South India migrated to the island and established their own kingdoms. The result was war for supremacy. The hero of the ensuing battles was Duttagamani, meaning Gamani the Enraged One, who by conquering the Tamils became the national unifier (r. 161-137 B.C.E.) and a symbol of an ethno-religious consciousness that has recently been revived in Sri Lanka.

---

[17]Alice Greenwald, "The Relic on the Spear: Historiography and the Saga of Dutthagamani," in *Religion and Legitimation of Power in Sri Lanka* (1978), 13-31; Roy Amore, "Peace and Nonviolence in Buddhism," in *The Pacifist Impulse in Historical Perspective* (1996), 252-253.

Gamani's war tactics seem the antithesis of Buddhist nonviolence. In his battles with the Tamils, he placed sacred relics of the Buddha on his lance, was accompanied into battle by 500 monks, and slew 31 Tamil kings. He even used a monk as a military general. All these actions appear to be contrary to the spirit as well as the letter of early Buddhism. Dutthagamini, having conquered the evil Tamil army, could rule without the aid of force and have his absolute power restrained by *dharma*. His nonviolence allowed Buddhist chroniclers to legitimate Gamani's violent conquest and political rule by appealing to the Buddha and Asoka.

Like Asoka, Dutthagamani showed sorrow for his violence after successfully conquering the island, but was assured by monks that because the men he slaughtered were not Buddhists, their deaths were equivalent to those of beasts and equaled only one and one half Buddhists. Dutthagamani proved even more contrite when he inadvertently ate a peppercorn and thereby broke a vow to eat only with monks. The King re-established his merit by building monasteries and donating to monks. Even so, he still over-reached his powers. When Gamani tried to preach the teachings, even though he had studied the scriptures and knew their contents, he was unable to talk. Clearly, only monks could interpret the Buddha's teachings.

Because Dutthagamini re-established the sacred order of the island, he could now be a monarch of nonviolence and justice whose merit would be reflected in the virtues of the people and would elicit the blessings of nature. In a sense, the king's battles and later support of the dhamma reenacted the primordial events in creating the island, by being like the Buddha in suppressing the evil in the island, like Asoka in restoring true kingship, and like Asoka's son in supporting true religion. The merit of the king would be so overwhelming that he would actually combine the functions of a Universal Monarch like Asoka and the merit of a saint and become a *bodhisattva*, a living Buddha. Thereby in Sri Lanka, his status would supersede even that of Asoka, who never gained such an exalted spiritual state.

What remains unclear is the historical basis for the Gamani stories. Scholars are unsure whether Gamini's conquest was justified by the chronicles because the legend of the Buddha and the mission of Asoka's son, Malinda, were already part of Sinhalese tradition. The alternative view is that the legends were created after the conquest as a method of legitimating Gamini's rule by invoking the prestige of the Buddha.

From a political perspective, it did not matter whether or not the connections of the Buddha and Asoka with Sri Lanka antedated Dutthagamini's reign, because soon these and other legends became a way of legitimizing wars for power and obedience to Buddhist rulers not only in Sri Lanka but also in Southeast Asia. Aspiring kings would legitimately employ realpolitik of the Kautilya's *Arthasastra* in their search for power because without a powerful king there would be anarchy, immorality, social chaos, and disturbances in nature. Once in power the king would be restrained by Buddhist notions of nonviolence and concern for the welfare of all peoples. The king by patronizing the monastic order would build up merit for himself and the kingdom, and this would result in peace and prosperity. The people would willingly obey a ruler who had prevailed because it was a sign of his superabundance of power *karma*. The monks would support the authority of the governing authorities so that they could pursue the monastic life in peace.

Buddhist kings in the areas of modern Laos, Sri Lanka, Burma, and Thailand for hundreds of years legitimated their rule as embodying Asoka charity and *bodhisattva* compassion. Such an ethos should have restrained their tyranny. However, the alleged realities of politics described by Kautilya allowed princes to initiate wars to establish and preserve their kingdoms; indeed, even to make holy wars against other Buddhists. They fought for land, for trade routes, even to weaken the power of schismatic Buddhists. By being founder, warrior, and saint Duttagamini reshaped a tradition and created an image that would endure for centuries. Historian Trevor Ling, who studied the pre-colonial history of war and peace in Burma and Thailand, concluded that kings "would fight men of any religion or none, if opportunity or occasion demanded it." "Loyalty to the state has come first and common interest with Buddhist co-religionists a poor second."[18]

IV. Japanese Buddhism: Zen and Samurai

In its formative period, Indian Buddhism incorporated into its teachings earlier Hindu beliefs in reincarnation and *karma* and accepted various Hindu deities as *bodhisattvas*. A similar amalgamation of earlier religious beliefs and customs occurred when monks introduced Buddhism to China. The Mahayana Buddhism that spread widely in China contained an elaborate pantheon of gods surrounding the Buddha who appeared as Siddhartha the man, a cosmic force in nature, and as a savior figure who allowed a monk by meditation to achieve his Buddha-nature or *Nirvana*.

Brought to China by missionary monks, Buddhism gained there a Taoist cosmology of ultimate emptiness that could be gained through meditation. The Chinese identified the achievement of Tao or Way of Heaven with realizing the Buddha-mind inherent in each person. Neither Tao nor *Nirvana* could be described in language, only experienced. The Tao sage Lao Tzse insisted that even to pose the question of the nature of Tao indicated that a person did not know its meaning.[19] Chinese Buddhism also combined ancestor worship with the Confucian ethics of morality, public service, and obedience to the Emperor, who by performing rituals ensured the continuation of the mandate of heaven bringing peace, prosperity, and power. When various forms of Mahayana Buddhism teachings reached Japan in Tendai (Heavenly Platform) or Shingon (True Word), in addition to the teachings of Siddhartha and stories of him in various human incarnations, there was the Buddha as a divine figure in heaven surrounded by a

---

[18]Trevor Ling, *Buddhism, Imperialism and War: Burma and Thailand in Modern History* (1979), 135-147. Paul Demiéville, "Le Bouddhisme et la Guerre" (1973), 354 argues that Buddhism did not lead to pacifism in ancient Japan and China.
[19] Winston King, *Zen and the Way of War* (1993), 11.

pantheon of gods and *bodhisatvas* bringing the promise of deliverance from this karmic existence into *Nirvana*.[20]

Buddhism came to Japan in the sixth century as a gift from the emperor of Korea to the Prince Regent Shotoku of Japan. The Japanese viewed their new religion as providing a means of ensuring the prosperity and strengthening the power of their kingdom by allowing the emperor in his priestly functions to perform rituals that would bring the favor of the Buddha and the gods. However, Japan never became a Buddhist *dharma* realm like Sri Lanka with only one official religion because the state cults remained religiously diverse, incorporating what would later be termed Shinto - traditional folk religions of spirits or *Kami*, nature worship, and legends of the imperial dynasty being founded by the sun goddess Amaterasu. Though there was opposition to Buddhism from advocates of Shinto and clans adopted either religion for political advantage, Buddhism became a permanent feature of court life and eventually the Japanese combined or at least did not emphasize the divergent beliefs of the two systems. For example, Amaterasu and the Buddha became conflated and the Shinto war god Hachiman became a *bodhisattva*.[21]

Japanese Buddhism originated and remained for its first five centuries a state-sponsored-and-controlled, political religion. Opposition to war and nonviolence did not appeal to the court or emperor. Emperor Shotoku founded some two hundred monasteries throughout Japan and saw Buddhism as a means of extending royal influence. Still, early Japanese Buddhism remained essentially a foreign import based in Chinese practices and centered on the court. Neither nobility nor monks sought to extend teachings or practices to commoners living in outlying areas. Within two centuries a few monasteries near the capital Kyoto had become major landowners that engaged in maneuvering at court for political

---

[20] Documents showing the different schools of Buddhism in Japan are in Ryusaku Tsunoda et al, *Sources of Japanese Tradition*, (1964), chs. 5-11.
[21] Winston King, 33, 177. This is the most comprehensive account of the influence of Zen on the samurai.

advantages. Because they had been exempted from taxation, the monasteries became virtually autonomous and powerful rivals to the crown.

Within the monasteries, monks studied texts, performed rituals, and sought for individual enlightenment but generally did not emphasize the Buddha's teachings upon compassion and non-killing. As the centralized authority of the emperors weakened, some monasteries became fortified castles and armies of monks not only defended their property but supported different warring factions. There was no affinity between the Buddhist-dominated court with its elaborate manners and esoteric knowledge and the uncouth warriors or *samurai* (literally "retainers") living in the countryside.

Monks dissatisfied with what they viewed as lax practice in Japanese monasteries journeyed to China to study Buddhism and returned to Japan seeking reforms or a reinvigoration of pure religion. One of these reform movements, called *Ch'an* by the Chinese, is more commonly known by its Japanese name Zen Buddhism.

The introduction of Zen during the twelfth century came at the same time as Japan entered its feudal age with the decline of the imperial influence and the rise to dominance of *shoguns*. The emperor remained important as a symbol of cultural unity and as a kind of high priest or intermediary to the gods, and his appointment of the shogun conferred political legitimacy. However, shogun supremacy came only after a series of bitter wars among rival clans, and violence emerged periodically until Japan became unified and pacified around 1600.

The shoguns dominating Japan came from the warrior class and would rule Japan from 1200 until 1868. Disdaining what they saw as the effete life style of the court, the shoguns established their capital a distance from Kyoto first at Kamakura and later at Edo (Tokyo). The shoguns soon became advocates of Zen, which became a kind of semi-official religion for the warrior class.

The shoguns' power rested upon a military force of samurai. Like European knights, the samurai belonged to a distinct upper class whose karmic destiny was to provide service, including doing battle, for the lord. So in spite of

Siddhartha's teachings about nonviolence, there was no questioning of the morality of war. For example, a warrior preparing to kill a noble justified his act to the intended victim by karmic destiny: "Please console yourself by remembering that all things are the result of the deeds of the previous life."[22] The shoguns and other lords (*daimyo*) bestowed lands upon samurai who in return owed military service. The vassal's first duty was absolute obedience to the lord and he should be prepared to die in service. Relations between daimyo were opportunistic with no disgrace attached to shifting loyalty for advantage in struggles to dominate the emperor or control land. Samurai, by contrast, should never waiver in loyalty, should never presume to advise the lord unless asked, though one could kill an evil adviser to the lord but then be prepared to commit suicide (*seppuku*). Unlike the monks who had earlier become advisers to the emperor, Zen monks who became officials for the shoguns did not engage in court intrigue or seek advantage for their religious practices. A follower of Zen could seek enlightenment equally well in a monastery or as a court official because his quest did not depend upon outward surroundings but individual qualities. So an emperor could become a monk or a samurai, a poet.

In battle, samurai wore distinctive armor depending upon their degree (there were 33 different ranks all of which should receive deference from merchants and peasants) and served as the mounted cavalry in feudal armies. There was considerable expense to equipping a warrior and furnishing a horse and so the warriors became a hereditary caste, each of whom was given enough land (at least in theory) to produce sufficient rice to maintain himself. The distinctive arms of each samurai were a long and a short sword, a long bow plus a few arrows, and a halberd or spear. The initial function of samurai in battle was to shoot arrows, followed by a cavalry charge to disrupt the formation of the opponent. Then he would dismount and engage in individual combats. There was no glory in killing a common soldier. Rather, the warriors' goal was to kill a skilled samurai,

---

[22] Quoted in Kenneth Kraft, *Eloquent Zen: Daito and Early Japanese Zen* (1992), 17.

then behead him, and carry off the head as a war trophy. On occasion, after such a duel, the victor might allow the loser to kill himself (*hari kari*) by plunging a knife into his lower chest to escape the disgrace of being killed. Wars normally were skirmishes, but on occasion when regional warlords sought national supremacy, there would be major battles with heavy casualties.

Becoming a samurai took long and arduous training. To be able to accurately shoot an arrow from a galloping horse at a target the size of a man's hat took months of practice (and a steady horse). Even more important was swordsmanship, which became a deadly art form. A warrior needed to master the correct offensive and defensive strokes, to be able to anticipate and counter an opponent's thrusts (even a surprise attack), to keep his balance, being prepared to move to escape a blow while striking the enemy. Success required skill and the ability to concentrate only on the battle at hand with no fear of death and a willingness to die because life or death was ultimately irrelevant.

Zen techniques helped a warrior in battle. The discipline of Zen allowed the clearing of the samurai's mind of all extraneous thought so that the warrior and his sword became a unity centered on the task at hand. Zen also allowed the samurai to become "a mirror" so that he could understand an opponent's mind and, thereby, anticipate his move. Note that for the samurai Zen practice was not concerned with the ethics of fighting or the cause of the quarrel. Obedience and indifference to death were the cardinal virtues.

The samurai's relation with his sword became religious as they in effect became a fused entity in battle. In many cultures the sword symbolized power with special mystical significance in its creation and use. (For example, when the boy Arthur pulled the sword Excaliber from a stone, it signified that he was the true king of England.) In Japan one of the three sacred regalia of the emperor is a sword. Swordsmiths who had mastered the difficult and delicate art of creating a hardened sword capable of breaking an opponent's weapon or cutting bone invoked the power of the gods and engraved sacred symbols (as well as their own names) on the blade. Schools of swordsmanship taught various techniques as well as the mind control necessary for success. Not all samurai were wealthy, and poor ones would often travel around seeking to prove their skills against local champions so that a lord would enlist their services.

Zen appealed to shoguns and samurai because it was a simplified and anti-intellectual Buddhism, which made them better warriors but placed few restrictions on other areas of life, though random killing of peasants was frowned upon. But if an unarmed peasant or merchant showed disrespect to a samurai, then he should be killed. Zen had no elaborate ritual or detailed commentaries upon the canonical writings as in esoteric Buddhism. Unlike other rival popular forms of Buddhism (also introduced from China and popular in the twelfth century) there was no concentration upon meditation on the *Lotus Sutra* to envision heaven as in Pure Land Buddhism or using chants as a means to salvation by faith as in *Amida*. There were no elaborate temples filled with carvings.

The austerity in Zen practice appealed to warriors. Zen Buddhist monasteries featured an unornamented meditation hall where the monks sat for hours on raised platforms in the lotus position (the way they normally sat) under the discipline of Zen masters, men whom earlier masters had certified as having achieved Buddha-mindedness. The vigorous give and take between the masters and the novices that could include slapping or other violent forms may have appealed to the warriors. Zen favored an oral transmission from masters who had gained enlightenment and traced this heritage back to the Buddha. After being satisfied that the novice had sufficient skills, the master would give a certificate entitling him to teach.

Zen practitioners sought neither mystical experience nor intellectual understanding because enlightenment could come only after a breaking down and transcending of the normal thought processes. This was accomplished through spending hours meditating (*zazan*) on cryptic utterances termed *koans*. Here is one spoken by the Buddha: "If you try to see me through form// or hear me through sound,//nothing you see or hear//is where I am." Other earlier examples used in training samurai were: the story of a monk asking a master "Does a dog have Buddha-nature or not." Chao-chous said, "Mu." (No). The novice should concentrate on that "No." A *koan* designed for warriors asked: "If you were surrounded by a hundred enemies, how would you manage to win without fighting or surrendering?"[23]

The purpose of spending hours over many months in meditation on a single *koan* in an unornamented room with other devotees under the supervision of a Zen master was to break down the illusions of common sense and reason in this *samsara* existence of interconnectedness. For example, one must understand the meaninglessness of distinguishing you and I, or I and the world, or mind and body, or life and death. A devotee must achieve a new form of consciousness so that even to pose these dualities became absurd. Any verbalization or learned intellectual or social system or beliefs or behavior pattern must end, because all concepts are non-Buddha mind. The final result – *Nirvana* or Buddha-nature – cannot be communicated. It transcends words and sense experience to achieve a final enlightenment in the void, not a void of utter nothingness, but a cosmic void.[24]

> The No-Mind is the same as the Right Mind. It neither congeals nor fixes itself in one place . . . The No-Mind is placed nowhere. When the No-Mind has been well developed, the mind does not stop with one thing nor does it lack any one thing. It is like water overflowing and existing with itself."[25]

Zen required a totally disciplined austere existence in which a monk devoted his lifetime to seeking individual enlightenment (*satori*). "Satori is emancipation, moral, spiritual, as well as intellectual. When I am in my isness, thoroughly purged of all intellectual sediments, I have my freedom in its primary sense." Even when living in a community and meditating in a group, the goal was self-obliteration. Zen required no social ethic, even to ask about ethics showed

---

[23] Kraft, 60-61.
[24] There are verbalizations in Zen, but they violate all the rules of linguistics. Daisetz T. Suzuki, *Zen and Japanese Culture* (1959), 6.
[25] Winston King, *Zen and the Way of War* (1993), 167-8.

illusion.[26] The ultimate goal, and even using moral language to describe it is meaningless, was to achieve transcendence, to imitate the Buddha who after his enlightenment devoted himself to communicating the truth.

What was the appeal of so forbidding a teaching to samuri warriors? First, there was an anti-intellectualism and de-emphasis upon ritual and book learning. Enlightenment did not come from studying the varieties of Buddhism or engaging in elaborate rituals. Enlightenment came from mindlessness, meditating upon a *koan* until it was like a hot iron in the belly that consumed one's existence until there was no self. There was also an austerity, analogous to a soldier's life. For the samurai warrior, Zen offered the prospect of total mindlessness so that in battle total concentration would blot out any fear of death or other extraneous factors. The warrior and his sword could become one focused entity in striving to defeat an enemy. After all, victory might depend upon a small quick movement that might make the enemy's sword stroke miss and throw him off balance.

Whether the ideal of the Zen samurai ever became pervasive is difficult to determine. Certainly, not all samurai went to a monastery and not all observed the rigorously ascetic life required.[27] Yet the emphasis upon total loyalty, the willingness to accept death in service to a lord as part of one's karmic destiny, and the importance of single-mindedness became central features of Japanese life. Zen's emphases on simplicity, order, and economy permeated many facets of Japanese life - in paintings, gardens, architecture, and the tea ceremony - from medieval times until the present.

Zen also influenced one of the most remarkable achievements of Japanese history. In the sixteenth century, the Japanese acquired guns from the Europeans and soon after learned how to make their own, even making improvements. Soon lords equipped their soldiers with arquebuses, which led to devastating effects on

---

[26] Daisetz T. Suzuki, *Zen and Japanese Culture (1959)*, 17, 47. 61-63. Zen "may be found wedded to anarchism, or fascism, communism or democracy, atheism or idealism, or any political or economic dogmatism."
[27] Martin Colcutt, "The Zen Monastery in Kamakura Society," in *Court and Bakufu in Japan*, ed. Jeffrey Mass (1982), 192-193.

the mortality of sword-fighting samurai. To fire a gun effectively, a warrior needed neither long training nor self-control. However, after the reunification of Japan under the Hojo shoguns in 1600, Japan gradually stopped using guns and continued until the mid-nineteenth century to rely upon samurai swords and bows and arrows.[28] The process of disarmament (more accurately, "disgunament") was done gradually with little discussion, with Hideyoshi (the first unifier of Japan) ordering the collection of guns from peasants in order to melt them down in order to create a massive sculpture of the Buddha.[29] In Japan, unlike Europe, a cultural imperative to value the sword and to preserve the samurai class triumphed over the destructive potential of the gun.

A second major change after 1600 was the transformation of the samurai from warriors into bureaucrats. After the unification of Japan, there was no need for soldiers. The Zen ideal of disciplined life and service to a lord became the ethos for secretaries and functionaries of the government. Samurai wrote poetry and painted as well as practicing swordsmanship. The craft of making swords continued as samurai prized them for their hardness and decorative fashion. The practice of swordsmanship (often carried on with wooden swords) evolved into an art form. The martial arts like *kung fu* and *jujitsu* became ways to gain mental self-control and self-defense, not to kill an opponent. Japan became a realm of peace, threatening neither internally or externally. Zen proved as adaptable to preserving peace as it had formerly been for making war.

As happened in the West when Roman emperors and kings became Christians, the Buddhists' adapting or taming of religious insights advocating peace and opposing violence into legitimating war was an uneven process. Monks who accommodated the teachings of the Buddha to the needs of monarchy facilitated the survival and spread of Buddhism. In return kings who still made war to obtain power would support religious institutions, publicly accept the teachings, and use

---

[28] Noel Perrin, *Giving Up the Gun: Japan's Reversion to the Sword, 1543-1849* (1979).
[29] Mary Elizabeth Berry, *Hideyoshi* (1982), 3, 148, 150.

them to justify their reign, pacify the population, and promote morality. The resulting social stability created conditions that would allow devout men and women, living in monasteries or in the secular world, to transcend politics and to seek *Nirvana.*

VII.
Islam in War and Peace

In 610 in Mecca, a forty-year-old Arabian merchant named Muhammad experienced a series of visions in which the angel Gabriel revealed the nature of God. Muhammad proclaimed that there was only one God, Allah, and the prevalent polytheism practiced in Arabia was idolatry that would lead to judgment and damnation. Each person's duty was to worship the one true God and to follow His moral commandments.

Muhammad demanded that the believer yield to God (Islam literally means "to submit"), and by so doing would obtain peace, or *salaam*. This peace attained in this life would be within the *umma*, or community of believers. Because peace was an absence of violence and also a political social order characterized by a justice in which all submit to God, all earthly peace required an Islamic ruler and law. There was also an eschatological dimension to peace that the believer would experience after death in the next life. Abraham would welcome all the faithful to heaven with a greeting of "Peace." Islam was and is an attempt to bring the peace of God to all creation, and such bliss will be achieved by worship and obedience to God's law. Such a peace is not an imposition on the earth, but a fulfillment of the natural order created by Allah. So Islamic law embodies a universal natural law binding upon all persons.[1]

This chapter is divided into six sections: the first deals with Muhammad, whose teachings and practices established the norms all Muslims affirm. Parts II,

---

[1] John Esposito, *Islam: The Straight Path* (1989) is a readable introduction to Islam. There are three good introductions to the Islamic traditions of war and peace. Written from the standpoint of comparative social ethics are John Kelsay, *Islam and War* (1993), and James Turner Johnson, *The Holy War Idea in Western and Islamic Traditions* (1997). Both of these books reflect the experiences of the Gulf War and recent encounters of Muslims with the West. An older book that treats Islam by itself is Majid Khadduri, *War and Peace in the Law of Islam* (1955). The discussion of Islam in the *Encylopaedia of Religion* contains a good summary of recent scholarship.

III, and IV discuss the expansion of the realm of Islam from Arabia into an empire. The caliphs faced problems of maintaining political and religious unity, particularly the divergence between Sunni and Shi'a. Under the Abbasid dynasty, Islamic jurists created laws of war and peace dealing with right conduct before, during, and after a war; for the first time the implications of the teachings on *jihad* were formalized. Part V, concentrating upon the writings of the influential historian Ibn Khaldun, shows that Islam was compatible with a realistic interpretation of the reasons for the rise and fall of dynasties. Part VI discusses the impact of the crusades from the perspective of Islam.

Our focus is twofold: what in the traditions of Islam fosters peace and legitimates war and how Muslims deal with the ethics of fighting. All religions deal with these issues and we need to see what is common among them as well as to understand what is unique to each. Islam follows the teachings and example of Muhammad as interpreted by followers seeking to apply the counsel of God in cultures from Indonesia to Morocco.

I. The Prophet

Muhammad did not consider himself and is not considered by devout Muslims to be a god or divine being; rather, he was a human whose actions exemplify perfect obedience to God's will and who became the messenger of Allah. After 610 for the rest of his life, a period of twenty-two years, Muhammad would periodically receive communications or visions from God, and he dictated these to a secretary or they were written down and preserved by his followers. There is a not-universally-accepted tradition that Muhammad was illiterate, so the beauty in style of the Arabic writings of God's counsel supposedly represents the perfection of Allah, not the learning of man. These dictations, written down in Muhammad's lifetime on scattered sheets, were put into a standardized form in the *Qur'an* within a generation of the Prophet's death.

The *Qur'an*, meaning "recitation" because it is a holy act to memorize and say the words, has a more exalted status in Islam than the *Bible* in Christianity. Muslims believe that the *Qur'an* contains the very words of God; its form as well as content is the revelation of Allah. In contrast, to most Christians the *Bible* represents as revelation the actions of God in the deliverance of Israel from Egypt or the life, teaching, and resurrection of Jesus of Nazareth. The *Bible* is stories about acts of God in history; the *Qur'an* also assumes God's actions in history, but it is fundamentally a book of instructions encompassing all of life dictated by God through Muhammad, rather than a collection of stories.[2]

The *Qur'an* contained all the revelations given by God to Muhammad on various occasions, and the *suras*, or chapters, were organized roughly by length rather than chronologically. There was, however, a section labeled Medina and another for Mecca that contained God's directions for Muhammad when he lived in these cities as a private citizen and later as ruler. The revelations addressed concrete situations, and the advice given could vary over time depending upon the context, and a *sura* could contain revelations given at different times. Later commentators distinguished between early and later revelations and particular and general commands; that is, a command which served well in one instance but which was subordinate to a more universal demand. Neither believers nor scholars doubt that the *Qur'an* contains the words of Muhammad. Muslims believe that all the revelations in the *Qur'an* are true and inerrant. The *Qur'an* contains the whole counsel of God for all life, and its truth is eternal.

While Islam has sought for the ideal of one faith and one politics, and all Muslims legitimate themselves through the teachings of Muhammad, divisions of practices and interpretations are almost coterminous with the death of the prophet in 632. The *Qur'an* was standardized early in an effort to prevent schisms. Even so, a fragile Muslim unity was obtained only after a series of wars against apostasy.

To understand the historical evolution of Muslims attitudes to war, it is necessary to juxtapose events in Muhammad's life with the *suras*, or chapters, of

---

[2] A good way to approach the *Qur'an* is to use Kenneth Craig, ed. and tr., *Readings in the Qur'an*, London, UK: Collins, 1988, which lists all verses on a subject. I have also used *The Qur'an: The First American Version*, tr. and commentary T. B. Irving (1985).

the *Qur'an*. Early, there grew up stories about the Prophet, termed *hadith*, that described events and sayings of the Prophet. The faithful use these stories as guides to conduct, because Muhammad exemplified faithful obedience to God. Unlike the *Qur'an*, which took its present form by ca. 650, stories of the Prophet continued to appear, and medieval Muslim scholars recognized many as legendary and attempted to distinguish the true from false. Still, modern scholars both within and outside the faith insist that there is far more historical information available about Muhammad than either Jesus or the Buddha.

For the first twelve years after proclaiming his initial vision, Muhammad stayed in Mecca and attracted a few followers. His strict monotheism seemingly threatened the economic welfare of the city because Mecca was a pilgrimage site for the nomadic Bedouin tribes who came to worship during the truce months at the *Ka'ba* shrine. The building housing the *Ka'ba*, a rock, contained statues of various deities, all of whom could be worshiped. The only unity among the tribes on the Arabian Peninsula was in the pilgrimage and common adherence to a cult of manliness meaning bravery in battle, sexual prowess, and loyalty to tribe.[3]

Muhammad's strict monotheism and moral rectitude, division of the world between his followers and those who did evil, and his unwillingness to compromise his visions from Allah made him enemies, even in his own clan. He attracted the support of a few Mecca inhabitants, most notably Abu Bakr, who would later become the first caliph. After the death of Muhammad's wife and his protector in his clan in Mecca, his position became untenable and he welcomed the opportunity to go to Medina, a trading community close-by, as an arbitrator between factions. During his journey to Medina in 622, actually a flight from his persecutors, the Prophet was saved through miracles from enemies who sought to kill him. This trip is now termed the *hajj* and is year one in the Muslim calendar.

During his sojourn in Mecca, Muhammad mainly emphasized spiritual renewal. *Jihad*, for example, literally meaning "effort" or "striving," was used to

---

[3] Kelsay, 18.

describe an interior struggle between faith and the forces of evil. There can be a *jihad* of the heart (moral reformation), of the tongue (proclaiming God's word abroad), and of the hand (works done in obedience to the law).[4] *Jihad* as a state of war is referred to as a "lesser" *jihad*. *Jihad* always is a struggle against evil, and the form depends upon circumstances. The first biography of Muhammad says that at the time of the flight from Mecca to Medina the revelation changed and allowed the use of the sword. Early *suras* show that the first military *jihad* was in response to the forced exile from Mecca:

> Those who have been wronged are permitted to fight [back] - since God is Able to support them - any who have been driven from their homes unjustly, merely because they say 'Our Lord is God [Alone] ... Fight those who fight against you along God's way, yet do not initiate hostilities. Fight in God's way and know that God is Alert, Aware.[5]

At Medina Muhammad moved rapidly from arbitrator to political religious leader. This development is of fundamental importance in understanding the difference between Christian and Islamic attitudes to politics and war. Jesus disdained political power, and because Christianity began as a movement of the disinherited, his followers did not face the responsibility for ruling until the reign of Constantine. In western Europe, there always remained a distinction between the spiritual/churchly realm and politics. An emperor or king was not, and could not become, a bishop. By contrast, Islam began with a merger of politics and religion; for Muhammad there was only one realm, that of obedience to God's law. The authority of God's law is based on revelation in the *Qur'an* and reason through natural law. So all are obligated to obey God's law, and Muhammad and his successors, the caliphs, had a divine mandate to govern and to reform society. Muhammad succeeded because he was not only a visionary but also a skilled politician. In his concern for a right ordering of politics and refusal to distinguish

---

[4] Johnson, 19.
[5] Kelsay, 21. *Qur'an* 22:40; 2:190, 243. There was also a pre-Islamic monotheism and a view of Allah as the chief god in Mecca. Richard Eaton, "Islamic History as Global History" in *Islamic and European Expansion* (1993), 5-8, 34.

the realm of politics from religion, Muhammad resembled Moses and Joshua more than Jesus or Buddha.

During his stay in Medina Muhammad had to deal with internal and external enemies. To protect and spread the faith, he authorized the use of force against unbelievers and led the army himself. There were about ninety expeditions or raids that followed the traditional pattern of caravan raids for booty now joined with a new imperative to avenge former religious persecution and to spread the new faith: "You who believe, fight any disbelievers who hem you in so they may find out how tough you are." "O believers, fight those unbelievers who are near you, and let them find a roughness in you."[6] The *Qur'an's* Medina *suras* exhort shirkers to join the battle for Islam. They promise life in heaven to those who die, provide instructions on when and how to pray on the battlefield, tell when hostilities can begin, define who the enemies are, and provide guidelines for the treatment of hostile warriors who are to be killed or, if converted, enslaved. Woman and children are not to be killed.[7] The Qur'anic commandment is a clear statement, earlier than anything in the West, but not India, of the immunity of at least some non-combatants.

The entire framework of war was placed in a context of God's personal intervention. When the Muslim forces won a battle even though outnumbered, God had acted. When they experienced a setback, God willed the defeat. Allah's counsels were at times inscrutable to mortal humans. Still, the ultimate victory would be God's, and the rhetoric of the *Qur'an* and the *hadith* at times portrayed Allah as actually engaged in the fighting.

Muhammad did not neglect the material wishes of his warriors. He authorized raids on caravans and promised four-fifths of the booty to the warriors. His one-fifth was spent on relief for the poor and orphans. He also provided subsidies for allies or to buy the neutrality of potential enemies. An

---

[6]W. Montgomery Watts, "Islamic Conceptions of War" (1976), 143. *Qur'an* 9:123/4.
[7] For example, "Raid, do not embezzle spoils, do not act treacherously, do not mutilate, and do not kill children."

incentive for nomadic warriors to become Muslim was that the raids were conducted only on non-believers. Muhammad thereby became a leader of a tribal federation whose warriors became a force for his conquest of Mecca and the later expansion of Islam.

The *Qur'an* distinguished the treatment given to polytheists from that of people of "the book" or the *Bible*. There was a fundamental difference in the attitudes to each other of Islam, Judaism, and Christianity. Both Judaism and Christianity were intolerant of other religions; truth was one, and each held that the worship of God outside its respective religious institutions (synagogue or church) was idolatry. Muhammad agreed that all polytheism was idolatry, but he recognized the legitimacy of both Judaism and Christianity and instilled into Islam an acceptance of religious diversity that over the centuries resulted in far more tolerance in the realm of Islam than in Christian Europe. To some extent, such a policy was a necessity because Muslims early began ruling areas populated by Christians and Jews, and it would have been impractical, perhaps even impossible, to have expelled them. By contrast, Christians did not begin to rule areas with Muslim inhabitants until almost a thousand years later.

Muhammad had some limited firsthand knowledge of Christian and Jewish practices, since both religions were practiced in Arabia.[8] He saw Islam as carrying on the essential teaching of both of those religions, of adapting these faiths for Arabs. Abraham became the founder of all three faiths, because before Moses, before the law, he had practiced the worship of God. Just as Christianity identified the Old Testament Lord God with the New Testament Trinity, so Islam identified God with Allah. Muslims asserted that the differences between Islam and the teachings of Judaism and Christianity came because later disciples had distorted the essential meanings of the founders. Moses and Jesus were prophets

---

[8] William M. Watt, *Muslim-Christian Encounters: Perceptions and Misperceptions* (1991), ch. 1-2. The *Bible* had not been translated into Arabic, and Muhammad's knowledge of Judaism and Christianity may have come from merchants or practitioners with only a limited understanding of these faiths. Islamic traditions see a radical disjunction between Mohammed and pre-Islamic societies. Some scholars agree, but others see a more evolutionary process. Eaton, 7-8.

like Muhammad, only the latter presented the teachings about God in their pure form. Islam rejected the divinity of Christ or trinitarian Christianity because that divided the unity of Allah.

In temper Islam was close to the Nestorian or monophysite Christianity that downplayed the humanness of Jesus and that prevailed in Egypt and the eastern Mediterranean.[9] This similarity may help explain why Islam could so easily become the dominant religion in these areas after centuries of Christian rule. Moreover, there is evidence that Muhammad originally saw himself as preaching a new or reformed Judaism and Christianity, and initially prayers were to be said facing Jerusalem. He thought of Islam as capturing for Arab peoples the essence of Judaism and Christianity. The Prophet expected the Jews in Medina to join his new religion. When some clans of Jews resisted the new political/religious order, he had them expelled from Medina, allowing them to take their property with them. On a later occasion, he ordered executed members of an opposing clan of Jews in Medina who opposed his rule.

The policy enunciated in the *Qur'an* for both Christians and Jews (and later expanded to include Zoroastrians in Persia and Hindus in India) was that these religions were legitimate and should be tolerated. There would be no persecution of either Jews or Christians in the realm of Islam, but there would also be no political power because both groups had departed from the truth. Christians and Jews, if they acknowledged the political authority of Muhammad or later Muslim rulers and paid a special tax, would be allowed to practice their religions in peace. The poll tax was a mark of inferiority, but the minority religious communities would be allowed to regulate their own members according to their precepts. These groups were, therefore, unlike polytheists or pagans who had no right to practice their religion. Islam was always in a state of strife or war

---

[9] Christianity was identified with the Byzantine Empire and those who seemed to deviate from Orthodoxy faced persecution. So Christians whom the Byzantines saw as heretics may have welcomed Muslim deliverance as allowing them more freedom. In addition, attacks from the Vandals and pagans and migration meant that, except for the Copts in Egypt, there were few Christians remaining in North Africa. Watts, *Muslim-Christian Encounters,* 61-62.

(*jihad*) with pagans, although there could be intervals of truce. The tolerance of Muhammad for people of "the book" is important to remember: from 600 until 1948, Jews experienced better treatment in Muslim territory than in Christian Europe.

Muhammad ruled Mecca for only two years, and at his death in 632 the area under his control did not even include all the tribes in Arabia. Still by marriages, astute diplomacy, and military conquest, Muhammad gradually obtained ascendancy over other towns and Bedouin tribes on the Arabian Peninsula. Looked at from the standpoint of political science, Muhammad slowly transformed a group of tribes or clans into a religiously based state.

II. The Spread of Islam

The Prophet had laid the political and religious foundation for attack upon the Byzantine Empire's possessions in the Fertile Crescent and the Sasanian Empire in Persia, two kingdoms already weakened by their wars against each other. Within a hundred years after 632, an Islamic realm stretched from the Atlantic Ocean to India. Arab warriors, fighting a *jihad*, defeated the forces of the Byzantine Empire in North Africa, Palestine, and Syria, and even initiated the first of several unsuccessful sieges of Constantinople in 669. The Byzantine Empire managed to survive by fighting the forces of Islam, first the Arabs and later the Turks. A remnant of the eastern Roman Empire endured until 1453, and through constant struggle and intermittent war protected eastern and northern Europe from Islamic conquest. The heartland of the Byzantine Empire would remain the Christian Orthodox, Greek-speaking population in what are now Turkey, Greece, and the southern Balkans.

Islam's initial knowledge of the theory and practices of Christian warfare came in battles against the Eastern Empire. Both the Byzantine Romans and Arab Muslims saw their causes as vindicated by God and fought a series of holy wars. There is no certainty as to whether holy war was invented several times because this was a normal response to religious fervor or was a product of cultural transmission learned by trade, the *Bible*, or fighting. Based on chronology, one could argue that Byzantine holy war came first and influenced Islam's *jihad*, and both led to medieval Europe's crusades. Whatever the origins of the practice, Islam and Christianity engaged in holy wars against pagans and each other in attempts to defend and to spread the faith.[10]

The Arab expansion threatened Europe also from the west and the south. By the end of the tenth century, Islam gained a toehold on Sicily, controlled some areas of Italy, conquered Spain, and conducted raids into France. The Franks halted İslam's advance into western Europe at the battle of Tours in 753, an event that had more significance for the northern Europeans than the Muslims, who thought the area of little value. In the east, the Arabs conquered the Sasanian Empire of what is now Persia. Later the Mongols, Genghis Khan's successors who after devastating much of Persia had converted to Islam, would conquer India. Christianity, which had earlier seemed the religion of the Mediterranean world, now was confined to part of Europe, and in both area and numbers seemed overwhelmed by Islam. No wonder the chroniclers of the Byzantine world saw the rise of this new religion as the reign of the anti-Christ, a time of troubles caused by the sins of the people, and a sign that the world would end soon.[11]

From the Islamic perspective, events looked much better. Muslims saw their conquests as vindication of Allah, a sign that Islam would become the dominant world religion and that the successors of Muhammad would rule a politically and religiously united realm. The pilgrimage center of the Muslim world remained Mecca and Medina, but after the conquest of what is now called the Middle East, the Umayyad dynasty transferred the political and religious capital from Arabia to Damascus and, after 750 with the establishment of a new dynasty of Abbasids, to Baghdad. Muslim conquest was made easier because

---

[10] Michael Davis Bonner, *Aristocratic Violence and Holy War: Studies in the Jihad and the Arab-Byzantine Frontier* (1996), 1-3. Fred M. Donner, "The Religious Foundations of War, Peace, and Statecraft in Islam," in *Just War and Jihad: Historical and Theoretical Perspectives on War and Peace in Western and Islamic Traditions* (1991), 31-70. See also the discussion in Watt that concentrates upon the Medina period.

peoples in the conquered lands, most of whom had long been accustomed to living in an empire and having no voice in government, were not required to convert, only to pay special taxes. All that was necessary was for the rulers to be Muslims and to rule according to God's law. There was no persecution of the Christian Copts in Egypt or Marionites in Lebanon, and the only people who initially converted in large numbers were the Berbers of North Africa, whose desire to share in the spoils of an expanding empire aided their religious motives. In later years, the majority would become Muslims.

The Umayyad dynasty (661-750) controlled a larger area but with fewer people than Rome at its height. Under the first four Caliphs and then the Umayyad, expansion became such a dominant feature of foreign policy that one historian has termed the empire a "*jihad* state."[12] Historians list many factors as motivating the drive to conquer: a religious desire to increase the lands controlled by Muslims, the economic need for booty that would fill the treasury of the Umayyads and allow all Islamic warriors to achieve economic equality, a means of diverting the energies of those discontented with the Umayyads away from rebellion. Successful *jihads* would demonstrate to the Muslim world that the Umayyad clan, which earlier had opposed Muhammad, enjoyed the favor of Allah. The initial campaigns brought overwhelming success against two weak and unpopular regimes, the Byzantines in North Africa and Palestine and the Sasanians in Persia. Later *jihads* against the Sind kingdom in India and the Visigoth kingdom in Spain also brought victories and wealth.

During the reign of Hisham (724-743) the Muslims encountered tougher opponents, a revitalized Byzantine Empire fighting in its heartland, nomads in central Asia, and the Franks in western Europe. The result was a series of major

---

[11] The Byzantines, though they had frequent contact with the Muslims, seemed to have made few efforts to find out accurate information and, instead, created a few negative stereotypes that have had a long-lasting influence on Europeans. Watts, *Muslim-Christian Encounters*, 70-71, 83.

[12] Khalid Yahya Blankinship, *The End of the Jihad State: The Reign of Hisham Ibn 'Abd al-Malik and the Collapse of the Umayyads* (1994), 1-4. The Umayyads also fought three civil wars (*fitna*) plus wars against Berbers and Kharijites. G. R. Hawting, *The First Dynasty of Islam: The Umayyad Caliphate AD 661-750* (2000), 66-67, 90.

defeats resulting in a weakened dynasty, rebellions, and the conquest by the Abbasids. The Abbasids, who moved the capital to Baghdad, were never able to control Spain and within a century semi-independent kingdoms emerged in Egypt and North Africa. The Abbasids placed more emphasis upon consolidating the empire than upon *jihad* expansion. Ironically, only under the Abbasids would jurists develop the theory of *jihad*.

Under the Abbassids the contributions of an urbanized Islamic civilization surpassed the faded Roman glories of Italy and the Byzantine Empire, let alone the remote barbarian-controlled northern Europe. Muslim scholars, who for religious reasons chose to remain almost totally ignorant of the religious writings of Latin Christianity, preserved and utilized the scientific and philosophical writings of the Greeks and Romans, served as a conduit for contributions from India and China, and made fundamental advances in mathematics, astronomy, medicine, and technology. The depth, variety, and sophistication with which eighth-century Islamic thinkers approached the problems of war and peace equaled or surpassed the contributions of classical civilization or early medieval Europe.

Muhammad's successors, termed caliphs, like him combined political and religious authority, although they made no claim to direct visions of God or spiritual equality with the Prophet. Still later generations cited the actions of the early caliphs who knew Muhammad as precedents for actions of the faithful, secondary only to the *Qur'an* and the practices of the Prophet. Islam had no sacerdotal priesthood to mediate the experience between God and the believer, relying instead upon men of deep piety who spent their lives studying the sacred scripture, the *hadith*, and the religious practice of the community. These scholarly commentators helped define the *shari'a*, or law, that provided the faithful with the correct interpretations of the traditions of the faith. The ruler or *Imam* should consult with the *umma* or community of pious scholars in determining correct policies. In contrast with the Jewish emphasis on talmudic stories and the Christian stress on theology, in Islam the most important intellectual activity has been the exposition of the *shari'a*. The *Qur'an* itself fosters an emphasis upon law for, unlike the *Bible* or the *Bhagavadgita*, it contains few stories and many detailed prescriptions for correct behavior.[13] Muslims believe that the *shari'a* is eternal, but interpretations of it are not, thereby allowing flexibility in practice and, through analogies, adjustments to new circumstances. Islam began as a reform movement, and the *shari'a* is more a prescription than a description of Muslim life. Since the reality never measured up to the ideal, Islam has a built-in emphasis upon reform of society.

A codification of faith and adjustment to government occurred within the first centuries after Muhammad's death similar to that occasioned in the Christian movement first by the delay of Christ's return and later by the conversion of Constantine. The first converts to Islam were provincial Arabs, the inhabitants of trading towns and nomads. With the expansion of Islam, by conquest but also by peaceful preaching, the religion had to be adapted to an urban population conversant with Greek, Roman, Persian, and Egyptian civilization. The Arab Muslim rulers were often a small minority, and they influenced and learned from their subject populations. So Muslim rulers resembled Byzantine, Persian, or Indian kingship. Conquest need not require conversion, because the Prophet insisted the adherence to Islam be voluntary. At the end of the first century of conquest, Muslims are estimated to have been about ten percent of the populations they ruled.[14]

Muhammad left no directions on how to choose his successor. The first sultan, Abu Bakr, had been an early follower of Muhammad and a relative through marriage. In time disputes occurred over whether the new caliph should come from the immediate family of Muhammad or from the Umayyad clan and climaxed in a bitter division of the Muslim community into two factions: the Sunni or

---

[13] Law here is not used in the sense of a state's legislation, but as series of mandates on attitudes and behavior. Many of the mandates in the *Qur'an* are beyond the purview of statutes. Islam began as a reform movement and the *shari'a* is more a prescription for, than a description of, Muslim life.

[14] Peter Partner, *God of Battles: Holy Wars of Christianity and Islam* (1997), 42.

orthodox party which controlled the caliphate, against the Shi'a, who were driven from power.

The Shi'a recognized neither the Umayyads nor Abbasids as true caliphs, believing that the succession should go through Muhammad's daughter Fatima to Ali and his sons, both of whom were killed in battle, and their descendants who are the true Imams. The assassination of Ali's son Hussein is communally re-enacted each year at Muharran. The Shi'a believe the other descendents of Ali went into hiding. The last of the twelve true Imams went into occultation or a kind of supernatural concealment in 874 and will return again at some future date. So for the Shiites there is a distrust of the reigning authorities and hope for an eschatological return of the hidden Madhi or Imam who will purge evil and restore Muhammad's unity between religion and ruler. Shi'a believe that only a true *Imam* or caliph can declare an offensive *jihad,* so this kind of a war is no longer possible. However, all Muslims are required to fight in a defensive *jihad.*

Unlike the Sunni who rest the authority of right interpretation upon the consensus of the *ulema,* the Shi'a insist that holy men, also termed *Imam* declare the infallible teachings of the law. In a sense, they have become successors of the Prophet. Such *imams* have great prestige and, after death, the burial places of these holy men become shrines of worship. Such teachings have allowed the Shi'a a cult of saints, much to the scandal of conservative Sunni who are warned against veneration at the tomb even of the Prophet as detracting from the homage due Allah. For the Shi'a there is one supreme jurist in every generation, but other scholars of the law - termed *ayatollahs* - also provide authoritative interpretations. The Sunni in theory froze the canon of acceptable beliefs or *Ijma* as interpreted by the *ulema,* but the Shi'a allow continuing revelation by infallible teachers.

Shi'a beliefs and practices attracted those who were estranged from the Umayyads, including many non-Arabs who felt they received second-class treatment. The Abbasids were no more sympathetic, but eventually Shi'a dynasties emerged in North Africa and Persia and even obtained the sanction from the caliph in Baghdad. Shiite influence remains dominant today in modern Iran and Iraq. Egypt, Saudi Arabia, and most of North Africa remain Sunni. The Shi'a division was only the first of many schisms in Islam, and there are many sects of Shiites, for example the Ismailis and the Druzes in Lebanon.

Those Muslims called Kharijites, who opposed both Caliph Ali and the Umayyads, saw only Allah as their king and defined themselves as in a constant state of rebellion. They often reacted violently against the luxurious lifestyle associated with the caliphs. The Kharijites believed that any devout Muslim could become caliph and, although they were suppressed, they initiated a tradition of reform movements that could become rebellions against political leaders who have allegedly betrayed Islam. Unlike the Sunni, who depended upon the caliph to declare a *jihad,* the Kharijites made holy war an obligation on the individual, almost a sixth pillar of the faith.

A complete contrast in response came from the Sufi, who also reacted against the lifestyle of the courts at Damascus and Baghdad. Sufism attracted those desirous of a mystical union with God. Sufis disliked the legalism associated with the jurists and tended to be apolitical, stressing asceticism and various meditation techniques as a way of arriving at truth. Some Sufi became hermits; others entered into monastic orders or brotherhoods and became politically powerful. In the nineteenth century Sufi orders helped lead resistance to European imperialism.

The ideal of the unity of Islam, insisted upon by Muhammad and still proclaimed by all his followers as a necessity for peace, is as illusive in practice as agreement among Christians.[15] While continuing to strive for a political/religious unity, eventually both religions had to adjust to the problems posed by spiritual and political divergence. Islam became a civilization with many local cultures and Arabs as a minority.

---

[15] There is a saying attributed to the Prophet that "differences of opinion among the community are a blessing." Among the Sunni this saying has allowed for tolerance of diversity with apostasy being only for renouncing the unity of God or the prophetic role of Muhammad.

III. *Siyars*: The Theory of War and Peace

The holy warriors responsible for the rapid political expansion of the realm of Islam saw themselves as fulfilling Muhammad's demand for a *jihad* against polytheists and religions of "the book," but their activities preceded the creation of a systematic theory of war and peace. In 750 the Umayyad dynasty was overthrown by the Abbassids. Some Muslims who had opposed the compromises the Umayyads had allegedly made sought to purify the actions of the caliphate. The new dynasty, whose hereditary claim to the caliphate was weak, therefore encouraged a reexamination of Muslim statecraft that might reflect negatively on its predecessor.[16] One result was the first creation in history of a detailed coherent doctrine of what actions were permissible in war.

The scholar and jurist al-Shaybani (750-804 or 805) was an important formulator of the Sunni Muslim theory of *siyar*, best defined as the rules binding on the state in its relation to other communities, and that includes the code of conduct for warriors. Shaybani, whose work built upon the commentaries of earlier scholars, treated *siyar* as an independent subject of study. Shaybani's work was long used as a textbook because of the clarity of his organization and writing; his *siyar* in addition to citations of passages of the *Qur'an* and *hadith*, also offered similar and contrasting interpretations from earlier teachers. He saw his method as deriving from two sources: traditions and analogy. The traditions were teachings and practices of Muhammad and the first caliphs; analogy was used to apply principles derived from the traditions to new situations. Analogy required an exercise of reason as an important tool in the discovery of truth. Since there were different responses to similar situations within the *Qur'an* and the practice of Islam, Shaybani distinguished between the universal principles and incidental usage applicable only in the original instances.

---

[16]The Abbassids' hereditary claim came through the Prophet's uncle. The army changed from a Bedouin force where every male served under the Prophet to a professional army for the Umayyads and Abbasids. Hugh Kennedy, *The Armies of the Caliphs: Military and Society in the Early Islamic State* (2001), 96.

Shaybani's most illustrious successor was the philosopher, physician, and judge Ibn Rushd, known to the west as Averroes (1126-1198). Ibn Rushd, an adherent of a different school of interpretation than Shaybani, served the Almohad princes of Spain. His methods of interpretation, juxtaposing the conclusions of various commentators, distinguishing between particular instances and general rules in the life and teaching of the Prophet, and blending in original insights, resembled Shaybani's treatises. Since Ibn Rushd distinguished those areas of war and peace where there was no debate from those issues where scholars differed, his work enables us to watch the ongoing Islamic encounter with the morality of war and peace.

Shaybani's *siyar* reflected the rapid increase in the realm of Islam; in fact, he assumed that the recent successes would continue indefinitely until the religion would conquer the entire world. So he wrote within the context of the Abbasid Empire. Consequently, a territorial state played no role in Shaybani's theory of war, because he assumed rather than justified the crucial distinction between the realm of religion (the *dar al-Islam*) and the abode of strife of war (the *dar al-harb*). The abode of war is where Muslims have neither political nor religious authority, and true peace can come only if they have both. So Islam was in perpetual struggle against all non-Muslim peoples and nations. This struggle or *jihad* could entail missionary activities or involve a war proclaimed by the caliph.

For Shaybani the only justified cause of war was religion: to preserve Islam and to conquer non-Islamic states, i.e., defensive and offensive *jihad*. It followed that there could be only one legitimate ruler of the world and he was the Abbasid caliph. Even though Ibn Rushd wrote long after political authority in Islam had been divided, he shared with Shaybani all the assumptions about the *dar al-Islam* and the *dar al-harb*.[17]

---

[17]Muhammad ibn al-Hasan al-Shaybani, *The Islamic Law of Nations*, ed. and tr. Majid Khadduri (1966), 17; *Jihad in Mediaevel and Modern Islam: The Chapter on Jihad from Averroes 'Legal Handbook ' Bidayat Al-Mudjtahid*, tr. Rudoph Peters (1977), 10-11, 19-20.

The spread of Islam need not require military force. The Prophet commanded, "Combat those who disbelieve in God." But actual fighting could occur only after the polytheists had been offered the chance to convert. "If they do so, accept it and let them alone. You should then invite them to move" to the territory of Islam. Jurists debated if one offer were sufficient or if another were required if there had been a lapse in fighting or a truce. Obviously the duty of *jihad* weighed more heavily on those living on the frontiers of Islam, and for them to begin a *ribat* was particularly meritorious.[18]

If the caliph negotiated a truce, it was because the temporary end of warfare was for the advantage of Islam. The example often cited was the necessity for a truce against external enemies because of an internal civil war. Once a truce had been negotiated, the caliph was bound to preserve its terms. If the enemy broke the truce, the caliph no longer had to abide by its terms, but he must inform the enemy before resuming war. Muhammad had once offered a truce, and later jurists debated the amount of time it lasted as a precedent. Commentators disagreed on the length of an allowable truce, with the maximum extending from one to ten years. The truce could involve either paying or being paid tribute. The truce could be proclaimed only by the *Iman (caliph)*. Converts could become part of the realm of Islam, and thereby join the *jihad* and gain booty.

Commentators distinguished between an offensive and defensive war. A defensive war, protecting the *dar al-Islam* from attack, was a duty incumbent upon all Muslims.[19] However, only the caliph could proclaim an offensive *jihad* and only selected individuals were eligible to fight. The caliph began the *jihad* with an offer to the enemy to convert, which would entail coming under his political authority. Once the offer to convert had been rejected, no additional declaration of war was required and the army could "attack by night or by day and it was permissible to burn [the enemy] with fire or to inundate them with

---

[18] "Djhad," *Encylopedia of Islam* (1965), II, 538-39.

water."[20] Ibn Rushd contrasted the Prophet's deeds, which allowed a surprise attack, with his words, which did not. Commentators differed on whether the words or deeds should be the general rule. Shaybani's *siyar*, in contrast to similar writings later on, did not consider the onset of war to be an important issue. He concentrated instead upon conduct in war.

Only adult able-bodied males could fight in a *jihad* war. All soldiers should be free, out of debt, and have parental permission. The war was to be fought against other adult males, and the enemy's choices were either to submit or die. An enemy prisoner of war who converted would be enslaved and not killed. The rules of war distinguished between Muslims and non-Muslims. Even a Muslim who fought for the enemy should not be enslaved or killed after the war.

Basing his conclusions upon the precepts of Muhammad, Shaybani insisted that war was not waged against children, women, the old, and insane. Also, he cited a saying of the Prophet sparing Christian monks. Ibn Rushd concurred that there was "no disagreement about the rule that it is forbidden to slay women and children."[21] Shaybani did not provide an underlying principle for this prohibition, but the probable rationale was whether or not a person carried arms, because women who fought in the battle lost their immunity. Ibn Rushd expanded the immunity list to peasants, hermits, the old, the chronically ill, and the insane, but he noted that not all commentators agreed with his conclusions. A modern scholar, seeking a rationale for children's immunity, suggests that until the age of puberty, the young were incapable of making an informed decision whether to become Muslims.[22]

---

[19] Some commentators said *jihad* applied only to offensive war that is to spread Islam. A defensive war to protect property or life is instinctive in man (and animals), so it is not a religious duty.

[20] al-Shaybani, 95.

[21] Averroes, 15-16. "Do not slay the old and decrepit, children or women." Abu Bakr, the first Caliph said, "Do not slay women, nor infants, nor those worn with age." There was a controversy as to whether peasants should also be immune.

[22] Kelsay, 62-64, notes that children could be enslaved and that the immunity was strongest if they were captives. In a city under siege, the children belong to parents who are resisting and, as an unintended consequence, might be killed.

The issue of non-combatant immunity was complicated by the verse in the *Qur'an* where the Prophet told his followers to slay all the polytheists; did he intend to include women and children? According to Ibn Rushd, the difficulty in arriving at a normative principle was that the practice of the Prophet and the early caliphs who normally spared noncombatants was inconsistent with this verse.

Which then took precedence: unbelief as a cause for death or inability to fight? For Shaybani, the immunity did not apply to any male; for Ibn Rushd, it still applied to noncombatant males, and he complained that "the source of this controversy [was found] in the fact that in a number of traditions, rules are given at variance" with both the *Qur'an* and the practice of the Prophet.[23] For our purposes, the debate among many Muslim commentators shows that for Muhammad and his successors religion limited the cause and the practice of war.

The presence of women and children or even of Muslim prisoners of war in a city did not change the strategy in dealing with the town. If the inhabitants of the city used Muslim women and children as a shield, the warriors should not desist attacking, but attempt not to aim directly at the children. The underlying principle was that, if it was necessary to besiege a city, the Muslim army could not be hampered by lesser evils concomitant to that attack.

There was little discussion in either source on the actions permissible in war. The commentators knew that early practices varied, and it was difficult for them to determine whether it was permissible to destroy fruit trees and buildings outside a besieged city. Should peasants be left some goods, or was all to be subject to the captors? Both commentators found a clear directive from the Prophet that animals were not to be slain nor maimed. The only issue discussed on permissible weapons was whether mangonels (catapults for throwing stones) could be used in a siege even if women and children were in the city, and the practice of the Prophet established that it was legitimate.

---

[23] Averroes, 15. He also noted that some commentators believed that captives should not be slain.

In the event of victory, females and children were to be enslaved and the males killed, enslaved, or ransomed, depending upon the interest of their Muslim captors. Polytheists, Christians, and Jews who by force resisted the political control of Islam could be enslaved. A male polytheist who opposed Islam could be killed; not so a female. No Muslim in the *dar al-Islam*, however, could be enslaved. A male captive who became a Muslim should not be killed but was still subject to slavery; he would have the same status as a Muslim who, because he was living in the *dar al-harb*, could become a spoil of war. The theory was that any Muslim living in the *dar al-harb* had the responsibility to move to the *dar al-Islam*. Unlike Shaybani, Ibn Rushd noted major disagreements upon the treatment of captives. The issue was whether they should be slain, and early practices were at variance with *Qur'anic* verses.

Although Muslim holy war was for the faith and not for riches, Shaybani's devoting more space to a technical discussion of the rules concerning divisions of the spoils in war than to any other issue shows the importance of booty in the warrior code. Following the Prophet's practice, the *Imam* received one-fifth of the spoils and the warriors four-fifths. Spoils were to be divided only upon return to the *dar al-Islam*, not in the field of battle. The *Imam* divided the land among the warriors, who also received a share of cattle, horses, and other animals, but any surplus goods or animals were to be destroyed: "They should not leave anything that the inhabitants of the territory of war could make use of."[24] The division of booty was complex, with certain shares going to cavalry and lesser amounts to foot soldiers. There were rules for those who died before the battle; who were absent the day the battle was fought; or who, besides being soldiers, were also slaves, merchants, minors, women, or prisoners. The Umayyads favored Arab Muslims in the distribution of spoils; this policy that caused resentment and favored the growth of the Shi'a changed under the Abbasids who did not discriminate against non-Arab converts.

---

[24] Shaybani, 99.

The range of issues discussed in Shaybani's *siyar* shows the complexity of relations between Muslims and outsiders. He provided a code of permissible acts for a merchant while in the *dar al-harb* either trading or seeking to recover women or property seized by the infidels. There were different rules for a Muslim man living in the *dar al-harb* depending on whether only he or his wife and children also were believers. For example, an adult male could not be enslaved, but his unbelieving adult children or wife could be; some but not all of his property could be taken. A Muslim who had been enslaved by a non-believer in the *dar al-harb* could kill his master and suffer no consequence, because a Muslim cannot be a slave. If a non-Muslim entered the realm of Islam on a safe-conduct, he had obligations and protections; there were additional stipulations on what he could carry with him on his return to the *dar al-harb* (nothing that could be used as a weapon). Non-Muslim emissaries to the court could also enter the *dar al-Islam* under a safe-conduct. Any Muslim who was not a slave could in theory grant a safe-conduct; it was debated whether women had the same right, with Ibn Rushd noting that the issue hinged on "whether women are to be put on a par with men."[25]

Special regulations dealing with Christians and Jews in the *dar al-Islam* stated who would be subject to taxation (not women, children, and the blind), their property rights within their community, and their rights in case there was a dispute with Muslims. There were even provisions on visits of relatives outside the *dar al-Islam* to their co-religionists. Other regulations dealt with peace treaties with unbelievers. If, for example, an improper person made a truce with a Christian ruler, the *Imam* was obligated to inform the ruler that the truce was invalid before he authorized a *jihad*. If the *Imam* who granted a safe-conduct died, that safe-conduct became invalid.

Because Islam united governmental and religious authority, protest movements accused caliphs and kings of apostasy and advocated a return to pure

---

[25] Averroes, 14.

Islam. The authorities used alleged betrayal of the true faith as an excuse to suppress schismatics. Shaybani devoted a long section to the legal status of those who committed apostasy. Because being an apostate meant war against true Islam, any Muslim who committed apostasy lost all legal rights, forfeited marriage and property rights. It was no crime to kill him. Even if the apostate converted to Christianity, he still could be executed. Such severe penalties applied only to apostate men; an apostate wife should be divorced and imprisoned, but not killed. Unlike the male, she was also allowed to retain property. The distinction between men and women came from the Prophet's prohibition of killing unbelieving women in war. A male slave who became apostate should be killed if he refused to recant. A slave woman should be imprisoned if she refused to recant, but not executed.

Sunni commentators took a jaundiced view of rebellion, seeing it as an act against Allah, but were also unwilling to rule it out unconditionally in case the caliph neglected the *shari'a*. Then the faithful could engage in an act of resistance if their legitimate demands were ignored and they then could mobilize a group. Being a rebel was a legal category. Rebellion (unlike apostasy) required acts of resistance by an organized group with considerable support within the Muslim community, and its actions must be supported by a serious (but not necessarily correct) interpretation of the traditions.[26] If all the five tenets of Islam were observed, then differences in unessential matters of the faith per se were not cause for war. In addition, the caliph should not initiate hostilities, but wait until the act of resistance occurred. In a war of rebellion both sides should seek a negotiated settlement and follow the example of the Caliph Ali who met with his opponents in order to seek a peaceful resolution. (The story of Ali, who was later assassinated, might not have been a very persuasive example.) If a battle should occur, opponents still retained certain rights by being Muslims and should be treated accordingly, i.e., not enslaved. However, there was no legitimacy for an

---

[26] Kelsay, 88-91.

individual to engage in political assassination, no matter what the offenses of the caliph.

IV. The Practice of War and Peace

In Islam as in other religions, there was often a gap between daily practice and the normative teachings on war with unbelievers and peace within the *dar al-Islam*. Certainly it would be a mistake to assume constant holy war or even hostility between Islam and its neighbors or harmony among Muslims within the realm. Within the *Qur'an* there was ambiguity as to whether the *jihad* or struggle was primarily an internal battle for purity and obedience to Allah or the attempt to spread the faith of Islam through preaching and practice. The expansion of Islam had often occurred through the exhortations of those who preceded or accompanied armies. The other pillars of Islam (prayer, alms giving, recitation of the *Qur'an*, pilgrimage to Mecca) were purely personal acts, but, as interpreted by the jurists, an offensive *jihad* as an act of war was the sole responsibility of the *Imam*. Individuals could take responsibility only in a defensive *jihad* to protect the faith, but even this was normally left to the state.

In addition, there were different kinds of war. The *Qur'an* more often used the word *qital* rather than *jihad* in referring to actual fighting. Islam distinguished between holy wars and various other kinds of wars between rulers. Intra-Muslim war was generally not a *jihad*. Even rebellions and battles against alternating versions of Islam would not be considered a *jihad*.[27] Originally, to become a member of the Muslim community meant to accept an obligation to fight, even though Muhammad utilized slaves and non-Muslims. Pay of soldiers was in booty; in time, substitutes could be hired and the Umayyads erected a professional army. Under the Abbasids, petty warlords gathered soldiers for expeditions, often with the caliph's authority. The personal involvement of the caliph in proclaiming and leading *jihads* did not develop until ca. 800 and was a

---

[27] The Shi'a could conduct a defensive *jihad* because unbelief made one a *kaffir*. There could be no offensive *jihad* until the return of the *Imam*.

response to conditions on the frontier with the Byzantine Empire. It is this definition of *jihad* that is codified into *siyars*.[28]

After the initial spread of Islam, the political/religious rulers sought for stability and preservation of the existing order. Small armed groups might seek to spread the faith with the implicit blessing of the caliphate, but Baghdad was far from the frontiers, and Islamic civilization neither desired nor needed much from the outside world. The caliphs paid more attention to important, and often more divisive, policies leading to costly wars over disagreements within the realm on the requirements of the faith and to what extent the differences threatened the integrity of the faith. In some ways, occupying roles analogous both to the pope and the emperor of the Byzantine Empire, the caliph, in theory, was the source of all political/religious authority, and local rulers or sultans sought for his sanction. However, individual regions were often autonomous. By the tenth century the Abbassid dynasty in Baghdad was Sunni, but the Fatimid rulers of Egypt and the Almoravids of North Africa were Shi'a. At the time of the Crusades, the Fatimid sultan of Egypt - determined by heredity - was Shiite, but effective authority often rested with the *vizier*, who was a Sunni and needed the approval of the caliph in Baghdad. Ibn Khaldun was a Muslim scholar whose experiences showed him that more than the *Qur'an* and the *siyars* were necessary to understand why unity could not be achieved, why dynasties rose and fell, and why the forces of Islam did not always prevail.

V. Muslim Realism: Ibn Khaldun

Ibn Khaldun (1332-1406) has been called the most original social scientist between Aristotle and Machiavelli, recognized as a pioneer sociologist who in a "science of culture" attempted to discover the laws governing the rise and fall of governments, and praised as a most profound Arab philosopher of history who brought realism to the understanding of politics.[29] He saw himself as a devout

---

[28] Bronner, 41, 68, 96-101; Partner, 45-46.
[29] Walter Fischell, *Ibn Khaldun in Egypt: His Public Functions and His Historical Research, 1392-1405* (ca.1967), 1-2. Muhsin Mahdi, *Ibn Kaldûn's Philosophy of History*, (1957), 5-6, 10.

Muslim, a diplomat, a judge, a teacher, and an historian seeking to decipher the relationship between the will of Allah and worldly success and failure. For our purpose of understanding the relationships between religion, war, and peace, Khaldun shows that within Islam there was a tradition of analyzing public affairs as social phenomenon explainable by natural processes.

Khaldun received his education in North African Muslim schools; one of his earliest works was a commentary on Averroes, and his history cited many earlier Arab and Persian historians, the *Bible*, and Aristotle. In addition, Khaldun drew upon his experiences as a courtier and diplomat first in the Maghreb, then in the kingdom of Granada in Spain, and finally in Cairo. By the end of the fourteenth century the Islamic kingdoms of Granada and North Africa were weaker, and there was dynastic instability. Ibn Khaldun sought to understand why kingdoms arose, flourished, and declined. As a devout Muslim, he believed that Allah determined events, could directly intervene in events through a prophet or miracles, yet Khaldun analyzed the dynastic history of the classical, biblical, and Arab worlds according to natural principles. By seeking to understand social forces, he broke with other Arab historians who focused on the significance of individuals.

Khaldun regarded the appearance of Muhammad and the spread of Islam through the conquests of the early caliphs as miracles not to be duplicated. So while recognizing the role of their religious fervor bringing to power later caliphs, he tended to treat contemporary interventions of God as an individual mystical rather than political factor.[30] For him natural causes explained the breakdown of the political unity of Islam under the Umayyad, Abbassid, and Turkish caliphs, the dynastic rivalries, the displacement of Arabs by Turkish rulers, the destructive success of the Mongol invasions, and the weakness and constant changes in the Maghreb kingdoms he sought to serve.

---

[30] Ibn Khaldun, *The Muqaddimah: An Introduction to History*, tr. Franz Rosenthal (1958), lxxii-lxxiii.

Ibn Khaldun argued that war was "natural among human beings. No nation and race is free from it." The origin of war was the desire of a group to take "revenge" upon another because of "jealousy and envy, or hostility." The war could be waged in behalf of God, or royal authority, or in an attempt to found a kingdom. Humans were not innately good; they would "eat each other if they could." There were four types of war: one among "neighboring tribes and competing families;" a second by "savage nations living in the desert" who raided others for property, but without a desire to create a state; a third was a *jihad* or holy war; and the fourth was "dynastic war against seceders and those who refuse obedience." "The first two are unjust and lawless, the other two are holy and just wars."[31] This perfunctory acknowledgment based upon the *Qur'an* was the only discussion of the ethics of war in the entire history.

Ibn Khaldun tended to sanctify the existing powers as the only legitimate authority. Yet his analysis of cycles of how kingdoms rose, endured, and fell was purely naturalistic, seeing legitimacy as arbitrary and more a product of habit of obedience than of right and wrong.

Like other Arab historians, Ibn Khaldun sought to base his history upon deduction from principles as well as observations. His account of rise of one dynasty would show how all dynasties were created. Humans were social beings, and -- based on kinship -- they established unity to form a community and to protect each other. Eventually, due to the qualities of a leader, one clan within the group or community would dominate. The group's solidarity was the key to its rise to power. Initially the group would have crusading zeal brought about by religious purity and simplicity of living. Its unity, a willingness to strive hard and to sacrifice, could be contrasted with the lax moral standards, desire for luxury, and reliance on bureaucracy of any long established kingdom. So the army of the challenger - motivated by religious zeal, group solidarity, and a desire to reform corrupt practices - would prevail. At first the new dynasty's power rested on the

---

[31] Ibid., II, 74.

army. As the dynasty sought to rule an expanded empire, the original clan or group members became city dwellers and were attracted to the civilized customs and material riches around them. Khaldun argued that the advances of civilization took place in cities; concentration of population allowed for improvements in artisan crafts and scholarship. In a short time, the new dynasty absorbed the ways of living of the previous rulers. Inevitably, its moral purity, religious fervor, and group solidarity declined as the rulers became accustomed to luxuries, ruled through a bureaucracy, and neglected the hard simple life that created good soldiers. The army no longer seemed crucial; the desire for easy living overcame self-sacrifice for the good of the group. Within three generations the cycle of dynastic decline would bring a new set of challengers.

Ibn Khaldun did not envisage the history of a state as existing separately from a dynasty; that is, there was not a territorial entity. At the beginning and the end of the dynasty, the army had an exalted role, because initially the army had to create the state and at the end, to preserve the state. While the charismatic leader was crucial in the formation of the dynasty, the character of later leaders was less crucial. For neither their piety and intelligence nor lack of these qualities had lasting effect upon the processes at work. Having an intelligent and dynamic leader in the later life of a dynasty would only increase the amount of tyranny because an able leader would see what was wrong, attempt to change it, and end by coercing his people to no good result.

Ibn Khaldun's discussion of the tactics used by the military, the functions of soldiers in a state, and the necessity of fortifications ignored ethical considerations. It was not that he approved of violations of Muhammad's standards for fighting; rather, he was appalled by the atrocities of Tamerlane and the Mongol invaders. Yet the victories and defeats of the Arabs, Turks, and Mongols could be explained by natural causes. Ibn Khaldun was not widely known in the West until the mid-nineteenth century, but intellectuals in the

Turkish Ottoman Empire that endured until after World War I continued to rely upon his naturalistic interpretation of the rise and fall of dynasties.[32]

VI. The Crusades

The Islamic response to the attack from the Crusaders beginning in 1085 shows the interaction of religious commitment, political calculation, and internal division. During the First Crusade beginning in 1095, Muslim authorities had so little knowledge of Western Europe that they could not differentiate between the Franks, English, and Germans and saw all as a part of the Byzantine Empire. So they also saw nothing distinctive about the Crusade, viewing it not as a Christian holy war but as a part of the ongoing struggle with the "Romans" (their term for Byzantium) over control of the lands bordering on the eastern Mediterranean. The Muslim political authorities in the various city-states of Damascus, Antioch, and Jerusalem were so distrustful of each other that there was no cooperation against the Christians. There was also no aid furnished Muslims in the Holy Land from the Fatimid dynasty in Egypt or the Abbassid sultan, neither of whom saw their vital interests threatened. The result of this disunity was that a relatively small number of western knights succeeded in conquering several cities on the route from Constantinople to Jerusalem and eventually created a Latin Kingdom in the Holy Land.

The Muslim rulers were horrified by the brutality of the Christians, particularly in the massacre of inhabitants of Jerusalem following its conquest. But once the Latin Kingdom was created, neighboring states arrived at working relationships with the Christians, which could involve truces, paying tribute, or even alliances against other Muslim areas. Their governing principle was not the purity of Islam or *jihad*, but the preservation of the ruling dynasty and virtual independence of each small area.

The existence of the Latin Kingdom on land that once had belonged to the *dar al-Islam* and the subordination of and even persecution of Muslims clearly

---

[32] Ibid., lxvii.

went against basic teachings of the *Qur'an*, but the religious response developed slowly. Only after the Latin Kingdom sought to enlarge itself, even attempting an invasion of Egypt and sinking a ship of pilgrims to Mecca, did the Muslim rulers become convinced that there could be no modus vivendi with the Christians.

Eventually two charismatic Muslim leaders, Nur al Din (1146-74) and Saladin (in power 1163-93) - known for their piety as well as their political astuteness - proclaimed a defensive *jihad*. They claimed that Islam had been debased by the actions of the tritheists who put crosses and church bells on mosques, ate pork and profaned sanctuaries by driving pigs into them (Muslims did not eat pork), and limited access to holy places. Jerusalem, previously not very significant to Muslims, now became a third holy city, a place of pilgrimage, ranking behind only Mecca and Medina. Allah had punished Islam for its disunity and lack of piety. For both Nur al Din and Saladin, proclaiming a *jihad* was a method for purifying the faithful as well as driving the infidel away.

While the proclamation of a *jihad* met with a sympathetic response from the faithful, it brought no outpouring of support of troops or money from either the caliph or other Islamic states. In part this was because the *jihad* could be used to camouflage dynastic ambitions, and both Nur al Din and Saladin spent more time and money fighting to conquer other Muslim cities and rulers than in attacking Christians. But their actions may not have exemplified a lack of piety so much as an awareness that they had to have a united area of support before fighting the Latin Kingdom. And as Saladin came to threaten Christians, so also he threatened the independence of various Muslim cities whose rulers engaged in alliances and sometimes fought alongside the Christians. The intricate maneuverings of many Christian and Muslim leaders resembled an attempt to create a balance of power rather than a Crusade or *jihad*. Saladin, a Kurd whose lack of noble birth distressed the European kings who eventually had to deal with him, used his position as a commander of an army of Nur al Din to become *vizier* of Egypt; after Nur al Din's death, Saladin undermined the son of Nur al Din and, after many battles, succeeded in unifying Egypt and Syria under a new dynasty controlled by members of his clan. Eventually, with his flanks secured against other Muslim states, Saladin moved decisively against the Latin Kingdom and re-conquered Jerusalem in 1187. His successful *jihad* against the Christians did not endear him to the caliph in Baghdad who feared that Saladin's strength might jeopardize his own position.

When Christian Europe counterattacked with the Third Crusade led by the Germanic Holy Roman Emperor and the Kings of France and England, other Islamic lands did not rally to provide Saladin with troops or money. After several bitter battles and the long siege of Acre, both sides realized that they were stalemated. No matter what the ideology of crusade and holy war, Richard the Lion Hearted and Saladin signed a truce leaving Christians in possession of certain cities along the coast, guaranteeing the rights of pilgrimage to Jerusalem, and allowing Christian control of certain sacred sites, including the Church of the Holy Sepulchre, built on the alleged site of Jesus' tomb.

The Third Crusade (1187-1192) exemplified the interaction between chivalry and religion. Both Saladin and Richard the Lion Hearted became identified as noble warriors. They evinced the juxtaposition of cruelty and compassion that characterized these wars. For example, after the siege of Acre, the Christians captured some three thousand Muslims whom they held for ransom. At the surrender of Acre, the terms for their release were for Saladin to pay some 200,000 dinar. But the negotiations stalled over technicalities, and King Richard had the three thousand civilians executed. After initial outrage, Saladin continued to negotiate with Richard. His modern biographer speculates that the three thousand were commoners, and perhaps the 200,000 dinar were more important to him than three thousand lives.[33] Yet, during the siege of Acre, Saladin, when he learned that a Christian mother had crossed the lines to plead for his help because her baby had been kidnapped, had the baby restored to her, and

---

[33] M.C. Lyons and D. E. P. Jackson, *Saladin: The Politics of the Holy War* (1982), 332-333; Gertrude Slaughter, *Saladin* (1955) 153-4, 218, 229; Andrew Ehrenkreutz, *Saladin* (1972), 201-203.

sent the mother and child back to the Christian camp with a generous reward. The Crusades on both sides were filled with such anomalous actions. The Muslims admired the faith of the Christians that would make them undertake such arduous military adventures; Christians in the Latin Kingdom's cities surrendered to Saladin because they knew that he would enforce treaty obligations and treat them honorably. Yet there were numerous examples of massacres by both sides, and leaders of crusade and *jihad* alike combined religious zeal with a willingness to let their soldiers seek booty.

Jihad functioned during the Crusades, as it has often done in the history of Islam, as a vehicle for religious renewal and purity, a means to unite the faithful, and a weapon to use against the religious and political power of allegedly corrupt Muslims or infidels. The rulers utilized the *jihad* as an instrument of domestic control or way of confronting outside opponents, and both contemporaries and historians have difficulty in untangling its ambiguous relationship to dynastic ambition and the self-interest of religious/political reformers. Saladin's invoking of the *jihad* reinvigorated Islamic holy war, but its use by the Berber Almoravids in Spain, the Mamluks in Egypt, and the Seljuk Turks tended to be selective and directed at other Muslim states, rebels, or Christians. Religious-political revivals characterized by holy war were followed by long periods of truces, accommodations, and alliances between Christians and Muslims. Still, the ideal of *jihad* persisted.[34] The Ottoman Turks saw their expansion of the realm of Islam that brought their armies to the gates of Vienna in the sixteenth century as a *jihad.*

Crusades as military expeditions authorized by the pope to retake Jerusalem came to an ignominious end in 1291 with the loss of the last European controlled city. During the next centuries, the Crusades appeared of little lasting significance to life in the Muslim world, though they would emerge after the creation of Israel in 1948 as a symbol of the hostility of the West to Islam. The main lasting effect of the Crusades was in European attitudes. Crusades as a

---

[34] Partner, 97, 99, 121-24.

Christian mentality that saw Islam as an inferior religion to be countered by force continued in Spain until 1492 and in the Austrian and Russian wars against the Ottoman Turks.

The Islamic *jihad*, like the Christian crusade and Just War, has undergone changes since the Middle Ages. The most basic would be a recognition of the plurality of Islamic kingdoms and legitimacy of non-Islamic states. In 1536 the Ottoman Sultan Süleymann entered into a treaty with King Francis I of France that allowed a continuing status that was not war.[35] Since the Ottomans had conquered Constantinople, the Balkans, and were threatening Austria, the Sultan's recognition of the legitimacy and permanence of France was not out of weakness. It was the same kind of implicit recognition of the sovereignty of national states made in western political theory during the Renaissance. Even so, European leaders did not recognize any Arab state as civilized and entitled to full diplomatic equality until the mid-nineteenth-century.

From the seventh century until the present the Islamic, Jewish, and Christian peoples of the Mediterranean world have had close economic and cultural contacts, sometimes peaceful but often hostile. Whether acknowledged or not, all three religions shared a heritage of classical culture and their similarities are striking. All three religions acknowledge that they pray to the same God; all are exclusive in that they recognize their distinctive revelation as final and oppose paganism or polytheism. All believe that God requires worship, prayer, charity and moral conduct. Also, all agree that God intervenes in history, protects his people, and authorizes war. All insist on the congruence of their precepts with reason and natural law, with Muslims insisting that Islamic law was an embodiment of natural law. So in Islam, as in post-Constantinian Christianity, obedience to God brought the only true peace, and divine law regulated the causes and conduct of war.

---

[35] Charles Frazier, *Catholics and Sultans: The Church and the Ottoman Empire 1453-1923* (1983), 24-28. The treaty was kept secret because the Pope still wished a crusade and Francis I did not wish to be excommunicated.

VIII.
Medieval Europe

Within a hundred years after his death in 430, the Roman world of Augustine had become only a memory of a longed-for ideal of peace with its connotations of order, law, and stability. The Church offered glimpses of a heavenly peace through the sacraments or through escape into a monastery, but had inadequate resources to reform society or build an earthly peace. For theologians the primary function of a civil peace, if such an entity were attainable in this imperfect world poised between the death of Jesus and an imminent return of Christ, was to protect churches and monasteries where God's peace could be attained.

To survive without the Roman Empire, the Church needed to convert the barbarians and to control their ways of making war. This chapter describes the emergence of medieval Christian Europe. By the eleventh century, the Church had enough power to launch a major reform program consisting of the Peace and Truce of God, Just War theory and - aided by knights - chivalry and Crusades. The success of the Church in structuring the new civilization brought opponents who insisted that the price of power was a compromise of the Jesus' peace mission. The Middle Ages provides a test case of the power of religion to influence war, the theme of this book.

I. The New Rulers of Europe

The Western Empire succumbed to succeeding waves of invading peoples from eastern Europe and Asia - during the fourth century the Visigoths, Germans, Franks, Vandals, and Lombards - and after these had settled down - beginning in the ninth century, the Magyars, Normans, and Slavs. The Romans had looked upon the Germanic tribes as barbarians. Still, they had frequently allowed the

Germans to settle within their borders and had employed them as mercenaries and utilized their military skills to defend the Empire.

Rome declined not just because of internal decay, but also because of new military tactics. "Horse Warriors" whose skills in riding allowed for a rapid offensive and then retreat had gained skills on the steppes of Eurasia and then had been pushed west. They were lightly armed with a composite bow made of several kinds of wood whose arrows were accurate at 300 yards and could penetrate armor at 100 yards. Not just Rome's legions but China's infantry proved no match for the Horse Warriors.[1] From 300 until 1400 cavalry would be the dominant form of warfare used by Christian, Muslim, and Mongol warriors. The Byzantine Empire diverted the first wave of Germanic tribes by bribery, but later emulated their tactics and even enlisted them for the cavalry. The Byzantines continued and bequeathed to Europe a tradition of a war without mercy, which Christians used against barbarians, rebels, and later against Muslims.

The Germanic invaders admired and adopted certain Roman customs. For example, the Lombard and Visigothic kings imitated the Roman court rituals and the practice of victory parades after battles, and they ascribed their successes to the intervention of God or the gods. Nevertheless, the urbanized, literate, and centralized society of Rome disappeared as the Empire was carved up into small decentralized warring areas or kingdoms whose leaders sometimes espoused what most Catholic bishops saw as heretical Arian doctrines.[2]

The Roman Catholic Church, the only large-scale institution surviving in the West, increasingly stood separate from Byzantine civilization and Orthodox Christianity and claimed a spiritual primacy based upon an apostolic succession beginning with St. Peter. In the Eastern Empire centered in Constantinople, the Orthodox Church remained subject to the emperors whose wars it blessed as holy.

---

[1]John Keegan, *A History of Warfare* (1993), 177-190. Philippe Contamine, *War in the Middle Ages* (1984), particularly 251-302, which can serve as a model of integration of intellectual and military history.

In the West the Roman Catholic Church emerged as an independent religious and political force. Pope Leo's negotiations with Attila the Hun in 452, which avoided a sack of Rome, symbolized the increased status of the papacy in religious and political affairs. The monastery system became the depository of the classical learning preserved in Western Europe. The Church began the task of converting and civilizing the Germanic hordes.

The Germanic tribes who had broken up the Empire and whose new lands had been acquired and maintained only by force were not likely to be converted to an anti-war Christianity. And the Church, which felt itself threatened first by the barbarians, then by the pervasive disorder, and after 700 by the Muslims, was not likely to repudiate either offensive or defensive war in its behalf. So just as third-century Christianity had merged elements of the Jewish, early Christian, Greek, and Roman beliefs and practices, so now did medieval Christianity synthesize Germanic and Roman Christian elements to produce a new civilization with a revised justification for war.

The Germanic tribes who converted to Christianity had glorified fighting and the heroism of the warrior. War, not peace, was the highest value and esteemed as the normal condition of life. The Germans had triumphed in the name of the god Wotan. In their sagas, men who died on the field of battle won an eternal but rather strenuous life in heaven. Every evening as the sun set, the warriors earned the right to drink mead (an alcoholic beverage), cavort with servant girls termed Valkyries, and join in a perpetual battle and slaughter. Being killed or wounded in this nightly battle resulted in no lasting damage. The Germanic cult of the warrior fit in easily with classical ideals of the hero and honor. The en masse conversion of the Franks after 496, brought about partially because Christianity seemed to bring success in battle, changed the language but not the content of the glorification of war. Wotan's sanctuaries became Christian churches; Wotan

---

[2]Arianism saw Jesus as a divine figure, but not co-equal or of the same substance as God the Father.

became Michael the Archangel whose earlier role in apocalyptic war now sanctified earthly battles. Before battle, warriors attended mass, and they carried into the fight victory-giving talismans and relics of Christianity - bones of saints, nails allegedly from Jesus' cross, pictures of the Virgin or the angel Michael.[3]

The papacy supported and utilized the fighting skills of the most powerful Frankish king, Charlemagne, against the kingdoms of heretical Arian-German Christians and the Muslims. In 800 the Pope crowned Charlemagne Holy Roman Emperor, a title aimed at making Charlemagne the western equivalent of the Byzantine emperor with a duty of supporting the church. Charlemagne utilized the Roman technique of no mercy in his wars with pagan Germans and equated his victories with Christian peace.[4]

After Charlemagne's death, his realm, including most of modern-day France, the Low Countries, Germany and northern Italy, lost even its small degree of political unity when divided among his sons who proved unable to keep order. Central government again disintegrated, and the authorities could provide no effective defense against the attacks of the Norsemen and the Hungarians who, after terrorizing much of Europe, eventually followed the practices of the earlier Germanic tribes, occupied land, and settled down. Even so, Western Europe remained a violent society characterized by incessant personal feuds, tribal vendettas, and plunder. Force even determined "justice" as disputes between two individuals were settled not by law but by personal combat, with God allegedly giving victory to the person in the right. In 1215 the Church denounced ordeal by combat as based upon superstition, but the custom did not immediately end.

II. Feudal War

By the tenth century, Europe became organized for defense through areas owned ostensibly by a feudal lord - whether Holy Roman Emperor, king, duke,

---

[3]James Aho, *Religious Mythology and the Art of War: Comparative Religious Symbols of Military Violence* (1981), 80-81.
[4]John France, *Western Warfare in the Age of Crusades, 1000-1300* (1999), 11.

count, or bishop - who provided land to a local magnate in return for his service during war. The local authority allowed the common people or serfs to produce food for themselves with a share going to the local lord. In return the lord owed them security. The serfs grew the food but were not armed, and all fighting was, in theory at least, reserved to the noble class, though the accompanying retainers were often commoners or slaves. A monastery whose lands made it a vassal to a king might furnish knights who were its vassals. Kings could also levy special taxes or tribute on the Church to support feudal wars. At first the arrangement between lord and vassal was simply land for service, but by the fourteenth century the knight might also receive some payments for his mandatory service.

Medieval European governments had insufficient taxing authority to provide for a disciplined infantry and supplies for a long campaign; the armed cavalry became the basic fighting force, and the fortified location the best defense. By 1000 the mounted elite fighting force had evolved into the knight in armor, and the fortified stronghold became the castle. Since it was costly to equip a knight with full armor and the noble warriors were among the most valuable members of this hierarchical society, pitched battles among large numbers of knights tended to be rare, though when they did occur, as at Agincourt (1415), the casualties could reach forty percent. The basic strategy was for a charge by knights, then a countercharge, followed by a melee. By the thirteen century, England's Edward III had dismounted knights carrying lances flanked by angled rows of archers with longbows, a tactic successfully used at Crécy and Agincourt.[5] Edward also managed to pay much of his army, which made them more controllable and less dependent on plunder.

The normal response to an invasion was to retreat to a fortified place or castle. A castle with moat, towers, and multiple walls and defended by men with

---

[5]Clifford Rogers, "'As if a New Sun Had Arisen: England's Fourteenth-century RMA," in *The Dynamics of Military Revolution 1300-2050*, eds. MacGregor Knox and Williamson Murray (2001), 26-34; David Hall, *Weapons and Warfare in Renaissance Europe* (1997), 12-15. France, 12-14.

crossbows could successfully withstand a long siege. Since invading armies had few supplies and had to live off the land, after a short time they generally moved on after devastating an area. Wars tended to drag on, maintained by small bands nominally in the service of the king but really out for private profit gained by foraging through the countryside. For example, the Hundred Years War (1337-1453) between England and France had comparatively few major battles but many inconclusive skirmishes by groups of knights and mercenaries. Devastation occurred by such marauding groups more interested in booty and living off the land than in any grand strategy.

European wars were not often battles to the death with enormous amounts of zeal for one side and hatred for the other. Rather, by the tenth century war tended to be a profit-making activity designed for a special class, the knights. The society that exalted the status of the knight did not intend to have its important nobles killed in the incessant struggles of the time. One reason to dress the knight in heavy armor was so that he was relatively invulnerable so long as he stayed on his horse.[6] Of course, the heavy armor also restricted his freedom of movement and made it unlikely that he could do much damage to anyone else similarly equipped. Medieval warfare was a means of earning a profit through pillaging and ransoms, and, like sports contests in our own day, resembled a ritual or game for the chosen few. There were no maps and often no overall strategy beyond the cavalry charge. The object was not to kill but to capture one's opponent so that he could be held for ransom.

The Church, a vulnerable institution seeking security on earth as well as peace in heaven, shared the concern of kings with ending the frequency and easing the cost of warfare both for the aristocracy and also for the serfs, who were most often the victims of the marauding bands. The Church during the so-called Dark

---

[6]The class of the warrior was shown even in weapons. Commoners used missiles (arrows) and aristocrats, blades. A sword was a more discriminating weapon, which could be used in a moderate fashion if the knight wanted to take a prisoner for ransom or show magnanimity. Hall, 15.

Ages had become the largest landowner in western Europe but felt vulnerable because it needed to rely upon local lords who might be more interested in plunder. The emergence of the prince-bishop, often a younger son of noble birth who had become a priest in order to reserve family lands for the eldest son, combined church and political authority in his person, which meant a divided allegiance. While the lower clergy were not to fight, the prince-bishop had an obligation to aid his lord by either furnishing knights or serving himself. Monasteries and bishops often controlled lands, requiring them to be vassals of a king and responsible for furnishing armed knights to the liege lord. During barbarian invasions, monks defended monasteries and accompanied troops. Later, in Spain and northern Germany orders of fighting monks defended fortresses or attacked Muslims and pagans. A bishop or archbishop, as the governing authority in a town, felt responsible for its defense. At times, either because of duty or inclination, the bishop and even the pope wore armor and led the troops in battle. In Italy the papacy became a state as well as a spiritual entity and authorized wars on behalf of its worldly possessions.

Because the Church provided the only unity Western Europe had, it had a strong interest in keeping the peace and security. Because disorder and war seemed ineradicable, the Church sought to control and direct rather than to end all fighting. The objective was to preserve and reform the general society with which it was so closely identified. So the Church's attempt to limit and to humanize war coincided with the interest of kings who wished to expand their control of the country by substituting the rule of law for private fighting, but also to receive assurances that killing in a justified war was acceptable to God and that if they should be killed in battle, they would not go to hell.

III. The Church's Peace Program

Ambrose and Augustine defended the legitimacy of war for laymen within the framework of the Empire, but only as a mournful necessity. There long remained a distrust of military killing, and those who shed blood often had to undergo a prolonged period of penance; for example ten years after the Norman conquest of England in 1076 a church council at Winchester issued the following requirements: a soldier who killed a person must do penance for a year; if he had wounded an assailant whose recovery was unknown, penance for forty days was required; those who did not know if they had killed should do penance one day a week the rest of their lives; all archers, who presumably could not be sure of the extent of their complicity in a person's death, should do penance for forty days.[7] There are other instances as late as the Renaissance of requiring purging of guilt by those who shed blood. The broader canonical practice was to require penance in cases of fighting with wrong intention.

After Augustine's time, the pacifist witness of the early Church remained reserved to priests, monks, and nuns - those who took special vows of Christian life but whose prayers for peace or for victory in war were thought to have more efficacy than outward force. The dilemma for those seeking to reform society to create a peaceful order was that a Church program aimed at building voluntary restraint secured by an oath would work only with those willing to be obedient. Others who continued to fight might need to be coerced into keeping the peace. So a peace effort might require war. Fighting for a Church-initiated peace had a high ethical value and could even pave the way for a holy war.

In the eleventh century, in an effort to quell disorder, particularly the devastation by bandits or renegade knights, the Church initiated a peace program as part of a general reform of parish and monastic life inspired by the monastery at Cluny and its famous abbot, Bernard of Clairvaux (1090-1153). The Cluniac reform aimed at tightening standards of clerical behavior in both the monastic and parish clergy, improving the conduct of the general society, and insuring that those in holy orders did not engage in war.

---

[7]Even though William the Conqueror invaded England in 1066 with papal support, his men were required to do penance after the battle of Hastings. Erdmann, *The Origins of the Idea of Crusade* (1997), 80-81; Bainton, *Christian Attitudes toward War and Peace* (1960), 109; Contamine, 266-67.

Under Popes Gregory VII (1073-1085) and Innocent III (1198-1216), the Church attempted to claim papal supremacy over the temporal as well as the spiritual realm through the "two swords" theory.[8] Medieval theorists insisted that the two swords referred first to a political sword belonging to the monarch who was responsible for worldly order and second to a spiritual sword belonging to the Church. Both magistrate and priest had supremacy in separate spheres. As the Church gained authority, her claims for supreme jurisdiction magnified. Pope Gregory VII insisted that the spiritual sword, because its jurisdiction was over matters of eternal importance, had the right to bestow the political sword, and that the Holy Roman Emperor and monarchs of Europe should be subordinate to the papacy. Naturally enough, the emperors did not agree, and the struggle between papacy and empire, termed the Investiture Controversy, occasioned a struggle that became an armed conflict. The popes claimed the right to judge whether the activities of the various kings, including their wars, met acceptable Christian standards. The papacy's assertion meant that neither kings nor emperor were absolutely sovereign, that above them was the Church, responsible for the welfare of all western Christendom.

Obviously if the papacy were to enforce correct notions of war not only on the monarchs but all medieval Europe, it would need clear standards of acceptable causes and practices in war. And since the Church claimed to encompass everyone in Western Europe, it would need a policy dealing with church personnel, kings, knights, serfs, merchants, women and children. The Church would also set policy to be used with outsiders: heretics, Jews, and Muslims. Although elements of the Church program had separate origins, in retrospect we can see the result as a comprehensive theory of war and peace created in the eleventh century and derived from but very different from the Augustinian formulation. The main elements in the Church's peace program were the Peace of God, the Truce of God, Just War theory, chivalry, the Crusades, and

---

[8] Luke 22:36-38.

the Inquisition. In the following discussions of each of these reforms, we must remember that they developed together, not in chronological sequence.

IV. The Peace and Truce of God

The tenth-century peace programs marked an attempt to expand the mission of the Church from being primarily concerned with heavenly to focus on earthly peace. Support came from three sources: the church hierarchy interested in protecting its property as well as the poor; kings seeking more control over their realms, and townspeople seeking security. The reform also tapped into popular piety of those who contrasted the ideal of Christendom with the sordid reality of constant fighting.

The Peace of God, lasting from 975 to 1025, attempted to isolate selected personnel from war selected: the clergy, merchants, peasants, and pilgrims.[9] Churches and church property should not be plundered; the possessions of merchants and serfs also were not subject to seizure. However, the ban on pillaging was not absolute; it applied only during a feud or against marauders, but not in a duly proclaimed Just War. So the Peace of God did not inhibit the powerful high nobility and monarchies that fought recognized wars, but only unauthorized troublemakers -- disturbers of the peace. Still, the Peace of God was the first recognition in the West of some distinction between those who were part of the fighting force and some noncombatants.

Those who agreed to abide by the Peace of God took an oath that made maintaining secular peace a religious duty. Townspeople formed themselves into peace militias to enforce the oath and often engaged in fighting for what they saw as a holy cause. In this sense, the Peace of God can be seen as a step away from

---

[9]Udo Heyn, *Peacemaking in Medieval Europe: A Historical & Bibliographical Guide* (1997), prints the Peace and Truce documents, provides an introduction to major themes, and includes a bibliography on the Church's and kings' attempts to create peace. Elizabeth Magnov-Nortier, "Enemies of the Peace, 500-1100," in *The Peace of God*, ed. Thomas Head and Richard Landes (1992), 68, concludes that the peace was not directed at private wars but to defend church lands against the laity.

the Augustinian formulation of war as a mournful duty and towards a crusading mentality in which people warred for God.

The same spirit of controlling but not abolishing warfare used in the Peace of God motivated the Truce of God, an attempt to limit when wars could be fought and to direct warlike energies away from Europe. The truce applied to all wars among Christians, but was not used in the Crusades against the Muslims, and there were many, including Thomas Aquinas, who questioned whether it should be applied in Just Wars. The Truce of God drew upon the widespread belief that special times of religious observances were holy and should be dedicated to God. Making war on these days was incompatible with God's peace. Certain seasons, the forty days of Advent and Lent, before Christmas and Easter, for example, holy days, and from Friday to Monday were set aside for the Lord. Fighting should cease on those occasions. A knight's oath might obligate him to observe both the Peace of God and the Truce of God.

Compliance with the Peace and Truce of God initiatives was spotty at best, depending on whether the bishop had the power or could rely upon other political authorities. In France and Germany in the eleventh century, peace militias composed of lay people and clergy attempted to enforce peace even though they had to fight to do so. The main immediate effect of this first facet of the peace movement was to prompt monarchs to suppress unauthorized violence and to reserve legitimate force for themselves. Because both the Peace and Truce of God would be incorporated into canon law, the Church had for the first time officially committed itself to working towards a limitation of conduct in war.

V. Justified War

Medieval theologians and canon lawyers sought to limit the incessant violence of the Middle Ages by providing clear guidelines as to when fighting was ethically permissible. The result, known as Just War theory, contained two distinct but related emphases: 1. justice in the cause of war, and 2. justice in the conduct of war. Rather than a theory, we might better describe the theologians' deliberations as creating justified-war traditions, because there was much variation in topics of interest and in conclusions on major as well as small matters. For example, unlike the canon lawyers who provided a detailed justification for the re-conquest of Jerusalem, Thomas Aquinas' treatment of war devoted little attention to the issues raised by the Crusades. The canon lawyers and decretalists, so termed because they commented on papal decrees, dealt with specific case studies. The decretalists advised a bishop on moral conduct when he faced the necessity of paying taxes to the king who was engaged in an unjust cause.[10] By contrast, Thomas Aquinas and other theologians were abstract, dealing with underlying principles. A consequence was that their theological insights could remain relevant even in a radically different political context. The Just War theories, moreover, evolved over time because of the changing nature of medieval society and practices of warfare. In its origins Just War theory assumed a society where warfare was the monopoly of a privileged class who were deeply concerned that their actions be pleasing to God.

The Just War theorists aimed not to create new truth, but to make clearer and spell out the implications of previously established truths, whether found in the *Bible*, St. Augustine, or pagan philosophers. They began with the truth of revelation contained in the Old and New Testaments, which they read ahistorically; Joshua, Moses, and David became like contemporary dukes and kings. Around 1140 the monk Gratian made a compilation of the writings of Augustine on many topics, including war and peace. So for the first time, theologians could see all his thoughts on war. Just War theories derived from Augustine's conclusion that there was no incompatibility between following Christ and waging war for the sake of peace. The third major source was the classics: Plato, certain Roman writers, and, after his reintroduction into Western Europe in the thirteenth century, Aristotle.

---

[10]Good beginning places for Just War theory in the Middle Ages written from the perspectives of an historian and a social ethicist are Frederick Russell, *The Just War in the Middle Ages* (1975) and James Johnson, *Ideology, Reason, and the Limitation of Wars: Religious and Secular Concepts 1200-1740* (1975).

The scholastic method of demonstrating truth was to state a proposition, then to list authorities and provide arguments supporting what will turn out to be the wrong answer, and finally, to provide other authorities and reasons to refute the first conclusion. The method was deductive, to arrive at new truths by drawing out the implications from older well established truths. Revelation buttressed by reason could provide answers to the dilemmas posed by war. The result would be a carefully argued series of true propositions.

The Just War advocates accepted the Augustinian perspective that war and fighting could be made compatible with Christian teachings. They reserved the pacifist insights of the early Church to a special class, the priests and monks, or a special place, the next world. They argued that for a prince and his knights to fight with clear conscience, the war had to be just in both cause and conduct. Thomas Aquinas' (1225-1774) *Summa Theologica*, which sought to provide a comprehensive statement of all Christian thought, has remained the single most important work by a Roman Catholic theologian and still occupies a privileged position in Roman Catholic thought. An exposition of Aquinas' thought on the ethics of war will show the strengths and weaknesses of medieval Just War theories.[11]

Aquinas first established that war was not always a sin, unlike schism, strife, and sedition. Following Augustine, Aquinas argued that the Sermon on the Mount meant self-defense involving no more than two persons. The New Testament anti-war texts had no applicability to a situation involving punishment rather than self-defense, or to a case involving government officials, or to a context involving moral responsibility for third persons. The Sermon on the Mount and other New Testament anti-war texts were about attitudes, not external actions,

[11]Relevant documents are printed in Holmes, 92-117; Leroy Walters, *Five Classic Just War Theories* (1971) contains an excellent analysis of Aquinas' contributions. A convenient compilation relating Thomas' political theory to his discussion of war is Paul Sigmund, ed., *St. Thomas Aquinas on Politics and Ethics* (1988).

and were counsels of perfection reserved for the few rather than moral precepts for all.

Thomas reaffirmed Augustine's attitude to peace and vision of the common good. For both, true peace was an orientation towards the truly good but not the absence of violence. Peace was a personal and community harmony, and Just Wars aimed at creating and preserving justice by destroying an evil or false peace. War for the sake of creating a true peace was a legitimate, even Christian, activity. War was not for Thomas an inherently evil activity, and he paid little regard to war as a mournful activity, a sign of original sin. For Aquinas a moral war must be just in its circumstances (who, what, when, where, by what means, why, in what manner) and end.

A basic issue in the Middle Ages was who had the right to wage war. Did it belong only to the Holy Roman Emperor, the papacy, kings, great nobles, or every baron? What about the newly emerging city-states like Venice? What was the relationship between the natural right of all to self-defense and restrictions on the right to wage war? Thomas limited legitimate war-making capacity to the prince, thereby pointing the way to strengthening the powers of the various monarchs who waged war within their realms ostensibly to preserve order and externally for self-defense. Although supporting kingship as the best form of government, Thomas did not wish to strengthen tyranny, arguing that this was the worst form of government.[12] Still, Thomas' theory did declare unjust most of the incessant violence that made life miserable during the Middle Ages.

Aquinas argued that the Church through the pope or his legate could counsel the princes on making war, but its legitimate authority to initiate a war was limited to a Crusade. But even a Crusade was required to have a just cause

---

[12]Thomas thought tyranny more likely to come from the rule of many, rather than one. In *On Kingship*, tyranny was to be endured as to avoid greater evils. In a *Commentary on the Sentences of Peter Lombard*, Aquinas said that a tyrant committed sedition and therefore it was permissible to "reject that rulership" and a person "who kills a tyrant is to be praised and rewarded." Quoted in Sigmund, 65-66.

separate from religious differences. Following Aristotle and Cicero, Thomas insisted that all humans had the capacity to understand natural law and that the order in all societies reflected a common law of peoples. A non-Christian king was a legitimate ruler if he kept order and preserved the peace. However, if a pagan ruler sought to expand his rule over Christians, or persecuted them, or interfered with the practice of Christianity, then he dishonored God and these actions constituted just cause for war.

Thomas, following Aristotle, insisted that the good of the republic was the highest form of human good, and that the prince had the obligation to direct, defend, and correct his subjects. Coercive law, part of the law of peoples, was a human addition to natural law for the utility of man. All rulers, whether Christian or not, had an obligation to use law, and a ruler's unbelief did not justify rebellion so long as order and domestic peace were preserved. So the existence of a Muslim state was legitimate and not a grounds for war, because faith was a spiritual activity.

The prince used law internally to preserve the society; externally he used war in a law-like or judicial manner. Only the prince could make war or kill people. Thomas agreed that there was a natural right of proportionate self-defense for protection of one's person, but this right did not extend to the intentional killing of the aggressor. However, if the killing was an unavoidable by-product, a person need not sacrifice his or her life. Normally a common citizen could use the system of court justice to defend his rights. No matter what the grievance, even with a tyrannical prince, the common citizen never had the right to initiate war. The full responsibility for justice in war lay with the prince who initiated it.

The prince waged war after his opponent committed a major intentional fault. The focus was on subjective guilt, which deserved punishment. In addition to the guilt, there must be an injury that resulted in substantial harm. Note that for Thomas, Just War did not begin with a major fault on both sides. Instead, his thought was judicial since there must be a relatively innocent and an overwhelmingly guilty party. The following would be just causes: 1. defending the commonwealth from external enemies; 2. salvation of the fatherland; 3. preserving the temporal peace of the commonwealth; 4. assistance of neighbors; 5. defense of the poor and oppressed. Only reason two requires explanation. Aquinas was willing to tolerate Jewish rituals within a Christian state, but there was no such liberty for heretics. Again, Thomas followed the postulates of Augustine, who was willing to use the power of the state to coerce heretics for their own good. Augustine, however, had defined faith as a spiritual matter and so had not sanctioned the killing of heretics solely because of erring beliefs. Thomas argued that heretics who corrupted the faith of others deserved punishment. He did not link the Crusade against Muslims to a Crusade against heretics, but the decretalists argued that heretics forfeited all civil rights and a war against them was just. Thomas did insist that schism was always a sin and that true Christians should always have the right to proselytize. He argued for allowing Muslim worship in Christian lands so that Christians could have similar privileges in Muslim kingdoms and might convert the Saracens.

Aquinas did not rank his five categories, nor did he provide any guidance of how to choose among them. The result was that in this, as in many subjects, the abstract nature of his advice provided little concrete guidance in the ambiguities of daily existence. He also was not concerned with the difference between offensive and defensive war.

Technicalities involved in the beginnings of war received little attention from Thomas because he was most concerned with intention. Even with just cause, a war begun and fought with wrong intention was unjust. The ultimate intent had to be to do good and to obtain justice. If the intent was to gain wealth or to revel in destruction, the war was unjust. Like other Just War theorists, Thomas disliked mercenaries. Booty was legitimate in a Just War, but if the knights' intent was to gain booty, that made the war sinful. Martyrdom in a Just War brought heaven; death in an unjust war brought hell. What if a knight, through ignorance, had right intention but fought in an unjust war? This was a "material" but not "formal" error and would not affect his status. The responsibility was the prince's, not the knight's. If the circumstances were reversed, the cause of the war would still be just, but the conduct unjust, and the knight would be responsible for his actions. A rapacious knight would be responsible for returning all booty, even though the war was just, because his intent was like robbery.

Aquinas had relatively little to say about conduct in a war. Citing the traditional precedent of Joshua's ambush, he defended actions that would allow the enemy to draw a wrong conclusion. However, he forbade lying to or violating one's pledge to the enemy. On the treatment of captives, there could be no just enslavement in an unjust war. Thomas said that a knight should not be enslaved in a Just War, because that was against his noble nature. He did not address the issue of the treatment of common soldiers.

At several places in his writings, Thomas insisted that the innocent should not be punished for someone else's crime and that there should not be indirect or unintentional killing of innocent persons. By analogy, Thomas should have supported noncombatant immunity. Yet his only stipulation of immunity applied to priests and churchmen because their functions were spiritual. He did hint at what would later be expanded into the doctrine of proportionality; that is, the harm done by the fault should be greater than the evil resulting from the correction.

What Thomas Aquinas summarized were three basic criteria for Just War: just authority, just cause, and just intent. By the fifteenth century insights within Just War theory building upon premises within Thomas would stress noncombatant immunity, law of double effect, and proportionality. There would be more discussion of the differences between offensive and defensive war, and the locus of correct authority would move from the prince to the sovereign state. Thomas Aquinas would influence intellectuals; knights and kings were more likely to read manuals of chivalry. The long-lasting contributions of chivalry to western ethical ideals on war were two: noncombatant immunity and international law.

VI. Chivalry

The Church's role in chivalry was also a response to the incessant warfare and failure of the political authorities to curtail it. The origins of chivalry were complex, stemming from the practices of soldiers on the battlefield, the Germanic celebration of the warrior, and classical concepts of heroism, courage, and honor. The medieval kings and nobility admired the accomplishments of the great warriors of antiquity and sought to emulate Roman military practices.

Chivalry was a mechanism of class control; in theory to become a knight, a man needed to be of noble birth and to have been trained or already have engaged in acts of war. Prowess in war and/or wealth allowed some commoners to gain knighthood. The Merovingian kings Charles Martel and Charlemagne rewarded those who fought by entrusting them with lands in return for military service. The lord conferred knighthood on an individual, often just before a battle, and battlefield dubbing remained one method. The origins of knighthood might lie in the king's bestowing of arms upon young men. The higher the rank of the one who bestowed knighthood, the greater the prestige. By the eleventh century, when western Europeans had mastered the art of riding a horse using stirrups (originally a Germanic contribution), the knight was defined as an armored cavalryman who proved his nobility by practicing chivalry. So chivalry became a set of Christian and secular ideals for behavior in war and peace for knights. As in the Peace and Truce of God and Just War theories, the Church again sought to control the warrior class.

The Church attempted to make knightly ordination almost an eighth sacrament. The candidate, on the night of Christ's resurrection, confessed his sins, took a purificatory bath, placed his sword on the altar, and conducted a vigil through the night, meditating upon his sacred vow. The next morning after a prayer, the knight said his vows and was dubbed either by the bishop or a king.' Yet for all its attempts to make knighthood a Christian vocation, the Church only succeeded in blending religion with other secular emphases.[13]   For example, in creating a mythical history for knighthood, medieval writers found three ideal knights from the classical world: Hector, Alexander, and Caesar; three from the Hebrew world: Moses, Joshua, and Judas Maccabeus; and three from the Christian world: Charlemagne, King Arthur, and Godfrey of Bouillon - the latter a leader of the First Crusade and first Christian king of the Latin Kingdom of Jerusalem. Making such varied men into models for Christian warriors required considerable shading of history.

The legends of King Arthur created a golden age of medieval chivalry: all Arthur's knights did good deeds such as rescuing fair maidens and killing dragons; a few knights quested for the Holy Grail; others sought the favors of a lady under the cult of courtly love; asceticism vied with sumptuous display at Camelot; all except villains showed strength, courage, good manners, and loyalty. The Knights of the Round Table proved their nobility of birth by courtesy and virtuous deeds and gained fame by their exploits of strength in tournaments and battle. The equality of those at the round table contrasted with the multitude kept out. Tournaments, the Crusades, legends, the poetry of the troubadours, and manuals of chivalry spelled out the ideals of noble behavior. Our concern is not with techniques of courting women or politeness in court, but behavior in war.

VII. Chivalry and War

The manuals of chivalry reflect how the concerns of the canonists and theologians on war and peace were translated into popular guidebooks. Honoré Bonet (fl. 1378-1398), *The Tree of Battles (L'Arbre des Batailles)* and Christine de Pisan (ca. 1364-1431), *Book of Fayttes of Armes and Chyualrye* - both written in the vernacular for use by knights, rather than in clerical Latin, and translated into several languages - were two of the most important chivalry guidebooks of the late

---

[13]Maurice Keen, *Chivalry* (1984), 64-82.   This is an excellent introduction to the origins and evolution of chivalry and the Church's role.

Middle Ages. (Both authors were contemporaries of Chaucer.)[14] Christine de Pisan acknowledged how unusual it was for a woman to be writing about war and asked the reader's indulgence, but her compilation had few indications of its feminine origin. She also wrote romances and poetry about courtly love that were about knightly manners, but did not include such topics in her *Fayttes of . . . Chyualrye*. Because of limitations on book production and number of readers in the fourteenth century, these two manuals reached a limited number of readers, but they did circulate at court, and were later printed. Like many medieval books, these manuals did not aim at originality.

Both writers assumed the inevitability of war, a knowledge of Just War theory (derived from common parlance rather than theologians or canon lawyers), and Christian knights devoted to upholding the ethics of chivalry. War in these two manuals was a holy enterprise, ordained by God. The first war, argued Bonet, was fought in heaven when the angel Lucifer rebelled against God. Consequently, all disorder on earth echoed the original conflict in heaven. God had fought for the Israelites, and he continued to determine the victors in war. In addition to the divine law contained in Scripture, the laws of nature and the laws of people also showed the inevitability of war. Different species of animals always fought, for example, dogs and wolves; humans had contrasting temperaments and their differences led to conflict and fighting.[15]

Chivalry made war a Christian enterprise. War was not an evil, but a "good and virtuous" activity that God "ordains." The supposed evils in war came from "false usage," the abuses of individuals. A chivalrous man fought only in Just Wars, and the criteria of Just War duplicated those of the theologians. That is, war was for the execution of justice and permitted only to sovereigns. The prince could justly fight for the Church, his patrimony, his vassals, an ally, the needy, and the oppressed. "For in cas of diffence al werre is gode." All wars of

---

[14]Honoré Bonet, *The Tree of Battles of Honoré Bonét* (ca. 1394), 1949; Christine de Pisane, *The Book of Fayttes of Armes and Chyualrye* (1408).

vengeance and aggression were unjust.[16] In addition, religious differences would not justify a war against either Jews or Muslims, but since Palestine had once belonged to Rome and had been seized unjustly, the pope could issue an indulgence to those seeking the reconquest of the land.

In advance of initiating a war, the prince had to consult with his counselors, and chivalrous advisers would always speak the truth. Before beginning fighting, the prince must tell his opponent the wrong, allow him to provide redress, and also seek arbitration. Even if he had just cause, the wise prince might not fight. Wars were blunt instruments and always resulted in evil done to inferiors. The prince must calculate his resources, estimate the enemy's strength, and decide whether it was better to endure than to begin the war; wisdom often lay in waiting, because in war a predicted success might be derailed by "fortune."[17] Fortune or luck allowed medieval people to affirm that God helped the virtuous to prevail and to understand catastrophe, often caused by their miscalculations or sins, but not always, because - as the Hebrews and Augustine learned - God's purposes remained mysterious.

The knight's profession was making war for just causes, and he was not to trade, till the soil, or be a scholar. He should be willing to run a prudent risk for worthy goals, but never appear foolhardy. If killed in battle in a Just War while protecting his fellow knights, that was praiseworthy. He should never be the first to retreat nor ever betray his lord, but it would be stupid to stand and fight if a retreat was necessary. While he might profit from a Just War, he was not a mercenary or warring for money and should never pillage. An army should bring its supplies and not live off the land, which required taking the products of noncombatants. The only excuse for such practices was dire necessity, and even then, the knight should take only enough for immediate needs and leave sufficient resources for the peasants. Capturing an opposing knight for ransom was

---

[15]Bonet, 81, 118-19.
[16]Bonet, 125-6; Christine de Pisan, 200-01.

permissible, but the ransom must be moderate, not reducing a fellow noble to penury. Women, children, the blind, and sick were not to be ransomed.

In tone, the chivalry manuals resembled the canon lawyers and decretalists who dealt with specific problems rather than the more abstract theologians. For example, Bonet and Christine de Pisan debated: if a knight aided a widow in distress militarily, could he charge her for his services? The answer: No, but she should be prepared to reward him. (Both manuals ignored the courtly-love motif prevalent in poetry.) If a man was vassal to two kings (as often happened during the Hundred Years War between the French and English) and both summoned him, what should he do? He should not divide his forces between them. In what probably appeared a rather unhelpful conclusion, de Pisan suggested that the vassal should attempt to arbitrate between them, choose the just side, or - if he did not know who was just - serve the king to whom he was most indebted. A knight could never serve an excommunicated lord nor one making war against the Church.[18] Bonet insisted that religious differences would not justify making war against Jews or Muslims.

Topics ranged widely: proper conduct in tournaments, truces, safe conduct, diplomatic immunity, whether a prisoner of war could escape (no, if he had given his word, but yes, if he was treated cruelly), coats of arms (what if two knights showed up with the same crest), heralds, trial by ordeal (condemned, but rules provided on how to do it), and the rights of scholars (an English boy could study at the University of Paris even in wartime and could be visited by his parents). The problems were those faced by medieval knights, and Bonet followed good scholastic form in giving the arguments for both alternatives before his conclusions. He used many examples, some from classical antiquity and the *Bible* but others from recent events.

---

[17]Christine de Pisan, 13-15.
[18]Christine de Pisan, 198-99; Bonet, 156-68.

Bonet and Christine de Pisan discussed the rights of prisoners of war and civilians. They argued that although the practice of putting prisoners of war to death was allowable by the laws of people and natural law, Christianity established a higher principle followed by chivalrous knights. No knight could put a prisoner of war to death because the war itself was the punishment for his wrong. Only a higher authority like the prince, acting as a judge, had that right. A knight who later captured an opponent who earlier had wounded him could not inflict any bodily harm on him. That would be an act of vengeance, not war. If an opponent had been wounded in war, his adversary could not pursue and kill him after the battle was over. Christian knights, though in theory having the right, also did not enslave their opponents. Reflecting that medieval warfare often required ransoming of prisoners, the manuals established standards on who could be held captive and how prisoners of war should be treated.[19]

The manuals do not state clearly that all non-combatants are to be spared; yet the prohibitions seem to lead to this conclusion. For example, by law all churchmen were protected; the "ancient custom of noble warriors" exempted from pillage "the widow, the orphan and the poor." Safe-conduct should be granted "all husbandmen, and ploughmen with their oxen" pursuing their business, a custom that it would be "expedient and convenient" to extend to "all sorts of people" who "cultivate the soil" and who "live off their labour" because "they have no concern with war or with harming anyone." Yet if civilians supported either of the warring parties, the exemption ended.[20] So as applied at Agincourt, the French could attack civilian baggage handlers because they aided soldiers and Henry V would have been wrong to order the execution of French prisoners in retaliation.

The chivalry guidebooks assumed that rules of conduct limited the actions of both sides at the beginning, during hostilities, and afterwards. This ideal of a higher law based upon revelation, natural law, and the law of peoples and

---

[19]Bonet, 152-58.
[20]Bonet, 188-89, 168, 185.

transcending nationality would by the sixteenth century become the foundation of international law.

The manuals of chivalry provided standards that kings could use to discipline soldiers. Bonet and Christine de Pisan wrote within the Just War tradition, but their prescriptions should be seen as a critique of the medieval practice of war rather than as a description of actuality. In the fifteen century, as mercenary armies and gunpowder made warfare more destructive, nobles in ornate armor staged pageant-like jousts and the English printer William Caxton published a history of King Arthur - both were attempts to exalt the ideals of chivalry as a way of contrasting a romantic past with a sordid present.

VIII. The Crusades

The enthusiastic response to the First Crusade, proclaimed by Pope Urban II in 1095, required two prerequisites: widespread acceptance of the concept of a holy war declared by and pursued on behalf of the Church and a special class of knights prepared to fight for Christ. The graft of Christianity onto knighthood bore fruit in the Crusade that, like the Arthurian quest for the Holy Grail, was the ultimate test of proving devotion to God through acts of war. The Crusade merged traditional vows of pilgrimage to Jerusalem with Christian war. The pilgrim received certain immunities and privileges after taking a vow to visit the holy places; after the conversion of Constantine such a visit was a meritorious act that had become popular. Failure to fulfill the vow could bring excommunication.[21] Fighting for Christianity was also no new thing; apologists for the later Roman Empire and Byzantium for centuries had claimed to be God's warriors against heathens, schismatics, and Muslims.[22] In the West the papacy had proclaimed holy wars to enable Norman invaders to recruit a force to

---

[21] James Brundage, *Medieval Canon Law and the Crusader* (1969), 30, 65, 114-38, 151.
[22] It is possible, though no one has demonstrated it, that the Byzantine holy war influenced Muslim holy war that influenced Western Europe's Crusades. See Albrect Noth, *Heiliger Krieg und Heiliger Kamp in Islam und Christentum* (1966).

re-conquer Sicily from the Muslims; in Spain there was an ongoing struggle between Christians and Moors. "The Song of Roland," a medieval epic recounting the battles of Charlemagne's warriors against Muslims, was the French equivalent of the King Arthur sagas. Bernard of Clairvaux had emphasized that monastic spirituality required a Christian battle against the devil. The rhetoric of being a soldier for Christ was old. New in the Crusades were the papacy's proclamation, the promise of remission of sins and immediate salvation if killed in battle, and the knight's vow to take up the cross and reconquer Jerusalem.

Jerusalem had a special status for Christians as the Holy City, God's dwelling place, the center of the world, the place where Jesus had taught, was crucified and rose from the dead, the area where Christ was king, and that would be the heavenly city when Christ returned to judge the quick and the dead. As the year 1000 approached, many Europeans anticipated the end of the world and return of Christ, who would inaugurate a millennial kingdom. That holy Jerusalem was now in Muslim hands seemed a direct affront to God. A war to recapture Jerusalem was also just, because that land had once been Christian, and therefore to retake it was to right a wrong, to engage in self-defense. Roman Catholic Europe could aid Orthodox Byzantium against Muslims, re-conquer the Christian lands of Asia Minor on route to Jerusalem, maybe even gain the wealth of Egypt, and reunify Christendom. Clearly here was a quest for the most intrepid Christian knights.

The First Crusade began with a sermon of Pope Urban in 1095 to knights who had taken oaths to abide by the Peace and Truce of God:

> Now that you have promised to maintain the peace among yourselves you are obligated to succour your brethren in the East, menaced by an accursed race, utterly alienated from God. The Holy Sepulchre of our lord is polluted by the filthiness of an unclean nation. Recall the greatness of Charlemagne . . . Let all hatred depart from among you, all quarrels end, all

wars cease. Start upon the road to the Holy Sepulchre to wrest that land from the wicked race and subject it to yourselves.[23]

The Pope was a reformer who wished to quicken the spiritual life of the Church. In addition, Urban may have wished to aid the Byzantine Empire, recently defeated by Muslims in a major battle, and to strengthen Roman Catholic influence in Orthodox Christian areas. Some believe his underlying motive was to divert knights from fighting each other into attacking the Church's external enemies. The Crusades are often accurately described as holy wars because the Church authorized the war and promised forgiveness of sins to all who took the vow and eternal life for those killed in the fight to retake the Holy Land.

The reaction to Urban's sermons was more than he anticipated or even welcomed, for he wished to appeal to knights only and wanted an orderly expedition under Church authority. Instead, the common people rose up to fight God's enemies, but the first result in Germany was a pogrom against the Jews. When the poorly organized rabble led by Peter the Hermit encountered the Muslims, they were overwhelmingly defeated and given their choice of conversion and slavery or death.

Knights took the crusading vow for many reasons - penance, greed, wanderlust, escapism, but most often, religious fervor. They and often their relatives contributed the money to outfit the knights and provide supplies for a several years' campaign. The typical military campaign in Europe ended in winter because of logistic difficulties. Now an army, after journeying to Constantinople, was supposed to fight its way through hostile territory filled with fortified cities

---

[23]Bainton, 112. The text of Urban's proclamation is based on later recollection. Christopher Tyerman, *The Invention of the Crusades* (1998), 19-25 stresses the diversity and changes over time and reviews the historiography about Crusades. A good collection of documents on the Crusades is Margaret Shaw, ed., *Chronicles of Crusades* (1966); J.C.S. Riley Smith, *The First Crusade and the Idea of Crusading* (1986) and *The Crusaders* (1987) are good introductions. John France concluded that for the gentry, "the kinds of rules in the West applied . . . notwithstanding the rival clash of Crusade and *jihad*. There were terrible exceptions" and both sides could use ransom for high-ranking soldiers. *Western Warfare in the Age of Crusades*, 227-29, 233.

in what is now Turkey, Lebanon, and Israel. Knights could expect to be gone for years, and most never returned. Those who anticipated wealth and fame were rarely satisfied. Still, the army of knights overcame internal divisions, near starvation, and several disasters; and against incredible odds, overcame a multitude of cities, climaxing in 1099 in the conquest of Jerusalem and creation of a series of Latin kingdoms.

In later years, after the Muslims recaptured Jerusalem in 1187 and additional Crusades failed to retake the Holy City, Christians stressed the miraculous nature of the First Crusade. The army of the First Crusade has been compared to a monastery on the move. Mass was celebrated every day; before battles, there would be a fast and solemn blessings of the soldiers; several knights had visions of Mary or Christ. Soldiers went into battle carrying sacred relics and shouting *"Deus hoc vult"* (God wills this) or *"Deus adjura"* (God aid us). The crusaders saw themselves as re-enacting the song of Miriam, Joshua's conquest of the Holy Land, and the Maccabees' victories. After conquest of the Muslim cities, Orthodox churches that had been turned into mosques would solemnly be reconsecrated according to Latin rites. Beneath the altar of the church at Antioch, the crusaders claimed to have discovered the lance that pierced Jesus' side during the crucifixion.

The papacy wanted the crusading knights to fight for St. Peter, but the soldiers saw themselves as engaged in a supernatural war for Christ. Neither the Peace nor Truce of God nor the restraints of chivalry applied to a war against Muslims. Since the Christian participants saw the war as a personal vendetta against the forces of evil personified by Muslims, massacres could have been anticipated - though these were not common. The most egregious case was after the conquest of Jerusalem when the crusaders massacred Muslims and Jews alike, and "in the temple and portico of Solomon, men rode in blood up to their knees and bridle reins."[24] The Muslims thought the Latin Christians barbarians. The Byzantines who had been fighting the Muslims for centuries found the blood lust and zeal of the Latin invaders abhorrent.

The Christianization of war reached its apogee with the creation of military orders to defend Jerusalem. The Knights Templar began in Jerusalem in 1128. The Templars were a consecrated fighting force, a combination of monk and knight whose members took pledges of chastity, poverty, and obedience, wore a special white tunic with a red cross, and were dedicated to the defense of the Holy City. They were joined in 1154 by the Hospitallers, who began as a group to provide charity for pilgrims and became a military order to protect those making pilgrimages to the Holy Land. The Teutonic Knights, founded in 1190 as an order to care for the sick, added fighting the infidel to their duties during the Third Crusade. The dedication of the members of the crusading orders is shown by the numbers who died while defending the Holy Land or on various Crusades. Over time, however, rivalry among the various orders and their increasing wealth changed their ideals. The Templars, for example, became influential in European banking and financial arrangements. Still, the orders provided the standing army for the crusading states.

The Crusades were a strange melee of idealism and crassness. Chivalry and political calculation lay behind the decisions of the Kings of England and France and Emperor of Germany to lead the Third Crusade (1187-1192), a response to the fall of Jerusalem. While succeeding in strengthening the Latin states, it failed in its objective to take Jerusalem and ended with a truce guaranteeing the right of pilgrims to visit Jerusalem. The Fourth Crusade (1198-1204) did not fight Muslims at all, but was diverted by its leaders and the Venetians into attacking, seizing, and sacking Constantinople. Partially in revulsion against this betrayal of idealism and believing that the failure of the Crusades was due to the wealth and political manipulation of the leaders, those

---

[24] Ibid.

behind the Children's Crusade of 1212 stressed that the innocence of children would guarantee God's intervention and a successful military campaign. The political authorities and the papacy never endorsed this Crusade but took no decisive steps to prevent it before the Crusade ended in disaster, with some children dying, others returning home, and many sold into slavery. Sensible Europeans knew that successful wars took planning and warriors. Those who heard the stories of the Hebrews' conquest of the Holy Land uncritically assumed that God would again intervene directly. The Children's Crusade marked the appropriation by many medieval commoners of Joshua's Yahweh's war.

The crusading ideal proved long-lived and adaptable to European needs. It helped motivate the Spanish conquest of the Iberian Peninsula, which finished in 1492 with the fall of Granada and the forced conversion or expulsion of all Jews and Muslims from Spain. The Teutonic knights used the Crusade in the expansion of Christian Europe against the pagans who inhabited the area that is now the Baltic States. The French king, seeking to expand his power, had the papacy proclaim a Crusade, lasting from 1120-29, against Christian heretics, Albigensians, who inhabited southern France and Catalonia. The papacy used Crusades against its political opponents in Italy and Germany. Innocent III, who proclaimed the Fourth Crusade and the Crusade against the Albigensians, was also responsible for proclaiming war against heretics. A Crusade against Jerusalem might be called defensive, a reconquest of lands originally Christian, though four hundred years of occupation could as easily be seen as giving Muslims just title. However, the Teutonic knights' Crusades to expand the area of Roman Catholicism against the pagans in eastern Europe (Poland, the Baltic states) were clearly offensive wars.[25] Here conversions were forced and religious and political authorities used Christianity as a means to power.[26] Monks who in Spain and

---

[25]John France, 203, describes the Northern Crusade versus pagans as "harsh and brutal," "the scale and horror of atrocity," and "savagery."

[26]Eric Christiansen, *The Northern Crusades: The Baltic and the Catholic Frontier 1100-1525* (1980), 68-69, 85, 92, 118-127.

Poland fought to expand Christian-controlled lands showed how the crusading zeal undermined traditional prohibitions.

The Crusades have been accurately described as both a modification of the Just War or a new kind of holy war. Either way, it meant a repudiation of an ancient Christian testimony that even killing in a necessary war was an evil that should be an occasion for penance. Crusades also seemed to negate the Church's program for peacemaking expressed in the Peace of God and Truce of God.

In later years the papacy transformed the vows to go to Jerusalem into moneymaking devices (termed indulgences) to gain remission of the penalties for sins. A knight who repented of a rash vow to go to Jerusalem could buy his way out or a merchant guilty of some major sin could gain a shortening of time served in purgatory through financing the outfitting of a crusader or even a large contribution to the Church. In addition, the failure to hold Jerusalem and the popes' involvement in temporal affairs tended to discredit the notion of a special kind of holy war, particularly a war that was lost. The *Bible* showed that God had enabled the Israelites to prevail when they were faithful but to be destroyed for their sins. Was God passing a similar judgment on Christian Europe, and should Christ's Vicar, the Pope, be engaged in declaring Crusades against Muslims or heretics when the Gospel message was of peace?

IX. Heretics: Persecution and Pacifism

Kings had long assumed all of Europe should profess one faith, but there had been little direct involvement of Church and political authorities in the persecution of heretics. In 385, a bishop suspected of Manicheism was handed over to authorities and executed on a charge of witchcraft; the pope was furious and excommunicated the bishop's accusers. There were no other western Europeans executed as heretics for 650 years. The medieval popes interested in reforms within the Church also sought unity within the faithful. In theory, the baptism of all children imposed an obligation upon them after they became adults and upon church authorities to maintain Christian truth. Church reform, persecution of heretics, and the growth of challenges to orthodoxy after the tenth century can be seen as attempts to purify the faith.

The age of the Crusades was also the beginning of a policy of executing heretics, and the papacy took the lead in pressuring secular authorities to act. When exhortations from clerical authorities proved insufficient, the papacy in 1231 created the Inquisition - staffed by Dominicans and Franciscans who specialized in preaching to the laity - to conduct investigations, determine who were heretics, and hand them over to the secular authorities for punishment. The accused was furnished a lawyer, and the object was confession and reclamation, but those who remained obdurate faced imprisonment, torture, and sometimes death. Heretics forfeited their property, which could be seized by the state.

For our purposes in understanding the Church's position on war, the Albigensian rejection of war marks a crucial change. The Cathari or Albigensians, who flourished in southern France in the twelfth and thirteen centuries, dissented from Catholic views on war. Their beliefs, ironically, had been learned by participants in the Second Crusade who imported the dualistic and nominally Christian beliefs back with them to southern France. The Albigensians restricted nonviolence to a few visible saints, termed *perfecti*, leaders who were celibate and vegetarians. More ordinary believers, who could receive salvation through receiving the merits of the *perfecti*, could use force to defend this elite. By contrast, the Waldensians, also originating in the twelfth century, though anti-clerical, remained Catholic in doctrine. The Waldensians used the example of Jesus against what they saw as the wealth and corruption of the Roman Church. Following Jesus meant swearing no oaths, living in voluntary poverty, and no shedding of human blood. All believers should observe nonviolence. By the fifteenth century, after centuries of persecution, Waldensian pacifism had evolved into a limited Just War theory that allowed self-defense. Pacifism for both

Albigensian and Waldensian was a by-product of a world view rather than a defining feature of these two sects.[27]

The medieval Church had contained pacifism by making its counsel of perfection applicable for those who retreated from the world into monasteries or the priesthood. From the twelfth century on, there were always some Christians in western Europe, belonging to groups the Roman Catholic Church termed heretics, who rejected the Constantinian synthesis and insisted on what they saw as a literal interpretation of the teachings and example of Jesus. In all these groups (and most of the information about them comes from hostile sources), there was a persistent stream of Christian pacifism. The Waldensians in Switzerland, the Lollards in England, and the Czech Brethren or Taborites in Bohemia criticized the wealth and power of the medieval Church and rejected Just War doctrine, chivalry, and Crusades. They insisted that Christians were called to radical obedience, which meant no taking of life either by law or war. So a Christian could not be a soldier.[28] The pacifist sects had little influence on Roman Catholicism or the courts of Europe, which remained committed to Just War doctrines. So long as western Europeans insisted that the religion of the realm must be one and that one was Roman Catholic, the sects would be persecuted.

In England from 1337 to 1485 a second form of anti-war protest came during the Hundred Years War and later dynastic struggle termed the War of Roses. Complaints against Just War theory and chivalry and paeans to peace came from poets like Chaucer, churchmen, and anonymous writers of popular literature who contrasted papal and scholastic pronouncements on justice in the cause and conduct of war with actual events. In actuality, they argued, there was neither justice in the cause of most of the wars nor moderation in conduct.

---

[27]Malcolm Barber, *The Cathars: Dualist Heretics in Languedoc in the High Middle Ages* (2000), 93ff, 120; Susanna Treesh, "The Waldensian Recourse to Violence," *Church History* (1986), 294-299. Euan Cameron, *Waldenses: Rejections of Holy Church in Medieval Europe* (2000), ignores pacifism as a significant belief. Malcolm Lambert, *Medieval Heresy: Popular Movements from the Gregorian Reform to the Reformation,* 3rd edition *Reformation,* (2002), 83-84, 120, 149, 174.
[28]Peter Brock, *Pacifism In Europe to 1914* (1972), 25-58.

Knights were mercenary thieves preying upon peasants and merchants. The critics did not deny the legitimacy of the English kings' claim to the French throne; instead, they focused on the results of the repeated invasions of France: high taxes, the pillaging of the countryside, and the deaths of soldiers and civilians.

The anti-war advocates continued a post-Augustinian perspective that peace was an individual spiritual quality, but unlike earlier writers insisted that this inward peace could be sought more easily when the country was tranquil. Peace also had a secular value in that the absence of war brought prosperity and the end of knightly brigandage.[29]

The critique of the Catholic Church's role in wars by the poets, clerics, and pacifist sects laid the foundation for a humanist and Anabaptist analysis of war during the Catholic and Protestant Reformations. By 1520 the introduction of gunpowder, the rise of mercenary armies, the increased power of states and monarchs, and a change in the role of the nobility ended the age of knights.

The medieval Church had more direct influence over western society than before or after the Middle Ages. So of crucial importance to the themes of this book is whether the Church's program on war promoted peace, prevented war, and changed the conduct of men in war? Or, to rephrase the question: would medieval war have been worse without the Church's efforts? Any answer to the "what if" question has to be very tentative, because changes in the nature of war were also influenced by political change and technology, i.e., the introduction of gunpowder and better armor and healthier horses.

The Crusades promoted war; chivalry sought to restrain conduct; Just War sought to outlaw aggressive war while making the practice of war more humane. The Church's dilemma was that making war more moral made it easier for kings to defend going to war, and an ethic based upon intentionality of soldiers is difficult to judge. Most likely, the Church's program did influence in a positive manner the way the upper classes made war, reduced the legitimacy of private wars, and by so doing helped civilians. It is doubtful that the teachings helped common soldiers or restrained kings. The Church's teachings on heretics were used to whitewash cruelty. By compromising because it saw the preservation of medieval society as a good and, thereby accepting an imperfect peace, the Church retained influence with those who wished to make war without losing the possibility of salvation.

---

[29]Ben Lowe, *Imagining Peace: A History of Early English Pacifist Ideas* (1997), 141-146.

IX.
Splintering of Christian Traditions

Between 1480 and 1648, all Europe never enjoyed a year of peace. Similar conditions prevailed in the Middle Ages, but then the incessant turmoil resembled internal anarchy or civil strife. This strife was replaced by dynastic wars of monarchs seeking to consolidate or expand their realms, battles of Christians against the Turks, and religious conflict between Protestants and Catholics. The increased security within kingdoms contrasted with the vulnerability of those living in small weak states or on the borders of powerful monarchies.

Although European courts proclaimed their intent to seek arbitration and to begin a war only to right wrongs, the primary causes of war remained, in the words of the Italian Lorenzo Valla in 1440, "desire of glory," "hope of booty," "fear of incurring disaster later, if the strength of others is allowed to increase," and "avenging a wrong and defending friends," or as summarized by historian J. R. Hale "greed, fear and altruism."[1] Altruism was the least important of these. So Europeans fought over the land even though the revenues of new lands rarely covered the cost of even a successful war.

When a king decided on war, he and his advisers found no shortage of grievances. Borders between states were ill-defined; and dynastic marriages brought convoluted kinship ties and gave constant claims that could be cited as just causes for war. The ambitions of the Habsburg monarchs - controlling Spain, the Netherlands, Austria, and the Holy Roman Empire - clashed with those of the Valois and Bourbon kings of France, who feared encirclement, so they fought over control of middle Europe or Italy. Peasants staged unsuccessful revolts against rapacious nobles; nobles struggled against monarchs curtailing feudal rights. The

---

[1] J. R. Hale, *War and Society* (1985), 22.

decentralization of 1200 that caused war evolved into the tyranny of 1600 that also brought war.

Our theme in this chapter is that the evolution in the purpose and nature of war brought changes in the ethical evaluation of war, a splintering of traditions that has continued to the present. Just War theories based upon Christianity and natural law remained the official position of Catholics and Protestants, but faced criticism from advocates of humanism, nonresistance, and realpolitik. Part I is a brief history of the wars over religion and changes in the nature of war. Part II summarizes the response to unceasing war by intellectuals drawing upon a heritage of classics and Christianity.

I. Wars of Religion

According to the Just War theories espoused by Christian princes and theologians during and after the Reformation, religious differences per se were not sufficient causes for war nor should the faith be spread by force. Yet for the next 150 years, religion played a major role in causing European conflicts as Protestants fought Catholics with both assuming that salvation depended upon adherence to "true" Christianity. Religion had long been seen as a just cause for war against heretics and kings who corrupted their peoples from true to false religion. So technically at least the conflicts could be considered Just Wars and not Crusades, even though the participants often saw their side as fighting a holy war. Even devout rulers - Spain's Philip II, Austria's Ferdinand II, Sweden's Gustavus Adolphus, and England's Oliver Cromwell - who saw their wars as battles for God always invoked a rationale based in Just War theories.

Rulers equated religious dissent with political opposition, churchmen invoked the power of the state to deal with alleged heresy, and fanatics acted citing biblical precedents, while a few theologians rationalized the assassination of kings. The Scottish Calvinist theologian John Knox (1514-1572) using Old Testament examples provided a theological defense of tyrannicide of England's

Catholic Queen Mary Tudor.[2] One assassin wounded the Protestant leader of the Netherlands William of Orange in 1582 and another killed him in 1584. After the pope excommunicated Elizabeth I of England, the papal secretary wrote that because she "was the cause of so much injury to the Catholic faith and loss of so many million souls, there is no doubt that whosoever sends her out of the world with the pious intention of doing God service, not only does not sin but gains merit."[3] The French and Spanish ambassadors plotted Elizabeth's murder in order to bring the Catholic Mary Stuart to the throne. Still, the so-called religious wars differed from medieval crusades in that political leaders, not the churches, authorized them, although with the full support of the clergy. With the exception of Cromwell's New Model army during the Puritan revolution, most soldiers were mercenaries rather than the devout.

Religious differences accentuated existing tensions and provided an additional compelling reason to fight. However, religious acrimony was only one of many causes of disorder, such as struggles between nobility trying to preserve local prerogatives versus kings seeking to centralize power, economic and social dislocation caused by inflation, population growth, the emergence of a market economy, expansion into the Americas and Indies, and the consolidation of estates by wealthy landlords. Dynastic rivalries, the Dutch and Swiss seeking independence, and the efforts of the Jesuits to recover lost lands and the Calvinists to extend their influence also caused war.

The initial jockeying between Lutherans and Roman Catholics within the multitude of German kingdoms and city-states ended with the Peace of Augsburg (1555), which recognized that the unity of Christendom had ended and initially eased conflicts by decreeing that the religion of the prince determined that of his domains (*cujus regio ejus religio*). The major religious wars came later - the French wars of religion (1562-98), the Thirty Years War in Germany (1618-48), and the Puritan Revolution in England (1641-1649).

---

[2] Jasper Ridley, *John Knox* (1968), 272-80.
[3] John Neal, *Queen Elizabeth* (1934), 258.

In the dynastic struggle in France, Catholics and Calvinists (Huguenots) fought over which creed would be dominant. The predominant image of this struggle is massacre and assassination. After a failed assassination attempt by the Catholic de Guise family, Catherine de Medici, acting regent, authorized in 1572 what has come to be known as the St. Bartholomew's massacre of leaders of the Huguenots gathered in Paris to celebrate a wedding of her daughter with the Protestant Henry of Navarre. It was supposed to be an occasion of reconciliation between the two religious factions. Believing that killing Calvinists had the sanction of the Crown, mobs in Paris and other French cities rampaged, killing men, women, and children. They savagely desecrated the bodies of victims as if they were purging the land of pollution. Five thousand died in violent rites patterned after Catholic rituals. In general Calvinists targeted priests and religious people (friars, nuns), while Catholics killed anyone, and neither group felt guilty afterwards. The winner of the succession struggle was Henry of Navarre, a Protestant who became a Catholic, although there is no documentary evidence for his famous rationale explaining the change of faith that "Paris is worth a mass." His religious settlement ensured that at end of the wars the prevailing ethos remained as at the beginning: "one king, one faith, one law." Henry IV's Edict of Nantes guaranteed to the Huguenots the right to worship (except in Paris) and civil rights. A Roman Catholic assassinated Henry IV in 1610.[4]

The Thirty Years War (1616-1648), originating as a religious and civil struggle, became an international conflict among Denmark, Holland, Sweden, France, and major German principalities. It started as a revolt of Protestant Bohemia against a crusading Catholic Holy Roman Emperor, Ferdinand II, but the war soon turned into his attempt to crush Lutherans throughout Germany, restore Catholic lands to the Church, and also increase Habsburg power. The fortunes of

---

[4]Michael Holt, *The French Wars of Religion, 1562-1629* (1995), 86-94,153, 163-65; Natalie Zemon Davis, "The Rites of Violence," *Society and Culture in Early Modern France* (1975), 158-59, 173.

the Catholic Church became linked with those of the Habsburgs, which meant that the slim possibilities for compromise evaporated.

At the time, observers blamed the religious fervor of monarchs, clerics, and people for the duration and brutality of the Thirty Years War, even though many princes operated on the basis of self-interest or balance of power and shifted alliances with little regard for religious purity. For example, after the Habsburgs invaded Italy, even the papacy opposed pro-Catholic Austria. And, towards the end of the struggle, the Roman Catholic Cardinal Richelieu, whose lack of a morally consistent policy was rationalized as *raison d'état*, brought France into the war on the side of the Protestants to weaken Austria.

Armies laid waste to lands as they fought with a ferocity that brought the economic decline of every section in Germany and a significant population loss, estimated at 15-20 percent. Historian C. V. Wedgewood's classic account summarized the war's results: "Its effects, both immediate and indirect, were either negative or disastrous. Morally subversive, economically destructive, socially degrading, confused in its causes, devious in its course, futile in its result, it is the outstanding example in European history of meaningless conflict." A recent evaluation says that the war did solve many issues, including establishing the religious boundaries of central Europe, but still concluded, "The war was the longest, most expansive, and most brutal war that had yet been fought on German soil" with a loss of people that was "proportionally greater than World War II." It was "an unprecedented catastrophe for the German people."[5]

The Treaty of Westphalia in 1648 formally recognized the independence of Switzerland and Holland, restored the religious boundaries of Germany as of 1624, gave Calvinism the legal right to exist, and reiterated the Augsburg formula allowing each prince to determine the religion of the inhabitants without outside interference.

---

[5]"The War and German Society," in *The Thirty Years War*, ed. Geoffrey Parker (1997), 189-193; C.V. Wedgwood, *The Thirty Years War* (1939), 526.

The last stages of the Thirty Years War coincided with the last religious war fought in England, the Puritan revolution against Charles I. This war originated in a struggle for supremacy between an absolutist-leaning king supported by Anglican bishops against Parliament controlled by Calvinists. As their name indicates, the Puritans wanted to purify the Church of England of what they saw as Catholic remnants. Religious and political reforms became mixed and eventually led to a successful (albeit temporary) revolution with the execution of the king, abolition of bishops and the aristocratic House of Lords, ascendancy of Oliver Cromwell, restructuring of the Church of England, and limited religious toleration. Even after the restoration of Charles II in 1660, religious tensions divided the country as Crown and Parliament sought to compel everyone to worship in the Church of England. In 1688 Protestants united in what they called a "Glorious Revolution" to overthrow the Roman Catholic James II and install Protestants William and Mary on the throne. The revolutionary settlement confirmed the supremacy of Parliament and resulted in the toleration of all Protestants but made public worship by Roman Catholics illegal.

The era of religious turmoil that began with the Lutheran reformation of 1517 ended with the Treaty of Westphalia and the Glorious Revolution. Throughout western Europe confessional politics had become so disreputable that states no longer either claimed or practiced the right to intervene in another country's affairs because of religious differences. The Treaty of Westphalia is generally recognized as the first formal recognition that a state is absolutely sovereign within its borders and that all states are legally equal, irrespective of size. The Westphalia system of autonomous states still remains the foundation of international relations.

Conduct of War

The methods used to fight each other in 1500 were far more destructive than in 1300. When the crossbow, whose steel-tipped arrows could pierce mail armor was introduced, the Church protested - probably not just because of the deadliness of the new weapon but because more nobles would be killed. When the more effective gunpowder-propelled shot from cannon and arquebus came into general use after 1400, there was no complaint by churchmen or nobles. The kings and city-states of western Europe, including the Papal States, hastened to equip their soldiers with the new weapons, even though maintaining supplies of cannon, guns, shot, and saltpeter and a corps of trained gunners dramatically increased the financial burden of war. Europeans rushed to improve the qualities of firearms, and by 1600 the basic technology of muskets and cannons reached a level of sufficient complexity that there would be no basic change in weaponry until the mid-nineteenth century.[6]

The composition of armies and tactics changed accordingly. Mounted armored cavalry declined in importance relative to infantry equipped with either pikes or guns. The Swiss perfected a moving formation of armed pikemen, similar to the Greek phalanx, that proved very useful against cavalry. Although Swiss mercenaries gained a reputation for ferocity and barbarity because they did not take prisoners, European monarchs and popes vied and paid well for their services.

Military tactics reflected the limits of technology. Cannon were very heavy and difficult to maneuver in the field, so they were most useful in sieges to batter walls. Until the introduction of the flintlock, an arquebus took about one minute to fire and required powder and a source for a spark (that could cause an explosion.) So infantrymen could not stand too close together and needed to be protected from cavalry charge by pikemen. With no standardized size or bore of cannon or shot, accuracy in shooting at any distance was impossible, and the most effective fighting strategy was to have a line of infantrymen who fired together. It was assumed that somewhere in that hail of shot a target would be hit. Then the first line would step back and reload while the second line of men fired. Since

---

[6]Bert S. Hall, *Weapons and Warfare in Renaissance Europe* (1997), 65-66. Before 1400, guns had more psychological effect than use on the battlefield. Cannon helped the Turks conquer Constantinople and the French drive the English from the continent. Nearly as important as the gun was the invention of the three-masted caravel, a ship that made possible the expansion of Europe to the Americas and the Indies.

powder and shot were expensive, soldiers did not practice gunnery. There was also no drill because armies were generally patched together at the last moment, so commanders found it difficult to maneuver the armies during battle.

Attracting good men for armies was difficult because soldiers were poorly qualified, poorly trained, and poorly paid. Zeal for religion brought many volunteers in a few struggles, such as the Puritan Revolution and the Thirty Years War.[7] However, in an era when there was some folk consciousness (i.e., the sense of being English, or Italian, or German) but no nationalism, the quarrels of the monarchs did not inspire hundreds to enlist. Yet the monarchs' needs for soldiers were greater because the size of armies more than doubled; a fighting force of 20,000 was not unusual and the largest armies, on paper at least, had from 50,000 to 100,000 men. So monarchs used a variety of tactics to raise armies. They hired mercenaries, appealed to their nobility to become officers, and forced local officials to meet a quota of men. Added to a few enlistees who listened to the recruiters about how soldiers enjoyed fame, fortune, and women were many whom town fathers saw as undesirables. Vagabonds, landless laborers, those who had transgressed the law - these were the expendable flotsam of society. Once in an army, a man served for life. Because of popular disdain for a soldier's life, an army became a separate society for officers with its own rules and etiquette, though for common soldiers whipping, maiming, and the gallows enforced discipline. No wonder contemporaries feared the presence of an army of either friend or foe as a fate almost equal to the presence of the plague, and of course armies killed far more of their own members and their enemies by spreading disease than by fighting.

The vestiges of chivalry survived in the officer corps and in the desire by a few to gain glory by deeds of valor not as a knight on a quest for the Holy Grail but as an officer in service of his king. Aristocrats and lesser nobility could have easier lives and exercise more influence in serving at court than in the army.

---

[7] Parker, *The Thirty Years War*, 173.

Younger sons became officers, particularly if they could afford to equip a company. Birth and favoritism brought high rank and even command of a company. There was no merit system of promotion within the army for either officers or men.

Kings made war for glory and power; merchants enjoyed the profits from supplying armies with the food and munitions necessary for fighting. Soldiers could hope for the booty taken from the successful capture of a town or after a rout of an enemy army. Yet whatever the rationale for engaging in war, the support of soldiers in peace and war strained national treasuries. There was never enough money, even in the Spain with the gold and silver flowing in from the New World, to train, equip, feed, and pay armies adequately. Taxation levels (and graft) were high, almost oppressively so. Governments rarely calculated accurately the cost of fighting a long war, and their exaction of money and food strained societies almost to the breaking point.

Civilians showed little enthusiasm for war except during times their cities were under siege when the normal animosity between soldiers and civilians lessened and men and women supported the defense. Of course, their involvement meant that, if the enemy took the town, civilians would experience severe reprisals - the murder of men, the rape of women, the pillaging of the town. The atrocities committed during the sack of Rome in 1527, done by Catholic soldiers, were paralleled by those after the fall of Antwerp in 1576 and by both sides during the Thirty Years War. Of course, townspeople knew that new weapons favored a strategy of defense and that a negotiated surrender would provide protections for civilians.

Europe strained, taxed, starved, expanded, and fought incessantly between 1480 and 1648. And when all the effort and blood had been shed, the geographical map of the continent at the end of the period looked little different from in the beginning. Not so the intellectual map by which Church, state, and individuals dealt with the moral issues posed by the new manner of war.

After 1500, Europeans adapted traditional approaches to war to deal with two new phenomena: religious diversity and a powerful state. Part II of this chapter will concentrate upon five approaches used by early modern Christians to deal with the ethics of war: Christian humanism (Erasmus), realpolitik (Machiavelli and Hobbes), nonresistance (Anabaptists), Just War (Luther and Suarez), and international law (Grotius). Each approach will be illustrated by dealing with one or more leading figures, most of whom were contemporaries but whose thoughts are presented not in chronological order but as exemplars of contrasting approaches to war and peace. Although there is an antique flavor to the formulations of each of these alternatives, all of these perspectives remain viable options for contemporary Americans.

II. The Traditions

Christian Humanism: Erasmus

Desiderous Erasmus (1466-1536) of Rotterdam pondered why Just War theories no longer seemed to restrain either the initiation or practice of wars among those who professed to be Christian. Erasmus was one of the many sensitive souls within the Church who saw the survival of medieval practices as hampering the reform of European society and the Roman Catholic Church. He sought to persuade by writing satires, schoolbooks, philosophy, theology, and new translations of the *Bible* and the Church fathers. His influence was enormous because of his genius as a writer and editor, but also because he had available a revolutionary way of reaching a wider audience - the printed book.

Erasmus came to symbolize a movement called Christian Humanism - an attempt to reintroduce into Europe the best of the classical world, to eradicate the superstition and corruption of medieval Christianity, and to persuade princes and people of the value of an imitation of Christ.[8] He contrasted the ethics and practices of Jesus and the early Church with those of contemporary princes and

---

[8]The best survey of the Christian humanist response to war is R. P. Adams, *The Better Part of Valor: More, Erasmus, Colet, and Vives* (1962). Good biographies of Erasmus include J. Huizinga, *Erasmus* (1924); Roland Bainton, *Erasmus of Christendom* (1969).

churchmen. He decried what he saw as the artificial barriers erected by Aquinas and the scholastics that interfered with seeing the New Testament accurately. The humanist vision of the moral life drew on themes derived from Stoicism: affirming the common ties of all humanity, using reason as a way of achieving truth, and living in accordance with nature. Christ came to bring life, peace, and love; war brought hatred, death, and destruction. Plato had opposed Greek fighting Greek. How much worse was it for Christian to fight Christian?[9]

Erasmus' critique of war began by re-examining the traditional exegeses of the love-your-enemies, be-content-with-your-wages, two-swords, and give-unto-Caesar passages used by Just War theorists. He concluded that the rationale for war using these passages destroyed the clear message and intent of Christ. The New Testament teaching and example of Jesus were clear: Christians could not kill their enemies as a way of loving them. The Old Testament teachings on war had been superseded by Jesus' ethic of love. The early Church fathers had opposed war; only with the changes of the Church in the post-Constantinian era had Christianity become corrupted.

Just War theory, argued Erasmus, did not restrain the starting of wars because it allowed individual princes to judge the rightness of their cause. The predictable result was that, although princes asserted the rightness of their cause, in actuality virtually all wars were unjust. Kings and their advisers camouflaged their real motives by proclaiming faults or grievances - many of which were trivial, even centuries old - as a pretext to begin a war. Before beginning a war, the prince should calculate the costs of the war versus the potential gain. Erasmus complained that the princes overestimated the chances for victory and underestimated the difficulties of ending the war successfully. Neither the costs

---

[9]Erasmus' comments on war are scattered throughout his writings. His perspective is summarized in "The Complaint of Peace" reprinted in John Dolan, *The Essential Erasmus* (1964); in the last section of *The Education of a Christian Prince* (1516), tr. Lester Born (1968), 249-257, and "The Soldier's Life" in the *Colloquies in Essential Works of Erasmus*, ed. W. T. H. Jackson (1965), 117-120.

nor results of battles could be accurately forecast, for, once wars started, they tended to drag on, often to an inconclusive ending with both sides impoverished.

Soldiers in battle, according to Just War theory, practiced moderate conduct. Unfortunately, Erasmus lamented, the nature of battle precluded restraint, and armies neither protected civilians nor respected property rights of either non-combatants or the Church. Just War theory attempted to link reason to war, yet reasonable men would not be engaging in war in the first place. Morality and war, the very concept of a Just War, was an oxymoron, for war undermined morality and destroyed justice.

Monarchs liked fighting because they had imbibed the false doctrines of chivalry. Erasmus translated a Latin treatise where the hero journeyed to Hades and found the skull of Helen of Troy; was this the remains of the beautiful adulteress who caused the Trojan War? Achilles, Hector, Alexander the Great, Julius Caesar -- neither these nor their medieval successors like Lancelot and Roland were fit heroes for Christian men. The favorite sport of kings was hunting wild animals. Erasmus saw a cause of war in the blood lust awakened by hunting and killing animals. Killing for sport created a restless spirit that would be satiated only through the excitement of battle. The incessant demand for blood awakened by the tournament and hunt brought out the bestial nature of humans; only, mused Erasmus, to compare men and beasts was unfair to the animals that killed neither their own kind nor destroyed for frivolous causes nor used all their ingenuity creating weapons. Men at war, he concluded, acted worse than beasts.

Erasmus was unhappy with the emergent absolutist states in Europe. His *Adages* proclaimed, "The King and the fool are born such."[10] Although aware that monarchs had complete freedom to declare war, Erasmus remarked that the state existed for the welfare of the people. He disliked tyranny and saw war as an exercise of tyranny by a king on his people. Few of the population wanted to fight, particularly over matters of concern only to the ruling dynasty. So the kings

---

[10] *Adages,* No. 1301; Adams, *Better Part of Valor,* 88-118.

had to coerce their men into serving in the military where they were horrendously treated. The result was a coarsening of behavior that meant soldiers could not be reintroduced into normal society when the war was over.

For Augustine war, caused by man's sin that brought God's answering justice, was an inevitable consequence of living in the earthly city. Erasmus was more optimistic, or at least had more confidence that humans could be educated: "Men are not born but made." War was a part of human fatuity and such folly could be conquered by reforming two crucial institutions of Europe: the monarchies and the Church. Erasmus wrote treatises to influence the education of princes and their advisers, recommended teaching the monarchs to rely on statecraft and not war, and sought to end the glorification of military life. He sought to de-glamorize war, to make the real hero the king who abstained from war and brought his people the blessings of peace. To be a success, defined as achieving honor, fame, and nobility, a king combined moral virtue with Christian piety and never authorized an act of injustice.[11]

The Catholic Church should aid princes in the pursuit of peace. The pope as vicar of Christ should imitate Him by becoming a peacemaker, concerned with arbitrating disputes among princes. As a young monk Erasmus had been in Italy when Pope Julius II, dressed in armor, led the victory parade of the papal army at the conquest of Bologna. Julius had personally led the troops in his wars to increase the size of the Papal States in Italy. Erasmus was horrified and later wrote a funny satire with Pope Julius after death appearing in armor with his army at the gates of heaven. St. Peter failed to recognize him. The ensuing dialogue between Peter and Julius showed the Pope's militaristic spirit and led to his being refused admission.[12]

Though Erasmus opposed the wars of the European princes, he was not an absolute pacifist. He defended as necessary a war that was truly for self-defense.

---

[11]Quentin Skinner, *The Foundations of Modern Political Thought, I, The Renaissance* (1978), 231-242.
[12]*The Julius Exclusus of Erasmus* (1514), tr. Paul Pascal (1968), 48, 77-79; Adams, 94.

When the Ottomans conquered Hungary and laid siege to Vienna, Erasmus supported a war against the Turks, but it was to be a war to protect Europe and not a crusade against the Saracens. Even the Church could support such a war. Still, he preferred a pamphlet war to a physical battle, for education was better than force to convert an opponent.

Erasmus was a Christian Humanist; that is, his vision was of peoples' essential rationality and piety. Leaders could be educated to see that all humanity was linked, that peace was in everybody's best interest. Erasmus' vision of a united Europe had much in its favor: rationality, common sense, and moderation. He thought its wisdom would be apparent to those who studied history, particularly to the monarchs who paraded their Christian faith. His motto can be summarized as "Sweet is war to those who know it not."[13]

Machiavelli: Realpolitik

In the summer of 1513, Niccolo Machiavelli, an Italian diplomat who had lost his position when the republican government of Florence ended, sought to regain the favor of the newly restored de Medici rulers by writing a treatise on the government of principalities. *The Prince* was presented to the Medici ruler probably in 1516, the same year Erasmus published his treatise *On the Education of a Prince*. Resembling Erasmus in the depth of learning, excellence of style, and variety of his writings, Machiavelli was editor of the classics, historian, poet, dramatist, and political theorist. Both men were scholars, committed to bringing the lessons of classical and recent history to bear on contemporary issues; they both opposed superstition in the Church and saw humans as engaged in an unceasing pursuit of folly. Machiavelli described *The Prince* as presenting "useful" facts based on history and disdained the advice of Erasmus and his clerical predecessors as "fantasies" based on speculation.[14]

---

[13]Adams, 94.
[14]Niccolo Machiavelli, *The Prince*, eds. Quentin Skinner and Russell Price (1988), 55. Skinner, 181-2 argues that Machiavelli drew upon a long tradition of political thought and that his originality was in the value of class conflict or faction and divorcing *virtù* from Christian virtues. Harvey Mansfield, *Machiavelli's Virtue* (1996), 200 agrees with the anti-Christian emphasis but

Machiavelli opposed virtually everything Erasmus recommended as policy for a prince. Erasmus sought for his prince to be a peacemaker. Machiavelli's prince "should have no other objective and no other concern, nor occupy himself with anything else except war and its methods and practices."[15] Erasmus opposed hunting because it created a warlike disposition; Machiavelli wanted the prince in peacetime to be engaged in hunting so as to harden himself for war. Machiavelli esteemed as heroes Cyrus the Persian, Alexander the Great, and Moses because they were war leaders who created nations. Erasmus sought to imitate the peaceful Jesus of Nazareth; Machiavelli wanted his prince to be like David. Erasmus' prince sought to be a good Christian; Machiavelli's leader sought the reputation of a Christian, could even be a good Christian, but only insofar as it served his political purposes. For a prince, piety, like morality and cruelty, was the means to a higher goal and should be used or neglected according to "necessity." Pope Julius II's warlike campaigns appalled Erasmus; Machiavelli admired the audacity and success of Julius. In 1515 with a new Medici ruler of Florence and a newly elected Medici as Pope Leo X (the successor to Julius), Machiavelli hoped that the combination of Church and state could lead to a unified Italy prepared to do battle against the barbarian French, Germans, and Spanish.

The contrast between Erasmus and Machiavelli resulted from many differences: a monk versus a diplomat, a strict Catholic and a lax one, a scholar-moralist who put Christian duty first against a scholar-observer who had watched success and failure firsthand. Most important, Erasmus most of his life dwelt in strong states with secure dynasties, while Machiavelli's laboratory was an Italy overrun by foreign armies.

In the late fifteenth century, Italy was divided among Venice, Florence, Milan, Naples, and Rome including the papal domains. These states' constant

---

sees *virtú* as involving acquisition and necessity with a successful end serving to justify any means. In all his writings, Machiavelli never uses terms like soul, natural law, or natural right.
[15]Ibid., 51-52. For general information on the context of *The Prince*, in relation to all of Machiavelli's works, see Sebastian De Grazia, *Machiavelli in Hell* (1989). A recently proposed

squabbles preserved an order through balance of power diplomacy aimed at preventing any one of them from obtaining hegemony. Then, beginning in 1494 with a French invasion, the Spanish, Germans, and French fought over and occupied Italy's weakened small states. Machiavelli had represented republican Florence at the courts of the Holy Roman Emperor and France and had observed the attempt of Pope Alexander VI and his son Caesare Borgia to create a powerful state controlling all of central Italy. Borgia, by a combination of ruthlessness and shrewdness, had nearly succeeded before the death of his father and his own illness at the same time brought his downfall. Fate or *fortuna* rather than the providence of God or punishment for sin doomed Caesare Borgia.[16] Machiavelli hoped that the right combination of actions, fortune, and necessity would allow the de Medici to succeed where Borgia had failed. *The Prince* would provide a blueprint for a new ruler of a new territory.

Machiavelli's view of man (not women) was as pessimistic as Augustine's. Men are "ungrateful," "dissembling," "avoiders of danger," "eager for gain," "excessively self-interested," "treacherous," "naive," and "gullible."[17] The passions of men can be controlled through habits, laws, religion, and fear. The prince should be prepared to use all of these, to appeal to his subjects' noble as well as base aspirations. All cities or kingdoms divided into two groups: the nobles who wanted to tyrannize and oppress the people, and the people who did not want to be dominated or exploited. The ruler had to satisfy and control both of these groups through two methods: good laws (or order) and good armies. Both were necessary to restrain people, because the Italians at present were "corrupt" and "effeminate" and could be restrained only by fear - fear of God, fear of laws, fear of the ruler. The first requisite for a successful state everywhere, but

---

theory sees *The Prince* as satire; if so, Machiavelli was too clever because for 500 years the public and scholars misinterpreted the work.

[16]Augustine in the *City of God* argued that making events determined by the god *fortuna* denied the providence of God. Machiavelli and Italian humanists initially viewed man as having the power to change events: fortune favors the brave. Skinner, I, 91-9; Mansfield, 18, 189-90.

[17]*The Prince and the Discourses* (1950), 9, 13, 19, 22, 61, 64-66; DeGrazia, *Machiavelli in Hell*, 87.

particularly in Italy, was not good laws but a good army, because a weak ruler like a weak state would soon be conquered. All neighboring states were potential enemies.

Internal and external enemies endangered the prince. If the internal faction prevailed, the result was anarchy; if the external opponent dominated, the result was conquest, destruction, and the loss of freedom. For Machiavelli, as for Cicero, no state would willingly commit suicide. The prince, whose welfare was tied to that of the state, had as his primary responsibility to gain and protect power by whatever means suited the time. Machiavelli did not delight in evil; he strongly condemned unnecessary cruelty in the prince and evil in the people. Evil in the people must be restrained. The best situation for a strong prince was to be loved by a virtuous people; here, the prince could appear to be moral. Still, respect tinged with fear gave more security than love, and respect could be gained by power - even power tinged with harshness.

History proved that there were only three possible conditions for a state: a dangerous peace, war, worse than war (loss of freedom, conquest). A long peace weakened a state by allowing evil characteristics of men to flourish that would result either in factions or a softness that made them unwilling to fight. Because peace was risky did not mean that war should be begun for frivolous reasons, because wars brought a multitude of ills, and success in battle depended upon skill and luck. For Machiavelli a constant readiness was the only way to postpone war, and the most effective fighting force was an infantry of citizens. Mercenary troops were dangerous because they did not have the welfare of the state at heart, so they preferred maneuver to battle. If they should succeed, their power could threaten the existence of the government. Italy had lost its freedom because of its reliance upon mercenaries.[18]

---

[18]Many Italian humanists disliked mercenaries. Machiavelli believed citizen soldiers to be more willing to risk their lives in a total battle. It is an example of his admiration for republican Rome, but the policy failed when used for Florence. Contemporaries hired professional soldiers because being an expert helped infantrymen in using the new weapons of war. C.C. Bayley, *War and Society in Renaissance Florence* (1961), 240-276.

For Machiavelli, the Just War was a necessary war - that is, without a war the situation would worsen and threaten the existence of the state. Yet at times Machiavelli wrote that to be healthy the state must continually expand. His state must be in constant activity; incessant striving kept fit the individual, the state, and the civilization. Like Plato, Machiavelli saw the ultimate cause of war in the insatiable desire of men for more goods, power, and fame. Peace was only a nonviolent war by fraud. So war was an inescapable part of civilization.

Before beginning a war, the prince plus his wise advisers should calculate their power and that of their adversaries and determine the wisdom of the war. Diplomacy worked well when it proceeded from strength and decision; temporizing in war or diplomacy because of weakness was a recipe for disaster. A postponed war would in the future become a more dangerous one. The prince should be constantly working to strengthen his state. There was no set formula for success in this endeavor, because the right actions depended upon the character of the prince, his relationship to the nobles and the people, and the nature of the threat. Whether he armed the people, built fortresses, conciliated or executed potential internal rivals varied according to circumstances. But his best security could come through the support of an armed people secure in their property who were not taxed to pay for his extravagances.

Machiavelli's prince did not stay at home in war, but led his armies into battle. Soldiers were unruly and must be controlled; therefore, all military leaders must be harsh. Machiavelli believed that in war men are most bestial. After all, rational men could be controlled by laws without war. So in war Machiavelli's leader must act the beast, to have the shrewdness of the fox and the strength of a lion.

The Prince divorced the *virtú* necessary for political success from Christian virtue, and yet Machiavelli was not irreligious. He believed in heaven and hell and strongly condemned evil in the people and a prince's unnecessary cruelty to the people. God, he asserted, left to humans the ability to shape their lives. The moral reason for the state's existence, and for all of the prince's actions, was the welfare of the citizens. God treasured the political community and the common good.

Since the conversion of Constantine, Christian theologians asserted that the ethics of Jesus and the needs of the state could be reconciled. God's ruling providence controlled happenings in church and state. Machiavelli did not in theory deny the providence of God, but his treatise argued that men and fate shaped destiny with regard to competence but not piety. Too much Christian virtue would weaken the Prince and risk the safety of the people. Within the state, the religious vision prevailed as a pattern of life for the common people. Externally, the international realm was anarchy with the ultimate determiner of survival being the intelligent application of power. The prince had to live by different standards from normal folk, for he must willingly be dishonest, calculating, and harsh for the good of the people. No matter what his tactics, he would be judged a good king (with fame, honor, and *virtù*) if he preserved and strengthened his realm and a bad king if he jeopardized its survival.[19]

Protestant Just War: Luther

The sixteenth-century Protestant Reformation destroyed the religious unity of western European Christianity, but the leaders associated with the churches linked to the state and requiring religious unity - Lutherans, Calvinists, and Anglicans - continued to approach war using categories derived from medieval Just War traditions. Martin Luther (1483-1546) became the single most important figure in creating a Protestant tradition of Just War theory.

Luther, an Augustinian monk and professor of biblical theology at the German University of Wittenberg, attempted to reform the Roman Catholic Church with the publication of his ninety-five theses or debating topics in 1517. Although continuing to think of himself as a Catholic reformer, Luther by 1519 diverged from Roman Catholic doctrine on the nature of grace, sacraments, church,

---

[19]Mansfield, 26-27. Mansfield argues that for Machiavelli, religion was a "weakness that can give strength, but only if it is well used by a prince." Religion sanctifies the outcome as a good because ordained by God.

priesthood, the papacy, and monasticism. Luther did not treat political theory as a discipline separate from theology. Rather, his political insights grew out of his view of Christian life and changed in response to rapidly changing political situations caused in part by the Reformation.[20]

Luther, whose portrayal of Christian life derived from an Augustinian interpretation of St. Paul, saw humans as so flawed by original sin that they could be saved only by God's free and merciful act of bestowing grace; no work of a person earned or merited salvation. The wiping out of sin or justification occurred when persons responded in faith to God's act of atonement through the sacrifice of Christ on the cross. God accepted and imputed Christ's righeousness to them and through grace created a new person in unity with Christ. God's loving act saved the person, but he or she remained flawed until death, so that the person in this life remained both saint and sinner.

God instituted government to restrain sinners who otherwise would act like beasts and devour each other. In order to prevent anarchy that would destroy the good of society, God gave natural law - which Luther summarized as the Ten Commandments, golden rule, and Jesus' command to love God and love neighbor - and the faculty of reason for the guidance of government. No form of government was divine, and there could be no Christian state. Government had limited functions: to bring order and to preserve internal peace necessary for the functioning of the Church. However, the magistrate's authority stopped at the church door because government could not lead men to salvation. After disorder erupted within the churches, Luther allowed the prince, not in his role as prince but as a Christian layman, to bring order as an interim bishop. Luther accepted the rule of a prince and never discussed whether monarchy was better than

---

[20]Thompson Cargill, *The Political Thought of Martin Luther* (1984). The most readable biography remains Roland H. Bainton, *Here I Stand: A Life of Martin Luther* (1950). Henrich Bornkamm, *Luther's World of Thought* (1958) is a convenient summary of many facets of Luther's theological and social thoughts. A good summary showing how Luther's thought evolved and the differences in interpretation is in Erwin Iserloh, Joseph Glazik and Hubert Jedin, *Reformation and Counter Reformation, History of the Church* (1986), V, 213-224.

aristocracy or democracy. He showed little understanding of the emergent sovereign territorial entity we call the state, concentrating instead upon the personal qualities of the leader.

Without government to secure peace and order, Christians would be like sheep led to slaughter. In one sense the true Christian was a free person above government, delivered through grace from bondage to outward law to become a loving servant to all. Yet because he or she was still a sinner and a minority in the society, God ordained government to restrain the corrupt actions of the individual and of the majority. All Christians lived in God's two realms: a physical kingdom ruled by force and a spiritual kingdom ruled by love.

The spiritual kingdom, whose physical manifestation was the Church, rested on free consent and had no power of outward coercion. The Church as a gathering of the faithful existed to proclaim the Word of God through preaching and sacraments; the magistrate had no power here.[21] Until the mid-1520's, Luther argued that there should be no persecution for heresy because religion was an inward disposition, but he always insisted that natural law required the magistrate to stop blasphemy. As he grew older, his definition of blasphemy expanded to include both Roman Catholics and Anabaptists.

Because the state preserved the necessary order, it was a good and should be preserved, even if force was required internally to restrain evil persons and externally to deter aggressors. These were essentially the same act, the only difference being that one occurred inside and the other outside the realm. So for Luther, the magistrate waged war to punish the aggressor's sin. War was a product as well as a symptom of sin.

God required all to serve Him in their place, whether magistrate, maid, butcher, lawyer, or soldier. Luther's priesthood of all believers proclaimed that

---

[21]The basic themes of Luther are spelled out in treatises published in 1520, "Open Letter to the German Nobility," "Babylonian Captivity of the Church," and "Treatise on Christian Liberty" and "On Secular Authority, To What Extent It should be Obeyed," in *Works of Martin Luther*, II, III, eds., C. M. Jacobs and Albert Steinhaeuser, (1915), (1930).

because God's grace saved men and women, their spiritual worth was equal. Priests and monks did not have a higher calling. Though priests still did not become soldiers, there was no taint to being in the military. The soldier's calling was to serve God while making war. A Christian as a child of grace living in God's kingdom on earth had nothing to do with war, but the Christian as sinner living on earth also had a calling ordained by God through His natural law. In his calling the person obeyed natural law, and natural law allowed coercion. So at the request of the magistrate, a Christian whose calling was a soldier could pick up the sword to protect his fellow citizen. That his profession involved killing was irrelevant. Luther spelled out his understanding of war in a treatise that positively answered his question: "Can a Soldier be Saved?"[22] The necessity of right intent, so emphasized by Aquinas, played little role, probably because Luther insisted that no work done by natural man merited salvation. Still, in his overall conclusions linking the military to natural law, seeing a war as analogous to a judicial punishment, and justifying a Christian's fighting as a necessary way of preserving peace, Luther's doctrine echoed Augustine and Aquinas. Luther even cited the same scriptural passages from the New Testament used by Augustine and the scholastics.

Luther's doctrine of the two realms meant that the Church did not have political authority, and that the prince derived his authority directly from the will of God, not through the Church. After being excommunicated by the Roman Catholic Church, he broadened his attack upon the papacy, eventually coming to see it as the Antichrist. The devil had inspired the mingling of spiritual and political in the papacy. For Luther there should be no papal states and no religious war. The Church had no authority to proclaim or wage a crusade, and the Emperor had no religious obligation to fight the Turks. If, however, the Turks invaded the Emperor's realm, he had an obligation to defend his subjects.

---

[22]Reprinted in Holmes, 141-64. Luther's major treatises on war are "The Admonition to Peace: A Reply to the Twelve Articles of the Peasants in Swabia," (1525), "Against the Robbing and

Luther denied categorically the right of revolution for any reason. God placed the king on the throne. Though he recognized that a wise prince "is a rare bird in heaven"[23] and that monarchs often became tyrants, Luther - basing his conclusions on Paul's demand to be subject to the "powers that be" - denied any right of rebellion. God would punish a tyrant, and the subject's duty was to accept suffering. Still, Luther did not allow the king to define right and wrong. That was the Church's prerogative, and Luther defended and often exercised the priest's right of criticizing the actions of princes. The subject's right of resistance was limited to passive disobedience. That is, he should not obey a commandment against God, no matter what.

Luther applied passive disobedience to the issue of war. If the king embarked upon an unjust war, a soldier who knew that the king did wrong should not serve. He had no right to take action against the unjust war even if the king punished his passivity. Luther recognized the right of what has come to be known as selective conscientious objection. That is, that the subject should willingly participate only in a Just War. If the subject did not know whether the war was just, he should serve, trusting that God would punish the king, not the soldier, for the fault.

Except for outlawing the crusade, Luther's doctrine of just cause echoed earlier formulations. A war for self-defense among equals was permissible; an aggressive war was immoral; a war of inferior versus superior was also unjust. "A rebellious nobleman deserves to have his head cut off just as much as a rebellious peasant." The prince had a duty to wage war against rebels, and he should do so without mercy. For the prince here acted for God, and rebellion was a sinful defiance of God's anointed. When in 1524 peasants rose in rebellion against the German nobility, Luther - who had earlier condemned the authorities' treatment of the peasants - told the authorities to be prepared to show no mercy but to "hew,

---

Murdering Hordes of Peasants" (1525), "Whether Soldiers, too, Can be Saved" (1526), and "On War Against the Turk" (1529) in *The Works of Martin Luther* (1930), III, IV.
[23]Luther, "Secular Authority: To What Extent It Should Be Obeyed," III, 184, 258, 265.

stab, slay, and lay about him as though among mad dogs." "For rebellion is a crime that deserves neither court nor mercy."[24] When criticized, Luther insisted that he was addressing a Christian magistrate who would spare the innocent but bring justice to the hardened rebel.

Luther originated what would later be called the first shot tradition, a major change in Just War theory. Aquinas, Suarez, and Grotius allowed a preventive war to forestall an attack. By contrast, Luther argued that because all aggressive war was evil, the only legitimate war was in self-defense. To determine whether the war was aggressive or in self-defense: see who took up arms first. Preventive or anticipatory war was unjust war. Waiting for the aggressor to begin the war would not lead to defeat, because God in his providence would punish him. Luther, in essence, made Just War theory more legalistic by simplifying what self-defense meant. The implication to his position was that there was a radical difference between every other act a monarch could take against his enemy and war. No action except aggressive war could justify taking up arms.

The threat from Anabaptists and the papacy caused Luther to modify his views on religious war. He argued that both Anabaptists and the papacy committed blasphemy, and, therefore deserved to be suppressed. Moreover, after the Catholic Holy Roman Emperor mobilized his forces against the Lutherans, Luther in 1530 reconsidered his position whether disobedience of inferior to superior magistrate might be allowable. For example, the German electors were also powers ordained by God with a responsibility of preserving a just order. The issue, as Luther now re-defined it, was whether the Emperor in attacking the Protestants was becoming the servant of the Pope and, thereby, the devil's agent. In this case resisting the evil of the Antichrist might be allowable.[25]

---

[24]Luther, "An Open Letter Concerning the Hard Book Against the Peasants," IV, 269, 278.
[25]"Dr. Martin Luther's Warning To His Dear German People," in Luther's Works, XLVII, 19, 30, 33-35. Quenton Skinner, *Foundation of Modern Political Thought, II, The Reformation*, 194-207, argues that Lutherans endorsed the idea of resistance to magistrates earlier than the Calvinists and utilized ideas of constitutionalism and private law first developed by the canonists and conciliarists and later used by Calvinists.

Even though Luther began with categories derived from Augustine and Thomas Aquinas, his final conclusions differed markedly from earlier Just War theories. In essence he strengthened absolutism by a denial of the authority of the Church over the monarch, reluctant acquiescence in the prince's right to bring order into the Church, and refusal to allow any rebellion. His doctrines of calling of a soldier, separation of the realm of the Christian from that of the citizen, and the natural-law basis of self-defense legitimated war. Yet his affirming of selective conscientious objection, endorsing passive disobedience, and denouncing of aggression kept an anti-war tradition alive in Protestantism. His downplaying of right intent and emphasis upon the first shot allowed a more legalistic interpretation of Just War theory to emerge. Even before Luther's death, Protestant princes latched onto his rationale for war while ignoring his paeans to peace, strictures about tyranny, and bemoaning of the evils of war.

Neither Luther nor his Calvinist successors accepted religious disunity within the state. They assumed that there would be one state and one religion and that religious disunity would lead to political weakness. With what seems today to be incredible naïveté, they also asserted that all right-thinking people would come to the same interpretation of scripture and accept identical theological dogmas as authoritative. For the next century, countries willingly waged war for these axioms. Unfortunately for the peace of Europe, religious unity was elusive, and in Germany, Low Countries, France, and England, the ruler's religion might differ from that of some portion of his subjects. Luther died without having to confront the issue of an idolatrous ruler directly. Members of the Reformed or Calvinist persuasion, because they were a minority with Catholic monarchs in France, the Netherlands, and Scotland, created a theory of justifiable revolution and debated the issue of assassination of a ruler.

Calvinism and Rebellion

The Reformed justification of resistance to the prince came about because of historical circumstances, not because of lack of reverence for established authority. The Reformed Churches began in the cities just over the French border

- Zurich, Geneva, Basel, and Strasbourg - spread from there to southern France, Holland, Scotland, and eventually England and New England. Ulrich Zwingli, the initial leader of the Reformed movement, was killed in 1531 when as chaplain he accompanied troops in battle.

John Calvin (1509-1564) became the primary codifier of the Reformed traditions. Calvin, a Frenchman educated in the classics and law, sought at first to reform the Roman Catholic Church from within but in 1534 became a Protestant, publishing the *Institutes of the Christian Religion*, a compendium of his theology, that he expanded in several later editions. In 1536 while visiting Geneva, he was asked to stay first as lecturer and then as minister, and he remained there, except for one three-year interval of exile, until his death. Calvin in Geneva became a decisive voice in state affairs, yet he was only one of many ministers in the city, never held political office, and always insisted on a separation of function between minister and magistrate. His program of reform depended upon the support of the elected Town Council. Geneva's Town Council listened to Calvin and followed his program of strict regulations; only in this limited sense can Geneva be termed a theocracy. Certainly it became a model for Reformed Protestants everywhere.

Calvin, like Luther, subordinated political theory to theology. Both demanded religious uniformity in the state, separated functions of Church and state, and sought for autonomy of the Church. Unlike Luther, Calvin gave a positive role in fostering the correct worship of God to the magistrate. The conduct of kings of Israel in reforming Jewish practices served as a role model for the actions of princes in encouraging the Church. Both men saw the magistrate as ordained by God, detested rebellion, and believed God rather than men should punish unjust rulers. Yet as the hostility of the king of France to the Protestants in his realm grew, Calvin added a justification to resist a tyrannical king. In the last revision of the *Institutes*, written in 1559, allowed a right of resistance to the "fierce licentiousness of kings" to inferior magistrates, but not the people.[26] Using

---

[26]John Calvin, *Institutes of the Christian Religion*, II, ed. John T. McNeill; trans. Ford Lewis Battles (1960). Denis Crouzet, "Calvinism and the Uses of the Political and Religious (France,

examples of "ephors" from Sparta and tribunes from Rome (both elected officials), Calvin declared that non-sovereign magistrates had the duty to defend the "freedom of the people" against kings who "violently fall upon and assault the lowly common people." Note that the authorization is for a defensive struggle, only magistrates can resist, and the word religion is not mentioned. However, Calvin's exegesis of the book of Kings II recounted as an example Jehu, whom God commissioned to kill King Joram and his mother Queen Jezebel by treachery because of their idolatry.

In the debate that accompanied the religious wars, Calvinist theologians allowed the right of rebellion on two grounds. One was constitutional: the king in his coronation oath made certain promises. If he violated them he could be deposed. The second was that, historically kingship originated for the sake of the people. If the king sought to foster false religion or to persecute true religion, then he had violated the original contract or covenant and could be deposed. Calvinists used the first provision in the Ten Commandments that forbade worshipping false gods against Catholic monarchs in France and Scotland and the Protestant king of England.

Calvinists in France were a minority attempting to gain support from the king and moderate Catholics. So they stressed the traditional and natural law justifications for limited resistance. In Scotland, where the Reformers had mass support, theologians drew more radical conclusions. A king's coronation oath had obligations to the people, and they, not just the magistrates, had the right to resist. And the potential fault was not just over false religion, but could be purely political. A king was a minister to serve the people, who could revoke his covenant after he violated natural rights. The king then became a private citizen,

ca. 1560-ca. 1572)" in *Reformation, Revolt, and Civil War in France and the Netherlands 1555-1585* (1999), 99-103.

and an individual had a right of self-defense. Only a few took the next step and granted to a person the right to assassinate a king.[27]

Nonresistance: The Anabaptists

The Anabaptists attempted to found a church embodying Erasmus' call for a recreation of the primitive church, obedience to the strict mandates of the *Bible*, imitation of Christ, and nonresistance. However, they repudiated Erasmus' commitment to reform within the Roman Catholic Church and also separated from the new state-linked Lutheran and Calvinist churches. Scholars label the Anabaptists as the Radical Reformation or a third force of the Protestant Reformation and see them as continuing selected Protestant emphases along with the purist and other-worldly impulses of medieval heretical groups like the Waldensians, Albigensians, and Czech Brethren. Like these groups, there was a strong lay component, anti-clericalism, and willingness to defy political-religious authorities at the cost of lives. A minority wherever they lived, the Anabaptists experienced persecution by those who saw them as a threat to the established pattern of church and society. Only once did the Anabaptists respond to force with force. Otherwise, they sought peace and accepted martyrdom as the price of discipleship.[28]

The Anabaptist movement first gained prominence during a public debate in 1524 in Zurich, Switzerland, over the baptism of infants. The Anabaptists or re-baptizers insisted that only adults, who understood the implications of faith for conduct, should be baptized because infant baptism was not scriptural and had no validity. Re-baptism was also the visible sign of a revolutionary doctrine of the church. The Anabaptist churches neither took responsibility for the whole

---

[27] Quenton Skinner, *A History of Political Theory*, II, 218, 228-232, 236, 310, 325-335, 341.

[28] James Stayer, *Anabaptists and the Sword* (1972) and "Anabaptists and the Sword Revisited," in *The Pacifist Impulse in Historical Perspective* (1996) should be contrasted with John Howard Yoder, "Anabaptists and the Sword Revisited: Systematic Historiography and Undogmatic Nonresistants," *Zeitschrift für Kirchengeschichte*, 85(1974), 270-83 and "Christian Attitudes to War, Peace, and Revolution: A Companion to Bainton, 165-201. Putting the varieties of Anabaptist teachings on war into a wider context are Peter Williams, *The Radical Reformation* (1962), and Claus-Peter Clasen, *Anabaptism: A Social History* (1972).

society nor supported the state. They advocated a free or believers church joined by adults on a voluntary basis.

Anabaptists argued that using force in religious matters destroyed truth. All authority came from the *Bible* through the Holy Spirit, which created a unity and community among believers. A member who disrupted or violated church teachings and refused to accept admonition could be opposed only through use of the ban or shunning. That is, the recalcitrant member, after being excommunicated, would be ignored, and even his family would refuse to speak to the person or do business with him. Isolation from the people of God should foster repentance, but there would be no physical coercion. Christians gained and retained authority through an inward spiritual experience expressed in surrender to the will of God.[29]

The Anabaptists also opposed the Constantinian linkage of Church and state that legitimated Christian war. The Anabaptist church neither took responsibility for the whole society nor supported the state. They agreed that magistrates might use force in civil society against lawbreakers, could even wage war. However, Anabaptists insisted that such activity was not Christ-like and so could not be engaged in or supported by followers of Christ. The two swords referred to incompatible and separate realms. Defending one's neighbor with the sword destroyed true Christianity: killing was not love. Augustine had argued that defending one's neighbor even in war showed Christian love, insisting that even in war death was not the ultimate evil because heaven was humans' true home, the only realm of true peace. Anabaptists agreed that death was not the ultimate evil and that heaven was a Christian's destination. However, Christ accepted crucifixion rather than fighting, so in imitation of Christ the Anabaptists embraced nonresistance, even at the cost of their lives.

---

[29]The most famous statement of Anabaptist pacifism is the Schleitheim Confession (1527) reprinted in Hans Hillerbrand, ed., *The Protestant Reformation* (1968), 129-37.

Diversity characterized the Anabaptists from the beginnings.[30] There was no centralized authority or common creed or one dominant personality who shaped the movement. Humble men and women secretly proselytizing faced constant persecution of imprisonment, torture and at worst hanging, drowning, or burning at the stake.[31] Anabaptists obeyed the magistrate when the law did not violate Christianity. They saw themselves as subjects and obeyed the authorities, except when taking oaths, which they saw as contrary to Jesus who said, "Do not swear at all" (Matthew 5:33).

For a few Rhineland Anabaptists, the Peasants' Rebellion, persecution, turmoil, and famine that characterized life in the 1530s signified the time of troubles before the end of the world. Christ or the Archangel Michael would soon return to lead his oppressed followers in a war against Antichrist. At a town of Münster in what is now Germany in 1534, apocalyptic Anabaptists gained control and sought to help Christ extirpate evil and inaugurate the millennium. When Catholics and Protestants laid siege (both hated militant Anabaptists), the Münster Anabaptists defended themselves, drove out opponents, instituted communism, and practiced polygamy - in imitation of Old Testament patriarchs. The orthodox Christians overran the town, took bloody reprisals on the Anabaptists, and restored order. During the next two hundred years most Protestants and Catholics used Münsterite as a smear word almost synonymous with Anabaptist.[32]

---

[30]Just who was an Anabaptist is a matter of some debate. Luther lumped the peasants who revolted in 1526, Anabaptists, and Thomas Muntzer as fanatics (*Schwarmer*). Since Muntzer never criticized infant baptism and did not advocate rebaptism, he should be viewed as an apocalyptic Protestant rather than as an Anabaptist. The peasants, who were joined by many urban dwellers, had been restive for some time and applied Luther's critique of the power of the papacy and Church to the nobles. Erwin Iserloh, *Reformation and Counter Reformation. History of the Church*, V, 116, 128-143,

[31]J. van Braght Thielemen, *The Bloody Theater, or, The Martyr's Mirror* (1660), tr. Joseph Sohn, reprinted 1975 contains the stories of the martyrs. Brad Gregory, *Salvation at Stake: Christian Martyrdom in Early Modern Europe* (1999) compares Protestant, Catholic, and Anabaptist views of martyrdom. Anabaptists debated whether there was a distinction between crucial and less important beliefs that a person should be prepared to renounce to avoid martyrdom. Many recanted. Most persecution ended after 1576.

[32]Other Anabaptists never saw the Münsterites as martyrs, but often saw rulers as persecutors and thought the only hope was for an apocalypse. Gregory, 216-17, 230.

After the Münster debacle, most Anabaptists repudiated taking up the sword for any reason. Menno Symons gathered scattered congregations of Swiss and German Anabaptists into a sect dedicated to nonresistance, biblical authority, and separation from the world. Within a close-knit church community, Mennonites cultivated an intense biblically based piety and simple lifestyle. Barred from learned occupations, many Mennonites engaged in trade and generally prospered. By contrast, the Hutterites, another Anabaptist sect, accepted as normative the description in Acts when individuals in the early Church gave up private property. So the Hutterites practiced a form of communism and found refuge on the estates of Austrian noblemen who valued their hard work and quiet existence. The Anabaptist vision of pacifism was almost monastic. That is, nonresistance was a way of life for the select few who elected to follow Christ.

After an early controversial existence in which they attempted to spread their beliefs throughout Europe, Anabaptists retreated from active confrontation with the world in an attempt to preserve sectarian purity. Mennonites settled in Holland and others in eastern Europe; after persecution at the end of the seventeenth century, some left Switzerland to seek refuge in Pennsylvania. Hutterites created communities on the estates of Austrian nobles until, in the nineteenth century, they migrated to America and Canada.

Catholic Just War Theory: Suarez

Just War theories survived the Catholic and Protestant Reformations, religious wars, and absolutist monarchies because their adherents sought to reform rather than to abolish state sponsored fighting. As in the Middle Ages, Just War theorists continued to outlaw certain kinds of violence, to legitimate other causes of war, and to limit practices in war. Today, most striking are not the differences but the similarities of Luther, Calvin, Vitoria, and Saurez. That agreement later allowed Hugo Grotius and natural-law theorists to downplay the roles of revealed religion in creating international law.

Francisco Suarez (1561-1617) became the most influential Jesuit theologian and legal commentator of the seventeenth century, serving as advisor to the pope and to the king of Spain. His discussion of the law of war was a part of the charity section of a *Work on the Theological Virtues: Faith, Hope and Charity.* Suarez's studies of war used familiar categories as normative: the revealed law of God, the natural law, and the laws of peoples or customary law. He was learned in, but not a slave to, the writings of the Church fathers, Augustine, and Aquinas, as well as canon and Roman laws. In form his treatises resembled the scholastics; that is, he summarized the reasoning of earlier and contemporary Just War writers, presented his own conclusions on controversial issues, and showed why his views were congruent with natural law and Christian charity.

For Suarez the issue was not war or Christian peace, but war against a false peace that destroyed the good of the people. God had placed upon the prince an obligation to maintain the safety of his realm against external enemies. Only a sovereign, as a ruler from whose decisions there was no appeal, could proclaim a Just War. The prince had an obligation to consult with his advisers, and God would hold both parties responsible for their decision. (Their liability was even greater than that of a priest who exhorted soldiers to fight for valor and justice, but who need not make inquiry into the justice of the war.) Suarez knew that often neither the prince nor his advisers could be absolutely certain of the justice of their cause, and so he devoted considerable space to the problem of doubt. In truly doubtful situations, the wise course was to avoid war.

A Just War could begin when the prince, after an impartial investigation, concluded that the other king had committed a substantial fault. He then had to offer the errant ruler a chance to make redress. Suarez recognized the dangers, but saw few alternatives, of having the prince be both plaintiff and judge. He hoped that in doubtful cases the disputants would submit to arbitration from foreign judges of the Church, but thought this unlikely given most princes' suspicions of foreign authorities. Because war brought many evils, the presumption was for peace, and war should be begun only in case of necessity.

Suarez's categories for a Just War derived from natural law, not revealed religion. Neither religious differences, idolatry, nor a desire for wealth, glory, and power was a legitimate cause of war. However, a prince leading a faithful people to idolatry did commit a fault allowing war. Just causes were a significant injustice, a "molestation," a seizure of property and refusal to restore it, denial of common rights in trade or transit, and "grave injury to reputation or honor" -- most of which Cicero had stated long before. A war of self-defense "to hold enemies in check" was always just, and an "aggressive" or preventive war could also be just; that is, a preemptive war could begin when the prince learned that the opponent was preparing to initiate war against him.[33]

Just War theory allowed a right of intervention to support one's allies if an enemy committed a substantial fault against them. Suarez insisted that if the ally intended to accept the fault without armed resistance, there was no right for a third party to intervene. Only if the ally were prepared to fight could another nation intercede on its behalf.

Suarez's criteria for a Just War - ostensibly the same as Aquinas' - placed far greater emphasis upon weighing of evidence, and the decision was far more legalistic. The same outward emphasis characterized Suarez's discussion of the conduct of soldiers. He never discussed the motives of soldiers or why they fought, emphasizing instead conduct during the war (showing courage, not fleeing), treatment of civilians during and captives after a war, and legitimate booty.

Proportionality, implicit in earlier theories, now received additional significance. The prince in deciding upon war must consider the welfare of the people. Even if success seemed likely, the prince had to calculate the destruction of the war against the fault. If the cost of vindication in lives or money or in the "communal welfare" was disproportionate to the evil done or to the gain to be achieved, the prince should not go to war.[34] The Catholic theologian Cajetan (1469-1534) insisted that the prince had to be certain of victory; Suarez said such confidence was impossible, but there had to be a probability of success.

---

[33]Francisco Suarez, "A Work on the Three Theological Virtues: Faith, Hope, and Charity," (1621) in *Selections from Three Works* (1944), 815-21.
[34]Ibid., 819, 821.

What if, after the prince had issued a public proclamation of war, an individual had doubts? Both advisers and generals, if asked by the king, must make diligent inquiry of the claims of both sides. If they determined that the war was wrong, they should not fight. Neither nobles nor generals need make such an investigation if the prince did not request it, but a general might be obligated by Christian charity to do so in order to warn the monarch. Mercenary troops (which Suarez did not condemn) had an obligation not to fight for any unjust side. The officers of mercenary troops should conduct an investigation before selling their services to a monarch. A common soldier who was ignorant as to whether the war was just need not make inquiry. But if he doubted the facts in dispute, he should consult prudent men. If then, he still was uncertain, he should trust the prince and serve. The prince had responsibility for the justice of the war, and only the clearest evidence allowed a man to disobey the ruler. Suarez never discussed the consequences of refusing to fight in a war proclaimed just by the monarch. Still, allowing generals, mercenaries, and soldiers to investigate and base their actions on their conclusions in doubtful cases opened the door to the doctrine of selective conscientious objection. Suarez defended the right or obligation for an individual who would serve in a Just War to refuse to fight in an unjust war.

Suarez had read Francisco de Vitoria's analysis of Spain's conquest of the West Indies. Since the Middle Ages, popes as successors to Peter had claimed the pastoral right to send missionaries to heathen and Muslim countries. Persecution of missionaries in these lands gave the papacy the right to proclaim a crusade, not to convert the inhabitants but to protect the missionaries so that the heathen could hear the gospel and freely choose Christianity. Vitoria insisted that neither pope nor emperor had any jurisdiction in the New World and that Spain had no right by virtue of religion nor superior civilization to conquer the Indians, who according to natural law exercised domination over land and people.

The Indians were also required to obey natural law; specifically, to allow free travel and free trade. The Spanish claimed a natural right to visit the West Indies and to establish forts or settlements for trading. If the Indians attacked, the

Spanish had a natural right to self-protection - even if that required conquest of the islands. Vitoria argued that a Spanish war against the Indians should be conducted with mildness, because of the ignorance of the natives. Vitoria's treatise could be read as an indictment of Spanish practices and defense of the conquest of the New World. Just War theory could rationalize the European rule of the Americas.[35]

In a passing comment, Vitoria compared the ignorance of the Indians to that of the French in denying the Emperor a right to the lands of Burgundy. Vitoria implied that, because of ignorance, both sides could be fighting a Just War. Vitoria's caveat had in practice become the standard in Europe. Unlike Vitoria, Suarez insisted that there could not be two just sides in a war and, that if the situation was so doubtful, there should not be a war and the two monarchs should seek a compromise. Yet he also recognized that both sides could believe themselves in the right, and each would follow the precepts of Just War.

The doctrine of non-combatant immunity was already firmly implanted in Just War theories. Suarez listed as "innocent" women, children, the sick, old, and clergy.[36] Such people should not be attacked or plundered. However, there were exceptions. Innocents in a city under siege would undoubtedly suffer. Suarez enunciated what has come to be known as the law of double effect. That is, if the goal was to take the city and some civilians were hurt, that was a permissible though regrettable action. But if the primary goal was to hurt civilians, that was wrong.

The victor in a just war could take many forms of compensation. An evil leader could be executed, or the enemy might pay reparations for the original evil plus the costs of the war. Such reparations should come from the leaders, but if

---

[35]Vitoria quoted in Holmes, 130-135; James Muldoon, *Popes, Lawyers, and Infidels: Popes, Lawyers, and Infidels* (1979) recounts the history of the Catholic Church's dealings with outsiders from Innocent III to the Spanish debates. James Johnson, *Ideology, Reason, and the Limitation of War: Religious and Secular Concepts 1200-1740* (1975), and *Just War Tradition and the Restraint of War: A Moral and Historical Inquiry* (1981) show the transition from a right and wrong side in war to the acceptance of kings' right to make wars in which both sides were treated equally.

these proved insufficient, both permanent and moveable goods from civilians could be taken. The prince was not to enslave captives, that would be against Christianity but not natural law, or to leave the citizens without the means to subsist. Legitimate spoils taken by soldiers constituted part of their pay and would not count as part of the reparations. "A prince who has obtained a just victory may do everything with the property of the enemy that is essential to the preservation of an undisturbed peace in the future, provided that he spare the lives of the enemies."[37] In reparations as in the conduct of war, proportionality was crucial. The victory must weigh the seriousness of the fault, the cost of the war, the involvement of the citizens in helping the unjust effort.

Suarez did not recognize the right of a faction to commit sedition or foment revolution against a prince. If the kingdom divided into two forces, justice lay with the prince. However, if a prince became a tyrant, the entire kingdom could legitimately rise up together and defend themselves. The rationale was that a tyrant prince had already committed war against his people and there was an inherent right of self-defense.

Hugo Grotius and International Law

Hugo Grotius (1583-1645) in the nineteenth century gained a reputation as the father of international law. Now scholars recognize the long gestation period for this law and the contributions of many thinkers, several of whom have been previously discussed in this book. Grotius' achievement was to have summarized the insights of many earlier writers about Just War theories and to have attempted to provide a systematic summary of dealings among states. *The Law of War and Peace,* printed in 1625, had an immense intellectual impact, being reprinted in forty-five Latin editions before 1800 and translated into English, French, German, and Dutch. Whether Grotius actually restrained the causes and reformed the practice of war or made peace more prevalent as he intended remains doubtful. His main accomplishment was to add prestige and coherence to traditional Just

---

[36]Suarez, 845-46.
[37]Ibid., 850.

War theories, ease the transition from a theological to a natural-law system in dealing with what we now term international affairs, and make accessible a codification of allowable practices.

The book's success came from many factors. Grotius, though devout, was not a clergyman and did not bury his thoughts on war in a theological treatise. Rather, he was an erudite lawyer and awed his contemporaries by citations from historians, philosophers, theologians, and soldiers from the biblical, classical, medieval, and modern period. Also, Grotius was a Dutch Protestant at the time of Holland's greatest influence, and he dedicated the book to the French Roman Catholic king. So the book was neither Protestant nor Catholic but reflected Grotius' Erasmus-like desire to end the controversies over religion, a task to which he devoted many years of his life. Suarez used a neo-scholastic form of reasoning and as a Jesuit had not endeared himself to Protestant monarchs by defending the claims of the papacy and justifying tyrannicide for heretic rulers. *The Law of War and Peace,* by contrast, logically organized like a law book, denounced the assassination of rulers, even those who were tyrants, and denied the legitimacy of war over religion - though with several caveats on the dangers from heretics. Grotius died during the Thirty Years War and on the eve of the English Puritan revolution. Many European intellectuals sympathized with Grotius' desire to foster peace or at least to ameliorate the destructive tendencies of war.

When he wrote *The Law of War and Peace,* Grotius had escaped from a Dutch prison (in a chest supposedly filled with books) and was a Protestant living in exile in France with a stipend from the French King. He hoped to be able to return to Holland and resume a diplomatic and scholarly career. Consequently, the ideas of many of the most important and controversial figures of his own time rarely appeared in the lists of sources: Luther, Calvin, and Machiavelli were never quoted; Erasmus, only once, even though he was a hero of Grotius; perhaps because Spanish Jesuits were unpopular in Holland, Suarez was mentioned only four times. By contrast, he cited forty-four different works of Cicero and his *On Duties,* eighty-one times. The antique flavor of Grotius' conclusions added authority because he seemed to be summarizing the wisdom and showing the relevance of classical Greece and Rome.

Finally, the book appealed to European monarchies because of its acceptance of absolutism, denial of the right of rebellion, and ambiguous language caused by Grotius' conflicting norms, since he saw the general customs of war as legally permissible while specifying which practices of war received the sanction of being morally right. Grotius' scholarship and caution forced him to confess that on major issues there were often different interpretations; in practice, such disagreements allowed nations to justify whatever policy served their self-interest.

The Law of War and Peace reflected the changed religious and political situation of seventeenth-century Europe. Grotius denied any special role to the Holy Roman Emperor or the papacy in keeping the peace of Europe or in dividing up the New World, a conclusion that caused the papacy to keep the book on the index of forbidden reading for two centuries. He also recognized that there was no institution above sovereign princes to enforce world law. Consequently, arbitration, though recommended as a way to avoid war, played little role. Because a unified Christendom no longer existed, the sovereignty of each principality or state meant that the source for internal law would be different from that for the law of war and peace among states. Grotius' most original contribution was to demonstrate that religious division made no difference in the conduct of foreign policy, for there was still a community of states bound by law, an international order above each political community.[38]

The Sources of International Law

The Law of War and Peace began by refuting the claims for pacifism and for realpolitik. If Jesus had intended to outlaw war, argued Grotius, he would have provided a clear denunciation of it. Verses commanding to go the second mile, avoid courts, and give your enemy a cloak were about small matters in domestic life, not war. Against the realist argument that the essence of politics

---

[38]G.I.A.D. Draper, "Grotius' Place in Development of Legal Ideas About War," in *Hugo Grotius and International Relations*, ed. Hedley Bull, et al. (1990), 177-208.

was a self-seeking power, Grotius invoked the Stoic belief in a God-given human nature created for society, the existence of natural law, and the universal testimony of those not blinded by ignorance.[39] He concluded that war was a necessary social phenomenon by which states could settle their differences.

Grotius sought to demonstrate that there was a "law" above princes, analogous to domestic law, useful in adjudicating the difficulties among states. It was law without a sovereign to enforce it in this world at least, but there were incentives to obey. Serving justice brought "peace of conscience" and God's approval; injustice brought ill effects. God had so designed the world and humans that obedience to justice brought advantage: "For the very nature of man, which even if we had no lack of anything would lead us into the mutual relations of society, is the mother of the law of nature."[40]

Grotius argued for the existence and contents of a law among nations, valid in war and in peace, with the type of a priori certainty gained in mathematics and a posteriori proof obtained through experience. To gain the first kind of certainty, he used reason to demonstrate the existence of a natural law deducible from the first principles of self-defense and sociability and embodying "security of property, good faith, fair dealing, and a general agreement between the consequences of men's conduct and their desserts."[41] These principles of natural law underlay the just laws in all societies, traditionally termed the law of peoples. To demonstrate the a posteriori certainty, Grotius used examples from history and quotations from wise men to prove universal agreement in the laws of peoples.

A third form of certainty came from revelation in the *Bible*. Finally, there were some customs of nations, established by practice, which did not have the certainty of any of the other three sources of law, but became valid through the will of princes or the states that observed them. Many conventions of war, like a

---

[39]Hugo Grotius, *Of the Law of War and Peace,* tr. Francis Kelsey (1925), 17, 661-76. A good introduction is Christian Gellinek, *Hugo Grotius* (1983).
[40]Grotius, 15-16.

public declaration of causes, had created a kind of common law of nations. In addition, not having the status of law, but nevertheless important in ameliorating the harshness of war was Christian charity. When his observations of the practice of war and natural customary law allowed extreme severity, Grotius pleaded with the monarchs of Europe to act with reasonable moderation befitting followers of Christ.

The complexity and ambiguity of *The Law of War and Peace* stemmed from Grotius' lists of actions allowed by different types of law and his failure to specify which standard to employ to evaluate conduct. In short, the reader could be confused because Grotius' intellectual conclusions as a lawyer/historian were often at variance with what he wished would happen as a humane Christian.

Just Cause

In *The Law of War and Peace,* war was a normal part of human society, legitimated by all forms of law and custom, not a disease to be eradicated. Within society, courts redressed wrongs; outside, among nations, war took the place of courts and a Just War punished or redressed wrongs done. Citing Aristotle, Cicero, Augustine, and Aquinas, Grotius listed the permissible causes of war: self-defense, defense of property, defense of allies unjustly attacked. A preventive war was allowable as a last resort, but only if the intent of the enemy was unmistakable, and he had already done some wrong. Neither fear, balance of power, wealth, prestige, bad government, nor vengeance was a legitimate cause for war. Right intent was important, because even if there was just cause, a war seeking wealth or honor was still unjust.

The custom of declaring war enabled the public to decide whether there were just cause. If soldiers were certain the war was unjust, they should refuse to fight. If uncertain, they should rely on the prince's wisdom and leave the judgment to God. Those engaged in unjust war were guilty of robbery. Grotius

---

[41]Quoted in George Sabin, *History of Political Theory*, (1937), 423.

insisted that Islam, Judaism, and Christianity agreed that all actions done in an unjust war were "moral injustices." [42]

If a prince were not absolutely sure of his rightness, or if the fault of the opponent were not of crucial importance, then he should refrain from war. Rulers had to use the same kind of care in determining the justice of their cause that courts used in trials. Even if there were a just cause, the wise ruler would often refrain from war because of the grievous ills it brought. After all, "warfare has no place among the useful arts."[43]

Luther's confidence that the just side would prevail was not shared by Grotius, for God's actions might be determined by many unknown factors. Like Saurez, Grotius knew that both sides could believe themselves just, even though one side was mistaken. In such cases, the soldiers on both sides should be treated as legal equals, and the wars should be pursued with more moderation than usual.[44] Inadvertently, Grotius reinforced the tendency in European wars to assume that laws on the conduct of war applied equally to soldiers on both sides whatever the justice of the cause. By the mid-seventeenth century, international law no longer conditioned the rights of soldiers and civilians in war on just cause. Just cause language ceased to have legal consequences, and was used as a way to gather popular support for the war or to motivate soldiers to fight harder.

During the wars of religion the Just War theorists debated if there were a right of rebellion. Even though Grotius as a Hollander defended the Netherlands' battle for independence against the Spanish, he denied any right of revolution by the people. Instead, he argued that the Dutch had long exercised certain rights of self-rule and that the Spanish had attempted to usurp or change the original form of government of the ancient Batavian Republic. Like Calvin, Grotius insisted that the character of government was founded on the original contract between leader and people that could not be changed without both parties' consent.

---

[42]Grotius, 547-55
[43]Ibid., 585.
[44]Ibid., 108, 138, 435, 508, 587-92.

However, Grotius denied the Calvinist assertion that inferior magistrates had a right to defend the traditional government against a usurping monarch. Unlike Luther, he did allow for certain private wars; these were for self-defense in cases of necessity and were not designed to kill the opponent. A Christian might decide that it would be better to risk or lose his or her life rather than engage in self-defense, but the law of nature did allow self-defense. The "contending by force" in private wars and rebellions could best be dealt with by the municipal law of a state; the international laws of war applied only when a sovereign, after finding a just cause, openly declared war and applied coercion.

Justice in Conduct of War

Within war, there were certain rights established by nature, others by the law of nations. For example, the law of nature did not sanction slavery, except as a punishment for certain crimes; by the law of nations, the defeated soldiers and civilians fighting in an unjust war could be enslaved and all their property passed to the conquerors. This, after all, had been the custom of the ancient world. Grotius did not rank his sources so that a precedent from Rome had as much relevance to establishing the law of nations as a practice in Renaissance Italy. As a result there remained a static quality to his sense of law, and he cited history without acknowledging the chasm between seventeenth-century France and ancient Athens. Because they reflected the nature of God and man, the law of nature and the law of peoples were unchanging. Consequently, according to Grotius, slavery was still a legal way to treat all the subjects conquered in a Just War. Yet during the Middle Ages, western Europeans stopped killing or enslaving their Christian captives in war. Therefore, Grotius concluded, drawing upon the customs of Muslims as well as Christians, that the practice of not enslaving fellow believers came from revelation. Christianity here provided a higher standard, but not one that applied to heathen black Africans.[45]

---

[45]Ibid., 690-96.

Just War theory allowed the right side to do what was both moral and necessary to win. Utility could justify laying waste the lands of the population of the unjust side as a way of punishing them and weakening their source of supplies; however, moderation and mercy required keeping such depredations to a minimum. Not natural law, but the customs of Europeans guaranteed the rights of civilians not to be prime targets.

Since the practice of nations in war through history had been anything but mild, Grotius relied upon the customs of European states toward each other. This meant that there would be standards for civilized warfare among Europeans that might not apply to war with allegedly uncivilized peoples - the Native Americans, the peoples of the East, and even perhaps the Muslims. In this differentiation between Christians and non-civilized peoples as well as his defense of right of transit and trade, Grotius provided a rationale for European imperialism, even though he refused to permit wars to expand religion and accepted Vitoria's arguments about the natural rights of native peoples. Grotius did not wish cruelty to be used on non-Europeans but, in the absence of a legal prohibition, had to rely on the prince's and soldiers' commitment to Christian moderation, feelings that had proved to be of short supply in the Spanish conquest of Mexico and Peru and the Thirty Years War.

Grotius spelled out the rules for many contingencies: the rights of neutral powers, the obligations on prisoners of war, the immunities of ambassadors, the justification for booty and reparations, the validity of treaties, the rights of enemy civilians behind enemy lines when war began, succession to kingdoms, when sovereignty was extinguished, the inalienable rights of slaves, acts absolutely forbidden under any circumstances (rape), immune noncombatants (children, women, old men, farmers, merchants, scholars, and religious occupations). He distinguished between what was wrong, what was just and good, and what was just and better. The laws of war, for example, gave soldiers the right to kill other soldiers without punishment, but this did not mean that killing was morally right. "The duty of a Christian," "moderation," "justice," "humanity," and "mercy" mitigated such harshness.[46] Ultimately, like Erasmus, Grotius relied upon his religious vision of a Christian prince and soldiers moved by considerations of honor, humanity, and justice to enforce his ideal of the law that structured the relations of civilized nations in war and peace.

Thomas Hobbes: The Normalcy of War

Unlike Thucydides, Caesar, Ibn Kaldun, and Machiavelli whose realism about war and diplomacy drew upon practical experiences, Thomas Hobbes was never a soldier, diplomat, or politician. The son of a poor English curate, Hobbes attended Cambridge and became a tutor for a nobleman's son. An armchair philosopher who delighted in good conversation and hated disorder and civil war, Hobbes read the classics and translated Thucydides, but sought to prove his conclusions by the authority of reason, not quotation of experts. Born in 1588, the year of the Spanish Armada, he claimed that his mother bore "twins, me and together with me fear."[47] But he was not fearful in pursuing the implications of his thought to what many contemporaries saw as extreme conclusions on religion and politics, first publishing his political theories on the eve of the English Puritan revolution and then expanding them in the *Leviathan,* published in 1651 after Oliver Cromwell's and the Puritans' triumph.

Hobbes was a strong defender of royal authority, denouncing as absurd Parliament's defenses of regicide and use of religion to legitimate rebellion. His strong commitment to royal authority resulted in being exiled to France, but the royalist supporters of King Charles disliked the implications of Hobbes' political theory. During his lifetime opponents, and there were few defenders, denounced Hobbes as an atheist and defender of tyranny, and the term "Hobbean," like that of a "Machiavel," became a way to describe an opponent as unscrupulous and power-mad.

Hobbes spelled out the implications of his premises clearly, but neither his contemporaries nor modern scholars agree upon the nature of Hobbes' religion or

---

[46] Ibid., 643, 733-34, 744.
[47] A. P. Martinich, *Hobbes: A Biography* (1998), 2.

its role in his thought. Was Hobbes a secularist whose discussion of God was camouflage, or was Hobbes a Calvinist Anglican seeking to prop up a weak central government and diminish the role of religion in fomenting civil war?[48] Was the existence of God necessary to Hobbes' reliance on natural law or was natural law a product of autonomous reason?

If Hobbes were a Christian, he certainly was an unconventional one. Like Grotius, Hobbes wanted to create a philosophy of certainty based upon axiomatic premises and deductions, like geometry, and saw himself as a Euclid of political theory. His universe was deterministic and mechanistic, with all activities including thought portrayed as matter in motion. There was no mind-body dualism, for all was matter; even God and angels were material. Galileo, whom Hobbes admired, argued that a body in motion would remain in this state except for an opposing force. Hobbes reversed Aristotle's insight that human beings were basically peaceful and war was unnatural; for Hobbes war (i.e., a body in motion) was the natural state and peace the anomaly. So the task for political theory was to explain how humans ever created peace.

Political philosophers of the seventeenth century contrasted the present civilization with a mythical state of nature before there was a state. For Jews, Christians, and Greeks the original age of humanity was a golden age of peace. Neither Hobbes nor other such theorists did any research as to what a state of nature might really have been like, although they thought that American Indians lived in one; rather, they used the primitive condition as a metaphor so they could have a beginning place to isolate the essential features of government.

Hobbes saw humans in the state of nature as essentially equal; that is, a person's divergences in strength or intellect were not enough to allow him to dominate his fellows. In the beginning, each person desired individual survival; Hobbes thought Aristotle and Augustine were wrong to posit a basic drive to

---

[48]A. P. Martinich, *The Two Gods of Leviathan: Thomas Hobbes on Religion and Politics* (1992), 1-16; David Gauthier, *The Logic of Leviathan* (1969), 178, 204-06.

sociability as the beginning point for society. Humans in this pre-state existence were neither sinful nor law-breakers because there was no sovereign to make law. So their natural inclinations could prevail, which for Hobbes meant seeking self-preservation, avoiding dangers, and desiring the glory of self-esteem or reputation. These innate attributes were, for Hobbes, the "causes of quarrel." Above all, humans feared death and so sought security by power, material possessions, and reputation. Whatever quantity of these an individual acquired in the state of nature, he would still be insecure because the state of equality meant all others were in competition for the same limited goods. So a neighbor's increase in power would threaten his own security. Because all humans were in direct and unlimited struggle for power and security, the result was a constant state of war and life was "solitary, poor, nasty, brutish, and short."[49]

In describing what human existence was like before a state, Hobbes used the international realm as an analogy. Here there was no law; monarchs sought unceasingly for advantages to make their realms secure. They built fortresses, entered alliances, and fought wars. Even when they were ostensibly at peace, they were in bitter competition. Because there was no sovereign over states, there could be no condition of law among them. Open or secret, hot or cold war remained an inescapable condition of a state's external life. So it was with an individual in the original state of nature.[50]

The state could not escape from its predicament, but an individual could because man was a rational creature with a natural desire for peace. Christian theologians saw peace as a sign of salvation, an indication of the human's true destiny under God. For Hobbes, peace was simply the absence of war. Peace resulted after rational humans calculated that it would serve their well-being; security came when they contracted to surrender their natural equality to a sovereign. The sovereign guaranteed internal peace to the inhabitants in return for

---

[49]Thomas Hobbes, *Leviathan or the Matter, Forme and Power of a Commonwealth Ecclesiasticall and Civil*, ed. Michael Oakeshott (1997), Ch. 13.
[50]Peter Caws, ed., *The Causes of Quarrel: Essays on Peace, War, and Thomas Hobbes* (1969).

absolute power. Hobbes exalted the status of the leader or monarch by calling him the *Leviathan*, a term taken from the book of Job where it refers to the whale.

Hobbes' Leviathan, like his God, is absolute, not responsible to his subjects, but he rules for good. The monarch, using principles derived from a natural law based upon reason and the Bible, established statute law. The ruler, as God's lieutenant on earth, was responsible for all law and order and right religion. The king had the sole responsibility to determine the correct religion for the realm; never could there be either a justifiable religious or constitutional ground for revolt against a sovereign. A bad king was not one who trampled on his subjects' rights or allowed false religion, for the people had surrendered to him full power in the original contract. Rather, a bad monarch weakened the state's authority and exposed it to civil war from within and invasion from outsiders.

Hobbes devoted nearly half of *Leviathan* to a discussion of religion and why it should not be allowed to disrupt a state. He affirmed his belief in God, Jesus as Redeemer, and miracles and insisted that correct Christian doctrine and practice were biblically based and confirmed by reason. Revelation and reason confirmed the validity of natural law. Personal revelation might be authoritative to an individual, but could never serve as the basis of the religion of a state. The almost irreconcilable combination of Hobbes' conventional Christian piety with his determinist, mechanistic, and pessimistic view of natural men has occasioned the scholarly debate as to whether Hobbes was a secularist or a Christian trying to reconcile traditional belief with new scientific information.[51] For our purposes the congruence of Christianity with Hobbes' account of natural law or the state of nature is not as important as his pessimistic view of humanity as prone to war and international relations as anarchy.

Hobbes became an important political theorist because his vision of humanity reversed the traditional priorities of the origin of monarchy and the duty

---

[51] Thomas Hobbs, *Leviathan*, ch. 12 on the origins of religion and parts 3 and 4; A. Martinich, *The Two Gods of Leviathan: Thomas Hobbes on Religion and Politics;* and Deborah Baumgold. *Hobbes' Political Theory* (1988) offer contrasting views.

of a king. However, his stark view of natural humanity was founded upon equality and psychology, not original sin. The political processes involved in creating and sustaining a state were natural; no providence or intervention by God was required. For Hobbes, unlike Machiavelli, war was the opposite of civilization; human creativity in the arts and sciences came only after the primitive war ended with the establishment of a state. His writings offered what most Europeans, even defenders of monarchy, saw as an unpalatable solution to the problem of anarchy: the creation of an absolutist government. For the pervasive problem of external war Hobbes offered no solution.

By 1700 after surveying the disastrous effects of war over differences in faith, statesmen and intellectuals concluded that it was ridiculous to make war over theology, although states continued to rely upon an alliance of monarch and church and to use the church to sanctify their struggles. The new absolutist states provided financial support for the clergy and built churches; in response, the clergy muted critiques of war. England and Holland accepted religious divisions within the state. Spain, Italy, and France (which under Louis XIV repudiated toleration for the Huguenots) would not accept religious divisions but would not fight or even justify wars as caused by the heretical beliefs of the opponent. But if war did break out, the struggle could still be portrayed as holiness versus evil. The decline of religion as a factor in international politics did not mean that the people became more or less devout, but that the institutional churches rather than politics became the focus of those seeking spiritual solace. After 1648 the religious map of Europe would be frozen, but the intellectual map filled with the voices of realpolitik, pacifism, Just War theory, and international relations. All of these perspectives are echoed in contemporary America.

Western Europe as a civilization unified by a common Roman Catholic faith was no more. Instead European unity came from a belief in Christendom whose common culture, at least as compared with India or the Ottoman Turks, was undergirded by natural law. Clergy might still issue calls for peace and theologians might debate Just War theories, but the most influential commentators on justice in the conduct of war would be jurists like Samuel Pufendorf (1632-94). The most profound evaluations of war during the eighteenth century came not from monks like Erasmus or jurists like Pufendorf but from the new class of *philosophes* who proclaimed themselves to be men of reason.

X.

WAR AND PEACE IN THE AGE OF REASON

Royal absolutism and the Enlightenment characterized European history between 1648-1789. Kings made war as they saw fit, with the major check upon their quest for wealth and power being other monarchs. Religious differences no longer caused wars among European states, although Spain, Portugal, France, and England all used the need to spread Christianity to benighted heathen as a rationale for colonial conquests. The kings of Europe insisted that their enemies' faults brought war, but in actuality just cause of war ceased to be an important criterion for either side. Instead, during the war, irrespective of who began it, each of the self-proclaimed civilized Christian states conformed to usages based upon custom, natural law, Just War theories, or what was now called international law. Crucial for this book's central theme of assessing religion's influence on war is whether Christian morality restrained conduct in war.

The age of absolutism was also the age of reason or enlightenment. Independent thinkers, most notably Voltaire, termed *philosophes*, basing their judgments upon reason, provided critical evaluation of kings and their wars. Isaac Newton's discovery of the laws of gravity led to the confidence that a scientist by using mathematics could discover how a law-abiding universe functioned. The *philosophes* sought to improve society by applying reason to religion, ethics, politics, and war, and contrasted the progress brought by free intellectual inquiry with the unceasing wars caused by institutions steeped in superstition, like the churches and hereditary monarchies. For the first time in human history, a few thinkers asked whether war was an inescapable part of human destiny caused by inherent flaws or if new institutions could be established that could end war. Our concern is with the Enlightenment's moral analysis of war and secularization of peace; that is, with seeing peace on earth as a political goal rather than a religious vision.

This chapter will first look at the Enlightenment critique of wars, using Voltaire's *Candide* as a case study, then examine the conduct of war in the age of absolutism, and, finally, look at two possible approaches to achieving peace: creating institutions to solve disputes, or having no army. Creating peace while keeping the military seemed possible because England achieved several periods of armed peace. For seventy years colonial Pennsylvania provided for Voltaire and other *philosophes* an example of an unarmed country enjoying peace with Indians.

II. Voltaire

Voltaire's *Candide,* written in 1759 during a major European war and published anonymously, is a satiric tale excoriating the suffering caused by incessant war, bad government, religious fanatics, obtuse philosophers, and the foibles, pretensions, greed, and cruelty of humanity. In the early chapters, Candide, an innocent youth, after being expelled from a castle portrayed as an earthly paradise, is duped into joining the Prussian army by recruiters who give him a few pennies and propose drinking a toast to the king. Candide is now a virtual prisoner, and the recruiters force him to wear leg irons on the march to camp so that he will not flee. In the army he learns rote drill and the manual of arms, being beaten with a stick when he is slow.

When the naïve hero tries to take a walk away from the camp, he is seized, charged, and convicted of attempted desertion and offered the choice of six bullets in the brain or running a gauntlet in which the entire company will beat him. Barely surviving, Candide, who like his fellow soldiers knows nothing of politics, participates in a battle where soldiers of both sides line up in a tight formation and first fire muskets at each other, then engage in hand-to-hand combat, resulting in thirty thousand being killed. Towns falling to either side are pillaged and burned, the men killed and the women raped. Such practices, says Voltaire, are allowed by the immemorial custom and the laws of war. Later Candide watches a naval battle between two ships after which the victorious side cheers as their opponent's vessel sinks and the men drown.

Candide described eighteenth-century armies as mercenary scum, claiming that in two armies of sixty thousand men preparing to do battle, there would be twenty thousand cases of venereal disease on each side. Voltaire also condemned the impressment of hundreds of unwilling young men and the poverty that drove others to enlist: "A million drilled assassins go from one end of Europe to the other murdering and robbing with discipline in order to earn their bread, because there is no honester occupation." In *Candide*, the destruction of civilians and pillaging were integral parts of war.

Candide described war whether between Prussia and Austria or Christians and Muslims as an absurd activity. The tale, written during the war for empire between France and England called the French and Indian War in America, described the struggle as "madness ... You know these two nations are at war for a few acres of snow in Canada, and that they are spending more on this fine war than all Canada is worth."[1] Like Erasmus but without his piety, Voltaire blamed wars on the greed and stupidity of monarchs and insisted that wars were a form of theft, a committing of murder in order to rob. Princes began war, the people paid, the realm was impoverished, and the conquests were of short duration.

Organized religion - whether Catholicism, Calvinism, or Islam - incited men to war and absolved them of their atrocities. The clergy, Voltaire charged, preached against all vices except war. Princes who wanted power, not piety, used religion to camouflage ulterior purposes. The Church, which was supposed to bring peace, blessed this murderous enterprise by fostering recruitment and singing *Te Deum* masses for victory. Just War theory served only to strengthen men in their hypocritical love of war. Voltaire belittled the premise of justice in the cause

---

[1]Francois-Murie Arouet de Voltaire, *Candide or Optimism*, tr. Norman Terry (1946), ch. 3: 20, 22; 7: 69, 84. For critical evaluations, see *Candide*, ed. Robert Adams (1966). Theodore Besterman, *Voltaire* (1969), is a good biography.

of war, claiming there had only been one Just War in all history, the revolt of the slave Spartacus against the Romans.

Voltaire's emotional and intellectual desire for peace and scorn for war expressed in *Candide* and many other writings conflicted with his view of the necessity of war as a fruit of the natural right of self-defense. Animals fought, so also did humans, who made their fighting more destructive because they applied reason. The flaws in human nature made wars inevitable. While his tales excoriated war, Voltaire's personal letters to monarchs softened his criticism of their wars. He praised the victories of Louis XV, Frederick the Great, and Catherine of Russia, designed a war chariot that he hoped would be used by the armies of France, Prussia, and Russia, and proclaimed the virtues of a crusade against the Turks as a way to stop Europeans from fighting among themselves.[2] His inconsistencies were not simply a by-product of hypocrisy or social climbing, but reflected his attraction to and repulsion for the glory of war, an ambivalence about his society, and a desire for and pessimism about the chances for meaningful change.

Voltaire's critique of war using themes enunciated by Erasmus was echoed by other eighteenth-century intellectuals. The Englishman Jonathan Swift in *Gulliver's Travels* showed the foolish causes and consequences of war in the Lilliputian kingdom. The French *philosophes* in the *Encyclopaedia* denounced wars as profitless activity caused by the greed of kings. Thomas Paine, pamphleteer of the American Revolution, reiterated the anti-war theses of Voltaire and the other *philosophes* in blaming George III for waging war on his subjects. None of these anti-war intellectuals was a pacifist, and all supported the wars of their countries.

Monarchs, who claimed to be Christians and to have their authority given by God for the common good, had the final responsibility for decisions on war. Their generals and advisers, also all Christians, as were the nobility, bishops, and upper classes knew of the requirements for justice in war. If Christian Just War theory were ever able to regulate war, the eighteenth-century should serve as a test case.

Historians comparing European wars between 1650 and 1789 with those that came before and after see the era as one of restraint in the conduct of war.[3] What caused the restraint? At issue in the next section is whether Voltaire or the Just War theorists provide a better description of war during the age of absolute monarchs. We will answer this question by assessing, first, the accuracy of Candide's encounter with the army, second, the method of fighting, and, third, the results of one hundred twenty-five years of incessant war.

III. Eighteenth-century Wars

Voltaire was generally accurate in describing the composition of armies. The royal governments provided quotas to local authorities who impressed into service the poor, misfits, and petty criminals. Those who volunteered for service tended to be the very poor or the adventurous for whom the army provided an opportunity for sustenance or escape, or both. Service was unpopular and desertion on the way to the regiment or in service common. The Prussians did on occasion put irons on recruits to keep them from deserting. Even in wartime, many soldiers fled. During the War of Spanish Succession, the French army lost one of every four soldiers by desertion. Generals had to adapt tactics to the unpopularity of service; marches and battles had to be in tight formation, because dispersal of troops in the woods would lead to mass desertion. Once in the army, a soldier served until peace or until he died of wounds or fever.[4]

Like Voltaire , most intellectuals viewed common soldiers as the dregs of

---

[2]Henry Meyer, "Voltaire on War and Peace," in *Studies on Voltaire and the Eighteenth Century* (1976), 144.
[3]M. S. Anderson, *War and Society in Europe of the Old Regime, 1618-1789* (1988), 180, 187-195; Geoffrey Best, *Humanity in Warfare* (1980), ch. l.
[4]Anderson, 129-130, 165. This section is based on André Corvisier, *Armies and Societies in Europe 1494-1789*, tr. Abigail Siddall (1979); Russell Weigley, *Age of Battles: The Quest for Decisive Warfare from Brietenfeld to Waterloo* (1991); Azar Gat, *The Origins of Military Thought from the Enlightenment to Clausewitz* (1989).

society, and few cared if they lived or died. In Prussia and Russia the nobility furnished the officer class and received great prestige. Elsewhere in Europe, officers were more likely the second sons of the family. A would-be officer in peacetime might buy both his rank and a regiment; the government would provide money for equipment and provisions to the ranking officer who would purchase supplies, often making profit for himself at the expense of the common soldier. Because the officer had a financial stake in the regiment, he would not wish to risk battle unnecessarily, for a defeat might entail a considerable monetary loss. Governments founded special academies to train officers and gunners. Civility in war was mainly confined to the relationships between officers on both sides. Gentlemen did not try to kill other gentlemen during battle.

Eighteenth-century soldiers were better trained, equipped, and disciplined than earlier armies. Soldiers began to march and wore distinctive uniforms, the *redcoats* of the British for example. The Prussian army pioneered a rigorous drill and severe discipline that became famous and imitated throughout Europe. Towards the end of the century governments attempted to provide separate barracks for troops, a development allowing more discipline, esprit de corps, and a separate code of behavior for soldiers to become more common.

Voltaire's representation of the mercenary character of armies is also accurate. In early eighteenth-century warfare, captured soldiers might join the opposing army. The cause did not matter so long as the pay was adequate. If the wages and supplies fell short, and this frequently happened, then the troops might riot. As the eighteenth century progressed, there were better logistics and more national feeling in armies, but throughout the period, soldiers rarely understood or identified with the goals of war. The British, with the smallest standing army and a channel to protect them, brought the art of hiring mercenaries to perfection. Because Scotland and Ireland were poor, their young men composed a substantial element in the French armies of Louis XIV.

Battles occurred when opposing lines of troops in formation stood around a hundred yards apart and in synchronized movements loaded and fired their muskets. It was easy to fire cannon shots (rounded balls of iron) into the massed troops, but loading a gun with grapeshot spread the destruction. The only debate on the morality of weapons concerned whether it was permissible to fire red-hot cannon balls. Victory came when one formation of soldiers broke under a cannonade or cavalry onslaught and the opponents charged with bayonets. When battles of this kind occurred, casualties were heavy, up to one-fourth of the men in some regiments, but victories were rarely decisive because armies moved so slowly.

Armies remained the scourge of the civilian population, for they attempted to save supplies by living off the surrounding population. While those who sold the army supplies might prosper, famine and starvation of the civilian population also resulted. Fed with meager rations and lacking sanitary procedures, armies transmitted diseases of all kinds wherever they were stationed, with far more soldiers and civilians being killed by disease than in battles. The historian André Corvisier described the effects of an army upon enemy civilians: "The people were at the mercy of the victor. The idea of citizen's rights was established only with great difficulty, and it was probably hindered by universal military obligation. The soldiers felt that they were not bound to respect civilians who took part in acts of war."[5] Peasants would take their revenge upon a defeated army or wounded soldiers. The population of a town that resisted a siege could, according to the laws of war, be pillaged with all moveable goods subject to seizure. Atrocities in such cases were common. Louis XIV in the Palatine and Peter the Great during the Swedish invasion of Russia practiced a scorched-earth policy, thereby depriving both the enemy and the civilian population in the war zone of food and shelter. Such acts came under the doctrine of military necessity.

---

[5] Corvisier, 78.

Thus far the picture of eighteenth-century war drawn by Voltaire in *Candide* seems only a slight exaggeration of conditions, but his conclusions require some modification. *Candide* takes place in Westphalia, an area that suffered much, yet most of Europe away from disputed borders was relatively untouched by war. The respectable inhabitants of the major cities of Europe felt the presence of war chiefly through increased taxes and the disruption or channeling of trade. The outfitting of ships, the supplying of food and uniforms, the need for more and better guns created economic opportunities for a few. Eighteenth-century war was much less destructive than the Thirty Years War. However, the crusading vigor and atrocities that marked that struggle continued in the wars of Austria and Russia against the Ottoman Turks and in those of English colonists and Native Americans.

The limited wars of the late seventeenth and eighteenth centuries applied only to certain states and certain areas, primarily the wars of France, Spain, England, Prussia, Russia, and Austria against each other. As their names show, the causes of many of these were dynastic: The War of Spanish Succession, the War of Polish Succession, the War of Austrian Succession. Other wars involved attempts of states to expand: France to the Rhine, and Sweden to create an empire in Poland and the Ukraine. England and Holland fought over trade; France and Great Britain fought over their empires in North America, the Caribbean, and Asia.

Eighteenth-century Europe resembled Hobbes' state of nature, with nations preparing for, fighting, or recovering from a war. And these wars did make a difference: the emergence of Russia and Brandenburg Prussia as major states, the rise and decline of Sweden, the failure of Spain, Holland, Austria, and the Ottoman Empire to sustain great power status, the carving up of Poland, and the British expulsion of the French from North America and India. The balance of power used previously against the Habsburgs now provided the sinews for an alliance of states against France's attempt to be the hegemonic power in Europe.

Western European war resembled an elaborate game of toy soldiers manipulated by the monarchs for their personal amusement. There was considerable devastation in those areas where the armies maneuvered, but because a normal daily march was five miles, the areas were rather small. Although Europeans planned for major decisive battles, they fought very few - only the Battle of Poltava where Russia wiped out the Swedish invading force had major consequences.

The art of war was to avoid fixed battles whenever possible, attempting to gain advantage by outmaneuvering one's opponent. One of France's greatest marshals, de Saxe, claimed that the best way to victory was to avoid pitched battle.[6] Most wars consisted of siege operations involving strong fortifications and miles of earthworks created by the attacking force. Strategists planned the layout of forts scientifically, with geometric diagrams showing the best places for cannons and how to dig ever closer to the walls. Sieges took enormous amounts of money for supplies and tied up troops for months, but led to relatively few casualties in battle. If the town saw that defense was hopeless, it might surrender. And if the town surrendered, terms might be worked out among armies for protecting civilians. Fighting to the death was against the prevailing ethos of war. In general, prisoners of war were neither enslaved nor ransomed. Rather, when a truce of peace was signed, elaborate exchanges of prisoners occurred. Now Europeans professed outrage at the custom of the Barbary pashas of North Africa of seizing ships and holding crews and passengers for ransom.

Maintaining the military was the most costly endeavor of eighteenth-century governments, even in peacetime taking up nearly 40% of the total revenues, and in war up to 80%.[7] Holland and Sweden declined because they did not have the population and resources to match major powers. Russia and Prussia became powerful because their whole societies became militarized at very heavy

---

[6]Maurice de Saxe, *My Reveries on the Art of War* (1732), in *Roots of Strategy*, ed. Thomas Phililips (1940), 298.
[7]Anderson, 98.

cost to their peasants and serfs. Even major commercial powers like England felt the strain of military expenditures.

No one maintains that eighteenth-century wars stayed within the bounds of justice in the cause of war, but the practice of war was restrained. Still debated is whether this limited warfare resulted from modest objectives, logistical weakness, class-consciousness, or religious and ethical guidelines. The last explanation appears less important than the first two. The monarchs kept the military within bounds as a support for their society, partially because the army also served as the police. Among the officer class there was mutual respect and a code of honor. However, during battle there was no awareness among soldiers that they were fighting in inconclusive battles and long sieges because of the ethical qualms of their superiors. The mixture of restraint and barbarism in eighteenth-century wars shows that, at best, ethical considerations remained a minor factor in decisions on the conduct of war.

When evaluating all the results from the incessant wars between 1660 and 1789, the historian M. S. Anderson concluded that "The average European ... would probably have lived better, and would certainly have been less heavily taxed and enjoyed greater physical security, if none of the great international struggles of the period had been fought."[8]

IV. Peace Makers in Early Modern Europe

Until the eighteenth century, war seemed to be an inescapable part of life caused by evil, resulting in more evil, and endured by the common people as a punishment for sin. The Reformed, Lutheran, and Roman Catholic teachings on original sin had undermined hope about the perfectibility of humans and the reform of their institutions. The only sustained critique of necessity of war came from Erasmus and Christian humanists in the Renaissance. Later events had not weakened the potency of Erasmus' opposition to war, but seemed to show that his view of human goodness was naïve. However, Erasmus' ideals found

---

[8]Ibid., 156.

particular resonance in England, an island that had escaped invasion after 1066 and had seen no need to build a large standing army.

The English had a long tradition of recognizing the need for peace. In the Middle Ages John Wycliff and the Lollards had opposed the Crusades, belittled Just War theory, and criticized the Catholic Church's support of wars. Medieval and Renaissance poets extolled the blessings of peace which they contrasted to the poverty and death brought by even successful wars. In addition, the British distrusted a large standing army, a fear accentuated by the role of the Puritan army under Cromwell's government. Finally, and perhaps most important, England enjoyed several long periods of peace under Henry VII, Elizabeth until 1588, James I and Charles I from 1602 until 1640, and after the peace of Utrecht from 1713 until 1739. So to the British government a policy that could successfully preserve peace seemed attainable. War no longer seemed an unavoidable act of God, but a product of human arrangements.

Those who advocated war, sometimes the same individuals who on other occasions extolled the blessings of peace, needed to prove the wisdom of fighting to the people. The English often became belligerent, but their leaders came to believe that nations could control international relations. By 1700 British diplomacy relied for security upon support for the balance of power, maintenance of a strong navy, and subsidies for foreign mercenaries.[9]

The practice of balance of power seems to occur naturally whenever there are many independent states that fear domination by one country. Examples include the alliance against Athens, the maneuverings of Italian city states in the Renaissance, the French against the Habsburgs and - after France became the dominant power in Europe under Louis XIV - England, the Netherlands, and Austria. European diplomatic history from 1648 on has revolved around the balance of power.

---

[9]Ben Lowe, *Imagining Peace: A History of Early English Pacifist Ideas* (1997), 69-71, 141-46, 179; Martin Ceadal, *The Origins of War Prevention: The British Peace Movement and International Relations, 1730-1854* (1996), ch. 2-3.

A nation could practice balance of power politics either by increasing its own power or by joining with other states, but the end result was always what is now referred to as a zero sum game. That is, one's power was always considered relative to another state. So an increase in French power would lead to a decrease in English; if both gained power, there would be no difference in the ratio. Of course, the difficulty has always been to calculate what power means in relation to military success in battle. How does a leader determine the morale of an enemy, or the stability of a dynasty, or the value of a navy versus an army? The result of such uncertainty has often been competition leading to war, because war is the only accurate method by which one nation can prove that it is more powerful than its neighbors. The rationale behind balance of power was of an almost natural mechanism that would lead to peace if the right equilibrium could be found. Unfortunately, as Immanuel Kant noted, the balance of power was like a house built in so fragile an equilibrium that it would collapse if a sparrow lighted on it.[10]

Unceasing wars caused a few European intellectuals to seek a new foundation for peace beyond the balance of power. These men sought to create an institutional mechanism to settle disputes by drawing upon their understanding of how peace had been maintained in antiquity and the Middle Ages. Rome had provided a peace through empire; several medieval thinkers, of whom Dante remains the most famous, hoped that a general peace could be created through the power of the Holy Roman Emperor. When at his ascension in 1519, Charles V as Holy Roman Emperor and King of Spain united the realms of Spain, the Low Countries, Austria, and much of Italy, the result of his overwhelming power was war with France. Even supporters of the Habsburgs soon realized that a creation of peace through empire was not a realistic solution in sixteenth century Europe.

An alternative way of obtaining peace would be to have an impartial arbitrator. During the Middle Ages, the popes sought to be the arbiter of disputes among kingdoms by virtue of their claim to hold the spiritual keys to all kingdoms.

---

[10]Immanuel Kant, *Perpetual Peace*, 65.

In the seventeenth century, neither Catholic nor Protestant kings trusted a papacy interested in expanding power in Italy to mediate their disputes. Still, the ideal persisted of an impartial authority to settle the rights and wrongs in controversy.

A few thinkers wondered about the possibility of creating a new institution termed a senate, diet, or alliance that would provide the all-inclusiveness of the old Roman Empire and the exalted status of the medieval papacy so that it could adjudicate disputes among nations. Reformers could point to examples of such leagues in Germany, Switzerland, and the Netherlands, although these federations united similar peoples. Because the new European parliament or diet would have as members separate sovereign states, some means needed to be found to convince monarchs to accept limitation on their powers to wage war in the interests of general peace.

The advocates of an international order are more accurately described as "peace planners." Several envisaged force either in the creation or the enforcement of arbitration. Two of the planners were French priests (Emeric Crucé and Charles de Saint-Pierre), two were English Quakers (William Penn and John Bellers), and three were philosophers (the French Jean Jacques Rousseau, the German Immanuel Kant, and the English Jeremy Bentham). The most famous peace planner was King Henry IV of France, whose plans were published after his death by his chief minister, the Duc du Sully. Sully claimed that, as special envoy for Henry IV, he had gained the support of Queen Elizabeth of England. Historians dispute Sully's assertion and believe that Sully was the real author of the plan, using the prestige of the assassinated French King and Queen Elizabeth to gain attention for his proposal. Still, Sully's fraud was successful until the mid-nineteenth century.[11]

---

[11]"Sully's Grand Design of Henry IV," in *Peace Projects of the Seventeenth Century,* eds. J. R. Jacob and M.C. Jacob in the Garland Library of War and Peace (1972). The Garland Library republished all of these early peace plans. A general history of these proposals is Sylvester J. Hemleben, *Plans for World Peace Through Six Centuries* (1943). See also A. C. F. Beales, *A History of Peace* (1931) and Elizabeth Souleyman, *The Vision of World Peace in Seventeenth and Eighteenth-Century France* (1941).

The peace plans discussed in this section span one hundred seventy-five years, beginning with Crucé's published in 1623 in the midst of the Thirty Years War and ending with those of Kant and Bentham created in the early stages of the French Revolution. Moreover, all these writings should be considered products of the Enlightenment because their authors shared a faith in the ability of reasonable people to create institutions to solve problems.[12] Unlike Augustine and Hobbes, they did not see war as an inescapable reality caused by a flawed humanity.

The authors shared the views of Erasmus and Voltaire of the frivolity of most causes of war and the stupidity of fighting as a method of solving disputes. Moreover, they also asserted that there were characteristics of the international order that made even peace-minded rulers incline to war. For example, since all nations constantly strove against each other for power, there could be no meaningful peace, only truces in their constant war. So a state could never feel secure. In spite of their Hobbesian view of the international realm, the peace planners argued that the immediate issues that led to war were negotiable and manageable.

None of the planners appealed to the people to pressure or supersede existing governments as a way of ending war. Instead, they assumed that the monarch or an equivalent authority in republics (Switzerland and Venice) would make all essential decisions. Although they hoped for a pious king devoted to pursuing Christian peace, they relied on the ruler's self-interest. Monarchs initiated wars to right wrongs or to increase their security, and yet battles were an irrational way to achieve such objectives because there was no guarantee that justice would prevail in the settlement or that security would be increased. The only certain result was that people would be impoverished and soldiers would suffer and die during the war.

---

[12]Martin Ceadal, following F. H. Hinsley, sees these plans as pre-modern because they required the consent of princes, not peoples, and did not recognize Europe as a collection of independent states. *The Origins of War Prevention*, 64. I see them as modern because they advocate creating new kinds of political institutions to resolve problems among states.

An institution that would free the monarch from external and internal threats and protect all his just rights could end the need for war. Then kings could devote their time and money to increasing trade, supporting the arts, and improving government. The assumption behind all the proposals was that kingdoms and republics would approve of an arrangement in which self-interest, the good of the realm, reason, and Christianity coincided.

Most of the peace planners wanted to create a diet or parliament composed of ambassadors from sovereign states who would adjudicate disputes. William Penn's plan proposed a system of weighted voting according to the wealth of member states; the Abbé de Saint-Pierre envisaged the equality of states with each having one vote, with preliminary decisions based upon a plurality, but final determination requiring either three-fifths or two-thirds, a figure that he hoped would ensure that the primary factor would be justice rather than politics. Most of the plans, even those by Quakers, saw the need of some kind of collective security arrangement by which all states together would enforce the parliament's decision on a recalcitrant member.[13]

The earliest plan, that of Crucé in 1623, was also the most ambitious, advocating the membership of all European states, including Turkey and Russia. Crucé hoped that the benefits of his parliament would be so apparent that states in Asia and other areas would organize similar peacekeeping assemblies. Other plans limited membership to the Christian nations of Europe, arguing that here similarity of culture would provide a unity.

The Henry IV - Sully plan took the most cognizance of power and war. Sully saw the cause of war in the overwhelming power of the Habsburg ruler of Spain and the Holy Roman Empire who aimed at total domination in Europe. However, if the boundaries of European states could be adjusted so that they became more equal in size, then, he argued, they would be less interested in war.

---

[13]Charles de Saint-Pierre, "A Shorter Project for Perpetual Peace," in *Peace Projects of the Eighteenth Century* (1974), 43-55. William Penn, "An Essay on the Peace of Europe," in *Peace Projects of the Seventeenth Century*, 6, 10.

Sully's plan was to create a federation of fifteen mostly equal European states by taking territory from the Habsburg's German possessions. Initially, a coalition of France and smaller states would make war against the Habsburgs in order to strip them of possessions in central and northern Europe, but leaving them Spain with its New World possessions in America and Asia. France, to show it was not self-interested, would claim no new territory for itself, but would like to have restored several areas allegedly unjustly taken by the Habsburgs. Of course, outsiders might have suspected that the end result might have made France rather than the Habsburgs the hegemonic power. The smaller states of Europe (Switzerland, Venice, the Papacy) would all gain sufficient territory to become more equal. Sully gave no weight to any consultation of people of the former Habsburg states who would receive new rulers. Peace would be created by balancing the power of all states that would join in a federation to keep the peace.

The resulting federation of European states could keep the peace in Europe by having a combined army that could be directed against the Turks, Russians, and other Asiatic nations. In Europe, warfare over religion would end since the ruler's decision on religion would be binding on the state. The federation of Protestant and Catholic states would include hereditary monarchies, elective monarchies, and republics. There would be no interference by the federation in any state's internal affairs. Sully was vague on how the federation would actually solve disputes or how it would operate. Because of the plan's association with Henry IV, it became the starting place for other thinkers less concerned with guaranteeing French interests and more devoted to ending all wars.

The Abbé de Saint-Pierre, whose plan was first published in 1713, placed his hopes for peace in a parliament able to mediate, but, if that proved unsuccessful, to institute binding arbitration. After all, princes proclaimed the justice of their causes and the faults of their opponents. So they should be willing to submit their claims to an impartial tribunal. Unlike Sully, the Abbé advocated no change in existing boundaries. He attempted to remove boundary disputes as a cause of war because each state upon joining the parliament would ratify the borders of the European states as lain down in the Peace of Utrecht ending the War of Spanish Succession in 1713. Formerly uncertain borders had often provoked war, because the rights of princes were so vague. Now the moral authority of the tribunal would be sufficient that enforcement of its decisions on borders would rarely require force.

Any army of the parliament would be small, and each nation would reduce its military because there would be no need for frontier fortresses and no external security threats. Saint-Pierre wanted the Grand Alliance to have no army of its own, but to be able to requisition troops (and the money to pay for them) when needed. The federation troops would be under a commander responsible to the Alliance, and all its forces would be ad hoc, so there would never be a federation standing army to threaten the security of any state. The plan guaranteed the security of each dynasty against any internal rebellion.

Immanuel Kant's essay *On Perpetual Peace* (1795) seems the most relevant of these plans, because he recognized the relationship between the form of government and foreign policy. Kant argued that a despotism - whether in the form of monarchy or democracy - would lead to war because those who made the decisions for war would not be affected. The kings who made the decisions for war did not suffer death, or poverty, or famine. So the necessary state for peace would be a republic, by which he meant that there would be a separation of powers between the legislature and the executive. An executive's power would be restricted to enforcing the law.[14] In a republic, in which all citizens were guaranteed their natural rights, the legislature would reflect the wishes of the people. Because the people experienced the horrors of war, they would work for peace, and the legislature would reflect their wishes.

Kant argued that republics would in time become the universal form of government because this was what nature or fate or providence decreed. A republican government, either a monarchy or democracy, fitted the moral nature of humanity and would eventually prevail. Then peace would come gradually, as first two nations and then more, after seeing the practical benefits of harmony, guaranteed the borders of each other, stopped trying to dominate their neighbors by force or money, entered into treaties without secret reservations for future force, reduced armies, and increased trade. The result would be a "pacific federation" based upon the "law of nations."[15] Kant had no illusions about ending humanity's proclivity to violence, but thought that money was a more effective force than armaments. Prosperity, trade and increased contacts would link nations together. Eventually republics would join in a federation that was not nor could become a sovereign government, but a joining of states that had pledged to keep the peace.

No European state paid much attention to the peace planners. Even their proponents wondered whether they were visionary, and contemporaries saw many weaknesses. Voltaire dismissed Saint-Pierre's schemes as daydreams and feared that the Abbé's desire to forbid rebellion would also promote tyranny. Jean Jacques Rousseau was more sympathetic, reissuing Saint-Pierre's proposals in a more concise and clearer format without the geometric jargon that the Abbé had used to make his proofs more mathematical. Although Rousseau sought to demonstrate that the advantages of such a diet were "immense, obvious, undeniable," he also recognized that most intellectuals saw a European parliament as an "absurd dream" and wondered whether the revolution required to implement the plans "might perhaps do more harm all of a sudden than it could prevent for centuries."[16]

The early plans had no method by which states could slowly adopt a new scheme. They also had no conception of peace other than the absence of war, and argued but did not demonstrate that wars were not profitable and did not increase

---

[14]Kant, "Eternal Peace," 76-80. W. B. Gallie, *Philosophers of Peace and War* (1978), 9-36 is a perceptive analysis of Kant's proposals.
[15]Ibid., 84-85, 90
[16]Rousseau, "A Project of Perpetual Peace," in *Peace Projects of the Eighteenth Century* (1974), 97, 131.

security. So even if Europe as a whole might lose from war, a monarch might wage a war not for victory abroad, but to increase his power at home. Finally, the advocates assumed that once a mechanism was in place, politics and the jockeying of states for advantage would cease. They did not recognize that there might be as many wars to enforce a diet's decisions as already existed, and nations would be unwilling to make the sacrifices for a remote war to keep a peaceful international order.

The peace planners were important not for what they accomplished or their specific proposals but for their understanding of the newly emergent international system of sovereign states. They saw nations as trapped in a system that required them to prepare for and often wage war irrespective of the qualities of the ruler. And war resulted in wasting men, taxes, and people with little real achievement. The peace planners thought that humanity could improve the status quo by building new institutions to solve problems. They occupied a middle position between those who thought all war was evil and so refused to participate and those who agreed that war was wrong but necessary and so sought to limit its ill effects.

V. An Experiment in Peace: Colonial Pennsylvania

Europeans saw in the New World a place to discover what humanity allegedly had been in an original state of nature and an empty land for experiments to improve society. Without much accurate information on "Indians," they romanticized them as noble savages representing the perfection of natural humanity without the overlay of artificial civilization. Yet the Spanish and Puritan settlers also created a counter-image in order to justify conquests whereby the indigenous people proved the natural barbarity and savagery of peoples without Christianity. Voltaire in *Candide* contrasted the cruelty of the Spanish Inquisition and European war with a perfectly peaceful and dull society, termed El Dorado, existing in an inaccessible region in the middle of South America.

The North American colonies offered a place for the English to create several versions of utopia: a new society whose success might offer a pattern to reform Europe while providing a refuge for those whose dissenting religions brought persecution, like the Puritans of New England and the Quakers or Friends in Pennsylvania. Voltaire found in colonial Pennsylvania his real El Dorado where peace, prosperity, and toleration were achieved with no monarchy, no priests, and no army.[17]

Early Pennsylvania was an anomaly in the English empire, a colony created and controlled for nearly a century by members of a pacifist religious group. Like the Hutterite settlements in central Europe, it would be a part of a larger governmental unit. Unlike them, the pacifist group would exercise political power over non-pacifists. Pennsylvania owed its unique combination of practices and ideas to the Quakers and William Penn, for it was a profit-making enterprise, sectarian community, and rational commonwealth.

Quakers or Friends originated in the 1650's during the religious ferment accompanying the Puritan revolution against King Charles I. Before 1660 war and peace played only a subordinate role in their religious beliefs; some Friends served in Oliver Cromwell's New Model Army while others refrained on religious principles. During its early years the new faith devoted most attention to proselytizing its most distinctive religious teachings: that all could experience inwardly the Light of God and obedience to that Light was all that was required for salvation. Friends proclaimed the spiritual equality of men and women, defended liberty of conscience, refused to take oaths, and denounced what they saw as immoralities and luxuries. Early Friends resemble the Anabaptists in their attempt to take literally Jesus' commandments and the Puritans in their activities to seek members and to reform society. Their rapid growth, criticism of the English government, and radicalism made conservatives fear the Quakers as

---

[17]Edith Philips, *The Good Quaker in French Legend* (1932); Voltaire, *Letters Concerning the English Nation* (1733), 28-32.

potential revolutionaries before and after the restoration of the monarchy under Charles II in 1660. The Peace Testimony became part of Quakerism only after an uprising by radical sectarians Fifth Monarchy in 1661. Then Friends announced that they would not be involved in any uprising or war.[18]

Seeing the cause of the Civil War in non-Anglican worship, the Restoration Parliament and the Church of England persecuted all dissenters, with the brunt of repression falling on Quakers, who refused to compromise or curtail their activities. Because King Charles II saw the opportunity to pay a large debt and rid England of a troublesome population at the same time, he gave the power of government and a colossal grant of land in 1681 to William Penn, the Quaker son of England's greatest seventeenth-century admiral.

William Penn, well-educated, wealthy, and a friend of monarchs, was a radical Quaker whose emphases on reason and moderation showed his commitment to early phases of the Enlightenment. He gave no signs of ever doubting his experience of the Inward Light, yet his treatises arguing for religious toleration and his plan for a European parliament were based upon self-interest, utility, and reason. For him, Pennsylvania was to be a New Jerusalem shaped by religious pacifist people living under a rationally planned Frame of Government and laws.[19]

At no time was the English government sympathetic to Penn's religious vision of creating a colony with no military forces in the midst of potentially hostile Indians and French. Before 1690 England was at peace, and Quakers controlled Pennsylvania's government, so within the colony there was not even discussion of the military. Between 1690 and 1763 England and France were frequently either preparing for or at war, the British government was obsessed with defense, and Pennsylvania had no militia or fortifications. After 1690

---

[18]Peter Brock, *The Quaker Peace Testimony, 1660 to 1914* (1990) is the best general account of Quaker pacifism, but for the early period see Meredith Weddle, *Walking in the Way of Peace: Quaker Pacifism in the Seventeenth Century* (2001).

English law required a governor to take an oath, so all the governors were non-Friends and received royal instructions to create a militia. There was also a non-Quaker element in the population, a minority dominated by Anglican spokesmen before 1720, and an overwhelming majority of at least two-thirds by the mid-1740's. Few of the new German Lutheran and Scots-Irish Presbyterian immigrants shared the Quaker pacifist perspective. By promising low taxes, religious freedom, and no militia the Quakers managed until 1755 to obtain an absolute majority in the Assembly, often more than two-thirds of the members, and to frustrate the governors' call for a militia.

Friends sought to keep Pennsylvania a pacifist haven by two strategies. The first was to treat the Native American with justice. William Penn journeyed to his new colony in 1682, met with the Lenni Lenape (or Delaware) Indians, and established a policy of purchasing all lands from them. The Quaker settlers and the early governors established a tradition of listening to and seeking to redress the Native Americans' grievances. Most of all, according to the Indians, Penn treated them with respect, perhaps because of his Quaker-inspired belief that all peoples could experience the Light of God in their consciences.

The Quakers and Indians established a peace that endured for seventy years in contrast to the bloody Indian wars in the South and New England. Friends saw the harmony between Penn and the Indians as a vindication of their pacifist principles, a sign of the providence of God. Voltaire, who like other *philosophes* had a favorable opinion of Friends' pacifism and lack of clergy, praised the alleged agreement between Penn and the Indians as the only treaty never sworn to and never broken.[20] Peace with the Indians was largely a domestic colony issue, not a prime concern to the English government.

---

[19]There is no good biography of Penn. The most scholarly account is in the notes and introductions to the *Papers of William Penn*, I-IV, ed. Richard Dunn and Mary Dunn (1981-1987).

[20]W. H. Barber, "Voltaire and Quakerism: Enlightenment and Inner Light," *Studies on Voltaire*, XXIX (1963), 81-109.

Pennsylvania's lack of militia and fortification against the French brought constant controversy within the colony and in Britain. Pennsylvania's Quakers dealt with demands from the English government, non-Quaker governors, and those colonists who saw the necessity for defense - particularly as the province became prosperous. Friends in the Assembly had to confront the issue of whether pacifism was compatible with control of the colony's government.

To the issue of minority/majority rights, Quakers in the Assembly argued that Pennsylvania was theirs by "birthright." Charles II and later settlers before migrating knew that a testimony against war was a Quaker belief. Friends had accepted the expenses and taken the risks in developing Pennsylvania and should not, therefore, become dissenters in their own land. However, if the inhabitants decided Quaker principles endangered the province, they should vote Friends out of the Assembly during the next election. Quakers in the Assembly reminded governors that there was no law against those who wanted a militia from forming a company on their own, although all attempts to create such a force had been failures. Those citizens who wanted to buy cannon could do so by private subscription. Finally, the Assembly gave reluctant acquiescence to specific demands from the English government for money to wage war, though always with some specification that the money be used for aid to Indians or grain.[21]

The Assembly's arguments camouflaged the fact that Quaker politicians who were pacifist for religious reasons employed mostly pragmatic reasons for their peace policy and that its continuation depended upon worldly success. The Anabaptists defended pacifism by ignoring such success, trusting the providence of God, and embracing the possibility of suffering and martyrdom. By contrast, Pennsylvania Quakers argued that the colony's peace as evidenced by good relations with the Indians depended upon obedience to God, which brought the Almighty's special protection, freedom, and prosperity. So long as they remained

---

[21] J. W. Frost, *A Perfect Freedom: Religious Liberty in Pennsylvania* (1990), ch. 2.

the servants of God, Pennsylvania would be at peace, a peace serving as a symbol of the truth of Quaker understanding of Christianity and wisdom in governing.

VI. War Comes to Quaker Pennsylvania

By the mid-eighteenth century, the British had colonized the coastal regions from New England to Georgia, and settlers began pushing westward. The French settled Canada and Louisiana and began to follow the St. Lawrence west and the Mississippi north to unify their empire with a fort at the mouth of the Ohio River at a place now called Pittsburgh. In 1755 a force of French and Indians defeated an English army, commanded by Major General Edward Braddock who intended to seize the French fort. Seeing the weaknesses of the British and desirous of pushing back the expansion of the colonists, the Delaware Indians began raiding the frontier settlers of Pennsylvania.

The Quaker-dominated Assembly did not wait for help from England. They voted a tax to support a war against the Indians and authorized the creation of a militia, though beginning the law with a statement that most Assemblymen opposed military force and providing that all conscientious objectors need not serve. Such a law seemed insufficient to opponents of Quakers who sought to persuade the English government to bar (by requiring an oath) all Quakers from the Assembly. The main body of Delaware River Valley Quakers were appalled at the pro-war actions of Quaker Assemblymen and sought to persuade them to resign. In time, a sufficient number did not stand for re-election so that the Quaker majority in the Assembly ended. An informal agreement with the English government specified that pacifist Friends would no longer serve in the Assembly in wartime. A few Friends who believed in the necessity of defensive war remained in the Assembly, even though Friends officially disapproved their actions.

The massacres of settlers caused Quakers to rethink their role in Pennsylvania, and they concluded that God was punishing Pennsylvanians for two sins in particular. One was the injustice done by the non-Quaker sons of

William Penn and the Scotch-Irish frontiersmen in defrauding the Indians of lands. A restoration of peace could come by redressing the Indians' grievances, not by putting bounties on scalps and killing the Native Americans as the governor wished. Quakers would serve as observers in negotiations between the Indians and the Pennsylvania governor to make sure that the Indians received justice. The second sin was slavery. Quakers had long had misgivings about slavery because Europeans justified enslaving Africans by claiming that according to Just War theory the captive in an unjust war merited death or slavery. Friends did not accept Just War theory and regarded slavery as a way for whites to make money by oppression. Philadelphia Yearly Meeting, the official body of Friends, denounced slavery in 1755 and began working against the slave trade and seeking to persuade Quakers to free their slaves.

Friends also sought to show their love of God by more strictly observing what they defined as His commands and questioning whether they might be called upon to suffer rather than to prosper. A group of reformers refused to pay war taxes and sought to persuade other Quakers that there was a fundamental incompatibility between obedience to God and serving in government either as a magistrate or assemblyman. In 1755 the reformers remained a minority within the Delaware River Valley Quaker community, but all American Quakers would adopt their recommendations during the Revolutionary War.[22]

The interval between the Peace of Paris in 1763 and the war of the American Revolution, beginning in 1774, was traumatic for Pennsylvania Quakers. Almost fifty percent of the Assembly members remained Friends, and although most Quakers still voted, many devout members refused to be Assembly members. The English government had vetoed the 1755 militia law as too democratic (enlisted men elected their officers) and too sympathetic to pacifists.

---

[22]Robert Davidson, *War Comes to Quaker Pennsylvania 1682-1756* (1956), concentrates on political events; a more rounded perspective emphasizing the effect on Quakers is Jack Marietta, *The Reformation of American Quakerism, 1748-1783* (1984). Focusing on the conflict with Native Americans is Francis Jennings, *Empire of Fortune: Crowns, Colonies, and Tribes in the Seven Years War in America* (1988).

So Pennsylvania's militia during the rest of the French and Indian War existed with no statutory authority. No new militia would be created until 1775, even though the so-called Pontiac's Rebellion terrified western Pennsylvanians.

When the crisis over British taxation of the colonies erupted in 1763, Pennsylvania Quakers sought to uphold American rights by peaceful protests and petitions to the king and Parliament. In the eighteenth century, English Friends had prospered in overseas trade, banking, and iron manufacturing and their wealth brought them prestige. American Friends wrote to their co-religionists to use their influence to persuade the English government to change policies. While this tactic succeeded against the Stamp Act, it did not prevent Parliament from passing the Townshend duties in 1767 or the Tea Act in 1772. Quakers joined the American boycotts of English goods, but disliked the patriots' use of violence to coerce dissenters. Friends opposed the destruction of property in the Boston Tea Party, the severity of the English government's response in the Intolerable Acts, and the rigidity of the patriot demands in the First Continental Congress of 1774. [23] After Lexington and Concord, the Pennsylvania Assembly again created a militia.

The issue was now focused: maintaining political power meant sacrificing the testimony for peace. Quakers now called on all members to refrain from voting, and to resign political office or be disowned from membership. Before July 1776 Philadelphia Yearly Meeting supported royal government as ordained by God and declared that Friends opposed all rebellions. After independence, Friends proclaimed their neutrality from both sides and announced that they would do no action to support either side in the war. That meant that they would not serve in the military, not pay for substitutes to serve for them, not pay war taxes, nor take an affirmation of loyalty to either side. Instead, Quakers - like the Anabaptists - would accept sufferings as the experience of those who attempted to follow Christ. During the war, the Revolutionary government disenfranchised

---

[23] Arthur Mekeel, *Quakers and the American Revolution* (1996), should be supplemented by the account in Jack Marietta.

Friends, distrained property, and exiled a few Quaker leaders to western Virginia. After 1776 never again would Quakers exercise political power in Pennsylvania.

Penn's "Holy Experiment" of pacifist government was weakened in 1755 and ended in 1776. Friends sought to dominate government before the French and Indian War and then to influence society by doing charitable deeds, working for the end of slavery, and treating Indians justly. That Quaker Pennsylvania had endured for nearly a century resulted from the anomalous policies of an inefficient British regime that tolerated policies it thought foolish and dangerous. Scholars disagree as to whether the colonial Pennsylvania experiment proved the viability of pacifism, or if pacifism were truly attempted, or if political power undermined Quaker religious principles. They debate whether the partial withdrawal from the Assembly in 1755 was a sellout or a worthwhile compromise. Quaker Pennsylvania was an accident of history made possible only in a disorganized empire. Unlike royal governments, the new democratic revolutionary governments of America and France would never tolerate pacifists in power. William Penn's experiment in peace ended with a democratic experiment created by a revolutionary war.

XI.

Revolutions as Just War

Just War theorists feared revolution and opposed tyranny. The Old Testament and Apocrypha described how God had raised up righteous rebels, and classical sources recounted the overthrow of tyrants, so Aquinas, Suarez, and Calvin had allowed inferior magistrates to resist a tyrant by protecting traditional rights. Augustine, Luther, and Grotius denied any right of revolution. The monarchies of early modern Europe did not recognize a right of rebellion by anyone and acted as if limitations on right conduct in war did not apply to rebels. Since between 1500 and 1700 virtually all the monarchies of Europe experienced major insurrections and used armies to suppress them with extreme harshness, the failure of Just War theories to legitimize or limit civil wars was a major blind spot.

The theme of this chapter is how three successful revolutions, the English in 1688, the American in 1776, and the French in 1789, added to Just War theory a natural right of rebellion against tyranny. The English revolution was conservative in preserving the existing monarchical structure and Parliament's power to legislate; the American and French were radical, repudiating monarchies, proclaiming the equality of all men, and insisting that the only legitimate government was a republic. Peoples' armies fighting for nationalism, liberty, and revolution posed serious issues about proper conduct in war.

Religion influenced the pattern of events in these three revolutions. In Great Britain, the fear by Protestant nobles and clergymen of the political implications of having a Roman Catholic monarch who also seemed to be undermining traditional English liberties led to a bloodless revolution against James II. James' Catholicism was a major factor in his overthrow, in the adherence of the Irish to the Stuart cause, and in the severe repression of the Irish by the English after the Battle of the Boyne. The events of 1688 intensified English and Scottish anti-Catholicism. Here, in a reversal of the pattern on the continent, the people's religion determined that of the king.

In the origins of the American and French revolutions the religion of the kings played a negligible role. In the colonies fears of the potential political impact of having Anglican bishops and rivalries between Anglicans, Presbyterian-Congregationalists, and Quakers shaped events before 1776, but the patriots' primary grievances were political and economic, not religious. After 1776, American preachers justified defying Great Britain by linking republicanism and religious purity. Before 1789 anti-Catholicism was not a major factor in the origins of the French revolution, but the coming to power of anti-clerical radicals led to disestablishment of the Catholic Church, followed by persecution of priests and nuns, and influenced how opponents within and outside the country viewed events.[1] All three revolutions seem modern because secular politics rather than religious fervor motivated the rebels. So the focus of this chapter is not upon the churches per se but upon the defenses of the right of revolution in changing Just War theory, the lessened impact of organized religions, and the new role of nationalism on conduct in war.

II. John Locke and the Glorious Revolution

In 1688 the English in a bloodless *coup d'état*, later described by the victors as a Glorious Revolution, deposed the Catholic King James II and crowned his daughter Mary and her husband William of Orange as queen and king. The supporters of the new government sought for a defense of their actions, which would justify the new dynasty but would not legitimate a second Puritan revolution. John Locke's two treatises on government, written before but published after 1688, provided a rationale for the revolutionary settlement.[2]

---

[1] The de-christianization of French society in the eighteenth century and the de-sacralization of the king did undermine confidence in the royal government. Roger Chartier, *The Cultural Origins of the French Revolution* (1991), ch. 5-6.

[2] John Locke, *Treatise of Civil Government and A Letter Concerning Toleration*, ed. Charles Sherman (1937); the implications of Locke's political theory for international relations are spelled out in Richard H. Cox, *Locke on War and Peace* (1960).

Locke symbolized a kind of Copernican revolution in political theory because power now came from below - the people - rather than being bestowed by God on a monarch. Locke utilized the traditional argument that government by providing peace and security existed for the common good of the people. He sought to demonstrate that all governments originated with the consent of the people to protect their inherent or natural rights of life, liberty, and property. A monarch did not derive authority from a patriarchal arrangement initiated by God in which the king became the father of his people. Because God bestowed the inherent rights of all men, government retained a religious sanction.

Locke's state of nature, where government originated, managed to be both Aristotelian and Hobbesian. Like Aristotle, Locke saw humanity in its original state as living in an Edenic innocence inclined to peace and sociability and observing a law of nature whose first premise was self-preservation. Yet he also saw the original equality of humans dwelling in a peaceable condition as very brief, quickly undermined by corrupt mankind. The resulting conditions of insecurity and danger resembled Hobbes' portrait of pre-state life as constant conflict, and so humans contracted to institute government in order to escape from insecurity. The contract obligated both government and people and, like a business arrangement, could be terminated by a revolution if the conditions were not fulfilled. A ruler who violated the original covenant in essence made war on the people and returned them to the state of nature. A revolution in such a case was an act of defense against a tyrant, a way to end a war.

The terms of the original compact limited the state. Locke insisted that humans' inherent, God-given rights made them the ultimate sovereigns who instituted government for their benefit. If the rulers violated the original contract, the people could create a new government. For earlier thinkers, the state of nature had existed only in remote antiquity; for Locke that state of nature was always potentially present and could be returned to by the people to defend their inalienable rights against a tyrant. They could not return to a state of nature for a prolonged period, for then all the liabilities of anarchy would again emerge. So only on rare occasions should the people reassert their original equality and create a new government to preserve their rights. Except for his warning that a government should not be changed lightly or without overwhelming evidence of tyranny, Locke provided no clear guidelines as to how a people could determine when the existing government became intolerable or how they could unite as one to overthrow a tyrant without succumbing to the dangers of a civil war.

Like Hobbes, Locke believed that external relations among nations remained always in a state of nature; that is, a temporary peace succumbing to insecurity and chaos. Even so, foreign affairs should be governed by natural law. Just as in a state of nature God created all people equal, so under natural law all sovereign nations had equal rights. Unfortunately, said Locke, there neither was nor could be an all-encompassing mechanism to enforce natural law on sovereign nations. The resulting anarchy, wars, truces, and treaties reflected constant competition among nations with no possibility of real peace.

Locke's view of the inability of natural law to bring order to foreign relations diminished the emergent field of international law symbolized by Hugo Grotius. Although natural law provided norms and a standard of right and wrong in international affairs, there was no positive law among nations because there was no mechanism of enforcement except war. The history of war, where on most occasions the strong oppressed the weak, demonstrated the irrelevance of natural law in the international conduct of nations.

Locke's definition of the contents of a binding but unenforceable natural law of nations, of the right and wrong in war, was traditional, except on property rights. He argued that Just Wars were those waged for defense or to punish attacks on people or property and that the state had a duty to protect its subjects, but only a weak obligation to redress other wrongs. Because wars were between governments, not their peoples, the rights of civilians were to be observed. The just side could levy reparations for the cost of the war on the unjust side, but all reparations must be moderate and should not impoverish the civilians and could not include the seizure of land. Locke disliked any reparations on the property of civilians because the ruler, not they, caused war. A conqueror might take the rent on property for a few years, but conquest never provided just title. So a state created by conquest without the consent of the people never became legitimate or de jure.[3]

Remembering the Puritan Revolution and wars over religion, Locke reiterated the traditional view that religious differences could not provide a just cause for war. Instead, he insisted, and his emphasis recognized the religious diversity of England, a state should accept a religious diversity which did not threaten the public weal. So the Puritans had no just cause to revolt against Charles I, but England after 1688 need not tolerate public worship of Roman Catholics who owed allegiance to a foreign power, the papacy. Because the papacy did not recognize the distinction between church and state, Catholics need not be tolerated.[4]

For Locke, religion should remain a private individual matter. Note that his conclusion brought a radical interpretation of significance to society of religious belief, making faith a matter of a person's conscience and divorcing it from institutions, whether church or state. A logical implication, that the church should have no say over how a state made war, was not addressed.

Locke specified that a country unjustly conquered in violation of natural laws could make an "appeal to heaven."[5] How one interprets this phrase will determine how modern or secular Locke's political theories were. Those commentators who argue that Locke meant an appeal to force as the only arbitrator in international affairs make him a successor to Machiavelli and Hobbes. Yet the "appeal to heaven" could also harken back to the Christian view that God was the sovereign of the world and would enforce his wrath on those who flout his law. Here Locke becomes far more traditional, compromising his modernity.

---

[3] Ibid., ch. 16 "Of Conquest," 119-31.
[4] Andrew Murphy, *Conscience and Community: Revisiting Toleration and Religious Dissent in Early Modern England and America* (2001), ch. 4, argues that Locke's contribution to toleration debates are over-estimated and that the radical religious sects were more important.
[5] Ibid., 15, 113, 120.

Locke's treatises on government justified a change in personnel in the dynasty without undermining the structures of English society. However, when in 1776 the American patriots concluded that the policies of Parliament and George III aimed at establishing a tyranny, they invoked Locke's natural right of revolution.

III. A Republican Just War: the American Revolution

By almost any standard, the English settlers in the thirteen North American colonies had more freedom that any European population, and the most oppressed group, the slaves in the South, received no benefit from the Revolution. How then could the patriots prove that their struggle was a defensive Just War against tyranny? The Americans interpreted events in England through a set of ideological blinders provided by an opposition group of early eighteenth-century English writers, termed Radical Whigs, who saw British liberty as endangered by monarchs whose alliances with members of Parliament allowed corruption to flourish and subverted the will of the people. The Radical Whigs insisted that only a vigorous defense of traditional rights could preserve British freedom.[6]

Like the Radical Whigs, the American colonists saw the British government's new taxes as one of a series of measures of a corrupted Parliament attempting to destroy liberty and reduce them to slavery. At the conclusion of the French and Indian War in 1763, the British government sought to tax the colonies to help pay for the war that had driven the French from Canada and Louisiana. The colonists protested that they were being deprived of their equal rights as Englishmen, that Parliament's taxing of Americans without their consent was making a distinction between British subjects in England and America.

The Americans declared for independence only after an agonizing search for an alternative solution. For the first ten years of their struggle after 1765, the colonists aimed at restoring the old English Empire. Patriotic boycotts, petitions, and resistance were defensive reactions to unjust laws. After fighting began with

Lexington and Concord in 1775, the patriots expanded their justification of what was now an armed rebellion from a defense of English liberties to a struggle for freedom of all humankind. In early 1776, the American Revolution became part of a God-ordained cosmic struggle against monarchy and for republican government.

The churches of America had supported the protests against taxation without representation, but there was no unanimity when the issue became not constitutional liberty within the British Empire but war and independence. The Presbyterian and Congregational clergy supported the war as a defensive struggle. The Quakers and pacifist sects opposed the war and withdrew from political activity. The Anglican laity in the South favored the patriot position, but their clergy, who had taken an oath of loyalty to the Crown, hesitated. Some endorsed the American position; a few became loyalist and still attempted to serve congregations, and many fled to England. Since after July 1776 the patriots did not allow freedom of thought to those who favored remaining British, those clergy and laity who dissented either kept quiet or claimed to be neutral. The Presbyterian and Congregational clergy who defended the war likened the Americans, as a new chosen people, to the Hebrews who resisted bondage in Egypt. The American cause was just, even holy, and strict moral legislation would guarantee Jehovah's support for liberty.[7] New England's troops and later the Continental Army sang:

> Let tyrants shake their iron rods
> And slavery clank its galling chains.
> We fear them not; we trust in God.
> New England's God forever reigns.[8]

---

[6] Bernard Bailyn, *The Ideological Origins of the American Revolution* (1967) is the most influential account of the radical Whig interpretation of the Revolution.

[7] J. W. Frost, *A Perfect Freedom: Religious Liberty in Pennsylvania* (1980), ch. 4; Charles Royster, *A Revolutionary People at War: The Continental Army and American Character*, 12-23, 152-177, 224-230.

[8] William Billings hymn "Chester" quoted in Steven Woodworth, *While God is Marching On: The Religious World of Civil War Soldier* (2001), 7.

In 1776 Thomas Paine and Thomas Jefferson used the same concepts as the clergy in proclaiming a God-bestowed natural law to freedom. Thomas Paine's *Common Sense*, published in early 1776, made explicit the radical implications that could be drawn from the thoughts of humanists, Locke, Radical Whigs, and *philosophes* in declaring that the *Bible* and Just War theory required independence and a republican form of government. In order to prove that religion opposed monarchy, Paine cited the anti-monarchical sentiments expressed in Judges and I Samuel, reiterated the biblical indictments of Israel's kings, and recounted England's history of rebellions and wars caused by monarchy. Kings caused unnecessary foreign and civil war and continually sought to expand their powers, so monarchy as a system destroyed internal and external peace. Paine, following Locke, concluded that a government that could not provide peace and security had no right to exist. Therefore, America had returned to a state of nature and could create a republic to guarantee the rights of free men. In addition, monarchy and British rule of America violated nature in two ways, argued Paine; it was absurd, first, to entrust rule to a man or woman whose only claim to power was heredity and, second, for a little island to rule an enormous land three thousand miles away.[9]

Unlike warlike monarchies, asserted Paine, a republic, because it rested upon the will of the people would be peaceful. America would have harmony with Europe because its connection with foreign nations rested on trade, and commerce fostered harmony. An independent America would trade freely with all nations and, therefore, would remain at peace with them. Although republics were inherently peace-loving, their peoples now would reluctantly unite to oppose a tyrant who was already waging war against them. America's cause was God's cause because the colonists fought for all humanity. So for Paine, the American Revolution was, in a sense, a war to end war.

---

[9]Thomas Paine, "Common Sense" in *Political Writings*, ed. Bruce Kuklick (1989), 15, 20, 26.

Thomas Jefferson's Declaration of Independence reasserted themes proclaimed by Paine and derived from Locke. God created men equal and endowed them with certain "unalienable rights" including "life, liberty, and the pursuit of happiness." They instituted government to provide security to property and person. However, when a government violated this covenant, a people could return to the state of nature and institute a new government.

Using the radical Whig interpretation of history, the longest section of the Declaration sought to prove that George III (Parliament that had passed most of the laws was ignored) had become a tyrant. The colonists, said the Continental Congress, had acted over the last years with forbearance, but ultimately had to "acquiesce in the Necessity" of separation. The list of grievances proving that George III had forfeited his right to government by becoming a tyrant concluded with denouncing the English government for initiating and then waging an unjust war:

> He has plundered our seas, ravaged our Coasts, burnt our towns, and destroyed the Lives of our people. He is at this time transporting large Armies of foreign Mercenaries . . . He has constrained our fellow Citizens taken Captive on the high Seas to bear Arms against their Country, . . . He has excited domestic insurrection amongst us, and has endeavored to bring on the inhabitants of our frontiers, the merciless Indian Savages, whose known rule of warfare, is an undistinguished destruction of all ages, sexes and conditions.[10]

The Declaration did not say that the "domestic insurrection" was an offer of freedom to slaves to join the British, or that Americans had failed in an attempt to enlist the aid of Native Americans.

A Just Republican War

America was born proclaiming the validity of natural law and Just Wars theory. The implication was that a republic would observe restraint in war. At

---

[10]*Sources and Documents Illustrating the American Revolution and the Formation of the Federal Constitution*, ed. Samuel Morrison (1967), 157-162.

issue was whether a revolutionary war against Britain and a civil war at home involving mobilization of the people could be fought observing the restraints of eighteenth-century western European war. Was the American Revolution "just" in its conduct? To what extent did it inaugurate a revolution in warfare? The aim, independence, was unlimited.

Both sides attempted to fight a conventional European war, with a Continental Army led by Washington opposing a mixed British and mercenary force under Sir William Howe. The standing armies (not the state militias) on both sides resembled earlier eighteenth-century armies; that is, officers came from the upper classes and the soldiers from the dregs of society. The American recruits, after an initial burst of enthusiasm in early 1776 faded, were lower class or immigrants, who enlisted for bounties and often deserted.[11] A Prussian officer, the self-proclaimed "Baron" Von Steuben trained the army to exacting drill, and discipline, though mild by German standards, was still harsh. When in 1780 the New Jersey line threatened mutiny because of inadequate supplies and shortage of pay, Washington had the dissidents surrounded by loyal troops and two leaders killed by a firing squad of their comrades.[12] Both armies used flogging as punishment for dereliction of duty. Even so, the ability of Americans to coerce enlistment was limited, and officers tempered the treatment of men because desertion was easy. State militias and a Continental Army of patriots fighting for liberty by their very nature added an ideological thrust to the war.

Recognizing that the eventual success of the American cause rested upon the good will of the people, the army made considerable efforts and generally succeeded in not alienating civilians. Washington ordered that supplies extracted from farmers should be paid for, although the Continental paper money used

---

[11]John Shy, "American Society and Its War for Independence," in *Reconsiderations on the Revolutionary War,* ed. Don Higgenbotham (1978), 78-80, 86; James Kirby Martin, "A 'Most undisciplined, Profligate Crew': Protest and Defiance in the Continental Rank, 1776-1783" in *Arms and Independence: The Military Character of the American Revolution,* (1984), eds. Ronald Hoffman and Peter Albert, 124-125.
[12]Martin, 132-37. Charles Royster, *A Revolutionary People at War: The Continental Army and American Character, 1775-1783* (1979), 295-306.

his army in the field in spite of chronic problems of supply, and the British proved unable to translate victories into effective control of the countryside.

Facing the task of pacifying an area as large as western Europe, Lord Howe fought a conventional eighteenth-century war. He occupied all major cities (Boston, New York, Charleston), seized the capital (Philadelphia), and defeated Washington's army in all the pitched battles. The British army moved slowly (it took from July 23 to Aug 25 to sail from New York to Pennsylvania) and did not fight during the winter. (The Americans crossed the Delaware River to attack Trenton on Christmas Day.)

Howe sought by mild treatment of civilians to make loyalists active supporters and win over those who were neutral or lukewarm. He also issued strict rules for good treatment of civilians and, on occasion, hanged soldiers caught plundering farmers. The British paid in gold for supplies, and - considering the logistic difficulties of maintaining an army so far from Europe - remained well supplied. In spite of Howe's efforts, on every occasion that there was prolonged contact with the American population, the British army alienated civilians by the harshness of their efforts.[13] Americans did not like to have British soldiers quartered in their houses, stealing their livestock, and using churches as barracks. The soldiers vacillated between treating people as rebels and erring brethren to be reformed through military force.

The commanders of both sides attempted to treat prisoners in accordance with conventions of the time, which meant that the prisoners' care should be paid for by their own army. Officers, who gave their word of honor they would not escape, could be paroled so that they could walk around the town. Even so, abuses of prisoners by both sides caused animosity. Howe and Washington engaged in mutual recrimination while each constantly sought to improve the conditions for prisoners. After negotiations, the rebels and British exchanged

---

[12]Martin, 132-37. Charles Royster, *A Revolutionary People at War: The Continental Army and American Character, 1775-1783* (1979), 295-306.
[13]John Shy, *A People Numerous and Armed* (1976), 190-92; Martin, 132.

prisoners. Each side attempted to enlist deserters and prisoners of war into its own army. Overall, the main armies of the revolutionaries and British observed the conventions of eighteenth-century war.

Civility broke down in areas where there were pre-existing disputes or where neither side had effective control: examples are the Wyoming Valley in Pennsylvania, the lower Hudson Valley, New Jersey between the American and British lines, and the South.[14] Here, in addition to guerrilla wars waged between loyalists and patriots, groups of irregulars or bandits who fought for plunder rather than politics terrorized civilian populations. South Carolina paid its militia in slaves seized from the British, and North Carolina offered a bounty for Indian scalps.

The British sought to enlist the Native Americans as allies, and Indian wars were never fought with the approved tactics of European wars. The Indians specialized in surprise attacks on backcountry settlements and farms; the American response was to burn Indian crops and towns, and women and children were often not spared. The Americans took few prisoners in Indian wars. Virtually all of what could be described as the flagrant atrocities of the Revolution occurred in Indian, guerrilla, and irregular warfare. The ferocity of fighting by irregular partisans in disputed areas showed that the revolution really was a civil war, and a greater percentage of the population emigrated from America than left from France during her revolution.[15] Tories could have their property confiscated and experienced a variety of restrictions and punishment, but no one was executed by either side just because he or she was a loyalist or a patriot.

The American Revolution showed that a rebellion involving large-scale mobilization of the population in the militia and Continental army could follow the limits of eighteenth-century warfare. The importance of a conservative officer class in keeping control of the Americans and the tactics of the British who sought

---

[14]*An Uncivil War: The Southern Backcountry During the American Revolution.* eds. Ronald Hoffman, Thad Tate, and Peter Albert (1985), 126-129, 232-3, 329-330; John Shy, *A People Numerous and Armed,* 183-192.

to conciliate as well as to conquer brought restraint. The French alliance and the turning of the American struggle for independence into a general European war also helped ensure that the conduct of the war remained traditional. Without the French navy and supplies, there would have been no American victory at Yorktown in 1781.

If the Americans had decided to oppose the British by guerrilla warfare rather than a standing army, and if the British had been successful in fomenting slave revolts, or utilized loyalist regiments and Indian allies more effectively, or managed to destroy Washington's army, then the mutual restraint would have been eroded.[16] In contrast with the French Revolution, the war for American independence seems old-fashioned, a rational and disciplined rather than a romantic and all-devouring struggle. America exported to Europe the example of restraint in a republican revolution.

IV. The French Revolution

The European age of absolute monarchy from 1648 until 1789 began and ended with major wars that devastated much of Europe. Like the Thirty Years War, the French revolutionary wars involved power and ideology, although the basic motivation was republicanism versus monarchy rather than Protestant versus Catholic. Our initial concern in this section is, first, to summarize enough historical information on the revolutionary wars to provide a basis to see why and where the eighteenth-century consensus on limited war endured and broke down and, second, to assess the role of religion in these conflicts, discussing first France and then England.

The members of the Estates General, summoned by Louis XVI in 1789 because the state was bankrupt, hoped for moderate reforms to curtail the power of the king, end many prerogatives of the aristocracy, and reduce the privileges of the higher clergy and French Roman Catholic Church. Inspired by a vision of the

---

[15]R. R. Palmer, *The Age of Democratic Revolution* (1959-65), I, 188-90.

philosophes that bad kings caused war and that the people were peace-loving, the leaders of France saw themselves as inaugurating a new European society. Neither the moderates, who wanted an English-like constitutional monarchy, nor republicans expected war. The new France's wars would be in self-defense and fought observing all the conventions of Just War theory, including the rights of civilians on both sides. An aggressive war for territory would be a relic of the past. The revolutionary reforms of French society should change her foreign relations and reduce the frequency and brutality of war. Moderates in England shared in this vision of a new world order.

During the four years after 1789, the Girondists replaced the moderate monarchists, and then they lost out to radical Jacobins. France became a republic, and in 1791 the radicals executed the king and queen and initiated a Reign of Terror against aristocrats and moderates. The traditional alliance between Crown and Church changed into bitter hostility between republicans and Roman Catholics as the Jacobins turned anti-clericalism into anti-Christianity, with the state confiscating Church property, stopping the tithe, abolishing monasticism, ending Catholic control of education, and virtually eliminating the power of the papacy over the Gallic Church. The papacy, the bishops and many of the lower clergy became foes of the revolution.[17]

In 1792 France wanted to export republicanism; the Habsburgs, to restore the Bourbon monarchy. So France declared war on Austria and Prussia and, after an initial defeat, the French the next year created a new mass army transforming

---

[16]Don Higginbotham, "Reflections on the War of Independence, Modern Guerrilla Warfare and the War in Vietnam," in *Arms and Independence: The Military Character of the American Revolution*, 1-24.

[17]The opposition of the bishops was predictable, since the king appointed them and of 135 in 1789 only 1 was a commoner. William Doyle, *The Oxford History of the French Revolution* (1989), 33-36, 117, 132-46 argues that the 1790 Civil Constitution by reducing papal authority, requiring lay election of bishops and parish clergy, and requiring an oath alienated Catholics, polarized the nation, and created the counter-revolution. Only eight bishops took the oath, and parish priests either took or refused the oath depending on the attitude of the people. The radicals regarded non-subscribers as treasonous. See also Robert Holtman, *The Napoleonic Revolution* (1956), 132. Adrien Dansette, *Religious History of Modern France, From the Revolution to the Third Republic*, I (1961); Owen Chadwick, *The Popes and European Revolution* (1981).

military strategy, and soon French victories in Belgium, the Rhineland, and Italy threatened the balance of power. Britain and Spain joined the war against France. In France a conservative reaction in 1794 ended the power of the Jacobins but not internal oppression, the war, or expansionism into Holland and Italy. A Directory of leaders had formal authority, but power gravitated to the military, in particular to a young Corsican general, Napoleon Bonaparte. Napoleon became a member of the Directory and then overthrew it in 1799. Soon he would be First Consul and then Emperor, with a goal of subduing all Europe militarily. He almost succeeded, waging war successfully against every major power in Europe, controlling either directly or through alliances all of western Europe except England. Britain and Napoleon waged all-out war, but neither could prevail until France invaded Russia in 1812. Then the allies defeated and exiled Napoleon to the island of Elba and restored the Bourbon monarchy. Napoleon's brief return from Elba showed that the French were still willing to wage war, but his defeat at Waterloo in 1815 ended the French empire.

In all, the wars of the French Revolution lasted with only a few brief truces for twenty-five years, with devastation over large areas. One estimate is that France lost 400,000 men in the wars of the Revolution and another million under Napoleon; since mortality rates in the Russian army were estimated at 50% every year, its losses dwarfed those of France.[18]

The French Revolution as a Just War

The French attack upon monarchy and their desire to preserve and spread republicanism caused and became the justification for war beginning in 1792. The war was a consequence of radical measures; that is, external and internal threats to the republic allowed extremists to seize the government, suppress domestic revolts, and execute opponents. They justified the suppression of civil liberties as

---

[18] Geoffrey Best, *War and Society in Revolutionary Europe, 1770-1870.* (1982), 45, 114. Many of the soldiers in Napoleon's armies were from elsewhere in Europe, either fighting for France because they believed in republicanism or were furnished by their governments as a kind of tribute.

the only means of preservation. Yet the severe measures prompted more unrest in France. When the Austrians appeared victorious at first and invaded France, the National Convention responded in 1793 by attempting to mobilize the entire population:

> Article 1 From this moment until that in which our enemies shall have been driven from the territory of the Republic, all Frenchmen are permanently requisitioned for service in the armies.
>
> Young men will go forth to battle; married men will forge weapons and transport munitions; women will make tents and clothing, and serve in the hospitals; children will make lint from old linen; and old men will be brought to the public squares to arouse the courage of the soldiers, while preaching the unity of the Republic and hatred against kings.[19]

Here was the first declaration of total war in modern history. War, no longer a plaything of a monarch, involved a people rising to defend their nation. With all males between eighteen and twenty-five eligible to serve in the army, the French enlarged their armies and this numerical superiority allowed them to overwhelm their opponents. For a brief period in 1793-94 military service became popular as the citizens from many classes rallied to the defense of the patria. The "Marseillaise," still the French national anthem, expressed the new conception of war.

> To arms, citizens!
> Form your battalions.
> Let us march, let us march!
> That their impure blood
> Should water our fields. [20]

Initially the French could argue that they were acting in self-defense and had the right to choose their form of government. Although they continued to

---

[19] Quoted in Weigley, *Age of Battles,* 290.
[20] Claude-Joseph Rouget de Lisle (1792).

label their wars as defensive, their expansion of the realm far beyond what even Louis XIV saw as natural borders required a new rationale. Now they proclaimed that the spread of republicanism constituted just cause because all authority existed for the benefit of the people, and, therefore, all monarchies should be overthrown to provide better government.[21]

Republicanism also could justify the systematic pillaging of conquered lands because the French claimed an additional advantage for expanding good government: since the peoples under monarchies would benefit from French liberation, they should be asked to bear the cost of the war. Just War theorists had said that those who began an unjust war could be charged reparations. For French republicans, all their wars became just, and so it was legitimate to charge the cost of the war to the peoples they liberated.

Even had it wished to do so, inadequate roads, a disorganized bureaucracy, and economic difficulties meant that the French government could not adequately supply its enormous armies fighting major battles long distances from home. Instead, it became official policy for the French to turn their soldiers loose to ravage occupied territory. What was not taken from cities or conquered provinces by plunder could be extorted by fines and requiring provisions from cities or conquered provinces. Troops foraged in the surrounding country, sometimes buying but often just taking what they wanted with no consideration for the needs of the inhabitants. In rich areas like northern Italy, the policy caused distress; in Spain, a poor country, it brought suffering so intense that the populace rose up against the French. Under Napoleon, the French by levying huge demands upon conquered lands turned making war into almost a profit-making activity. The plunder was not just for the army. Official policy was to expropriate works of art; the first national art museum in the world, the Louvre, was a former palace turned into an art gallery in 1793 to show the public the treasures gathered by kings and the republican armies.

---

[21] Geoffrey Best, *Humanity in Warfare* (1980), ch. 2.

Under the Directory and then under Napoleon the rationale for expansion changed from exporting republican values into a war for hegemonic control of Europe. The French people's enthusiastic participation and total mobilization for war also declined after 1795. Universal conscription continued, though there were ways of avoiding service.[22] Napoleon forced conquered lands to supply men for his armies, and foreigners constituted a majority of the French army that invaded Russia. Still, by controlling information in the French press, issuing propaganda extolling his achievements, staging festivals, suppressing opponents, and winning victories, Napoleon managed to maintain popular support for his wars.[23]

Modern nationalism began with the French Revolution. A dictionary definition of nationalism is "an attitude, feeling, or belief characterized by a sense of national consciousness, an exaltation of one nation above all others, and an emphasis on loyalty to and the promotion of the culture and interests of one nation." A nationalist identifies himself as a member of a state having a unique culture that is determined by boundary lines. All ethnic groups within the state owe primary allegiance to the nation, and the preservation of that state becomes the greatest value. The belief that the nation constitutes a unique culture and that, for example, all Frenchmen are alike and should live in a nation is a product of recent history. The belief is romantic and irrational, based upon a geographic determinism ignoring the arbitrary nature of boundaries and the varieties of culture and peoples within most states. Yet the nation-state has become the primary actor in international affairs, and nationalism, when allied with religion, has become a dominant force in the world. [24]

---

[22] Alan Forest, *Conscripts and Deserters: The Army and French Society During the Revolution and Empire* (1989), 5; Robert B. Holtman, *The Napoleonic Revolution* (1981), 45-46. Because of the exemptions and early marriages, the population of France increased during the wars.
[23] Robert B. Holtman, *Napoleonic Propaganda* (1950).
[24] *Webster's Third New International Dictionary* (1971), II, 1505. Contrasting views as to whether nationalism was primarily an intellectual revolution or was a response to a new stage in social development are in E. Kedourie, *Nationalism* (1993) and Ernest Gellner, *Nationalism* (1997). Conor Cruise O'Brien, *God Land: Reflections on Religion and Nationalism* (1988), sees land-nationalism as beginning with the ancient Hebrews.

The French first took advantage of enlisting the sentiments of the entire nation to wage a people's war, but Napoleon's armies later encountered national feelings used against them by Spanish, English, Germans, and Russians. Although Americans began the process, the French Revolution had a profound effect in adding nationalism as a just cause for war. People had long had a sense of themselves as French, English, or Spanish, even though regional or local loyalties might be more important. For Germans and Italians, the sense of peoplehood was distinct from statehood. So long as monarchs made war for dynastic reasons and armies were composed of derelicts and mercenaries, there was no reason for a people's or an army's firm loyalty to the state. During the French Revolution people identified their welfare with the policies of their government, resisted being ruled by foreign rulers, and insisted on being self-governed - in a word, became patriotic. European monarchies often controlled diverse peoples: the Habsburgs ruled Austrians, Hungarians, and Poles. Neither the Germans nor Italians comprised a state. The weakness of France at the beginning of the Revolution allowed Austria, Prussia, and Russia to carve up Poland. The newly-minted right of self-determination meant problems for transnational monarchies when ethnic groups assumed that having a coterminous state and nationality was a good, and the denial of an ethnic group's right to statehood was just cause for a revolution.[25]

V. The Practice of War

There were three fundamental changes in warfare after 1789: in size and organization of armies, degree of mobilization of people, and the frequency of major battles. The evolution in battle strategy was not caused by new technologies, because there were only minor improvements in the weapons of war. A massed volley from a line of soldiers remained the only way to compensate for inaccuracy. Reloading muskets before each shot remained a multi-step

---

[25]Napoleon, a native of Corsica who became a French nationalist, was in many ways still a classicist; that is, he attempted to impose his reformed version of French law on Holland, Italy, and parts of Germany and redrew the map of Europe with little regard to ethnic differences. The Congress of Vienna in 1815 also often ignored nationality in redefining the countries of Europe.

phenomenon, although one key to French successes was a more rapid rate of fire. Napoleon increased the number of cannons and concentrated their fire at the most vulnerable spot of an opponent's line. With the use of newly invented "shrapnel" by 1814, artillery caused 20% of battle casualties. Victory came when the cavalry or soldiers with bayonets broke the line of the opponents, often after an encircling movement. French generals stressed speed in both marching and maneuvering, sought for decisive battles, placed less emphasis upon fortification and sieges, and willingly accepted heavy casualties in pursuit of victory.[26] After the Austrians and Russians adopted Napoleon's strategies, war casualties on both sides mounted: at Wagram, 33,000 French and 37,000 Austrians; at Borodino, 80,000 casualties by French and Russians caused by firing 2.09 million projectiles.

Civilians not in the immediate vicinity of a battle ran more risk of being plundered than attacked, and the French army showed no mercy to male civilians, who could be despoiled of goods, and females, who became targets for rape. The officer corps on all sides professed allegiance to and attempted to observe the limitations required by the laws of war. If in assessing their success we use as a standard the limited western European wars of the eighteenth century, the revolutionary wars significantly eroded non-combatant rights and civility. Yet looked at from the standpoint of the twentieth century, officers fought the Napoleonic wars with restraint.[27]

Two important innovations in warfare increased civilian destruction: guerrilla tactics and economic blockades. Guerrilla warfare (we still use the Spanish name) first occurred in Spain after Napoleon removed the incompetent Bourbon king and placed his brother Joseph on the throne. The regular Spanish army had been and continued to be ineffectual, but heavy depredations and the French reputation for infidelity occasioned a popular resistance movement

---

[26]A brief analysis of Napoleon's military strategy is in Holtman, *Napoleonic Revolution*, 35-64, and Geoffrey Wawro, *Warfare and Society in Europe 1792-1914* (2000), 1-22. More detailed analysis is in Best, *War and Society in Revolutionary Europe* and Weigley, *Age of Battles.*
[27]Gunther Rothenberg, "The Age of Napoleon," in *The Laws of War*, ed. Michael Howard, et al. (1994), 87-90.

affirming Spanish culture and Catholicism. The lower clergy and independent peasants led the resistance, and the guerrilla fighters had not been trained in the classic rules of civilized warfare. The peasants, who wore no uniforms, were not regular soldiers and, unless they had superiority in numbers, avoided pitched battles and attempted surprise attacks. After battles, they blended into the regular population who supported them. Since the guerrillas had no secure area of control, they could not keep or exchange prisoners of war. So they killed prisoners, including French soldiers wounded or left behind in hospitals. The French, who were appalled at the guerrilla ways of fighting (so were the British, the ally of the Spanish), reacted savagely. Since the guerrillas resisted the representatives of the French people, then the French would retaliate against Spanish people. The guerrillas were fighting from a position of weakness and could not defeat the regular French army, yet they, along with Wellington's English troops, caused Spain to become "Napoleon's bleeding ulcer" and made it impossible for the French to exercise effective control of the land. The Spanish monarch in exile was not happy with the arming of peasants, a reluctance shared by other European states.

Elsewhere the closest approximation to guerrilla warfare occurred during Napoleon's retreat from Moscow in 1812. The Russians had followed their customary policy of dealing with invasion by retreat (partially because Napoleon's army of 600,000 was larger and more powerful) and a scorched-earth policy that denied supplies to the aggressor. So Russian serfs had experienced severe conditions. They satisfied their desire for revenge with guerrilla-like attacks on the starving and/or wounded retreating French soldiers. As in Spain, such atrocities were the policy of irregulars; when the main Russian army invaded France, officers kept the soldiers under strict control. Only the Prussian army behaved barbarously in 1813 in its desire for vengeance on the French people. Neither monarchies nor regular armies approved of the tactics of guerrilla fighters during the Napoleonic era or later, and, except for the British, European nations did not create militias. After seeing republics close-up, the monarchies feared giving the people arms that could be used against their authority, and the regular soldiers recognized that an enemy could be weakened but wars would not be won by badly trained militias or guerrillas. Except briefly after the Franco-Prussian War of 1870, Europeans would not utilize guerrilla tactics again until World War II.

The second innovation in warfare involved the targeting of civilians and grew out of the battle for European hegemony between Britain and France in which each sought to destroy the opponent's government. So unlike the restrained war between the monarchies before 1789, Napoleon's war aims were unlimited. Between 1805-12 Napoleon reigned supreme after having defeated or neutralized all continental powers, redrawn the outlines of states, put his relatives on thrones, and enlisted all Europe in his battle with Britain. Napoleon with the best army ruled on land; England protected by a channel only twenty-one miles wide at its narrowest place had the best navy in the world. So each side attempted to use its weapon - control of land, control of sea - in waging economic warfare against its opponent. They could not defeat each other's primary military weapon, so they sought to attack civilians through denial of trade, even of food.

Both nations sought to end the other's foreign commerce. Britain declared that all ships going to the continent, even to neutral countries, must first stop in England and pay duties. Any ship that did not could be seized as a spoil of war. Neutral America and Denmark protested that free ships made free goods and that a trade normal in peacetime could not be outlawed in war. Parliament debated whether the British designed the Orders in Council to win the war or to enable its merchants to control and tax all trade to the continent. According to the rules of war, a legal boycott had to be enforced, not be just a paper declaration. The British could not control all the ports of Europe, but British privateers could harass neutral ships.

Napoleon responded in his Milan and Berlin decrees, insisting that any ships trading with England could be seized. Since his navy was inferior, his boycott was a clearly a paper declaration and he proved willing to conciliate neutral grievances. Britain and France made exceptions when they served their purposes. For example, Napoleon allowed the export of grain to England after he levied a heavy duty on it. The French army wore uniforms made of British cloth. According to the laws of war, stopping supplies from entering into a town during a siege was legitimate. What was new was the expansion of this concept to a whole country; to say, in effect, that wartime necessity allowed depriving the civilians of France and its allies of all imported foodstuffs. The populations of both Britain and France suffered during the war, although the near-famines that occurred in England resulted from bad harvests rather than Napoleonic blockades. In 1793 the French attempted to mobilize the entire population to win the war. The issue posed by the blockades, which would reappear in 1914 and 1939, was whether mobilized civilians were a legitimate target in war.

VI. The Church and War

A formal declaration of war continued to be the norm, but other restraints upon just cause disappeared. After 1789, war was between peoples, and neither European sovereigns nor the French republic/empire wanted public dissent. Under revolutionary and wartime conditions, neither the Church nor her representatives managed to maintain enough independence to influence the decisions of government. Even the clergy's ability to speak out varied according to the society.

The French Church, particularly its hierarchy, had been strong supporters of the monarch who, according to a treaty with Rome, nominated bishops to be confirmed by the pope. So bishops tended to be aristocrats and to have little in common with lower clergy or the populace. The moderates wished to stay on the good side of the Church, not so the Girondists and Jacobins, who learned their anti-clericalism from the *philosophes* and demanded toleration and separation of church from state. Soon the revolution was anti-Catholic, attempting to replace orthodox Christianity with celebrations in Notre Dame (renamed the Temple of Reason) to the Supreme Being of reason and natural law. The Church responded with hostility, fomenting revolution against the republic in the Vendée and supporting the Austrian armies against France.[28] The internal war in France against opponents of the republic was very much a religious war; only now the issue was Catholicism versus deism or atheism. Many bishops and clergy who opposed the revolution left France, and those who stayed needed to be circumspect even in carrying on pastoral functions, for republicans suspected them of being monarchists. With the papacy and the hierarchy firmly on the side of autocracy, the Catholic Church in France had no influence in restraining either the Terror or the war.

Napoleon claimed to have no religion, but saw faith as useful to the state. He viewed the open hostility of the Roman Catholic Church to the Revolution as weakening the power of France to make war and so sought a compromise allowing religious practice, restricting political influence, and giving the government control over the clergy. In 1801 he signed a Concordant with Rome allowing the legitimacy of Roman Catholic worship and the consecration of new bishops, but not restoring the Church's temporal power. The state would now pay the clergy who would take an oath of loyalty and preach obedience to the government. The clergy who earlier witnessed the virtual destruction of French Catholicism viewed Napoleon as a messenger of God (a new King David with France as a new Israel fighting a holy war against barbarism) and continued to support him.[29] Napoleon's relations with the papacy soon degenerated, however, and in 1808 he imprisoned the pope and abolished the Papal States in Italy. Napoleon enlisted the power of the state to stage-manage news and did not allow church leaders or anyone else to criticize his policies openly. Instead, his government issued orders for the bishops to celebrate *Te Deum* masses for his victories and even instructed them as to the contents of pastoral letters. The bishops and clergy acquiesced with no protest. They either justified the Napoleonic wars under the theory that France

---

[28] John McManners, *The French Revolution and the Church* (1969), 64-5, 82-85, 94-95.
[29] J. P. Berthe, "Naissance et Elaboration d'une 'Theologie' de la Guerre chez les eEveques de Napoleon," in *Civilisation chrétienne XVIII-XX Siécle*, ed. Jene Derre (1975), 95-99.

was threatened or maintained silence, insisting that their duty was to serve the spiritual needs of the congregation.

The French Revolution marked a basic reorientation of the role of Christianity. Before 1648 wars occurred over which form of Christianity the state would espouse. Now republicans and radicals opposed Christianity and wanted the state separate from the church.

Elsewhere in Europe the traditional attitude of the churches of voicing support for all government wars continued unchanged or was strengthened by the wars against France. Europe's autocrats had never allowed lower clergy free political expression and powerful prelates, like France's Cardinal Richelieu, had identified closely with the purposes of the monarchy. So before 1789, there was no tradition of Luther-like condemnation of the policies in war or peace. The revolutionaries' desecration of churches, executions of priests and monks, and official anti-Christianity appalled Catholic, Presbyterian, and Lutheran clergy. French anti-religious expression remained common in the Napoleonic Empire and in his army even after Napoleon's Concordant. Protestants and Catholics saw their countries' armies defeated by the French, witnessed the creation of puppet regimes like the new Batavian Republic replacing Holland, and experienced Napoleon's financial extortion of defeated countries. Napoleon's transparent ambition to dominate all Europe meant that any war against him could be seen as defensive. So after 1792, the European clergy enthusiastically endorsed their governments' anti-France war policy.

VII. Great Britain

Britain with its limited monarchy, hatred of Bourbon absolutism, anti-Catholicism, religious toleration for Protestants, and two-party parliamentary system might have been expected to sympathize with French republicanism. And this was true initially; even after Britain declared war, there was always a vocal peace party. So the English reaction varied, and it is necessary to distinguish the government's position from that of the war opposition, termed the Friends of Peace.

Before 1789, Britain, because of its parliamentary system, moved toward acceptance of open political dissent against government policy, even allowing open discussion of war and peace. After 1765, during the years of colonial constitutional protest and even after fighting in the American Revolution began in 1775 members of Parliament, journalists, and pamphleteers expressed sympathy for the colonists, though not for an independent America. Initially the Whig opposition saw the Americans as defending British liberties against a corrupt monarchy/aristocracy. Dissent from British war policies continued until the peace treaty was signed in 1783.

Agitation for political reforms in England continued, and the new prime minister, William Pitt the Younger, came to office in 1784 with the reputation as a reformer. Many Britons greeted the beginnings of the French Revolution as a positive step. Protestant Englishmen contrasted their heritage of religious liberty and parliamentary government with French absolutism and Roman Catholic intolerance, so there was widespread approval for the initial declarations of the French for a constitutional monarchy, religious freedom, and peace.[30] Pitt's government changed its mind after the imprisonment and execution of the king and queen, French successes in the war with Austria leading to the occupation of the Netherlands, the revolutionaries' desire to export republicanism, and the beginnings of the "Reign of Terror." After a vigorous public debate on events in France, England went to war in 1794.

The government's position was that this was a necessary war to protect Britain's king and church. French republicanism and infidelity struck at the very basis of civilized existence, and her aggression upset the balance of power in Europe. Fearing the spread of a revolutionary contagion to England, the government attempted to discredit all political reformers as Jacobin republicans seeking to subvert the constitution. Pitt and his Tory Party embraced repression

---

[30] Roland Bartel, "English Clergymen and Laymen on the Principle of War, 1789-1802," *Anglican Theological Review* (1956), 235-38

at home as the way to quarantine the republican virus. They were successful in defeating the reformers and persuading the English to support constant war with France.

Not only were there no electoral or other reforms at home (except for ending the slave trade) but, unlike continental powers, there were also no basic changes in the navy or army. Sixty percent of the navy men were impressed, with many others being vagabonds or convicts.[31] The government ignored popular protests against its "recruiting" methods and even claimed the right to board neutral ships to impress British subjects serving on them. Within the navy, discipline remained harsh, and conditions on ships were so appalling that in 1797 and 1803, with Napoleon threatening invasion, there were major mutinies in the Channel fleet. Britain also continued to use eighteenth-century methods of conducting land war: subsidizing allied forces, utilizing foreigners in its own army, reserving commands for members of the upper class and, most of all, relying on its navy. Unlike Napoleonic France, the government could not control the press or manage the news to avoid unfavorable comment. In spite of barbarous treatment of its soldiers, the British soldiers and sailors proved patriotic. Charismatic leaders like Admiral Nelson ("England expects every man to do his duty") and competent generals like Wellington could draw upon anti-French feeling and nationalism to motivate their men.

The clergy of the Church of England supported the government's repression at home and the war efforts. A study of the established Church's attitude even during the initial stages of the Revolution when there was sympathy for France found no clergyman caught up in the euphoria for peace.[32] Later only a few clergymen openly criticized the government's policies or conduct in waging the war. Instead, the Anglican clergy sought to persuade men to enlist in the army or navy, held services for consecrating war flags, preached repentance on fast days

---

[31]Best, 146.
[32]Bartel, 238-41.

so that God would help the British, and thanked God for English victories. When others denounced England's destruction of neutral Denmark's fleet to keep it from falling into the hands of Napoleon, the Church of England uttered no protest. It is fair to conclude that the Anglicans spoke what and when the government wanted. Like other established churches, the Church of England was a prop for the monarchy.

A small but vocal peace party existed throughout the long years of war with supporters within the minority Whig Party in Parliament, republican reformers, manufacturers interested in free trade, and the clergy of dissenting churches - primarily Unitarians, old dissenters (rationalistic Congregationalists and Presbyterians), and Quakers. Only the Quakers were pacifists; the others willingly endorsed self-defense on the two occasions when the French threatened to invade England. The peace party consisted of respectable middle-class people who were critics of the ruling class but not revolutionaries nor interested in the working class or poor.

The Friends of Peace based their protest on Christian moral teachings and traditions of English liberty.[33] Like Erasmus, whose anti-war essays they republished, the Friends saw Christianity as opposed to war. Like the French *philosophes* they viewed humans optimistically, as creatures whose reason could solve problems without fighting. They saw war with France as unnecessary, a result of the follies of monarchies and wealthy classes who initiated and continued wars as a method of increasing their own power and curtailing liberty.

The peace party insisted that the French had the right to choose their own government, and that Britain was fighting on the side of absolute monarchy and Roman Catholicism. They wondered if Pitt really remembered what Bourbon kings were like, agreed that there were excesses in the French Revolution, but insisted that the *ancien régime* in France was so evil that violence was necessary.

---

[33]J.E Cookson, *The Friends of Peace: Anti-War Liberalism in England 1793-1815* (1986).

The Friends of Peace denounced the war as immoral in its effects. The dissenting clergy in the peace party used fast days to condemn the failures of the government and saw the war as a punishment for England's sins. Opposition newspapers printed poems featuring the gore of battle, the death of soldiers far from home, and the suffering of fatherless children and widows.[34] The Friends of Peace insisted that moral standards applied to individuals and nations. Rather than fight Napoleon to the death, the government should aim at compromise and a peaceful solution.

The Friends of Peace sought to demonstrate that the war enriched a few at the expense of many. Great Britain between 1790 and 1815 suffered not only from war but from the reordering of the economy under the beginnings of the Industrial Revolution. Manufacturers of the new factories disliked the restrictive Orders in Council on trade. They asserted that the war caused the high price of grain and near-famine conditions in 1797 and proclaimed the thesis that would become the credo of liberals in the nineteenth century: trade creates peace.

The propaganda of the Friends of Peace had little immediate impact on England's conduct of the war with Napoleon, but was destined to play a major role in nineteenth-century peace organizations and, with the increase in power of manufacturers and parliamentary reform in Britain, became a constant element in political debate. An organized peace movement made rapid headway as soon as the war was over, and the English realized the price they had paid to defeat republican and imperial France.

After 1815 the established churches and monarchies of Europe attempted to deny that the French Revolution had taken place, still insisting that rebellion was against God. In the early nineteenth century the people in France, Spain, Austria, and Italy continued to insist that Just War theory allowed revolution against kings. Because the Roman Catholic Church supported monarchy, the

---

[34]Betty T. Bennett, *British War Poetry in the Age of Romanticism: 1793-1815* (1976), 20-21, 236, 361.

rebels tended to be anti-clerical and to base their actions on reason and natural law. Christian Europe rejoiced when the Greeks overthrew Turkish rule and declared independence. The French ideal of the distinctive genius of a people, a national identity, which should take a political form was now applied by Italians, Germans, Poles, Hungarians, and Serbs - groups who claimed to be a nationality and desired self-rule in their own states. The denial of this right also became a just cause for war.

Even though Napoleon subverted the ideal of French republicanism when he had himself crowned Emperor, his defeat meant the overthrow of French ideals of liberty and citizenship. Still there would be lasting military effects: the concept of a nation in arms, nationalism, a cult of the citizen soldier, a fascination with military genius, and a taste for military glory. Through the rest of the century European intellectuals would be fascinated and repelled by French military prowess. The revulsion against the carnage of Napoleon's wars created the modern peace movement. Yet his almost re-creation of a new Roman Empire through conquest stimulated a new appreciation of militarism and realpolitik.

XII.
Religion, Nationalism, and War in the Nineteenth Century

In 1800 neither Prussia nor the U.S. counted for much on the world's stage; by 1900 they had emerged as industrial giants and great powers. The major focus of this chapter is on religious attitudes to war of these two influential but very different governments: autocratic Prussia and republican America. Our theme is the influence of Christianity on nationalism and nationalism on Christianity. The Church, once the handmaiden of kings, now proved equally usefully in emergent nation-states. Prussia will be treated first because its intellectuals pioneered a new attitude to the state and war. An ideology linking nationalism, religion and militarism flourished in a country that remained at peace from 1814 until the 1860's. Then in the next decade, Prussia created a united Germany by conquest and came to dominate central Europe. The United States by purchase and also by conquest after 1800 expanded to the Pacific Ocean and then through war created a new national unity between 1861 and 1865. Unlike Prussia, America's ideology was anti-war and pro-peace; yet from 1812 to 1880 it was very active militarily, with three major wars and numerous battles or undeclared wars against the indigenous population. The historian Geoffrey Perret correctly labels the United States "a country made by war."[1]

The fusions of Christianity and nationalism used to unify nations could be applied to overseas conquests. After 1870 Germany and America joined Britain and France in the scramble for colonial empires. Since the age of Columbus, spreading Christianity had provided a rationale for conquest. Our interest is in the

---

[1]Geoffrey Perret, *A Country Made by War: From the Revolution to Vietnam - The Story of America's Rise to Power* (1990).

response of missionaries to the nineteenth-century wars of imperialism in Africa and Asia. Europeans waged brutal wars against those who resisted foreign rule.

In their struggles for unity, the United States and Prussia joined religion and nationalism and regarded themselves as superior peoples favored by God. Yet their very different histories require dissimilar treatment. An understanding of new German attitudes to war and peace can be arrived at by treating three early nineteenth-century intellectuals: the philosopher George Frederick Hegel, the theologian Frederich Schleiermacher, and the military theorist Carl Clausewitz. All were profoundly affected by the Napoleonic Wars and helped define German attitudes to the state and war. American attitudes are better seen through an analysis of popular responses to three wars: the War of 1812, the Mexican War, and the Civil War.

I. The European Context

The defeat of Napoleon and the victor's arrangements worked out at the Congress of Vienna gave Europe forty years of relative peace until 1860. The monarchies of Europe led a reaction against the liberalism and nationalism associated with the French Revolution and in alliance with the established churches - whether Protestant, Catholic, or Orthodox - worked against republican and democratic ideas. Contrasting with the triumph of absolutism in government and revival of religious orthodoxy were enormous economic, social, and intellectual changes caused by the industrial revolution, the rapid growth of cities, and the increasing power of the bourgeoisie. The cosmopolitan rationalism of the Enlightenment succumbed to a romantic nationalism.

In Europe's only great-power war, Britain and France fought a limited war against Russia in the Crimea in 1854-1856 in order to preserve a balance of power by preventing Russian expansion at the expense of the weak Ottoman Empire. The main Russian demand was religious: the preservation of Orthodox rights in churches in Jerusalem. Ironically, the Tsar's initial willingness to meet French-English complaints did not avoid a war. Although historians have labeled the Crimean War an unnecessary war, there was almost no opposition within the churches of the three states. English churches proclaimed that their men fought for the sake of Christian civilization, a remarkable conclusion since the British fought in alliance with a Muslim empire that Europeans generally condemned as barbaric, against a state with an established powerful Church. English newspapers proved to be remarkably chauvinistic in portraying the few who opposed the Crimean War as traitors.[2] In France Emperor Napoleon III had no difficulty in enlisting the support of Catholics who wanted to wrest control of sacred sites in the Holy Land away from the Russian Orthodox Christians. Although willing to fight in the Crimea to preserve Turkey as a buffer against Russia, Britain and France undermined what remained of Turkish control in North Africa as they sought to carve out spheres of influence in Egypt and Algeria.

Italy's and Germany's struggles for national unification were the most important European wars of the nineteenth century. Italian unification depended upon driving Austria from northern Italy, overthrowing the Kingdom of Naples, and ending papal rule of the central area including Rome. Many Italian patriots merged anti-Austrian and anticlerical themes in opposing the temporal claims of the Roman Catholic Church. The papacy's opposition to the unification of Italy under the House of Savoy stemmed from its claim to temporal powers, not religious differences. After the defeat of Austria and proclamation of an Italian state, French troops protected a papal state at Rome until 1870, when they were withdrawn to fight Prussia. Rome then became the capital of Italy, and the pope proclaimed himself a captive within the small territory surrounding the Vatican and St. Peter's.[3] Official Roman Catholic opposition to the Italian state continued until after World War I, though with minimal effect.

---

[2]H. Daniel-Rops, *The Church in an Age of Revolution 1789-1870* (1965), 267; an interpretation stressing the religious motivation of the Tsar is David Welch, *Justice and the Genesis of War* (1993), 48-75. Norman Rich, *Why the Crimean War? A Cautionary Tale* (1985), 10-12; Kingsley Martin, *The Triumph of Lord Palmerston: A Study of Public Opinion in England before the Crimean War* (1963), 18-20, 202-208.
[3]Anthony Rhodes, *The Power of Rome in the Twentieth Century: The Vatican in the Age of Liberal Democracies, 1870-1922* (1983), chs. 1, 2.

Religious factors played little role in Prussia's wars with Protestant Denmark, Catholic Austria, and Catholic France. Lutheran/Reformed churches in Prussia had long functioned as an arm of the state, and pastors following Luther's doctrine of two spheres confined their role to the spiritual realm. As will be seen shortly, the romantic apotheosis of the Prussian state also precluded criticism of German unification.

In comparison to the titanic wars of the late eighteenth and early twentieth centuries, the Italian and German wars produced few casualties. Germany, for example, defeated Austria in six weeks and France in a few months. So most Europeans remained ignorant of how costly a long war by industrialized countries could become, partially because they chose to ignore the lessons of the American Civil War. After 1870, with Germany and Italy united and France defeated, there were no major wars in Europe for forty years, although the Balkan states fought each other and Turkey. European countries engaged in the Anglo-Boer War in South Africa and the Russo-Japanese War in the Orient. Although class conflict, colonialism, nationalism, and arms races posed serious challenges to the European concert of powers, diplomats seemed able to solve problems peacefully, and reformers dreamed that civilized Europe had entered a new era of peace.

II. Prussia

Prussia was repeatedly humiliated during the wars of the French Revolution. The Prussian army was generally considered to be the best fighting force in Europe during the long reign of Frederick the Great (1740-1779). One generation later, Napoleon at the battles of Jena and Auerstädt completely routed the Prussian army, occupied Berlin, and forced a treaty requiring forfeiture of territory, an indemnity, and furnishing of troops for his invasion of Russia. The Prussian reaction to French domination created new attitudes to the state and military which can be illustrated by contrasting Frederick the Great's reactions to Machiavelli's *The Prince* with those of Hegel.

Eighteenth-century Prussia has been described as an army in search of a state. Prussia aspired to be a great power, yet it was surrounded by three more powerful states (France, Russia, and Austria) and had no well-defined historic, cultural, or natural borders. So its ruler had to practice carefully diplomacy and war.

Frederick was absolute monarch, warrior, and *philosophe* - a practitioner of power politics who sought to be a man of reason. Early in his life, just before becoming king, he wrote a pamphlet entitled *Anti-Machiavel* that rejected the amoral politics advocated by the Renaissance courtier. Frederick proclaimed the necessity of a prince's actually being a trustworthy person: "It is thus not power, force, or wealth which win the hearts of men, but personal qualities, goodness, and virtue." Morality was necessary for a king's primary duty, promoting the welfare of his subjects. In his rejection of the virtue of making war and being a conqueror whom he labeled as having the character of a "thief," Frederick's catalogue of the evils of war read like that of his friend Voltaire.[4] However, almost immediately after becoming king, Frederick engaged in a surprise attack on Austria in order to seize Silesia and provoked a general European war. In his later life Frederick agonized over his conduct and expanded and qualified but never repudiated his initial stand against Machiavelli. Perhaps seeking to justify his own conduct, he did stress a monarch's need to break treaty obligation during rare instances of necessity when the welfare of the people (not that of the dynasty) would benefit. Still, he insisted that an enlightened monarch would normally keep his word. A comparison of the young Frederick's theory with his later actions shows that he did not recognize how quickly he would come to resemble Machiavelli's ideal prince.

Frederick was not a nationalist. He did not stress the importance of the German culture or *volk* or language or the bond between the people and the soil,

---

[4]Frederick of Prussia, *The Refutation of Machiavelli's 'Prince' or Anti-Machiavel,* ed. Paul Sonnino (1981), 40-41, 54, 106, 116. A discussion of the influence of *raison d'état* on

nor did he attempt to appeal to national sentiment. Frederick remained the cosmopolitan man of reason devoted, paradoxically, to increasing the power of Prussia. Ready on occasion to practice power politics, he rejected Machiavelli's idea that the essence of the state was power and fought a series of limited eighteenth-century wars. He bequeathed a state (not a nation) ill-equipped to deal with the French Revolution.

Napoleon's open practice of realpolitik coupled with his success prompted his opponents to reassess the value of morality in foreign policy. Prince Metternick of Austria recalled a conversation in which Napoleon stated that he did not "give a hang about the lives of a million people." Talleyrand, the bishop who served as Napoleon's foreign minister, described Napoleon as the embodiment of Machiavelli's Prince. Napoleon's cavalier attitude toward keeping his treaties, the ruthlessness with which he dealt with opponents, and his welcoming of war reminded the Prussians of *The Prince*. He seemed to possess the *virtú, fortuna*, and genius requisite for a successful Prince. Machiavelli's treatise called for such a man to lead a disunited and demoralized Italy against the foreign invaders, including the French.[5]

Prussian intellectuals saw their situation as analogous to that of Renaissance Italy. The German-speaking populations - split among Prussia, Austria, and dozens of small principalities - were easy prey to France. Germans needed a Napoleon, a new Prince, to unify them and to drive out the French. In situations of extremity, morality and reason did not seem to help. What was needed was success, and, as in Renaissance Italy, the methods must be adopted to the time. Prussian intellectuals fused Machiavellian realpolitik, glorification of war, and a religiously based nationalism into an ideology to counter Napoleon and to unify the Germans.

Frederick, Hegel, etc. is in Friedrich Meinecke, *Machiavellism: The Doctrine of Raison d'état in Modern History*. tr. Douglas Scott (1957), 272-369.
[5]Gerhard Ritter, *The Prussian Tradition 1740-1890*, I *The Sword and the Scepter 1740-1890* (1969), 41-44.

The philosopher George Frederick Hegel (1770-1830) pioneered the re-evaluation of Machiavelli. To Hegel, Machiavelli had correctly described the need of the state to survive and identified its essential ingredient as power. The Germans, wrote Hegel, had learned that their rich cultural heritage was inefficacious against Napoleon. Hegel admired Napoleon, saw him as one embodiment of the Spirit or Reason that determined the course of world events, and did not morally condemn him. For Hegel, what Prussia needed to learn was how to make war like Napoleon, because war was the defining essence of the state at its purest and highest: "War has the deep meaning that by it the ethical health of the nations is preserved and their finite aims uprooted."[6]

The intellectual issue for Hegel was how to combine religious values with sordid reality. Frederick had professed moral restraint while practicing realpolitik. Hegel sought to show that even evil contributed to ultimate good. He recognized that the methods of war and those of international power politics seemed on the surface unethical. But, he argued, ethics for a state were not the same as for a person. So the state's use of deception was not an immoral act, because the existence and survival of the state was an ethical good. Hegel saw the interaction of the moral and immoral elements in statecraft as creating a larger synthesis of good, a working out of Spirit or God in history that had climaxed in the creation of the Prussian monarchy.

The complex philosophical rationale behind Hegel's optimism is not as important for our purposes as his assertion that the state became the prime source of value. Frederick's advocacy of *raison d'état* depended upon the good of the people; Hegel's, on the value of the state. Hegel in essence brought realpolitik out of the closet and justified its practice as contributing to the greater good.

A second element in the re-evaluation of Machiavelli was a new emphasis upon an organic and historical appreciation of the state. Ever since the Greeks,

---

[6] W. F. Georg, "The Philosophy of Law," in *Hegel Selections*, ed. Jacob Loewenberg (1957), 436, 438, 443-48, 464-68.

those who appealed to reason stressed its universality. Because human nature was always the same, a detailed knowledge of any individual event was unnecessary. At the beginning of the nineteenth century, German thinkers individualized reason, insisting that one person's or nation's reason need not be identical with universal reason. Instead, a nation, like an organism, developed through time, and each nation became an entity with a distinct culture and destiny. The successes and failures of the nation became those of its inhabitants, not just those of the ruling dynasty. So it became important for the German folk to be in a German state because a nationality defined the essence of a political entity. A state's borders and a nationality's borders should coincide. Machiavelli's *The Prince* allegedly discovered Italian identity and nationality and advocated unity to drive out the foreigner. Prussia should do the same.

The theologian Frederich Schleiermacher (1768-1834), the most significant German theologian since the Reformation, merged religious devotion and the new sense of national feeling. Product of a pietist background, Schleiermacher found emotional intensity in love of God and service of the state. For example, he wanted to separate church and state schools because church schools, following the Sermon on the Mount, could not adequately teach the history and necessity of war and inspire patriotism. In Berlin as a professor of theology and eloquent preacher, Schleiermacher became an advocate for a holy war against the French and a promoter of German unity. He hoped that a great popular uprising against the French would create a definition of German national unity. The monarchy remained fearful that an uprising against the French might later be directed against the king.

Schleiermacher preached that Germany had a right to be a nation, that French successes came because the people had forgotten Prussian traditions, that foreign domination destroyed freedom and religion, and that God would favor a German war of liberation. Service to God was linked to service to the state because God blessed the cause of nationalism. The casualties of war became bearable because God had destined the Germans to be a free people. Schleiermacher interpreted the defeat of Napoleon in the battles of 1812 and 1813 in messianic fashion, giving God the credit for victory, though recognizing patriotism as playing a role: "in Him is that nation trusting which means to defend at any price the distinctive aims and spirit which it has had implanted in it, and is thus fighting for God's work."[7]

Like Hegel, Schleiermacher saw the Prussian monarchy as an ideal form of government that bound king and people in a unity sanctified by tradition. The state became "the supreme fulfillment of the individual's life;" the emotional bond between the individual and God through the Church which gave meaning to life was analogous to the link between the individual and the state.[8] God created not just women and men, but Germans, Frenchmen and Italians. Each people would glorify God in its distinct way and would create a state expressive of the national culture. The corollary to Schleiermacher's emphasis upon national spirit was expressed by his brother-in-law Ernest Moritz Arndt (1769-1860). Arndt insisted upon the purity of German language and race and the rejection of foreign elements: "I hate all Frenchmen without distinction in the name of God and of my people ... I teach this hatred to my son, I teach it to the sons of my people."[9]

III. Clausewitz

Carl von Clausewitz's *On War*, published in 1832, after his death, became the single most influential treatise on war ever written, partially because the Prussians recommended it, and they created the best army in Europe. First used by the Prussians in the mid-nineteenth century, adopted by the French after 1870, later employed by the Japanese, praised by Communist Frederick Engels and later Lenin, recommended by American General George Marshall to the young Dwight Eisenhower who read it many times, *On War* is now standard reading in military academies around the world. Some of its influence may be due to the ambiguities

---

[7] Jerry Dawson, *Friedrich Schleiermachner: Evolution of a Nationalist* (1966), 98, 103.
[8] Hans Kohn, *The Idea of Nationalism* (1946), 249.
[9] Quoted in ibid., 259-60.

in the text, because Clausewitz was engaged in a major revision at his death and had completed only the initial chapter. So the published manuscript contained two major and perhaps incompatible descriptions of war: one exalting violence and the other stressing the relation of war and politics.

Equally important to its longevity, the text is less concerned with tactics, how one fights a given battle, than strategy, how one wins a war. Clausewitz wanted to know why Alexander the Great, Caesar, Frederick the Great, and Napoleon were successful. When should a nation go to war? What were the advantages of offense and defense? When should a people fight a guerrilla war? Unlike the *philosophes*, Clausewitz insisted there was no science of warfare, for there was constant contingency in battle. *On War* provided a series of case studies drawn from ancient and modern history to illustrate underlying principles.[10]

Clausewitz was obsessed with Napoleon. He had fought against the Emperor and been taken prisoner. Later, while Prussia was still an ally of the French, Clausewitz had joined the Russian army to oppose Napoleon and had participated in the final campaigns in which Prussia joined to defeat him. Clausewitz knew Hegel, participated in the surge of German nationalism, and praised Machiavelli's understanding of the importance of power for a state. Christianity, the Just War tradition, and morality played no role in his system. Instead of a condemnation of war or its effects, the book assumed that all states engaged in constant war, that survival of the state remained the paramount value and could be assured only by victory in war.

Clausewitz's first definition of war was "an act of force, and there is no logical limit to the application of that force." "Moderation" in the "theory of war" was a "logical absurdity." That is, the essence of war was power with no

---

[10] Clausewitz, *On War,* ed. Michael Howard and Peter Paret (1976). The easiest way to read *On War* is to begin with Bernard Brodie's "Guide to the Reading of *On War,*" 641ff. Peter Paret, *Clausewitz and the State* (1978) shows the evolution of his ideas; more theoretical analyses are in Michael Howard, *Clausewitz* (1983), and Raymond Aron, *Clausewitz* (1985).

limitation, although in reality war never existed in this simple form because the battle was complicated by "friction." Friction in war is the tendency of everything to grind to a halt, to dissipate energy without function. Weather, food supply, the enemy, the morale of the army, even fate could conspire against maximum utilization of violence. Each army, in addition to fighting the enemy, had a constant struggle against friction. The successful commander and army first overcame friction and then defeated the opponent.[11]

Escalation worked against friction in war. As an act of violence, war had a tendency to increase in severity because when both sides attempted to prevail, each added to its resources in order to overwhelm the opponent. So the war became fiercer. Eventually the side won that brought the most force to bear on a critical objective - a major city or an opposing army. Striking quickly, with overwhelming force brought to bear, on the enemy's "critical mass" gave victory. Clausewitz stressed the advantage of a surprise attack with concentration of force upon the enemy's most vulnerable spot. In the resulting victory, the enemy was disarmed, lost his will to fight, so that the conqueror could impose his will on him.[12] War was, moreover, a kind of "duel" or "gamble" because an unforeseen "friction" would upset plans.

Great commanders - like Napoleon and Frederick the Great - by acts of will overcame friction to inspire men and forced the army to victory. The commander should not fear war or rush to battle precipitously. Clausewitz, with only a rudimentary vocabulary of psychology at his disposal, fell back upon the term "genius" as the attribute of a successful general. Genius combined intelligence, cunning, audacity, courage, and perceptiveness. He must know his objectives and the weaknesses of his opponent and vary his tactics according to conditions. One of those conditions was the political situation.[13]

---

[11] Clausewitz, *On War,* 75-77, 119.
[12] Ibid., 77, 85.
[13] Ibid., 100, 112.

Clausewitz's second definition seems less belligerent: war was a "continuation of policy with other means." Here politics and war were not separated and a state's interest determined the value of the goal and set the way it fought. In a political war, victory could have a different meaning: buying time, diverting an enemy, compromising objectives, or solving a difficult internal problem. War as a division of politics allowed for limited wars, guerrilla wars, and de-escalation. Clausewitz read about the peoples' uprising against the French army of occupation in Spain and observed Napoleon's army retreat from Russia. He saw that popular uprisings by people who could not win in a set battle could tie down large armies. Guerrilla warfare was a strategy for the weak who knew the country and could meld into the general population. Such tactics could not win a war, because they were adaptations to weakness. Eventually, after the guerrillas had drained the opposing army sufficiently, they had to confront the enemy in open battle to obtain a victory. Because his criteria was success in battle, not morality, Clausewitz analyzed and did not condemn the "atrocities" that were an inevitable part of guerrilla war.[14]

Clausewitz died before his treatise could be adjusted to take full account of his second definition of war. So many observers stressed only the emphases upon attack, morale, and total violence. In retrospect, *On War*'s great weakness was its reliance on ancient and recent history. There had been for several centuries no basic changes in transportation or weaponry; the industrial revolution's impact on furnishing enormous quantities of war supplies was not apparent to Clausewitz. So he popularized the notion of a total war assuming that war had reached its limits in the Napoleonic battles.

Prussian history between 1815 and 1860 illustrates that an ideology of militaristic nationalism blessed by religion is not in itself a sufficient cause of war. The glorification of war and the apotheosis of the German state found in Hegel, Schleiermacher, and Clausewitz initially had little immediate impact on German

---

[14]Ibid., 69, 87, 480-83.

policy. In the aftermath of the Napoleonic Wars, Prussia followed a conservative policy of staying out of war, keeping arms out of the hands of the masses, countering revolutionaries, and supporting the status quo.

Prussia emerged from the Napoleonic wars with new non-contiguous Roman Catholic provinces and a minority who wanted a constitutional monarchy with a parliament. The state had a substantial Polish population, and neighboring Austria had traditionally been the cultural and often political leader of all German-speaking peoples. Prussia's two kaisers, Frederick William III and IV, who reigned from 1798-1860, forced the unification of the Reformed and Lutheran Churches in 1817 into the Prussian Evangelical Church. Fearful of revolution, the monarchy used the rituals of the Church along with myths of early Germans and festivals to oppose sentiments for democracy. The kaisers cooperated with Russia, Austria, and the papacy in opposing revolution in 1830 and 1848.

A decisive change began in the 1840s as Prussia began to industrialize, experienced population growth, and modernized its army. A new chancellor, Otto von Bismarck (1861-1890), determined to unify Germany not through liberal policies but war. Though he professed to be an awakened Christian, Bismarck did not allow his religion to interfere with realpolitik. With victories over Denmark, Austria, and France between 1864 and 1870, the new German empire emerged as the most powerful state in Europe, created, as Bismarck proclaimed, not by democracy but by "blood and iron." Still, German self-identity remained a potent mixture of Christianity, pagan myths, German legends, and history, and nationalism first synthesized in the wars against Napoleon and later symbolized by Richard Wagner's operas.

IV. The United States

The United States of America ended her revolutionary era glorying in war and proclaiming a desire for peace. Her success in obtaining independence from the greatest military power in Europe strengthened Americans' belief that God had selected the United States for a unique, almost messianic, destiny. Americans were a new chosen people with a mission to proclaim to the world the benefits of republican government. However, the mission to Europe and Latin America was to promote the benefits of political democracy and religious liberty by good example and not by war. Ambassador to France, Secretary of State, and President, Thomas Jefferson argued that governments of the people, as distinct from monarchies, were peace loving, so republics would not fight over frivolities like honor or to expand their borders.

The United States also proclaimed a commitment to Just War theory in both cause and conduct. In 1776 God had favored America over Britain because her struggle was defensive. Later as a weak nation whose navy was not powerful enough to force opening of markets for shipping, America relied heavily on treaties, international law or custom to secure neutral trading rights. Washington's 1796 "Farewell Address" had called upon Americans to stay out of Europe's wars, a need made pressing because of the impact of the French Revolution. Americans liked France's republicanism, but not its anti-religious ideology or Reign of Terror, and wished to trade with England and France and to avoid irritating either. So America, along with neutral Denmark, proclaimed a right to trade with both belligerents.

Federalists and Jeffersonian Republicans favored different sides in the European wars, but at home both sought to extend America's power by treaty or coercion over lands claimed by Europeans and/or occupied by Indians. By the Treaty of Paris in 1783, the United States gained all territory east of the Mississippi River. By purchase, it acquired the Louisiana Territory in 1803. So the United States with a small population had more territory than any European nation except Russia. Yet Americans soon wished to expand to include Canada, Florida, Texas, California, and Oregon, and they debated whether such lands could be obtained peacefully by purchase or treaty or by force and if their government should accept limitations imposed by adherence to theories of Just War or natural rights or natural borders - however ambiguously such terms were defined.

The first test of republican principles was over the rights of the aboriginal inhabitants, termed "Indians" by the Europeans. The United States government treated Native Americans as sovereign governments with which to sign treaties, but also regarded them as uncivilized or savage beings who should be removed from lands desired by American citizens. Europeans and white Americans did not care that many of these lands had not been conquered or even seen by Europeans and that their native inhabitants had never alienated sovereignty nor consented to be ruled by outsiders.

Since the fifteenth century, Europeans ruled lands in the New World theoretically according to an alleged right of discovery of empty lands or safe sojourn in order to trade, but in actuality, force accompanied by effective settlement determined legitimacy. Spain, France, Sweden, Holland, and England seized New World lands and the country that defended successfully gained title, irrespective of the wishes of even white inhabitants. So in 1763 Canada became English; Louisiana was first French, then Spanish, French again, and finally American. It made little difference that according to the rules of Just War theory the lands actually belonged to Native Americans.

Religion served to justify the wars fought by the U.S. and the Indians. The Americans had so fused religion and culture that they insisted that conversion of the natives to Christianity meant that the males should stop hunting and begin farming while women did housework and children attended school. Indian rituals exalting the hunt and war were devil worship. The Native Americans, whose language had no word for "religion," defended as their traditional way of life dancing, hunting, waging war, and possessing the lands bestowed by the Great Spirit.

Throughout the nineteenth century, Americans posited many rationales to justify dispossessing the native inhabitants. Indians were migratory and did not farm. (Actually, women in all tribes did farm.) The *Bible* told Americans to "be fruitful and multiply." The Indians were uncivilized savages, and, as Aristotle said, natural superiors must rule inferior peoples. When in the 1830's the Cherokees became sedentary farmers and drew up a constitution, the government of Andrew Jackson argued that such behavior was against their nature.

Missionaries protested against Jackson's policies.[15] Religion motivated a few people, generally living far away from the frontier, to complain about America's policies even while insisting upon the need for the Indians to assimilate. However, those who for the sake of conscience opposed the exploitation, greed, racism, and land hunger driving U.S. policy consistently failed to restrain the settlers' westward migration or to persuade the government to set aside adequate good lands on reservations so that the Native Americans could preserve their traditional customs. In essence, U.S. power forced treaties granting legitimacy, and avarice by speculators and farmers brought settlements. Often the colonization preceded the treaties. When the Indians resisted, Americans fought what they called defensive wars to preserve their property rights. When it came to the lands, the settlers neither knew nor cared about Just War theories on permissible cause and both sides ignored the stipulations regulating the conduct of war. The result was a demographic disaster for the Native Americans, so catastrophic that some scholars have called the results genocide.[16] A pious rhetoric about God's chosen and civilized people camouflaged the realpolitik that governed the American march from "sea to shining sea."

V. War of 1812

The War of 1812 has been correctly described as a second war of independence against Great Britain. In terms of number of casualties or size of

---

[15]William McLoughlin, *Cherokees and Missionaries, 1789-1839* (1984) and *Cherokee Renaiscence in the New Republic* (1986); Bernard Sheehan, *Seeds of Extinction: Jeffersonian Philanthropy and the American Indian* (1973) and Robert Berkhofer, *Salvation and the Savage.* Still useful for the entire period is Albert Weinburg, *Manifest Destiny: A Study of Nationalist Expansion in American History* (1935), which can be supplemented by more recent work focusing on the racism involved in expansion. See for example, the essays in *Manifest Destiny and Empire: American Antebellum Expansion,* ed. Sam Haynes and Christopher Morris (1997).

[16]The Native Americans' susceptibility to disease, chiefly smallpox, more than war was responsible for the declining numbers. Demoralization caused by loss of native lands, the destruction of wildlife, and susceptibility to alcoholism also contributed. Even the well-meaning efforts of Christian missionaries often contributed to the breakdown of traditions and weakening of tribes. After the Revolution, the Indians in the Old Northwest were defeated; the major wars between 1812 and 1860 were with the Creeks and Seminoles. The Plains Indians were forced onto reservations after the Civil War.

armies the war could not compare with the Napoleonic battles in Europe. For our purposes of assessing the impact of religion on battle, the War of 1812 was significant because in America, for the first time since Constantine, respectable institutional churches were separate from the state, and the variety of religious responses provides an opportunity to assess the role that independent churches could play.

The causes of the war stemmed from British contempt for the weak new republic and policies opposing Napoleon: impressing of sailors on American ships, restricting neutral America's trade to the European continent, and stirring up Indians in the Northwest Territory. British actions encountered an assertive United States nationalism determined to resist humiliation and desirous of expansion into Canada. Ironically, strongest support for the war came from the South and West, areas least affected by British trade restrictions, while the maritime states in the North opposed.

Convinced that war was an irrational way of settling disputes and determined to defend American rights by economic coercion, the Jefferson and Madison administrations hoped that a boycott of European trade would make Europeans more amenable. The duplicity of Napoleon, whose pro-American proclamations meant little, and the recalcitrance of England in refusing to ease its Orders in Council and impressment policies caused America's policy of economic sanctions to fail.

Before and during the war, there was a vigorous debate on its desirability, with opposition led by the non-pacifist Federalist politicians and Congregationalist clergy from New England. The American churches divided over the wisdom of war, partially by denomination and region. Methodists and Baptists, dominant in the South and West, defended the war. The issues first debated in the War of 1812 have since often recurred in America: the nature of Just War, the meaning of defeat, the clergy's right to offer moral advice on war, the limits of dissent in a war, and the U.S.'s role in the world.[17]

The opposition clergy insisted that they were not politicians, but as Christians had the right to offer moral advice. They learned that anti-war preaching in wartime was a political act that earned criticism. Outside of New England, being pro-war was not controversial. Whether pro- or anti-war, the churches' role remained subordinate to political realities with the clergy acting as cheerleaders or naysayers but having little influence on government actions.

The Congregationalist clergy, who tended to be Federalists, saw themselves as declaring God's will on religious and civil matters. They contrasted Protestant Britain, of evangelical Bible and missionary societies, fighting a defensive war against an atheistic and aggressive France, and attacked the anti-Christian deism alleged of President Madison and the Republicans. The Americans' projected invasion of Canada would be an offensive war, and the war itself was a sign of God's punishment of America for her people's sins and the irreligion of its leaders. The clergy used President Madison's call for observance of a Fast Day to confess sins and ask God's blessing on America's armies to condemn the administration and to argue that New England should stand apart from the war effort.

Proponents of the war, supporters of the Democratic-Republican Party, denounced the Federalist clergy as meddling in politics. Baptist and Methodist clergy saw America as receiving a special mandate from God because of its republican government and religious freedom. Fighting this war was a religious duty and God would help the American cause because it was defensive, i.e., just. Drawing upon a reservoir of anti-British thought, pro-war spokesmen portrayed a despotic, corrupt England engaged in a series of acts against America, supporting paganism in India, and Roman Catholicism and absolutism in Europe.

---

[17]William Gribben, *The Churches Militant: The War of 1812 and American Religion* (1973); James Banner, Jr., *To the Hartford Convention: The Federalists and the Origins of Party*

The war ended in a stalemate, with Americans claiming a victory because Andrew Jackson repelled a British invasion of New Orleans after the signing of a peace treaty that addressed none of the initial grievances. The end of the Napoleonic wars took away the need for trade restrictions that had caused the war. Still, the Union had endured with a legacy of assertive American nationalism prevailing over anti-war politicians and clergy.

The war showed the limitations upon the role of American churches during a war. Because of religious pluralism, the churches did not agree on whether the war was justified. During wartime, patriotism overwhelmed the moral qualms of the clergy, and everywhere Britain's invading forces encountered a people united to oppose them. The ambiguities of struggle neither reduced America's appetite for war nor for displacing Indians nor for expansion. Most Americans came to accept that Canada would not be conquered and, if the northern neighbor eventually were to join the American experiment, it would have to be on the basis of free consent - which was what Americans stood for anyway.

VI. Peace Societies

A few evangelical Christians and Quakers in Britain and America, after surveying the destruction of the Napoleonic wars, concluded that civilized nations needed a better way of settling disputes, and so they founded voluntary organizations to work for peace. The societies debated whether all members or only the officers had to oppose all wars or only offensive wars. The Quakers, who tended to dominate and to provide the finances for these organizations, opposed even defensive wars as unchristian. However, most members while supporting alternatives to war were not willing to rule out the need for some defensive wars. On the European continent, the public's disapproval of conscientious objection to all wars and approval of defensive war meant that there was little appeal for secular peace societies.

Politics in Massachusetts 1789-1815 (1970), 26-29, 154-55; J.W. Frost, *A Perfect Freedom: Religious Liberty in Pennsylvania* (1980), 116.

Even in Britain and America, only a small minority of the middle class - mostly clergymen, evangelicals, Unitarians, and Quakers - supported the peace societies. These groups first began working together to end the slave trade and abolish slavery and now joined in seeking other reforms. The emergent nondenominational peace societies built upon the intellectual legacy of the Enlightenment and Friends of Peace, the new enthusiasm for voluntary societies to reform evils, and Erasmus' interpretation of Christian ethics.

There was little originality in the peace societies' critique of war. The New Testament, reason and morality stood against wars caused by an inordinate passion for glory, power, and wealth. Even so-called Just Wars created poverty and suffering all out of proportion to any gain. Armies were nurseries of vices and soldiers victims and victimizers. The pacifists remained optimists, believing that under the influence of civilization and religion humans would learn to solve problems without fighting. When queried about the practicality of opposing all war, the Societies tended to rely upon the doctrine of particular providence; that is, God would protect any nation trusting in His mercy and prepared to abolish its military.

By the 1830's Britain's peace societies increasingly emphasized secular utilitarian arguments, such as replacing traditional alliance systems with international arbitration and congresses of nations. Under the influence of political reformer Richard Cobden, peace reform became linked with repeal of the Corn Laws and free trade. Commerce would create personal links among nations and thereby foster friendship. Ultimately the economic ties would become so strong that disrupting trade for war would become too costly. Reducing the taxes used to maintain the military would allow commerce to flourish.

The historian Martin Ceadel argues that by 1850 the English peace movement had gained political influence in the Whig party by denouncing offensive wars and proclaiming the necessity of reforming the international system. Those who opposed all wars provided the money and the dedication for the peace movement, but these people had little political clout. Instead, those who used the anti-war arguments of the peace movement put on the defensive those who glorified the military and members of the Tory party who believed that the best way to preserve peace was to prepare for war. The "dissenter conscience" would oppose imperialism and demand that Britain's foreign policy consider morality, not just balance of power or realpolitik.[18]

In America, the radical abolitionists who supported William Lloyd Garrison's call for immediate emancipation for slaves also criticized the conservatism and emphasis upon international reform of the American Peace Society. To the radicals peace was less a political reform than a personal moral stance of nonresistance in which the individual pledged never to use force. By contrast, the peace societies promoted their goals through education, relying primarily upon tracts and lecturers. Elihu Burritt (1810-1879), distressed by the many defensive war proponents in the American Peace Society, founded the Universal Brotherhood in 1846 and lectured in America, England, and on the Continent in an effort to persuade people to make a pledge not to serve in the military or to support a war. The highest estimate is that by 1850 100,000 people in America and Britain had signed, but a signature alone did not mean a deep commitment to nonresistance. When tensions with Great Britain and Mexico developed in the 1840s, the American peace societies proved to have little political impact.[19]

VII. The Mexican War

In 1846 America's desire for additional territory led to an aggressive war with Mexico. Texas, originally colonized by Spain and now a province of the Republic of Mexico, had become attractive to westward migrating Americans. Conflicts between Mexico and American inhabitants of Texas resulted in a revolt, a struggle marked by atrocities including the execution of prisoners of war that

---

[18] Martin Ceadel, *The Origins of War Prevention: The British Peace Movement and International Relations, 1730-1854* (1996), 122, 246, 270, 336, 348-49, 354, 379, 412, 516. Peter Brock, *Pacifism in Europe to 1914* (1972), ch. 9-10.
[19] Peter Brock, *Pacifism in the United States from the Colonial Era to the First World War* (1968), chs. 6, 8-16.

resulted in independence, but with the southern border of the Republic of Texas in dispute. Texans applied for admission as a state. In spite of strong Mexican opposition and misgivings within the United States, the Democratic Party elected James K. Polk president in 1846 on a platform advocating admitting Texas and asserting a strong claim to Oregon with the slogan "54° 40' or fight." Facing possible war with both Britain and Mexico, Polk struck a deal drawing the Oregon boundary at the 49th parallel - thereby ending one crisis.

After Congress admitted Texas to the Union, Polk sent American troops to land in the disputed border area and, after Mexican troops seized an American border patrol with eleven killed, proclaimed that Mexico had now shed "American blood on American soil." Then Congress with overwhelming majorities in both Houses declared war. The President and the military insisted that the war was not against the people of Mexico, but its corrupt and tyrannical government.

The ease of victory surprised most foreign observers. For all her belligerent rhetoric, the United States entered the war almost totally unprepared and facing what appeared to be a more numerous and better equipped Mexican army. Yet from the first battles near the Rio Grande River, America won an unbroken series of military successes, conquering northern Mexico, seizing by force and without consulting the inhabitants New Mexico and California, invading the heartland of Mexico and occupying Mexico City.[20] General Winfield Scott's campaign in Mexico continued the traditions of eighteenth-century warfare by maneuvering to avoid pitched battles whenever possible in order to avoid casualties by either side. By the peace treaty signed in 1848, Mexico ceded one-third of her territory, with America paying $15,000,000 and assuming claims of citizens against Mexico.

Unitarians, Congregationalists, and Quakers saw the conflict as caused by America's desire for land, exposed Polk's "first shot" manipulations, and opposed the addition of California and New Mexico. Abolitionists saw the war as part of a conspiracy to create slave territory. America's Whig Party saw the war as unnecessary, but felt compelled to vote supplies for the troops and still found that its reservations allowed Democrats to charge it with aiding the enemy. Still, with the Whig Party professing skepticism and second-guessing Polk's policies, there was sufficient freedom for both clergy and the popular press to have registered opposition. Yet a historian concluded that the anti-war movement "had little effect on the war's duration, outcome, or final terms."[21]

Unlike the War of 1812, the Mexican War was generally popular. Even those who saw the war as unnecessary believed in supporting the government, and early victories tended to silence dissenters. Polk managed to fund the war without raising taxes. Every state met the national government's quota for enlistments with no difficulty. The high level of literacy among enlisted men also allows insights into their views of the war. The soldiers, most clergyman, and journalists (newspapers used war correspondents who for the first time accompanied an army) used similar concepts defending America's conduct in a Just War.

Americans defined themselves as a religious people in a special relationship to God's providential order, which mandated spreading their ideals of religion and government. The victories proved once again that God favored them. Except in New England, the churches supported the war, with the clergy drawing upon Old Testament analogies to prove that this was a holy war, a new crusade. Yet for all their boasting of their superiority to Mexico, Americans also found in war a cure for their deep-seated insecurities. They worried that their country had become too materialistic and individualistic and had betrayed the heritage of the Revolution. The war served as a crucible to purge an incessant pursuit of wealth

---

[20] Russell Weigley, *The American Way of War: A History of Military Strategy* (1973), 59-76, and T. Harry Williams, *The History of American Wars from 1745 to 1918*, (1981), 144-85.
[21] John Schroeder, *Mr. Polk's War: American Opposition and Dissent, 1846-1848* (1973), 62, 71-72, 92, 107, 162.

and an effeminate love of luxury and allegedly proved that her young men could be motivated by idealism, self-sacrifice, altruism, and heroism.[22]

Americans pictured their role in Mexico through a haze of nineteenth-century romanticism derived from reading the novels of Sir Walter Scott and histories of the conquests of Cortez. Although not knowing much about either the conquistadors or knights, the soldiers saw themselves and were seen by the popular American writers as imitating the knights of old on a chivalric mission for justice, truth, and right. So heroic American soldiers would not pillage or attack civilians, and there would be no plundering of Mexican cities.[23] The American military claimed that fair treatment of Mexican civilians would make a negotiated settlement more likely. Ignoring the contradictory nature of explanations for their military successes, Americans ascribed Mexico's defeats to God's providence, the skill of America's citizen soldiers (not the West Point graduates who led them), and the inferiority of the Mexicans.

Many Americans thought that it would be the United States' destiny as a superior people to rule Mexico, though most assumed that this process would come by natural attraction rather than conquest. Still, those senators who opposed the final peace treaty wanted to incorporate Mexico into the United States. Victories brought an outpouring of sentiments about the inevitable destiny of Anglo-Saxons to rule Mexicans; allegedly, Americans as a superior race with better institutions also deserved New Mexico and California. America's supposed altruism was mixed with contempt for the Mexicans as an inferior race. After all, Mexico had had a succession of unstable governments and military coups since independence; the Catholic Church had too much power and did not believe in religious toleration, and poverty was everywhere. Being defeated and occupied by the American army would provide a lesson to the Mexicans about how republics should function.

---

[22] Robert W. Johannsen, *To the Halls of the Montezumas: The Mexican War in the American Imagination* (1985), 48-50. Clayton Summer Ellsworth, "American Churches and Mexican War," *American Historical Review* (1940), 301-26.

Did the war with Mexico vindicate the American claim that republics followed civilized rules of warfare? Because the administration wanted a treaty with Mexico, the army was under strict orders to treat Mexican civilians well. American troops did not need to plunder Mexicans for food, because civilians willingly sold what was needed. General Winfield Scott rejected a plan to storm the city of Veracruz because of the presence of women and children, but he did order the shelling of the city in spite of humanitarian pleas from European consuls residing there. The regular army behaved rather well, but General Zachary Taylor could not control the behavior of troops like the Texas Rangers who used the war as a pretext for banditry. The Mexican rancheros had a similar reputation. Considering that wars are always accompanied by abuses, by and large the war was fought by soldiers on both sides according to the rules of war. [24]

The Mexican War proved that republics could be as greedy and expansion-minded as monarchs. In spite of a popular press and free churches, the government could manipulate the right of self-defense and Just War theory in Machiavellian fashion. A few dissenters in the popular press and churches provided no block upon a democratic government's ability to wage war. In fact, some opposition strengthened self-righteousness by proving the existence of freedom and, thereby, strengthened America's claim that she fought to expand the area of freedom and democracy against Mexican despotism. A people who believed themselves superior in religion, race, and government cared very little about the rights of other nationalities.

Finally, the Mexican War showed that a democratic country could manipulate natural law, natural rights, and natural boundaries in the interest of national destiny. At the end of the Revolution, the new United States jumped the Appalachian Mountains to claim lands to the Mississippi River. Even after the Louisiana Purchase, America laid claim to Florida and Texas. War with Mexico allowed her to jump the Rocky Mountains and seize California and to rule from

---

[23]Ibid., 32, 71.

ocean to ocean. At the end of the nineteenth century, even the oceans were not sufficient natural boundaries as imperialistic America leaped over the Caribbean for Puerto Rico and the Pacific Ocean for Hawaii and the Philippines.

VIII. Civil War

Americans used the same themes cited to show their superiority to Mexico in 1848 against each other in the Civil War. Clergy, writers, and politicians again talked of God's providential relationship to his chosen people, America's special destiny, the heritage of the Revolution, the mystic bounds of the Union, holy war, the nature of democracy, a superior and inferior civilization, a distinctive way of life, and the barbarity of the opponent. All these themes were reinterpreted in relation to the underlying cause of the war, Afro-American slavery. In essence, the war involved a disagreement of evangelical Protestants in the North and South over the morality of slavery.[25]

To the South after 1840, slavery was a moral institution, legitimated by the *Bible*, guaranteed by the Constitution, and necessary to preserve a superior economic and political way of life. Slavery's expansion into new territories of the West was necessary to keep the balance of power against a rapidly industrializing North. In order to protect its "peculiar institution," the South prepared to fight a defensive war against Yankee aggression.

Northerners saw themselves as defending a superior way of life based upon free labor against an aggressive slaveholding conspiracy. Believing that the Constitution restricted the power of the Federal government over slavery in states where it existed, the Republican Party sought to prevent the expansion of slavery into the territories. In 1860 Lincoln's election brought secession of seven states in the Deep South and no clear response from the North. In April after Lincoln

[24] Ibid., 36-38, 100-03, 133.
[25] James McPherson, *The Battle Cry of Freedom: The Civil War Era* (1988), is a standard and very readable one-volume history. Chapter 4 deals with the religious-moral causes, but the book ignores the roles of religion during the war. The best way to gain the flavor of the Civil War is to read the documents compiled by Henry S. Commager, ed. *The Blue and the Gray: The Story of the Civil War as told by Participants* (1950).

notified the South that he would re-supply non-military materials at Fort Sumter in Charleston harbor, the Confederates decided to act quickly and they fired the first shot. The earlier deeply-divided North now showed the power of nationalism in rallying to preserve the Union. To a minority of Northerners in 1861 and a majority by 1864, slavery threatened the Union and America's special role in world history. The War Between the States initiated to save the Union became a war to end the immoral institution of slavery.

The churches of North and South played a major role in creating sectional identity, defining the issues, and inspiring the people to fight.[26] Before 1850 Methodists, Presbyterians, and Baptists divided into northern and southern branches over the issue of slavery; Episcopalians and Roman Catholics managed to stay together only by officially ignoring "the peculiar institution." The separation of the largest Protestant denominations allowed the Southern churches to define the South as a distinct people pledged to the preservation of slavery.

Both sides invoked the *Bible* as justification for their contrasting views of slavery. The South defended the origins of slavery by relying on two *Bible* stories in Genesis where, after murdering his brother, Cain's brow was darkened as a judgment and, second, the condemnation of Ham for looking upon Noah's nakedness "a servant of servant shall you be." Southern clergymen insisted that both Testaments assumed slavery and neither Moses, the prophets, Jesus, nor Paul ever condemned the institution. The defense of slavery solidified the South's commitment to a biblically based evangelical religion. Northerners countered that neither the curses of Cain nor Ham mentioned race and that the *Bible* never discussed racial slavery. Unable to prove that the letter of the *Bible* opposed

---

[26] "Without the clergy's active endorsement of succession and war, there could not have been a Confederate nation." Harry Stout and Christopher Grasso, "Civil War, Religion, and Communications: The Case of Richmond," in *Religion and the American Civil War*, ed. Randall Miller, Harry Stout, Charles Wilson (1998), 318, 346. The sixteen essays in this book deal with many facets of the role of religion as cause and sustainer of the war. Steven E. Woodworth, *While God is Marching On: The Religious World of Civil War Soldiers* (2001), contains many examples of the varieties of interpretation of the religious significance of the war, some orthodox and others not. Ch. 14 argues that defeat of the South did not change its belief in the

slavery, abolitionists insisted that following the Golden Rule was contrary to slavery. Slavery resulted in the sexual abuse of black women, destroyed marriages by separating families in the slave trade, led to physical violence by masters, and negated Blacks' God-given natural rights.

Before 1860 the South had become a closed society allowing no debate on the truths of religion or the beneficence of slavery. The clergy served as spokesmen for the region, defending slavery as a moral good, denouncing Northern reformers, abolitionists, and industrialists, and - after much hesitation in 1860 - pronouncing God's blessings upon secession and the war. The Confederates stood as the new children of Israel against the irreligion and materialism of the North. Prayer and moral living would guarantee God's intervention on the side of the South, his new chosen people. Religion and regionalism combined to create a new civil religion in which God would bless the South and intervene in an almost miraculous fashion to preserve it.

Northern writers portrayed the regions differently, describing Southerners as poor, badly educated, and lazy. Planters made money by ruthlessly exploiting their slaves. The lash and the brothel, not the family, symbolized the slave system. Free labor, economic opportunity, a spirit of reform, a commitment to democracy, and the piety of its people made the North prosper. Long before the Civil War, the North wanted to remake the South in its own image. Until 1860 the Union held together because the moral qualms of many Northerners about slavery paled against their racism, love of nation, fear of war, and qualms about jeopardizing the source of cotton for the mills of Pennsylvania and New England.

Interpreting the War

When the war came, the clergy on both sides defended the righteousness of their causes. Each prayed to have God's help in waging a holy war, denounced the enemy's conduct as unjust aggression, and claimed to be fighting a defensive

---

righteousness of the cause. The book shows the impact of Protestant Christianity on the war but also leads to caution about simplifying the relations of religion and war.

action. During the course of the struggle, both armies experienced religious revivals. The North and South had to learn to cope with defeat, to explain why Jehovah did not allow the forces of right to prevail, and to come to terms with the enormous number of casualties. To preachers, defeats meant that God was chastising people for their sins, which could be reformed, but should not be interpreted as a sign of God's pleasure in the other side. The North and South saw the war as purifying their societies, strengthening idealism, and affirming true manhood.[27]

The South never really had a good war song. "Dixie" was full of nostalgia for the past, "good times there are not forgotten," and foreboding, "to live and die in Dixie." In contrast, Julia Ward Howe's "Battle Hymn of the Republic" tapped into the religious and moral fervor by drawing upon biblical images of the apocalypse, redemption, and freedom. "Mine eyes have seen the glory of the coming of the Lord" (millennialism); "He is tramping out the vintage where the grapes of wrath are stored" (judgment against an aggressive Southern slavocracy is implied). "As He [Jesus] died to make men holy, let us die to make men free." (Our atonement is for freedom; our task is to fight). God was present in this struggle: "I have seen him in the watchtowers of a hundred circling camps." And the Union would triumph, "Glory, glory, hallelujah," because right could be established by steel. "His truth is marching on." The "Battle Hymn" was a great fight song.

A restrained and thoughtful analysis of the war came in Lincoln's Gettysburg and Second Inaugural addresses. Because of the similarity of the occasion - a commemoration of the war dead - to Pericles' funeral oration, a comparison of the two speeches illustrates common themes. Both orators contrasted the insignificance of words with the deeds: "the world will little note nor long remember what we say here, it will never forget what they did here."

---

[27] Essays by Eugene Genovese, Bertram Wyatt-Brown, and George Fredrickson, in *Religion and the American Civil War* (1998), 74-130.

They invoked the heritage of the ancestors: "Four score and seven years ago our forefathers;" praised the valor of the soldiers: "brave men living and dead," and drew upon religious language: "who have consecrated" this battlefield. Thucydides made palatable the deaths of the men by the survival of Athens, a kind of death/rebirth motif. Lincoln, similarly, found ultimate moral purpose in the sacrifice of lives for democracy: "that government, of the people, by the people, and for the people shall not perish from the earth." Lincoln here also invoked the special destiny of the American people; Americans believed that if the republican experiment failed, democracy would disappear "from the earth." So there was a cosmic importance to the Civil War. Note that nowhere did the words "victory" or "slavery" or "union" or even "Gettysburg" appear in the Gettysburg Address.[28]

Lincoln and Jefferson Davis proclaimed days of fasting and prayer during the war to beseech the aid of the Almighty; on October 3, 1863, Lincoln decreed a day of Thanksgiving for the successes at Vicksburg and Gettysburg. Moved to the last Thursday in November, Thanksgiving Day would become a national holiday.

Lincoln's "Second Inaugural," delivered in April 1865 when victory was in sight, sought to understand the reason why a good God had allowed so much suffering in the war. Both sides "read the same *Bible* and pray to the same God, and each invokes His aid against the other … . The prayers of both could not be answered fully. That of neither has been answered fully." Lincoln stressed the guilt of both sides in the slave system. Because slavery was a moral offense perpetuated by North and South, the justice of God might require the struggle to continue until "all the wealth piled by the bondsman's two hundred and fifty years of unrequited toil shall be sunk and until every drop of blood drawn with the lash shall be paid by another drawn with the sword." Lincoln here reaffirmed a providential interpretation of history as old as the Hebrew Scriptures. In spite of the calamity of war, Americans as a religious people still believed that God's judgments were "truth and righteous," and the nation's duty was to do the "right, as God gives us to see the right." Lincoln's Second Inaugural was a call for forgiveness and reconciliation, an affirmation of God's justice amid the carnage of war.[29]

The Nature of the War

Military historians describe the Civil War as the first modern war, with weaponry and tactics revolutionized by industrial and scientific progress. Replacing muskets, rifles could be shot quicker, with more accuracy at twice the distance. Most casualties came from rifle fire, not artillery. Heavy artillery played an important role, particularly in sieges, but the smoke of battle restricted its usefulness because gunners had to fire blindly. Cavalry offered mobility to scout, but the horsemen dismounted in order to fight with rifles. Normally armies could not live off the land and were supplied by train, but Lee's invasion of Maryland and Sherman's "March to the Sea" proved that adequate foodstuffs could be obtained by plunder. War materials could be moved easily to the front by railroad, but battlefield maneuvering was much slower. European observers thought the loose formations and flexibility of Confederate soldiers stemmed from a lack of training; yet it may have also reflected a survival impulse against increased firepower. Grant's use of telegraph to keep in constant touch with subordinates, his reliance upon staff, and his constant care for details of supply were like a modern army. Yet the Civil War was also traditional. Initially, generals tried to use Napoleonic strategies and colonels still led the troop charges. Above all, the Civil War showed the costliness in lives of modern war. The battle of Antietam alone cost more casualties than the combined totals of the War of 1812, the Mexican War, and the Spanish-American War and four times the

---

[28]Garry Wills, *Lincoln at Gettysburg: The Words that Remade America* (1992) 54-55, 90, shows the impact of classical ideals, particularly Pericles' speech, on the orations.
[29]Ronald White, "Lincoln's Sermon on the Mount: The Second Inaugural," in *Religion and the American Civil War* (1998), 208-223.

numbers lost at D-Day. More soldiers died in the Civil War than in all of America's other wars combined.[30]

The North had overwhelming superiority in manpower and supplies, and it proceeded to expend them and to crush the South in what evolved into a grinding war of annihilation. There were sixty major battles, most of them indecisive. At Gettysburg, Lee lost one-third of his total army; Mead, one-fourth of the Union forces. In the Wilderness campaign in which Grant sought to isolate Richmond, the soldiers fought in bloody trench warfare unable to see each other because of the smoke. Casualties in the final battles between Lee and Grant were so high that before Cold Harbor, Union soldiers wrote their names on slips of paper and pinned them to the backs of their coats in order to make identification of the bodies easier.

In 1863 Lincoln issued a code designed to establish rules of conduct for U.S. armies' treatment of enemy soldiers and civilians without, however, conveying recognition of the Confederate government. This General Order Number 100, written by German immigrant Francis Lieber, drew upon the "common law of war." One premise originating with Plato was that war was not for the sake of war but "the means to obtain great ends of state;" another stemming from chivalry was that "men who took up arms against one another in public do not cease on this account to be moral beings responsible to one another and to God."[31] So a uniformed soldier killing enemy soldiers in a war was permissible, but "unnecessary or revengeful destruction of life" was not. All civilians, particularly women and children, were not permissible targets; the wounded and prisoners of war received special protections. These protections also applied to ex-slaves, because the laws of war did not recognize race. This provision was needed because the Confederates threatened to kill any Afro-American Union soldier who became a prisoner. Articles provided rules for flags

---

[30]McPherson, 544, 854. Soldier deaths were ca. 620,000 and there are no reliable estimates of civilian deaths.

of truce, armistices, sieges, paroles, and spies, and exempted from harm schools, churches, libraries, and hospitals. A blockade of food was declared legal. In dire circumstances, military necessity allowed the suspension of part of the code. Most important, the code was to be observed by both sides and violations by either side could be punished as war crimes by the Union armies. Lieber's code served as a foundation for later attempts to create an international law of war.

To what extend did the two armies observe Order 100? With so many battles and cavalry maneuvering, civilians were bound to be hurt, but neither side deliberately targeted civilians or plundered cities. However, protection of civilians eroded during the later stages of the war. The battles in the Shenandoah Valley and between bandit-like guerrilla forces of William Quantrill opposing the Jayhawkers in Missouri resulted in massacres and a scorched earth policy. In the last stages of the war, Union General Sherman determined to destroy all property in his path useful to supply the Confederate armies in order to break the will of the enemy to continue the war. He rationalized that undermining civilian morale would help end the war quickly. On his march from Atlanta to the ocean Sherman's men created an eighty-mile wide stretch of destruction. In South Carolina the destruction was even greater because its people seemingly bore special responsibility for starting the war, but the pillaging stopped when Sherman's army reached North Carolina. Sherman proclaimed that "war is hell," and his tactics helped make it more so.[32] Most surprising, considering the bitterness of the war, were that the regular armies rarely killed civilians and, in the aftermath, that the leaders of the Confederacy received mild punishment.

During the war Northerners and Southerners acted as though they were two separate peoples. The farm boys who populated the armies of the North and South had much in common, and there were frequent occasions for camaraderie.

---

[31]General Order Number 100, 1863; Francis Lieber, *Guerrilla Parties Considered with Reference to the Laws and Usages of War* (1862).
[32]Charles Royster, *The Destructive War: William Tecumseh Sherman, Stonewall Jackson, and the Americans* (1991), shows that a willingness to expand the nature of permissible targets was common in both North and South, 39, 87-89, 108-9, 117. McPherson, 784.

Yet for all their similarity, these soldiers willingly fought hard, slaughtered the enemy, and sacrificed their lives. The churches, which had helped bring on the war, blessed the killing as a holy struggle.

IX. Colonialism

Since 1500 Europe has owed the expansion of its influence over the rest of the world to its superior military technology and ability to mobilize resources.[33] By 1920 Japan, Thailand (Siam), Turkey, and Ethiopia had managed to escape colonial rule; China was too big to conquer, so outsiders created spheres of influence within or enclaves on the border like Macao and Hong Kong. Elsewhere whites ruled either as settler-colonizers in North and South America, Australia, and South Africa, or as imperial masters in sub-Saharan Africa, Indonesia, and Vietnam, or through indirect domination of indigenous rulers as in India, North Africa, Iran, and the Middle East. Religion provided a motive to resist: Christianity in Ethiopia versus Italy, Islam in Algeria and Senegal against France, and the native religion (Hongo snake cult) in Tanganyika anti Germany. The U.S., Russia, and Austria-Hungary annexed contiguous lands, but for other major powers the conquered areas were distant lands. The native peoples did not welcome outside rule and atrocities marked the wars to subdue. The Zulus in South Africa, the Sepoys in India, the Sufi brotherhoods in Chechnya and the Sudan, and the Indians of North America utilized their religions to inspire resistance to the cruelties of imperialism. Our concern here is not with the opponents or with the native merchants and rulers who often collaborated and made the imperial systems work, but with the Christians whose nations claimed the right and had the power to rule the world. The motivations for conquests have been summarized as God, glory, and greed.[34] Our concern is with God, because

---

[33] William H. McNeill, *The Pursuit of Power: Technology, Armed Force and Society since A.D. 1000* (1982), chs. 4, 7 and "The Age of Gunpowder Empires, 1450-1800" in Michael Adams, ed., *Islamic and European Expansion* (1993), 103-140.
[34] Dana Robert, "Christianity in the Wider World" in *Christianity: A Social and Cultural History* (1998), 525-580 is a brief history of the impact of Christian missions. Bruce Vandervort, *Wars of*

the desire to convert and civilize backward peoples - Kipling's "white man's burden" - provided a crucial rationale.[35]

The nineteenth century witnessed an enormous expansion of Christianity into Africa and Asia brought about by Protestant and Catholic missionaries. The missionaries' response to the Chinese Opium War (1845-48) showed why their presence rarely served as a check upon European military expansion. Here was a clear-cut moral issue with Europeans clearly in the wrong. Economic issues caused the war. The British had an unfavorable balance of trade because China desired little that the West produced. So the British encouraged the production of opium in its colony India as a cash crop to be exchanged for Chinese exports of tea, silks, and fine porcelain. The Chinese willingly accepted silver in exchange, but that would have increased Britain's unfavorable balance of trade. The war began after the Chinese government forbade the importing of opium and sought to crack down upon smuggling, done mostly by British merchants. The British used their superiority in naval armaments to force the Chinese government to open its markets and to allow trade in opium. In exacting a humiliating treaty of peace, the British also acquired Hong Kong.

The Christian missionaries residing in China knew the causes and witnessed the war. Missionary efforts had thus far produced few converts, and the Chinese government had restricted accessibility to most of the country. The missionaries (and the British government and the general public) knew by 1850 that opium was a dangerous narcotic. In the debates in Parliament, petitions of missionary organizations of Wesleyans, Congregationalists, and Baptists criticized the opium trade. But other missionaries and the British government overlooked

---

Imperial Conquest in Africa (1998) 42, 58, 75, 104, 123, 138-9,158, 185-7, 196-202, stresses the complexity of motives in different countries with the initiatives for military conquest often coming from military commanders in Africa. Before 1880 European successes depended upon African disunity and most colonial armies had a majority of Africans. Control was limited to coastal areas. During partition, Europeans had overwhelming technological superiority. Still, most casualties came in rebellions. For example, German tactics in the Hiero uprising in 1904 resulted in 15,000 out of 80,000 surviving.

the human cost of the opium trade and supported the war as a means of opening China to Christianity and trade. In other words, the moral evil of forcing the opium trade could be justified as part of a greater good. (The Opium War also serves as an ironical commentary upon the liberal argument that free trade fostered peace among nations.)[36]

In the scramble for colonies in Africa and the Far East after 1880, missionaries saw Christianity as part of the superior civilization that Europeans were bringing to the rest of the world.[37] Yet missionaries in the field often complained about the behavior of traders and colonial administrators and wrote to their supporters back home to bring pressure on governments to change policies. Native rulers found that enlisting the aid of missionaries gave a voice against discriminatory policies. Colonial officials found missionaries difficult to control and feared their activities would upset native rulers. Initially, those who attended missionary schools became the clerks who made the colonies functions, but they later led the movements for independence.

Christianity gained from colonial conquests, but its identification with outside rulers was often a mixed blessing. Many churches desired "spiritual free trade" in which all religions competed equally. British missionaries complained that the French favored Jesuit efforts in their colonies of Madagascar and Tahiti. In China, the unpopularity of European powers caused some evangelists to attempt to go alone, while others wanted their nations to pressure the Empress' government to open more areas for evangelism and to protect them, particularly during and after the Boxe uprising of 1900. After anti-foreign Chinese, termed

---

[35] Michael Adams, "'High' Imperialism and the 'New' History," *Islamic and European Expansion*, 311-344 is a historiographical review of recent interpretations of imperialism that manages to ignore religion.
[36] Peter Ward Fay, *The Opium War 1840-1842* (1975), 330-332; Jack Beeching, *The Chinese Opium Wars* (1976), 60-61, 161.
[37] Missionaries sometimes advocated European intervention to improve the lives or to end wars. The conquest could come through native rulers, but a threat of force was in the background and the wars were often brutal.   See essays on the Western Sudan, European partition, and establishment of colonial rule in *History of West Africa*, ed. J. F. A. Ajayi and Michael Crowder (1974), 380-483.

"Boxers," killed 181 foreign missionaries and 32,000 converts, the missionaries of many countries supported the use of force against the Chinese government. (A decade later a revolution created a Chinese Republic that was sympathetic to missions.) During the Boer War (1899-1902) in South Africa, British missionaries supported the war against the Boer settlers and favored the expansionist policies of the imperial government as likely to help the native Africans. German missionaries following the policy of their government supported the Boers. In the Congo Free State created in 1884, after non-Belgian missionaries invited by King Leopold criticized the appalling treatment of the black inhabitants, the King sought to find more quiescent ones.[38] Non-Belgian missionaries, particularly American and British, provided evidence of abuses used by E. D. Morel, British consul Roger Casement, and the Congo Reform Association. The exposure of the exploitation resulted in the Belgian government's takeover of the colony in 1904.[39]

In West Africa, "European rule derived ultimately from military conquest" both in its establishment and in putting down revolts, or as Hilaire Belloc observed: "Whatever happens we have got// The Maxim gun and they have not."[40] The missionaries' moral sensitivity to Islamic slavery did not extend to European-initiated colonial wars, except to condemn indigenous leaders like the Mahdi, who invoked their religious traditions as a means of opposing the Europeans. Britain's Prime Minister Gladstone ran for office denouncing Ottomans' cruelties in suppressing Christians in the Balkans, but never criticized the even greater cruelties of the Russians' campaigns against Muslims in the southern Caucasus.

There was no one response of missionaries to late nineteenth-century wars of colonial expansion. The relationships between missionaries and colonial powers depended on many factors: time sequence (if the missionaries were in the

---

[38]James Greenlee and Charles Johnson, *British Missionaries and Imperial States 1870-1918* (1999), 10, 21-22, 34-35, 40-41, 47, 66-68, 80. Ironically, Leopold had justified the creation of his state as a means to suppress the slave trade.

[39]Roger Anstey, *King Leopold's Legacy : Congo under Belgian Rule 1908-1960* (1966), 33-36; Ruth Slade, *King Leopold's Congo* (1962), 178-92. C. P. Groves, *The Planting of Christianity in Africa* (1964), III, 124, 129-134, 267-271.

area first or came after conquest), relations between missionaries and native rulers, stability or conflict in the region, whether the missionaries came from the rulers' country or were outsiders, and whether Europeans deemed the area suitable for settlement. The personalities of the colonial officials, merchants, and missionaries, the theologies and traditions of different churches in the mother country, and the missionaries' view of their responsibility to converts and inhabitants - all influenced how the churches viewed war between Europeans and natives. The conclusion of a historian of Christianity in Africa is that wars between Europeans and Africans hindered the missionary work.[41] The missionaries provided the reports used by critics of imperialism. However, opposing colonial wars was rare, because the natives used Islam or indigenous beliefs as a rallying force against Europeans, and most missionaries believed in the superiority of Christian civilization.

[40]A. E. Afigbo, "The Establishment of Colonial Rule, 1900-1918," in *History of West Africa*, II, 424-434.
[41]Groves, *The Planting of Christianity in Africa*, III, 254, 261. One result of the wars was that the colonial authorities prohibited missionary activities in some areas.

XIII.
A CIVILIZED WAY TO PEACE

The participants in the peace movement of the late nineteenth century forecast with uncanny accuracy the strategy and effects of a coming major European war. Jan Gotlieb Block, a Polish railroad magnate, published in 1898 a six-volume study that argued that the coming war would be long, involve enormous armies, and end by virtually bankrupting Europe. After a long struggle of attrition, almost a stalemate, everybody - even the nominal winner -would lose. During battle soldiers would attempt to escape the lethal artillery barrages by digging trenches and would face murderous machine gun fire when trying to advance. Deaths would number in the millions. The fighting would be marked by atrocities, as nations that saw their survival threatened would employ any means. The war would precipitate social revolution, the decline of Europe, and create ascendancy for the United States and Japan.[1]

Unfortunately for Europe, the peace groups' descriptions of a coming major war proved more perspicacious than those of generals and admirals, who belittled civilian Block's writings and prophesied instead a short, easy victory. However, Block's diagnosis confirmed the peace workers' fears and motivated their actions after they concluded that a cataclysmic war was the inevitable result of the policies of the major states. So they set out to convince the people that traditional patterns of statecraft were obsolete.

The peace workers' hopes for progress in ending war came in spite of their knowledge of contemporary trends. They warned of the increased risk of war brought about by the advent of a new imperialism and of the enormous increase in

---

[1]I. S. Block (Jan Gotlieb), *The Future of War in Its Technical, Economic, and Political Relations* (1899); Sandi E. Cooper, *Patriotic Pacifism: Waging War on War in Europe 1815-1914* (1991), ch. 6.

destructiveness in armaments resulting from new technology and industrialism. They saw clearly the dangers of virulent nationalism exemplified by a jingoist popular press, chauvinistic schoolbooks, a rigid alliance system, and an arms race.

In the late nineteenth century, reformers first used the term "militarism" to condemn the preponderant attention given to building the strength of the army and navy and to ridicule those who welcomed war as a means for the young men or nations to prove their idealism and build character.[2] Militarists allegedly saw international relations as a power game, with war as the ultimate court of disputes and morality as irrelevant.

The reformers who opposed militarism called themselves "pacifists;" this term was also first used in this period and will be employed in this chapter to describe those who contrasted war as unreasonable and a disaster with peace among nations as a normal condition allowing economic, social, and moral progress. The pacifists' optimistic premise was that by changing the international order, war could be ended. Neither God, Darwinian natural selection, nor culture destined humankind to inevitable war; rather, it was a product of the evolution of human society and had now outlived its usefulness.

Although in private statesmen often accused their opponents of acting in terms of realpolitik and responded accordingly, no government officially espoused such a philosophy, and all responsible leaders professed to be committed to resolving disputes peacefully. Europeans saw themselves as civilized beings and condemned brute force as a relic of the barbarians, even while they used force to carve up Africa, nibble away at the Ottoman Empire, and create spheres of influence and colonies in China and Southeast Asia.

---

[2]The first use of "militarism" was in 1864, "pacifism" in 1902, and "pacifist" in 1906. Militarist originally had its pejorative meaning and was soon applied to Prussia; pacifism's meaning was more nebulous and could refer to anyone seeking peace. *Oxford England Language Dictionary* (2d ed., 1989), IX, 766; XI, 38; on English usage before World War I, see A. J. Anthony Morris, *Radicalism Against War 1906-1914: The Advocacy of Peace and Retrenchment* (1972), 198-199; Michael Howard, *War and the Liberal Conscience* (1978), and "The Causes of War." V. R. Berghahn, *Militarism: The History of an International Debate 1861-1979* (1982).

In the late Victorian and Edwardian eras, powerful states engaged in an incessant, even frantic, emphasis upon seeking security through weapons and alliances and holding congresses to redraw the map in the Balkans and Africa. Not ignored, but marginalized by conciliatory gestures, was a diffuse popular peace movement attempting to make changes in the behavior of nations so that humans living in small and large nations could enjoy security.

Peace is a moral and religious imperative, but creating effective organizations and policies has proved extraordinarily difficult. This chapter seeks to explain why. The focus of this chapter is on the peace movement from 1870 until 1914, a time when pacifism reached its apogee, having, by one estimate, a million actively committed adherents.[3] The first section will describe the social composition and power of the peace movement in different countries; the second will describe the ideas; the third the projects, and the final assess why the peace movement failed to prevent World War I. Even in failure, the period witnessed accomplishments: the creation of the Red Cross, the Geneva Conventions, the first multi-state arms control conferences, and an international movement working for peace.

II. Peace Activity in Europe

The peace movement between 1870 and 1914 was largely a European-American phenomenon. Peace conferences did not allow advocacy of freedom for a colonized European nation like Poland (at the time divided among Prussia, Russia, and Austria-Hungary), so also there would be no hearing from colonial non-European peoples like the Egyptians and Vietnamese. Even though a few intellectuals believed that the Buddha and Muhammad had original insights about war and peace, the West assumed that contemporary representatives of colonized non-Christian lands had no insights worth discussing.

The peace movement had the strength to be a political force only in Great Britain, the United States, and France. These countries accepted open criticism of

---

[3]Howard, 53.

the government, advocated religious toleration, and elected representatives who passed legislation. Here the peace movement was a legitimate pressure group, like other political associations seeking to influence the government. However, even in the democracies, elites in the executive branch controlled foreign policy and as a matter of policy often kept parliaments ill-informed. Freedom for the peace movement did not translate into political power.

In contrast with the liberal democracies were the three autocracies in central and eastern Europe. In Russia, the Tsar exercised absolute control of all policies; in Germany and Austria-Hungary representative assemblies legislated on domestic matters, but foreign and military policy remained the prerogative of emperors. Here peace societies seeking to reform foreign policy or de-emphasize military force could be labeled subversive, not just scorned as naïve.[4] So pacifists had to agitate with circumspection and insist that their activities were non-political.

The German peace movement faced opposition from a successful military that between 1863 and 1870 defeated Denmark, Austria, and France and was now recognized as having created the most powerful army on the continent. Consequently, pacifists remained on the defensive and had little impact upon a pro-military government. The Kaiser, the churches, the universities, the lawyers, the press, government officials, and the military opposed peace reforms. The peace movement attracted the support of a few intellectuals, small merchants, primary-school teachers and assorted individualists.[5] German pacifist support was localized in Alsace-Lorraine, whose inhabitants feared being the location of the next war, and south Germany - areas far from the locus of power.

---

[4] Essays by Richard Laurence, "Peace Movement in Austria," Solomon Wank, "Diplomacy Against the Peace Movement: The Austro-Hungarian Foreign Office and the Second Hague Peace Conference of 1907," and Roger Chickering, "Problems of a German Peace Movement 1890-1914," 42-54 in *Doves and Diplomats: Foreign Offices and Peace Movements in Europe and America in the Twentieth Century*, ed. Solomon Wank (1978).

[5] Roger Chickering, *Imperial Germany and a World Without War: The Peace Movement and German Society 1892-1914* (1975), 172-3, 216-217.

The bourgeoisie, who dominated the small German peace movement, sought to keep a privileged position while reforming international relations. The leaders maintained a distance from the workers and socialists, who also talked about peace but desired fundamental changes of society as well. So the powerful socialist movement in Germany, with the largest political party in the Reichstag before World War I, showed little interest in the middle-class peace movement. The historian Sandi Cooper compared the status and intellectual isolation of a peace reformer in early twentieth-century Germany with that of being a communist in America at the height of the Cold War.[6]

France was the only major power on the European continent with a strong peace movement. Crushed in the 1870 war with Prussia, France had experienced invasion, endured a military occupation, paid reparations, and lost the border territory of Alsace-Lorraine to the newly proclaimed German Empire. Aware of the human cost of modern war, many French sought for an alternative way to solve international disputes. They wanted to regain Alsace-Lorraine, but feared that Germany's more numerous population, rapid industrialization, and strong army made a military victory unlikely. So perhaps holding a plebiscite was the best way of acquiring Alsace-Lorraine. The French also argued that international law forbade the annexation of territory without the consent of the inhabitants, although they did not apply this restraint to their own colonial empire. While listening to and hoping for positive results from the peace movement, the French Third Republic's governments rebuilt their army, sought for alliances with Russia and Britain to counter German power, engaged in colonial expansion in North Africa and Indo-China, planned for war, and hoped for revenge.

The French peace movement did not originate in the Roman Catholic Just War tradition, nor was it religiously inspired. The government of Emperor Louis Napoleon III, which led the French to defeat in 1870, had been very pro-Catholic. The liberal supporters of the Third Republic inherited a perspective of free

---

[6] Cooper, 69.

thought and anti-clericalism originating in the Enlightenment and the French Revolution. The French peace movement wanted to prove its case for international reform by reason, history, and science, basing its conclusions upon facts rather than religious sentiment.

The press, intellectuals, schoolteachers, government officials, and the Protestant minority supported a French peace movement claiming 300,000 members living throughout the country.[7] Those favoring the peace reform opposed the army's and the Church's role in the Dreyfus affair, a false persecution of a Jewish officer by the military from 1894-1906, and saw the militarization of society as weakening of democracy. As in Germany and Britain, but unlike America, the French peace movement had two loci of support, the middle class and the socialists, who represented its cause in the National Assembly. In spite of different views on most economic and political issues, peace advocates in the bourgeoisie, the radical, and socialist parties created a working alliance.[8]

Socialist Peace

Socialists had long been critics of nationalism and the wars caused by a capitalist-dominated state system. By 1914 there were three million socialists in Germany, a million in France and in Austria-Hungary, and 500,000 in Great Britain who believed "that the International shall be the human race." Yet they also believed that true peace could come only after violent revolutions that would take place in individual states, after which workers throughout the world would create a socialist utopia of freedom.[9]

Karl Marx's 1848 *Communist Manifesto* proclaimed that true peace would come only after the triumph of the working class, but he devoted little attention as to how this utopian vision would be realized. Instead, he focused on the present class struggle between workers and capitalists, in which the triumph of the workers could come suddenly after violent revolution. Since most Marxists

---

[7] Ibid., 66.
[8] Ibid., 64; Chickering, *Imperial Germany,* ch. 8, 327-83.

emphasized the violent struggle between classes, they played little role in the peace movement. At the time of the First Communist International in 1868, Marx denounced the peace societies' program as failing to deal with oppression, poverty, and exploitation, which actually caused war.[10] Until after the coming transformation of society, Marx regarded all wars as between the ruling elements of societies, symptomatic of the contradictions in capitalist society, and of little concern to the workers, who were exploited in the production of war materiel and as cannon fodder in battle.

Before World War I, left-wing Marxists showed little interest in a pacifist movement that ignored class struggle and internal revolution and wished only mild reform in domestic affairs and a gradual improvement of the international order. Lenin, for example, saw the struggles for colonial empires of the late nineteenth century as exemplifying the capitalist search for new markets - a prelude to the increasing contradictions in capitalist society that would result in war, after which the workers could prevail. Those socialists who worked for violent revolution ignored the peace movement.

Revisionists at the gatherings of International Socialists during the 1890s presented themselves as Social Democrats who saw no necessity of a violent revolution. Before his death in 1883, Marx constantly reformulated his teachings; his colleague Frederick Engels also pondered the problems of the workers' relations to issues of war and peace and concluded that in certain societies the proletariat could triumph peacefully. The suppression of the Paris Commune at the end of the Franco-Prussian war showed that violent revolution might not succeed, but elections of socialists to parliaments in Germany, France, and Britain opened another avenue to power. In these countries, socialist theoreticians and political and labor-union leaders reinterpreted Marxist thought, stressing the

---

[9] R. Craig Nation, *War on War: Lenin, the Zimmerwald Left, and the Origins of Communist Internationalism* (1989), 3, 21.
[10] W. B. Gallie, *Philosophers of Peace and War: Kant, Clausewitz, Marx, Engels and Tolstoy* (1978) 66-99; Cooper, 36.

possibilities in and linkage between domestic and international reform, and speculating about whether in democratic countries the triumph of the workers could come peacefully.

Revisionist socialists also questioned the Marxist perspective that capitalism inevitably would cause wars that would lead to the revolution. An alternative perspective was that internal reforms could prevent external wars. English socialists, for example, criticized their government's search for markets abroad and saw in military spending a diversion of resources that might be used to improve the conditions of the poorer classes. They denounced the arms race as a product of the greed of arms manufacturers who sought to sow distrust among nations as a way of increasing their own sales and profits. Capitalists used arms races, imperialism, and wars to distract the workers from their true destiny.[11]

For the revisionist socialists in France and Britain (and to a lesser extent in Germany), worker solidarity was the way to preserve the peace. Following Marx, they insisted that the workers' primary allegiance was to their class, not the nation. Socialist solidarity would prevent war, because in the event of war the suppressed classes would neither make guns nor serve in armies. Instead, Europe would be paralyzed by mass strikes, and governments would have to make peace. Socialist Democrats in France sought to join hands with their class-mates in Germany, Holland, Belgium, and Britain.

Bourgeois peace workers joined revisionist socialists in the French National Assembly in advocating international law and arbitration and stressing the peaceful nature of democratic societies. By 1910 socialists and radicals in France and Britain agreed with peace societies in championing international law and arbitration, and they joined liberal democrats in claiming that military spending hurt social programs and strengthened reactionary aristocracies. An alliance of workers and bourgeoisie working for peace would surely prevent war.

Great Britain

The most powerful European peace movement was in Great Britain, where a Liberal Party government repeatedly stressed its commitment to reducing military expenditures, disarmament, and arbitration of international disputes. Pro-pacifist Radical Whigs and Labour (socialist) members composed about one-third of the ruling coalition from 1906 until 1914 and had significant support from major newspapers like the *Manchester Guardian*, trade unions, socialist intellectuals, free trade manufacturers, Quakers, dissenting churchmen, lawyers, and supporters of the Whig Party (now renamed Liberals) who had earlier opposed the expansion of empire and the Boer War.[12]

The traditional Whigs saw additional colonies as a drain upon resources. These men wished to avoid getting involved in war on the continent, and put their trust in the British navy to protect their island and the Empire. The Liberals sought good will with all European states, and particularly with France and America, on the theory that democratic states should work together because the people, as distinguished from economic interests, were inherently peace-loving.

Still, even with the Liberals in power and a sympathizer serving briefly as prime minister, the pacifists did not control the foreign office, admiralty, and army, whose ministers had little sympathy with pacifist emphases. The pacifist back-benchers could threaten to oppose policies, but they knew that voting against the government risked causing the downfall of the Liberal Party and the return to power of the Tories, who scorned pacifism, favored alliances, and increased military spending. In Britain, as in all European countries, the press - often controlled by very conservative businessmen - labeled the peace movement as either pro-communist or foolish.

The Church of England traditionally opposed pacifism. The Church hierarchy had long supported the Tory Party, and bishops still exercised

---

[11] The Radicals views were summarized in John Atkinson Hobson's influential *Imperialism* (1902).
[12] A. J. Anthony Morris, *Radicalism Against War, 1906-1914* (1972), 5-12.

considerable power in the House of Lords. Until after 1907 when the Second Hague Conference met, the bishops and clergy of the Church of England showed little interest in the peace movement.[13] Then, convinced of the estrangement between Germany and Britain, a few bishops participated in cultural exchanges between the two countries.

As a result of Britain's fear of German power, in spite of back-bench protests by the pacifists, the Liberals created a triple entente with France and Russia and engaged in a naval arms race with the Germans. Until August 1914, leading ministers affirmed that Germany and Great Britain remained friendly and that danger of war was remote.

III. The United States

In America, pacifism was a non-partisan reform attracting influential politicians, big businessmen like Andrew Carnegie, and newspaper and magazine editors who sought to reform big business. The peace movement's foci appealed to different constituencies, some of whose other aims were incompatible, but who agreed on the possibility and desirability of creating a more peaceful world by applying features of the American system of government worldwide. Much to the annoyance of Europeans, Americans kept advocating a world court, like the U.S. Supreme Court, a world parliament, like the Congress, and a code of world law, like the Constitution.

The American peace movement never controlled either major political party, but its aims received public support from presidents, secretaries of state, and many members of Congress.[14] Within the Republican Party, some of the most conservative politicians supported the movement for international law and arbitration, seeing in these a stabilizing influence. They wished to apply their

---

[13] Albert Martin, *The Last Crusade: The Church of England in the First World War* (1974), 61-67.
[14] C. Roland Marchand, *The American Peace Movement and Social Reform, 1898-1918* (1972) David S. Pattern, *Toward a Warless World: the Travail of the American Peace Movement 1887-1914* (1976); Charles DeBenedetti, *The Peace Reform in American History* (1980), chs. 4, 5.

own reverence for law and order and the status quo to the international sphere, to create a constitution for the world.

A second impetus of the American Peace Movement came from those involved in the Progressive movement, people who wanted to use the powers of government to solve social problems, including regulation of big business, workmen's compensation for injuries suffered on the job, and protective legislation for women and children. Believing that too little democracy caused many of the ills of American society, pacifists supported the direct election of senators, popular referendums, and recall of public officials. The peace movement's emphasis upon democracy, education, and the goodness of the people echoed Progressive themes.

Women's suffrage was the most important Progressive reform directly related to the peace movement, since it was widely believed that giving women the vote was a step toward a peaceful foreign policy. Women would bring a moral focus to international politics because they would be reluctant to send their sons to war. Peace reform attracted women who opposed obtaining the vote as destructive of the family, as well as those who saw the suffrage as a means of protecting the family. Because peace work could be presented as a continuation of women's traditional maternal role, all classes of women could support it. Of course, putting peace within the feminine orbit weakened its appeal to supposedly hardheaded politicians dealing with sordid reality.

For its Progressive supporters, the peace movement was one of several good causes, and for most it was not their primary focus. Rather, they saw foreign affairs as susceptible to the same impulses to efficiency, democracy, fair play, and morality they were applying to domestic problems. The Progressive movement became the dominant political mood of America between 1900 and 1917, attracting to the peace movement the support of university professors, small businessmen, lawyers, feminists, social workers, and labor unions.

Historians attach the label the "Social Gospel" to the religious impulse in the Progressive movement. The Social Gospel was an attempt to apply the moral teachings of Jesus to the wider society through the power of government. Evangelical and Modernist clergy and laymen cooperated in a crusade against evil, whether symbolized by distillers or arms merchants. In addition to the longtime peace churches, Methodists, Presbyterians, Congregationalists, and Baptists supported peace reform.[15] The newly formed Federal Council of Churches, the first flowering of the ecumenical movement in America, established a commission on peace and arbitration. The Social Gospelers saw Jesus as a bringer of peace and denounced war as an anti-Christian activity. Nations professing Christianity should be able to create mechanisms so that they could solve their disputes without fighting. The pro-religious perspective of American peace workers often distressed their more secular European counterparts who, for example, refused to open international conferences with prayer because it would discredit the proceedings.

The Russian novelist Leo Tolstoy proclaimed a radical religious alternative to the gradual reform supported by peace societies and the social gospel. Leo Tolstoy advocated a pacifist Christian anarchism that he saw as similar to the nonresistance of American abolitionists like William Lloyd Garrison. Tolstoy advocated total nonresistance based upon following without reservation Jesus' teaching in the Sermon on the Mount. The truth of nonresistance did not depend upon the *Bible*, which was full of unintelligible doctrines, but upon "knowledge of goodness, that is God, directly through reason and conscience." In a series of essays published between 1893 and 1909, Tolstoy condemned personal and institutional violence found in government, the law, and private property. He opposed socialists and scientists for a reductionist understanding of the true nature of humanity, scorned nationalism as betraying the unity of peoples, and attacked the Christian churches for emphasizing false dogma and supernaturalism.

---

[15] Marchand, 323-80, stresses that most of the clergy involved in the pre-war peace movement were not pacifists and that different groups were active depending upon the immediate issues. Roland White, Jr., and Howard Hopkins, eds., *The Social Gospel: Religion and Reform in Changing America* (1967), and Donald Gorrell, *The Age of Social Responsibility: The Social Gospel in the Progressive Era 1900-1920* (1988) are general summaries of the movement.

He dismissed Just War theories as contrary to the love that was the true essence of Jesus' teaching. Christian "love is not a necessity to be adapted to anything, but is the essential nature of man's soul. Man does not love because it is advantageous for him to love this man or those men, but because love is the essence of his soul - because he cannot help loving."[16] Any form of violence destroyed this love. War, he proclaimed, had a simple solution: citizens should refuse to take up arms, or, as recently summarized: "What if they had a war and nobody came."

For most American pacifists, Tolstoy's perspectives were too radical. Instead, they utilized his anti-war teachings while joining peace societies that seemingly offered a viable median between an anarchist apolitical Christianity and Just War theory. For a few nonresistants, pacifism rose out of a religious commitment that denied the primacy of the secular world and insisted upon taking the Sermon on the Mount literally. The nonresistants played a relatively minor role in the European and U.S. peace movements, but Tolstoy's ideas would later influence Mohandas Gandhi's thought on nonviolence.

American peace workers joined in many organizations, often with an interlocking directorate, designed to change school curricula, foster international exchanges, support arbitration, and define international law. The Carnegie Endowment for International Peace sponsored scholarly conferences and publications, issuing scholarly translations of the writings of Grotius, Suarez, Pufendorf, and other commentators on international law. The Endowment subsidized American and European peace societies and their publications. Carnegie provided funds for a building for the World Court at The Hague in Holland and the Pan-American Union Building in Washington, D.C. American peace workers participated in meetings of the Interparliamentary Union (for members of legislatures) and the Universal Peace Congresses held in major European cities and once in Boston. With support from many politicians,

---

[16]Leo Tolstoy, *The Kingdom of God and Peace Essays* (1960), ix, 129; Peter Brock, *Pacifism in*

academics, feminists, clergy, union leaders, and publishers of magazines and newspapers, the American peace movement was in a stronger position to influence national policy than pacifists in any other state.

In comparison with Europe in 1900, the American military establishment was weak. Europeans had one of every ten citizens in the army; American one of 1,800.[17] Even in comparison with Britain's army, let alone those on the continent, the size of the American army was negligible, but the U.S. had created a modern navy. To cynics, the peace movement's power came because the United States was bordered by two oceans and two friendly and much weaker neighbors. Even so, the peace movement had powerful enemies in the military, the State Department, and the press. President Theodore Roosevelt, who won the Nobel Peace Prize for mediating a war between Japan and Russia, had private scorn for the Hague Conferences. Roosevelt's combination of belligerent and pro-pacifist public utterances earned him a reputation as the Dr. Jekyll and Mr. Hyde of the American peace movement. In America, as in England, generalized public support of the peace movement did not stop imperialism or reliance upon a powerful navy. Still, Presidents William Howard Taft and Woodrow Wilson and their secretaries of state remained strong supporters of the goals and methods of the peace movement and made arbitration a central focus of foreign policy. Americans remained less worried about arms races, security, and becoming involved in a European war than in showing their commitment to a moral and civilized way of solving international disputes.

IV. An Agenda for Peace

August 1914 showed the inadequacy of the conventional wisdom of relying on arms and balance of power to keep peace. The war also showed the inability of the peace movement to change governments' policies. The issue to be considered here is whether that failure was due at least in part to weaknesses in the peace movement's understanding of war or tactics. To what extent was a lack

Europe to 1914 (1972), 453-64. Gallie, *Philosophers of Peace and War*, 100-132.

of power due to ideological shortcomings? What alternatives did the peace workers provide? Were they as uncomprehending of the nature of politics as their opponents charged?

A portrait of the peace movement should recognize changes over time and in different countries. Before 1900 the movement's leaders attempted to refrain from criticizing any nation or discussing social structure. After 1900 conferences openly talked about imperialism's legacy and debated freedom for subject peoples in Europe as well as overseas. [18] The earlier movement was male-dominated; later, British and American women identified their struggles for suffrage with work for peace.[19] Even within one country, the aims of organizations and prominent leaders varied. For example, in America Jane Addams, William Jennings Bryan, and Andrew Carnegie agreed on the need for peace but little else. The peace movement was extremely decentralized, and congresses were often endangered by the delegates' national differences. Still, there were enough shared perspectives to refer to a peace movement.

A common thread was patriotism. The peace workers condemned the excesses of nationalism, but they saw themselves as strengthening their countries by decreasing the likelihood of war. Before 1900 leaders at the international peace conferences, fearing walkouts, tried to avoid issues like Alsace-Lorraine that would alienate delegates or subject participants to recriminations after they returned home. Even later those who found their countries singled out for criticism often became defensive and allowed love of country to supersede their commitment to international justice. The willingness of peace societies to subordinate the international themes of peace and reconciliation to national needs robbed the movement of its potential for radical opposition. Or, to phrase it

---

[17] Cooper, 121.
[18] Exposés of the barbarous tactics used in putting down the Boxer Rebellion, the American suppression of guerrillas in the Philippines, and the Boer War, during which the English invented concentration camps, and the economic exploitation of the Belgian Congo prompted peace conferences to discuss cruelty in colonial expansion and to begin to assert the right of self-determination for non-European peoples. Cooper, 61-62, 174-180.
[19] Harriet Hyman Alonso, *Peace as a Women's Issue* (1993), chs. 2, 3.

another way, political leaders knew that the pacifist critique could be blunted by appeals to nationalism.

A second general belief came from a secularized and generalized Just War theory. The peace workers insisted on reserving to all nations the right of self-defense. The peace movement sought to abolish aggressive war, to reduce the prevalence of war, but defending the homeland was legitimate. No government and very few peace workers showed an interest in unilateral disarmament. Mutual disarmament or arms control or placing some kind of limits upon military spending evoked public support, but different security needs for each country made any kind of agreement on the form of arms limitation difficult even for the peace workers.

Third, most peace reformers, even in autocratic nations, believed in democracy and in the goodness of people. In genuinely democratic systems, they argued, the people would easily detect unworthy motives and refuse to fight. The leaders of democracies also learned how to compromise differences by listening to divergent perspectives. By contrast, autocracies fostered war because princes did not like opposition, and often subordinated the welfare of subjects to power politics. The emperors of Europe had reason to be suspicious of the peace movement, for its view of good government would drastically reduce their power over foreign policy. The peace movement argued that diplomacy should not be reserved to an elite accustomed to making secret treaties. Instead, "open covenants openly arrived at," to use Wilson's later phrase, would prevent war. France and Britain, traditional enemies, now were friends because both nations had become democracies; that their new friendship rested upon hostility to Germany was an inconvenient fact.

The peace movement also had confidence in the judgment, if not in the policies, of the important leaders, even of the autocracies. Christian gentlemen who knew what they were doing and who were committed to peace led all the major European nations. These well-educated men were skilled in negotiating strategies. Only in Russia could foreign ministers ignore public opinion, but even it boasted of Christian civilization. Elsewhere parliaments and newspapers could make their wishes known. The peace advocates trusted that their political leaders' core values would not allow them to lie to the people. These leaders, all openly professing to abhor war and to be working for peace, would not risk the horrors of modern war lightly. The series of crises in the Balkans and North Africa that Europeans had overcome since 1870 proved the prudence and skill of the diplomats.

Peace reformers shared many cultural values with other Europeans. They distinguished between civilized and barbarous peoples and asserted that there was a common western heritage previously termed Catholic Europe and now called Christendom. While a common culture had not prevented wars in the past, the peace reformers hoped that now Europeans had outgrown such immature behavior. Men of reason knew how to settle disputes without bashing each other over the head. All Europeans could appreciate Shakespeare, Goethe, Beethoven, Newton, Raphael, and Kant. Academic associations, cultural events, and intellectual movements crossed national boundaries, making Europe one civilization more than it had ever been before.

The peace reformers also maintained that the changing conditions of economic life made war less likely. They noted that Great Britain's trade with Germany dwarfed that of either nation with any one colony. The bankers and capitalists who invested in other countries had an interest in preventing war. The industrial revolution linked the nations of Europe in a common enterprise, and any nation beginning a war risked losing more than it could gain. In fact, calculations by any intelligent businessman or government would show the unprofitableness of going to war. Norman Angell's very popular *The Great Illusion* (1910) argued that the economies of great nations were so firmly linked that a great war would soon paralyze them. For nearly a hundred years English liberals had preached that free trade was good for business and good for peace.

Finally, the peace reformers had confidence in man's ability to understand and control society. The late nineteenth century witnessed the professionalization of the social sciences, a repudiation of laissez-faire economics, and the beginnings of the modern welfare state. Economics, sociology, history, and political science sought to discover the rules or laws of human behavior, one of which was that war had outlived its usefulness. The social sciences sought to borrow some of the prestige of science and technology by doing research and making deductions from facts to support ideas. Peace reform, a product of the social sciences, was not utopian or mystical, but offered a factual analysis of the causes of war and the methods to prevent it. All that was required was to convince the politicians and diplomats that the right formulas had been found.

The peace workers showed their optimism in their preference for education and disdain for politics as controversial and divisive. If only the peace message could get into the newspapers, magazines, and schoolbooks, they reasoned, the people would rally to their cause and the politicians would fall into line. With a constant barrage of pamphlets, lectures, conferences, and books, the peace movement tried to persuade the people, although the people turned out in practice to be the middle classes. Why workers could be reached only through the socialist and labor union movement and the reasons for their general lack of commitment to the cause remained a mystery to the peace societies. In Europe some older leaders said to educate the elite and the people will follow. In America this was also the approach of the Carnegie Endowment. The peace movement's public relations efforts did educate sufficient people to make the politicians pay attention.

V. Programs: Arbitration and Limiting War

The peace workers proposed a course of actions that, they believed, if accepted could avoid war. The program had already proved its efficacy at the end of the Civil War. The United States had a series of grievances with Great Britain over the depredations of the ship *Alabama*, a Confederate steamer built in an English port, that had later attacked the Union's shipping. In 1872 America and Britain submitted their dispute to binding arbitration and both nations accepted the result, with Britain paying a $15,000,000 penalty. Arbitration had also eased conflicts between America and Latin American countries over debts and in 1896, had solved a boundary dispute in Venezuela. The number of successful arbitrations rose constantly: between 1820-1880 eighty-two cases, 1880-1900 ninety cases.[20]

After 1900 there was a vogue for treaties of arbitration with over 150 being signed. The Liberal government in Britain favored them. Britain and France cemented their entente with an arbitration treaty. Britain and the United States negotiated such a treaty, with significant loopholes, but the Senate refused to ratify it as an encroachment upon its powers. The Taft administration (1908-12) made arbitration treaties a keynote of its foreign policy, negotiating bilateral arrangements with Latin American nations. The Latin American nations welcomed arbitrations as a method of preventing invasions by the United States or European powers to collect debts. Virtually all European nations signed many arbitration treaties, with the exception of Germany, whose Kaiser thought they were silly. Most arbitration treaties had reserve clauses, allowing each state to act unilaterally on matters of self-defense and national honor. Even so, peace advocates saw these weak treaties as the beginning of a process that would not infringe upon sovereignty while making war less likely. They also hoped that the bilateral arrangements would serve as a stepping stone to a general arbitration treaty among all nations.

A second major project of the peace movement was an attempt to enforce limits on the conduct of war. During the Civil War, Abraham Lincoln had instructed Franz Lieber, a German immigrant, to draw up a code governing permissible practices in war. Lieber's code became the basis for later European attempts to create conventions - derived from Grotius - as to treatment of civilians in wartime, the status and treatment of injured and uninjured prisoners of war, and neutral rights.[21]

---

[20] Marrin, 67; different figures in Cooper, 91.
[21] Frank Freidel, *Francis Lieber: Nineteenth-century Liberal* (1947), 323-341; Sheldon Cohen, *Arms and Judgment: Laws, Morality, and the Conduct of War in the Twentieth Century* (1989).

Nations also sought better treatment of wounded soldiers. During the Crimean War, Florence Nightingale became a Victorian heroine for her work in nursing the wounded soldiers, and her later testimony as to the conditions in British hospitals led to greater concern for medical treatment of soldiers. A Swiss businessman, Henry Dunant, saw the carnage and appalling treatment of the wounded at the French-Austrian battle of Solferino in 1859. Dunant's crusade to persuade European nations to improve conditions of injured soldiers resulted in the creation of the Red Cross in 1863-64.[22] At the Geneva Convention, fifteen nations agreed that a wounded soldier would not be treated as an enemy. Now hospitals, ambulances, and medical personnel (including civilians) would not be a legitimate target of war. Dunant's vision of neutral medical personnel having access to the battlefield did not survive. Instead, each country created its own national Red Cross to minister to its soldiers. The International Red Cross remained separate from these national societies and accountable only to the Swiss government that appointed its board. It attempted to coordinate the work of the national Red Cross organizations, but its most famous task became the inspection of prisoner of war camps.

The Red Cross was both pro- and anti-military. The Geneva Convention diplomats asserted the supremacy of a humanitarian ideal above military needs. Yet the military welcomed better treatment of wounded soldiers who then could fight again. Governments also approved of the decision of the Red Cross to inform them but not to publicize the results of its investigations into POW camps. From the military's perspective, the humanitarian impulse of women and conscientious objectors could now be enlisted in a war effort. The existence of the Red Cross would also reassure civilians that their sons, since universal conscription was now the norm, would receive good medical care. The Geneva

---

[22] Martin Gumpert, *Dunant: The Story of the Red Cross* (1938), 125, 133, 139. Caroline Moorehead, *Dunant's Dream: War, Switzerland and the History of the Red Cross* (1998).

Conventions marked a legalization of an earlier custom of recognizing the special status of a wounded soldier.[23]

The Lieber code, the Geneva Conventions of 1868 and 1888, and the Red Cross drew upon the Just War theories that insisted that natural law and/or the laws of peoples created universal norms to be observed by all nations in peace and in war. The task of the practitioners of the new academic discipline of international law was to codify the new laws of war and to embody them in treaties among nations. Then in a dispute nations could turn to impartial arbiters or judges to settle the matter fairly.

The Hague Conferences

After 1870 the impact of the peace movement varied greatly, with influence coming in the 1880s, a subsequent loss of momentum resulting from the British and American wars of the 1890s, and a revival of interest and great visibility occurring after the first Hague Conference in 1899 and continuing until 1914.

The Hague Conferences made the peace movement intellectually respectable. In 1898 Tsar Nicholas I of Russia, worried about the increased cost of armaments, called for a conference involving all nations to meet at The Hague in Holland to discuss disarmament. The peace movement was delighted with the Tsar's proposal, for here was a major European power, and an autocrat as well, intent on settling the problems of the arms race. In spite of the great reluctance and skepticism of the major powers, the Conference opened in 1899 with twenty-six nations in attendance. Forty-seven nations sent delegates to the second Conference held in 1907, with the increase coming from Latin America. A third Hague Conference was scheduled for 1915.[24]

---

[23] Geoffrey Best, *Humanity in Warfare* (1980), remains the best survey of the impact of the movement for limitation in war on the conduct of war.
[24] William I. Hull, *The Two Hague Conferences and their Contributions to International Law* (1908), and Calvin Davis, *The United States and the First Hague Conference* (1962) and *The United States and the Second Hague Conference: American Diplomacy and International Organizations* (1975).

At the two Hague Conferences, the major powers made no serious efforts at disarmament or arms control on either armies or navies. Their militaries had veto power over most nations' actions, because the civilian governments insisted that military power was the way to preserve the peace. So the Hague diplomats passed euphonious statements about arms control. At the first Conference the Germans and Americans, both of whom were expanding their fleets, made sure that navies were not on the agenda. Even though the British, French, and Americans prepared to discuss disarmament at the second Conference, the Germans threatened a walkout if the subject were even on the agenda.

Believing that having no accomplishments from the Conferences would be a public relations disaster, the diplomats spent most of their time revising the laws of war. The nations agreed (each nation had one vote and decisions required unanimity) to outlaw a few weapons, like dum-dum bullets and projectiles dropped from balloons, which none of the military staffs thought were significant weapons. They revised the Geneva Conventions insisting that wounded soldiers were to be considered neutral, a category different from prisoners of war. The attention of the second Conference focused on naval rights, a subject made relevant because of the invention of the dreadnoughts or battleships. Although the Conference did recommend new conventions defining contraband, spelling out the rights of neutral shipping, and prohibiting the bombardment of undefended places, differences among continental military and naval powers, would-be belligerents and neutrals, and large and small states meant that highly significant and controversial issues could not be resolved.

At both Conferences, the delegates disappointed the peace movement by rejecting any treaty providing for binding arbitration. The Conferences did authorize each nation's appointing judges to a panel of arbitrators to be constantly available and a Judicial Arbitration Court. The Conferences recommended an arbitration before going to war and the necessity of a declaration of war before beginning hostilities, though the delegates could not agree on how long an interval was required between the declaration and hostilities.

Peace workers complained that the diplomats spent more time deciding what was allowable in war than in creating the mechanisms to preserve the peace. Still, they hoped that the process of meeting had a momentum and that, after additional education, the Hague Conferences would tackle the difficult issues. In retrospect, the Hague Conferences created the first permanent international organization and served as the forerunners of the League of Nations and the United Nations.

Careful observers noted their disappointment in the Hague Conferences, but insisted that just having the two meetings had started a process that would in time bring real disarmament, limitations on the conduct of war, and better protection for neutral rights and the civilians of warring nations. After all, with the pacifist belief in progress, civility, and leaders, it was only a matter of time until nations of the world would see the advantage of law over brute force.

In retrospect we can find many subjects the peace movement could have stressed more: the vested interests in an arms race, the relations between internal instability and external adventures, the dangers in the alliance system, and the cost of realpolitik. They could have learned from the socialists that capitalism's search for markets led to imperialism and increased the dangers of war. Still, there seems to be no reason to assume that a change of strategy or a broadening of the perspective would have given the peace movement any prolonged successes.

The leaders of the late Victorian and Edwardian peace movement were not clergymen or theologians and did not rely upon Just War theory or religious feelings as a method of influencing people. These secularized idealists distinguished modern pacifism from the sentimentalism of peace reformers of earlier periods who relied upon good will or individual religious feelings. They saw themselves as practical men and women, not willing to condemn defensive war as evil, but working to create institutions and mechanisms for the international community of nations. For all their scientific practicality, there was a strong element of moralism in their attitudes and many believed that humans were basically good and that, with the help of God, progress was certain. Their optimism was a weakness, for it led to complacency even in the face of Block's dire forecast.

Since the Napoleonic era, the "concert of Europe" had prevented a general war, even though individual nations had fought. Conferences held in Berlin in 1881 and 1893 sought to solve issues arising from Balkan nationalism and war and the partition of Africa to the great powers' satisfaction. The Russian Tsar, British prime minister, and American presidents made public declarations in favor of international arbitration and disarmament. Trusting in the providence of God and the ability of statesmen, Europeans and Americans forecast that the twentieth century would witness the triumph of peace.

Bibliography of Works Cited
and Suggestions for Further Reading

Introduction: The Past in the Present

Bennett, Olivia, Jo Bexley, and Kitty Warnock, eds. *Arms to Fight: Arms to Protest: Women Speak Out About Conflict.* London: Panos, 1995.

Black, Jeremy. *Why Wars Happen.* New York: New York University Press, 1998.

Bramson, Leon, and George Goethals, eds. *War: Studies from Psychology, Sociology, And Anthropology.* New York: Basic Books, 1994.

Campbell, L. B. *Shakespeare's Histories.* CA: Huntington Library, 1947.

Diamond, Jared. *Guns, Germs, and Steel: The Fate of Human Societies.* New York: Norton, 1999.

Ehrenreich, Barbara. *Blood Rites: Origins and History of the Passions of War.* New York: Metropolitan, Henry Holt, 1997.

Elshtain, Jean. *Women and War.* New York: Basic Books, 1967.

___ and Sheila Tobias, ed. *Women, Militarism, and War.* Savage, MD: Rowman and Littlefield, 1990.

Foakes, R. A. *Shakespeare and Violence.* Cambridge, UK: Cambridge University Press, 2003.

Fussell, Paul. *Wartime: Understanding and Behavior in the Second World War.* New York: Oxford University Press, 1989.

Girard, René. *Violence and the Sacred.* Trans. Patrick Gregory. Baltimore, MD: Johns Hopkins, 1977.

Gregor, Thomas, ed. *Natural History of Peace.* Nashville, TN: Vanderbilt University Press, 1996.

Gregor, Thomas and Leslie Sponsel, ed. *The Anthropology of Peace and Nonviolence.* Boulder, CO: Rienner, 1994.

Haas, Jonathan, ed. *The Anthropology of War.* Cambridge, UK: Cambridge University Press, 1990.

Harris, Adrienne and Ynestra King, eds. *Rocking the Ship of State: Toward a Feminist Peace Politics.* Boulder, CO: Westview, 1989.

Hattaway, Michael. "Blood is their Argument: Men of War and Soldiers in Shakespeare and Others." *Religion, Culture and Society in Early Modern Britain: Essays in Honor of Patrick Collinson.* Ed. Anthony Fletcher and Peter Roberts. Cambridge, UK: Cambridge University Press, 1994.

Holinshed, Raphael. *Holinshed's Chronicles As Used in Shakespeare's Plays.* New York: J .M. Dent, 1940.

Howell, Signe, and Roy Willis, eds. *Societies at Peace: Anthropological Perspectives.* London: Rutledge, 1989.

Jorgensen, Paul A. "Moral Guidance and Religious Encouragement for the
    Elizabethan Soldiers." *Huntington Library Quarterly,* XIII, 1950.
___. "Theoretical Views of War in Elizabethan England," *Journal
    of the History of Ideas,* XIII (1952): 469-481.
Juergensmeyer, Mark. *Terror in the Mind of God: the Global Rise of Religious
    Violence.* Berkley: University of California Press, 2000.
Kohn, Carol. "Sex and Death in the Rational World of the Defence
    Intellectual," in Laslett, Barbara, ed. *Gender and Scientific Authority.*
    Chicago: University of Chicago Press, 1996.
Lincoln, Bruce. *Death, War, and Sacrifice: Studies in Ideology and Practice.*
    Chicago: University of Chicago, 1991.
Lorentzen, Lois Ann, and Jennifer Turpin, eds. *The Women and War Reader.*
    New York: New York University Press, 1998.
Low, Bobbi S. *Why Sex Matters: A Darwinian Look at Human Behavior.*
    Princeton, NJ: Princeton University Press, 2000.
Lowe, Ben. *Imagining Peace: A History of Early English Pacifist Ideas.*
    University Park: PA: Penn State Press, 1997.
O'Connoll, John. *The Ride of the Second Horseman: The Origins of War.* New
    York: Oxford University Press, 1995.
Otterbein, Keith F. *Feuding and Warfare: Selected Works of Keith F. Otterbein.*
    War and Society Series, I. Amsterdam, Netherlands: Gordon and Breach,
    1994.
Pierson, Ruth, ed. *Women and Peace: Theoretical, Historical, and Practical
    Propositions.* New York: Croom Helm, 1987.
Reyna, S. P. and R. E. Downes, eds. *Studying War: Anthropological Perspectives*
    War and Society Series, vol. II. Amsterdam, Netherlands: Gordon and
    Breach, 1994.
Ruddick, Sara. *Maternal Thinking: Toward a Politics of Peace.* New York:
    Ballantine, 1990.
Saccio, Peter. *Shakespeare's English Kings: History, Chronicle, Drama.* New
    York: Oxford University Press, 2000.
Smoker, Paul, Ruth Davies, and Barbara Munske, eds. *A Reader in Peace
    Studies.* New York: Pergamon Press, 1990.
Sponsel, Leslie E. and Thomas Gregor, eds. *The Anthropology of Peace and
    Nonviolence.* Boulder, CO: Lynne Reiner Publishers, Inc., 1994.
Tanner, Kathryn. *Theories of Culture: A New Agenda for Theology.*
    Minneapolis, MN: Fortress Press, 1977.
Turner, Paul and David Pitt. *The Anthropology of War and Peace: Perspectives
    In the Nuclear Age.* New York: Bergin and Garvey, 1989.

I. The Hebrew Scriptures and War

Beale, G. K. *The Use of Daniel in Jewish Apocalyptic Literature and in the
    Revelation of St. John.* Lanham, MD: University Press of America, 1984.

Blenkinsopp, Joseph. *A History of Prophecy in Israel: From the Settlement in the Land to the Hellenistic Period.* Philadelphia, PA: Westminster Press, 1983.

Burns, J. Patout, ed. *War and Its Discontents: Pacifism and Quietism in the Abrahamic Traditions.* Washington, DC: Georgetown University Press, 1996. Essays by Michael Broyde, Everett Gendler, Yehada Mirsky, and Naomi Goodman.

Christensen, Duane. *Transformations of the War Oracle in Old Testament Prophecy: Studies in the Oracles Against the Nations.* Missoula, Montana: Scholars Press, 1975.

Collins, John Joseph. *Daniel, First Maccabees, Second Maccabees: With an Excursus on the Apocalyptic Genre.* Wilmington, DE: Michael Glazier, 1981.

Craigie, Peter. *The Problem of War in the Old Testament.* Grand Rapids, Michigan: Eerdmans, 1978.

Dozeman, Thomas B. *God at War: Power in the Exodus Tradition.* New York: Oxford University Press, 1996.

Friedman, Richard Elliott. *Who Wrote the Bible?* San Francisco, CA: Harper, 1997.

Jones, G. H. "The Concept of Holy War" in *The World of Ancient Israel: Sociological, Anthropological, and Political Perspectives.* Ed. R. E. Clements. Cambridge, UK: Cambridge University Press, 1989.

Kaiser, Otto. *Isaiah 1 - 12: A Commentary.* Trans. John Bowden. Second edition. Philadelphia, PA: Westminster Press, 1983.

___. *Isaiah 13 - 39: A Commentary.* Trans. R. A. Wilson. Philadelphia, PA: Westminster Press, 1974.

Lind, Millard. *Yahweh Is a Warrior: the Theology of Warfare in Ancient Israel.* Scottsdale, PA: Herald Press, 1980.

Miller, Patrick. *The Divine Warrior in Early Israel.* Cambridge, MA: Harvard University Press, 1973.

Nardin, Terry, ed. *The Ethics of War and Peace.* Princeton NJ: Princeton University Press, 1996. Essays by Michael Walzer and Avierzer Ravitzky.

Niditch, Susan. *War in the Hebrew Bible: A Study in the Ethics of Violence.* New York: Oxford University Press, 1993.

Perdue, Leo G. and Brian W. Kovacs, eds. *A Prophet to the Nations: Essays in Jeremiah Studies.* Winona Lake, IN: Eisenbrauns, 1984.

Rad, Gerhard von. *Holy War in Ancient Israel.* Trans. Marva Dawn. Grand Rapids, MI: Eerdmans, 1991.

___. *Message of the Prophets.* Trans. D. M. G. Stalker. New York: Harper, 1972.

___. *Studies in Deuteronomy.* Trans. D. M. G. Stalker. London: SCM, 1953.

Smend, Rudolph. *Yahweh War and Tribal Confederation: Reflections upon Israel's Earliest History.* Nashville, TN: Abington, 1970.

Stolz, Fritz. *Yahwes und Israels Kriege: Kriegstheorien und Kriegserfahrungen im glauben des alten Israel.* Zurich, Switzerland: Theologischer Verlag, 1972.

Thompson, J. A. *The Book of Jeremiah.* Grand Rapids, MI: Eerdmans, 1980.

Yoder, Perry B. and Willard M. Swartley, eds. *The Meaning of Peace: Biblical Studies.* Louisville, KY: Westminster/John Knox Press, 1992.

II. The New Testament and War

Bammel, Ernst, and C. D. F. Moule, eds. *Jesus and the Politics of His Day.* Cambridge, UK: Cambridge University Press, 1984.

Brandon, S. G. F. *Jesus and the Zealots: A Study of the Political Factor in Primitive Christianity.* New York: Scribners, 1967.

Cadoux, C. J. *Early Christian Attitudes to War: A Contribution to the History of Ethics.* London, UK: George Allen, 1940.

Cassidy, Richard J. *Jesus, Politics, and Society: A Study of Luke's Gospel.* Maryknoll, New York: Orbis, 1978.

___ and Philip Scharper, eds. *Political Issues in Luke-Acts.* New York: Orbis, 1983.

Crossan, John Dominic. *The Historical Jesus: the Life of a Mediterranean Jewish Peasant.* San Francisco: Harper, 1991.

___ and Jonathan Reed. *Excavating Jesus: Beneath the Stones, Behind the Texts.* New York: Harper San Francisco, 2001.

Cullman, Oscar. *Jesus and the Revolutionaries.* Trans. Gareth Putnam. New York: Harper and Row, 1970.

Duling, Dennis and Norman Perrin. *The New Testament: Proclamation and Paranesis: Myth and History.* Fort Worth, TX: Harcourt Brace, 1994.

Ferguson, John. *Politics of Love: The New and Non-Violent Revolution.* Cambridge, U.K.: J. Clarke, 1973.

Fredriksen, Paula. *From Jesus to Christ: The Origins of the New Testament Images of Jesus.* New Haven, CT: Yale University Press, 1988.

Hengel, Martin. *Was Jesus a Revolutionist?* Trans. William Klassen. Philadelphia: PA, Fortress Press, 1971.

Horsley, Richard. *Jesus and the Spiral of Violence.* San Francisco, CA: Harper and Row, 1987.

Kee, Howard. *Understanding the New Testament.* Englewood Cliffs, NJ: Prentice Hall, 1983.

Macgregor, G. H. C. *The New Testament Basis of Pacifism.* London, UK: J. Clarke, 1936.

Mack, Burton L. *A Myth of Innocence: Mark and Christian Origins.* Philadelphia, PA: Fortress, 1988.

Meier, John. *A Marginal Jew: Rethinking the Historical Jesus.* 2 vols. New York: Doubleday, 1991.

Myers, Chad. *Binding the Strong Man: A Political Reading of Mark's Story of Jesus.* Maryknoll, NY: Orbis, 1988.

Yoder, John. *The Politics of Jesus: Vicit, Agnus Noster*. Grand Rapids, MI: Eerdmans, 1972.

Yoder, Perry and Willard Swartley, eds. *Meanings of Peace: Biblical Studies*, trans. W. Sawatsky. Louisville, KY: Westminster/John Knox, 1992.

III.   The Greeks and War

Adkins, A. W. H. *Merit and Responsibility: A Study in Greek Values*. Oxford, UK: Clarendon Press, 1960.

Aristotle. *Politics of Aristotle*. Trans. Ernest Baker. New York: Oxford University Press, 1958.

Aristophanes. *Five Comedies*. Trans. Benjamin Bickley Rogers. Garden City, NY: Doubleday, 1955.

___. *Peace*. Trans. Alan H. Sommerstein. Chicago, IL: Bochazy-Carducci 1985.

Bloom, Harold, ed. *Homer: Modern Critical Views*. New York: Chelsea House, 1986.

___, ed. *Homer's Iliad: Modern Critical Interpretation*. New York: Chelsea House, 1987.

Connor, W. Robert. *Thucydides*. Princeton, NJ: Princeton University Press, 1984.

Diogenese, Laertius. *Lives of Eminent Philosophers*. Trans. R. D. Hicks. Cambridge, MA: Harvard University Press, 1965.

Ducrey, Pierre. *Warfare in Ancient Greece*. New York: Shocken, 1985.

Dudley, Donald R. *A History of Cynicism from Diogenes to the Sixth Century A.D.* London, UK: Methuen, 1937.

Dyer, Gwynne. *War*. New York: Crown, 1985.

Euripides. *The Bacchae and Other Plays*. Trans. Philip Vellacott. Great Britain: Penguin, 1981.

Griffin, Jasper. *Homer on Life and Death*. Oxford, UK: Clarendon, 1980.

Hamilton, Edith. *The Greek Way to Western Civilization*. New York: New American Library, 1960.

Holmes, Arthur F., ed. *War and Christian Ethics*. Grand Rapids, MI: Baker, 1975.

Iliad of Homer. Trans. Richmond Lattimore. Chicago, IL: University of Chicago, 1951.

Inwood, Brad. *Ethics and Human Action in Early Stoicism*. Oxford, UK: Clarendon, 1985.

Keegan, John. *A History of Warfare*. New York: Knopf, 1993.

___. *War and Civilization*. Television documentary shown on Arts and Entertainment Network, Aug 2-5, 1998.

Lipsius, Frank. *Alexander the Great*. New York: Saturday Review Press, 1974.

Mikalson, Jon D. *Honor Thy Gods: Popular Religion in Greek Tragedy*. Chapel Hill, NC: University of North Carolina Press, 1991.

Ostwald, Martin. "Peace and War in Plato and Aristotle," in *Scripta Classica Israelica: Yearbook of the Israel Society for the Promotion of Classical Studies*, ed. Hannah M. Cotton, et al., vol. XV, 1996.

Pearson, Lionel. *Popular Ethics in Ancient Greece*. Stanford, CA: Stanford University Press, 1962.

Plato. *The Republic of Plato*. Trans. Francis Cornford. Oxford, UK: Oxford University Press, 1958.

Pritchett, W. Kendrick. *The Greek State at War*, vol. III. Berkeley, CA: University of California, 1974.

Reckford, Kenneth. *Aristophanes' Old-and-New Comedy* vol. I. Chapel Hill, NC: University of North Carolina Press, 1987.

Reesor, Margaret E. *The Nature of Man in Early Stoic Philosophy*. London, UK: Duckworth, 1989.

Rich, John and Graham Shipley, eds. *War and Society in the Greek World*. New York: Routledge, 1993.

Robinson, Charles Alexander. *Athens in the Age of Pericles*. Trans. Richard Dunn. South Bend, IN: Notre Dame University Press, 1973.

Rubino, Carl A. and Cynthia W. Shelmerdine, eds. *Approaches to Homer*. Austin, TX: University of Texas Press, 1983.

Sommerstein, Alan H., ed. *Comedies of Aristophanes*, vol. V, *Peace*. Chicago, IL: Bolchazy-Carducci, 1985.

Sophocles. *Sophocles*. Trans. Harold Lloyd-Jones. Cambridge, MA: Harvard University Press, 1994, 1996.

Taaffe, Lauren K. *Aristophanes and Women*. New York: Routledge, 1993.

Thucydides. *The Peloponnesian Wars*. Trans. Rex Warner. Great Britain: Penguin, 1959.

Weil, Simone. *The Iliad: A Poem of Force*. Trans. Mary McCarthy. Wallingford, PA: Pendle Hill, 1956.

Whitman, Cedric. *Aristophanes and the Comic Hero*. Cambridge, MA: Harvard University Press, 1961.

Zampaglione, Geraldo. *The Idea of Peace in Antiquity*. Trans. Richard Dunn. Notre Dame, IN: University of Notre Dame Press, 1973.

IV. Rome: Pagan and Christian

Alfoldi, Andrew. *The Conversion of Constantine and Pagan Rome*. Oxford, UK: Clarendon, 1948.

The Ante-Nicene Fathers. Translations of the Writings of the Fathers Down to A.D. 325. Latin Christianity: Its Founder, Tertullian, "Apology" and "On Idolatry," vol. III. *Origen,* "Celsus," vol. IV. Eds. Alexander Roberts and James Donaldson. New York: Charles Scribners, 1899-1903.

Augustine. *The City of God*. Trans. Marcus Dods. New York: Modern Library, 1950.

___. *The Political and Social Ideas of St. Augustine*. Ed. Herbert A. Deane, New York: Columbia University Press, 1963.

Barnes, Timothy D. *Constantine and Eusebius*. Cambridge, MA: Harvard University Press, 1981.

Baynes, N. H. and H. St. L. B. Moss. *Byzantium: An Introduction to East Roman Civilization.* Oxford, UK: Clarendon, 1949.

Bloom, Harold, ed. *Virgil: Modern Critical Views*. New York: Chelsea House, 1986.

Brown, Peter L. *Augustine of Hippo: A Biography.* London: Faber, 1967.

___. *Religion and Society in the Age of Augustine.* New York: Harper, 1972.

Caesar, Julius. *Seven Commentaries on the Gallic Wars*. Trans. Carolyn Hammond. New York: Penguin, 1960.

Camps, W. A. *An Introduction to Virgil's Aeneid*. Oxford, U.K.: Oxford University Press, 1979.

Caspary, Gerard E. *Politics and Exegesis: Origen and the Two Swords.* Berkeley, CA: University of California Press, 1979.

The Church and War: Papers Read at the Twenty-First Summer Meeting and the Twenty-Second Winter Meeting of the Ecclesiastical History Society. Oxford, Oxfordshire, UK: Published for the Ecclesiastical Historical Society by Basil Blackwell, 1983.

Cicero. *On Moral Obligation: A New Translation of Cicero's De Officiis*. Trans. John Higginbotham. London, U.K.: Faber, 1967.

Cochrane, Charles. *Christianity and Classical Culture: A Study of Thought and Action from Augustus to Augustine.* Oxford, UK: Oxford University Press, 1957.

Eusebius, Pamphilus. *The History of the Church from Christ to Constantine.* Trans. G. A. Williamson. Baltimore, MD: Penguin, 1965.

___. *The Life of the Blessed Emperor Constantine*. London: Samuel Bagster, 1845.

Evans, John. *War, Women, and Children in Ancient Rome.* New York: Routledge, 1991.

Figgis, John. *Political Aspects of Saint Augustine's "City of God."* New York: Longmans, Green and Co., 1921.

Harnack, Adolf von. *Militia Christi: The Christian Religion and the Military in the First Three Centuries*. Trans. David M. Gracie. Philadelphia, PA: Fortress Press, 1981.

Harris, William V. *War and Imperialism in Republican Rome 327-70 B.C.* Oxford, UK: Clarendon Press, 1979.

Helgeland, John, et al., eds. *Christians and the Military: The Early Experience.* Philadelphia, PA: Fortress, 1985.

Helgeland, John. "Roman Army Religion," in *Aufstieg und Niedergang der Romischen Welt,* 1470-1505. New York: De Gruyter, 1978,

___. "Christians and the Roman Army from Marcus Aurelius to Constantine," in *Aufstieg und Niedergang der Romischen Welt.* New York: De Gruyter, 1979.

Herrin, Judith. *The Formation of Christendom*. Princeton, NJ: Princeton University Press, 1987.

Hopkins, Keith. *Conquerors and Slaves.* Sociological Studies in Roman
   History, vol. I. Cambridge, U.K: Cambridge University Press, 1978.
Howard, Michael, et al., eds. *The Laws of War: Constraints on Warfare in the
   Western World.* New Haven, CT: Yale University Press, 1994.
Kee, Howard, et al. *Christianity: A Social and Cultural History.* New Jersey:
   Prentice-Hall, 1999.
Livy. *The War with Hannibal.* Trans. Aubrey de Selincourt and ed. Betty Radice.
   Reading, U.K: Penguin, 1986.
McCormick, Michael. *Eternal Victory: Triumphal Rulership in Late Antiquity,
   Byzantium and the Early Medieval West.* Cambridge, UK: Cambridge
   University Press, 1986.
Markus, R. A. *Christianity in the Roman World.* London: Thames and
   Hudson, 1974.
Mitchell, Thomas N. *Cicero: The Senior Statesman.* New Haven, CT: Yale
   University Press, 1991.
New Testament Aprocrypha. Gospels and Related Writings. Ed. Edgar Hennecke,
   et al. Philadelphia, PA: Westminster, 1963,
Origen. *Contra Celsum.* Trans. Henry Chadwick. Cambridge, UK: Cambridge
   University Press, 1965.
Raaflaub, Kurt and Nathan Rosenstein, eds. *War and Society in the Ancient
   And Medieval Worlds.* Center for Helenic Studies, Washington, D.C.
   Cambridge, MA: Harvard University Press, 1999.
Rich, John and Graham Shipley, eds. *War and Society in the Roman World.*
   New York: Routledge, 1993.
Stevenson, William, Jr. *Christian Love and Just War: Moral Paradox and
   Political Life in St. Augustine and his Modern Interpreters.* Macon,
   GA: Mercer University Press, 1987.
Swift, Louis, ed. *The Early Fathers on War and Military Service.* Wilmington,
   DE: Glazier, 1983.
___. "War and The Christian Conscience. The Early Years," in *Augsteig und
   Niedergang der Romischen Welt.* New York: De Gruyter, 1978: 835-68.
___. "War as a Moral Problem in the Early Church: The Historian's
   Hermeneutical Assumptions," in *The Pacifist Impulse in
   Historical Perspective.* Ed. Harvey L. Dyck. Toronto: University of
   Toronto, 1996.
Vegetius, Flavius. "The Military Institutions of the Romans," in *Roots of
   Strategy.* Trans. John Clark. Harrisburg, PA: Military Service, 1940.
Virgil (Publius Vergilius Maro). *The Aeneid.* Trans. W. F. Jackson Knight. New
   York: Penguin Books, 1984.
Wengst, Klaus. *Pax Romana and the Peace of Jesus Christ.* Philadelphia, PA:
   Fortress Press, 1987.
Williams, R. D. *The Aeneid.* London: Allen and Unwin, 1987.
Yoder, John Howard. *Christian Attitudes to War, Peace, and Revolution: A
   Companion to Bainton.* Elkhart, IN: Peace Resource Center, 1983.

V. The Religions of the East: Hinduism

Bandyopadhyaya, Banerjee Narayanchandra. *Development of Hindu Polity and Political Theory*. New Delhi, India: Munshiram Manoharlal, 1980.

Bhagavadgita. Trans. and ed. S. Radhakrishnan. New York: Harper, 1948.

Dikshitar, V. R. Ramachandra. *War in Ancient India*. Delhi, India: Motilal Banarsidass, 1944, reprinted 1987.

Drekmeier, Charles. *Kingship and Community in Early India*. Stanford, CA: Stanford University Press, 1962.

Dundas, Paul. *The Jains*. New York: Routledge, 1992.

Govind Tryambak. *The Art of War in Ancient India*. London, UK: Oxford University Press, 1929.

Gupta, S. P. and K. S. Ramachandran, eds. *Mahabharata: Myth and Reality, Differing Views*. Delhi, India: Agam Prakashan, 1976.

Heesterman, J.C. *The Inner Conflict of Tradition: Essays in Indian Ritual, Kingship, and Society*. Chicago, IL: University of Chicago Press, 1985.

Hiltebeitel, Alf. *The Ritual of Battle: Krishna in the Mahabharata*. Ithaca, NY: Cornell University Press, 1976.

Hindu Scriptures. Trans. and ed. Dominic Goodall. Berkeley, CA: University of California, 1996.

Hopkins, Thomas. *The Hindu Religious Traditions*. Belmont, CA: Wadsworth, 1971.

Katz, Rught Cecily. *Arjuna in the Mahabharata: Where Krishna Is, There Is Victory*. Columbia: South Carolina: University of South Carolina, 1989.

Klostermaier, Klaus K. *A Short Introduction to Hinduism*. Oxford, U.K.: One World, 1998.

The Mahabharata. Trans. and ed. Chakravarthi Narasimhan. New York: Columbia University Press, 1965.

Minor, Robert N., ed. *Modern Indian Interpreters of the Bhagavadgita*. Albany, NY: State University of New York Press, 1986.

The Rig Veda: An Anthology. Trans. Wendy Doniger O'Flaherty. New York: Penguin, 1981

Vettammani. *Puranic Encyclopaedia : A Comprehensive Dictionary With Special Reference to the Epic and Puranic Literature*. Delhi, India: M. Banarsidass, 1975.

Walker, Benjamin. *The Hindu World: An Encyclopedic Survey of Hinduism*. New York: Praeger, 1968

Zaehner, R. C. *Hinduism*. New York: Oxford University Press, 1970.

VI. Religions of the East: Buddhism
Buddhist Nonviolence and Statecraft

A Buddhist Bible. Trans. and ed. Dwight Goddard. Boston, MA: Beacon, 1994 edition.

Demiéville, Paul. "Le Bouddhisme et la Guerre," in *Choix D'Études Bouddhiques 1929-1970.* Leiden: Brill, 1973.

Dialogues of the Buddha. Part 1 in *The Sacred Books of the Buddhists.* Trans. T.W. Rhys Davids. (1899). This edition, London: Luzac, 1969.

Gokhale, Balrisha, G. *Asoka Maurya.* New York: Twayne, 1966.

Gombrich. "The Consecration of a Buddhist Image," *Journal of Asian Studies.* 26 (1966).

___. *Theravada Buddhism: A Social History from Ancient Benares to Modern Colombo.* New York: Routledge, 1991.

Ikeda, Daisaku. *Buddhism: the First Millennium.* Trans. Burton Watson. Tokyo, Japan: Kodansha, 1978.

Ling, Trevor. *Buddhism, Imperialism, and War: Burma and Thailand in Modern History.* Boston, MA: George Allen and Unwin, 1979.

The Middle Length Discourses of the Buddha. The Majjhima Nikaya. Trans. Bhikkhu Bodhi and Bhikkhu Nanamoli. Boston, MA: Wisdom Publications, 1995.

Sharma, Ram S. *Aspects of Political Ideas and Institutions in Ancient India.* Delhi, India: Motilal Barnarsidass, 1959.

Smith, Bardwell, ed. *Religion and Legitimation of Power in Thailand, Laos, and Burma.* Chambersburg, PA: Anima, 1978.

___. *Religion and Legitimation of Power in Sri Lanka.* Chambersburg, PA: Anima, 1978.

Strong, John. *The Legend of King Asoka: A Study and Translation of the Asokavadana.* Princeton, NJ: Princeton University Press, 1983.

Swearer, Donald K. *Buddhism.* Niles, IL: Argus, 1977.

___. *Buddhism and Society in Southeast Asia.* Chambersburg, PA: Anima, 1981.

Thapar, Romila. *Asoka and the Decline of the Mauryas.* Oxford, UK: Oxford University Press, 1961.

The Two Wheels of Dhamma: Essays on the Theravqada Tradition in India and Ceylon, Eds. Gananath Obeyesekere, Frank Reynolds, and Bardwell Smith. Chambersburg, PA: American Academy of Religion, 1972.

Walpola, Rahula. *What the Buddha Taught.* New York: Grove, 1974.

Japan

Berry, Mary Elizabeth. *Hideyoshi.* Cambridge, MA: Harvard University Press, 1982.

Collcutt, Martin. "The Zen Monastery in Kamakura Society," in *Court and Bakufu in Japan.* Ed. Jeffrey P. Mass. New Haven, CN: Yale University Press, 1982, 191-220.

Kraft, Kenneth. *Eloquent Zen: Daito and Early Japanese Zen.* Honolulu: HA: University of Hawaii Press, 1992.

King, Winston L. *Zen and the Way of the Sword: Arming the Samurai Psyche.* New York: Oxford University Press, 1993.

Lu, David J. *Japan: A Documentary History: The Dawn of History to the Late Tokugawa Period.* Vol. I. Armonk, New York: M.E. Sharpe, 1997.

McFarland, H. Neill. *Daruma: The Founder of Zen in Japanese Art and Popular Culture.* Tokoyo, Japan: Kodansha, 1987.

Perrin, Noel. *Giving Up the Gun: Japan's Reversion to the Sword, 1543-1879.* Boston, MA: Godine, 1979.

Turnbull, S.R. *The Samurai.* New York: MacMillan, 1977.

Suzuki, Daisetz T. *Zen and Japanese Culture.* London, UK: Routledge and Kegan Paul, 1959.

Tsunoda, Ryusaku, W. M. T. De Bary, and Donald Keene. *Sources of Japanese Tradition.* Vol. I. New York: Columbia University Press, 1964.

VII. Islam in War and Peace

Adas, Michael, ed. *Islamic and European Expansion.* American Historical Association. Philadelphia: Temple University Press, 1993.

Aho, James A. *Religious Mythology and the Art of War: Comparative Religious Symbolisms of Military Violence.* Westport, CN: Greenwood Press, 1981.

Al-Azmah, Aziz. *Ibn Khaldun: An Essay in Reinterpretation.* London, UK: Cass, 1982.

Blankinship, Khalid Yahya. *The End of the Jihad State: The Reign of Hisham Ibn 'Abd al-Malik and the Collapse of the Umayyads.* Albany, NY: State University of New York, 1994.

Bronner, Michael. *Aristocratic Violence and Holy War: Studies in the Jihad and the Arab-Byzantine Frontier.* New Haven, CT: American Oriental Society, 1996.

Donner, Fred McGraw. *The Early Islamic Conquests.* Princeton, NJ: Princeton University Press, 1981.

Ehrenkreutz, Andrew S. *Saladin.* Albany, NY: State University of New York Press, 1972.

Eposito, John. *Islam: The Straight Path.* New York: Oxford University Press, 1989.

Fischel, Walter J. *Ibn Khaldun in Egypt: His Public Functions and His Historical Research, 1392-1405: A Study in Islamic Historiography.* Berkeley, CA: University of California, 1967

Gauillaume, Alfred. *Islam.* Hammondsworth, UK: Penguin, 1966.

Gellner, Ernest, ed. *Islamic Dilemmas: Reformers, Nationalists and Industrialization: The Southern Shore of the Mediterranean.* New York: Mouton, 1985.

Halm, Heinz. *Shiism.* Trans. Janet Watson. Edinburgh, UK: Edinburg University Press, 1991.

Hawting, G. R. *The First Dynasty of Islam: The Umayyad Caliphate AD 661-750.* New York: Routledge, 1986. This edition, 2000.

Hodgson, Marshall. *The Venture of Islam: Conscience and History in a World Civilization The Classical Age* Vol. I. Chicago: University of Chicago Press, 1974.

Jandora, John W. *The March from Medina: A Revisionist Study of Arab Conquests.* Clifton, NJ: Kingsbury, 1990.

Johnson, James Turner. *The Holy War Idea in Western and Islamic Traditions.* University Park, PA: Penn State University Press, 1997.

Johnson, James Turner and John Kelsay, eds. *Cross, Crescent, and Sword: The Justification and Limitation of War in Western Islamic Tradition.* New York: Greenwood Press, 1990.

Kelsay, John. *Islam and War: A Study in Comparative Ethics.* Louisville, KY: Westminster/John Knox, 1993.

___ and Johnson, James Turner, eds. *Just War and Jihad: Historical and Theoretical Perspectives on War and Peace in Western and Islamic Traditions.* New York: Greenwood Press, 1991.

Kennedy, Hugh. *The Prophet and the Age of the Caliphates: The Islamic Near East from the Sixth to the Eleventh Century.* New York: Longman, 1986.

___. *The Armies of the Caliphs: Military and Society in the Early Islamic State.* New York: Routledge, 2001.

Khadduri, Majid. *War and Peace in the Law of Islam.* Baltimore, MD: Johns Hopkins University Press, 1955.

Khaldun, Ibn. *The Muqaddimah: An Introduction to History.* Trans. Franz Rosenthal. London: Routledge and Kegan Paul, 1958.

___. *An Arab Philosophy of History: Selections from the Prolegomena of Ibn Khaldun of Tunis.* Trans. Charles Issawi. London: John Murray, 1950.

Lewis, Bernard, ed. *Islam: from the Prophet Muhammad to the Capture of Constantinople, Politics and War* Vol. I. Oxford, UK: Oxford University Press, 1987.

Lyons, M. C. and D. E. P. Jackson. *Saladin: the Politics of the Holy War.* Cambridge, UK: Cambridge University Press, 1982.

Mahdi, Muhsin. *Ibn Khaldûn's Philosophy of Culture: A Study of the Philosophic Foundation of the Science of Culture.* Chicago, IL: University of Chicago, 1957.

___. *Ibn Khaldûn's Philosophy of History: A Study of the Philosophic Foundation of the Science of Culture.* Chicago, IL: University of Chicago, 1964.

Partner, Peter. *God of Battles: Holy Wars of Christianity and Islam.* Princeton, NJ: Princeton University Press, 1997.

The Qur'an. The First American Version. Trans. T. B. Irving. Brattleboro, Vt: Amana, 1985.

The Qur'an: Readings in the. Trans. and ed. Kenneth Cragg. London, UK: Collins, 1988.

Rushd, ibn (Averroes). *Jihad in Medieval and Modern Islam: The Chapter on Jihad from Averroes' Legal Handbook 'Bidayat al Mdjtahid.* Trans. Rudoph Peters. Leyden, Netherlands: Brill, 1977.

Shaybani, Muhammad ibn al-Hasan al. *The Islamic Law of Nations.* Ed. and trans. Majid Khaldduri. Baltimore, MD: Johns Hopkins University Press, 1996.

Watt, William Montgomery. "Islamic Conceptions of Holy War," in *The Holy War*. Ed. Thomas P. Murphy. Columbus: Ohio: Ohio State University Press, 1976.

___. *Muslim-Christian Encounters: Perceptions and Misperceptions.* New York: Routledge, 1991.

VIII. Medieval Europe

Adams, Robert P. *The Better Part of Valor: More, Erasmus, Colet and Vives, on Humanism, War and Peace 1496-1535.* Seattle, WA: University of Washington Press, 1962.

Aquinas, Thomas. *Introduction to Saint Thomas Aquinas*, ed. Anton Pegis. New York: Modern Library, 1948.

___. *St. Thomas Aquinas On Politics and Ethics,* ed. and trans. Paul Sigmund. New York: Norton, 1988.

Bainton, Roland. *Christian Attitudes toward War and Peace.* London: Hodder and Stoughton, 1960.

Barber, Malcolm. *The Cathars: Dualist Heretics in Languedoc in the High Middle Ages.* Harlow, UK: Longman, 2000.

Bonet, Honoré. *The Tree of Battles: an English Version.* Ed. and trans. G. W. Coopland. Cambridge, MA: Harvard University Press, 1949.

Brundage, James. *Medieval Canon Law and the Crusader.* Madison, WI: Wisconsin University Press, 1969.

___. *The Crusades, Holy War, and Canon Law.* Brookfield, VT: Gower, 1991.

Cameron, Euan. *Waldenses: Rejections of the Holy Church in Medieval Europe.* Oxford. UK: Blackwell, 2000.

Christiansen, Eric. *The Northern Crusades: the Baltic and Catholic Frontier,* Minneapolis, MN: University of Minnesota Press, 1980.

Christine de Pisan. *The Book of Fayttes of Armes and of Chyualrye.* Ed. A. T. P. Byles. Trans. William Caxton. London: Early English Text Society. Oxford University Press, 1932.

Contamine, Philippe. *War in the Middle Ages.* Trans. Michael Jones. Oxford, UK: Blackwell, 1984.

Copleston, Frederick C. *Medieval Philosophy.* New York: Harper, 1962.

Erdmann, Carl. *The Origin of the Idea of Crusade.* Trans. and foreword by Marshall W. Baldwin and Walter Goffard. Princeton, NJ: Princeton University Press, 1997.

France, John. *Western Warfare in the Age of Crusades, 1000-1300.* Ithaca, NY: Cornell University Press, 1999.

Hall, Bert S. *Weapons and Warfare in Renaissance Europe.* Baltimore: John Hopkins University Press, 1997.

Head, Thomas and Richard Landes, eds. *The Peace of God: Social Violence and Religious Response in France Around the Year 1000.* Ithaca, NY: Cornell University Press, 1992.

Herrin, Judith. *The Formation of Christendom*. Princeton, NJ: Princeton University Press, 1987.

Heyn, Udo. *Peacemaking in Medieval Europe: An Historical and Bibliographical Guide*. Regina Guides to Historical Issues. Claremont, CA: Regina, 1997.

Johnson, James Turner. *Ideology, Reason and the Limitation of War: Religious and Secular Concepts 1200-1740*. Princeton, NJ: Princeton University Press, 1975.

___. *Just War Tradition and the Restraint of War: A Moral and Historical Inquiry*. Princeton, NJ: Princeton University Press, 1981.

___. *The Quest for Peace: Three Moral Traditions in Western Cultural History*. Princeton, NJ: Princeton University Press, 1987.

Joinville, Jean and Geoffroi de Villehardouin. *Chronicles of the Crusades*. Ed. and trans. M. R. B. Shaw. Baltimore, MD: Penguin Books, 1963, reprinted 1977.

Keen, Maurice Hugh. *Chivalry*. New Haven, CT: Yale University Press, 1984.

___. *The Laws of War in the Late Middle Ages*. London: Routledge and K. Paul, 1965.

Knox, MacGregor and Williamson Murray, eds. *The Dynamics of Military Revolution 1300-2050*. Cambridge, UK: Cambridge University Press, 2001.

Lambert, Malcolm. *Medieval Heresy: Popular Movements from the Gregorian Reform to the Reformation*. 3rd edition. Oxford, UK: Blackwell, 2002.

Ladurie, Le Roy. *Montaillou: The Promised Land of Error*. Trans. Barbara Bray. New York: Braziller, 1978.

Lowe, Ben. *Imagining Peace: A History of Early English Pacifist Ideas 1340-1560*. University Park, PA: Pennsylvania State University Press, 1997.

Mayer, Hans Eberhard. *The Crusades*. Trans. John Gillingham. Oxford, UK: Oxford University Press, 1988.

Muldoon, James. *Popes, Lawyers, and Infidels: the Church and the Non-Christian World, 1250-1550*. Philadelphia, PA: University of Pennsylvania Press, 1979.

Murphy, Thomas Patrick, ed. *The Holy War*. Columbus, OH: Ohio State University Press, 1976.

Peters, Edward. *Christian Society and the Crusades, 1198-1229*. Philadelphia, PA: University of Pennsylvania Press, 1971.

Renna, Thomas. "The Idea of Peace in the West, 500-1500," *Journal of Medieval History* 6 (1980).

Riley-Smith, J. S. C. *The Crusades: A Short History*. New Haven, CN: Yale University Press, 1987.

___. *The First Crusade and the Idea of Crusading*. Philadelphia: University of Pennsylvania Press, 1986.

___. *The First Crusades 1095-1131*. Cambridge, UK: Cambridge University Press, 1997.

Russell, Frederick H. *The Just War in the Middle Ages*. Cambridge, UK: Cambridge University Press, 1977.

Shaw, Margaret R. B. *Chronicles of the Crusades*. Baltimore, MD: Penguin Books, 1963.

Theisen, Wilfred. "1022 and All That," *Occasional Paper* 39 (May 2, 1991).

Treesh, Susanna. "The Waldenesian Recourse to Violence." *Church History* 58 (1986): 294-305.

Tyerman, Christopher. *The Invention of the Crusades*. Toronto, Canada: University of Toronto Press, 1998.

Vale, Malcolm. *War and Chivalry: Warfare and Aristocratic Culture in France and Burgundy at the End of the Middle Ages*. Athens, GA: University of Georgia Press, 1981.

Walters, LeRoy Brandt. "Five Classic Just War Theories: A Study in the Thought of Thomas Aquinas Vitoria, Suarez, Gentili, and Grotius." Ph.D. diss., Yale University, 1971.

IX. Splintering of European Traditions

Adams, Robert P. *The Better Part of Valor: More, Erasmus, Colet, and Vives on Humanism, War, and Peace 1496-1535*. Seattle, WA: University of Washington Press, 1962.

Arkaksinen, Timo and Martin Bertman, eds. *Hobbes: War Among Nations*. Brookfield, VT: Avebury, 1989.

Bainton, Roland. *Erasmus of Christendom*. New York: Scribners, 1969.

___. *Here I Stand: A Life of Martin Luther*. Nashville, TN: Abington, 1950.

Baugmgold, Deborah. *Hobbes' Political Theory*. Cambridge, UK: Cambridge University Press, 1988.

Bayley, C. C. *War and Society in Renaissance Florence: The De Militia of Leonardo Bruni*. Toronto, Canada: University of Toronto Press, 1961.

Benedict, Philip et al., eds. *Reformation, Revolt and Civil War in France and the Netherlands1555-1585*. Amsterdam,Netherlands:Koninklijke Nederlandse Akademie van Weternschappen Verhandelingen, 1999.

Bornkamm, Heinrich. *Luther's World of Thought*. Trans. Martin Bertram. St Louis, MO: Concordia, 1958.

Bossy, John. *Peace in the Post-Reformation*. Cambridge, UK: Cambridge University Press, 1998.

Bull, Hedley; Benedict Kingsbury, and Adam Roberts, eds. *Hugh Grotius and International Relations*. Oxford, UK: Clarendon Press, 1990.

Calvin, John. *Institutes of the Christian Religion*. Library of Christian Classics, vol. XX. Ed. John T. McNeill. Trans. Ford Lewis Battles. Philadelphia, PA: Westminster, 1960.

Cargill Thompson, W. D. J. *The Political Thought of Martin Luther*. Brighton, Sussex, UK: Harvester Press, 1984.

Caws, Peter, ed. *The Causes of Quarrel: Essays on Peace, War, and Thomas Hobbes*. Boston: Beacon, 1989.

Clasen, Claus Peter. *Anabaptism: A Social History 1525-1618*. Ithaca, NY: Cornell University Press 1972.

Cooper, J. P., ed. *New Cambridge Modern History, The Decline of Spain and the Thirty Years War 1609-1648/59* Vol. IV Cambridge, UK: Cambridge University Press, 1970.

Daniel-Rops, Henri. *The Catholic Reformation*. Trans. John Warrington. Garden City, NY: Doubleday, 1964.

Davis, Natalie Zemon. *Society and Culture in Early Modern France*. Stanford, CA: Stanford University Press, 1975.

Edwards, Charles. *Hugo Grotius: The Miracle of Holland*. Chicago: Nelson-Hall, 1981.

Erasmus, Desiderius. *The Education of a Christian Prince*. Trans. Lester Born. New York: Norton, 1968.

___. *The Essential Erasmus*. Ed. John P. Dolan. New York: Mentor Omega, 1964.

___. *The Julius Exclusus of Erasmus*. Trans. Paul Pascal. Intro. J. K. Sowards. Bloomington, IN: Indiana University Press, 1968.

Fernández-Santamariá, J. A. *Reason of State and Statecraft in Spanish Political Thought, 1595-1640*. Lanham, MD: University of Maryland Press, 1983.

___. *The State, War and Peace: Spanish Political Thought in the Renaissance, 1516-1559*. New York: Cambridge University Press, 1977.

Fleisher, Martin. *Machiavelli and the Nature of Political Thought*. New York: Atheneum, 1972.

Gauthier, David P. *The Logic of Leviathan: The Moral and Political Theory of Thomas Hobbes*. Oxford, UK: Clarendon, 1969.

Gellinek, Christian. *Hugo Grotius*. Boston: Twayne, 1983.

Gentili, Alberico. *De Iure Bellis Libri Tres* Vol. XVI, pt. 2. Oxford: Clarendon Press, 1933.

Gilbert, Allan H. *Machiavelli's Prince and Its Forerunners: The Prince as a Typical Book de Regimine Principium*. Durham, NC: Duke University Press, 1938.

Gilbert, Felix. *Machiavelli and Guiccardini: Politics and History in Sixteenth Century Florence*. Princeton, NJ: Princeton University Press, 1965.

Grazia, Sebastian de. *Machiavelli in Hell*. Princeton, NJ: Princeton University Press, 1989.

Grotius, Hugo. *De Jure Belli Ac Pacis Libri Tres* Vol. II. Trans. by Francis Kelsey. Oxford, UK: Clarendon Press, 1925.

Hale, J. R. *War and Society in Renaissance Europe, 1450-1620*. New York: St. Martin's Press, 1985.

Hobbes, Thomas. *De Cive. The English Version*. Ed. Howard Warrenden. The Clarendon Edition of the Philosophical Works of Thomas Hobbes. Oxford, UK: Clarendon Press, 1983.

___. *Leviathan*. Introduction K. R. Minogue. New York: Dutton, 1976.

Holt, Mack P. *The French Wars of Religion, 1562-1629*. New York: Cambridge University Press, 1995.

Huizinga, John. *Erasmus*. New York: Scribners, 1924.

Iserloh, Erin, Joseph Glazik, and Hubert Jedin. *Reformation and Counter-Reformation. History of the Church* Vol. V. Trans. Anselm Biggs and Peter Becker. New York: Crossroad, 1986.

Lowe, Ben. *Imagining Peace: A History of Early English Pacifist Ideas.* University Park, PA: Penn State University Press, 1997.

Luther, Martin. *Works of Martin Luther* 6 Vols. Philadelphia, PA: A.J. Holman, 1915-1931.

___. *Luther's Works* Vol. XLVII. Philadelphia, PA: Fortress Press, 1971.

Machiavelli, Niccolo. *The Art of War* (1521). Trans. Ellis Farneworth. New York: Capo, 1965.

___. *The Prince*, ed. Quentin Skinner and Russell Price. New York: Cambridge University Press, 1988.

Mansfield, Harvey C. *Machiavelli's Virtue*. Chicago, IL: University of Chicago, 1996.

Martinich, Aloysius P. *The Two Gods of Leviathan: Thomas Hobbes on Religion and Politics*. Cambridge, UK: Cambridge University Press, 1992.

Muldoon, James. *Popes, Lawyers, and Infidels:The Church and the Non-Christian World 1250-1550*. Philadelphia, PA: University of Pennsylvania Press, 1979.

Parker, Geoffrey, ed. *The Thirty Years War*. 2nd edition. New York: Routledge, 1997.

Ridley, Jasper. *John Knox*. New York: Oxford University Press, 1968.

Sabine, George. *A History of Political Theory*. New York: Henry Holt, 1937.

Scott, James Brown. *The Spanish Origin of International Law*. London: Clarendon Press, 1934.

Skinner, Quentin. *The Foundations of Modern Political Thought V*ol. I, *The Renaissance*; Vol. II, *The Age of Reformation*. Cambridge, UK: Cambridge University Press, 1978.

Strayer, James. *Anabaptists and the Sword*. Lawrence, Kansas: Coronado, 1976.

Suárez, Francisco. *Selections from Three Works. DeTriplici Virtute Theologicca, Fide, Spe, et Charitate*, 1621 Vol. II. Trans. by Gwladys L. Williams. London: Clarendon Press, 1944.

Vitoria, Francisco de. *Francisci de Victoria De Indis et De Ivre Belli Reflectiones*. Ed. Ernest Nys. Washington, DC: The Carnegie Institution of Washington, 1917.

Wedgwood, C. V. *The Thirty Years War*. New Haven, CT: Yale University Press, 1939.

Williams, Peter. *The Radical Reformation*. Philadelphia, PA: Westminster Press, 1962.

Wolin, Sheldon. *Politics and Vision: Continuity and Innovation in Western Political Thought*. Boston, MA: Little, Brown, 1960.

The World of Hugo Grotius. Proceedings of the International Colloquium Organization by the Grotius Committee. 1983. Amsterdam: APA - Holland University Press, 1984.

X. War and Peace in the Age of Reason

Adams, Robert M., ed. *Voltaire, Candide, or Optimism.* New York: Norton, 1966.

Anderson, M. S. *War and Society in Europe of the Old Regime 1618-1789.* New York: St. Martin's, 1988.

Best, Geoffrey. *Humanity in Warfare.* New York: Columbia University Press, 1980.

Bloom, Harold, ed. *Jean-Jacques Rousseau, Modern Critical Views.* New York: Chelsea House, 1988.

Brock, Peter. *The Quaker Peace Testimony 1660-1914.* Syracuse, NY: Syracuse University Press, 1990.

Ceadel, Martin. *The Origins of War Prevention.* Oxford, U.K.: Clarendon, 1996.

Corvisier, André. *Armies and Societies in Europe, 1494-1789.* Trans. Abigail T. Siddall. Bloomington, IN: Indiana University Press, 1979.

Davidson, Robert. *War Comes to Quaker Pennsylvania, 1682-1756.* New York: Columbia University Press for Temple University, 1957.

Frost, J. William. *A Perfect Freedom: Religious Liberty in Pennsylvania.* New York: Cambridge University Press, 1990.

Gallie, W. B. *Philosophers of Peace and War: Kant, Clausewitz, Marx, Engels, and Tolstoy.* Cambridge, England: Cambridge University Press, 1978.

Gargaz, Pierre-Andre. *A Project of Universal and Perpetual Peace.* New York: Garland, 1973.

Gat, Azar. *The Origins of Military Thought from the Enlightenment to Clausewitz.* Oxford, UK: Clarendon Press: 1989.

Hemleben, Sylvester John. *Plans for World Peace Through Six Centuries.* Chicago, IL: University of Chicago Press, 1943.

Jacob, J. R. and Jacob, M. C., eds. *Peace Projects of the Seventeenth Century* comprising Sully's "Great Design of Henry IV," Hugo Grotius, "The Law Of War and Peace," and William Penn, "An Essay Towards the Present and Future Peace of Europe" in The Garland Library of War and Peace. New York: Garland, 1972.

Jacobs, M. C., ed. *Peace Projects of the Eighteenth Century* comprising Charles de Saint-Pierre, "A Shorter Project for Perpetual Peace," Jean Jacques Rousseau, "A Project of Perpetual Peace," and Jeremy Bentham, "A Project of Universal and Perpetual Peace" in The Garland Library of War and Peace. New York: Garland, 1973.

Jennings, Francis. *Empire of Fortune: Crown, Colonies, and Tribes in the Seven Years War in America.* New York: Norton, 1988.

Kant, Immanuel. *Eternal Peace and Other International Essays.* Trans. W. Hastie. Boston, MA: World Peace Foundation, 1914. The Garland Library reprints the 1903 edition by Mary Campbell Smith.

Marietta, Jack. *The Reformation of American Quakerism, 1748-1783.* Philadelphia: PA: University of Pennsylvania Press, 1984.

Mekeel, Arthur. *The Quakers and the American Revolution.* York: UK: Sessions, 1966.

Meyer, Henry. "Voltaire on War and Peace." In *Studies on Voltaire and the Eighteenth Century.* Banbury, UK: Voltaire Foundation, 1976.

The Papers of William Penn, Vol. I-IV. Ed. Mary Dunn and Richard Dunn. Philadelphia, PA: University of Pennsylvania Press, 1981-1987.

Rousseau, Jean Jacques. "L'État de Guerre," in *Political Writings of Jean Jacques Rousseau.* Vol. I. Ed. C. E. Vaughan. New York: Wiley, 1962.

Rowe, Constance. *Voltaire and the State.* New York: Octagon, 1968.

Vattel, Emer de. *Le Droit des Gens: ou Principes de la Loi Naturelle, Appliques a la Conduite et aux Affaires des Nations at des Souverains.* Washington, D. C.: Carnegie Institution of Washington, 1915.

Voltaire, Francois-Marie Arouet. *Candide or Optimism.* Ed. Norman L. Torrey. New York: Appleton-Century-Crofts, 1946.

___. *Candide or Optimism, translation, Backgrounds, Criticism.* Ed. Robert M. Adams. New York: W. W. Norton, 1966.

Weddle, Meredith B. *Walking in the Way of Peace: Quaker Pacifism in the Seventeenth Century.* New York: Oxford University Press, 2001.

Weigley, Russell. *The Age of Battles: The Quest for Decisive Warfare from Breitenfeld to Waterloo.* Bloomington, IN: Indiana University Press, 1991.

XI. Revolutions as Just War

Ashley, Maurice. *The Glorious Revolution of 1688.* New York: Scribner's, 1966.

Bailyn, Bernard. *The Ideological Origins of the American Revolution.* Cambridge, MA: Harvard, 1967.

Bartel, Roland, "English Clergymen and Laymen on the Principle of War, 1789-1802." *Anglican Theological Review* 38 (1956).

Bennett, Betty, ed. *British War Poetry in the Age of Revolution.* New York: Garland, 1976.

Best, Geoffrey. *War and Society in Revolutionary Europe, 1770-1870.* New York: St. Martin's, 1982.

Bertho. "Naissance et Elaboration d'une 'Theologie' de la guerre chez les Eveques de Napoleon." *Civilisation Chrétienne.* Ed. Jene Rene Derre. Paris: Editions Beuchesne, 1975.

Chadwick Owen. *The Popes and European Revolution.* Oxford History of the Christian Church. Oxford, UK: Clarendon, 1981.

Chartier, Roger. *Cultural Origins of the French Revolution.* Trans. Lydia Cochrane. Durham, NC: Duke University Press, 1991.

Cookson, J. E. *The Friends of Peace: Anti-War Liberalism in England 1793-1815.* New York: Cambridge University Press, 1982.

Cox, Richard Howard. *Locke on War and Peace.* Oxford, UK: Clarendon Press, 1960.

Daniel-Rops, H. *Church in an Age of Revolution 1789-1870*. Trans. John
    Warrington. New York: Dutton, 1965.

Dansette, Adrien. *Religious History of Modern France. From the Revolution to
    the Third Republic*. New York: Herder & Herder, 1961.

Doyle, William. *The Oxford History of the French Revolution*. Oxford, UK:
    Clarendon Press, 1989.

Forrest, Alan. *Conscripts and Deserters: The Army and Society During the
    Revolution and Empire*. New York: Oxford University Press, 1989.

Gellner, Ernest. *Nationalism*. New York: New York University Press, 1997.

Higgenbotham, Don, ed. *Reconsiderations on the Revolutionary War.
    Contributions in Military History #14*. Westport, CT: Greenwood Press,
    1978.

Hoffman, Ronald and Peter Albert, eds. *Arms and Independence: The
    Military Character of the American Revolution*. Charlottesville, VA:
    University Press of Virginia, 1984.

___, Thad Tate, and Peter Albert, eds. *An Uncivil War: The Southern
    Backcountry during the American Revolution*. Charlottesville, VA:
    University of Virginia Press, 1985.

Holtman, Robert B. *Napoleonic Propaganda*. Baton Rouge, LA: Louisiana State
    University Press, 1950.

___. *The Napoleonic Revolution*. Baton Rouge, Louisiana: Louisiana State
    University Press, 1967.

Hoppitt, Julian. *A Land of Liberty: England, 1689-1727*. New York: Oxford
    University Press, 2000.

Jackson, John W. *With the British Army in Philadelphia, 1777-1778*. San
    Rafael, CA: Presidio Press, 1979.

Kedouri, Eli. *Nationalism*. New York: Praeger, 1960.

Kohn, Hans. *Prelude to Nation-States: The French and German Experience,
    1789-1815*. Princeton, NJ: Van Nostrand, 1967.

McManners, John. *The French Revolution and the Church*. London: S.P.C.K.,
    1969.

Paine, Thomas. *Political Writings*. Ed. Bruce Kuklick. New York: Cambridge
    University Press, 1989.

Palmer, R. R. *Age of Democratic Revolution: A Political History of Europe and
    America 1760-1800*. Princeton, NJ: Princeton University Press, 1959-
    1964.

Paret, Peter, et al., eds. *Makers of Modern Strategy from Machiavelli to the
    Nuclear Age*. Princeton NJ: Princeton University Press, 1986.

Royster, Charles. *A Revolutionary People at War: The Continental Army and the
    American Character 1775-1783*. Institute of Early American History and
    Culture. Chapel Hill, NC: University of North Carolina Press, 1979.

Shy, John. *A People Armed and Numerous: Reflexions on the Military Struggle
    For American Independence*. New York: Oxford University Press, 1976.

Soboul, A. "Religious Sentiments and Popular Cults During the Revolution: Patriot Saints and Martyrs of Liberty," in Jerry Kaplow, *New Perspectives on the French Revolution: Readings in Historical Sociology.* New York: Wiley, 1965.

Tackett, Timothy. *Religion, Revolution and Regional Culture in Eighteenth-Century France: The Ecclesiastical Oath of 1791.* Princeton, NJ: Princeton University Press, 1986.

Wawro, Geoffrey. *Warfare and Society in Europe 1792-1914.* New York: Routledge, 2000.

XII. Religion, Nationalism, and War in the Nineteenth Century

Aron, Raymond. *Clausewitz, Philosopher of War.* Englewood Cliffs, NJ: Prentice-Hall, 1985.

Banner, James M., Jr. *To the Hartford Convention: The Federalists and The Origins of Party Politics in Massachusetts 1789-1815.* New York: Knopf, 1970.

Barclay, David. *Frederick William IV and the Prussian Monarchy 1840-1861.* Oxford, UK: Clarendon Press, 1995.

Beeching, Jack. *The Chinese Opium Wars.* New York: Harcourt, Brace, Jovanovich, 1976.

Brock, Peter. *Freedom from War: Nonsectarian Pacifism, 1814-1914.* Toronto, Canada: University of Toronto Press, 1991.

___. *Freedom from War: Sectarian Nonresistance from the Middle Ages to the Great War.* Toronto, Canada: University of Toronto Press, 1991.

Ceadel, Martin. *The Origins of War Prevention: The British Peace Movement and International Relations, 1730-1854.* Oxford, U.K.: Clarendon, 1996.

Chickering, Roger. *Imperial Germany and a World Without War.* Princeton, NJ: Princeton University Press, 1975.

Clark, Christopher. "The Napoleonic Moment in Prussian Church Policy," in *Napoleon's Legacy,* eds. David Lavid and Lucy Riall. New York: Oxford University Press, 2000.

Clausewitz. *On War.* Eds. Peter Paret and Michael Howard. Princeton, NJ: Princeton University Press, 1976.

Commager, Henry S., ed. *The Blue and The Gray: The Story of the Civil War as Told by Participants.* Indianapolis, IN: Bobbs Merrill, 1950.

Cooper, Sandi. *Patriotic Pacifism: Waging War on War in Europe, 1815-1914.* New York: Oxford University Press, 1991.

Dawson, Jerry F. *Friedrich Schleiermacher: The Evolution of a Nationalist.* Austin, TX: University of Texas Press, 1966.

Dunham, Chester A. *The Attitude of the Northern Clergy Toward the South 1860-1865.* Toledo, OH: Gray, 1942.

Dymond, Jonathan. *An Enquiry into the Acccordancy of War with the Principles of Christianity and an Examination of the Philosophical Reasoning by which it is Defended: With observations on Some of the Causes of War, and Some of its Effects.* London: Longman, Hurst, 1823.

Ellsworth, Clayton Summer. "The American Churches and the Mexican War," in *American Historical Review* 45 (1940).

Eyck. Erich. *Bismarck and the German Empire.* New York: Norton, 1968.

Fay, Peter War. *The Chinese Opium War 1840-1842.* New York: Norton, 1976.

Frederick II, King of Prussia. *The Refutation of Machiavelli's Prince or Anti-Machiavel.* Ed. Paul Sonnino. Athens, Ohio: Ohio University Press, 1981.

Friedrich, Carl J. *Constitutional Reason of State: The Survival of the Constitutional Order.* Providence, RI: Brown University Press, 1956.

Friedrickson, George. *The Inner Civil War: Northern Intellectuals and the Crisis of the Union.* New York: Harper and Row, 1971.

Gallie, W. B. *Philosophers of Peace and War: Kant, Clausewitz, Marx, Engels and Tolstoy.* Cambridge, UK: Cambridge University Press, 1978.

Gat, Azar. *The Origins of Military Thought: From the Enlightenment to Clausewitz.* Oxford, UK: Clarendon Press, 1989.

Gribbin, William. *The Churches Militant: The War of 1812 and American Religion.* New Haven, CT: Yale University Press, 1973.

Groves, C. P. *The Planting of Christianity in Africa* Vol. III, 1878-1914. London, UK: Lutterworth, 1964.

Hayes, Carleton Joseph Huntley. *Essays on Nationalism.* New York: Macmillan, 1926.

Hayes, Sam and Christopher Morris, eds. *Manifest Destiny and Empire: America's Antebellum Expansion.* College Station, Texas: Texas A & M Press for University of Texas Press, 1997.

Hegel, Georg Wilhelm. *Hegel's Political Writings.* Trans. T. M. Knox. Oxford, U.K.: Clarendon Press, 1964.

Howard, Michael Eliot. *Clausewitz.* Oxford, UK: Oxford University Press, 1983.

___. *War and the Liberal Conscience.* New Brunswick, NJ: Rutgers University Press, 1978.

Johannsen, Robert Walter. *To the Halls of the Montezumas: the Mexican War in the American Imagination.* New York: Oxford University Press, 1985.

Kohn, Hans. *The Idea of Nationalism: A Study in Its Origins and Background.* New York: Macmillian, 1946.

___. *Nationalism, Its Meaning and History.* Malabar, FL: Kreiger, 1982.

Levinger, Matthew. *Enlightened Nationalism: The Transformation of Prussian Political Culture 1806-1848.* New York: Oxford University Press, 2000.

Linden, W. H. van der. *The International Peace Movement 1815-1987.* Amsterdam, The Netherlands: Tilleul, 1987.

McPherson, James M. *Battle Cry of Freedom: The Civil War Era.* Oxford History of the United States. New York: Oxford University Press, 1988.

Martin, Kingsley. *The Triumph of Lord Palmerston: A Study in Public Opinion in England Before the Crimean War.* New York: Hutchinson, 1963.

Meinecke, Friedrich. *Machiavellism: Doctrine of Raison d'État and Its Place in Modern History.* New Haven, CT: Yale University Press, 1967.

Miller, Randall, Harry Stout, and Charles Wilson, eds. *Religion and the American Civil War.* New York: Oxford University Press, 1998.

Moorehead, James. *American Apocalypse: Yankee Protestants and the Civil War 1860-1869.* New Haven, CT: Yale University Press, 1978.

Mosse, George L. *Nationalization of the Masses.* New York: Fertig, 1975.

Paret, Peter. *Clausewitz and the State.* New York: Oxford University Press, 1976.

___, Gordon Craig, and Felix Gilbert, eds. *Makers of Modern Strategy: from Machiavelli to the Nuclear Age.* Princeton, NJ: Princeton University Press, 1986.

Perret, Geoffrey. *A Country Made by War: From the Revolution to Vietnam - The Story of America's Rise to Power.* New York, Vintage, 1990.

Rhodes, Anthony. *The Power of Rome in the Twentieth Century: The Vatican in the Age of Liberal Democracies, 1870-1922.* London: Sidgwick and Jackson, 1983.

Rich, Norman. *Why the Crimean War? A Cautionary Tale.* Hanover, NH: Hutchinson and Smith, 1985.

Ritter, Gerhard. *The Sword and the Scepter: The Problem of Militarism in Germany.* Vol. I, *The Prussian Tradition 1740-1890.* Trans. Heinz Norton. Coral Gables, FL: University of Miami Press, 1969.

Royster, Charles. *The Destructive War: William Tecumseh Sherman, Stonewall Jackson, and the Americans.* New York: Knopf, 1991.

Schroeder, John H. *Mr. Polk's War: American Opposition and Dissent, 1846-1848.* Madison, WI: University of Wisconsin Press, 1973.

Sheehan, James. *German History, 1770-1866.* Oxford History of Modern Europe. Oxford, UK: Oxford University Press, 1989.

Slotkin, Richard. *Regeneration Through Violence: The Mythology of the American Frontier 1600-1860.* Middletown, CT: Wesleyan University Press, 1973.

Wawro, Geoffrey. *Warfare and Society in Europe 1792-1914.* New York: Routledge, 2000.

Weigley, Russell. *The American Way of War: A History of American Military Strategy and Policy.* New York: Macmillan, 1973.

Wills, Garry. *Lincoln at Gettysburg: The Words that Remade America.* New York: Simon and Schuster, 1992.

Williams, T. Harry. *A Military History of American Wars: From 1745 to 1918.* New York: Knopf, 1981.

Woodworth Steven. E. *While God is Marching On: The Religious World of Civil War Soldiers.* Lawrence, KS: University Press of Kansas, 2001.

XIII. A Civilized Way to Peace

Alonso, Harriet. *Peace as a Women's Issue: A History of the U.S. Movement for World Peace and Women's Rights.* Syracuse, NY: Syracuse University Press, 1993.

Berghahn, Volker Rolf. *Militarism: The History of an International Debate, 1861-1979.* New York: St. Martin's Press, 1982.

Best, Geoffrey. *Humanity in Warfare.* New York: Columbia University Press, 1980.

Bloch, I. S. *The Future of War in its Technical Economic and Political Relations.* New York: Doubleday & McClure, 1899.

Booth, Ken and Moorhead Wright, eds. *American Thinking about Peace and War.* New York: Barnes and Noble, 1978.

Chambers, John W. II. *Eagle and the Dove: The American Peace Movement and United States Foreign Policy.* Syracuse, NY: Syracuse University Press, 1991.

Chatfield, Charles. *For Peace and Justice: Pacifism in America 1914-1941.* Knoxville, TN: University of Tennessee Press, 1971.

___. *The American Peace Movement: Ideals and Activism.* New York: Twayne, 1991.

Chickering, Roger. *Imperial Germany and a World Without War: The Peace Movement and German Society, 1892-1914.* Princeton, N J: Princeton University Press, 1975.

Cohen, Sheldon M. *Arms and Judgment: Law, Morality, and the Conduct of War in the Twentieth Century.* Boulder, CO: Westview, 1989.

Cooper, Sandi E. *Patriotic Pacifism: Waging War on War in Europe 1815-1914.* New York: Oxford University Press, 1991.

Crook, D. P. *Darwinism, War, and History: The Debate Over the Biology of War from the Origin of the Species to the First World War.* Cambridge, UK: Cambridge University Press, 1994.

Davis, Calvin DeArmond. *The United States and the First Hague Conference.* Ithaca, N. Y.: Cornell University Press, 1962.

___. *The United States and the Second Hague Conference: American Diplomacy and International Organization, 1899-1914.* Durham, NC: Duke University Press, 1975.

DeBenedetti, Charles. *Origins of the Modern American Peace Movement 1915-1929.* Millwood, NY: KTO Press, 1978.

Freidel, Frank. *Francis Lieber: Nineteenth-Century Liberal.* Baton Rouge, LA: Louisiana State University Press, 1947.

Gallie, W. B. *Philosophers of Peace and War: Kant, Clausewitz, Marx, Engels, and Tolstoy.* New York: Cambridge University Press, 1978.

Gat, Azar. *The Development of Military Thought: The Nineteenth Century.* Oxford, UK: Oxford University Press, 1992.

Gorrell, Donald. *The Age of Social Responsibility: The Social Gospel in the Progressive Era.* Macon, GA: Mercer University Press, 1988.

Gumpert, Martin. *Dunant: The Story of the Red Cross.* New York: Oxford University Press, 1938.

Herman, Sondra R. *Eleven Against War: Studies in American Internationalist Thought 1898-1921.* Stanford, CA: Hoover Institution Press, 1969.

Howard, Michael. *War and the Liberal Conscience.* New Brunswick, NJ: Rutgers University Press, 1978.

Hull, William I. *The Two Hague Conferences and their Contributions to International Law.* Boston: Ginn, 1908.

Marchand, C. Roland. *The American Peace Movement and Social Reform 1898-1918.* Princeton, NJ: Princeton University Press, 1972.

Marrin, Gilbert. *The Last Crusade: The Church of England in the First World War.* Durham, N. C.: Duke University Press, 1974.

Moorehead, Caroline. *Dunant's Dream: War, Switzerland, and the History of the Red Cross.* London: Harper Collins, 1998.

Morris, A. J. Anthony. *Radicalism Against War 1906-1914: The Advocacy of Peace and Retrenchment.* Totawa, N. J.: Rowman and Littlefield, 1972.

Nation, R. Craig. *War on War: Lenin, the Zimmerwald Left and the Origins of Communist Internationalism.* Durham, NC: Duke University Press, 1989.

Tate, Merze. *The Disarmament Illusion: The Movement for a Limitation of Arms to 1907.* New York: Macmillan, 1942.

___. *The United States and Armaments.* Cambridge, MA: Harvard University Press, 1948.

Wank, Solomon, ed. *Doves and Diplomats: Foreign Offices and Peace Movements in Europe and America in the Twentieth Century.* Westport, Ct.: Greenwood Press

XIV. World War I

Bailey, Charles. "The British Protestant Theologians in the First World War: Germanophobia Unleashed." *Harvard Theological Review* 77 (April, 1984).

___. " 'Got mit uns:' Germany's Protestant Theologians in the First World War." Ph.D. diss., University of Virginia, 1978.

Bartov, Omer and Mack, Phyllis, eds. *In God's Name: Genocide and Religion in the Twentieth Century.* New York: Berghahn Books, 2001.

Brock, Peter. *Twentieth-Century Pacifism.* New York: Van Nostrand Reinhold, 1970.

Bussey, Gertrude and Margaret Tims. *Women's International League for Peace and Freedom.* London: George Allen & Unwin, 1965.

Ceadel, Martin. *Pacifism in Britain 1914-1945.* Oxford, UK: Clarendon, 1980.

Chambers, John, ed. *The Eagle and the Dove: The American Peace Movement and United States Foreign Policy 1900-1922.* 2nd edition. Syracuse, NY: Syracuse University Press, 1991.

Chatfield, Charles. *For Peace and Justice: Pacifism in America, 1914-1941.* Knoxville, TN: University of Tennessee Press, 1971.

The Church and War: Papers Read at the Twenty-First Summer Meeting and the Twenty-Second Winter Meeting of the Ecclesiastical Society. Edited by W. J. Sheils. Studies in Church History, vol. XX. Oxford, UK: Blackwell, 1983.

Combs, Jerald A. *American Diplomatic History: Two Centuries of Changing Interpretations.* Berkeley, CA: University of California, 1983.

Fussell, Paul. *The Great War and Modern Memory.* New York: Oxford University Press, 1975.

Graham, Robert A. *Vatican Diplomacy: A Study of Church and State on the International Plane.* Princeton, NJ: Princeton University Press, 1959.

Hoover, A. J. *God, Germany, and Britain in the Great War: A Study in Clerical Nationalism.* New York: Praeger, 1989.

Hynes, Samuel. *A War Remembered: The First World War and English Culture.* New York: Atheneum, 1991.

___. *A Soldier's Tale.* New York: Penguin, 1997.

Keegan, Paul. *The Face of Battle.* New York: Viking, 1976.

Kissenger, Henry. *Diplomacy.* New York: Simon and Schuster, 1994.

Kraft, Barbara. *The Peace Ship: Henry Ford's Pacifist Adventure in the First World War.* New York: Macmillan, 1978.

Link, Arthur. *Wilson the Diplomatist: A Look at his Major Foreign Policies.* Baltimore: John Hopkins University Press, 1957.

Marrin, Albert. *The Last Crusade: The Church of England in the First World War.* Durham, NC: Duke University Press, 1974.

The Marshall Cavendish Illustrated Encyclopedia of World War I. Ed. Peter Young and Mart Dartford. Freeport, L. I., NY: M. Cavendish, 1984.

Papal Encyclicals (1903-1939). Ed. Claudia Ihm. Raleigh, NC: Consortium: McGrath, 1981.

Piper, John J., Jr. *The American Churches in World War I.* Athens, Ohio: University of Ohio Press, 1985.

Pierard, Richard V. "John R. Mott and the Rift in the Ecumenical Movement During World War I," *Journal of Ecumenical Studies.* (1986): 22.

Power, Samantha. *"A Problem from Hell": America and the Age of Genocide.* New York: Basic Books, 2002.

Stoessinger, John. *Why Nations Go to War.* 6th edition. New York: St. Martin's, 1993.

Tuchman, Barbara. *The Guns of August.* New York: Macmillan, 1962.

Wank, Solomon. *Doves and Diplomats: Foreign Offices and Peace Movements In Europe and America in the Twentieth Century.* Westport, CT: Greenwood Press, 1978.

Williams, John. *The Home Fronts: Britain, France and Germany 1914-1918.* London, UK: Constable, 1972.

Winter, J. M. *Socialism and the Challenge of War; Ideas and Politics in Britain, 1912-18.* Boston: Routledge and Kegan Paul, 1974.

XV. Searching for Peace, Finding War 1920-39

Europe and America

Alonzo, Harriet Hyman. *Peace as a Women's Issue: A History of the U. S. Movement for World Peace and Women's Rights.* Syracuse, NY: Syracuse University Press, 1993.

Barnes, Kenneth C. *Nazism, Liberalism, and Christianity: Protestant Social Thought in Germany and Great Britain 1925-1937.* Lexington, KY: University Press of Kentucky, 1991.

Benda, Julien. *La Trahison des Clercs.* Paris: B. Grasset, 1929.

Bilis, Michel. *Socialistes et Pacifistes 1933-1939: Ou L'Impossible Dilemme des Socialistes Francais 1933-1939.* Paris: Syros, (n.d.).

Binchy, D. A. *Church and State in Fascist Italy.* Oxford, U.K: Oxford University Press, 1941.

Biographical Dictionary of Modern Peace Leaders. Ed. Harold Johnson. Westport, CN: Greenwood, 1958.

Blinkhorn, Martin, ed. *Spain in Conflict 1931-1939: Democracy and Its Enemies.* Beverly Hills, CA: Sage, 1986.

Cannistraro, Philip V., ed. *Historical Dictionary of Fascist Italy.* Westport, CN: Greenwood, 1982.

Ceadel, Martin. *Pacifism in Britain 1914-1945: The Defining of a Faith.* Oxford, U.K.: Clarendon, 1980.

Chatfield, Charles. *The American Peace Movement: Ideals and Activism.* New York: Twayne, 1992.

___. *For Peace and Justice: Pacifism in America 1914-1941.* Knoxville, TN: University of Tennessee, 1971.

___ and Peter Van Den Dungen, eds. *Peace Movements and Political Cultures.* Knoxville, TN: University of Tennessee, 1988.

___, ed. *The Americanization of Gandhi: Images of the Mahatma.* New York: Garland, 1976.

Day, Dorothy. *The Long Loneliness: The Autobiography of Dorothy Day.* New York: Harper, 1952.

The Encylopedia of The Third Reich. Ed. Christian Lenter and Friedemann Bedurfig. Trans. Amy Hackett. New York: Macmillan, 1991.

Evans, Ellen Lovell. *The German Center Party 1870-1933: A Study in Political Catholicism.* Carbondale, IL: Southern Illinois University Press, 1981.

Fox, Richard. *Reinhold Niebuhr: A Biography.* San Francisco, CA: Harper and Row, 1987.

Helmreich, Ernst Christian. *The German Churches under Hitler: Background, Struggle, and Epilogue.* Detroit, MI: Wayne State Press, 1979.

Historical Dictionary of the Spanish Civil War 1936-1939. Ed. James W. Cortada. Westport, CT: Greenwood, 1982.

Ingram, Norman. *The Politics of Dissent: Pacifism in France 1919-1939.* Oxford, UK: Clarendon Press, 1991

Johnson, Eric. *Nazi Terror: The Gestapo, Jews, and Ordinary Germans.* New York: Basic Books, 1999.

Keynes, John M. *Economic Consequences of the Peace.* New York: Harcourt Brace and Howe, 1920.

Klejment, Anne and Nancy Roberts, eds. *The Catholic Worker and the Origins of The Catholic Church and Catholic Radicalism in America.* Westport, CN: Greenwood, 1996.

Lannon, Frances. *Privilege, Persecution, and Prophecy: The Catholic Church in Spain 1875-1975.* Oxford, UK: Clarendon, 1987.

McCarthy, Esther. "The Catholic Periodical Press and Issues of War and Peace: 1914-1946." Ph.D. diss. Stanford University, 1957.

McKercher, B. J. C., ed. *Arms Limitation and Disarmament: Restraints on War, 1899-1939.* Westport, CT: Praeger, 1992.

Maehl, William Harvey. *The German Socialist Party: Champion of the First Republic 1918-1933.* Philadelphia, PA: American Philosophical Society, 1986.

Meyer, Donald B. *The Protestant Search for Political Realism 1919-1941.* Berkeley, CA: University of California Press, 1961.

Miller, Robert Moats. *American Protestantism and Social Issues 1919-1939.* Chapel Hill, NC: University of North Carolina Press, 1958.

Muste, A. J. *Essays of A. J. Muste.* Ed. Nat Hentoff. Indianapolis, IN: Bobbs-Merrill, 1967.

Nutt, Rich. *Toward Peacemaking: Presbyterians in the South and National Security, 1945-1983.* Tuscaloosa, AL: University of Alabama Press, 1994.

Oliver, John. *The Church* [of England] *and the Social Order.* London, UK: A. R. Mowbray, 1968.

Passelecq, Georges, and Bernard Suchecky. *The Hidden Encyclical of Pius XI.* Trans. Steven Rendell. New York: Harcourt Brace, 1997.

Piel, Mel. *The Catholic Worker and the Origins of Catholic Radicalism.* Philadelphia, PA: Temple University Press, 1982.

Pollard, John F. *The Vatican and Italian Fascism 1919-1932: A Study in Conflict.* New York: Cambridge University Press, 1985.

Prado, Luis Aquirre. *The Church and the Spanish War.* Madrid: Servicio Informativo Espanol, 1965.

Preston, Paul, ed. *Revolution and War in Spain 1931-1939.* New York: Methuen, 1984.

Rhodes, Anthony. *The Vatican in the Age of Dictators.* London: UK: Hodder and Stoughton, 1973.

Sanchez, Jose M. *The Spanish Civil War as a Religious Tragedy.* Notre Dame, IN: University of Notre Dame Press, 1987.

Socknat, Thomas P. *Witness Against War: Pacifism in Canada 1900-1945.* Toronto, Canada: University of Toronto Press, 1987.

Swanberg, W.A. *Norman Thomas: The Last Idealist.* New York: Scribners, 1976.

Will, Herman. *A Will to Peace: Peace Action in the United Methodist Church: A History.* Washington, D.C: General Board of Church and Society of the United Methodist Church, 1984.

Winter, J. M. *Socialism and the Challenge of War: Ideas and Politics in Britain 1912-18.* London: Routledge & Kegan Paul, 1974.

Wolff, Richard J. and Jörg K. Hoensch, eds. *Catholics, the State and the European Radical Right, 1919-1945.* Boulder, CO: Social Science Monographs; Highland Lakes, N.J.: Atlantic Research and Publications; New York, 1987.

Wright, J. R. C. *"Above Parties": The Political Attitudes of the German Protestant Church Leadership 1918-1933.* Oxford, UK: Oxford University Press, London, 1974.

India

Ashe, Geoffrey. *Gandhi.* New York: Stein and Day, 1968.

Bennett, Scott. " 'Pacifism not Passivism:' The War Resisters League and Radical Pacifism, Nonviolent Direct Actions and the Americanization of Gandhi 1915-1963." Ph. D. diss., Rutgers University, 1998.

Bhagavadgita. Ed. S. Radhakrishnan. New Delhi, India: Harper Collins, 1993.

Borman, William. *Gandhi and Non-Violence.* Albany, NY: State University of New York Press, 1986.

Dalton, Dennis. *Mahatma Gandhi: Nonviolent Power in Action.* New York: Columbia University Press, 1993.

Gandhi, M.K. *Satyagraha* [Non-Violent Resistance]. Ahmedabad, India: Navajivan, 1958.

Gupta. S. P. and K.S. Ramachandran, eds. *Mahabharata: Myth and Reality, Differing Views.* Delhi, India: Agam Prakashan, 1976.

Heesterman, J. C. *The Inner Conflict of Tradition: Essays in Indian Ritual, Kingship, and Society.* Chicago, IL: University of Chicago Press, 1985.

Juergensmeyer, Mark. *Fighting With Gandhi.* San Francisco: CA: Harper and Row, 1984.

Katz, Rught Cecily. *Arjuna in the Mahabharata: Where Krishna is, There is Victory.* Columbia: South Carolina: University of South Carolina, 1989.

The Mahabharata. Ed. and trans. Chakravarthi Narasimhan. New York: Columbia University Press, 1965.

Minor, Robert N., ed. *Modern Indian Interpreters of the Bhagavadgita.* Albany, NY: State University of New York Press, 1986. Particularly essays by Stevenson on Tilak, Minor on Sri Aurobindo, and Jordens on Gandhi.

Sharp, Gene. *Gandhi as a Political Strategist.* Boston, MA: Sargent, 1979.

Seshachari, C. *Gandhi and the American Scene.* Bombay, India: Nachiketa, 1969.

Japan

Barnhart, Michael A. *Japan Prepares for Total War: The Search for Economic Security, 1919-1941.* Ithaca, NY: Cornell University Press, 1987.

Bix, Herbert. *Hirohito and the Making of Modern Japan.* New York: Harper Collins, 2000.

Cook, Haruoko Taya and Theodore F. Cook. *Japan at War: An Oral History.* New York: The New Press, 1992.

Fletcher, Miles. *The Search for a New Order: Intellectuals and Fascism in Prewar Japan.* Chapel Hill, NC: University of North Carolina Press, 1982

Hardacre, Helen. *Shinto and the State, 1868-1988.* Princeton, NJ: Princeton University Press, 1989.

Harries, Meirion and Susie Harries. *Soldiers of the Sun: The Rise and Fall of the Imperial Japanese Army.* New York: Random House, 1991.

Holtom, D. C. *Modern Japan and Shinto Nationalism: A Study of Present-Day Trends in Japanese Religions.* Chicago, IL: University of Chicago Press, 1947.

___. *The National Faith of Japan: A Study in Modern Shinto.* 1938. New York: Paragon Book Reprint Corp., 1965.

Iriye, Akira. *Power and Culture: The Japanese-American War 1941-1945.* Cambridge, MA: Harvard University Press, 1981.

Kitagawa, Joseph M. *Religion in Japanese History.* New York: Columbia University Press, 1966.

Mitchell, Richard H. *Thought Control in Prewar Japan.* Ithaca, NY: Cornell University Press, 1976.

Smethurst, Richard J. *A Social Basis for Prewar Japanese Militarism.* Berkeley, CA: University of California, 1974.

Suzuki, D.T. *Zen and Japanese Culture.* 1938. New York: Pantheon, 1957.

Takizawa, Nobulhiko. "Religion and the State in Japan," *Journal of Church and State* 30 (Winter, 1988)

Victoria. Brian. *Zen at War.* New York: Weatherhill, 1957.

Wetsler, Peter. *Hirohito and War: Imperial Traditions and Military Decision Making in Pre-War Japan.* Honolulu: University of Hawaii Press, 1969.

XVI. World War II: The Apotheosis of Barbarity

Bartov, Omer. *The Eastern Front, 1941-1945, German Troops and the Barbarisation of Warfare.* New York: St. Martins, 1986.

Bartov, Omer and Mack, Phyllis, eds. *In God's Name: Genocide and Religion in the Twentieth Century.* New York: Berghahn, 2001.

Bernstein, Barton, "Why the USA Dropped Atomic Bombs on Japanese Cities," in *Proceedings of the Forty-Five Pugwash Conference on Science and World Affairs (1995).* NJ: World Scientific, 1995.

Berry, Paul and Mark Bostridge. *Vera Brittain: A Life.* London: Chatto & Windus, 1995.

Bird, Kai and Lawrence Lifeschultz, eds. *Hiroshima's Shadow.* Stony Creek,
　　CN: Pamphleteer's Press, 1998.
Brill, Norman and Gilbert Beebe. *A Follow-up Study of War Neuroses.* U. S.
　　Veterans Administration Medical Monograph. Washington, DC, 1955.
Brittain, Vera. "Massacre by Bombing," Fellowship. X, No. 3 (March, 1944).
Brown, Seyom. *Human Rights in World Politics.* New York: Longman, 2000
Chadwick, Owen. *Britain and the Vatican during the Second World War.*
　　Cambridge, U.K.: Cambridge University Press, 1986.
Chandler, Andrew. "The Church of England and Nazi Germany 1933-1945,"
　　Ph.D. diss. University of Cambridge, 1990.
____. "The Church of England and the Obliteration Bombing of Germany in the
　　Second World War," *English Historical Review* 108 (1993).
Cohen, Marshall, et al., eds. *War and Moral Responsibility.* Princeton, NJ:
　　Princeton University Press, 1974.
Cook, Haruko Taya and Theodore F. Cook. *Japan At War: An Oral History.*
　　New York: New Press, 1992.
Cornwell, John. *Hitler's Pope: The Secret History of Pius XII.* New York:
　　Viking, 1999.
Dictionary of Military History and the Art of War. Ed. André Corvisier.
　　English ed. Julian Childs. U.K: Blackwell, 1994.
Djilas, Milovan. *Wartime.* Trans. Michael B. Petrovich. New York: Harcourt
　　Brace Jovanovich, 1977.
Dower, John. *Japan In War and Peace: Selected Essays.* New York: New Press,
　　1993.
____. *War Without Mercy: Race and Power in the Pacific War.* New
　　York: Pantheon, 1986.
Dunn, Joe Pender. "The Church and the Cold War: Protestants and
　　Conscription, 1940-1954." Ph.D. diss., University of Missouri-Columbia,
　　1973.
Dyer, Gwynne. *War.* New York: Crown, 1985.
Ellis, John. *World War II: A Statistical Survey: The Essential Facts for All the
　　Combatants.* New York: Facts on File, 1993.
Encyclopedia of the Holocaust, ed. Israel Gutman. New York: Macmillan, 1990.
Ewing, E. Keith. "The Pacifist Movement in the Methodist Church during World
　　War II: A Study of Civilian Public Service Men in a Nonpacifist Church."
　　M.A. thesis, Florida Atlantic University, 1982.
Falk, Richard, compiler. *Crimes of War.* New York: Random House, 1971.
____. *Reviving the World Court,* Charlottesville, VA: University Press of
　　Virginia, 1986
Fireside, Harvey. *Icon and Swastika: The Russian Orthodox Church under Nazi
　　and Soviet Control.* Cambridge, MA: Harvard University Press, 1971.
Furet, Francois, ed. *Unanswered Questions: Nazi Germany and the Genocide of
　　the Jews.* New York: Schocken, 1989.
Fussell, Paul. *Doing Battle: The Making of a Skeptic.* Boston: Little Brown,
　　1996.

___. *Wartime Understanding and Behavior in the Second World War.* New York: Oxford University Press, 1989.

The Gallup Poll. *Public Opinion 1935-1941.* Washington, DC: The Gallup Organization, 1972.

Goldhagen, Daniel. *Hitler's Willing Executioners.* New York: Knopf, 1996.

Gray, J. Glenn. *The Warriors: Reflections on Men in Battle.* New York: Harcourt, Brace, 1959.

Hafer, Harold F. "Evangelical and Reformed Churches in World War II." Ph.D. diss., University of Pennsylvania. Philadelphia, 1947.

Hallie, Philip. *Lest Innocent Blood be Shed: The Story of the Village of le Chambon, and How Goodness Happened There.* New York: Harper & Row, 1979.

Hamby, Alonzo. *Life of Harry S. Truman.* New York: Oxford University Press, 1995.

Harries, Meirion and Susie Harries. *Soldiers of the Sun: The Rise and Fall of the Imperial Japanese Army.* New York: Random House, 1991.

Hastings, Max. *Bomber Command: The Myths and Reality of the Strategic Bombing Offensive 1939-1945.* New York: Dial Press/James Wade, 1979.

Hersey, John. *Hiroshima.* New York: Knopf, 1946.

Howard, Michael, ed. *Laws of War: Constraints on Warfare in the Western World.* New Haven, CT: Yale University Press, 1994.

Hynes, Samuel. *The Soldiers' Tale: Bearing Witness to Modern War.* New York: Penguin Press, 1997.

Irving, David. *The Destruction of Dresden.* New York: Ballantine Books, 1963.

Johnson, Eric. *The Gestapo, Jews, and Ordinary Germans.* New York: Basic Books, 1999.

Kertzer, David. *The Popes Against the Jews: The Vatican's Role in the Rise of Modern Anti-Semitism.* New York: Alfred A. Knopf, 2001.

Klemperer, Victor. *I Will Bear Witness: A Diary of the Nazi Years 1933-1941.* Trans. Martin Chalmers. New York: Random House, 1998.

Koppes, Clayton R. and Gregory D. Black. *Hollywood Goes to War.* New York: Free Press, 1987.

Lloyd, Roger. *The Church of England, 1900-1965.* London: SCM, 1966.

Lukas, Richard. *Forgotten Holocaust: The Poles under German Occupation 1939-1944.* Lexington: KY: University of Kentucky Press, 1986.

McCarthy, Esther. "Catholic Periodical Press and Issues of War and Peace, 1914-1946." Ph.D. diss., Stanford University, 1977.

Maddox, Robert. *Weapons for Victory: The Hiroshima Decision Fifty Years Later.* Columbia, MO: University of Missouri Press, 1995.

Malaparte, Curzio. *Kaputt.* Trans. *Cesare* Foligno. New York: E. P. Dutton, 1946.

Marrus, Michael. *The Holocaust in History.* Hanover, NH: Brandeis University Press, 1987.

Mayer, O. J. *Why Did the Heavens Not Darken: The "Final Solution" in History.* New York: Pantheon, 1988.

Messenger, Charles. *"Bomber" Harris and the Strategic Bombing Offensive 1939-1945.* New York: St. Martin's, 1984.

de Montclos, Xavier, et al., eds. *Églises et Chrétiens in Deuxieme Guerre Mondiale.* Lyon, France: Press Universitaires de Lyon, 1982.

Newman, Robert P. *Truman and the Hiroshima Cult.* East Lansing, MI: Michigan State University Press, 1995.

Orser, William Edward. "The Social Attitudes of the Protestant Churches During the Second World War." Ph.D. diss. University of New Mexico, 1969.

Oxford Companion to World War II. Ed. I.C.B. Dear and M. R. D. Foot. Oxford, U.K: Oxford University Press, 1995.

Pagliaro, Harold. *Naked Heart: A Soldier's Journey to the Front.* Kirksville, MO: Thomas Jefferson University Press at Truman State University, 1996.

Passelecq, George and Bernard Suchecky. *The Hidden Encyclical of Pius XI.* New York: Harcourt, Brace. 1997.

Phayer, Michael. *The Catholic Church and the Holocaust, 1930-1965.* Bloomington, IN: Indiana University Press, 2000.

Power, Samantha. *"A Problem from Hell": America and the Age of Genocide.* New York: Basic Books, 2002.

Queen, Edward L., II. *In the South the Baptists Are the Center of Gravity.* Brooklyn, NY: Carlson, 1991.

Rhodes, Richard. *The Making of the Atomic Bomb.* New York: Simon and Schuster, 1986.

Roberts, Walter R. *Tito, Mihailovic and the Allies 1941-1945.* New Brunswick, NJ: 1973.

Robertson, Geoffrey. *Crimes Against Humanity: The Struggle for Global Justice.* London: Allen Lane, 1999.

Schmidt, Hans. *Quakers and Nazis: Inner Light in Outer Darkness.* Columbia, MO: University of Missouri Press, 1997.

Schulte, Theo. *The German Army and Nazi Policies in Occupied Russia.* Oxford, UK: Berg, 1989.

Sherwin, Martin J. *A World Destroyed: The Atomic Bomb and the Grand Alliance.* New York: Vintage, 1977.

Sittser, Gerald L. *A Cautious Patriotism: The American Churches and the Second World War.* Chapel Hill, N.C: University of North Carolina Press, 1977.

Stoltzfus, Nathan. *Resistance of the Heart: Intermarriage and the Rosenstrasse Protest in Nazi Germany.* New York: Norton, 1996.

Taylor, Telford. *The Anatomy of the Nuremberg Trials.* New York: Knopf, 1992.

Terkel, Studs. *"The Good War" An Oral History of World War II.* New York: Pantheon, 1984.

United States Strategic Bombing Survey. *Summary Report (Pacific War).* Washington, DC: U. S. Government Printing Office, 1946.

___. *Japan's Struggle to End the War.* Chairman's Office, 1 July, 1946.

Verrier, Anthony. *The Bomber Offensive.* New York: McMillan, 1969.

Walzer, Michael. *Just and Unjust Wars: A Moral Argument with Historical Illustrations.* New York: Basic Books, 1977.

Weinburg, Gerhard. *A World at Arms: A Global History of World War II.* Cambridge, UK; New York: Cambridge University Press, 1994.

Wills, Gary. "Vatican Regrets." *New York Review of Books* (May 25, 2000).

Wittner, Lawrence. *Rebels Against War: The American Peace Movement 1941-1960.* New York: Columbia University Press, 1969.

Woetzel, Robert. *The Nuremberg Trials in International Law.* New York: Praeger, 1960.

Yzermans, Vincent A., ed. *Major Addresses of Pope Pius XII,* Vol.II. *Christmas Messages.* St. Paul, MN: North Central, 1961.

Zaretsky, Robert. *Nimes At War: Religion and Politics in the Gard 1938-1944.* University Park, PA: Penn State University Press, 1995.

XVII. The Cold War - I
Conventional Weapons and Wars

Allison, Graham and Philip Zelikow. *The Essence of Decision: Explaining the Cuban Missile Crisis* 2nd edition. New York: Longman, 1999.

Anderson, Jervis. *Bayard Rustin: Troubles I've Seen: A Biography.* New York: Harper Collins, 1997.

Au, William. *The Cross, The Flag, and the Bomb: American Catholics Debate War and Peace 1960-1983.* Westport, CN: Greenwood, 1985.

Blight, James and David Welch, eds. *On the Brink: Americans and Soviets Reexamine the Cuban Missile Crisis.* New York: Hill and Wang, 1989.

___ et al. *Cuba on the Brink: Castro, the Missile Crisis, and the Soviet Collapse.* New York: Pantheon, 1993

Brown, Robert McAfee. *Religion and Violence: A Primer for White Americans.* Philadelphia, PA: Westminster, 1973.

Caputo, Philip. *A Rumor of War.* New York: Holt, Rinehart & Winston, 1977.

Clergy and Laity Concerned About Vietnam. *In the Name of Freedom: The Conduct of War in Vietnam by the Armed Services of the United States.* New York, 1981.

Chadwick, Owen. *The Christian Church and the Cold War.* New York: Penguin. 1992.

Crane, Conrad. *American Airpower Strategy in Korea 1950-1953.* Lawrence, KS: University of Kansas, 2000.

Cromartie, Michael, ed. *Peace Betrayed?: Essays on Pacifism and Politics.* Washington, DC: Ethics and Public Policy Center, 1990.

Cumings, Bruce. *The Origins of the Korean War.* Vol. I, *Liberation and the Emergence of Separate Regimes 1945-1947,* Vol. II, *The Roaring of the Cataract.* Princeton, NJ: Princeton University Press, 1981, 1990.

De Benedetti, Charles and Charles Chatfield. *The Antiwar Movement of the Vietnam Era.* Syracuse, NY: Syracuse University Press, 1990.

Dunn, Joe Pender. "The Church and the Cold War: Protestants and Conscription, 1940-1955." Ph.D. diss., University of Missouri, 1975.

Fitzgerald, Francis. *Fire in the lake: The Vietnamese and Americans in Vietnam*. Boston: Little, Brown, 1972.

Frady, Marshall. *Billy Graham: A Parable of American Righteousness*. Boston: Little Brown, 1979.

Gaddis, John. *The United States and The Origins of the Cold War 1941-1947*. New York: Columbia, University Press, 1972.

___. *We Know Now: Rethinking Cold War History*. New York: Oxford University Press, 1996.

The Gallup Poll. *Public Opinion, 1935-1971*. New York: Random House, 1972.

The Gallup Poll. *Gallup Opinion Index, "Public Opinion and the Vietnam War 1964-1967."* New York: Random House, 1967.

Garfinkle, Adam. *Telltale Hearts: The Origins and Impact of the Vietnam Antiwar Movement*. New York: St. Martin's Press, 1995.

Ginsberg, Robert, ed. *The Critique of War: Contemporary Philosophical Explorations*. Chicago: Henry Regnery Company, 1969.

Goldwater, Barry. *Where I Stand*. New York: McGraw Hill, 1964.

Greeley, Andrew. *The American Catholic: A Social Portrait*. New York: Basic Books, 1977.

Halberstam, David. *The Best and the Brightest*. New York: Random House, 1972.

Hall, Mitchell. *Because of Their Faith: CALCAV and Religious Opposition to the War*. New York: Columbia University Press, 1990.

Harris, Louis. *Anguish of Change*. New York, Norton, 1973.

Hebblethwaite, Peter. *Paul VI: The First Modern Pope* New York: Paulist, 1993.

Herr, Michael. *Dispatches*. New York: Knopf, 1977.

Herring, George. *America's Longest War: The United States and Vietnam 1950-1975*. New York: Knopf, 1979.

Hersh, Seymour. *My Lai 4: A Report on the Massacre and Its Aftermath*. New York: Random House, 1970.

Karnow, Stanley. *Vietnam: A History*. New York: Viking, 1983.

Leffler, Melvin. "Inside Enemy Archives." *Foreign Affairs* (1996), 120-34.

Lewy, Guenter. *America in Vietnam*. New York: Oxford University Press, 1980.

___. *Peace and Revolution: The Moral Crisis of American Pacifism*. Grand Rapids, MI: Eerdmans, 1988.

Lowe, Peter. *The Origins of the Korean War*. New York: Longman, 1997.

McNamara, Robert, et al. *Argument Without End: In Search of Answers to the Vietnam Tragedy*. New York: Public Affairs, 1999.

McNeal, Patricia. *Harder Than War: Catholic Peacemaking in Twentieth-Century America*. New Brunswick, N.J.: Rutgers University Press, 1992.

Meinertz, Midge. *Vietnam Christian Service: Witness in Anguish*. USA: Church World Service, 1976.

Mirsey, Jonathan. "The Never Ending War," *New York Review of Books* (May 25, 2000): 47.

___. "No Trumphets, No Drums," *New York Review of Books* (September 21, 1995): 42.

National Conference of Catholic Bishops. *In the Name of Peace: Collective Statements of the United States Catholic Bishops on War and Peace, 1919-1980.* Washington, DC: National Conference of Catholic Bishops, 1983.

Neuhaus, Richard John. "The War, The Churches, and Civil Religion," *Annals of the American Academy of Political and Social Science* 387 (1970): 128-40.

New Republic. 29 April 1985. (special issue on 10th anniversary of fall of Saigon.)

Nhat Hanh, Thich. *Love in Action: Nonviolent Social Change.* Berkeley, CA: Parallax Press, 1993.

___. *Fragrant Palm Leaves: Journals 1962-1966.* Berkeley, CA: Parallax Press, 1998.

O'Brien, Tim. *Going after Cacciato.* New York: Delacorte Press/S. Lawrence, 1978.

O'Brien, William V. *The Conduct of Just and Limited War.* New York: Praeger, 1983.

Osmer, Harold H. "United States Religious Press Response to the Containment Policy During the Period of the Korean War." Ph.D. diss., New York University, 1970.

The Pentagon Papers: The Defense Department History of the United States Decisionmaking on Vietnam. Boston: Beacon Press, 1971-72.

Podhoretz, Norman. *Why We Were in Vietnam.* New York: Simon and Schuster, 1982.

Quigley, Thomas, ed. *American Catholics and Vietnam.* Grand Rapids, MI: Eerdmans, 1968.

Quinley, Harold. "The Protestant Clergy and the War in Vietnam," *Public Opinion Quarterly* 34 (1970): 43-52.

Respectfully Quoted: A Dictionary of Quotations Requested from the Congressional Research Service. Ed. Suzy Platt. Washington, DC: Library of Congress, 1989.

Robinson, Lee Ann. *Abraham Went Out: A Biography of A. J. Muste.* Philadelphia, PA: Temple University Press, 1981.

Schroeder, Steven. *A Community and a Perspective: Lutheran Peace Fellowship and the Edge of the Church, 1941-1991.* New York: University Press of America, 1993.

Schulzinger, Robert. *A Time for War: The United States and Vietnam 1941-1975.* New York: Oxford University Press, 1997.

Small, Melvin and William Hoover. *Give Peace a Chance: Exploring the Vietnam Antiwar Movement.* Syracuse, NY: Syracuse University Press, 1997.

Smith, Tracey Dean. "Agitation in the Land of Zion: The Anti-Vietnam War Movements at Brigham Young University, University of Utah and Utah State University." M.S. thesis, Utah State, 1996.

Smylie, James H. "American Religious Bodies, Just War, and Vietnam, "*Journal of Church and State* 11 (1969): 383-408.

Sorenson, Theodore. *Kennedy.* New York: Harper and Row, 1965.

Starr, Jerold. "Religious Preference, Religiosity, and Opposition to War," *Sociological Analysis*, 36 (1975): 325-34.

Stehle, Hansjakob. *Eastern Politics of the Vatican 1919-1979.* Trans. Sandra Smith. Athens, OH: Ohio University Press, 1981.

Stone, Ronald and Dana Wilbanks, eds. *The Peacemaking Struggle: Militarism and Resistance.* Essays prepared for Advisory council on Church and Society of the Presbyterian Church USA. Lanham, MD: University Press of America, 1985.

Stueck, William. *The Korean War: An International History.* Princeton, NJ: Princeton University Press, 1995.

Tracy, James. *Direct Action: Radical Pacifism from the Union Eight to the Chicago Seven.* Chicago, IL: University of Chicago Press, 1996.

Tygart, Clarence E., "Social Movement Participation: Clergy and the Anti-Vietnam War Movement," *Sociological Analysis* 34 (1973): 202-11.

"Vietnam: A Television History." PBS documentary produced by WGBH, Boston; Central Independent Television, UK; Antenne-2 France and LRE Productions. 13 videocassettes, 780 minutes. 1993.

Weigel, George. *Tranquillitas Ordinis the Present Failure and Future Promise of American Catholic Thought on War and Peace.* New York: Oxford University Press, 1987.

Wittner, Lawrence. *Rebels Against War: The American Peace Movement 1941-1960.* New York: Columbia University Press, 1969.

Wuthnow, Robert. *The Restructuring of American Religion: Society and Faith Since World War II.* Princeton, NJ: Princeton University Press, 1988.

Yergin, Daniel. *Shattered Peace: The Origins of the Cold War.* New York: Penguin, 1990.

Zahn, Gordon. "The Scandal of Silence," *Commonweal* 95 (October 22, 1971): 79-85.

Zaroulis, Nancy and Sullivan, Gerald. *Who Spoke Up: American Protest Against the War in Vietnam 1963-1975.* Garden City, NY: Doubleday, 1989.

XVIII. The Cold War - II
Nuclear Weapons

Boyer, Paul. *By the Bomb's Early Light: American Thought and Culture at the Dawn of the Atomic Age.* New York: Pantheon, 1985.

___. *When Time Shall Be No More: Prophecy Belief in Modern America.* Cambridge, MA: Harvard University Press, 1992.

Byrne, Paul. *The Campaign for Nuclear Disarmament*. London: Croom Helm, 1988.

Chadwick, Owen. *The Christian Church in the Cold War*. London, U.K: Penguin, 1992.

Clark, Grenville and Louis Sohn. *World Peace through World Law*. Cambridge, MA: Harvard University Press, 1958.

Cohen, Marshall, Thomas Nagel, and Thomas Scanlon, eds. *War and Moral Responsibility*. Princeton, NJ: Princeton University Press, 1974.

Commission of the Churches on International Affairs and Pontifical Commission "Justitia et Pax," eds. *Peace and Disarmament:Documents Of the World Council of Churches and Roman Catholic Church*, 1982.

Commission on the Relation of the Church to the War in the Light of the Christian Faith of the Federal Council of Churches of Christ in America. *Atomic Warfare and the Christian Faith*. New York, 1946.

Commission to Study Bases of a Just and Durable Peace of the Federal Council of Churches. *A Righteous Faith for a Just and Durable Peace*. 1942.

Davidson, Donald. G. *Nuclear Weapons and the American Churches: Ethical Positions on Modern Warfare*. Boulder, CO: Westview, 1983.

Dougherty, James E. *The Bishops and Nuclear Weapons*. Hamden, CN: Archon, 1984.

Ellis, Jane. *The Russian Orthodox Church: A Contemporary History*. Bloomington, IN: Indiana University Press, 1986.

Falwell, Jerry. *Nuclear Weapons and the Second Coming of Jesus Christ*. Old Time Gospel Hour, 1983.

Ford, Harold P. and Francis W. Winters, eds. *Ethics and Nuclear Strategy?* Maryknoll, NY: Orbis Books, 1977.

George, Alexander and Richard Smoke. *Deterrence in American Foreign Policy: Theory and Practice*. New York: Columbia University Press, 1974.

Henriksen, Margaret. *Dr. Strangelove's America: Society and Culture in the Atomic Age*. Berkeley, CA: University of California Press, 1997.

Hoffman, Stanley. *Duties Beyond Borders: On the Limits and Possibilities of Ethical International Politics*. Syracuse, NY: Syracuse University Press, 1981.

Kahn, Herman. *Thinking About the Unthinkable*. New York: Avon, 1962.

Kaplan, Fred. *Wizards of Armageddon*. New York: Simon and Schuster, 1983.

Kennan, George. *American Diplomacy 1900-1950*. Chicago, IL: University of Chicago Press, 1951.

Kennedy, Edward and Mark Hatfield. *Freeze! How You Can Help Prevent Nuclear War*. New York: Bantam, 1982.

Krauthammer, Charles. "Morality and the Reagan Doctrine." *New Republic* 8 April 1986.

Lifton, Robert J. and Greg Mitchell. *Hiroshima in America: Fifty Years of Denial*. New York: Putnam's, 1995.

___ and Eric Markusen. *TheGenocidal Mentality: Nazi Holocaust and Nuclear Threat*. New York: Basic Books, 1990

Meyer, David. *A Winter of Discontent: The Nuclear Freeze and American Politics.* New York: Praeger, 1990.

Mujtabai, A. G. *Blessed Assurance: At Home with the Bomb in Amarillo, Texas.* Boston: Houghton Mifflin, 1986.

Murnion, Philip J., ed. *Catholics and Nuclear War: A Commentary on The Challenge of Peace.* The U.S. Catholic Bishops' Pastoral Letter on War and Peace. New York: Crossroads, 1983.

Musto, Ronald G., ed. *Catholic Peacemakers: A Documentary History.* 2 vols. New York: Garland, 1996.

Myers, Frank. "British Peace Politics: The Campaign for Nuclear Disarmament and the Committee of 100, 1957-1962," Ph.D. diss., Columbia University, 1965.

Newhouse, John. *Cold Dawn: The Story of SALT.* New York: Holt, Rinehart and Winston, 1973.

Nutt, Rick L. *Toward Peacemaking: Presbyterians in the South and National Security 1945-1983.* Tuscaloosa, AL: University of Alabama Press, 1994.

Potter, Ralph B. "The Responses of Certain American Christian Churches to Nuclear Dilemma 1958-1956." Ph.D. diss., Harvard, 1965.

___. *War and Moral Discourse.* Richmond, VA: John Knox Press, 1969.

Queen, Edward. *In the South the Baptists Are the Center of Gravity.* Brooklyn, NY: Carlson, 1991.

Quester, George. *Nuclear Diplomacy: The First Twenty-Five Years.* New York: Dunellen, 1970.

Ramsay, Paul. *The Just War: Force and Political Responsibility.* New York: Scribner, 1968.

___. The *Limits of Nuclear War: Thinking About the Do-Able and the Un-Do-Able.* New York: Council on Religion and International Affairs, 1963.

___. *Speak Up For Just War or Pacifism: A Critique of the United Methodist Bishops' Pastoral Letter "In Defense of Creation."* University Park, PA: Pennsylvania State University Press, 1988.

Rhodes, Richard. *Dark Sun: The Making of the Hydrogen Bomb.* New York: Simon and Schuster, 1995.

Rotblat, Joseph and Jack Steinberger, eds. *A Nuclear-Weapon Free World: Desirable? Feasible?* Boulder CO: Westview Press, 1995.

Schell, Jonathan. *The Fate of the Earth.* New York: Knopf, 1982.

Stehle, Hansjokob. *Eastern Politics of the Vatican 1917-1979.* Trans. Sandra Smith. Athens, OH: Ohio University Press, 1981.

Sussman, Glen. "Anti-Nuclear Weapons Activism in the United States and Great Britain: A Comparative Analysis." Ph.D. diss., Washington State, 1987.

Talbott, Strobe. *Deadly Gambits: the Reagan Administration and the Stalemate in Nuclear Arms Control.* New York: Vintage Books, 1985.

Taylor, Richard and Nigel Young, eds. *Campaigns for Peace: British Peace Movements in the Twentieth Century.* Manchester, UK: Manchester University Press, 1987.

Tucker, Robert W. *The Just War: A Study in Contemporary American Doctrine.* Baltimore, MD: Johns Hopkins Press, 1960.

___. *Just War and Vatican Council II.* New York: The Council on Religion and International Affairs, 1966.

United Methodist Council of Bishops. *In Defense of Creation: The Nuclear Crisis and a Just Peace.* Nashville, TN: Graded Press, 1986.

United Methodist Church Commission to Study the Christian Faith and War in the Nuclear Age. *The Christian Faith and War in the Nuclear Age.* Nashville, TN: Abington, 1963.

United Presbyterian Church, USA: The Peacemaking Project Program Agency. "Peacemaking: The Believers' Calling." New York: 1982.

Walsh, Michael and Brian Davies, eds. *Proclaiming Justice and Peace: Papal Documents from Rerum Novarum through Centesimus Annus.* Mystic: CN: Twenty-Third Publications, 1991.

Walters, Philip. "The Russian Orthodox Church." In *Eastern Christianity and Politics* Vol. 1, *Christianity Under Stress.* Ed. Pedro Ramet. Durham, NC: Duke University Press, 1988.

Walzer, Michael. *Just and Unjust Wars: A Moral Argument with Historical Illustrations.* New York: Basic Books, 1977.

Wasserstrom, Richard, ed. *War and Morality.* Belmont, CA: Wadsworth, 1970.

Webster, Alexander. *The Price of Prophecy: Orthodox Churches on Peace, Freedom, and Security.* Washington, D.C.: Ethics and Public Policy Center, 1993.

Weigel, George. *Tranquillitas Ordinis: The Present Failure and Future Promise Of American Catholic Thought on War and Peace.* New York: Oxford University Press, 1987.

Welsby, Paul. *A History of the Church of England 1945-1980.* Oxford, UK: Oxford University Press, 1984.

Wilbanks, Dana and Ronald Stone. "Presbyterians and Peacemaking: Are We Now Called to Resistance?" New York: Advisory Council on Church and Society, 1985.

___, eds. *The Presbyterian Struggle: Militarism and Resistance.* New York: University Press of America, 1985.

Will, Herman. *A Will of Peace: Peace Action in the United Methodist Church: A History.* Washington, DC: General Board of Church and Society of the United Methodist Church: 1984.

Wittner, Lawrence S. *One World or None: The Struggle Against the Bomb* Vol. I, *A History of the World Nuclear Disarmament Movement Through 1953,* Vol. II, *Resisting the Bomb 1954-1970.* Stanford, CA: Stanford University Press, 1993, 1997.

XIX. Religion and War in the Creation of Israel

Almog, Shmuel. *Zionism and History: The Rise of a New Jewish Consciousness.* New York: St. Martin's, 1987.

Almog, Shmuel, Jehuda Reinharz, and Anita Shapira, eds. *Zionism and Religion*. Hanover, NH: Brandeis University Press, 1998.

Avi-hai, Avraham. *Ben-Gurion, State-Builder: Principles and Pragmatism 1948-1963*. Wiley: New York, 1974.

Avishai, Bernard. *The Tragedy of Zionism: Revolution and Democracy in the Land of Israel*. New York: Farrar Straus Giroux, 1985.

Bregman, Ahron. *Israel's Wars: A History since 1947*. New York: Routledge, 2nd edition, 2002.

Cohen, Michael J. *Palestine and the Great Powers 1945-1948*. Princeton, NJ: Princeton University Press, 1982.

"Debate on the 1948 Exodus." *Journal of Palestine Studies*, 21, no. 81 (1991).

Elpeleg, Zvi. *The Grand Mufti: Haj Amin Al-Hussaini*. Trans. David Harvey. London, U.K.: Frank Cass, 1993.

Hazony, Yoram. *The Jewish State: The Struggle for Israel's Soul*. New York: Basic Books, 2000.

Louis, William Roger and Robert W. Stookey, eds. *The End of the Palestine Mandate*. Austin, TX: University of Texas Press, 1986.

Meir, Golda. *My Life*. New York: Putnam, 1975.

Morris, Benny. *The Birth of the Palestinian Refugee Problem, 1947-1949*. Cambridge, UK: Cambridge University Press, 1987.

New Encyclopedia of Zionism and Israel. Ed. Geoffrey Wigoder. Cranbury, NJ: Herzl Press Publication, Associated University Press, 1994.

Peretz, Don, ed. *The Arab-Israel Dispute*. New York: Facts on File, 1996.

Perlmutter, Amos. *Israel: The Partitioned State, A Political History Since 1900*. New York: Scribner's, 1985.

Prior, Michael. *Zionism and the State of Israel: A Moral Inquiry*. New York: Routledge, 1999.

Reinharz, Jehuda. *Chaim Weizmann: The Making of a Zionist Leader and The Making of a Statesman*. New York: Oxford University Press, 1985, 1993.

Rodinson, Maxime. *Israel: A Colonial-Settler State?* New York, Anchor Foundation, 1973.

Rubinstein, Amnon. *The Zionist Dream Revisited*. New York: Shocken, 1984.

Ruether, Rosemary Radford and Herman Ruether. *The Wrath of Jonah: The Crisis of Religious Nationalism in the Israeli-Palestinian Conflict*. New York: Harper and Row, 1989.

Said, Edward W. *The Politics of Dispossession: The Struggle for Palestinian Self-Determination, 1969-1994*. New York: Vantage, 1995.

Segev, Tom. *One Palestine, Complete: Jews and Arabs Under the British Mandate*. Trans. Haim Watzman. New York: Metropolitan, 2000.

Shimoni, Gideon. *The Zionist Ideology*. Hanover, NH: Brandeis University Press, 1995.

Shlaim, Avi. *The Iron Wall: Israel and the Arab World*. New York: Norton, 2000.

Sicker, Martin. *Judaism, Nationalism, and the Land of Israel*. Boulder, CO: Westview, 1992.

Silver, Eric. *Begin: The Haunted Prophet.* New York: Random House, 1984.
___. "Arab Witnesses Admit Exaggerating Deir Yassin Massacre." *Jerusalem Post,* 2 April 1998.
Sternhell, Zeev. *The Founding Myths of Israel: Nationalism, Socialism, and the Making of the Jewish State.* Trans. David Maisel. Princeton, NJ: Princeton University, 1997.
Sykes, Christopher. *Crossroads to Israel 1917-1948.* Bloomington, IN: Indiana University Press, 1973.
Teveth, Shabtai. *Ben-Gurion: The Burning Ground 1886-1948.* Boston: Houghton Mifflin, 1987.
Wheatcroft, Geoffrey. *The Controversy of Zion: Jewish Nationalism, the Jewish State, and the Unresolved Jewish Dilemma.* Reading, MA: Addison Wesley, 1996.

XX. Islam and Modern War: Iran and Iraq

Abrahamian, Ervand. *Khomeinism: Essays on the Islamic Republic.* Berkeley, CA: University of California, 1993.
Adas, Michael, ed. *Islamic and European Expansion.* Philadelphia: Temple University Press, 1993.
Gellner, Ernest, ed. *Islamic Dilemmas: Reformers, Nationalists and Industrialization: The Southern Shore of the Mediterranean.* New York: Mouton, 1985.
Halm, Heinz. *Shiism.* Trans. Janet Watson. Edinbugh, United Kingdom: Edinburgh University Press, 1991.
Hiro, Dilip. *The Longest War: The Iran-Iraq Military Conflict.* New York: Routledge, 1991.
Johnson, James Turner. *The Holy War Idea in Western and Islamic Traditions.* University Park, PA: Penn State Press, 1997.
Johnson, James Turner and John Kelsay, eds. *Cross, Crescent, and Sword: The Justification and Limitation of War in Western and Islamic Tradition.* Westport, CN: Greenwood, 1990.
Karpet, Kemal H. *The Politicization of Islam: Reconstructing Identity, State, Faith, and Community in the Late Ottoman State.* Oxford, UK: Oxford University Press, 2001.
Keddie, Nikki, ed. *Religion and Politics and Iran: Islam from Quietism to Revolution.* New Haven, CN: Yale University Press, 1983.
Kelsay, John. *Islam and War: A Study in Comparative Ethics.* Louisville, KY: Westminster/John Knox, 1993.
Kelsay, John and James Turner Johnson, eds. *Just War and Jihad: Historical and Theoretical Perspectives on War and Peace in Western and Islamic Traditions.* Westport, CN: Greenwood, 1991.
Kramer, Martin, ed. *Shiism, Resistance, and Revolution.* Boulder CO: Westminster, 1987.

Lewis, Bernard. *The Emergence of Modern Turkey.* 3rd edition. New York: Oxford University Press, 2002.

Menashri, David, ed. *The Iranian Revolution and the Muslim World.* Boulder, CO: Westview, 1990.

Munson, Henry, Jr. *Islam and Revolution in the Middle East.* New Haven, CN: Yale University Press, 1988.

Murphey, Rhoads. *Ottoman Warfare 1500-1700.* New Brunswick, NJ: Rutgers University Press, 1999.

Omid, Homa. *Islam and the Post-Revolutionary State in Iran.* New York: St. Martin's Press, 1994.

Roy, Olivier. *The Failure of Political Islam.* Trans. Carol Volk. Cambridge, MA: Harvard University Press, 1994.

Shaw, Stanford J. *Between Old and New: The Ottoman Empire under Sultan Selim III 1789-1807.* Cambridge, MA: Harvard University Press, 1971.

Sachedina, Abdulaziz Abdulhussein. *The Just Ruler in Shiite Islam: The Comprehensive Authority of the Jurist in Imamite Jurisprudence.* New York: Oxford University Press, 1988.

Said, Edward. *Orientalism.* New York: Vantage, 1979.

Sirreyeh, Elizabeth. *Sufis and Anti-Sufis: The Defence, Rethinking and Rejection of Sufism in the Modern World.* Richmond, Surrey, UK: Curzon, 1999.

Tripp, Charles. *A History of Iraq.* Cambridge, UK: Cambridge University Press, 2000.

Waardenburg, Jacques. "Islam as a Vehicle of Protest," in *Islamic Dilemmas: Reformers, Nationalists and Industrialization.* 1985: 22-48.

Watt, William M. *Muslin-Christian Encounters: Perceptions and Misperceptions.* London, New York: Routledge, 1991.

XXI. The Gulf Wars against Iraq

Anderson, Kenneth. "Who Owns the Rules of War?" *New York Times Magazine.* 13 April, 2003: 38.

Arnove, Anthony, ed. *Iraq Under Siege: The Deadly Impact of Sanctions and War.* Cambridge, MA. South End Press, 2000.

Bennis, Phyllis and Michel Moushabeck, eds. *Beyond the Storm: A Gulf Crisis Reader.* New York: Olive Branch Press: New York, 1991.

Blumberg, Herbert and Christopher French, eds. *The Persian Gulf War: Views from the Social and Behavioral Sciences.* New York: University Press of America, 1994.

Bumiller, "Religious Leaders Ask if Antiwar Call Is Heard." *New York Times,* 10 March 2003.

Elshtain, Jean et al. *But Was It Just? Reflections on the morality of the Persian Gulf War.* New York: Doubleday, 1992.

Goodstein, "Catholics Debating: Back President or Pope." *New York Times,* 6 March 2003.

"The Gulf War: Five Years After," *Frontline*, Public Broadcasting Co. 1996.

Hallett, Brian, ed. *Engulfed in War: Just War and the Persian Gulf*. Honolulu: Hawaii: Spark M. Matsunaga Institute for Peace, University of Hawaii, 1991.

Johnson, James Turner and George Weigel, eds. *Just War and the Gulf War*. Washington, DC: Ethics and Public Policy Center, 1991.

Kaplan, Robert. *Of Paradise and Power: America and Europe and the New World Order*. New York: Knopf, 2003.

Kelsay, John. *Islam and War: The Gulf War and Beyond, A Study in Comparative Ethics*. Louisville, KY: Westminster/John Knox, 1993.

The Lehrer Report, *News Hour*. March 3, 2003.

New York Times, New York. April 22, 2003.

Pew Forum on Religion and Public Life, "Iraq and Just War: A Symposium," September 30, 2002.

Pew Survey "Americans Hearing about Iraq from the Pulpit but Religious Faith Not Defining Opinions." March 13-16, 2003.

Pew Survey "Americans Struggle with Religious Role at Home and Abroad." March, 2003.

Pisatori, James, ed. *Islamic Fundamentalisms and the Gulf Crisis*. Chicago, Ill: The Fundamentalism Project of American Academy of Arts and Sciences. USA, American Academy of Arts and Sciences, 1991.

Rieff, David. "Were Sanctions Right?" *New York Times Magazine* 27 July 2003.

Smock, David. *Religious Perspectives on War: Christian, Muslim and Jewish Attitudes Toward Force After the Gulf War*. Washington, DC: U. S. Institute of Peace, 1995.

Stoessinger, John. *Why Nations Go to War*. 6th edition. New York: St. Martin's Press, 1993.

Tripp, Charles. *A History of Iraq*. Cambridge, UK: Cambridge University Press, 2000.

Vaux, Kenneth L. *Ethics and the Gulf War: Religion, Rhetoric, and Righteousness*. Boulder, CO: Westview, 1992.

Woodward, Bob. *The Commanders*. New York: Simon and Schuster, 1991.

XXII. The 1990s: Religious-Ethnic Wars

Abrams, Irwin. *Nobel Peace Prize and Its Laureates: An Illustrated History 1901-1987*. Boston: G. K. Hall, 1988.

Ackerman, Peter and Jack Duvall. *A Force More Violent: A Century of Nonviolent Conflict*. New York: Palgrave, 2000.

Appleby, R. Scott. *The Ambivalence of the Sacred: Religion, Violence, and Reconciliation*. Carnegie Commission on Preventing Deadly Conflict. Lanham, MD : Rowman & Littlefield Publishers, 2000

___. *Religious Fundamentalisms and Global Conflict*. Headline Series, no. 301. Foreign Policy Association.

Aronson, Geoffrey. *Israel, Palestinians, and the Intifadah: Creating Facts on the West Bank.* New York: Kegan Paul and Institute for Palestinian Studies, 1987.

Barak, Ehud, Benny Morris, Robert Malley, and Hussein Agha. "Camp David and After: An Exchange." *New York Review of Books.* 9 August, 2001: 13; June 2002: 42-47; 27 June 2002: 47-48.

Barash, David. *Introduction to Peace Studies.* Belmont, CA: Wadsworth, 1991. Press, 2000.

___, ed. *A Reader in Peace Studies.* New York: Oxford University Press, 2000.

Berryman, Philip. *Liberation Theology: Essential Facts about the Revolutionary Movement in Latin America-and Beyond.* Philadelphia, PA: Temple University Press, 1987.

Breadun, Deaglan de. *The Far Side of Revenge: Making Peace in Northern Ireland.* Wilton, Ireland: Collins, 2001.

Brown, Michael and Richard Rosecrance, eds. *The Costs of Conflict:Prevention and Cure in the Global Area.* Lanham, MD: Rowman and Littlefield, 1999.

Brown, Seyom. *The Causes and Prevention of War.* New York: St. Martin's Press, 1987.

Burton, John, ed. *Conflict: Human Needs Theory.* New York: St. Martin's Press, 1990.

___. *Conflict:Resolution and Prevention.* New York: St. Martin's Press, 1990.

___. *Conflict Resolution: Its Language and Process.* Lanham, MD: Scarecrow Press, 1996.

Catherwood, Christopher. *Why the Nations Rage: Killing in the Name of God.* London, UK: Hodder and Stoughton, 1999.

Davis, Scott, ed. *Religion and Justice in the War over Bosnia.* New York: Routledge, 1996.

Destexhe, Alain. *Rwanda and Genocide in the Twentieth Century.* Trans. Alison Marschner. New York: New York University Press, 1996.

Ellis, Marc H. *Unholy Alliance: Religion and Atrocity in Our Time.* Minneapolis, MN: Fortress, 1997.

Embree, Ainslie. *Utopias in Conflict: Religion and Nationalism in Modern India.* Berkeley, CA: University of California, 1990.

Esposito, John. *The Islamic Threat: Myth or Reality?* New York: Oxford, 1992.

Fisher, Roger et al. *Beyond Machiavelli: Tools for Coping with Conflict.* Cambridge, MA: Harvard University Press, 1994.

___ and William Ury. *Getting to Yes: Negotiating Agreement Without Giving In.* New York: Penguin, 1983.

Goldman, Francisco. "Victory in Guatemala." *New York Review of Books.* 21 May 2002: 77-79, 82-84.

Gopal, Sarvepalli. *Anatomy of a Confrontation: Babri-Masjid-Ramjanmabhumi Issue.* New York: Penguin, 1991.

Gourevitch, Philip. *We Wish to Inform You that Tomorrow We Will Be Killed with Our Families: Stories from Rwanda*. New York: Farrar, Straus, and Giroux, 1998.

Ganguly, Sumit. *The Crisis in Kashmir: Portents of War, Hopes of Peace*. Cambridge, UK: Woodrow Wilson Center Press and Cambridge University Press, 1997.

Geertz, Clifford. "Which Way to Mecca." *New York Review of Books*. 12 June 2000: 27-29; 3 July 2002: 36-39.

Hassett, John, Hugh Lacey, and Leo J. O'Donovan, eds. *Towards a Society that Serves Its People: The Intellectual Contribution of El Salvador's Wounded Jesuits*. Washington, DC: Georgetown University Press, 1991.

Hoffman, Bruce. *Inside Terrorism*. New York: Columbia University Press, 1998.

Holbrooke, Richard. *To End a War*. New York: Random House, 1998.

Huntington, Samuel, et al. "The Clash of Civilizations? The Debate." 1993 *Foreign Affairs Reader*. New York, 1996.

Ignatieff, Michael. *The Warrior's Honor: Ethnic War and the Modern Conscience*. New York: Metropolitan, 1998.

Jack, Homer A. *WCRP: World Conference on Religion and Peace*. New York: World Conference on Religion and Peace, 1993.

Jett, Dennis C. *Why Peacekeeping Fails*. New York: Palgrave, 2001.

Johnson, Douglas and Cynthia Sampson, eds. *Religion: The Missing Dimension of Statecraft*. New York: Oxford University Press, 1974.

Juergensmeyer, Mark. *The New Cold War: Religious Nationalism Confronts the Secular State*. Berkeley: CA: University of California Press, 1993.

___. *Terror in the Mind of God: The Global Rise of Religious Violence*. Berkeley, CA: University of California Press, 2000.

Hall, Harold and Leighton Whitaker, eds. *Collective Violence: Effective Strategies for Assessing and Intervening in Fatal Group and Institutional Agression*. Boca Raton, FL: CRC Press, 1999.

Kaminer, Reuven. *The Politics of Protest: The Israeli Peace Movement and the Palestinian Intifadah*. Brighton, UK: Sussex University Press, 1996.

Kepel, Gilles. *The Revenge of God: The Resurgence of Islam: Christianity, and Judaism in the Modern World*. University Park, PA: Penn State University Press, 1994.

___. *Jihad. The Trail of Political Islam*. Trans. Anthony Robert. Cambridge, MA: Harvard University Press, 2002.

Kriesberg, Louis. *Constructive Conflicts:From Escalation to Resolution*. Lanham, MD: Rowman and Littlefield, 2003.

Lawrence, Bruce. *Shattering the Myth: Islam Beyond Violence*. Princeton, NJ: Princeton University Press, 1998.

Lesch, Ann. *The Sudan: Contested National Identities*. Bloomington, IN: Indiana University Press, 1998.

Lowy, Michael. *The War of Gods. Religion and Politics in Latin America*. New York: Verso, 1996.

Mahmutcehogic, Rusmir. *The Denial of Bosnia.* Trans. Francis James and
Marina Bowder. University Park, PA: Pennsylvania State
University Press, 2000.

Mojzes, Paul, ed. *Religion and the War in Bosnia.* Atlanta, GA: Scholars Press,
1998.

Muslih, Muhammad. *Foreign Policy of Hamas.* New York: Council on Foreign
Relations, 1999.

Pandev, Gyanandra. *Remembering Partition: Violence, Nationalism and
History in India.* Cambridge, UK: Cambridge University Press, 2001.

Power, Samantha. *"A Problem from Hell": America and the Age of Genocide.*
New York: Basic Books, 2002.

Prunier, Gerald. *The Rwanda Crisis: History of a Genocide.* New York:
Columbia University Press, 1995.

Queen, Christopher and Sallie B. King, eds. *Engaged Buddhism: Buddhist
Liberation Movements in Asia.* Albany, NY: State University Press of
New York, 1996.

Rashid, Ahmed. *Taliban: Militant Islam, Oil, and Fundamentalism in Central
Asia.* New Haven, Yale University Press, 2000.

Rieff, David. *A Bed for the Night: Humanitarianism in Crisis.* New York: Simon
and Shuster, 2002.

Rotberg, Robert, ed. *Creating Peace in Sri Lanka: Civil War and Reconciliation.*
Washington D.C: Brookings Institution, 1999.

Ross, Marc H. *The Culture of Conflict: Interpretations and Interests in
Comparative Perspective.* New Haven, Yale University Press, 1993.

___. *Management of Conflict: Interpretations and Interests in Comparative
Perspective.* New Haven, Yale, 1993.

Ruperman, "Rwanda Retrospect." *Foreign Affairs.* 78 (2000): 94-118.

Sells, Michael. *The Bridge Betrayed: Religion and Genocide in Bosnia.*
Berkeley, CA: University of California Press, 1998.

Sela, Avraham and Moshe Ma'oz. *The PLO and Israel: From Armed Conflict to
Political Solution, 1964-1994.* New York: St. Martin's Press, 1997.

Sharp, Gene. *Civilian Based Defense: A Post-military Weapons System.*
Princeton, NJ: Princeton University Press, 1990.

___. *Gandhi as a Political Strategist: With Essays on Ethics and Politics.* Boston,
MA: Sargent, 1979.

___. *Making Europe Unconquerable: The Potential of Civilian-Based
Deterrence and Defense.* Cambridge, MA: Ballinger, 1985.

Shawcross, William. *Deliver Us From Evil: Peacekeepers, Warlords and a
World of Endless Conflict.* New York: Simon and Schuster, 2000.

Talbot, Ian and Gurharpal Singh, eds. *Region and Partition: Bengal, Punjab
and the Partition of the Subcontinent.* New York: Oxford University
Press, 1999.

Thompson. W. Scott et al., eds. *Approaches to Peace: An Intellectual Map.*
Washington, DC: U. S. Institute of Peace, 1991.

Tibi, Bassam. *The Challenge of Fundamentalism: Political Islam and the New World Disorder*. Berkeley, CA: University of California Press, 1998.

Van der Verr, Peter. *Religious Nationalism: Hindus and Muslims in India*. Berkeley, CA: University of California Press, 1994.

Weigel, George and John Langan, eds. *The American Search for Peace: Moral Reasoning, Religious Hope, and National Security*. Washington, DC: Georgetown University Press, 1991.

Yarrow, Clarence. *The Quaker Experience in International Conciliation*. New Haven, CN: Yale University Press, 1978.

Yoder, John Howard. *Nevertheless: Varieties of Religious Pacifism*. Scottsdale, PA: Herald Press, 1992.

Zimmerman, Warren, et al. *War in the Balkans*. A Foreign Affairs Reader. New York, 1999.

Index

*Individuals, movements and countries mentioned only once in the text are often not indexed.

STUDIES IN RELIGION AND SOCIETY